IMAGINING ASIA(S)

The **ISEAS – Yusof Ishak Institute** (formerly Institute of Southeast Asian Studies) is an autonomous organization established in 1968. It is a regional centre dedicated to the study of socio-political, security, and economic trends and developments in Southeast Asia and its wider geostrategic and economic environment. The Institute's research programmes are grouped under Regional Economic Studies (RES), Regional Strategic and Political Studies (RSPS), and Regional Social and Cultural Studies (RSCS). The Institute is also home to the ASEAN Studies Centre (ASC), the Temasek History Research Centre (THRC) and the Singapore APEC Study Centre.

ISEAS Publishing, an established academic press, has issued more than 2,000 books and journals. It is the largest scholarly publisher of research about Southeast Asia from within the region. ISEAS Publishing works with many other academic and trade publishers and distributors to disseminate important research and analyses from and about Southeast Asia to the rest of the world.

IMAGINING ASIA(S)

Networks, Actors, Sites

EDITED BY

ANDREA ACRI • KASHSHAF GHANI
MURARI K. JHA • SRAMAN MUKHERJEE

ISEAS YUSOF ISHAK INSTITUTE

Published in Singapore in 2019 by
ISEAS Publishing
30 Heng Mui Keng Terrace
Singapore 119614
E-mail: publish@iseas.edu.sg
Website: <http://bookshop.iseas.edu.sg>

ISEAS Library Cataloguing-in-Publication Data

Names: Acri, Andrea, 1981–, editor. | Ghani, Kashshaf, editor. | Jhā, Murārī K., editor. | Mukherjee, Sraman, editor.
Title: Imagining Asia(s) : Networks, Actors, Sites / edited by Andrea Acri, Kashshaf Ghani, Murari K. Jha and Sraman Mukherjee.
Description: Singapore: ISEAS – Yusof Ishak Institute, 2019. | Series: Nalanda-Sriwijaya Centre Series ; NSC29 | Includes bibliographical references.
Identifiers: ISBN 9789814818858 (paperback) | ISBN 9789814818865 (PDF)
Subjects: LCSH: Asia--Civilization.
Classification: LCC DS12 I31

Typeset by Superskill Graphics Pte Ltd

Contents

List of Contributors vii

Introduction 1
Andrea Acri, Kashshaf Ghani, Murari K. Jha, Sraman Mukherjee

Part I: Conceptualizing the Region: Past and Present

1. Locating Asia, Arresting Asia: Grappling with "The Epistemology that Kills" 17
Farish A. Noor

2. Imagining "Maritime Asia" 36
Andrea Acri

3. In Search of an Asian Vision: The Asian Relations Conference of 1947 60
Gopa Sabharwal

Part II: Conceptualizing Asia through the Prism of Europe

4. In Pursuit of Knowledge from Asia: François Valentijn on the Hindu Social Divisions in the Coromandel Region, c. Seventeenth–Eighteenth Century 93
Murari K. Jha

5. British Romantic Poetics and the Idea of Asia 125
Anjana Sharma

Part III: Networks of Knowledge Across the Indian Ocean

6. An Indian Ocean *Ribāṭ*: War and Religion in Sixteenth-Century Ponnāni, Malabar Coast 147
Mahmood Kooria

7. Travelling Spirits: Revisiting Melaka's *Keramat* from the Indian Ocean 175
Fernando Rosa

Part IV: Histories and Geographies of Pilgrimage in Asia
8. Transmissions, Translations, Reconstitutions: Revisiting Geographies of Buddha Relics in the Southern Asian Worlds 215
Sraman Mukherjee

9. The Politics of Pilgrimage: Reception of Hajj among South Asian Muslims 251
Kashshaf Ghani

Part V: Trans-Local Dynamics and Intra-Asian Connections across Space and Time
10. Sanskritic Buddhism as an Asian Universalism 275
Iain Sinclair

11. Interconnectedness and Mobility in the Middle Ages/Nowadays: From Baghdad to Chang'an and from Istanbul to Tokyo 334
Federica A. Broilo

12. Connecting Networks and Orienting Space: Relocating Nguyen Cochinchina between East and Southeast Asia in the Sixteenth and Eighteenth Centuries 358
Vu Duc Liem

13. The Highlands of West Sumatra and their Maritime Trading Connections 393
Mai Lin Tjoa-Bonatz

Index 425

ABOUT THE CONTRIBUTORS

Andrea Acri (PhD Leiden University, 2011) is *Maître de conférences* (Assistant Professor) in Tantric Studies at the École Pratique des Hautes Études (EPHE, PSL University, Paris) since 2016. Prior to that, he has held research and teaching positions in India (Nalanda University), Singapore (Nalanda-Sriwijaya Centre at the ISEAS – Yusof Ishak Institute, and Asia Research Institute at the National University of Singapore), Australia (Australian National University), and the Netherlands (International Institute for Asian Studies, Leiden). His main research interests include Shaiva and Buddhist tantric traditions in South and Southeast Asia, as well as wider cultural and historical dynamics of Intra-Asian connectivity.

Federica A. Broilo is currently an Adjunct Professor at the University of Urbino "Carlo Bo" where she teaches Islamic Art and Architecture. She has been Assistant Professor at the Department of History of Art at Mardin Artuklu University, Turkey until December 2015. She holds a PhD in Oriental Studies from Ca' Foscari University of Venice, Italy (2009). She is especially interested in the relation between water, light and architectural spaces in the Mediterranean world and beyond.

Kashshaf Ghani is currently Assistant Professor at the School of Historical Studies, Nalanda University, India. He specializes on premodern South Asia covering the years 1000–1800 CE. His research covers society, politics, religion and cultural interactions in this region, with a focus on the History of Sufism, its practices, rituals, and networks; Indo-Persian history; community interactions; cosmopolitan cultures; and South Asian languages. He also researches in areas of Asian interconnections; historical connections of South Asia with West and Central Asia; Muslim networks in Asia; and travel and transregionalism in Muslim societies.

Murari Kumar Jha is currently a Visiting Fellow at the Weatherhead Centre for International Affairs, Harvard University (2018–19). Earlier, between 2015 and 2018, Dr Jha worked as an Assistant Professor at the School of Historical Studies, Nalanda University. Prior to joining Nalanda, he was a Research Fellow in the Department of History, NUS, during 2013 and 2014. After completing his studies at Jawaharlal Nehru University, New Delhi, Dr Jha pursued his higher studies at Leiden University between 2006 and 2013, where he wrote his PhD dissertation, "The Political Economy of the Ganga River: Highway of State Formation in Mughal India, c.1600–1800". Dr Jha is currently working on a monograph tentatively titled "River and Empire: An Economic and Environmental History of the Ganga in Mughal India, c.1500–1800".

Mahmood Kooria is a postdoctoral researcher at Leiden University, the Netherlands. Earlier he was a research fellow at the International Institute for Asian Studies (IIAS) and African Studies Centre (ASC), Leiden and the Dutch Institute in Morocco (NIMAR), Rabat. He did his PhD at the Leiden University Institute for history on the circulation of Islamic legal ideas and texts across the Indian Ocean and Mediterranean worlds. With Michael N. Pearson he has edited *Malabar in the Indian Ocean World: Cosmopolitanism in a Maritime Historical Region* (Oxford University Press, 2018). He has published in several peer-reviewed journals such as the *Journal of the Economic and Social History of the Orient*; *Annales. Histoire, Sciences Sociales*; *Law & History Review*; *Oxford Journal of Law and Religion*; and *Itinerario*.

Sraman Mukherjee (PhD Centre for Studies in Social Sciences, Calcutta and University of Calcutta, 2010) is Assistant Professor in the Department of Visual Arts at Ashoka University (India). Trained as a historian of colonial and early postcolonial South Asia, his work explores the interface between the past and the present in the constitution of the disciplinary and institutional domains of art history, archaeology and museums; biographies of material traces (sites, objects, and monuments); and histories of the inter-Asian circulation of objects, ideas, and people. Before joining Ashoka University, Sraman held postdoctoral research positions at the International Institute for Asian Studies (Leiden), at the Royal Netherlands Institute for Southeast Asian and Caribbean Studies (KITLV, Leiden), and in the Department of Art History and the Institute for Advanced Study at the University of Minnesota (Minneapolis); and teaching positions in the Department of History at Presidency University (Calcutta, India) and in the School of Historical Studies at Nalanda University (Rajgir, India).

Farish A. Noor is Associate Professor at the S. Rajaratnam School of International Studies (RSIS) and the School of History, College of the Humanities, Arts and Social Sciences (COHASS), Nanyang Technological University (NTU), Singapore. His work has been focused on Southeast Asian history and politics, with a particular emphasis on the colonial era in the nineteenth century. His latest works include *America's Encounters With Southeast Asia 1800–1900: Before the Pivot* (Amsterdam University Press, 2018).

Fernando Rosa is a Brazilian anthropologist and historian who has worked on and lived in various Indian Ocean societies, particularly South Africa (Cape Town), India (Kerala and Goa), Peninsular Malaysia (mostly Kuala Lumpur and Melaka), Macau (China), and Indonesia. He has also lived and worked in Atlantic societies such as Brazil and parts of the Caribbean (including Martinique, Suriname, Aruba, and Curaçao). He is now a research affiliate with the English department, Stellenbosch University, South Africa. His mains fields are African studies and Indian Ocean studies. His research interests lie in the domain of oceanic intellectual networks and related languages (and their archives), as well as in processes of creolization and cosmopolitanism.

Gopa Sabharwal founded the undergraduate Department of Sociology at India's foremost liberal Arts college, Lady Shri Ram College for Women, in 1993. She was a Fulbright Scholar in Residence in 2006 at Chatham College for Women (now Chatham University), Pittsburgh. From 2010 to 2016, she served as founding Vice Chancellor of Nalanda University, entrusted with giving shape to the vision of establishing a new Nalanda for the twenty-first century—a unique international, research-focused postgraduate University with a focus on inter-Asian relations, an interdisciplinary curriculum, and a unique pedagogy. Her books include *Ethnicity and Class: Social Divisions in an Indian City* (New Delhi: Oxford University Press, 2006); *The Indian Millennium—AD 1000 to AD 2000* (Penguin India, 2000); and *India Since 1947: The Independent Years* (Penguin Random House India, 2017). Her research interests focus on ethnic identities, urban India, visual anthropology, and the history of society.

Anjana Sharma teaches at the Department of English, Delhi University. She was Founding Dean, Academic Planning at Nalanda University from 2011 to 2015. She was the recipient of a Fulbright Fellowship in 2001 and was Senior Fellow at the Nalanda-Sriwijaya Centre, ISEAS – Yusof Ishak Institute, in 2016. Her research interests span revolutionary print and visual culture, British literature of the late eighteenth and early nineteenth century, and questions of gender. Her most representative works are *The Autobiography of Desire: English Women Novelists of the 1790s* (2004), the edited *Frankenstein: Gender, Culture, and Identity* (2004), and the co-edited *Agamemnon's Mask: Greek Tragedy and Beyond* (2007). Her recent scholarship is related to examining the representation of the critical year 1947 in Indian history and the representation of MK Gandhi in English language newspapers. The Nalanda experience focused on the rich seam of inter-Asian interactions and resulted in the editing of two significant volumes: *Civilizational Dialogue: Asian Interconnections and Cross Cultural Exchanges* (2013) and *Records, Recoveries, Remnants and Inter-Asian Interconnections: Decoding Cultural Heritage* (2018).

Iain Sinclair is currently a Visiting Fellow at ISEAS – Yusof Ishak Institute. He has studied the art and literature of Sanskritic civilization for over two decades (MA Hons, 2000; PhD, 2016). His doctoral dissertation focused on the transitional period of tantric and monastic Buddhism in Nepal.

Mai Lin Tjoa-Bonatz is teaching Southeast Asian culture and archaeology in various universities. She has a PhD in Art History from Technische Universität Darmstadt, Germany, and an MA in Art History, Archaeology, and Southeast Asian regional studies from the Johann Wolfgang Goethe Universität in Frankfurt am Main. She was a Visiting Fellow with the Nalanda-Sriwijaya Centre at the ISEAS – Yusof Ishak Institute in Singapore and served as a research assistant for excavations conducted on Sumatra, Indonesia in 2003–8 and 2011–14. Her main interests are architecture, maritime cultural heritage, gold jewellery, settlement and missionary history in Southeast Asia.

Vũ Đức Liêm is Lecturer in History at Hanoi National University of Education (HNUE), Vietnam. He is finishing his dissertation on the early nineteenth century Vietnamese political history at Hamburg University, Germany. He previously obtained undergraduate and graduate degrees in History at HNUE, Chulalongkorn University (Thailand), and a graduate fellowship at the National University of Singapore. His area of research covers early modern Vietnamese warfare, geopolitics, and political history.

INTRODUCTION

Andrea Acri, Kashshaf Ghani, Murari K. Jha
and Sraman Mukherjee

This edited volume stems from the conference "Imagining Asia(s): Networks, Actors, Sites" held at ISEAS – Yusof Ishak Institute in October 2016, jointly organized by the Nalanda-Sriwijaya Centre (Singapore) and Nalanda University (India). This event, bringing together fourteen scholars from various countries, constituted a landmark for the collaboration between the two institutions and, we believe, also a gesture towards the academic and intellectual "rapprochement" between two regions of the world—South and Southeast Asia—whose deeply connected histories have been forgotten for a long time, and need now, more than ever, to be (re)conceptualized as an integrated phenomenon. Indeed, the intellectual agenda driving this conference has been an engagement with the idea of "Asia" in the frame of Area Studies scholarship and, at the same time, a commitment to the study of Intra-Asian networks and connections that has been the hallmark of recent scholarship, including the very series in which this volume has been published.

Asia has long been perceived as a clear and distinct geographical unit. As a continent lying to the east of Europe, it has been malleable to different imaginations and politics. Area studies scholarship, for example, has carved Asia into the seemingly self-contained regions of West and Central Asia, South and Southeast Asia, and East Asia. These regional configurations reflect more the changing (geo)political and economic interests in these areas rather than any of their historical or cultural roots. Recent scholarship, however, has presented Asia as a cultural entity produced through political imaginations located in specific historical contexts, and revealed the arbitrariness of the Area Studies divide.[1] More importantly, it has advanced the question as to what Asia is, and as to whether there existed one or many Asia(s).[2]

Following the lead of such scholarship, this conference sought to explore Asian societies as interconnected formations through trajectories/networks of circulation of people, ideas, and objects in the *longue durée*. Moving beyond the divides of conventional Area Studies scholarship and the arbitrary borders set by late colonial empires and the rise of post-colonial nation-states, this conference mapped critically the configuration of contact zones in which mobile bodies, minds, and cultures interact to foster new images, identities, and imaginations of Asia. Offering some historiographical reflections and, at the same time, presenting novel research trajectories, the conference addressed such questions as: When does the idea of Asia (and regions) come into being, and how far back in time can we trace these spatial imagination(s)? What are the logistical aspects governing the routes—overland and maritime—that linked up different regions of Asia? What roles did imperial formations (old and new, European and non-European) play in shaping Asia? Do ideas of nationalism and post-colonial nation-states fracture Asia?

The ancient Greeks employed the term Asia to denote the eastern inhabited world in their spatial imagination. More than being a geographic region located on the map, Asia is a broad concept that can meaningfully be understood to shed further light on the processes of globalization that signify the growing interconnections among regions, cultures, ideas, economies and polities. Prasenjit Duara (2010) and other scholars have highlighted the richness and polysemy of the category of Asia and its potential for understanding the contemporary world. Just as "Asia"—and its subregions of South, Central, Southeast, and East Asia—are construed as conceptual categories, a similar case can be made for the terms such as "Indies" or "East Indies" (*Oost Indiën*) often employed since the early-modern period. The term "India" or "Indies" covered many regions to the east of the Persian Gulf and included the Malay Peninsula and the Indonesian Archipelago.

---

[1] See, e.g., Ali (2009), Bose (2006), Chaudhuri (1993), Subrahmanyam (1997), Frank (1998), Lewis and Wigen (1997), Noor (2016), and Singh and Dhar (2014).

[2] Among the most recent contributions are Duara (2010), Subrahmanyam (2016 and 1997), Acharya (2013), Milner and Johnson (2001), and Frey and Spakowski (2015).

"India", and the phrase "the countries of the sea", were already employed by the Persia-based seafaring community of Nestorian Christians in the first millennium CE (Colless 1969, pp. 21–22). If Asia can be perceived as a hallmark of interconnections at multiple levels throughout eastern Eurasia, the East Indies can be understood as one of the core regions where such processes unfolded during the pre-modern, early modern and colonial periods. Historians of the Indian Ocean such as K.N. Chaudhuri (1985), and more recently Michael Pearson (2003) and Sugata Bose (2006), have shown how the Indian Subcontinent and the adjoining regions constituted the fulcrum around which much of the economic, cultural, and political contacts gravitated between East Africa and the China Sea.

Rather than giving primacy to an arbitrarily defined geographic category, Asia can be visualized as a zone or discursive field of intensified interconnections intertwining almost every aspects of human society. Any attempts to chart out an imagined geographical construct such as Asia inevitably "also make manifest the impossibilities and potential of mapping Global Asias, that conceptually determined site that insists on its own indeterminacy and plurality as much as its global expanse." (Chen 2017, p. vii). Conceptual impossibilities aside, a working geographical construct of Asia may be defined as including the continental landmass between "the Pontic Steppe, the Mediterranean Sea and the Sinai Desert in the West; Japan, the Philippines, and the Pacific Ocean in the East; the Arctic Sea in the North; and the Indian Ocean and Indonesian Archipelago in the South." (Fairey and Farrell 2018, p. 6). While this vast swathe of geography can be taken as indicative of the heterogeneity that the region recognized as Asia signifies, an exciting line of enquiry is to look for translocal phenomena including parallelisms, synchronisms, and processual continuities, or, to say it with Andrew Abalahin (2011, p. 664), to reframe "a series of world-historical developments that bring together histories that have customarily been viewed apart".

At our historical juncture characterized by growing globalization and regional integration, and at the turn of what is regarded to be the "Asian Century", scholarship is increasingly formulating alternative configurations to conceptualize Asian spaces and phenomena that are not bound to a static geographical model, let alone geopolitical contingencies, but that are rather the expression of dynamic processes of transfer through networks of human agents, flora and fauna, material objects, etc. Research focusing on such translocal relationships is not a new phenomenon: novel conceptualization of macro-regions, spaces, or cultural phenomena spanning across (and beyond) Asia that transcend the boundaries of the Area Studies paradigm have been developed on the basis of old ideas, namely the overland and maritime Silk Roads (von Richthofen 1877; Chavannes 1903), Monsoon Asia (Mus 1933), or Eurasia (McNeill 1963; Goody 2010); new or fine-tuned models include Sino-Pacifica (Abalahin 2011), Zomia (van Schendel 2002), Maritime Asia (Guillot, Lombard and Ptak 1998), and the Bay of Bengal Interaction Sphere (Gupta 2005), to name just a few. Innovative scholarship emphasizing a comparative perspective has also focused on social dynamics and their relationship to the human and natural environments, namely borderlands vs. centres, maritime and coastal communities (or "water civilizations") vs. highland communities, Insular vs. Mainland, state spaces vs. stateless peoples, etc.; the circulation and appropriation of languages and body of texts across Asia, such as the Sanskrit Cosmopolis and Vernacular Millennium (Pollock 2006), the Islamicate and Persianate worlds (Ho 2006), Sinosphere and Indosphere (Matisoff 1990); religious phenomena, such as the Axial Age (Jaspers 1953), the Śaiva Age (Sanderson 2009), the Pali Cosmopolis/Buddhist Ecumene (Frasch 2017), and the Demonological Cosmopolis (White 2012); the Indian Ocean (and the sea in general) as an unifying factor in Asian history (Chaudhuri 1985, Pearson 2003); and other historical dynamics such as networks and synchronisms (Lombard 1995), "strange parallels" (Lieberman 2003, 2009), convergence (Kulke 1990, 2014), etc. Also notable is the recent resurgence of temporal categories such as the "Medieval" and the "Early Modern" as tools to elaborate new models for global history (see, e.g., Holmes and Standen 2018; Strathern 2018), which are especially relevant in bringing out the interconnected and dynamic nature of Asia across time.

Situating itself within this intellectual agenda, the present volume challenges the set boundaries of Area Studies and sets out to explore Asian societies, cultures, and identities as interconnected formations through trajectories of circulation of people, ideas, and artefacts in the *longue durée*.

CONTENTS OF THE VOLUME

The collective body of work presented in this volume includes select papers from the conference, as well as two papers from invited contributors (Kooria and Rosa). Part I, "Conceptualizing the Region: Past and Present", groups three chapters setting the intellectual stage of the volume through a consideration of relevant theoretical and historiographical issues foregrounding the scholarly (re)conceptualizations of Asia on the one hand, and discussing the idea of Asia in the context of key events and cultural trends of the twentieth century that have had an impact on subsequent geopolitical and socio-cultural developments on the other.

Chapter 1, "Locating Asia, Arresting Asia: Grappling with 'the Epistemology That Kills'" by Farish Noor problematizes the modern and contemporary political boundaries of Asia drawn in the nineteenth century and appropriated by post-colonial states. In unpacking the issues of naming, identity, modernity, and postmodern global capitalism in the context of framing and imagining Asia(s), Noor reminds the reader of Todorov and Cohn's warning about the workings of an epistemology that kills and arrests, and the investigative modalities that have been used to fix the meaning of signifiers. Modern Asian history is as much a history of modernity as it is a history of Asia, and scholars cannot hope to situate themselves radically outside the discursive economy of modernity, despite the fact that today we are all too aware of the pits and traps that lie within its regulated parameters. The chapter suggests a possible way to discuss the meaning of Asia, and locates that object of discussion without locking it permanently within a grid of determined meanings and values that reduces and essentializes.

Chapter 2, "Imagining 'Maritime Asia'" by Andrea Acri tries to reconceptualize (i.e., reimagine) geopolitical configurations of Asia as framed by the current Area Studies paradigm though the prism of the socio-spatial construction of "Maritime Asia". Acri advocates a borderless history (and geography) of the largely maritime and littoral swathe of territory from the Indian Ocean littorals to the Western Pacific in the *longue durée* that takes into account long-distance connections and dynamics of religious interaction. Having surveyed the genealogy of the expression "Maritime Asia", Acri describes this dynamic macro-region of intersecting discursive fields across which networks of cultural brokers travelled since time immemorial, regarding it as forming—just like Eurasia—one interconnected network with a shared background of human, intellectual, and environmental history. The chapter then applies the concept of Maritime Asia to the study of the genesis and circulation of Sanskritic Buddhism(s) across the region from the third to the fourteenth century and beyond, and offers some concluding reflections situating the concept in the intellectual trajectory of such terms as "Eurasia", "Monsoon Asia", and the "Indian Ocean World".

Chapter 3, "In Search of an Asian Vision: The Asian Relations Conference of 1947" by Gopa Sabharwal captures the idea of Asia set forth at the 1st Asian Relations Conference that took place in New Delhi in March–April 1947, as a non-political and non-official event. The objective of the conference, attended by 250 delegates from thirty-three countries, including such leading personalities as Mr Gandhi, Pandit Nehru, Dr Sutan Sjahrir, and Mrs Sarojini Naidu, was "to bring together the leading men and women of Asia on a common platform to study the problems of common concern to the people of the continent". This was the first attempt in modern times of the countries of Asia to come together, and therefore all the speeches echoed the coming together of Asia.

Part II, "Conceptualizing Asia through the Prism of Europe", discusses the perception, and constitution, of Asia and ideas about Asia as formulated in European intellectual circles of the early modern and modern periods.

Chapter 4, "In Pursuit of Knowledge from Asia: François Valentijn on the Hindu Social Divisions in the Coromandel Region, c. Seventeenth–Eighteenth Century" by Murari K. Jha discusses the knowledge transfer between Asia and Europe along the trade networks of the Indian Ocean operated by the Dutch East India Company. More specifically, the chapter pays attention to the Western European curiosity to know the Eastern world and society. In post-Enlightenment Europe, such curiosity for the knowledge about Asia was deployed to understand and redefine the European self in contrast to the Asian Other. In doing this exercise, and by focusing primarily on the work of François Valentijn, Jha examines the activities of the Europeans to dig deeper in generating knowledge about the southeastern Indian society and how such knowledge was transferred to the European reading public.

Chapter 5, "British Romantic Poetics and the Idea of Asia" by Anjana Sharma explores how the "discovery" of Asia in the eighteenth century by the British forever altered the cultural and political aesthetics of writers, thinkers, philosophers and poets who began to constitute the Republic of Letters in Great Britain. As the British imperial juggernaut rolled on it sought to erase ancient civilizational pathways and began to very consciously recast Asia in terms of its own cultural, literary and political referentiality. Ideas of Asia took shape and were transmitted from imperial sites and were circulated transnationally. Consequentially, what emerged in the nineteenth century British imaginary was an Asia that was defined by geography yet transcended borders: an Asia that was fundamentally displaced from its core principles of cultural syncretism that coexisted within its robust multiple philosophical and literary traditions. Discussing key literary works, such as Coleridge's iconic *Kubla Khan*, the Bryronic "Eastern" tale *The Giaour*, Shelley's *Prometheus Unbound*, and Keats unfinished *Hyperions*, Sharma argues that the afterlife of the Romantic endeavour still shapes the idea of a monolithic Asia in global literary studies, despite the significant inroads made by Edward Said and others who have interrogated and dismantled these (mis)readings.

Part III, "Networks of Knowledge Across the Indian Ocean", groups two papers focusing on the fluid contact zone including the countries around the Bay of Bengal, which can be analysed as the theatre of cultural and material transfer since time immemorial. In so doing, it delineates a more coherent geography of knowledge transfer across geographical, ethnic, and linguistic boundaries. This perspective further highlights that post-war truncation of Asia into the area studies divisions such as South Asia and Southeast Asia is problematic and least useful for historical enquiry, as much as an arbitrary and reified distinction between "Asia" and "Europe".

Chapter 6, "An Indian Ocean *Ribāṭ*: War and Religion in Sixteenth-Century Ponnāni, Malabar Coast" by Mahmood Kooria explores the concept and practice of *ribāṭ* to understand the ways in which the Muslims perceived and conceptualized their conflicts in the sixteenth-century Indian Ocean. *Ribāṭ*, a term and concept originally derived from the central Islamic lands and texts, was used by the authors of jihadi-treatises in Malabar to identify their physical struggles as well as their locatedness in Islamic history. Based on treatises written in Arabic, Kooria examines how such a "peripheral" Muslim community imagined itself and its worldviews while living under non-Muslim rulers, the Zamorins, and cooperating with them in the warfront. Describing the concept of *ribāṭ* and its applicability to a non-Middle Eastern Indian Ocean context, and focusing on one particular and important micro-region within Malabar called Ponnāni, the author suggests that concepts like "frontier zones" do not make justice to the nuances of the coastal communities who fought against the Portuguese intrusions without being part of a larger frontier to an imperial centre.

Chapter 7, "Travelling Spirits: Revisiting Melaka's *Keramat* from the Indian Ocean" by Fernando Rosa takes a comparative look at *keramat* in Melaka and the Indian Ocean. Rosa uses theoretical insights from comparative religion as well as Indian Ocean histories, especially those connecting South and Southeast Asia, in order to understand local historic structures. In this wide-ranging chapter, he reinserts *keramat*—today seen as Islamic saintly shrines—within the ancient histories of the Indian Ocean and its broad religious networks. He also engages in an extended discussion of the meaning of *keramat* within certain streams of thought in the larger Islamic tradition, especially in the twentieth century. In particular, he examines the work of Abdul A'la Maududi, emphasizing in this way the wider framework of doctrinal objections to *keramat*. Moreover, on the basis of recent path-breaking work, Rosa indicates that the ancient Austroasiatic (and, perhaps, tantric?) religious and cultural matrix encompassing both South and Southeast Asia is importantly rooted in a shared notion of feminine power and deities. That notion survives in modern Nusantara, as suggested by Braginsky for Sumatra, but in a state of tension with doctrinal forms of Islam. Finally, Rosa suggests that the ancient, deep-rooted histories of creolization of South and Southeast Asia are relevant also as religious and cultural resources for today's predicament of globalized jihadist violence.

Part IV, "Histories and Geographies of Pilgrimage in Asia", includes two chapters exploring the role of pilgrimage in the complex dynamics that shaped intra-Asian connections, which could in turn contribute to question and reorient our contemporary perceptions about socio-cultural, religious, and ethnic identities across the regions of South Asia, Southeast Asia, and the Middle East in the nineteenth and twentieth centuries.

Chapter 8, "Transmissions, Translations, Reconstitutions: Revisiting Geographies of Buddha Relics in the Southern Asian Worlds" by Sraman Mukherjee traces the circulating lives of Buddha's relics across colonial South and mainland Southeast Asia. The chapter investigates the changing semantics, contexts, and contents of material reconstitution of Buddhist corporeal relics as they travelled from archaeological sites and museums to practising Buddhist temples. It develops around one particular case of a Buddhist corporeal relic and retraces its journey from an excavation site near Peshawar (presently in Pakistan) to its current location in a new relic temple in Mandalay (in Myanmar) in the opening years of the twentieth century. Mapping the changing institutional, cultural, and political locations of this and similar relics, Mukherjee explores how Buddhist corporeal relics accrued certain meaning, value, and visibility through a network of social relations created by gift, exchange, market economy, and political diplomacy. In so doing, he revisits the role of the modern state formations in shaping the domain of Area Studies scholarship.

Chapter 9, "The Politics of Pilgrimage: Reception of Hajj among South Asian Muslims" by Kashshaf Ghani discusses the growing trend among early twentieth-century Bengali Muslims to look beyond their immediate borders in an attempt to connect with Muslim societies in West Asia, particularly with regard to the Ottoman-supported Sharif administration and its policies towards the hajj pilgrims. Ghani looks into the multiple ways such events reflecting the political and religious environment in the Hejaz were being read and interpreted by Bengali Muslims. He argues that the community, though located at one far end of the Islamic world, could not isolate itself from the implications of such political turmoil on the holy ritual of hajj. Changes in the political climate attracted much reaction from within the community, and Muslim periodicals in Bengali played a leading role in carrying this news to the Muslim masses in Bengal. Two periodicals—*Chholtan* and *Ahl i-Hadith*—are taken into account in the chapter, in an attempt to read trends of transregionalism among Muslims in twentieth century Bengal.

Part V, "Trans-Local Dynamics and Intra-Asian Connections across Space and Time", closes the volume by grouping four chapters devoted to the registers of intra-Asian connections from the perspective of different disciplinary foci, such as religious studies, philology, history, art history, and archaeology, and marrying micro- and macro-historical analysis.

Chapter 10, "Sanskritic Buddhism as an Asian Universalism" by Iain Sinclair explores the ways in which Sanskritic Buddhism—a nontheistic, nonessentialist religion of universalist orientation—marked out its own distinctive territory across the parts of the world now called South, Central and Southeast Asia. Sinclair argues that regional expressions of Sanskritic Buddhism are much more weakly tied to parochial institutions than other forms of Buddhism, which follows from the fact that its canonical language, Sanskrit, is also a nonsectarian language that is standard across nation-state boundaries and is used for purposes other than religion. As Sanskritic Buddhism takes part in a technical discourse (*śāstra*) on semisecular subjects such as medicine, grammar and literary composition, it tends to coexist and be in dialogue with Brahmanism, without being predicated on it, and shares in the socio-religious milieu of Hinduism. However, its geographic extent far exceeds that of Hinduism, covering much of the Sino-Tibetan world and its diaspora, while at the same time, the unitary transnational character of Sanskritic Buddhism has often been obscured by the nationalist priorities of colonial scholarship and its globalist successors. The chapter highlights various stratagems used to construct a Buddhist transsectarianism on the discursive level.

Chapter 11, "Interconnectedness and Mobility in the Middle Ages/Nowadays: From Baghdad to Chang'an and from Istanbul to Tokyo" by Federica Broilo maps the active networks of circulation and exchange during the middle ages, arguing that cultural systems of the Abbasid Caliphate of Baghdad and Tang China were not inserted in sealed boxes. Chang'an and Baghdad were at that time two of the biggest cities in the world, marked by strong rule, successful diplomatic relationships, economic expansion, and a cultural efflorescence characterized by a cosmopolitan style. The comparative methodology of the chapter describes both entanglements and contacts among artistic and architectural practices belonging to different cultural systems that appear distant on the geographic chart, but are actually much closer than originally thought. The adoption of models moving within the broad borders of Asia is relevant to our days, when read together with other contemporary phenomena that are now affecting Asia again, such as the use of distinctive architectural icons coming from a specific part of Asia like Turkey into newly constructed buildings in Japan. Broilo engages in a comparison between those phenomena searching for a key to read them as part of the same process of interconnectedness and mobility from West Asia to East Asia and back.

Chapter 12, "Connecting Networks and Orienting Space: Relocating Nguyen Cochinchina between East and Southeast Asia in the Sixteenth and Eighteenth Centuries" by Vu Duc Liem examines the geographical configuration of early modern Vietnam through the prism of economic networks and political landscapes. It argues that the Nguyen Cochinchina had developed a unique perspective of geographical orientation along the frontier between East and Southeast Asia. The Nguyens were economically directed southward to their Southeast Asian neighbours, but culturally and politically northward to the Sino-world. Cochinchina thus offers a fascinating example of a polity standing at the crossroad of Asian networks, between the two geopolitical entities that we now label as East and Southeast Asia. Anthony Reid recognized that Southeast Asia is a space of "not China, not India", but was unable to precisely define what it is in the between. By following the networks and identifying the spatial aspects of political acclimatization, this chapter engages with the question of who were the agents "in the between", and how they defined identity and located themselves in space.

Chapter 13, "The Highlands of West Sumatra and Their Maritime Trading Connections" by Mai Lin Tjoa-Bonatz gives a first glimpse into the nature, role, and operations of the settlements in Tanah Datar, the heartland of the Minangkabau community in the highland of Western Sumatra, through a close examination of their material culture from the fourteenth to the seventeenth centuries. It is now possible to analyse different types of ceramic imports at these sites in the light of ongoing archaeological investigations, and advance some interpretations in connection with other historical and archaeological data on commercial interactions between the highland and maritime regions. The interconnection between the uplands and the lowlands had essential effects on the cultural and socio-economic conditions of the highlands. New excavation finds suggest that the hill site at Bukit Gombak represents the centre of King Ādityavarman's polity, the last Hindu-Buddhist king of Indonesia in the fourteenth century.

In discussing the issues of (trans)locality, mobility, and imagination in Asian contexts through a multi-site, multi-register, multi-actor approach, this volume hopes to contribute to an emerging field of scholarship that has begun to critically examine the framework set by Area Studies scholarship within the field of Asian Studies. At the same time, its wide-ranging historical and geographical approach aims at enriching our understanding of "Asia" as a fluid contact zone shaped by multidirectional circulatory dynamics characterized by connections and interactions.

Bibliography

Abalahin, Andrew. 2011. "'Sino-Pacifica': Conceptualizing Greater Southeast Asia as a Sub-Arena of World History". *Journal of World History* 22, no. 4: 659–91.

Acharya, Amitav. 2013. *Civilizations in Embrace: The Spread of Ideas and the Transformation of Power: India and Southeast Asia in the Classical Age.* Singapore: Institute of Southeast Asian Studies.

Ali, Daud. 2009. "Connected Histories? Regional Historiography and Theories of Cultural Contact between Early South and Southeast Asia". In *Islamic Connections: Muslim Societies in South and Southeast Asia,* edited by R. Michael Feener and Terenjit Sevea. Singapore: Institute of Southeast Asian Studies.

Bose, Sugata. 2006. *A Hundred Horizons: Indian Ocean in the Age of Global Empire.* Cambridge, Mass.: Harvard University Press.

Chen, Tina. 2017. "Context, Coordinate, Circulation: The Postrepresentational Cartographies of Global Asias". *Verge: Studies in Global Asia* 3, no. 1 (Spring): vi–xiv.

Chaudhuri, K.N. 1985. *Trade and Civilisation in the Indian Ocean: An Economic History from the Rise of Islam to 1750.* Cambridge: Cambridge University Press.

———. 1993. "The Unity and Disunity of Indian Ocean History from the Rise of Islam to 1750: The Outline of a Theory and Historical Discourse". *Journal of World History* 4, no. 1: 1–21.

Chavannes, Édouard. 1903. *Documents sur les Tou Kiue (turcs) occidentaux, Recueillis et commentés par Édouard Chavannes.* St. Petersburg: Commissionnaires de l'Académie impériale des sciences.

Colless, Brian E. 1969. "Persian Merchants and Missionaries in Medieval Malaya". *Journal of the Malaysian Branch of the Royal Asiatic Society* 42, no. 2 (216): 10–47.

Duara, Prasenjit. 2010. "Asia Redux: Conceptualizing a Region for Our Times". *Journal of Asian Studies* 69, no. 4: 963–83.

Fairey, Jack, and Brian P. Farrell. 2018. "Series Introduction: Reordering an

Imperial, Global, Modern Asia". In *Empire in Asia: A New Global History*, edited by Jack Fairey and Brian P. Farrell, vol. 1. London: Bloomsbury.
Frank, Andre G. 1998. *ReOrient: Global Economy in the Asian Age*. Berkeley: University of Calfornia Press.
Frasch, Tilman. 2017. "A Pāli cosmopolis? Sri Lanka and the Theravāda Buddhist ecumene, c. 500–1500". In *Sri Lanka at the Crossroads of History*, edited by Z. Biedermann and A. Strathern, pp. 66–76. London: UCL Press.
Frey, Mark, and Nicola Spakowski, eds. 2015. *Asianisms, Regionalist Interactions, and Asian Integration*. Singapore: NUS Press.
Goody, Jack. 2010. *The Eurasian Miracle*. Cambridge: Polity.
Guillot, Claude, Denys Lombard, and Roderick Ptak, eds. 1998. *From the Mediterranean to the China Sea: Miscellaneous Notes*. Wiesbaden: Harrassowitz.
Gupta, Sunil. 2005. "The Bay of Bengal Interaction Sphere (1000 BC–AD 500)". *Indo-Pacific Prehistory Association Bulletin* 25: 21–30.
Ho, Engseng. 2006. *The Graves of Tarim: Genealogy and Mobility Across the Indian Ocean*. Berkeley: University of California Press.
Holmes, Catherine, and Naomi Standen, eds. 2018. "Introduction: Towards a Global Middle Ages". Special Issue "The Global Middle Ages", *Past & Present* 238, Issue Supplement no. 13: 1–44.
Jaspers, Karl. 1953. "The Axial Period". In *The Origin and Goal of History*, by Karl Jaspers, pp. 1–25. New Haven: Yale University Press.
Kulke, Hermann. 1990. "Indian Colonies, Indianization or Cultural Convergence? Reflections on the Changing Image of India's Role in South East Asia". In *Onderzoek in Zuidoost-Azie. Agenda's voor de jaren negentig*, edited by Henk Schulte-Nordholt. Leiden: Rijksuniversiteit te Leiden.
———. 2014. "The Concept of Cultural Convergence Revisited. Reflections on India's Early Influence in Southeast Asia". In *Asian Encounters; Exploring Connected Histories*, edited by Parul Pandya Dhar and Upinder Singh, pp. 3–19. New Delhi: Oxford University Press.
Lewis, Martin W., and Kären Wigen. 1997. *The Myth of Continents: A Critique of Metageography*. London and Los Angeles: University of California Press.
Lieberman, Victor. 2003. *Strange Parallels: Southeast Asia in Global Context, c. 800–1830. Volume 1: Integration of the Mainland*. Cambridge: Cambridge University Press.
———. 2009. *Strange Parallels: Southeast Asia in Global Context, c. 800–1830*. Vol. 2, *Mainland Mirrors: Europe, Japan, China, South Asia, and the Islands*. Cambridge: Cambridge University Press.
Lombard, Denys. 1995. "Networks and Synchronisms in Southeast Asian History". *Journal of Southeast Asian Studies* 26, no. 1: 10–16.
Matisoff, James A. 1991. "Sino-Tibetan Linguistics: Present State and Future Prospects". *Annual Review of Anthropology* 20: 485–86.

McNeill, William H. 1963. *The Rise of the West*. Chicago: University of Chicago Press.
Milner, Anthony, and Deborah Johnson. 1997. "The Idea of Asia". In *Regionalism, Subregionalism and APEC*, edited by John Ingelson, pp. 1–20. Melbourne: Monash Asia Institute.
Mus, Paul. 1933. "Cultes indiens et indigènes au Champa". *Bulletin de l'École française d'Extrême-Orient* 33: 367–410.
Noor, Farish A. 2016. *The Discursive Construction of Southeast Asia in 19th-Century Colonial-Capitalist Discourse*. Amsterdam: Amsterdam University Press.
Pearson, Michael. 2003. *The Indian Ocean*. London: Routledge.
Pollock, Sheldon. 2006. *The Language of the Gods in the World of Men: Sanskrit, Culture, and Power in Premodern India*. Berkeley: University of California Press.
Von Richthofen, Ferdinand. 1877. "Über die zentralasiatischen Seidenstrassen bis zum 2. Jh. n. Chr.". *Verhandlungen der Gesellschaft für Erdkunde zu Berlin 1877*: 96–122.
Sanderson, Alexis. 2009. "The Śaiva Age: The Rise and Dominance of Śaivism during the Early Medieval Period". In *Genesis and Development of Tantrism*, edited by S. Einoo. Tokyo: Institute of Oriental Culture, University of Tokyo.
van Schendel, Willem. 2002. "Geographies of Knowing, Geographies of Ignorance: Jumping Scale in Southeast Asia". *Environment and Planning D: Society and Space* 20: 647–68.
Singh, Upinder and Parul Pandya Dhar, eds. 2014. *Asian Encounters: Exploring Connected Histories*. New Delhi: Oxford University Press.
Strathern, Alan. 2018. "Global Early Modernity and the Problem of What Came Before". *Past & Present* 238, Issue Supplement no. 13: 317–44.
Subrahmanyam, Sanjay. 1997. "Connected Histories: Notes towards a Reconfiguration of Early Modern Eurasia". In "The Eurasian Context of the Early Modern History of Mainland South East Asia, 1400–1800". Special Issue, *Modern Asian Studies* 31, no. 3: 735–62.
———. 2016. "One Asia, or Many? Reflections from Connected History". *Modern Asian Studies* 50, no. 1: 5–43.
White, David G. 2012. "Netra Tantra at the Crossroads of the Demonological Cosmopolis". *Journal of Hindu Studies* 5: 145–71.

Part I

Conceptualizing the Region: Past and Present

1

Locating Asia, Arresting Asia: Grappling with "the Epistemology That Kills"

Farish A. Noor

I. THE ARRESTING GAZE: ASIA IS FRAMED

Asia reveals itself, over iced coffee.

A few years I ago I found myself walking down Orchard Road in downtown Singapore. I walked past one of those generic coffee bars that serve beverages that purport to have some family resemblance to coffee; and chanced upon two tourists who were sitting outside as they enjoyed their iced caramel lattes. Both were male, Caucasian, and both were uniformly dressed in some kind of "Camel Trophy-Safari" kind of get-up (presumably to blend in with the background, if not each other). Then one of them said to the other: "I believe that here I have found the heart of Asia".

That Asia can reveal its heart over iced coffee in a high-street urban coffee bar is not surprising, for that is indeed the state of Asia today. Before proceeding any further, I would like to situate this discussion in the context of the here-and-now, which is a *modern* Asia that exists firmly in the modern era.

In this chapter I wish to raise a problem—*one that I have not been able to resolve myself*, and one which is itself a symptom of the modern times we live in. That we today are embedded in modernity seems fairly self-evident: Asia's political boundaries today are basically the same boundaries that were drawn in the nineteenth century, when the power of colonial capitalism was at its height. Our nation-states, built as they were on the foundations of colonies of the past (none of which were ever democracies, it could be added) are fundamentally modern constructs in the mould of the Westphalian model. Our epistemologies and vocabularies are likewise modern, replete with references to citizenship, economic agents, assets and commodities, territories, and spaces that are often taken as ontologically set and given. In terms of who and what we are, our sense of identity and what constitutes identities that are Asian are also predicated upon a binary logic where an oppositional form of dialectics is seen to be at work.

As a teacher who is interested in both the history and politics of Asia, I am struck by how *modern* our political concerns and praxis are today: here in Southeast Asia much of what passes as national and regional politics now comes in the form of contestations over identity and meaning; sometimes in the ways through which we have commodified our identities and claimed them as "national" identities, sometimes in the ways through which we have made claims on others and accused others of cultural/identity appropriation, etc. Jameson (1991), in his work on Postmodernity, has already noted the salient features of late industrial capitalism which we see all around us now: bricolage, commodification, and the politics of identity-difference. And in the ways through which we, Asians, today have come to know ourselves and represent ourselves to ourselves and others, we likewise replicate and reproduce the very same modalities of knowing and understanding that Cohn (1996) saw and documented during the colonial era of the nineteenth century.

In an Asia where "native identity" can be commodified, bought, and sold, a veritable market of the "authentic" has emerged since the postcolonial era which rests happily within the broader framework of market commodification in general; and where Asians can buy their identities at the mall and engage in different ways of merrily exoticizing themselves to their hearts content. Scholars such as Richter (1989) and Burns and Novelli (2007) have written at length about the political economy of tourism in Asia,[1] and how that industry has not only served as a source

[1] Richter (1989) has noted that "tourism is a highly political phenomenon, the implications of which have only been rarely perceived, and even less understood. Furthermore, it matters a great deal whether the public and key policymakers are able to grasp the fact that, although tourism has a carefree frivolous image, the industry is huge, highly competitive, and has

of state revenue but also as a means through which Asia's politics of identity has been reproduced and kept alive.[2] That same tendency towards ossification and arrest (of meaning) has been seen elsewhere by scholars like Talib Ahmad (2008), whose writing on the official historical narratives in some Southeast Asian countries has pointed to the tendency to narrowly select elements of the past to present a flattened-out, homogeneous, and static reading of history that is both nationalist and essentialist at the same time.[3]

---

acute social consequences for nearly all societies... Today tourism is the largest industry in the world and is expected to maintain that status at least up to the second half of the twenty-first century. In 1985 world-wide tourist expenditure was estimated to be around 1,800 billion dollars. Over 125 nations in the world consider tourism to be a major industry, and in nearly a third of those countries it is the major national industry, a top earner of foreign exchange and the major source of employment. Even in a country as affluent as the United States, tourism is the second major industry, the largest tradable service export, one of the top three sources of revenue for 39 out of the 50 states, and the employer of 6 million Americans, the country's second biggest employer." (pp. 2–3). Furthermore "for many governments the explicit impetus for encouraging tourism is economic. Tourism is sold by the international travel industry as a non-controversial way to accrue foreign exchange without losing non-renewable resources. Tourism is elastic in demand in the way that most agricultural products are not and as a service industry it is sometimes assumed, erroneously, that it is labour-intensive. It is argued that the tourist dollar, via a multiplier effect, infuses the local economy with several times the original dollar's value before its effect fades. Unlike other economic policies, tourism supposedly attracts foreign capital easily, requiring only the inducements most developing nations are willing to accept... But regardless of its initial motivation, the political impact of tourism is extremely important". (p. 14).

[2] Celebrating the indigenous may well end up being little more than marketing them for the sake of tourist dollars, and as Susan Keitumetse (2007) has argued, the theme of "primitive", "culturally pure" and "uncontacted" *indigeneity* is problematic for the simple reason that it requires the repetition and reproduction of stereotypes about the Other; in doing so, it permanently freezes the indigenous other in terms that are negative and further perpetuating the notion that the viewer/visitor is endowed with a higher moral consciousness and a superior rational sensibility. Be it in the case of African societies that were studied by Keitumetse or Asian societies, the celebration of ethnic indigenous identity is always problematic, particularly when it also comes under the rubric of the tourist and heritage industries (p. 110).

[3] Abu Talib Ahmad, in his study of the state museums of Malaysia and the representations of history in them, notes that in the case of the official state museums of Kelantan, Trengganu, Selangor, Kuala Lumpur, Penang and Sabah there is a tendency by the museum authorities to present an official account of the history of each respective state, but in a manner that conforms with the official history of Malaysia as described and narrated in the history textbooks of the country. Ahmad highlights the collusion between official

As noted by Tyson (2010), the net result of these processes has been a return to a politics of essentialized authenticity in some parts of Asia, where national identities have been anchored upon essentialized and reductivist readings of culture, and where becoming ("authentically") indigenous has assumed the status of a political-economic project, accompanied by its own political economy that revolves around a buy-off-the-rack mode of cultural production and where Asians can now self-exoticize themselves whenever they feel the need to "find themselves", in accordance with the hegemonic logic of the market.[4]

historians and museum curators (p. 46) and how both institutions effectively reinforce each other's somewhat narrow perspectivism, leaving students, readers, and museum visitors with a singular impression of Malaysia's historical development that allows no room for alternative readings of history or contingency in the progression of history. Furthermore, as Malaysia's official history came to be written by an increasingly closed-off coterie of historians who were themselves partisan to the needs and agendas of the ruling elite, these official histories (both in books and museums) reflected the narrow and monological perspective of the ruling elite in power. Therefore, as Ahmad notes, there are scant references to the role played by opposition movements and parties in the historical development of Malaysia, and in some of the state museums there are few references to the hybrid, fluid, and cosmopolitan origins of Malaysia: the long historical presence of communities such as the Orang Asli, Chinese, Indian, and Arab migrants who later settled in Malaysia to be neglected, marginalized, or left out entirely in many of the state museums he studied (pp. 51–52). Another interesting observation that Ahmad makes is that in some of the state museums there are few negative accounts of the Japanese occupation of Malaysia during World War II, and few references to the atrocities committed by the Japanese armed forces (particularly against the Europeans and Malayans of Chinese ethnic background). Ahmad contrasts this to the manner in which Singapore's museums have been more explicit and objective in their treatment of the Japanese occupation, regardless of how such accounts of Japanese atrocities were not keenly welcomed by Japanese tourists in Singapore (pp. 66–67.)

[4] Tyson's work looks at the revivalism of *adat* traditions in the outer island provinces of Indonesia following the fall of the Suharto regime in 1998 and the move towards decentralization of power from the political capital Jakarta to the local governments of the provinces. Many scholars have been critical of the process of decentralization in Indonesia for the reason that the advocates of decentralization have often been local elites who stand to gain the most from the dispersal and distribution of power and economic resources; and that many groups and movements that have pushed for further decentralization have couched their appeals on the discourse of native or local particularism and exclusivism, at times leading to the rise of local variants of micro-nationalism among ethnic communities that seek to reclaim power and territory on the basis of remedial rights and entitlements. In Tyson's work on the demands that were made by community leaders in Sulawesi he notes that the demands of the Toraja people of Tana Toraja were often linked to political demands for greater economic control and access to local resources, but these demands were also

These developments have naturally occasioned an academic response, and much work has already been done on the phenomena of commodified identities and its attendant political economy. Likewise scholars have looked at how identities—both ethnic-national and religious—have been policed by both state and non-state actors across Asia.[5] As the philosopher Zygmunt Bauman argued recently, "the question of identity has changed from something you are born with to a task: You have to create your own identity"[6] and in the process of making those identities, all manner of tropes, metaphors, and overdetermined signs have been put to work.

My own concern has less to do with the political economy of identity politics, or the manner in which identities are constructed and at times contested/claimed by various actors. Rather, my deeper concern lies in the manner in which we have come to know Asia, and been able to make epistemic claims of knowledge about Asia and Asians. For apart from the violence of exclusive claims and acts of (sometimes forceful) appropriation, I believe that there is an even deeper level of violence that needs to be addressed, as it strikes at the very heart of our work as teachers, artists, and writers. My own focus is not on identity-making and identity-contesting as bricolage, but rather on the violence of naming, and thus knowing. It is a problematic that was raised by Todorov in his important work, *The Conquest of America* (Todorov 1984).

II. THE FIRST ACT OF VIOLENCE: I NAME YOU, AND THUS I KNOW YOU

> Nomination is equivalent to taking possession.
>
> *Tzvetan Todorov, The Conquest of America* (1984)

---

catering to the needs of local political parties that no longer claim a national appeal and mandate, but rather that seek to "protect" their territories on the basis on nativist-essentialist claims to belonging and entitlement. As such, *adat* revivalism was more than an instance of "staged authenticity" and certainly more political in nature and intent.

[5] An instance of such policing was seen recently, when a minor scandal broke out in Thailand over a tourist ad that featured elements of Thai history as well as historical personages who are regarded as being almost sacrosanct in Thailand today. As a result of the furore that ensued, the ad was eventually taken off TV. See BBC, *Thai Tourism Video Stirs Cultural Heritage Debate*, http://www.bbc.com/news/blogs-news-from-elsewhere-37484447.

[6] Re Interview with Zygmunt Bauman, *Social Media Are a Trap*, in *El Pais* English edition, 19 January 2016, http://elpais.com/elpais/2016/01/19/inenglish/1453208692_424660.html.

Todorov's *Conquest of America* is instructive for us today, for it was in this work that Todorov wrote at length about what he called "the knowledge that kills". In his account of the European conquest of America, Todorov argues that long before the massacres that decimated and destroyed the civilization of the native Americans came another form of violence that was equally catastrophic, and it was in the form of a desire to *know* the Other. Todorov's Columbus was not merely an explorer who was bent on appropriating the lands and riches of others for his monarch, but an enquirer "who performs a 'finalist' strategy of interpretation" ... where "the ultimate meaning is given from the start". Columbus does indeed come to conquer and subsequently know the land and people he has conquered, but "he knows in advance what he will find", for the Other was already defined in dialectical terms as the constitutive Other to Europe even before he set off on his journey (Todorov 1984, p. 17). As Columbus and his men fought their way into the interior of America, he begins to build his own order of knowledge and power through the act of naming the places he visits and planting his flag. Todorov argues that "others' words interest him very little", as Columbus sought to rename places according to the typological ordering that he introduced, and which made sense to him, according to his own register of signification and meaning (ibid., p. 27). The up-shot of this enterprise is the *epistemology that kills*; an epistemology that does come to know the world, but from a singular perspective that does not admit the validity of other epistemologies. The foundational act of violence was the *naming* of *America* itself, for with that singular act an entire continent and all the communities in it were made knowable while rendered voiceless at the same time.

America may have been a nominal construct to the Europeans who conquered it, but it was no mere nominal construct like "mountains" and "hills", "traffic jams" and "political crises" are. America was both a sign and signifier that was loaded with meaning from the outset, and that meaning was subsequently imposed upon both the land and the people who were named.

The relevance of Todorov's work for our own concerns lies in the way he has identified the root of the problem itself, which lies in the violence that is inherent in the act of *naming*. Granted that we cannot possibly escape language, and that any understanding/experience of the world around us is mediated through language—*one of the premises of discourse analysis being the claim that reality is discursively constructed*—we are still left with the moral and philosophical burden of knowing, and how to know *anything* without doing violence to the thing itself. What holds true for

America also holds true for Asia; and if the foundational act of violence meted out upon America came with its naming, then would that not be the case as well for Asia, whose naming was the first step in the process of arresting it and rendering it a simple and fixed idea?

As we grapple with the complex project of imagining and reimagining Asia/s today, it is important to understand how and why we ended up with this predicament in the first place. It might, therefore, be useful for us to return to the beginning, and look at how that singular notion of Asia came about, and how a thing as complex, multifarious, and fluid as that could be brought within the arresting gaze of violent scholarship. And like many foundational myths, the etymological roots of "Asia"—as it was seen and defined by Western scholars—was likewise rooted in myths as well.

In 1520, Johannes Boemus published his *Omnium Gentium Mores, Leges et Ritus*, which is regarded as the first work of ethnography produced in the Western world.[7] Translated into other major European languages and republished throughout the sixteenth and seventeenth centuries, the work was considered an authoritative account of societies beyond Europe at the time. Asia appears in the second part of the work, and from the outset is described in terms both mythical and monumental:

> Asie (Ἀσίη), the seconde part of the thre wherin to we haue said that the whole erth is diuided; tooke name as some hold opinion, of the doughter of Oceanus and Tethis, named Asia (Ἀσία), the wife of Iaphetus, and the mother of Prometheus. Or as others affirme, of Asius, the sonne of Maneye the Lidian. And it stretcheth it self from the South, bowtyng by the Easte into the Northe: hauyng on the Weste parte the two flouddes, the Nilus and Tanais, and the whole Sea Euxinum, and parte of the middle earth sea. Vpon the other thre quarters, it is lysted in with the Ocean, whiche where he cometh by Easte Asie, is called Eous (as ye would saie toward the dawning) by the South, Indicus (of the countrie named India) and after the name of the stoure Scithiane, vpon the northe Scythicus. The greate mounteine Taurus ronnyng East and West, and in a maner equally partyng the lande in twaine:

[7] So influential was Boemus' work that many other editions were produced, translated into other European languages. In 1555 William Waterman translated the work and had it published under the title *The Fardle of Facions,* and in 1611 Edward Aston issued a second version under the title *The Manners, Lawes and Customs of all Nations.*

> leaueth one parte on the Northe side, called by the Grekes the outer Asie: and another on the South, named the inner Asie.[8]

Having advanced from classical Hellenic sources, Boemus' account of Asia extended it beyond the limits that had been set by Herodotus, for whom Asia had stopped at Anatolia and the Persian Empire. Boemus lists amongst Asia's peoples the Medeans, Parthians, Persians, Scithians, Tartars, and Indians. Of the Indians "of Ynde", he claims that there lived among them some tribes where the people "have no neckes, and have their eyes in their shoulders" and others with "dogges heades"[9]—descriptions that would later be taken up and repeated in the writings and engravings of Sebastian Munster, whom Boemus obviously influenced and inspired. Muster's *Geographia* (1540) and *Cosmographia* (1544) would borrow many of the themes of Boemus' work, and the maps that accompany his writings were full of images of Asians of all sorts, including the famous dog-headed Asiatics and headless men whose faces were found on their chests instead.

That "Asia" emerges from within the corpus of classical Western mythology is telling, for it means that Asia—though cast and framed as the Other beyond the pale of Europe—was never radically outside the discursive economy of Western mythology. And because the Other is always an "internal Other" that is bound within the oppositional dialectics of identity and difference, there is never a radically exterior Other that can be known/spoken of. From the outset, Asia is framed in dialectical terms as Europe's constitutive Other, and can only be known thus, in dialectical terms.

The framing of Asia as Europe's Other becomes readily apparent in the writings on Asia that followed in the wake of Boemus' work. For scholars like Theodorus de Bry (and his sons Theodore and Israel de Bry), the encounter with Asia—that was depicted for the first time in their work which offered among the first glimpses of life in India and Java (1601)—was problematic, for it meant having to recognize an Asia that was both civilized and yet different (or more explicitly, non-European) (De Bry and De Bry 1601). De Bry found it easier to depict the New World that

---

[8] From the English translation of the work by Waterman (1555): ebooks.adelaide.edu.au/h/hakluyt/voyages/.

[9] Ibid.

was being discovered in the fifteenth to sixteenth centuries, for there it was possible to frame America in terms that made sense according to the logic of revealed knowledge and scripture: in his work on America there are copious references to the rites and rituals of the native Americans that were described and illustrated in a manner that confirmed the logic of differentiation that separated Europeans from the "heathens and savages" of the New World, all of which confirmed—in the eyes of de Bry and his readers—what scripture had foretold and which reinforced the distinction between a Eurocentric-Christian understanding of civilization and what was regarded as pagan barbarism.

Asia, however, could not be depicted and understood in the same manner that the New World had been framed. In de Bry's work, we see some of the first images of India and Java which revealed a complex, dynamic, and prosperous Asia whose socio-cultural landscape was likewise complex and rich: In the engravings of the port-city of Bantam (Banten) in Java, we see different communities engaged in trade and politics; ships of all kinds and sizes that hail from different parts of Asia; soldiers and citizens whose dress and accoutrements point to active local industry. Yet despite the complexity of socio-economic life that we see captured in these early images, Asia resists exoticization for the simple reason that much of the dynamism that is captured in de Bry's work also happens to be mundane: trade and commerce, governance and administration, are at work here.

Notwithstanding the fact that Asia was populated by Asians who were every bit as mundane and ordinary as the next European, the tendency to frame Asia as a place that could be known in exotic and extraordinary terms would continue in the writings of subsequent authors, such as Walter Raleigh (1614). Raleigh's account of the history of the world takes off from premises that were biblical and European, and in his work an eschatology of sorts can be seen, where Asia marks both the beginning and end of human endeavour. With compass in hand, Raleigh sets off to find the exact location of Paradise, which he argued could be located precisely:

> Of the feate and place of Paradife, all ages haue held difpute; and the opinions and iudgements haue been in effect, as diuers, as among thofe that haue written vp on this part of Genefis, as vpon any one place therein, feeming moft obfcure: fome there are, that haue conceiued the being of a terreftrial Paradife, without all regard to the worlds Geographie and without any refpect to Eaft and Weft, or any

> confideration of the place where Mofes wrote, and from whence he directed the way how to finde out and iudge, in what region of the world this garden was by God planted, wherein he was exceeding refpective and precife. (Raleigh 1614, Book I, Chapter 3.I. p. 33)

Through a combination of deft reasoning and some selective appropriation of facts, Raleigh comes to the conclusion that Paradise is real, that it is on earth, and that it is located in the Indies. The maps that accompany his work include references to places that already existed and were real enough, such as Bengal, Malacca, Sumatra, Pegu, and parts of maritime Southeast Asia; but also pinpoint the exact location of the garden of Eden somewhere in present-day Iraq. But here again it can be seen that Asia can only be understood and rendered knowable to Western eyes from a Western perspective, as the background to a larger cosmic drama taken from Old Testament sources. Nowhere in Raleigh's work does Asia speak for or of itself, and nowhere in the work are any concessions made to the possibility that Asia and Asians may have their own cosmologies and belief-systems that locate the region and its people—both geographically and epistemologically—according to registers that are different.

As a nominal construct, Asia had meaning, and was made meaningful in works such as Raleigh's. In the centuries that followed, Asia's importance and meaningfulness was amplified even further in the writings of Europeans who came to see it as a place that was distinct from Europe, a mirror-inversion and constitutive Other to what Europe was, could be, and was meant to be. In both fictional and non-fictional works, Asia was examined and its meaning expanded further: Thomas de Quincey's *Confessions of an Opium-Eater* (1822)—being itself a biographical work that straddled the fuzzy boundary between non-fiction and the delusional—is a case in point, where Asia is conjured up in the dreams of the opium addict as a place that was overdetermined in meaning and where the Occidental Self was dwarfed in comparison. After a chance encounter with a mysterious Malay who popped up seemingly from nowhere, Quincey writes about how the encounter had triggered in him a succession of nightmares of an Asia that was vast and overpowering:

> This Malay, partly from the picturesque exhibition he assisted to frame, partly from the anxiety I connected with him image for some days, fastened afterwards upon my fancy and that upon my dreams, bringing with him other Malays more worse than himself who ran am-muck at me, and led me to a world of nocturnal troubles… That

> Malay has been a fearful enemy for months. Every night, through his means, I have been transported into Asiatic scenery… Southern Asia, in general, is the seat of awful dreams and associations. As the cradle of the human race, if on no other ground, it would have a dim, reverential feeling about it. The mere antiquity of Asiatic things, of their institutions, histories, above all their mythologies—is so impressive that to me the vast age of the race and name overpowers the sense of youth in the individual. Man is a weed in those regions… The vast empires, also into which the peoples of Asia have been cast, give a further sublimity to the feelings with Oriental names and images. (de Quincey 1822, p. 95)

And if Asia could be imagined by de Quincey as the seat of vast empires that overpowers the sense of youth in the individual, then a similar view of Asia as a land of boundless opportunity and untold wealth could be read of the pages of other modern European writers whose framing of Asia (and Asians) conformed to the logic of racialized colonial-capitalism as it developed during the era of the militarized colonial companies. Confining ourselves here to scholarship on Southeast Asia, we can see that in the works of men like Johan Nieuhof (1682), Wouter Schouten (1708), John Stockdale (1812), Stamford Raffles (1817), John Crawfurd (1829, 1830), John Anderson (1826), etc., Asia was not simply any nominal construct, but one that was imbued with meaning and value.

The most important difference that we need to take note of, however, is that by the time we get to the late eighteenth to nineteenth centuries, Europe's understanding and framing of Asia was no longer couched in a discourse that was rooted in Western mythology, theology, or metaphysics, but rather a modern, rational, scientific (and often also pseudoscientific), and instrumentalist discourse that found its home in the very real structures of colonial-capitalism and colonial power. The nineteenth century framing of Asia was a modern one, where all the tools and discourses of modernity were in attendance, ranging from pseudoscientific theories of racial difference to a thoroughly modern mindset that set out to arrange the world (soon to be colonized almost entirely) according to typologies and violent hierarchies that made sense and were meaningful to those who worked within the belly of the colonial enterprise.

The modern turn in Europe occasioned the secularization of Western society and the Western worldview as well; and as Europe's power expanded globally so was this push towards desacralization extended worldwide. By the nineteenth century the religiously informed worldview of the likes of de Bry and Raleigh were long forgotten, and with that went the sacred geographies and cosmologies of both the West and Asia: the modern colonial-companies of Britain, Holland, and France were less concerned about the location of Paradise and the garden of Eden, and more interested in coal deposits, paddy fields, and rubber plantations. The understanding of land and nature, space and territoriality that emerged from the nineteenth century onwards changed how Asia was seen, and how space and the landscapes/seascapes of Asia were configured as well: landscapes became territories to be occupied and commodified, and seascapes became vectors for maritime power-projection. Empire rendered the whole world a battlefield, and Asia became contested territory.

In the course of this transformation we are all familiar with the ways through which Asia and Asians were reinterpreted and redefined again, to meet the ends of militarized colonial-capitalism. Looking at the region of Southeast Asia, we can see that not only was Southeast Asia identified, located, placed, and defined, but so were its constituent parts: Raffles (1817) framed Java and the Javanese as a land of antiquity trapped in a past that had to be conquered in order to be curatored and brought into the order of Western historiography; Crawfurd (1829) had framed Burma and the Burmese as a land and people oppressed by Asiatic tyranny and who needed to be rescued by the forces of the British navy and the army of the East India Company; Anderson (1826) in turn presented Sumatra as a land of boundless natural wealth that could be liberated by colonial-capitalism; while Borneo was seen and cast as the den of pirates and head-hunters, whose potential would only be realized after the arrival of the gunboat. In all these cases, Asia was known and made knowable; but through every act of knowing-naming, the Other was disabled as well.

That Asia was framed and defined is, in itself, not the core problem which deserves our attention; for if Asia is to be understood in any way it would undoubtedly be framed in one way or another. And though the definition and framing of Asia did involve the dialectics of identity-difference, and employed the use of typologies and violent hierarchies, I would argue that this needs to be understood in the context of East-West relations and differentials of power that were the norm in the colonial era.

My own concern here lies in the baser, simpler question of whether we—as scholars who work on Asia today—can ever situate ourselves outside a discursive economy where such modalities are at work, and how we—today—can try to reframe and rethink "Asia" in a manner that avoids or lessens the violence that seems embedded in the act of knowing-naming.

If we are to attempt such a thing, we should perhaps begin by accepting the fact that such a project is situated in the here-and-now of Modernity, and that we ourselves are trapped within, and defined by, the same logic of Modernity as well.

III. OUR POST-EMPIRE IMPERIAL EPISTEMOLOGIES

> Power is the ability not just to tell the story of another person, but to make it the definitive story of that person.[10]
>
> *Chimamanda Ngozi Adichie, The Danger of A Single Story* (2009)

> We all have to accept reality, yes, that's true. But just to accept reality and do nothing else: that is the attitude of human beings who have lost the ability to develop and grow, because human beings also have the ability to create different realities.
>
> *Pramoedya Ananta Toer*

I do not think that I (or anyone) need to apologize for being opposed to Empire, but I also do not think that we—as modern subjects—have been able to exceed the limits of Empire that easily either. On the contrary I do feel that we—again, as modern subjects—continue to live and labour under the long shadow of the nineteenth century, and in so many ways our worldviews, epistemologies, and vocabularies of today are also the worldviews and vocabularies that we have inherited from the recent past.

That the vocabularies and epistemologies of Modernity and colonialism continue to inform us, and continue to frame Asia and Asians in terms that are debilitating, can be seen everywhere: their workings can be seen in our political economies, our statecraft, our modes of governance, and the ways through which we understand, present, and re-present ourselves. Traces of this vocabulary are found all around us, from our tourist ads—where invariably Asia can only be presented in terms exotic—to our history books, where the postcolonial nation-state takes centre stage as the primary (and often only) actor on the stage of history, and our histories are invariably national histories cast and written in a distinctly Westphalian mould.

[10] Chimamanda Ngozi Adichie, *The Danger of A Single Story*, TEDGlobal 2009, July 2009. http://www.ted.com/talks/chimamanda_adichie_the_danger_of_a_single_story/transcript?language=en.

The problem seems to be the very vocabularies that we have inherited, and which happen to be the vocabularies that we use today in modern academic work. A cursory overview of the histories that have emerged in and across postcolonial Asia would show that in many ways we—scholars of Asia today—are still caught in what could be called an "imperial epistemology" where the very words we use to describe, frame, and name phenomena have had their meanings set since the nineteenth century. Consider, for example, the manner in which the postcolonial "official" national histories of Asia have been written, and how they foreground the nation-state as the primary actor. The national histories of many postcolonial Asian countries have the tendency to backdate the presence of the postcolonial nation-state to a past when nation-states did not even exist; as a result of this, we have the history of Indonesia being backdated to the era of Majapahit and Srivijaya, and even earlier, despite the fact that it could be argued that those who built the temples of Prambanan and Borobudur did not toil away in the Javanese sun with the idea of the Indonesian Republic of the future as their goal.

And when describing political phenomena of the past to a present-day audience, it can be seen that the only vocabulary we have at our disposal is one where signifiers like "empire", "hegemony", "power", etc., are already sedimented and defined in terms that were set by the nineteenth century. Postcolonial Asian historians write about the glorious past of great Asian civilizations and empires like the Cholas of India or the Ming of China, but in terms that strike me as surprisingly modern and contemporary. But if these were indeed "empires" (as we understand "empires" today), then pray tell—where are the fortresses, garrisons, and barracks of these so-called empires that had (supposedly) such hegemonic power over the rest of Asia? If the Chola "empire" did indeed extend all the way to Southeast Asia as some historians suggest, then can we unearth concrete evidence of the kind of imperial mode of governance and power-projection that we would associate with, say, the Roman empire, or the British empire?[11]

[11] As an aside, I would like to address one of the more interesting developments we have seen in recent times, namely India's "Look East" policy and its attempts to re-establish socio-cultural and economic bonds with the nation-states of Southeast Asia. Contemporary India's "Look East" policy may be old news by now, and several attempts have been made by successive Indian governments to reactivate the residual memory of South Asia's long-term impact on Southeast Asia. But what has hampered such initiatives is the tendency of

On the contrary, I would argue that signifiers like "empire" are wholly inappropriate when we try to describe the socio-political-economic realities of Asia before its encounter with Western modernity, and to use such terms today would entail a flattening out, and homogenization, of all kinds of socio-economic-political life in Asia that would conform to a particular Western historical model.

One of the reasons why we have not been able to escape this modern vocabulary is because the very tools of analysis and description that we use are themselves *modern*. And the way that our histories, sociological and anthropological research, cultural studies, etc., today tell the history of Asia is often a modern recounting of the tale. Our research—much of it analytically and methodologically sound and bona fide—is nonetheless *modern* research, and consequently reveals the workings of modernity at play. This is true of some of the best works on Asia we have seen since the post-war era, and works like Steinberg's (ed.) *In Search of Southeast*

many postcolonial historians, both in India and Southeast Asia, to write national histories that are narrow and compartmentalized, and which foreground the nation-state as the primary actor in history. The problems with this are manifold, not least the simple fact that any retrospective reading of Indian history that goes back to a time when the very signifier "India" was not in use is itself erroneous and misleading. Additionally I find that many of these initiatives have taken off from the premise that India once had "empires" whose territorial reach and cultural influence extended all the way to and across Southeast Asia, which is likewise problematic, for the simple reason that these were not "empires" in the sense of the British empire, with colonies that were under military occupation and direct political control. Chaudhuri (1990) was correct in the manner that he depicted Asia as a patchwork of economic-cultural centres that were in constant engagement and dialogue with one another, and when he argued that political-economic influence then (in the premodern era) was more indirect and informal, that came in the form of trade, movement, migration, and settlement instead. Thus when we look at the long-term cultural imprint of South Asia's Indic culture on Southeast Asia—that is manifest in the traces of its Hindu-Buddhist architecture and plastic arts, material history, languages, and mythology—we should perhaps see this as a result of long-term cultural borrowing and adaptation between individuals and communities, rather than states or the result of state policy. Equally important is the need to understand and appreciate the fact that movement, migration, and contact across Asia in the premodern era occurred without the attendant vocabulary of states, national identities, and borders, and as such did not bring with it any sense of "cultural expansion" or political-hegemonic purpose. If South Asian mystics, merchants, and migrants moved to Southeast Asia then, it was to attain a range of objectives: to preach and convert, to trade, to settle, etc. To speak of the "Indianization" of Southeast Asia, on the other hand, suggests a sense of common national purpose that may never have been there in the first place.

Asia: A Modern History (1987) come to mind: thorough though the scholars of that edited work were recounting of the history of Southeast Asia, they were nevertheless working within the parameters of nation-states as ontologically given entities that were/are clear and distinct. The history of Southeast Asia that we find in Steinberg's edited work is one that traces the development of Southeast Asia to the era of nation-states, but one that also compartmentalizes the criss-crossing histories, geographies, and cosmologies of the peoples of the region within set political borders; and as a result—driven as it was by a teleology—the work leads us "naturally" to the modern era of nation-states while inadvertently relegating to the silenced margins the communities that straddled borders, communities without borders, and those communities that-might-have-been.

In fields such as International Relations and Political Theory (both of which impacted upon Area Studies and Asian Studies in so many ways), states, borders, territories (both terrestrial and maritime) were, and remain, ontologically given things that are deemed valid objects of analysis. And it is in those domains that we see "Asia" well and truly fixed as an ontological object that is identifiable and locatable, notwithstanding the discursive construction that went into the idea of Asia itself.

At the same time, scholars who reside in other domains of the humanities have grown increasingly concerned and critical about the manner through which Asia has been nominated, labelled, and categorized, and historians in particular have gone to great lengths to show how Asia's location (as a discursive construct) has never been an accidental or innocent one. Awareness of the fact that the framing and labelling of Asia in terms that are exotic, strange, alluring, etc., has always been part and parcel of the dialectics of naming where Asia was named by others, and we have also seen attempts by scholars to reverse or overturn the violent hierarchies that have located Asia and Asians in a negative position, as the constitutive Other to the West/universal norm. Some of these attempts, however, have led to a mere overturning of violent hierarchies without ending those hierarchies instead; and have come in the forms of nativist-essentialist scholarship that extols Asian identities as positive (such as the "Asian values' debate of the 1980s) while keeping the logic of binary oppositions intact. On a personal note I would like to state clearly that in my opinion such strategies do not work, and in fact do a disservice to scholarship in the long run; for such projects have often led to the production of self-serving and self-referential nationalist narratives that are reductivist in nature, and where everything Asian is seen as positive and everything Western is cast in a negative light.

I raise these points here not as an excuse to avoid speaking about Asian history or politics, and certainly not as an appeal to any kind of Asian "authenticity" or difference couched in essentialist terms. Rather my concern is far more mundane and basic, and it lies in my deep disquiet that our very vocabulary may be a disabling one which does not capture the complexity of a premodern Asia as was mapped out in the work of scholars like Chaudhuri (1990). But how else can we speak of Asia without recourse to a vocabulary that is replete with signifiers like "states", "territory", "sovereignty", and so on? And can we ever conceptualize Asia without there being an Other to it? Are we, in short, destined to forever repeat this cycle of violent nomination/naming and the violence of Othering the Other?

Granted that we cannot simply step (radically) out of the discursive economy of modernity, we can still interrogate it from within and perhaps even try to upset some of forms of binary logic we see at work there.

Living and working as we do in the poststructuralist era where we no longer regard texts as canonical and binding, and where the death of the author has already been proclaimed by Barthes, our own readings of the works on Asia written in the past can likewise be complex and nuanced. A text that comes to mind is Raffles' *History of Java* (1817), which, as Bastin has noted, was even then regarded as a work of propaganda. But as I read that work today, I am less interested in Raffles' account of Java—for frankly I find very little of that—but more interested in the perspective of the author, which becomes blatantly, even painfully, clear at times. Raffles' *History of Java* is, for me, less a history of Java and more a history of Raffles himself, the company he served (East India Company) and the country he belonged to. Less a history of Asia, that same work can, and perhaps should, be read as a history of the West and of Western imperialism across Asia. It tells us more about the norms and values of the men of Empire, and of the workings of Empire's complex of power-knowledge that can be critically assessed and exposed along Foucauldian lines today. By doing so, we do not eradicate or nullify the powerful dyads and binary logic that is at work in Raffles' writing, but we expose them for what they are: discursive strategies that were put to work in the project of creating a nominal construct called "Java" (and "Javaneseness").

The same strategies can be employed in the work that we—scholars of Asia—do, and we already see instances of this kind of critical thinking taking place in contemporary deconstructive history, in the human-centric geographies we are doing, in the emphasis on subregional studies where localities and "home" need not be confined and determined by the borders of modern nation-states. Asia is not about to go away, and it will always remain as a domain of interest and study. But what we need to recognize is that the very tools we have used to study Asia in the recent past—conventional histories and geographies, political economic analyses of states as units, etc.—are wanting and evidently inadequate.

The modern state is ill-equipped to deal with the complexity that is everywhere to be seen in Asia today, but I pin my hopes on the social sciences and humanities, where critical theory now holds sway and where a healthy incredulity of meta-narratives and grand/official narratives are seen. But all of this takes off from the here-and-now, and by us admitting to the fact that we ourselves are embedded in a Modernity we cannot escape from, but can interrogate further.

Bibliography

Abu Talib Ahmad. 2008. "State Museums and their Representations of the Past in Malaysia". *Journal of the Malaysian Branch of the Royal Asiatic Society* 82, pt 2: 45–70.

Anderson, John. 1826. *Mission to the East Coast of Sumatra in MDCCCXXIII, under the Direction of the Government of Prince of Wales Island.* London: William Blackwood, Edinburgh, and T. Cadell Strand.

De Bry, Johan Theodore, and Johann Israel De Bry. 1601. *Icones Sive Expressae Et Artifitiosae Delineationes Quarundam Mapparum, Locorum Maritimorum, Insularum, Urbium, & Popularum: Quibus & Horundem Vitae, Naturae, Morum, Habituumque Descriptio Adiuncta est: Veluti Haec Omnia, In India Navigatione Versus Orientem Sucepta, diligenter Obseruata, Adeoque Tribus Hisce Indiae Orientalis Descriptae libris inserta funt.* Frankfurt.

Chaudhuri, K.N. 1990. *Asia Before Europe: Trade and Commerce in the Indian Ocean from the Rise of Islam to 1750.* Cambridge: Cambridge University Press.

Cohn, Bernard S. 1996. *Colonialism and Its Forms of Knowledge: The British in India.* Princeton: Princeton University Press.

Crawfurd, John. 1829. *Journal of an Embassy from the Governor-General of India to the Court of Ava.* London: Henry Colburn.

———. 1830. *Journal of an Embassy from the Governor-General of India to the Courts of Siam and Cochin-China.* London: Henry Colburn and Richard Bentley.

Grafton, Anthony. 1992. *New World, Ancient Texts: The Power of Tradition and the Shock of Discovery.* Cambridge, Mass.: Belknap Press of Harvard University Press.

Jameson, Fredric. 1991. *Postmodernism, Or the Cultural Logic of Late Capitalism.* Durham: Duke University Press.

Keitumetse, Susan. 2007. "Celebrating or Marketing the Indigenous?". In *Tourism and Politics: Global Frameworks and Local Realities*, edited by Peter M. Burns and Marina Novelli. Amsterdam and Oxford: Elsevier Press Advances in Tourism Research Series.

Nieuhof, Johan. 1682. *Zee- en Lant-Reise door verscheide Gewesten van Oostindien, behelzende veele zeldzaame en wonderlijke voorvallen en geschiedenissen. Beneffens een beschrijving van lantschappen, dieren, gewassen, draghten, zeden en godsdienst der inwoonders: En inzonderheit een wijtloopig verhael der Stad Batavia.* Amsterdam: de Weduwe van Jacob van Meurs.

de Quincey, Thomas Penson. 1948. *Confessions of an English Opium Eater.* London: Folio Society. 1st published in *London Magazine*, 1821; London: Taylor and Hessey, Fleet Street, 1822.

Raffles, Thomas Stamford. 1817. "Regulations of 1814 For the More Effectual Administration of Justice in the Provincial Courts of Java", appended in *The History of Java.* London: Black, Parbury and Allen, publishers for the Honorable East India Company, Leadenhall Street; and John Murray, Albemarle Street.

Raleigh, Sir Walter. 1614. *The Historie of the World. In Five Bookes.* London: Printed by Walter Burre.

Richter, Linda K. 1989. *The Politics of Tourism in Asia.* Honolulu: University of Hawaii Press.

Schouten, Wouter. 1708. *Voiage de Gautier Schouten aux Indes orientales, Commencé l'An 1658. & fini l'An 1665. Où l'on void plusieurs Descriptions de Païs, Roiaumes, Isles & Villes, Sièges, Combats sur terre & sur mer, Coutumes, Manières, Religions de divers Peuples, Animaux, Plantes, Fruits, & autres Curiositez naturelles.* Paris: Pierre Mortier. [Republished in several editions, e.g., Wouter Schouten, *Reys – Togten naar en door Oost-Indien*, Amsterdam: Gerrit Tielenburg en Jan 'Tlam. 1740.]

Steinberg, David Joel, ed. 1987. *In Search of Southeast Asia: A Modern History.* Honolulu: University of Hawaii Press.

Stockdale, John Joseph. 1812. *Sketches, Civil and Military, of the Island of Java and Its Immediate Dependencies, Comprising Interesting Details of Batavia and Authentic Particulars of the Celebrated Poison-Tree.* London: Printed for the author, Pall Mall.

Todorov, Tzvetan. 1984. *The Conquest of America.* New York: Harpers Collins.

Tyson, Adam D. 2010. *Decentralisation and Adat Revivalism in Indonesia: The Politics of Becoming Indigenous.* London: Routledge.

2

Imagining "Maritime Asia"

Andrea Acri

INTRODUCTION

The question as to what Asia is, and as to whether there existed one or many Asia(s), has been asked many times over the past two decades or so.[1] Yet, in spite of a recent wave of studies foregrounded by "borderless"/global history, and focusing on intra-Asian connections, today's mainstream histories and geographies of Asia are largely the result of colonial and post-colonial national narratives, or of post–World War II global academe, which has framed the "Area Studies Paradigm" and (arbitrarily) divided Asia into the quadrants of South, Central, Southeast, and East Asia.

In this chapter I propose to reconceptualize (i.e., reimagine) Asia by widening the geo-historical framework through which the complex mosaic of cultural and religious phenomena linked by a shared deep history are to be investigated. I begin by offering a historiographical survey tracking the history of the concept of "Maritime Asia", and exploit it to theorize the long-distance maritime connections and dynamics of interaction among societies throughout the swathe of territory stretching from the Indian Ocean littorals to the Western Pacific. I then apply this perspective to the study of the genesis and spread of Sanskritic Buddhism across Maritime Asia from the third to the fourteenth century CE.

[1] Among the most recent contributions are Duara (2010a), Subrahmanyam (2016 and 1997), Acharya (2010), and Milner and Johnson (2001).

THE IDEA OF MARITIME ASIA

Maritime Asia can be conceived as a dynamic macro-region of intersecting discursive fields across which networks of cultural brokers travelled since time immemorial. From the early centuries of the Common Era, this macro-region constituted an integrated system of littorals and hinterlands connected by the sea routes governed by the seasonal monsoon winds. Influenced by similar environmental and climatic factors, Maritime Asia formed an ideal theatre for the circulation of crops, people, goods, languages, beliefs and ritual systems, and ideas.[2] Spreading across the superimposed geopolitical boundaries of modern nation-states, and transcending such equally arbitrary and historically constructed geographical entities as South/Southeast/East Asia, I imagine Maritime Asia as forming a single interconnected network, and arguably even an integral cultural ecumene with a shared background of human, intellectual, and environmental history. More than a mere (and static) geographical expression, Maritime Asia is a metaphor representing dynamic social networks that may help us to make sense of complex historical processes, like for example the circulation of Indic religions—most notably, tantric traditions—across Asia.[3]

A recent trend in contemporary scholarship on Asia has been the emphasis on translocal, cosmopolitan phenomena focusing on large-scale processes of socio-cultural and economic integration. Such concepts as Subrahmanyam's "connected histories", favouring flexible and fluid cultural zones rather than "civilizational" fixed representations,[4] have laid the foundations for a new wave of historical scholarship focusing on circulatory processes of cultural transfer. Research produced in the

[2] Duara (2010b, p. 1028) points out that this circulation was largely peaceful, thereby suggesting a model of Asian connections that is "weakly-bounded, network-oriented, pluralistic, multitemporal".

[3] The choice of not including a map in this chapter is deliberate: a static map, representing a mere geographical container, would not do justice to the dynamic, pulsing, multi-layered, and fluid character of the Maritime Asia model. In the absence of an interactive and dynamic digital model/computer interface, an act of the imagination is required to visualize the fluid and constantly evolving nature of this network, within (but also beyond) its geographical boundaries in the *longue durée*.

[4] See Subrahmanyam's (2016, p. 22) critique of the four civilizations existing across the Indian Ocean region, namely "Islam", "Sanskritic India", "South East Asia", and "Chinese", distinguished by Chaudhuri (1991, pp. 49–66).

past two decades has increasingly relied on the concept of "networks" to elucidate the dynamics of inter-Asian cultural transfer on the one hand, and reoriented the geographical focus towards a maritime/Indian Ocean dimension on the other.

The idea of an interconnected maritime space linking the Indian Ocean to the China Sea appears to have been developed in maritime history circles in France and Germany in the 1990s.[5] As far as I am aware, the descriptor "Maritime Asia"[6] has been first used in a systematic way in a series of volumes edited by German Sinologist Roderich Ptak—some of which jointly with French (maritime/Southeast Asia) historians like Denys Lombard and Claude Guillot[7]—on (East) Asian and global maritime history appeared in the late 1990s.[8] Geoffrey Wade (2003) uses the expression several times in a working paper reviewing European studies on the "Premodern East Asian Maritime Realm"; depending on the context, it appears to be synonymous with "maritime East Asia", "maritime Southeast Asia", or to denote the maritime space between Japan, Taiwan, and Southeast Asia, or again represent a neutral (and vague) expression akin to "maritime Europe" (denoting Europe's "maritime space").[9] Along similar lines,

[5] The preface to the volume *From the Mediterranean to the China Sea: Miscellaneous Notes*, edited by Claude Guillot, Denys Lombard, and Roderich Ptak (1998), mentions a second "Franco-German initiative on Maritime Asian History", which culminated in a symposium held in Paris in 1997.

[6] The expression is often printed as "maritime Asia" (with the "m" of "maritime" in lower case), but occasionally, "Maritime Asia" is also used, such as in the Preface to Guillot, Lombard and Ptak (1998).

[7] Ptak is apparently "inspired by the work of Denys Lombard on Southeast Asian concepts of maritime space, which in turn was inspired by Fernand Braudel's famous work on the Mediterranean" (Willis 2005).

[8] Cf. the Series *South China and Maritime Asia*, edited by Ptak, which includes, among other publications, *Asia Maritima: Images et réalité 1200–1800* (Lombard and Ptak 1994), and the above-mentioned volume by Guillot, Lombard, and Ptak (1998). See also the edited volume *Maritime Asia: Profit Maximisation, Ethics and Trade Structure* (Sprengard and Ptak 1994). In a more recent monograph, Ptak (2007) uses the term "*Die Maritime Seidenstraße*". The legacy of this intellectual tradition has been furthered in recent studies by Angela Schottenhammer (see Schottenhammer 2007; Antony and Schottenhammer 2017).

[9] This appears to be the case in a number of contributions in the field of East Asian Studies and International Studies, where "maritime Asia" would seem to reflect a Sino-centric bias: see, e.g., Leonard (1972), Brook (2017), and Busch (2013).

Robert Antony (2017) uses the descriptors "East–Southeast Asian Maritime", "Maritime Silk Road", "South China Sea World" and "Maritime Eastern Asia" as applying primarily to "the whole of Eastern Asia—from Korea and Japan in the north to Sumatra and the Celebes Islands in the south", and forming "a huge intra-regional system… an immense area [that] transcended political, linguistic, ethnic, and cultural boundaries" (ibid., p. 11).

While the denominator Maritime Asia remains relatively marginal in the panorama of Area Studies and global knowledge, which prediliges the expression "Maritime Silk Roads"[10] to denote a supra-national, sea-focused conceptualization of Indian Ocean–China Sea connectivity, it seems to have become popular in the jargon of recent publications in the fields of Strategic and International Studies, especially from China and Japan.[11] As such, it has fared much less well than the—in several respects cognate—term "Eurasia", which is now commonly used in mainstream historical scholarship, Area Studies, International Relations and, indeed, public discourse. Both terms Eurasia and Maritime Asia have contingent origins, and have not been used in a consistent way by scholars; yet, according to Hann (2016, p. 2), Eurasia "remains the best term available to denote the largest landmass of the planet, including large islands such as Great Britain and Japan". In the same way, Maritime Asia (or Oceanic Asia) may be one of the best terms to describe the southeastern rim of Asia, or the swathe of maritime and mainland territory from the Indian Subcontinent to Japan.[12] As the word Eurasia was coined to correct an ancient bias implying and separation between Europe and Asia (ibid., p. 1), so Maritime Asia seems to have been coined to correct the bias of

[10] The conceptualization of "Silk Roads of the sea" might go back to French scholar Chavannes (1903, p. 233). Sen (2014a, p. 39) argues that the labels (Maritime/Overland) "Silk Road(s)/Route(s)" are misnomers, for "Silk from China was neither the earliest nor the most commonly traded commodity. The early history of maritime trade indicates the prevalence of beads, precious stones, and pearls as the main merchandise; during the later periods, bulk goods, such as incense, pepper, spices, and porcelain dominated the trading activity" (cf. Whitfield 2007, pp. 208–10; Antony 2017, p. 1). However, since the terms "Silk Road(s)/Route(s)" have become part of the modern global parlance, I will not refrain from using them here.

[11] Wade (2003) refers to a symposium held on the occasion of the 10th Anniversary of the Japanese Research Group of Maritime Asian History, "The Potential of Maritime Asian History", Naha, Okinawa, Japan, on 1 November 2003.

[12] The other being "Monsoon Asia": see below.

landmass-based history, as well as arbitrary boundaries set by Area Studies and metageography.

Ptak and other (maritime) historians have refrained from embarking on a precise definition of Maritime Asia, considering it as a chain of spaces and exchanges rather than a continuum or unity; indeed, to my knowledge, the expression has never been defined and contextualized so as to represent a coherent heuristic device to reframe our current conceptualizations of Asia as a region.[13] An attempt to move towards that direction is Barbara Andaya's short study "Oceans Unbounded: Transversing Asia across 'Area Studies'" (2007).[14] Capitalizing on the recent endorsements on the centrality of maritime history, Andaya attempts to "transverse the academic divides separating the study of 'South', 'East' and 'Southeast' Asia", and widen the discourse to global history by using the expression "maritime Asia". It is worth quoting some key paragraphs here:

> ... envisaging an interconnected maritime Asia[15] that is not subservient to the boundaries of area studies and modern nations, and yet does not descent to the simplistic and overly general, is a formidable challenge. A number of studies have tracked trading diasporas and economic linkages, but the place of the oceans in the cultures of Asia's littoral societies has received much less attention. (ibid., p. 1)
>
> It is the human dimension that makes this interlocking relationship between land and ocean such a compelling teaching device. If we insist

[13] Duara occasionally mentions the expression in his work, yet without giving a clear definition of it (cf., e.g., 2010b, pp. 1027–28, where, having referred to Jack Goody's persuasive argument about the interconnectedness of the Eurasian world, moves on to describe maritime Asia as a model of de-militarized Asian connectivity). Similarly, Willis (1993) does not define its usage (and, like Duara and others, avoids the use of the capital "M" in "maritime"). Antony (2017) uses the descriptor "Maritime Asia" in the title of Chapter I of the edited volume *Beyond the Silk Roads* ("Integrating Maritime Asia with World, Transregional, and Local History: An Introduction"); however, while making a strong case for the need of a paradigm-shift that disentangles Asian maritime history from Eurocentric or Sinocentric models, he nowhere employs, let alone define, the expression "Maritime Asia" in the chapter itself.

[14] The version printed in the *Asia-Pacific Journal/Japan Focus* is a modified version of the one published in the *Journal of Asian Studies* 65/4, November 2006, pp. 669–90. Both reproduce her presidential address to the annual meeting of the Association for Asian Studies (AAS) in San Francisco, 6 April 2006.

[15] The 2006 version of the study reads: "interconnected Asia". The expression "maritime Asia" occurs, however, on p. 674.

> that the sea and those who live with the sea deserve a more prominent place in our study of Asia, we will take an important step in developing the framework required for any comparative overview. In turn, this framework will go a long way towards overcoming the confines of so-called area-studies while redressing the scholarly preoccupation with land-based societies that has so informed the presentation of Asian cultures. (ibid., p. 3)
>
> The "transocean" standpoint may enable us not merely to work with a larger canvas, but to capture something of the human encounters that underwrite the communication between areas and between peoples. Although there is probably no way we can be what Rhoads Murphey once termed a "complete Asianist" (Murphey 1988), we can do our best to think across the boundaries of disciplines, areas and a presentism that privileges the land. As we work ever harder to bring Asia into the academic mainstream, an understanding of the ocean and of how it shaped the lives of real people may open up new perspectives on the intertwined histories that should be integral to our projection of "Asia". (ibid., p. 18)

As challenging as it may be to arrive at a definition that is not overly general and simplistic, I conceptualize Maritime Asia as the largely maritime geographical expanse, encompassing Monsoon Asia[16] and the Indomalaya Ecozone,[17] spanning the eastern littorals of the Indian Subcontinent (and their hinterlands) in the west[18] to the South China Sea littorals (and their hinterlands), the Philippine islands, Taiwan, Korea, the Ryukyus and Japan in the northeast. The fulcrums of this region are the littorals of peninsular and mainland Southeast Asia, and the Malay-Indonesian Archipelago. Borrowing the metaphors of "cores" and "edges" applied by Wang Gungwu (see Ooi 2015, p. 121) to describe the system formed by the Eurasian

[16] A historiographical appraisal of this idea, coined by Jules Sion in the 1920s and further developed by Paul Mus in the 1930s, is Acri forthcoming.

[17] See Figure 10.1 in Sinclair, this volume.

[18] In fact, the westernmost limits could perhaps be extended to the island of Socotra between the Indian Ocean and the Red Sea/Eastern Africa (see Sinclair, this volume, p. 291). As pointed out by Subrahmaniam (2016, p. 19), for the Portuguese "there seems to have been no great desire to distinguish maritime Asia from East Africa, which for them formed a part of the same navigational continuum, and was also comprehended under the same administrative title of the *Estado da Índia*".

continent on the one hand and the Mediterranean Sea and North Africa on the other, I regard the Western Asian littorals on the Indian Ocean, the Persian Gulf and Red Sea, the Eastern African littorals, inner continental (North) India and China, Korea and Japan, the Western Pacific (i.e. Papua New Guinea and Melanesia), and even the Australian northern shores as "appendices" or "edges" linked to the sea- and land-based networks of economic, cultural, and religious exchange that collectively shaped Maritime Asia. It is worth mentioning here Lieberman's (2009, p. 10) conceptualization of premodern Eurasia as part of a coherent, integrated Ecumene connected to Southeast and East Asian "appendices" that, through comparative study, reveals parallel but independent social adaptations, climatic shifts, and commercial links—what he calls "strange parallels", i.e., synchronous developments between geographically distant regions in Southeast Asia and the wider Eurasian area. Paraphrasing and coalescing Lieberman's (2009, p. 10) set of questions on premodern Eurasia, I ask: in what ways and to what extent can we regard (the cores of) premodern Maritime Asia as a coherent ecumene?

Maritime Asia may be conceptualized not only as a world region, but also as a "socio-spatial grouping" (Lewis and Wigen 1997) constituted by a pattern of ever-changing relations dominated by basic underlying affinities.[19] This region comprised a web of coastal and inland polities connected to each other through a network of cosmopolitan port-cities across the Bay of Bengal/Indian Ocean and the South China Sea/Western Pacific Ocean, forming a "single ocean" (Wolters 1999, pp. 44–45) or, rather, a "Two-Ocean Mediterranean" (Wang Gungwu in Ooi 2015, pp. 57–93). Following an increasing recognition of the predominant role played by the sea routes or Maritime Silk Roads in shaping premodern intra-Asian connectivity, it seems appropriate to study cosmopolitan cultural phenomena as participating in complex circulatory processes involving economic/mercantile, diplomatic, and religious networks moving across the maritime and littoral expanse encircling the southern rim of Asia. The emphasis on the maritime routes—which were fundamentally interlinked with overland routes (see Whitfield 2007, pp. 206–8)—reflects the need to reposition them as keys in shaping intra-Asian connectivity. For instance,

[19] For Lewis and Wigen (1997, pp. 186–88), "world regions" cannot be defined on the basis of the idea of political and ecological boundaries, but on the basis of historical processes that yield an "assemblage of ideas, practices, and social institutions".

Ray (2013, p. 13) rightly notes that "though the seas have been important for the five millennia of human history, they are also the most glossed over in historical discourse, which has tended to focus on predominantly land-based national histories". Indeed, we need to realize that the Indian Ocean was not a physical and intellectual barrier between South and Southeast Asia, but rather a space favouring exchange and interaction. Already in 1933, Mus described the sea as a unifying factor in the region of Monsoon Asia:

> The wide distribution over the surface of the globe of the regions I have just mentioned is not as absolute a barrier as you might be tempted to believe at first. For too long, ethnography has proceeded by purely continental groupings.... A hundred, two hundred or a thousand kilometres of sea, especially where there are prevailing winds, are a distance much less considerable than a hundred, two hundred or a thousand kilometres of land, divided by mountains, forests and hostile tribes ... whenever sea lanes establish communication, it is reasonable to expect a cultural unity.... (Mus 1975, p. 9 [1933]).

Here I also think about Pearson's insight that the societies inhabiting the Indian Ocean littorals might have "more in common with other littoral societies than they do with their inland neighbours" (2006, p. 353). Cutting across the natural boundaries and barriers of continental topography, sea-based routes formed a network of conduits that led to the formation of translocal cultural phenomena such as the "Sanskrit Cosmopolis" (Pollock 2006) and the "Pali Cosmopolis" (Frasch 2017). Several scholars have highlighted the interconnected and cosmopolitan nature of the premodern Indian Ocean trade network. According to Kauz (2010, p. 1), this network emerged as a "largely coherent structure, and has been a space which served as a huge stratum connecting the various kingdoms and cultures adjacent to it, causing interchanges in all possible fields and certainly mutual influences". Asking whether the history of the civilizations around and beyond the Indian Ocean exhibit any intrinsic and perceptible unity, expressed in terms of space, time, or structures, Chaudhuri has found "a basic underlying structure, the ground floor of material life, which remained invariant while displaying variations within certain limits" (1993, pp. 1, 7). According to him (1985, p. 23), the unifying factor that "brought the whole [Indian Ocean rim] area within the operation of a single local variable" was the cyclical monsoon wind. By following the rhythms of the monsoons, sailors were forced to wait for months in foreign ports for the contrary winds that would take them back home, thus becoming agents and recipients of cultural transactions.

The physical and human unit that Chaudhury calls the "Indian Ocean system" was not limited to the sea, but included the hinterlands—even when they are far away from the shores—as its integral part (1985).[20] Similarly, Pearson (2003) has stressed the "deep structure" underlying the Indian Ocean, including climatic and physical factors. Andre G. Frank (1998) has considered the Indian Ocean area as extending to the South China Sea, and as having been central in global history for at least five millennia up to about 1800. Even more importantly, Andaya (2007, p. 6) has argued against treating the Ocean as a mere "transport surface", or a neutral medium by which goods and people moved from a place to another. Highlighting the need to imagine "the human reality that initiated and sustained commercial exchanges along ocean pathways", she views the sea "as a space for creative human activity". A scholarly desideratum is, therefore, to evaluate the impact of the sea in shaping a "maritime imaginary". As a matter of fact, most of Southeast Asia's population lives in coastal areas, and is thus subjected to a high degree of marine influence on social mores and material and immaterial culture (ibid., pp. 9–12). Linguistics and archaeology have confirmed this situation: witness the boat-shaped coffins found throughout Maritime Asia (often even at a remove from the coasts), the synonymy of the words "boat" and "coffin", the "boat-shaped" roofs of house architecture, and terms to denote social and political elements calqued on navigational jargon. Across the vast Indo-Pacific zone, boats and navigation techniques were not only connected to material technology, but also to bodies of knowledge about geography, astronomy, atmospheric phenomena, tidal and current patterns, fauna, etc. It would be unreasonable not to assume that some of those bodies of knowledge did not interact with—in the sense of both influencing and being influenced by—the beliefs, mythologies, and rituals that contributed

[20] This aspect is also stressed on Project Mausam's (see below, p. 53) official website: "The central themes that hold Project 'Mausam' together are those of cultural routes and maritime landscapes that not only linked different parts of the Indian Ocean littoral, but also connected the coastal centres to their hinterlands" (http://ignca.gov.in/project-mausam-3/project-mausam, accessed 29 June 2019). The aspect of Indian Ocean-hinterland connectivity is effectively highlighted in the edited volume on the Northern Bay of Bengal before colonialism by Mukherjee (2011).

to shape the cultures of the communities living in the maritime space that covers about a half of the earth's surface. Furthermore, it is becoming increasingly clear that communities living in coastal regions (and their connected hinterlands) experienced cosmopolitan dynamics, which can be contrasted to the more conservative and isolated communities living on mountains—some sort of "uplands-lowlands" dichotomy or "vertical geography" that has been invoked, for example, to make a case for the existence of the area of Zomia (Perdue 2013, p. 379).

Keeping in mind the above, it seems to be high time to revisit the deep past of Maritime Asia from the perspective of geoenvironmental history and maritime connectivity, and advocate a new approach that will explore the correlations between the physical environment and the multidirectional dispersal of people, goods and ideas. More evidence of prehistoric contacts between South Asia, Southeast Asia, and East Asia has turned up in recent years. The presence of jar burials, Dongson drums, Sa-Huynh ornaments, and agate and carnelian beads along the Indo-Pacific arc (Theunissen, Grave and Bailey 2000; Calò 2014) suggests the possibility of interactions and transfer of religious ideas and practices from East to South Asia, while studies on the distribution of ceramics, cowries, cultigens, and nautical terms and devices, have highlighted the regular maritime links between early farming communities in South, Southeast Asia, and East Asia since at least the first millennium BCE (Gupta 2005, p. 22; Hoogervorst 2013, p. 102; Selvakumar 2011; Yang 2014). In a series of recent studies, Bellina (2014, 2018) and Favereau and Bellina (2016) discuss Maritime Southeast Asian populations' socio-political and economic developments when the region became part of the Maritime Silk Roads system, highlighting long distance interactions and processes of globalization cross the South China Sea–Indian Ocean networks in the late prehistoric and early historical period. Building on archaeological evidence and biological and linguistic reconstructions (Bellwood 2011), as well as such ideas as Solheim's (2006) "Nusantao" linguistic and cultural network in the South China Sea,[21] Bellina (2018) presents new data on technology and material culture that suggests the existence of a prehistoric Maritime Southeast Asian "cultural matrix" prior to and during the region's integration into the wider trans-Asiatic

[21] According to Solheim, the Nusantao Maritime Trading Network covered the vast region from Japan to Madagascar and was established in 5000 BC.

maritime networks. A religious matrix extending over Monsoon Asia in the pre- and early historical period has been theorized by Dentan (2002, 2017), and discussed further by Acri (2017).

Gupta (2005, p. 21) distinguishes interactive, long-distance "processes of human dispersals and techno-cultural diffusions (including the Neolithic expansion from southern China into Southeast Asia) and short-term movements of men and material inspired by trade opportunities", arguing that the latter were usually effected through conduits opened by earlier expansions. As noted by Hoogervorst (2013, p. 12) along similar lines, there is an increasing awareness that "literary references to commercial activities between these state-level societies [across the Indian Ocean] only reveal the culmination of much older networks", which in the case of South and Southeast Asia go back to at least the second half of the second millennium BCE—thus well before the beginning of the phenomenon of "Indianization". Nephrite artefacts from Southeast Asia and Taiwan, dating to between 3000 BCE and 500 CE, have been unearthed through much of mainland Southeast Asia and the Philippines, thus providing evidence for extensive sea-based trade networks across the South China Sea (Hung et al. 2007). Long-range contacts between North China and the South China Sea or even the Indian Ocean are suggested by the findings of shell cowries in elite burials of Northern China as early as the second millennium BCE (Li 2003; Liu 2004). Certain "Austronesian" cultural and religious features have been detected in premodern Japan (Abalahin 2011, pp. 661, 676), while an argument (still preliminary, and controversial) in favour of an early direct influence from pre-Indicized Southeast Asia (and Java in particular) to Japan has been made by some scholars (Kumar 2009; Kumar and Rose 2000; Toichi, 1974; Waterson 1990, pp. 15–17).[22] Cameron (2017, pp. 25–26) has produced new archaeological evidence on the existence of a "Prehistoric Maritime Silk Road" constituting "one of a series of interaction spheres that dovetailed into other interaction spheres in the Indian Ocean extending all the way to the Indian subcontinent" from ca. 3000 BCE onwards. Blench (2013) has hypothesized an "arc of

[22] The existence of these trade and cultural networks is supported by environmental factors, namely, the currents linking Southern Japan and the Ryukyus islands to Taiwan and the Philippines (Andaya 2007, p. 6). Strikingly enough, the chant of a priestess in a royal Ryukyu anthology of 1531 "summons the spirits of Japan, China, Java and 'the southern seas'" (ibid.).

vegeculture" as early as 10,000 BP, characterized by tubers, Musaceae, sago exploitation and sugar-cane stretching between Melanesia and Eastern Nepal, correlated with linguistic evidence as well as a suite of material culture items and, perhaps, ideas. Significant instances of global (maritime) interconnections—especially in the realm of material culture—in the ancient world have been invoked by Holmes and Standen (2018, pp. 10–11) to make a point about the heuristic validity of the category "Global Middle Ages": for instance, the corals from Southeast Asia used in a ca. eleventh-century Buddhist reliquary from northeastern China, the visits of seafarers from Sulawesi to the islands or northern coast of the Australian land mass, Chinese pottery found in archaeological contexts in the Middle East, Africa, Southeast Asia and Australia, etc. It is a current desideratum for historians to connect all these findings, interpret them in the light of an overarching model, and integrate them into a new narrative, for which the category of Maritime Asia could provide a coherent geographical and socio-spatial framework.[23]

IMAGINING SANSKRITIC BUDDHISM(S) IN MEDIAEVAL MARITIME ASIA

Buddhism was an important unifying factor in Asian history. It partook of, and had an impact on, the imaginaries and related practices characterizing the Sanskritic continuum that shaped many regional sociocultural contexts in Maritime Asia, thus becoming a phenomenon of enormous importance for global history of ideas.[24]

The spread of Buddhism, and especially of its Sanskritic varieties, across Asia has been mainly studied from a perspective focusing on transmission through the overland routes or "Silk Roads", and emphasizing Central Asia as an important transit corridor and contact zone between South and East Asia. However, recent scholarship has recognized the contribution of the southern rim of Asia—especially South India, Sri Lanka, and Southeast Asia—to the genesis, transformation, and circulation

[23] An edited volume surveying evidence of pre- and proto-historical maritime cultural transfer within the geoenvironmental area of Monsoon Asia is Acri, Blench and Landmann 2017.

[24] See Sinclair's chapter on Sanskritic Buddhism in this volume.

of various forms of Buddhism(s).[25] Applying the perspective of Maritime History, Indian Ocean Studies, and Global History to Buddhist Studies, and advocating the necessity to uphold a "geographically wide framing of almost every question that can be asked about Esoteric Buddhism" (Kim and Linrothe 2014, p. 2), a strong argument can be made for the important and constitutive role played by the sea and the Southern Asian littoral and insular regions in the genesis and circulation of Buddhism across the socio-spatial grouping of Maritime Asia from the third to the fourteenth century and beyond (Acri 2016, 2018).[26] This geographically wide, and chronologically extended, perspective emphasizes the maritime interactions that occurred across geographical and cultural boundaries in the region comprised a web of coastal and inland polities connected to each other through a network of cosmopolitan ports and entrepôts from the Bay of Bengal to the South and East China Seas. In so doing, it advances an alternative, and complementary, historical narrative that takes the "southern pathways", i.e., the sea-based networks, into due consideration, thereby revealing the limits of a historiography that is uniquely premised on land-based, "northern pathways" of transmission of Buddhism(s) across the Eurasian landmass. This transregional approach emphasizes the mobile networks of human agents, textual corpora, and visual/architectural models and icons, and also contextualizes the religious, historical, and socio-political dynamics—intervening on a local/regional as well as cosmopolitan/supralocal scale—that shaped these networks as

---

[25] A critique against the predominant land-based approach in the spread of Buddhism across Asia has been advanced by Sen (2014a, p. 40). In an earlier work, Sen (2003) has unveiled the multidirectional connections existing between Asian Buddhist centres in the seventh century and their integration in the wider Asian Buddhist world in the eighth century, characterized by overlapping networks of relations that were religious as much as economic, diplomatic, and political in nature.

[26] The primary chronological framework of my studies is the period that I define by way of convention as "mediaeval", i.e., the widely used periodization referring to the post-Gupta period of South Asian history (especially as per Davidson 2002; cf. 2015, pp. 372–73). I extend the application of mediaeval to the wider area of Maritime Asia, as done by Sprengard and Ptak (2004, p. vii), and also by Wong and Heldt (2014, p. 16) with respect to China, "as a gesture to a more global history" (ibid.)—compare Abu-Lughod's (1989) and Pollock's (2006) application of the term to the Eurasian world, as well as the recent, ground-breaking and promising contribution towards the conceptualization of the "Global Middle Ages" with a focus on dynamic connections and social interactions by Holmes and Standen 2018 (and several articles in the same special issue of the journal *Past & Present*).

they moved across different geographical and cultural worlds, in order to achieve a coherent and unitary narrative to account for this complex phenomenon of translocal cultural transfer.

Although Chinese records documenting long-distance transfer of Buddhism from its northeastern Indian cradle to the outlying regions of South India, Sri Lanka, Southeast Asia, and China via the maritime routes date back to the early centuries of the Current Era, it is from the fifth century onwards that written and material evidence becomes increasingly substantial, testifying to an efflorescence of long-distance maritime contacts that were to last for several centuries to come.[27] A significant number of Buddhist monks of different ethnicities travelled far and wide, moving along the maritime routes connecting South, East, and Southeast Asia. Those sea routes, established over the centuries by a steady flow of traders and seafarers, were also plied by pilgrims and religious specialists who crossed oceans and lands in search of knowledge, Sanskrit scriptures, relics, icons, and political sponsors.

As is shown by textual, epigraphic, and art historical materials—including icons, ritual accoutrements, *dhāraṇīs*, manuscripts, and monuments—Buddhist cults, imaginaries, and ritual technologies flourished across the vast swathe of littoral, island, and hinterland territory of Maritime Asia. Buddhist vestiges recovered from the Indian Subcontinent littorals, Sri Lanka, the Maldives Islands, peninsular and coastal mainland Southeast Asia, and what are now called the Indonesian Archipelago and the Philippine islands, speak in favour of the existence of pervasive and sustained multidirectional Buddhist exchanges among interconnected nodes linking South Asia and the Western Indian Ocean to China, Korea and Japan through the maritime routes. A polycentric,[28] geographically wide, and maritime-based approach is, therefore, an intellectual *sine qua non* to fully appreciate how religious, mercantile, and diplomatic networks acted as catalysts for transmission of Buddhism far and wide across Asia over more

[27] Of course, the Hindu and Buddhist networks took over earlier, pre- and early historical networks initiated by Austronesian- and Austroasiatic-speaking navigators (Sen 2014a, p. 40; 2014b, pp. 35–36).

[28] A strong case for a multicentric circulation of Buddhism rather than a monodirectional transmission from a South Asian "homeland" to Southeast and East Asian "peripheries" has been made by Sen (2003), while Neelis (2011) has advanced a "networks approach" or "networks model" to study early Buddhism and trade networks in northwestern India. This approach individuates the nodes, conduits, and hubs that facilitated the dynamic processes of exchange, thus going beyond the metaphors of cultural "influences" that have so far characterized the scholarly discourse.

than a millennium. This approach could rectify misconceptions such as the received idea that the southern regions of India and maritime Southeast Asia had a marginal role in the Buddhist Cosmopolis, combined with an overemphasis on the dominance of Theravāda/Pali Buddhism in Sri Lanka and mainland Southeast Asia. Prior to the thirteenth century, both Sri Lanka and Southeast Asia hosted important (and even predominant, in the case of the latter area) Sanskritic Buddhist traditions, and played a constitutive role in the genesis and transmission of both nascent and consolidated forms of Mahāyāna and Mantranaya Buddhism across Maritime Asia from the fifth to the thirteenth century. Rather than constituting mere stopovers and entrepôts for traders and voyagers, the two regions were frequented by monks and laymen alike to collect texts, relics, and icons, visit pilgrimage sites, acquire knowledge in institutionalized centres of higher learning or renowned individual masters, and receive patronage. The Malay Peninsula, Sumatra, and Java formed a strategic geographical area in the Maritime Silk Roads system that has yielded significant vestiges of its glorious Hindu and Buddhist past, yet is still under-represented in contemporary scholarship. Far from being a cultural backwater that passively received Indic influences, it held an integral place in the Buddhist world as both a crossroads and terminus of contacts since the early centuries of the Common Era. At any rate, while the contribution of the Austronesian-speaking region of Nusantara to the Indian Ocean trade network has been recognized in terms of providing superior shipping technology, nautical terminology, and ship crews, the creative and constitutive force of Southeast Asian agents and milieux in the transfer, transformation, and translocation of people, texts, notions, and artefacts in the Buddhist world remains to be fully appreciated. Indeed, a number of monks who travelled the sea routes and visited Southeast Asia—such as, e.g., Guṇavarman, Paramārtha, Yijing, Vajrabuddhi, Amoghavajra, and Atiśa—stirred up new developments in China as well as Tibet and the Indian Subcontinent.

While it is undeniable that the overland and maritime Silk Roads were fundamentally interlinked and complementary (Whitfield 2007), the combined archaeological and textual evidence points to a predominant role of the latter in enabling the mobility of Buddhist agents, artefacts, texts, and ideas over long distances from the early centuries of the first millennium CE. Maritime travel was the faster, most economical, and safest way to move people and goods in the ancient world. The sea was a connecting factor in Asian history since time immemorial, and around the first centuries CE, the seasonal Monsoon winds were exploited by maritime traders plying the routes connecting the ports in the Mediterranean Sea with those along the coastal and insular areas of South, Southeast, and East Asia. By the middle of the seventh century CE, factors such as a radical expansion of commercial maritime routes connecting South with East Asia, as well as the gradual decline of Buddhism and Buddhist exchanges in Central Asia following the Muslim conquest of Transoxiana and other socio-political contingencies, contributed significantly to the sea-based exchange not only of mercantile goods but also of Buddhist beliefs and ritual practices, and ultimately led to the formation of a global Buddhist Asia. Unlike the Central Asian ones, the interlocking maritime networks of Buddhism survived well past the thirteenth century into the nineteenth century, for instance the Bay of Bengal circuit linking Sri Lanka to Myanmar and Thailand, and the China Sea circuit linking China to Southeast Asia, Korea, and Japan (Sen 2014a, p. 55; 2014b, pp. 33–34).

CONCLUSION

Adhering to the intellectual agenda of the volume, and following the lead of recent scholarship revealing the arbitrariness of the Area Studies divide, in this chapter I have encouraged an "oceanic turn", a *longue durée* approach, and a widening of the geo-historical framework to the study of the translocal dynamics that govern historical processes transcending the boundaries of both nation-states and macro-regions as they are commonly framed in the current academe. I have also questioned the idea of Asia as a geographical continent constituted by clearly defined discrete "regions", and conceptualized it as a fluid space characterized by socio-cultural dynamics and environmental factors spanning across discrete histories and geographies.

In advocating the need for a unified historiography of the supralocal system of Maritime Asia, I should like to stress that I do not regard that concept as a "container" (i.e., a mere geographical expression), but rather as dynamic pattern, or "matrix", of linguistic, cultural, and material interactions and processes of adoption and rejection (or "homogenization" and "heterogenization") intervened over a vast—yet interconnected—area influenced by similar geo-environmental factors. In revisiting the theoretical framing of the idea of Maritime Asia by previous scholarship and reinterpreting it as a continuum—analogous to the "Indian Ocean world" or "Eurasia"—that could help us to make sense of complex interconnected phenomena in the *longue durée*, I have followed Subrahmanyam's concept of "connected histories" that favours flexible and fluid cultural zones rather than "civilizational" fixed representations, and also critiqued too a narrow-focused micro-history, "localized" ethnography and philology, and Area Studies compartmentalization.

It seems to me that the (not entirely unmotivated) negative perception towards the elaboration of grand narratives that has characterized academe from the last decade of the twentieth century, which has elevated "teleology and anachronism to the status of cardinal sins" and sometimes shown "an aversion towards asking basic questions about how we got where we are today" (Strathern 2018, p. 318), is now being problematized by a new trend of connective scholarship seeing comparative coherence to periods applied to a global perspective (for instance, the "Medieval" and the "Early Modern"). As summarized by Strathern (2018, p. 325) when discussing "Global Early Modernity", "if the diverse societies of the world are becoming more interconnected it makes sense that they will come to exhibit other comparable developments to the extent that there is some kind of loose holistic logic to their emergence". Inscribing my intellectual project in this perspective emphasizing comparativism and connectivity in the framework of temporal periodizations and spatial (re)configurations, I regard the metaphor of Maritime Asia as a powerful heuristic tool to capture the dynamics across space and time that connects seemingly disconnected phenomena, actors, geographies, and historical trajectories, to form a coherent narrative. This narrative may not be limited to definite "periods": for instance, it may be argued that the "new" Hindu and Buddhist networks of mediaeval Maritime Asia overlapped with the "old" networks of proto- and early historical Monsoon Asia, thereby creating a historical continuum. This continuum may extend from the Sanskrit Cosmopolis and the Pali Cosmopolis in Sri Lanka and Mainland Southeast Asia to the Persianate and Islamicate worlds across the Indian Ocean, Maritime Southeast Asia, and Central Asia. The Islamicate circuits overlapped with, and sometimes replaced, the Indic circuits of cultural exchange—witness the circulation of Tamil, Arabic, and Malay materials across South India, Sri Lanka, and the Malay-Indonesian world explored by Ricci (2011), or the movement of an Arabo-Malay diaspora across the Indian Ocean over the past 500 years studied by Ho (2006), or again the spread of Islam at the hands of Muslim traders across Monsoon Asia/Indian Ocean world discussed by Prange in his *Monsoon Islam* (2018).[29]

[29] Note that Prange uses the denominator "maritime Asia" multiple times in his book, along with the expression "Monsoon Asia".

In conclusion, a reframing and reorientation of the parameters of the current scholarly debate into the direction of a (truly) "connected" and "borderless" history of Asia through the metaphor of Maritime Asia has the potential to bear an influence on current global imaginaries—witness the impact of such concepts as "Silk Roads" and "Eurasia"—as well as on issues of identity and heritage construction across the world's most densely populated region. It may be apt at this point to quote Hann's (2016) opening and concluding remarks in his thought-provoking article on the idea of Eurasia:

> [...] to embrace Eurasia in the maximally inclusive sense corrects a long-term bias in the discipline [i.e. Anthropology] and at the same time gives it a fresh critical edge on the contemporary world. (2016, p. 2)
>
> I therefore argue for an inclusive conception of Eurasia in a double sense, socially and territorially. My expansive territorial usage would become universal if the establishment of a Eurasian political-economic unity were to be the prelude to a world society. If this remains utterly utopian, those fortunate enough to be able to make their living as scholars are nonetheless free to uphold such a concept, to explore its historical roots and probe its potential in the present. We are free to theorize and investigate empirically a Eurasian mental space—analogous to the way Europe is currently specified in the charters and treaties of the European Union. (2016, p. 8)

I would make an analogous point about Maritime Asia. It is perhaps significant in this context to mention a governmental undertaking recently inaugurated by India, i.e., Project Mausam (2014–2019), described as "an exciting, multi-disciplinary project that rekindles long-lost ties across nations of the Indian Ocean 'world' and forges new avenues of cooperation and exchange".[30] Its goals are, according to India's Ministry of Culture, to transcend the present-day ethnic and national boundaries, revive the lost linkages countries along the Indian Ocean shared with each other for millennia, as well as to constitute "a platform to connect discrete Cultural and Natural World Heritage sites across the Indian Ocean 'world' by providing a cross-cultural, transnational narrative".[31] By imagining Maritime Asia as a geographical arena with a shared history of human migration,

[30] http://ignca.gov.in/project-mausam-3/project-mausam (accessed 29 June 2019).

[31] https://www.iaspreparationonline.com/project-mausam (accessed 29 June 2019).

long-distance trade, linguistic contact and dispersal, and cultural transfer, we may be able to narrate highly fluid translocal dynamics and, perhaps, long-term continuities, which transcend metageography and geopolitical divisions that artificially fragment what were in origin shared cultural processes.

Bibliography

Abalahin, Andrew. 2011. "'Sino-Pacifica': Conceptualizing Greater Southeast Asia as a Sub-Arena of World History". *Journal of World History* 22, no. 4: 659–91.

Abu-Lughod, Janet. 1989. *Before European Hegemony: The World System A.D. 1250–1350*. New York: Oxford University Press.

Acharya, Amitav. 2010. "The Idea of Asia". *Asia Policy* 9 (January): 32–39.

Acri, Andrea, ed. 2016a. *Esoteric Buddhism in Mediaeval Maritime Asia: Networks of Masters, Texts, Icons*. Singapore: ISEAS – Yusof Ishak Institute.

———. 2016b. "Chapter 1: Introduction: Esoteric Buddhist Networks along the Maritime Silk Routes, 7th–13th Century AD". In *Esoteric Buddhism in Mediaeval Maritime Asia: Networks of Masters, Texts, Icons*, edited by Andrea Acri, pp. 1–25. Singapore: ISEAS – Yusof Ishak Institute.

———. 2017. "Chapter 3: Tantrism Seen from the East". In *Spirits and Ships: Cultural Transfers in Early Monsoon Asia*, edited by Andrea Acri, Roger Blench, and Alexandra Landmann. Singapore: ISEAS – Yusof Ishak Institute.

———. 2018. "Maritime Buddhism". *Oxford Research Encyclopedia of Religion* (Online resource). DOI: 10.1093/acrefore/9780199340378.013.638.

———. Forthcoming. "Revisiting the Monsoon Asia Idea". In *Monsoon Asia Reader*, edited by D. Henley and N. Wikramasinghe.

———, Roger Blench, and Alexandra Landmann, eds. 2017. *Spirits and Ships: Cultural Transfers in Early Monsoon Asia*. Singapore: ISEAS – Yusof Ishak Institute.

Andaya, Barbara. 2007. "Oceans Unbounded: Transversing Asia across 'Area Studies'". *Asia-Pacific Journal | Japan Focus* 5/4 (Number 0, April).

Antony, Robert J. 2017. "Integrating Maritime Asia with World, Transnational, and Local History: An Introduction". In *Beyond the Silk Roads: New Discourses on China's Role in East Asian Maritime History*, edited by Robert J. Antony and Angela Schottenhammer, pp. 1–24. Wiesbaden: Harrassowitz Verlag.

———, and Angela Schottenhammer, eds. 2017. *Beyond the Silk Roads: New Discourses on China's Role in East Asian Maritime History*. Wiesbaden: Harrassowitz Verlag.

Bellina, Bérénice. 2014. "Maritime Silk Roads' Ornament Industries: Socio-political Practices and Cultural Transfers in the South China Sea". *Cambridge Archaeological Journal* 24, no. 3: 345–77.

———. 2018. "Development of Maritime Trade Polities and Diffusion of the

'South China Sea Sphere of Interaction Pan-Regional Culture': The Khao Sek Excavations and Industries' Studies Contribution". *Archaeological Research in Asia* 13 (March 2018): 1–12.

Bellwood, Peter. 2011. "Holocene Population History in the Pacific Region as a Model for Worldwide Fod Producer Dispersals". *Current Anthropology* 52 (Supplement 4): S363–S378.

Blench, Robert. 2013. "Was There Once an Arc of Vegeculture Linking Melanesia with Northeast India?". In *Pacific Archaeology: Documenting the Past 50,000 Years: Papers from the 2011 Lapita Pacific Archaeology Conference*, edited by Glenn R. Summerhayes and Hallie Buckley. University of Otago Studies in Archaeology, no. 25, Dunedin: Otago University Press.

Brook, Timothy. 2017. "Chinese Charting of Maritime Asia". *Oxford Research Encyclopedia of Asian History*. https://doi.org/10.1093/acrefore/9780190277727.013.65.

Busch, Richard C. 2013. "An American Perspective on Maritime Asia". Draft paper as prepared for delivery at the 2013 East China Sea Peace Forum, 5 August 2013. The Brookings Institution. https://www.brookings.edu/wp-content/uploads/2016/06/05-american-perspective-maritime-asia-bush.pdf.

Calò, Ambra. 2014. *Trails of Bronze Drums Across Early Southeast Asia: Exchange Routes and Connected Cultural Spheres*. Singapore: Institute of Southeast Asian Studies.

Cameron, Judith. 2017. "A Prehistoric Maritime Silk Road: Merchants, Boats, Clots and Jade". In *Beyond the Silk Roads: New Discourses on China's Role in East Asian Maritime History*, edited by Angela Schottenhammer and Robert J. Antony, pp. 24–41. Wiesbaden: Harrassowitz Verlag.

Chaudhuri, Kirti Narayan. 1985. *Trade and Civilisation in the Indian Ocean: An Economic History from the Rise of Islam to 1750*. Cambridge: Cambridge University Press.

———. 1991. *Asia Before Europe: Economy and Civilisation of the Indian Ocean From the Rise of Islam to 1750*. Cambridge: Cambridge University Press.

———. 1993. "The Unity and Disunity of Indian Ocean History from the Rise of Islam to 1750: The Outline of a Theory and Historical Discourse". *Journal of World History* 4, no. 1: 1–21.

Chavannes, Édouard. 1903. *Documents sur les Tou Kiue (turcs) occidentaux, Recueillis et commentés par Édouard Chavannes*. St. Petersburg: Commissionnaires de l'Académie impériale des sciences.

Davidson, Ronald M. 2002. *Indian Esoteric Buddhism: A Social History of the Tantric Movement*. New York: Columbia University Press.

———. 2015. Review of *Making Sense of Tantric Buddhism: History, Semiology, and Transgression in the Indian Traditions* by Christian K. Wedemeyer. *History of Religions* 54: 371–75.

Dentan, Robert K. 2002. "'Disreputable Magicians', the Dark Destroyer, and the Trickster Lord". *Asian Anthropology* 1: 153–94.

———. 2017. "Fearsome Bleeding, Boogeyman Gods and Chaos Victorious: A Conjectural History of Insular South Asian Religious Tropes". In *Spirits and Ships: Cultural Transfers in Early Monsoon Asia*, edited by Andrea Acri, Roger Blench, and Alexandra Landmann, Ch. 2. Singapore: ISEAS – Yusof Ishak Institute.

Duara, Prasenjit, ed. 2010a. "Asia Redux: Conceptualizing a Region for Our Times". *Journal of Asian Studies* 69, no. 4 (November): 963–83.

———. 2010b. "Response to Comments on 'Asia Redux'". *Journal of Asian Studies* 69, no. 4 (November): 1027–29.

Favereau, Aude, and Bérénice Bellina. 2016. "Thai-Malay Peninsula and South China Sea networks (500 BCE–AD 200), based on a reappraisal of 'Sa Huynh-Kalanay'-related ceramics". *Quaternary International*, Elsevier, 416: 219–27.

Frank, Andre G. 1998. *ReOrient: Global Economy in the Asian Age*. Berkeley: University of California Press.

Frasch, Tilman. 2017. "A Pāli Cosmopolis? Sri Lanka and the Theravāda Buddhist Ecumene, c. 500–1500". In *Sri Lanka at the Crossroads of History*, edited by Z. Biedermann and A. Strathern. London: UCL Press.

Guillot, Claude, Denys Lombard, and Roderich Ptak, eds. 1998. *From the Mediterranean to the China Sea: Miscellaneous Notes*. Wiesbaden: Harrassowitz.

Gupta, Sunil. 2005. "The Bay of Bengal Interaction Sphere (1000 BC–AD 500)". *Indo-Pacific Prehistory Association Bulletin* 25: 21–30.

Hann, Chris. 2016. "A Concept of Eurasia". *Current Anthropology* 57, no. 1 (February): 1–27.

Ho, Engseng. 2006. *The Graves of Tarim: Genealogy and Mobility Across the Indian Ocean*. Berkeley: University of California Press.

Holmes, Catherine, and Naomi Standen, eds. 2018. "Introduction: Towards a Global Middle Ages". Special Issue "The Global Middle Ages", *Past & Present* 238, Issue Supplement no. 13: 1–44.

Hoogervorst, Tom. 2013. *Southeast Asia in the Ancient Indian Ocean World*. Oxford: Archaeopress.

Hung, Hsiao-Chun, Yoshiyuki Iizuka, Peter Bellwood, Kim Dung Nguyen, Bérénice Bellina, Praon Silapanth, Eusebio Dizon, Rey Santiago, Ipoi Datan, and Jonathan H. Manton. 2007. "Ancient Jades Map 3,000 Years of Prehistoric Exchange in Southeast Asia". *Proceedings of the National Academy of Sciences of the United States of America* 104, no. 50 (December): 19745–50.

Kauz, Ralph. 2010. "Preface". In *Aspects of the Maritime Silk Road: From the Persian Gulf to the East China Sea*, edited by Ralph Kauz. Wiesbaden: Harrassowitz Verlag.

Kim, Jinah, and Rob Linrothe. 2014. "Introduction: Buddhist Visual Culture". *History of Religions* 54, no. 1: 1–4.

Kumar, Ann. 2009. *Globalizing the Prehistory of Japan: Language, Genes and Civilization*. London: Routledge.

———, and Phil Rose. 2000. "Lexical Evidence for Early Contact between Indonesian Languages and Japanese". *Oceanic Linguistics* 39, no. 2: 219–55.

Leonard, Jane Kate. 1972. "Chinese Overlordship and Western Penetration in Maritime Asia: A Late Chi'ng Reappraisal of Chinese Maritime Relations". *Modern Asian Studies* 6, no. 2: 151–74.

Lewis, Martin W., and Kären Wigen. 1997. *The Myth of Continents: A Critique of Metageography*. London and Los Angeles: University of California Press.

Li Shuicheng. 2003. "Ancient Interactions in Eurasia and Northwest China: Revisiting J.G. Andersson's Legacy". *Bulletin of the Museum of Far Eastern Antiquities* 75: 9–30.

Lieberman, Victor. 2009. *Strange Parallels: Southeast Asia in Global Context, c. 800–1830*. Vol. 2: *Mainland Mirrors: Europe, Japan, China, South Asia, and the Islands*. Cambridge: Cambridge University Press.

Liu, Li. 2004. *The Chinese Neolithic: Trajectories to Early States*. Cambridge: Cambridge University Press.

Lombard, Denys, and Roderich Ptak, eds. 1994. *Asia Maritima: images et réalité 1200–1800*. Wiesbaden: Harrassowitz.

Milner, Anthony, and Deborah Johnson. 1997. "The Idea of Asia". In *Regionalism, Subregionalism and APEC*, edited by John Ingelson, pp. 1–20. Melbourne: Monash Asia Institute.

Mukherjee, Rila, ed. 2011. *Pelagic Passageways: The Northern Bay of Bengal Before Colonialism*. Delhi: Primus Books.

Mus, Paul. 1975. "India seen from the East: Indian and Indigenous Cults in Champa" (translation). *Monash Papers on Southeast Asia* 3. ["Cultes indiens et indigènes au Champa". *Bulletin de l'École française d'Extrême-Orient* 33 (1933): 367–410.]

Neelis, Jason. 2011. *Early Buddhist Transmission and Trade Networks: Mobility and Exchange Within and Beyond the Northwestern Borderlands of South Asia*. Leiden/Boston: Brill.

Ooi, Kee Beng. 2015. *The Eurasian Core and its Edges: Dialogues with Wang Gungwu on the History of the World*. Singapore: Institute of Southeast Asian Studies.

Pearson, Michael. 2003. *The Indian Ocean*. London: Routledge.

———. 2006. "Littoral Society: The Concept and the Problems". *Journal of World History* 17, no. 4: 353–73.

Perdue, Peter C. 2013. "Nature and Power: China and the Wider World". *Social Science History* 37, no. 3: 373–91.

Pollock, Sheldon. 2006. *The Language of the Gods in the World of Men: Sanskrit, Culture, and Power in Premodern India*. Berkeley: University of California Press.

Prange, Sebastian. 2018. *Monsoon Islam: Trade and Faith on the Medieval Malabar Coast*. Cambridge: Cambridge University Press.

Ptak, Roderich. 2007. *Die Maritime Seidenstraße: Küstenräume, Seefahrt und Handel in vorkolonialer Zeit*. Munich: Verlag C.H. Beck.

Ray, Himanshu P. 2013. "Introduction: Beyond National Boundaries". In *The Sea, Identity and History*, edited by S. Chandra and H.P. Ray, pp. 13–39. Singapore: Institute of Southeast Asian Studies; New Delhi: Manohar.

Ricci, Ronit. 2011. *Islam Translated: Literature, Conversion, and the Arabic Cosmopolis of South and Southeast Asia*. Chicago: University of Chicago Press.

Schottenhammer, Angela, ed. 2007. *The East Asian Maritime World 1400–1800: Its Fabrics of Power and Dynamics of Exchanges*. Wiesbaden: Harrassowitz Verlag.

Selvakumar, Veerasami. 2011. "Contacts between India and Southeast Asia in Ceramic and Boat Building Traditions". In *Early Interactions between South and Southeast Asia: Reflections on Cross-Cultural Exchange*, edited by Pierre-Yves Manguin, A. Mani and Geoff Wade, pp. 197–220. Singapore: Institute of Southeast Asian Studies.

Sen, Tansen. 2003. *Buddhism Diplomacy and Trade: Realignment of Sino Indian Relations 600–1400*. New Delhi: Manohar.

———. 2014a. "Buddhism and the Maritime Crossings". In *China and Beyond in the Mediaeval Period: Cultural Crossings and Inter-Regional Connections*, edited by D.C. Wong and G. Heldt, pp. 39–62. Singapore: Institute of Southeast Asian Studies; New Delhi: Manohar.

———. 2014b. "Maritime Southeast Asia Between South Asia and China to the Sixteenth Century". *TRaNS: Trans -Regional and -National Studies of Southeast Asia* 2, no. 1: 33–34 (31–59).

Solheim, Wilhem G. 2006. *Archaeology and Culture in Southeast Asia: Unravelling the Nusantao. With contributions from D. Bulbeck and Ambika Flavel*. Quezon City: University of the Philippines Press.

Sprengard, Karl A., and Roderich Ptak, eds. *Maritime Asia: Profit Maximisation, Ethics and Trade Structure*. Wiesbaden: Harrassowitz Verlag.

Strathern, Alan. 2018. "Global Early Modernity and the Problem of What Came Before". *Past & Present* 238, Issue Supplement no. 13: 317–44.

Subrahmanyam, Sanjay. 1997. "Connected Histories: Notes towards a Reconfiguration of Early Modern Eurasia". In "The Eurasian Context of the Early Modern History of Mainland South East Asia, 1400–1800". Special issue, *Modern Asian Studies* 31, no. 3: 735–62.

———. 2016. "One Asia, or Many? Reflections from Connected History". *Modern Asian Studies* 50, no. 1: 5–43.

Theunissen, Robert, Peter Grave, and Grahame Bailey. 2000. "Doubts on Diffusion: Challenging the Assumed Indian Origin of Iron Age Agate and Carnelian Beads in Southeast Asia". *World Archaeology* 32, no. 1: 84–105.

Wade, Geoffrey. 2003. "The Pre-Modern East Asian Maritime Realm: An Overview of European-Language Studies". Asia Research Institute Working Paper Series No. 16, December.

Waterson, Roxana. 1990. *The Living House: An Anthropology of Architecture in South-East Asia*. Singapore: Oxford University Press.

Whitfield, Susan. 2007. "Was there a Silk Road?". *Asian Medicine* 3: 201–13.

Willis, John E. 1993. "Maritime Asia, 1500–1800: The Interactive Emergence of European Domination". *American Historical Review* 98, no. 1 (February 1993): 83–105.

———. 2005. Review of Ptak, Roderich, *China, the Portuguese, and the Nanyang: Oceans and Routes, Regions and Trade (c. 1000–1600). Variorum Collected Studies Series*. Brookfield, VT, and Aldershot, Hampshire: Ashgate Publishing, 2004, *Itinerario* 29, no. 2 (July): 123–24.

Wolters, Oliver W. 1999. *History, Culture and Region in Southeast Asian Perspectives*. Singapore: Institute of Southeast Asian Studies. First edition 1982.

Wong, Dorothy C., and Gustav Heldt. 2014. "Introduction: Cultural Crossings". In *China and Beyond in the Mediaeval Period: Cultural Crossings and Inter-Regional Connections*, edited by Dorothy C. Wong and Gustav Heldt. Singapore: Institute of Southeast Asian Studies; New Delhi: Manohar.

Yang, Bin. 2004. "Horses, Silver, and Cowries: Yunnan in Global Perspective". *Journal of World History* 15, no. 3: 281–322.

3

In Search of an Asian Vision: The Asian Relations Conference of 1947

Gopa Sabharwal

In 1947, between 23 March and 2 April, New Delhi played host to the Asian Relations Conference[1] over ten days. Studying the newspapers of the time allows us to capture the minutiae of this first attempt to articulate an idea of Asia. The newspapers, an underutilized source of research, help us capture in some detail, the sentiment of the moment, the various conversations that emerged at the time, their trajectory and allow us to ponder whether what followed was inevitable.

March 1947 was four and a half months before the Indian nation formally came into being. The months leading up to the conference had witnessed the bloodiest communal riots in the eastern regions of Bengal and Bihar and more recently in Lahore, Amritsar, and surrounding areas

[1] The initial research for this paper emerged from a longer piece of academic work which is seeking to set out the events of 1947 as they unfolded, day by day, through English-language newspapers in five Indian cities. This is a multi-volume, interdisciplinary work co-authored with Anjana Sharma, Department of English, University of Delhi. The five newspapers are *Hindustan Times* (*HT*) Delhi, *The Statesman* (Calcutta), *The Times of India* (Bombay), *The Hindu* (Madras) and the *Civil and Military Gazette* (Lahore). For the writing of this piece, the *Dawn* (Delhi) had also been consulted.

of Delhi. In fact, there was ongoing unrest in and around Delhi and the Punjab during the conference—news that featured on the front pages of daily newspapers. The India to which the delegates arrived, had learnt, a few weeks earlier from the British Government on 20 February 1947 its plan for India's future—stating that they intend to leave India by June 1948. This statement and its ramifications were still being discussed in political and social circles as well as in the press at the time of the conference. The statement had also announced that there would be a change in Viceroy to oversee the transition. At the time of hosting the conference, no one had a clue that Indian independence was going to be fast-tracked from June 1948 to August 1947, and that the country would be partitioned at birth.[2] The light at the end of the tunnel of colonial rule was however visible and the country, led by Nehru, was working towards a future where India as a nation would have a global presence and establish independent relations with the other nations of the world.

Despite the volatile conditions and the acrimony characterizing Indian political life at that time, the Interim Government of India headed by Nehru went ahead with hosting the conference for which preparations had been underway for many months. The hosting of the first ever international Asian Relations Conference was viewed in the press and public in general as a unique and momentous event. The conference was deemed important enough to be covered by radio broadcast with All India Radio scheduling special programmes of recorded excerpts and eyewitness accounts.

The conference week itself was one of hectic activity on more than one front, witnessing the departure of Lord Wavell the Viceroy, who in his farewell address broadcast on radio said: "You have hard, difficult and dangerous years ahead. But you will overcome them".[3] Wavell left India on 23 March, the day of the plenary session of the conference. The new Viceroy Lord Mountbatten arrived on 22 March to take over charge and took oath of office on 24 March. There was also a change of Ministry in Madras and the boycott of the conference by the Muslim League, two days prior to the event. The All India Muslim League, led by Mohammad Ali Jinnah, which viewed itself as the sole voice of the Muslims of India, put out a statement declining the invitation to the conference on 19 March

---

[2] The announcement for independence being fast-tracked was made on 3 June 1947.

[3] "Wavell Wishes India Well", *Hindustan Times*, 22 March 1947, p. 1, col. 2.

1947, to which the Working Committee of the Asian Relations Conference put out a rebuttal clarifying the non-political nature of the conference—something that was repeated again and again in various contexts, throughout the deliberations in the days that followed. The organizers reiterated in their reply to the Muslim League that:

> the primary object of the Conference is to focus attention on social, economic and cultural problems of the different countries of Asia and to foster mutual contacts and understanding. Political problems, particularly of a controversial character or relating to the internal affairs of any participating countries are deliberately excluded from the agenda of the Conference … Mr Nehru … in August, 1946, … sought Mr Jinnah's support for the Conference and at the request of the latter, papers relating to the Conference were sent to him in Bombay. It is regretted that Mr Jinnah took no further notice of the scheme.[4]

The Muslim League statement reflected the stated political position of the League, which had been aired earlier and countered by those organizing the conference. The League said:[5]

> The so-called Asian Relations Conference which has been sponsored by the Indian Council of World Affairs, ostensibly for the purpose of fostering cultural relations between Asian countries, is a thinly disguised attempt on the part of the Hindu Congress to boost itself politically as the prospective leader of the Asiatic peoples. In convening this Conference … the Congress did not seek the co-operation of the Muslim League which alone represents the hundred million Muslims of India. It is absurd and ridiculous for a Hindu political party to pose as the sole cultural representative of this vast sub-continent, and its attempt to mislead Asiatic countries into accepting it as such is nothing short of a fraud.[6]

---

[4] "Asian Relations Conference: No Political Affiliations", *Hindu*, 21 March 1947, p. 6, col. 1.

[5] "True Character of 'Asian Conference' Exposed: League Assembly rejects Invitation", *Dawn*, 20 March 1947, p. 8, col. 1. The statement of the Muslim League, taken at a meeting of the Muslim League party of the Central Legislature, on 19 March 1947 was also reproduced by other newspapers such as the *Hindustan Times* and the *Hindu*.

[6] The *Dawn* newspaper, founded by Mohammad Ali Jinnah, had an item of on 7 March 1947, with a London dateline based on a "cable received by Indian Muslim League circles here" which suggested that the Arab States contemplating attending the forthcoming

> Nor is the present time, when internal conflicts of unprecedented magnitude are inflicting such tremendous wounds on the Indian body-politic and when the future shape of independent India is still to emerge from the welter of the present, opportune for getting together with other peoples of Asia either on the social, cultural or political plane…
>
> We regret that a number of organizations in Muslim countries should have been beguiled by the Indian Hindu Congress into consenting to participate in this conference by sending either delegates or observers. Indian Muslims are engaged at present in a struggle for their very existence with the Indian Hindu Congress at whose invitation these Muslim representatives from abroad have come ... Our Muslim brethren from abroad who have agreed to associate themselves with this move without ascertaining the views of Muslim India are unwittingly doing a disservice to the Muslim cause in India (ibid.).[7]

These views were recorded in the press and were not hidden from the public and the foreign delegates as they arrived in New Delhi, a few days before the conference. While the conference was widely publicized in the nationalist papers such as the *Hindustan Times* (HT),[8] it was subjected to bitter and sarcastic attacks in the Muslim League papers—particularly the

Inter-Asian Conference in India should reconsider the situation. The cable states, said the paper: "The Inter-Asian Conference is a political stunt and is a part of a Hindu plan to pose as the leaders of Asia .... As the Conference is not sponsored by the Government of India there can be no question of participation by Arab States as such. Their participation would be regarded by the Indian Muslims as an unfriendly gesture and would harm the Muslim cause in India". "Inter-Asian Conf. A Stunt: Arabs Asked Not to Join", *Dawn*, 7 March 1947, p. 1, col. 6.

[7] The conference committee had sent out an envoy Mr El Sayed Himmat el-Kureishy to the Middle East in February, to ensure Arab participation in the conference. The *Dawn* newspaper says that his objective is "removal of the misunderstanding that Zionists have been invited to the Conference". He carried a message from Mrs Sarojini Naidu, addressed to all official bodies and Women's Unions throughout the Middle East. "Congress Propaganda in Middle East", *Dawn*, 1 March 1947, p. 3, col. 4.

[8] The *Hindustan Times* published a ten-page Inter-Asian Conference Supplement on 23 March 1947 with articles by C. Rajagopalachari, Maulana Azad, Sarojini Naidu, K.P.S. Menon, Appadorai and others. There were columns devoted to who's who among the delegates, interviews with delegates, items on each country and special coverage of India–China relations.

Dawn.[9] The boycott, wrote Mansergh, chair of British Commonwealth relations at Chatham House, who attended the conference, brought the event into the political arena (1947, p. 302). These events did not however manage to dampen the spirit that prevailed at the moment, which seemed to echo the sense that the time was right for a homecoming of all Asian nations and for communal rejoicing, as bonds of brotherhood between nations would be renewed and established afresh. Despite what the Muslim League said, there was also a sense that India was taking its rightful place in Asia.

There is no clear information as to who first thought of hosting such a conference, and what its expected outcome was to be. The official publication that appeared after the conference, cites an interview that Jawaharlal Nehru gave to the correspondent of both the *Manchester Guardian* and *The Hindu* in December 1945, where he had explained how an Asian conference could help understand Asia's problems and promote co-operation among Asian nations. This idea was further strengthened following his tour of Southeast Asian nations in March 1946. In his inaugural address at the conference, however, Nehru shied away from taking the credit. He said "It so happened that we in India convened this conference … but the idea of such a conference arose simultaneously in many minds and many countries of Asia".[10] Observers at the conference both agree and disagree with this view (McCallum 1947a; Mansergh 1947).

In more formal terms, the responsibility of playing host to the conference had been accepted by the fledgling Indian Council of World

---

[9] "Genesis of the Asian Conference", *Dawn*, 21 March 1947, p. 4, col. 3, an edit page article by Tahir, calls the conference "a curious mixture of hush and fanfare". The reason for this he says is that the "nascent Hindu Imperialism which is staging this show is amateurish and is not perfectly sure of its ground". He traces the conference to the idea of the formation of an "Asiatic Federation", "sponsored by the 'Eastern Economist', the organ of Mr Birla" who was a businessman connected with the Congress Party, a view at complete odds with the official statement on the genesis of ICWA and the idea of the conference as put out by the Working Committee of the Asian Relations Conference.

[10] *Asian Relations being Report of the Proceedings and Documentation of the First Asian Relations Conference New Delhi, March–April 1947* (New Delhi: Asian Relations Organization, 1948), p. 1. The Report not attributed to any author, is referred to as *AR* in citations throughout this essay.

Affairs (ICWA), set up in 1943.[11] The council was "an unofficial and non-political body ... to encourage and facilitate the scientific study of Indian and international affairs" and did "not express an opinion on any aspect of Indian or international affairs" (Venkatasubbiah 1947). From the outset, as stated in the press statement to the Muslim League's charge, care was taken to uphold the assumption that the conference would be non-official and cultural and its main object would be to exchange ideas regarding the common problems faced by all Asian countries. The format chosen was that of the already established Pacific Relations Conference at Hotsprings, Virginia, which Vijaylakshmi Pandit and four others from India had attended in 1945 as representatives of ICWA, where the seeds of hosting such an event were planted in their minds.[12] The invitation issued by ICWA noted the aim of the conference as being "to provide a cultural and intellectual revival, and social progress in Asia, independent of all questions of internal as well as international politics" (McCallum 1947a, p. 13).

The topics for discussion or the agenda for the conference was initially intended to be settled by an Agenda Committee comprising representatives from all Asian countries—but given the shortage of time and the difficulties in contacting people, this idea was dropped. The conference Secretariat working through various committees took upon itself all the burden of all the tasks involved. In deciding topics to be discussed, the ICWA group took the view that "controversial issues relating to particular states, and issues which ... can only be solved at higher levels" (*AR* 1948, p. 4) were best avoided. Topics for discussion were assigned to round-table groups. These were bunched under eight heads as listed below. The categories reflect, as Noor (2014) would say, epistemologies that had been imprinted on the area by colonial regimes through a "language game" that enabled them to understand, describe, codify, and categorize their colonies (ibid, p. 56). These were now

[11] The organization is still in existence and as of 2001 has been officially taken over by the Government of India as per an Act; it is currently affiliated to the Ministry of External Affairs. Unfortunately, very few records, archives, and photographs of the Asian Relations Conference are in the Government's possession, and scholars have to look elsewhere for information on the conference.

[12] K. Santhanam, "Origin and Scope of Asian Conference", *HT*, 23 March 1947, p. 13, col. 1.

being incorporated into the discourse of the new nations, by the nations themselves as reflected in the list.

1. National Movements for Freedom
2. Racial Problems
3. Inter-Asian Migration
4. Transition from Colonial to National Economy
5. Agricultural Reconstruction and Industrial Development
6. Labour and Social Services
7. Cultural Problems
8. Status of Women and Women's Movements

On the question of invitees, there were two main issues: (1) which countries to be invited, and (2) who was to be invited from each country? It was decided to invite all Asian countries as well as Egypt, which was closely aligned to the Middle East. It was also decided to invite observers from cultural institutions in some non-Asian countries such as Australia, New Zealand, Britain, the United States, and the Soviet Union (see Table 3.1). Commenting on the invitation and the attendees at the close of the opening plenary, Nehru remarked: "there is hardly any country missing as far as I think, except one that has been prevented from coming to this Conference. One country, Japan, is not represented here—and that for reasons which are beyond Japanese control or ours" (*AR* 1948, p. 68). Nehru, in the course of an interview during the conference, clarified that he would have liked to see Japan represented at the conference, but he would not make any representations to General MacArthur or any other authorities over non-attendance of Japanese delegates invited to the conference. "It was a 'general rule'", he said, that the Japanese were not allowed to leave their country at present for such purposes … it is not as if any exception has been made in the case of this conference".[13] It is reported that the consensus of opinion of a majority of the delegates interviewed, barring one was that Japan could have attended the conference since it was of a non-political nature.[14] The *Dawn* however, reporting the same story quoting

[13] "Asian Relations Conference: Absence of Japanese Delegates", *The Hindu*, 29 March 1947, p. 5, col. 6. The only delegate quoted as having said "It is better if the Japanese should not be here" is the delegate from the Philippines. His reason was that they cannot so quickly forget the atrocities committed on their people.

[14] Ibid.

TABLE 3.1
List of Participating Countries and Organizations

Participating Countries in Alphabetical Order		*List of Observers*
1. Afghanistan	15. Kirghizia	1. Arab League, Cairo
2. Armenia	16. Korea	2. Australian Institute of
3. Azerbaijan	17. Malaya	International Affairs, Sydney
4. Bhutan	18. Mongolia	3. Australian Institute of
5. Burma	19. Nepal	Political Science, Sydney
6. Cambodia,	20. Palestine Jewish	4. India Institute, London
Cochin China	Delegation	5. Institute of Pacific
and Laos	21. The Philippines	Relations, Moscow
7. Ceylon	22. Siam	6. Institute of Pacific
8. China	23. Tadjikistan	Relations, New York
9. Egypt	24. Tibet	7. Royal Institute of
10. Georgia	25. Turkey	International Affairs,
11. India	26. Turkmenistan	London
12. Indonesia	27. Uzbekistan	8. United Nations
13. Iran	28. Vietnam	Organization, New York
14. Kazakhstan		

Source: *AR* (1948), pp. 263–64.

the news agency noted that "there is a wide divergence of opinions among delegates over the question as to whether or not the Japanese should have been present".[15] The criteria with regard to participation was set after much deliberation, and it was decided to invite:

(a) a joint delegation of sixteen from cultural associations and institutions in each Asian country and Egypt, the criteria of cultural body being applied with some flexibility;

[15] "Nehru Feels Japan's Absence in Asian Relations Conf.", *Dawn*, 28 March 1947, p. 8, col. 2. The story goes on to say that one "extreme point of view that was expressed by one observer was that while there was much talk at the Conference about the economic independence of Asia, and Britain, France and Holland were regarded as the big bad wolves ... there was little or no attention paid to the enormous physical destruction caused by the Japanese in various parts of China and South East Asia" (ibid.). The piece goes on to say that "a good many delegates do feel that the absence of Japan ... detracts from the fully representative character of the Asian relations Conference as Japan is in many ways one of the most advance of Asian Countries".

(b) individual scholars to supplement the representation from public associations; and
(c) four observers from the government of each Asian country (*AR* 1948, pp. 5–6).

In the end there were participants from twenty-eight countries and observers from another eight institutions. The total number of delegates was 190 and observers 45 (see Table 3.1). If we add to this the number of distinguished visitors and diplomats accredited to the Government of India, the number of attendees totals 400 (Mansergh 1947, pp. 296–97). The countries represented accounted for more than half of the world's population—a fact that was stated with pride by the Chairman of the Reception Committee in his welcome address. English was the official language of the conference, with interpreters available for Russian, French, Arabic, Persian, and Chinese. Some delegations like the Tibetan brought members who could act as interpreters. In one session during the conference, a lot of time was spent on the idea to develop a new world language that would serve as an auxiliary international language for Asia, and the merits and demerits of Esperanto as such a language were discussed in fair detail. The final conclusion was that English alone could be the international language of Asia (Talbot 1947). Attendance by representatives of almost all Asian nations is undeniably one of the remarkable achievements of the Conference, given the difficulties of distance, travel, and cost at the time.

In order to facilitate conference deliberations, some publications were prepared, the most significant of which was the book titled *Asia in the Modern World* which collated in one place political and economic information of varying levels of consistency about Asian countries. It is doubtful that this publication was used as a base document of any kind, and may just have ended up as a source book that few people used. There is no reference to it during any deliberations or in the report that was subsequently published, and some of the later reviews tend to point out the Asian-ethnocentrism of this publication attributing to Asia many virtues and blaming current backwardness on western imperialism (Price 1950).

Going by the public interest in the conference, the committee decided that in addition to group sessions for discussion of particular themes and the group plenary sessions for wider discussion, there should be some plenary sessions where the wider public may be allowed access to the conference delegates and their ideas. Thus, the plenary sessions planned for 23 and 24 March were public sessions while other business sessions were confined to the round-table groups. Five groups would deliberate on the topics assigned in sessions confined to delegates, observers, and some invited distinguished guests. The reports of the round table were discussed at group plenary sessions open to all delegates. At the end of the conference, on 2 April, there was a final public plenary session similar to the opening session. The detailed programme of the opening session was published in the newspapers, as also advertisements for selling tickets to the public events.[16]

Newspapers covered all details of the conference such as the detailed programme, ticket sales for public events, the entertainment being staged for delegates, the receptions by the Viceroy and Nehru, the various exhibitions from Art to Science at different parts of Delhi, and visits by delegations to parts of Delhi such as the Broadcasting House, the Central Assembly and to Birla Mandir (Temple) and the University of Delhi. The arrival of each delegation and its composition was reported by the papers. It makes interesting reading, revealing that special chartered planes were used to enable delegates to travel. A plane with the capacity for thirty-four passengers was sent to pick up delegates from Indonesia and Vietnam from Singapore. Another special plane was also sent from Delhi to enable Dr Shariar,[17] the Indonesian Premier, to arrive in time for the closing ceremony.[18] The Tibetan delegation made a twenty-one-day journey by varied means of transport including horseback and then by road, train, and finally plane. They were also described as one of the most picturesque delegation at the conference.[19] Others, like the East African delegates, arrived at Bombay by ship, before proceeding to Delhi. Newspapers also

[16] *HT*, 22 March 1947, p. 10, col. 6.

[17] There is a divergence in how Dr Sutan Shariar is referred to in the press. The spelling used in this essay is that used by the official publication of the conference.

[18] The newspapers also report that Dr Sutan Shariar would meet his wife Begum Maria Shariar, for the first time in twelve years, when he arrived in New Delhi. Begum Shriar was Dutch and was in Holland during the war. Post the war she was unable to travel to Indonesia due to "Dutch unwillingness and uncertain political relations between the Dutch and the Indonesian Republicans" ("Shariar Arriving in New Delhi Today", *HT*, 31 March 1947, p. 1, col. 3). She was flown into India by the India Office, anticipating Shariar's visit to India ("Shariar Will Meet His Wife after 12 Years", *Dawn*, 31 March 1947, p. 8, col. 3).

[19] "Tibetan Delegation Arrives in Delhi", *HT*, 20 March 1947, p. 3, col. 4.

carried pictures of delegates being received at the Willingdon Airport in Delhi. The media interest also extended to broadcasting the proceedings of the conference, especially the speeches in English, which were to be recorded on glass by the Mutual Broadcasting System of New York along with All India Radio.[20]

The opening plenary session, at 5 p.m. on 23 March 1947, at the Old Fort or Purana Qila grounds in New Delhi was conducted in a huge tented space specially created for the occasion. It was a fan-shaped auditorium that had ten thousand people in it. The delegates and the observers marched in a procession led by Mrs Sarojini Naidu, and the leaders of the delegation took their seats on the dais which was a hundred feet long. The dais had as its backdrop a large map of Asia especially prepared for the occasion, and the flags of Asian countries fluttered in the arena. Countries without national flags were represented by symbols. Since India too had not yet adopted a national flag, she was represented by a symbol designed by Ernest Joseph, interpreting the spirit of India.[21]

Jawaharlal Nehru, who at the time had the title of Vice President of India heading the Interim Government, gave the inaugural address after Mrs Naidu had delivered the presidential address and read messages from distinguished organizations and persons. Nehru first spoke in Hindustani for about ten minutes, before moving to deliver a prepared text in English. He began by addressing "Friends and Fellow Asians"[22] and evoked the shared historical past of Asia—the many linkages that existed between countries. He said:

> India always had contacts and intercourse with her neighbor countries … with the coming of British rule … these contacts were broken off and India was completely isolated from the rest of Asia. The old land routes ceased to function and our chief window to the outer world

[20] "Plan to Record Proceedings", *HT*, 19 March 1947, p. 4, col. 4.

[21] "Nehru's Stirring Call to the People of Asia", *HT*, 24 March 1947, p. 1, col. 1. The Indian symbol comprised five six-pointed stars on either side, symbolizing the high development of mathematics in India. Between these ten stars, was a seven-pointed star conveying universalism and India's spirit of absorption and assimilation. At the base were lines representing the five senses and above them a seven-petal lotus representing cultural development.

[22] Ibid., p. 20.

> looked out on the sea routes which led to England. A similar process affected the other countries of Asia also (*AR* 1948, p. 23).

Nehru was careful to focus on the future rather than the past and to stay with the theme of forging links for the times ahead. The dynamic Asia of the past, he said, became "static and unchanging" but is "again finding herself" (ibid., p. 21) and "after a long period of quiescence, has suddenly become important in world affairs" (ibid.). He also slipped in the statement:

> It is fitting that India should play her part in this new phase of Asian Development ... she is the natural centre and focal point of the many forces at work in Asia. Geography is a compelling factor, and geographically she is so situated as to be the meeting point of western and northern and eastern and southeast Asia (ibid., p. 23).

Not one to underestimate the moment, he also said:

> when the history of our present times is written, this event may well stand out as a landmark which divides the past of Asia from the future. And because we are participating in this making of history, something of the greatness of historic events comes to us all (ibid., p. 25).

He further voiced the essential agreement for all discussions, namely that,

> We shall not discuss the internal politics of any country because that is rather beyond the scope of our present meeting. Naturally we are interested in these internal politics because they act and react on each other, but we may not discuss them at this stage, for if we do, we may lose ourselves in interminable arguments and complications. We may fail to achieve the purpose for which we have met (ibid., p. 26).

In the next sentence, he set out one of those intentions: "I hope that out of this Conference some permanent Asian Institute for the study of common problems and to bring about closer relations will emerge; also perhaps a School of Asian Studies" (ibid., p. 26). Nehru referred to Gandhi who was on a village-to-village peace march in eastern India following bloody riots a few months prior, and hoped that he would visit the conference. "He is engrossed in the service of the common man in India, and even this Conference could not drag him away from it" (ibid., p. 26).

Gandhi, of course, did come to the conference in time for the closing plenary session—he had been summoned to Delhi following an urgent invitation from the new Viceroy Mountbatten for talks.[23] The talks took place on 31 March and a few days following that. Gandhi attended the conference on 1 April where he answered some questions from the delegates and formally addressed the plenary on 2 April. The other guest who arrived at the conference late (also on 1 April) was Dr Sutan Shariar, Indonesian Prime Minister, for whom it was his first public appearance at an international gathering. A message from him had been read during the opening plenary since he was in the midst of signing an agreement with the Dutch. That done, he was able to travel and was welcomed by Pandit Nehru, who introduced him to the delegates.

For the closing plenary, the crowds had increased to 20,000 visitors—and the arena had to be let out at the sides. The gathering cheered Gandhi, Nehru, Sutan Shariar, and Sarojini Naidu as they spoke at the final session. The radio coverage from Delhi and the eyewitness accounts included extracts from the speeches of Mahatma Gandhi and Dr Shariar. The radio columnist in *The Statesman* noted that this was the first time ever that Mahatma Gandhi's voice had been heard over All-India Radio (*The Statesman*, 6 April 1947, p. 5).

The general "feel good" factor and spirit of Asian co-operation that seemed to be the overarching theme of all deliberations at the conference was, however, precarious from the word go. To quote an observer at the conference:

> The cultural camouflage was something of a liability because it meant in practice that the politico-economic field was surveyed not as a whole, but only in those parts which could, in some way or other, be associated with culture … [the] one striking omission—there was virtually no consideration of strategic problems and their bearing on the new political order (Mansergh 1947, p. 295).

All the leaders of the delegations, speaking in alphabetical order of the country they represented, generally confined themselves to the broad themes, but there were references to certain political issues nonetheless. Bandaranaike from Ceylon, however, cautioned that it is

> a melancholy fact of history that when the petrifying effect of foreign rules disappears … so too at times baser motives of selfishness and

[23] "Gandhiji to Meet Viceroy", *The Hindu*, 27 March 1947, p. 4, col. 4.

> internal conflict and weaknesses rise to the surface. As Roman rule decayed and died in Europe, … [it] plunged into … the Dark Ages … We cannot allow that type of history to repeat itself (*AR* 1948, p. 40).

Despite the conference being "cultural", there was the expected reaction to separate invitations having been issued to China and Tibet. The press reported that informed sources in Nanking said that China protested informally to the Indian Embassy over the invitation from Pandit Nehru to Tibet to send delegates to the conference in Delhi in acceptance of the British Empire's Tibet policy. The Chinese Government felt that since Tibet was a part of China's sovereign territory, the Indian leader showed disrespect for the integrity of Chinese territory.[24]

While the interim government in India had very cordial relations with Nationalist China, this was not something that the Chinese would allow to pass. Yang (1987) writes that the probable leader of the Chinese delegation Dai Jitao, upset with this invitation to Tibet, declined to attend. He asked the Tibetan authorities to send their delegates to the conference along with the Chinese delegates and offered to pay for their passage—that too did not happen. Apparently, the delegates from both sides met on the plane to Delhi (ibid., p. 408).[25] Having got to New Delhi, upon entering the arena where the inauguration was to be held, the Chinese delegation was upset at seeing the map on the stage showing Tibet outside the national border of China. The Chinese Government observer, George Yeh, apparently approached Nehru and said that unless the map was corrected, the Chinese would withdraw. With the consent of Nehru, Yeh, who happened to be a calligrapher and painter, amended the map by painting Tibet in the same colour as China (ibid.). No source, other than the said article however seems to note or corroborate this incident.

As the two-day plenary came to an end, Nehru was chairing the last session and had to allow the delegate representing Egyptian women, Miss Karima El-Said to speak. She sought to respond to certain remarks in

[24] The *HT* reports in 21 February 1947, p. 4, col. 6 that Dr Carson Chang, the Chairman of the Democratic Socialist Party has accepted Nehru's invitation and applied for a passport to travel.

[25] This could at best be part of the Tibetan delegation since the papers report the arrival of the Tibetan delegation in Delhi and note that the Chinese delegation is to arrive almost a week later.

the speech delivered earlier by Professor Hugo Bergman of the Hebrew University of Jerusalem, leader of the Jewish delegation from Palestine, who referred to Palestine as the holy land for his community. Nehru remarked: "we have tried to avoid, for obvious reasons, raising and discussing controversial issues at this Conference … but some reference was made … I think it only right that she should have a chance" (*AR* 1948, p. 64). The lady delegate proceeded to state the following:

> We strongly object to any settlement in Palestine except for the Arabs …. Jews have been in Europe for the last eighteen centuries … Arabs have been in Palestine for the last fourteen centuries … we do not want British rule to be replaced by that of European Zionists … The Arabs must live in Palestine. Palestine cannot belong any more to its original inhabitants (ibid.).

The Jewish representative wished to reply, but the chairman refused permission on the ground that the conference did not permit extensive discussions on sensitive political matters. The Jewish delegates proceeded to walk out but were persuaded to return and peace was restored after hearty hand-shakes.[26] While bringing the proceedings of this closing session to an end, Nehru responded to the comments of the Egyptian delegate recognizing first that there were many problems that could be listed between nations and also within nations and if "we entered that question we would simply lose track of the real work before us here and lose ourselves in interminable arguments" (*AR* 1948, p. 70). He also hoped that "this question of Palestine itself will be settled in co-operation between them and not by any appeal to or reliance upon any outsider" (ibid.). The Arab League delegate, Taquiddeen Solh, also included a response to Bergman in his address which followed later, though the versions of what he said differ between the newspaper and the official publication. The next day, he along with the government observer from Egypt Dr Abdul Ahab Azzam issued a signed statement against Jewish designs on Palestine.[27]

The round-table sessions that then commenced comprised two sessions of deliberations and then a plenary session. Eight topics were discussed,

---

[26] "Tributes to India's Greatness", *HT*, 27 March 1947, p. 1, col. 6.

[27] "Jewish Designs on Palestine Will Be a Menace to World Peace", *Dawn*, 27 March 1947, p. 3, col. 1.

as listed in Table 3.2. The proceedings as set out in the official version make for largely predictable exchanges given that it had been agreed that there would be no resolutions passed at this conference. Despite that, there were awkward moments which the Chairpersons had to handle. The first group discussion on National Movements for Freedom, which focused largely on the need for Asian countries to end imperialism and economic exploitation and enforce the principle of self-determination, had a discussion on the use of Indian armed forces for the colonial subjugation of Burma, Ceylon, Malaya, and also possibly Indonesia. Also raised was the issue of economic and demographic aggression from India and China in smaller nations such as Ceylon, Burma, Malaya, and Indonesia.

Nehru, who was also in charge of the External Affairs in the Interim Government, made an intervention to say that the first step his Government had taken was to order withdrawal of Indian forces from Indonesia. The report adopted for this session recorded the view that "no Asian country should give any direct or indirect assistance to any colonial power in its attempts to keep any Asian country in subjection" (*AR* 1948, p. 81). The other view that seemed to emerge and gain support was the need to develop an Asian news agency so that Asian nations were to be no longer dependent upon Western news agencies for news in the region. This got expanded into an idea for the development of several national news agencies, something that subsequently happened all over the world.

The immediacy of the present was again brought to the fore by the Korean delegate who recounted that the Allied Powers had agreed that Korea should be free and independent after the war; however, when the Japanese surrendered "what the Koreans got was Allied occupation and a division of the country into two" (ibid., p. 86). With the Cairo and the Moscow declarations being unfulfilled, Korea was still waiting to get its independence. After the conference ended, leaders of the Indonesian and the Vietnamese delegations put forth a five-point programme of positive action to prevent colonialism. They said: "The Inter-Asian Relations Conference has strengthened our conviction that mutual support and actual co-operation between all Asian countries must be organized and brought into practice. Without this colonialism will always endanger the peace and prosperity of all peoples over the whole world."[28] The statement further

[28] *HT*, 6 April 1947, p. 1.

TABLE 3.2
The Round Table Sessions

Topics for Round Table	*Number of Sessions*	*Key Persons Involved*	
I: National Movements for Freedom	2	Chairman:	Mr Philip Hoalim (Malaya)
		Vice Chairman:	Sir N. Gopalaswami Ayyangar (India)
	Group A	Rapporteur:	Mr M.A. Raschid (Burma)
II: Racial Problems	2	Chairman:	Dr Wen Yuan-ning (China)
III: Inter-Asian Migration		Vice Chairman:	Sardar K.M. Panikkar (India)
	Group B	Rapporteur:	Dr Baron Haimendorff (guest: India)
			Mr Mohd Salleh Daud (Malaya)
IV: Transition from Colonial to National Economy	2	Chairman:	Mr SWRD Bandaranaika (Ceylon)
		Vice Chairman:	Mr D. Sjahroezah (Indonesia)
	Group C	Rapporteur:	Professor D.R. Gadgil (India)
V: Agricultural Reconstruction and Industrial Development	3	Chairman:	Mr David Hacohen (Palestine Jews)
		Vice Chairman:	Mr Bijaya Shum Shere Jung Bahadur (Nepal)
	Group C	Rapporteur:	Dr VKRV Rao (India)
VI: Labour Problems and Social Services	2	Chairman:	Mr N.M. Joshi (India)
		Vice Chairman:	Dr D.H. Lew (China)
	Group C +1 with Group E	Rapporteur:	Professor Humayun Kabir (India)
VII: Cultural Problems	3	Chairman:	Mr Phya Anuman Rachaton (Siam)*
			Mr V. Kupradze (Georgia)
	Group D		Dr Abdul Majid Khan (Afghanistan)
		Vice Chairman:	Mr R.P. Masani (India)
		Rapporteur:	Miss Leilamani Naidu (India)
			Mr K.G. Saiyidain (India)
VIII: Status of Women and Women's Movements	2	Chairman:	Madam Safiyeh Firous (Iran)*
			Madam Paz Policarpio Mendez (Philipines)
	Group E	Vice Chairman:	Rani Lakshmibai Rajwade (India)
			Lady Rama Rao (India)
			Mrs Renuka Ray(India)
		Rapporteur:	Miss Leilamani Naidu (India)
			Mrs Hannah Sen (India)

Note: * One session each.

pointed out that while colonialism is considered an international crime by all civilized countries, it is still operating in the homelands of the coloured peoples of Asia.[29]

The group discussions on Racial Problems and Inter-Asian Migration voiced issues that have continued to be important in the region during the ensuing decades. Much of the discussion centred upon the rights of large groups of migrants from other countries who had settled in different host countries. A division emerged between those who chose to take on the nationality of the host country and those who did not. Those who chose nationality could outnumber indigenous populations leading to other problems. The two largest emigrant countries in the region being India and China, issues such as the legal status of immigrant populations such as Indians in Burma and Ceylon, and Chinese in Malaya, Burma, and Indonesia were raised. Also discussed were dual nationality, naturalization of current immigrants, the fact that non-Burmese were outnumbering Burmese and the same was likely to happen in other smaller countries, tension and distrust amongst people, the feeling of exploitation among the local population, and the transfer of wealth to the countries of the immigrants; however, no binding declarations of any kind could be passed due to the unofficial nature of the conference.

For our present discussion, we do not need to go into a summary of every group discussion and the report adopted by each group. Certain general comments on the deliberations will suffice. As seen above, in the record of the two groups discussions, most deliberations went through the range of Asian experience in each of the areas listed for discussion. Unique situations, challenges that needed to be overcome, areas for inter-Asian co-operation, plans for furthering the growth of each country, combating poverty and other social indicators such as health, hygiene, housing and education, empowering women, the importance of universal adult franchise, building indigenous capacity in all fields be it agriculture, industrial production or creating institutions devoted to science and learning were issues that were discussed in detail.

While there was a fairly broad agreement that Asian nations needed to share information, resources, ideas, and cultural exchange, there were also moments of disagreement, and expected attempts to showcase the success

[29] Ibid.

of governance based on certain political ideologies as well as some rather bizarre ideas too. Thus, for instance, the participating republics of the Soviet Union were eager to show how the Soviet system had overcome nearly all of the problems being faced by the various nations at the conference. Kazakhstan declared that democratic reforms carried out in the organization of agriculture meant that all land now belonged to the peasants and the Government provided for the mechanization of agriculture. If Asian countries were to grow agriculturally, feudal elements needed to be deprived of their rights in land which should be handed over to the peasantry (*AR* 1948, pp. 132–33). On industry and labour issues, they said that "no strikes occurred in the Soviet Union … because industry belongs to society as a whole" (ibid., p. 165). Both Kazakhstan and Uzbekistan said that after the Revolution they had made remarkable achievements in education, which was free and compulsory (ibid., p. 194).

There were uncomfortable moments, such as when the delegate from Cambodia made a statement that Indo-China was made up of a number of countries and she "could not tolerate anyone other than these should speak in the name of her country" (ibid., p. 205). The Chairpersons and other delegates had to be alert at all times to not let anything unanticipated creep into the proceedings while letting speakers have the space to articulate their views in a frank and free manner.

In another session, the group was on the verge of passing a resolution against the rule adopted by the conference that no resolutions barring one setting up the permanent organization of the conference was to be passed. An Indian delegate actually questioned this rule and demanded to see it in writing, which led to the Steering Committee of the conference to call a meeting and pass the minutes of an earlier meeting which had recorded that no resolution would be placed or adopted by the conference, except possibly in respect of establishing a permanent institution for carrying on the work of the Asian Relations Conference.

The conference was nonetheless a euphoric moment amidst a range of predicaments that prevailed in all countries at the time. Delegates and the organizers tried to focus on the big picture and the way forward, which cannot be taken to mean that they were in denial of the pressing problems that they were all dealing with at home. These problems were of such magnitude that they were always present in the background, but there was always scope for discussion of ways to overcome them and to maybe do so with engagement from neighbouring countries.

In the case of India, the problems and reports daily featured in the newspapers for all to see, alongside the constant criticism of the conference coupled with some sensational headlines in the *Dawn*.[30] Gandhi, in a short address during the penultimate plenary session, could not keep himself from addressing this reality of the country. He said:

> I am sorry that I have to refer to the conditions that we see today. We do not know how to keep the peace between us and within ourselves. We do not know how to settle between ourselves in a humane manner … we … resort to the law of the jungle. It is a shameful thing and it is an exhibition which I would like you not to carry to your respective countries but bury here (*AR* 1948, p. 175).

In his address at the closing plenary, Gandhi used the word "carnage" to refer to the violence in India and repeated that it was a sorry and shameful thing: "Do not carry the memory of that carnage beyond the confines of India" (ibid., p. 244). Gandhi outlined the "message of the East, the message of Asia is not to be learnt through European spectacles, not by imitating the vices of the West, its gunpowder and atom bomb. If you want to give a message of importance to the West it must be a message of love" (ibid.).

Having been involved in restoring peace in riot hit villages in East India for the last few months, Gandhi said, that without humanism, or love or respect for truth, all ideas would remain just that. His speeches seemed somewhat out of place in the euphoria of the moment—Sarojini Naidu referred to that in her closing remarks when she said that the apostle of love and truth is feeble today:

> He is bent and tired with the tragic pilgrimage of his to solace the bleeding hearts of sufferers in Bengal and Bihar ... that frail body, those tired limbs, that almost inaudible voice is not Mahatma Gandhi. Gandhi is he who says, "love and forgive, love and create, love and be free". That is the message of India (ibid., p. 253).

Nehru, having bypassed the troubles in India in his speech at the opening plenary, referred to them briefly at the closing plenary and made two points—one, that this trouble does not frighten him who has to deal with

---

[30] *Dawn*, 31 March 1947, p. 1, col. 1, ran a headline "Nehru's Secret Deal with British Govt.; Accepts Dominion Status; Wants Britain to Hand Over Muslims to Him; Plan Under Consideration of Attlee's Cabinet". The source of the story is the diplomatic correspondent of a publication called *The People*. Nehru later dismissed this as "fantastic nonsense".

it officially; and secondly, that this was inevitable since one cannot have the birth of complete freedom without labour pains.

The conference thus came to a close after a bit over ten days with reasonable smoothness. The American observers from the Institute of Pacific Relations in an article on the conference wondered about "the extent to which this conference and its successors can deal in the future with Asia's needs" (Thompson and Adloff 1947, p. 97). That question does not have a simple answer. The conference, no matter what may be said about it, had a number of "firsts" to its credit. It was the first of its kind international gathering in Asia, and despite some hiccups, it did succeed in forging links—personal face-to-face links between Asian countries and their delegates. It served as a forum for Asians who had never before conferred together, to do so and to hear from each other about the prevailing conditions in their own countries. As Sutan Shariar said at the closing plenary attended by 20,000, people may question the motives for calling this assembly as well as doubt whether it will produce the desired results. What had brought Asian countries together was not a debate on the "capitalist system as opposed to … the Soviet economic system; nor was it a question of industry versus agriculture; but it was a compelling sentiment, a forceful sentiment which insistently sought expression in this Conference" (*AR* 1948, p. 240). This Asian sentiment he went on to add needed to be preserved as a holy flame which will spur all nations to greater endeavours.

The American observer Talbot wrote after the conference that "few conferences accomplish what they set out to do. Devising ways and means to keep this one under control despite explosive subjects on the agenda was a chore that had kept the Indian Planning Committee worrying nights" (1947). The observer from Britain concluded that

> Even though the Conference may not decisively influence the course of events in Asia, it was the outward and visible sign of Asia's new importance in world affairs. In placing on record the new status which the continent as a whole has assumed, the Conference has done something both to make Asian peoples politically more self-conscious and to encourage them to play a greater part in world affairs (Mansergh 1947, p. 295).

Talbot concluded by saying that "In this frankly exploratory conference many frayed and tangled threads of present-day Asian life found a chance to come together. Whether they will successfully form the warp and woof of a real continental fabric will be revealed by the progress of the new Asian Relations Organization." (1947).

The next Asian conference was to be held in China two years hence. This was announced by the Chinese delegate at the closing plenary as being the unanimous opinion of the delegates. History tells is that this conference never happened. This invitation to China may or may not have been the result of trying to assuage the feelings of the delegation on the separate invitation to Tibet. Some writers on the conference, however, seem to suggest that the Chinese delegation had been entrusted with the task of ensuring that "India did not run away with the leadership of the conference" (Thompson and Adloff 1947, p. 98). There seem to have been certain misgivings amongst the Chinese on the character and location of the permanent Asian organization. Thompson and Adloff report that lack of clarity on the form and substance of this organization "helped the Chinese in what seemed to be an undercover drive to make the permanent organization, if it must be formed, comparatively impotent and free from domination by India" (ibid.).

Mansergh summarized that the practical conclusions of the conference were threefold:

> It was decided in the first place to hold a similar conference within two years in China. It was decided in the second place to create a Provisional Council of which Pandit Nehru was to be President and on which all Asian countries were to be represented … The third decision was the recommendation of this Provisional Council that an academic institute should be set up in the capital of each Asian country with a view to studying the history and culture of Asia. These institutes would also help in a way that has not so far been clearly defined in the work of the Provisional Council (Mansergh 1947, p. 302).

Writing seventy years after the event, we know that the proposed Asian institution never quite came into being. Its establishment was announced at the closing plenary by none other than Nehru himself, who had been elected its President, but events probably overtook this initiative. Nations other than China too were not overly enthusiastic about the new organization since Southeast Asian nations were wary of both countries with Great Traditions—India and China— or, once home, post the euphoria and the oratory and confronted with more immediate and urgent tasks, most nations probably decided to tread with caution on the proposal. Amitav Acharya (2010) believes that the fear of both Indian and Chinese domination led a group of Southeast Asian country delegates to contemplate at the conference itself, and imagine a regional association of their very own—which could be regarded as a stepping stone to the formation of the Association of Southeast Asian Nations (ASEAN), which in his words again, has a better record of longevity than the Asian Relations Organization that emerged out of the 1947 conference (ibid., p. 36).

The Arabs states too seemed quiet, and were liable according to one commentator to regard the Arab League as their premier organization for action (Thompson and Adloff 1947, p. 99).The boycott by the Muslim League and Jinnah who remained in Bombay for the duration of the conference, and the fact that Jinnah had tried his best to ensure that Arab Muslims boycott the conference, all played a part in overwhelming the delegates. When the delegates arrived in New Delhi, they were "treated to such a torrent of propaganda that many of them worked hard trying to walk a tightrope" (ibid.). A controversy erupted on the very first day when the Egyptian observer Mustafa Momen, was quoted as having said on arrival in Karachi that he opposed the demand for Pakistan and that the Congress and the Muslim League should work in unison. Two days later, i.e., 22 March 1947, the *Dawn* ran a story charging the Hindu propaganda machinery of distorting the views of the Muslim visitor.[31] The *Dawn* made it its business to let the delegates from Islamic countries know that a hoax had been perpetrated on them by the Hindu Congress,[32] a message it repeated in very inventive ways.

---

[31] "Egyptian Visitor's Views Distorted: Hindu Propaganda in Action", *Dawn*, 22 March 1947, p. 8, col. 1. The story written by the *Dawn* political correspondent is based on a supposed meeting with the person concerned, who denied having made any such statement. It says that Mr Momen has written to Jinnah and other Muslim members of the Interim Government explaining he had been misrepresented. Post the conference, Mr Momen called on Jinnah in New Delhi and the 50-minute meeting got front page coverage in the *Dawn* ("Egyptian Leader's 50-minute Talk With Qaed-e-Azam", 5 April 1947, p. 1, col. 3), which quotes him as saying that Mr Jinnah is the first and foremost leader of Muslim India, and that the whole of the Muslim world feels the greatness of his personality. Both these bits of news do not appear in any of the other English newspapers.

[32] "A Fraud on Asia", Editorial, *Dawn*, 22 March 1947, p. 4: excuses the delegates for not knowing Indian reality with regard to the Muslims. "Nevertheless, the Muslim nation in this sub-continent offers them welcome—from afar. If the visitor's grasp the terrible Indian realities of the present, they will not misunderstand Muslim non-participation in this conference." (ibid). The editorial ends with a reminder to all Islamic delegates that there "is an imperishable bond and a spiritual kinship between one Muslim and another ...

On the day of the inauguration of the conference, 23 March, also observed by the Muslim League as Pakistan Day, the *Dawn* ran a story once again by its unnamed Special Correspondent, with the sensational headline "Foreign Muslim Visitors to Be Politically Doped: Congress Emissaries in Middle East Countries" (*Dawn*, 23 March 1947, p. 10). The story based on a plan purportedly being hatched by Sarojini Naidu, K.M. Pannikar and other Congressmen to invite Muslim delegates to a meeting at a Muslim venue in New Delhi where they will meet Muslim clergy and others who will prove to them that the Congress has Muslim support.[33] Caught in the crossfire of this heavy barrage of Muslim propaganda, it is no wonder that the Islamic voice was subdued. The Arab-Jew issue continued as a side show with newspaper coverage in the *Dawn*, of a press conference organized by Mr Mostafa Momen, leader of the Egyptian delegation, where he released the text of a letter written to the Chairman of the Organizing Committee of the Conference, protesting against the Jewish representatives from European countries participating as real representatives of Palestine, while the Muslim and Arab representatives of Palestine are absent. He demanded that these representatives be not allowed to speak at the closing session. He also pointed out that Egypt was the only one of eight Arab countries present at the conference.[34]

The message of striving for unanimity despite disagreement and to do so with amity and goodwill was an outcome that Nehru cited in his closing address. He compared this attempt to other similar attempts at internationalization and the pragmatic challenges they confronted. Talking of the United Nations he said:

---

which no propaganda by the enemies of Islam can sunder or alienate. We refuse to believe that there is a single Muslim among the delegates and observers … who when put to the test of the brotherhood of Islam, will be found wanting" (ibid.).

[33] "Foreign Muslim Visitors to Be Politically Doped: Congress Emissaries in Middle East Countries", *Dawn*, 23 March 1947, p. 10. The piece further states that hired "Maulvis" (Islamic expert) have been employed to keep Muslim delegates and observers constant company. It says that delegates of Egypt and Iran have become aware of how they are being "doped". It goes on to say that Sardar Patel misused the government departments under his control to send out emissaries to the Middle East to garner support for the conference.

[34] "Organizers' Open Anti-Arab Attitude: Mostafa Momen's Protest Against Jewish Propaganda", *Dawn*, 3 April 1947, p. 8, col. 1. No representative from the Palestine Jewish Delegation spoke at the closing session.

> We stand for the United Nations because therein lies some hope of world co-operation and world peace. Yet the United Nations have not functioned in an obviously united way. They have not set an example of peace and goodwill in their attempt to function together. I hope those are only the troubles of early beginnings which they will survive to lead us to a better and co-operative world. Therefore we support the United Nations (*AR* 1948, p. 248).

These words may also have been a guide for how he hoped the proposed Asian Relations Organization or ARO as it was being referred to, much like the UNO, would shape up.

It is also appropriate at this point to ask the question regarding what kind of idea of Asia emerged at this conference. There were two stated images of Asia that were put out by the organizers—one was the cartographic map of Asia on the stage at the public plenary venue, and the other was the description of Asia in the conference publication: *Asia in the Modern World* by Venkatasubbiah (1947), which also draws on the cartographic origins of the word Asia. This description is what the book opens with. It reads:

> The Greeks gave the continent of Asia its name. Actually Eurasia is a single continent, but it suited the Hellenic navigators charting the Aegean waters to call the land they saw at sunrise as Asia and the land they sighted at sunset as Europe—from the Greek root words, *asu* and *ereb*, which respectively mean the two phases of the sun (ibid., p. 1).

This explanation of the origin of the word Asia differs from the conception of Asia as set out in Boemus's account or that of Herodotus (Noor 2016, pp. 27–28). While there is no universal acceptance of the origin of this nomenclature, it does point to the more widespread idea of defining Asia in terms of separating the East from the West or Europe from Asia—a practice that gained currency in post-colonialism, the line being of course totally arbitrary. Situated as this conference was in the time that marked the beginning of the end of colonialism, what did the inhabitants of the landmass known as Asia—the participants at the Asian Relations Conference—put forth as an idea of Asia? Were there many ideas of Asia? Not to forget that the conference also invited Egypt, for they believed that while Egypt is "geographically part of the African continent its population wholly belongs to the Asian community" (Venkatasubbiah 1947, p. 17).

The speakers, almost all seemed to say something about Asian interrelations and not about the idea of Asia. For instance, there was a strong recognition of Asia being a region whose people once met frequently and were now meeting as strangers. The common ground of cultures that go back to antiquity and have encountered other cultures and have shown both resilience and change, were themes that were reiterated. The more eloquent speakers at the conference all had comments on defining Asia, Asian unity, and the Asian perspective in some way, for example, by drawing upon distinctive Asian history and contribution to the world. Nehru in his opening speech was careful to make the point that Asia as a whole owed much to China and the Arab countries, and still had much to learn from others who had made remarkable progress. He was also careful to state that the aim of the conference was not against any country or continent, but to establish that the "countries of Asia can no longer be used as pawns by others" (*AR* 1948, p. 24). He spoke of an Asian message to the world but said that "we cannot carry a message to others unless we know it ourselves" (ibid., p. 249): "Asia is not merely something on a map—a place for the rivalry of imperialisms or a region where there are large markets to be exploited, but … it consists of human beings with dignity and a long past behind them, … who are going to have a big future" (ibid.). He however confined himself to see this future common ground emerge from the Asian Relations Organization that was proposed at the conference and from the setting up of academies or schools for Asian studies.

Is this a subdued Nehru? May be so. But then he was speaking at a time and place where the world as a whole had just emerged from the ravages of war and the countries at the conference were almost all waging their own distinct struggles, with some like India on the threshold of becoming nations on maps with boundaries and frontiers that were being drawn by the very imperialists who had disrupted their lives two centuries ago. This was a time for realpolitik as opposed to big words, nostalgia, or grand ideas, and Nehru was no longer just a freedom fighter but someone who held political office as head of the Interim Government. His approach is suggestive of that role coupled with a recognition of the challenges India faced, the foremost being poverty. He was probably also desirous of bringing the conference to a peaceful close, having seen first-hand the many near misses on various political fronts which were indicative of how precarious relations between nations could be. There also seems to have been a written protest by some delegates just prior to the closing session demanding that the delegate from Cochin-China, Dang Ngoc Chanh,[35] from the Ministry of Interior, be not allowed to speak at the closing session. This incident finds mention in none of the papers barring the *Dawn* (*Dawn*, 3 April 1947, p. 1), which carries the full text of the letter addressed to the president of the organizing committee, protesting against the presence of French-sponsored delegates from Cochin-China, or southern Vietnam.[36] The concerned person did not speak at the closing session.

Sutan Shariar, the first Prime Minister of Indonesia, expressed his happiness to meet his "far flung Asian family—our spiritual and cultural brothers", and welcomed the conference as a chance "to provide Asians the opportunity to plan and execute orderly and co-ordinated development along humanistic and international lines" (*AR* 1948, p. 239). He touched upon the motivating factor behind this gathering and termed it "a forceful sentiment which sought expression in this Conference" (ibid., p. 240). This sentiment, he said, "is the result of centuries of humanitarian endeavour on the part of all Asians. We have cultivated it with such fervor that it is now a powerful force ... which widely used should help us realize not only the vision of the 'One World' we have been striving for, but also the dream of the oneness of mankind" (ibid., p. 241).

This "One World" will begin with "One Asia" of the Asian sentiment, ended Shariar. Nehru too had used the term "One World" in his inaugural speech and said that for it to happen Asian countries would have to co-operate. Nehru had said at the opening session that Asia is finding herself and it would be a fair to conclude that at this gathering, the idea of Asia was a work in progress and something that had to be constructed. To quote Nehru: "Strong winds are blowing all over Asia. Let us ... welcome them for only with their help can we build the new Asia of our dreams" (ibid., p. 27).

Sarojini Naidu, known for her eloquence and not hampered by holding political office, built on the idea from Nehru and evoked the essence

---

[35] The official publication *Asian Relations*, spells the last name as "Chanh" while the *Dawn* spells it as "Chang".

[36] "Delegates Protest against Viet-Nam Quisling's Participation in Asian Conference", *Dawn*, 3 April 1947, p. 1, col. 3. The letter requested the organizing committee "not to allow the notorious Viet-Namese quisling named Dong Ngoc Hang to speak at the closing session of the conference. By doing so the Conference will show itself faithful to the cause of the oppressed peoples and express the earnest wish of all the delegates." Names of all sixteen signatories are listed.

of Asia, namely its spirit that, though buried for centuries, was alive and ripe for a renaissance. What will Asia do with her renaissance, she asked, and concluded that it will redeem the world through compassion, love, and forgiveness. In her concluding remarks Sarojini Naidu said: "go back to your countries and say: 'We were mistaken … the heart of Asia is indivisible and one'." (ibid., p. 253). The message all around was for peace and to rebuild connections, countries, cultures, people, and hearts.

Gandhi, coming straight out of his tour of riot-hit villages, a tired and broken man, given the amount of violence and destruction he had seen in the previous few months, evoked the names of wise men from Asia—Zoroaster, Buddha, Jesus, Moses, and Mohammed—and said that Asia has to conquer the West with the message of love that these teachers have left. The West, he said, was despairing of the multiplication of atomic bombs and the world as a whole had to be delivered from wickedness and sin (ibid., p. 245).

Surprising as it may seem, it is evident that the "idea of Asia" articulated at this conference had yet to emerge and take form, but what the gathering sought to do is set the ground rules for this idea to be established. There was no mention of the Japanese idea of "Asia for Asiatics". The overwhelming sentiment at the conference was that while all efforts to recapture the dignity of Asia and its nations needed to be made, this identity need not be constructed as a binary to Europe or America or any other part of the world. Equally important was the plea for peace, for not starting violent recriminations for actions of the past but instead look ahead to make a new future. The theme of "One Asia" was a plea for Asian countries to maintain peace amongst themselves and for the larger ones like India and China to assure the other nations that they had no colonial or expansionist designs. To what extent that has happened and how much of an "Asian way" of handling issues, if there is such a way, has influenced Asian and world affairs is a story that is still unfolding. The past seventy years are indicative of how this idea was not a box to be ticked but something that will continue to form as nations mature and grapple with events on both the national and international stage.

Since 1947, various other regional subgroupings have been attempted, such as the Association of Southeast Asia (ASA) in 1961, which grew into the Association of Southeast Asian Nations (ASEAN) in 1967; the Asia-Pacific Economic Cooperation (APEC) in 1989, with the newest being the East Asia community or EAS (East Asia Summit) in 2005. Those groupings are flexible, as is best illustrated in the case of the EAS, which included India, Australia, and New Zealand in the group.

In doing so, Acharya says the grouping took a "functional rather that a geographic view of East Asia" (2010). The grouping is proving to be even more non-exclusive by subsequently inviting both the United States and Russia to join in 2011.

As an aside, the founding of the new Nalanda University in 2010 with the support of the EAS participating countries, and nurtured by leading scholars from the region, as an institution to focus on inter-Asian linkages, may just be an inadvertent step in fulfilling that last wish articulated by Nehru in his closing speech that India and indeed every Asian nation should have an academy or School for Asian Studies which will focus on Asian cultures, languages, and all other things pertaining to Asia. To what extent this institution will succeed in fulfilling this dream remains to be seen.

The idea of Asia is, if anything, a dynamic concept that will continue to be cast and recast over time. Asia, no matter how defined, will continue to be an object of analysis, enquiry and discovery. In fact, newer ways of mapping the region and its linkages have emerged—notions such as the Sanskrit Cosmopolis (Pollock 2006) and Monsoon Asia have emerged in addition to other ways of looking at Asia, including Emerging Asia (Duara 2010; Acharya 2010). These multiple signifiers each in their own way challenge the constructed identity of Asia as a unified space defined by "gunboat epistemology" (Noor 2014), but also put forth frameworks that may actually challenge, redefine and establish linkages that are deeper and more meaningful to the people of Asia.

The versatility of the concept and the varied shape it may be given is also demonstrated by the introduction of the Asian Games in 1951, in New Delhi, a venture that has stood the test of time. Moreover, the seventeen unbroken editions of the games have also served as a canvas for regional sports to make their bid for international recognition as seen in the introduction of judo and taekwondo in the 1986 Seoul games; kabaddi, sepak takraw and wushu in the 1990 Beijing games; karate in the 1994 Hiroshima games and pencak silat, sambo, jujitsu and kurash making their debut in the 2018 games in Jakarta–Palembang, Indonesia—the eighteenth edition of the games. Busan 2002 was the first time that all forty-four member countries of the Olympic Council of Asia participated in the games, a feat repeated in Doha (2006) where all forty-five member nations were present as they were in Guanzhou (2010) and Incheon (2014)—a much better record than many of the other regional groupings. Other subregional sporting activates like the South East Asian Games (SEA Games) emerged from the original Southeast Asian Peninsular Games in 1959 and the acceptance of sport for regional interaction has led to the creation of the smaller East Asian,

Central Asian, South Asian and West Asian games in 1993, 1995, 1984 and 1997 respectively, with varying degrees of success.

In the past seven decades, Asia and Asians have continued to connect in many ways beyond the established lines of trade and commerce and national boundaries and interests. These linkages are both actual and virtual between people, societies, products and ideas and have extended into newer and hitherto unexplored realms including food, music, movies and literature to name a few. In a world where the avenues of engagement with other cultures have expanded manifold, the resultant modes of experiencing and defining Asia are emerging anew and will no doubt provide yet new conceptions on how to map and evaluate interactions, interests and linkages. These newer engagements are also slowly gaining academic engagement both at the micro level and the theoretical or analytical level, marking a big shift from where we were in 1947 (Ho 2017; Harper and Amrith 2014). The forms it will take are difficult to predict but we may do well to remember that when cultures interact, the outcome could depend among other things on whether the stress is on similarities or differences.

Bibliography

Acharya, Amitav. 2010. "Asia Is Not One". *Journal of Asian Studies* 69, no. 4 (November): 1001–13.

Asian Relations. 1948. Report of the Proceedings and Documentation of the First Asian Relations Conference, New Delhi, March–April 1947. New Delhi: Asian Relations Organization.

Duara, Prasenjit. 2010. "Asia Redux: Conceptualizing a Region for Our Times". *Journal of Asian Studies* 69, no. 4 (November): 963–83.

Harper, Tim, and Sunil Amrith, eds. 2014. *Sites of Asian Interaction: Networks and Mobility*, Cambridge: Cambridge University Press.

Ho, E. 2017. "Inter-Asian Concepts for Mobile Societies". *Journal of Asian Studies* 76, no. 4: 907–28.

Mansergh, Nicholas. 1947. "The Asian Conference". *International Affairs* (Royal Institute of International Affairs 1944–) 23, no. 3 (July): 295–306.

McCallum, J.A. 1947a. "The Asian Relations Conference". *Australian Quarterly* 19, no. 2 (June): 13–17.

———. 1947b. "Personalities at the Asian Relations Conference". *Australian Quarterly* 19, no. 3 (September): 39–44 (accessed 23 June 2017).

Noor, Farish A. 2014. *The Discursive Construction of Southeast Asia in 19th Century Colonial-Capitalist Discourse*. Amsterdam: Amsterdam University Press.

Pollock, Sheldon. 2006. *The Language of the Gods in the World of Men: Sanskrit,*

Culture, and Power in Premodern India. Berkeley: University of California Press.

Price, Maurice T. 1950. "Reviewed Work(s): Asian Relations: Being Report of the Proceedings and Documentation of the First Asian Relations Conference, New Delhi, March–April, 1947". *Social Forces* 28, no. 3 (March): 349–50.

Talbot, Phillips. 1947. "As the As the British Empire Was Falling Apart, Gandhi Gave This Advice to the Rest of Asia". *New Republic*. 15 April.

Thompson, Virginia. 1948. "Regional Unity in Southern Asia". *Pacific Affairs* 21, no. 2 (June): 170–76.

——— and Richard Adloff. 1947. "Asian Unity: Force or Façade". *Far Eastern Survey* 16, no. 9 (7 May): 97–99 (accessed 5 September 2016).

Venkatasubbiah, H. 1947. *Asia in the Modern World*. New Delhi: Asian Relations Conference, Indian Council of World Affairs.

Yang, Yun-yuan. 1987. "Controversies over Tibet: China versus India". *China Quarterly*, no. 111 (September): 407–20 (accessed 29 September 2016).

Part II

Conceptualizing Asia through the Prism of Europe

4

In Pursuit of Knowledge from Asia: François Valentijn on the Hindu Social Divisions in the Coromandel Region, c. Seventeenth–Eighteenth Century

Murari K. Jha[1]

Asia is inhabited as far as India; but beyond this, it is all desert towards the east, nor is any one able to describe what it is. Such and so great is Asia (Cary 1848, p. 250).

INTRODUCTION

By examining some key texts written by the Dutch clergymen Abrahmus Rogerius, Philippus Baldaeus and François Valentijn, I discuss how knowledge about precolonial southeastern India was produced, disseminated,

[1] Faculty Development Allowance (FDA) of Nalanda University helped me to conduct research for this chapter at the British Library, London, during the summer of 2017. I am indebted to the Weatherhead Centre, Harvard University, where I finalized the manuscript in 2018. I thank my former supervisor Jos Gommans for reading and commenting on an early draft of the chapter. I also thank Paula Koning and Antonius Harmsen for checking my Dutch translation in the text. For the comments and questions, I thank the participants in the Nalanda University and Nalanda-Sriwijaya Centre joint conference held in Singapore in 2016. For any remaining mistakes, I am solely responsible.

and consumed. Although by their very nature these Dutch accounts are culturally mediated and coloured by religious presuppositions and agendas, an analysis of some of these texts may help the historian to evoke some prevalent Western ideas about the society in the Coromandel region in the early modern period (sixteenth to eighteenth century).

The need to create and improve upon the rudimentary knowledge about the East that was inaugurated by Herodotus in his *Histories* would continue in the Hellenistic and Roman worlds through the Renaissance and early modern Europe. For example, in the so-called Age of Explorations the European curiosity to learn about Asia metamorphosed into the systematic creation of tangible knowledge. In fact, the survival of the nascent states in the fiercely competitive, and religion-inspired and ideologically fragmented society of Western Europe depended on the creation and documentation of new knowledge (van Linschoten 1885).[2] For example, charting the sea routes, mapping regions, river estuaries or strategic ports, documenting commodities, and describing local populations and their belief systems, all constituted practical and usable forms of knowledge. In post-Enlightenment eighteenth-century Europe, knowledge about Asia was deployed not only for the strategic and commercial purposes but also to understand and define the European Self in contrast to the Asian Other. The creation, documentation, and dissemination of knowledge through the printing and publishing revolution also bequeathed important information about the functioning of social categories and "superstitious" beliefs on the different regions of the continent.

In this chapter I shall focus on Valentijn's writings about the social and religious aspects of Hindu society in southeastern India during his time. Before the Dutch came to the region, the Portuguese missionaries had tried to advance the cause of Christianity in the region. However, they found the existing caste structure a major impediment to make any meaningful progress towards their evangelizing goals. Although the Dutch were less enthusiastic about winning converts compared to their Iberian counterparts, they invested considerable energy and efforts to understand the Hindus' social organization and religious beliefs. Benefitting from the contemporary Dutch interests in such matters, I shall specifically discuss Valentijn's account of "heydendom" (implying Hinduism) in the

[2] Linschoten worked as Secretary to the Archbishop in Goa from 1584 to 1588/89, and successfully spied on the Portuguese secrets of trade in the East Indies, passing them on to their Protestant enemy and political rivals, the Dutch. See Toler, n.d.

Coromandel region along with his description of the normative division of society among Brahmans, Kṣatriyas, Vaiśyas, and Śūdras. The purpose is to describe and understand how such a social division was operating within the contemporary society. Although the British colonial rulers deployed the tools of censuses and surveys for enumeration and fixation of caste hierarchy, I should like to argue that the historical role and functions of the precolonial social institutions remained foundational to their subsequent evolution and sedimentation in the nineteenth and twentieth centuries.

Anthropologist Nicholas B. Dirks perhaps gives too much agency to the British colonial state's efforts and capability to intervene and shape the supposedly malleable Indian society when he argues that "caste (again as we know it today) is a modern phenomenon, that it is, specifically, the product of an historical encounter between India and Western colonial rule" (Dirks 2001, p. 5). Digging deeper than the surface of colonial rule, historian Sumit Guha has recently argued that many of the modern sociopolitical power relations had been operating through India's precolonial past. In a similar vein, historian Rosalind O'Hanlon writes that any formulation arguing for the colonial ingenuity in the "invention" of caste in fact "underestimates the degree of continuity into the colonial period, and portrays the vernacular critiques of caste developed in colonial India as essentially derivatives of colonial discourse" (Guha 2013, p. 16; see also O'Hanlon 2017, p. 443). Rather than providing a historiographical survey of the ongoing debate on the caste system in South Asia, this chapter examines Valentijn's text and appraises the information on the organization and functioning of different social groups or castes in precolonial southeastern India. Based on the data from the seventeenth and early eighteenth centuries, a case of continuity can be made between the precolonial and colonial periods, especially the way in which social hierarchy operated, caste differentiation made and upheld, and exclusion perpetuated. Information in Valentijn's volume dealing with southeastern India was based primarily on the writings of the Dutch clergymen Abrahmus Rogerius and Philippus Baldaeus who had lived in peninsular India for several years in the seventeenth century. Along with these works, Valentijn also utilized documents and papers that he obtained from the *Verenigde Oost-Indische Compagnië* (VOC) officials who had served the Company in the Coromandel and Bengal regions. Before discussing Valentijn's text on the Hindu social categories in the later part of this chapter, I shall begin by briefly alluding to the life history of our energetic but somewhat controversial protagonist François Valentijn.

LIFE AND WORK OF FRANÇOIS VALENTIJN

François Valentijn, the author of an encyclopedic yet allegedly plagiarized work in five volumes and eight parts *Oud en Nieuw Oost-Indiën*, was born on 17 April 1666 in Dordrecht in the Netherlands. His father, Abraham Valentijn, was a co-rector of the Grammar School at Dordrecht and his mother, Maria Valentijn, was a daughter of a *Predikant* or Minister of the Dutch Reformed Church. Belonging to an established middle-class Dutch family having good connections with the Calvinist establishment and the VOC officials in the Netherlands was certainly a social privilege that eased the way for the ambitious young François to realize a promising career. After completing his early education at his father's Grammar School, at the age of sixteen he went to study theology at the Universities of Leiden and Utrecht on a scholarship. When he was just eighteen years old, he qualified for the post of Minister of the Dutch Reformed Church in 1684. Soon he joined the VOC service to hold the position of the parish of Victoria Castle on the island of Amboina and reached Batavia in December 1685. He formally moved to Amboina, one of the first islands that came to be fully controlled by the VOC, towards the end of February 1686, less than two months short of his twentieth birthday.

He spent two terms in the East Indies: first, from 1685 to 1694, and second, from 1705 to 1713. His first stint was fruitful as he made rapid progress in learning Malay, acclimatized with the local environment while serving in the Amboina and Banda islands, and maintained an active social life as a resident in the Victoria Castle. The first term in the East Indies also proved to be rewarding for his personal enrichment and for advancing his academic interests. In 1692 he got married with Cornelia Snaats, the rich widow of Henrik Leydekker—a private Dutch citizen in Amboina who had owned ships and left behind his great fortunes. This marriage made available to Valentijn the wealth that Cornelia had inherited. As Cornelia came from a Dutch family that was long settled in the East Indies, she had an excellent command over the Malay language and could fluently read the Jawi script. She proved to be a great companion of Valentijn, helping his way in realizing the ambition to pursue his Malay studies. It has been conjectured that probably Cornelia would have been instrumental in translating the Bible into low Malay that Valentijn claimed to be his own. This Malay Bible became a source of controversy when Valentijn tried to publish it after he returned to Batavia for his second term of stay in December 1705 (see Beekman 1996, pp. 127–28). These controversies stemmed primarily from his soared relationship with the Batavian Church Council and Amboinese administration.

By the time Valentijn reached the East Indies for the second term, many things had changed in Amboina. The famous German-born botanist Georg Eberhard Rumphius (1627–1702), who was resident in Amboina during Valentijn's first term, died without being able to publish his great manuscript on Amboina's natural history. Two of Valentijn's step-children got married into the Rumphius family, and this marital alliance would have given him access to the manuscripts left behind by Rumphius. Since Valentijn was not in good terms with the civil and ecclesiastical establishments at Batavia, he was initially denied permission to return to the Netherlands. It was only after the death of Governor General Abraham van Riebeeck (1653–1713) that he was able to embark on a journey back home with his family members. He spent the last thirteen years of his life working on his multi-volume *Oud en Nieuw Oost-Indiën*, which was published between 1724 and 1726. He died in 1727 after seeing all his volumes out from the press (Arasaratnam 1978, pp. 1–14; Beekman 1996, pp. 119–44).

Valentijn's *Oud en Nieuw Oost-Indiën* contains an incredible amount of information on the East Indies and each volume is exhaustive in giving details of each region it deals with. However, the selection of regions discussed in it shows a haphazard arrangement, which does not follow any orderly sequence. As historian Sinnappah Arasaratnam has suggested, Valentijn kept on adding, compiling, and writing whatever materials came to his possession, without caring much to have any sequence in the arrangement of the volumes (Arasaratnam 1978, p. 16). For example, volume one deals with the Moluccas, volume two with the Amboina; volume three with the Amboina again, Banda, Macassar, Bali, Tonkin, Cambodia and Siam; volume four again goes to "Great Java" and Island Java, Surat and the Great Mughals, China and Taiwan. Finally, volume five discusses Coromandel (along with Pegu and Bengal), Persia, Malacca, Sumatra, Ceylon, Malabar, Japan, the Cape of Good Hope and Mauritius. On the other hand, his description of a particular region follows a well-organized sequence. For example, when he deals with the Coromandel Coast he begins with its geography, the political establishments therein, followed by the Dutch commercial settlements or what he calls "Comptoir" and political and commercial affairs on the coast, and finally he describes religion (*Van den Godsdienst der Kust van Choromandel*). In this section on religion, he describes Hindu, Muslim and Christian religions in a set order. These geographical and conceptual concerns remain at the heart of the descriptions of other regions as well. Having briefly touched upon Valentijn's life and work, an introduction to the region's contacts with the VOC will be in order.

VOC'S CONTACTS WITH THE COROMANDEL COAST

According to Valentijn, the Dutch early contacts with the Coromandel go back to 1603 when Jacob Pietersz, who had sailed to the East as a part of Admiral Wybrand van Warwyk's fleet, visited the coast (Raychaudhuri 1962, p. 15; see also Valentijn 1726b, p. 57). The Dutch discovered that the successful trading in the East Indies depended much on the procurement of cotton textiles produced in the Coromandel region. Thus, a regular Dutch factory or trading post was established at Petapuli and Msulipatnam in August 1606 with the permission of Mohammad Kuli (r. 1581–1611), the king of Golconda (Terpstra 1911, p. 34; Heeres 1907, pp. 45–46). The initial Dutch perception about the critical role of cotton textiles from the Coromandel Coast was shared by the Dutch explorer Hendrik Brouwer (the future VOC Governor General at Batavia), who in 1612 described the region as the "left arm of the Moluccas and the surrounding islands because without textiles that come from there, the trade in the Moluccas will be dead." (Heeres 1907, p. 154; Prakash 1998, p. 92). Within the first two decades of the seventeenth century at least four factories were established on the Coromandel Coast. While the Petapuli and Tirupapaliyur factories were closed by 1618 owing to local disturbances, the factories at Masulipatnam and Pulicat proved to be of enduring importance, so much so that Fort Geldria was constructed in Pulicat with the responsibility of a "government" (Prakash 1998, pp. 127–28).

In order to make a better sense of the Dutch observations on the region and society, it should be noted that the Dutch merchants did not always lead a coast-centric life in eastern India but they had established their settlements and residential quarters into the hinterlands. In 1613 they had a small residence in a village called Palakollu, surrounded by other weaving villages situated well into the interior. Later they erected a stone building which housed eight or ten VOC officials and around seventy Indian employees to assist them. They took this village on a lease which was subsequently confirmed by a royal *farman* issued in 1658 from the king of Golconda. Apart from purchasing textiles from the surrounding areas, the Dutch exploited the fertile rice fields of the Palakollu village and made an annual profit of 1,000 pagoda. According to Arasaratnam, in one of the suburban villages of Masulipatnam, the Dutch acquired a piece of land from the rulers and built residences where the officials retired for amusement and recreation (Arasaratnam 1978, p. 68). From these instances it is clear that the Dutch were active not only on the coast, they had penetrated well into the hinterlands. Opportunities to visit the hinterlands for trade and recreational activities allowed some of the keen Dutch observers to take note of the local cultural and religious practices, customs and norms, and the prevailing social order or hierarchy.

In the course of the seventeenth century, the Dutch commercial contacts with the Coromandel Coast further deepened as a result of the VOC's fast-expanding intra-Asian trade. Bewildering varieties of cotton textiles procured in the region became staple for the VOC's trade within Asia and towards the end of the century between India and Europe. The Coromandel Coast became intricately linked with Southeast Asia as well as the Chinese and Japanese trade networks of the Dutch East India Company. At the turn of the seventeenth century, when the export to Europe was gearing up, the VOC's investment in this region was well over a million guilders and in 1701 the figure reached 1.7 million guilders, remaining well over 1.5 million till 1703.[3] The commercial contacts were instrumental in facilitating other kinds of linkages, especially in social and cultural spheres, between the Dutch and the Coromandel Coast.

Many Dutch Predikants, i.e., the ministers of religion or clergymen, took keen interest in social and religious matters of the region. For example, Abrahamus Rogerius, Philippus Baldaeus, and Daniel Havart sought to understand and reflect on the dynamics of society and religion on the Coromandel Coast (Havart 1693). In spite of their obvious limitations such as being outsiders in the region, mostly relying on the data provided by informants belonging to a particular social category, the Dutch observers, moved by a half-hearted desire to win some converts, produced accounts that often help us to peep into the indigenous social and religious practices. They wrote their accounts primarily for the Dutch (and European) reading public, catering to the intellectual curiosity of those who were interested to learn more about Asia. The curiosity and interest of European public was

[3] Nationaal Archief, *Verenigde Oost-Indische Compagnië* (VOC), Inventaris Nummer 341, "Beschrijving van 's Comp:s handel en omslag mitsgaders derzelver bestaan ter Kust Choromandel, alles met betrekking tot den tegenwoordiger tijd door den Raad Ordinair Jacob van der Waeijen", f. 32.

founded on the need to define itself in the light of eastern knowledge. This construction of knowledge about early modern South Asian society cannot be solely interpreted as a hegemonic activity of an intellectually superior and politically powerful people who framed a weak and backward society at their will (Irschick 1994, p. 8).[4] The context in which such texts were written, the role of violence and counter-violence from the VOC and its South Asian counterparts animated the larger ambiance to which historian Sanjay Subrahmanyam calls "indeterminate equilibrium" (Subrahmanyam 2007, pp. 147–48). In such a context the knowledge produced in collaboration with the local informants was atrophied to produce larger metanarratives that catered to the needs of European audience. It is possible to categorize these descriptions as a sort of early Dutch "Orientalism", which contains grains of historicity. This early "orientalist enterprise" enables us to glean into the presuppositions, the context and thought processes that led to the construction of the Dutch accounts. With this basic theoretical premise in mind, we can turn to the work produced by Valentijn.

GENEALOGY OF VALENTIJN'S TEXT

Like many other Dutch travellers writing on the Eastern world, Valentijn also asserts that he is giving an accurate (*nauwkeurig*) account of the old and new East Indies. He posits that his account has a neat order or sequence. Valentijn follows mainly a descriptive style and fills his text with an incredible amount of information, although, as we already noted, the geographical arrangement and sequencing of his volumes are rather random. Apart from putting all the relevant information together, at times, he also synthesizes them in order to construct a coherent narrative. In the beginning of his description of *Heydensche Godsdienst* (pejoratively heathen's or Hindu's religion) Valentijn acknowledges the previous works of Abrahamus Rogerius and Philippus Baldaeus on this subject. However, he seems to be critical of both these authors' works when he says none of them in fact knew Sanskrit and could explore their sacred works, the Vedam

[4] Irschick (1994) has challenged Edward Said's proposition by arguing that, "we can no longer presume that the view of local or what later became Indian society was a product of an 'imposition' by the hegemonic colonial power onto a mindless and subordinate colonized society".

(the Vedas). As Valentijn put it, Rogerius's understanding of "paganism" depended on his friendly intercourse with Padmanābha, Damersa and other Brahmans. He stresses the need for a Predikant living in India to learn Sanskrit in order to read and translate the religious law books and form a scientific view of the religion exposed in them. After voicing this rather fleeting criticism, he declares that his intention is not to belittle or put any blame on Rogerius and Baldaeus; rather, he has reasons to praise their efforts as he himself has a direct experience of serving as Predikant in the Indies, where one gets little or no time to undertake such work of acquiring the necessary linguistic skills.

Valentijn's description of the Hindu religion follows a particular order. He begins by giving a general outline of the religion and then gradually breaks the theme into parts in a set order. For example, first he describes Brahmanism, followed by different sects within it; then he goes on discussing each sect's ritual practices and beliefs one after another. In discussing certain aspects of the religion, Valentijn has clearly borrowed from the works of Rogerius and Baldaeus. Rogerius's account relies primarily on his chief informant Padmanābha—a *smārta* or "orthodox" Brahman who gives a biased description of other currents within Brahmanism. Overall, it appears that Valentijn does not always copy the text from other authors but sometime really tries to go deeper into the issue after digesting facts he drew from different sources (Valentijn 1726b, pp. 84–85).[5] On certain occasions he attempts to improve the text and synthesizes analogous information found in other works.[6]

Abrahmus Rogerius's volume *De Open-Deure tot het Verborgen Heydendom* ("The open door to the hidden heathendom") has been organized in two parts. While the first part deals with four chief *geslachten* (literally "categories" but the term is often taken to imply castes) on the Coromandel Coast, no doubt following the established Brahmanic textual tradition of such normative social division, the second part gives particular

[5] One such instance is Valentijn's discussion on the issue of *sati* or widow-burning where he describes identical traditions found elsewhere and quotes texts in Latin.

[6] When, for instance, Valentijn talks about the measures of repentance taken by a person if he kills a Brahman, he seems to have completed Rogerius's description by adding that such person must build a temple for the God Eswara (*īśvara*) who had himself undergone such repentance after killing two *rākṣasa*s or demons who were the sons of Brahman (Valentijn 1726b, p. 73) and compare it with Rogerius (1651), pp. 3–4 and Baldaeus (1672), pp. 10–17.

attention to the God and the different modes of Hindu worship. The first part is organized into twenty-one chapters discussing myriad social and cultural practices of the Brahmans. The second part also has twenty-one chapters, discussing various Hindu Gods, pagodas or temples, the uses of the sacred Ganga water, and the question of life after death.[7] The rest of the book deals with the life of Barthrouherri (Bhartṛhari, whose dates are uncertain but who is assumed to have flourished around the fifth century CE) and his useful proverbs.[8] Rogerius follows, as Valentijn also does, a descriptive narrative style and systematizes his information in each section dealing with a particular theme. While Valentijn normally skips acknowledging his sources in the notes, Rogerius refers, by the means of footnotes, to the works of many previous authors such Johan van Twist (d.1643), Jan Huyghen van Linschoten (1563–1611), and others (Rogerius 1651, pp. 84–85). He often tries to go deeper into the matter and expand on it in the footnotes. Unlike Valentijn, Rogerius does not discuss the geography or the political settings of the region he has dealt with, and specifically focuses on the social and religious questions of the "heydendom". Rogerius's volume is in a small booklet form and the print format is very different from that of Valentijn's *Oud en Nieuw Oost-Indiën*.

Baldaeus's work is divided into three parts. The first part is titled *Naauwkeurige Beschrijvinge der Indische Kusten Malabar ende Choromandel* ("Accurate description of the Indian coasts Malabar and Coromandel"), the second part is a *Beschryving Van het Machtige Eyland Ceylon* (Description of the powerful island Ceylon), and the third part is called *Afgoderye Der Oost-Indische Heydenen zijnde een ware en nauwkeurige verhandelinge van den Godtsdienst der Indostansche, Choromandelsche, Malabarsche en Ceylonsche Heydenen, hoe de zelve afgebeelt en geëert werden* ("Idolatry of the East Indian Hindus being a true treatise of the religion of the pagans of Hindustan, Coromandel and Ceylon, how they are represented and honoured"). The volume was published in large folio size and the print format closely resembles that of the Valentijn's *Oud en Nieuw Oost-Indiën*.

---

[7] It has been argued that the division of Rogerius's work into two parts, one dealing with secular and the other with the religious spheres, was commonsensical and natural to Western ways of thinking. It, however, does violence to the unity of Hinduism and this separation is foreign and artificial to Hindu doctrines and rituals (Lach and van Kley 1993, p. 1030).

[8] On Bhartṛhari, uncertainties about his time and his works on morality (*Nîtiśataka*) and renunciation (*Vairāgyaśataka*), see Wortham (1886); Ingalls (1968), pp. 38–39.

Like Valentijn, Baldaeus has also included a number of sketching illustrating various themes. Thus, one may speculate that Baldaeus's volume-format has consciously or unconsciously influenced Valentijn as the latter's work bears a close resemblance with the former's. Baldaeus has dealt with a number of subjects and covered a wider geographical region, including Malabar, Coromandel, and Ceylon. Furthermore, in the beginning of the volume he has provided information on the political establishments, Dutch factories, commercial products that the region furnished, and trade along the western coast of India.

In the third section of his work, Baldaeus specifically talks about idolatry and religious matters of the *heydenen* or Hindus. This section has been further subdivided into two parts, of eight and eighteen chapters respectively. In the first part Baldaeus begins with *Van de algemeene kennisse Gods* ("Of the general knowledge of God") and goes on to discuss the Christian God and the ancient Gods and metaphysical aspects citing a number of authorities from the Greek and Roman traditions. After this introductory chapter discussing general religious matters, he moves on referring to Rogerius and enumerates six different sects of Brahmans (*Weistnouwas* [Vaiṣṇava], *Seivia* [Śaiva], *Smaerta* [Smārtas], *Schaerwaeka* [Cārvākas], *Pasenda* [Pāṣāṇḍa] and *Tschectea* [Śākta]) and the idol *Ixora,* i.e., Īśvara (Baldaeus 1672, p. 6). This part of the volume veers around the Ixora theme and discusses many other Gods of the Hindu pantheon described in the subsequent chapters. The second part of this section is chiefly devoted to the discussion of the God *Vistnum* or Viṣṇu and the stories about his ten incarnations in eleven out of the eighteen chapters. In the rest of the chapters, he discusses devil, the strength of the soul, the respect shown to the Pagodas by the heathens, and so on. In the descriptions found in all these chapters Baldaeus filters his narrative through the lens of a Dutch Reformed Predikant. In the "Preface to the discreet reader", he asserts his authority in matters of Hindu religion more than anyone else because he had lived and travelled through many places on the coasts of Malabar and Coromandel and in Ceylon (Baldaeus 1672).[9] Many of the descriptions from the works of Rogerius and Baldaeus found their way

[9] "That I had the courage to inform the critical reader, is mainly because I lived in many places, traveled around and I attended to important sieges and campaigns, so as a witness I am able to speak about this subject with authority." See preface in Baldaeus (1672).

into the text of Valentijn who reproduced them and at times enriched them with his own narrative and interpretive skills.

ANALYSIS OF VALENTIJN'S TEXT

Given the fact that Valentijn's work contains exhaustive information, more abundant than the data found in the above mentioned two works of Rogerius and Baldaeus, one may wonder as how and from where he accumulated the additional data. A close reading of his text makes it clear that his narrative is not a product of his creative imagination, but it in fact describes some actual facts from the specific regions of Asia he visited. As far as his adhering to the prevalent academic conventions of time is concerned, Valentijn acknowledges—albeit en passant and unsystematically—some authors who had already published their works such as Rogerius and Baldaeus, and he copiously (and often silently) borrows information on relevant social and religious aspects from them. Apart from the published sources, Valentijn seems to be relying on a number of unpublished manuscripts sourced from the former VOC officials who had been to the Coromandel Coast (Valentijn 1726a).[10] He obtained these sources either through corresponding with them or contacting the descendants of the former employees of the VOC.

In the "Foreword" of volume three, book one of the *Oud en Nieuw Oost-Indië*, Valentijn talks about many persons of high status who had provided him with drawings and maps along with other materials to complete his text. He claims to have utilized many neat maps and beautiful drawings which had been hitherto kept in secrecy, and whose publication in his volume would give more splendour and glory to his work (Valentijn 1726a).[11] Valentijn says that he procured these maps and drawings from

[10] In Voorbericht van den Schryver aan den Bescheiden Lezer or preface from the author to the discreet reader, Valentijn says, "No less help was given to me by the Honourable Daniël Bernard, who has been Governor of Coromandel for many years, with use of his documents concerning this government; and also his Honour has given me enlightenment with many letters, for which uncommon and generous benevolence I express my great thanks to his Honour." Apart from Daniël Bernard, he also acknowledges the papers of Joannes van Steeland who had been the member of Extraordinary Council of the Netherlands Indies and the Governor on the Coromandel Coast.

[11] See Voorbericht van den Schryver aan den Bescheiden Lezer. "… die Papieren weder een ongemeenen luister en çieraad aan myn Werk geven,".

those who had been to the East and were employed on the high positions in the service of the VOC. He mentions names of such officials such as Mattheus van den Brouke and Elias van den Brouke, who had been to Bengal and Coromandel respectively and who furnished "extremely neat and true papers of these regions" (Valentijn 1726a).[12] While talking about Nagapattinam and a massive flood that temporarily submerged the area in 1680, Valentijn refers to Heer Landvoogd (Governor) Jacob Jorisson's report sent to Batavia concerning the measures to be taken at Nagapattinam against such flooding. (Valentijn 1726a, pp. 4–5).

The density of information on the Coromandel Coast makes it clear that Valentijn had access to a diverse array of maps, drawings, reports and the letters of VOC officials employed in the southeastern part of India. Some of Valentijn's accounts are certainly based on these documents. One may criticize Valentijn for not giving in footnotes the proper citations or references to the manuscript sources, which leads to the impression that he was just copying or "plagiarizing" the works of others. However, the charges of plagiarism are difficult to hold against authors who were writing in the early modern period because the texts produced by them may not always distinguish "between proper and improper intertextuality" (Thomas 2000, p. 279).[13] On the other hand, according to the prevailing norms of the period, a manuscript always belonged to its master or possessor and it was the master's discretion to use it the way the author wished. Even the copyright of a book could be bought and published by the buyer as an author in a brand-new packaging (Van Eerde 1976, p. 46).[14] Indeed, Valentijn was an enthusiastic collector of manuscripts and he may have passed some of these without crediting their creators. Moreover, it was largely an accepted norm for that age to use the manuscript if the possessor had acquired it by one or the other means.

---

[12] See *Voorbericht van den Schryver aan den Bescheiden Lezer.*

[13] Another such example might be the Royal Geographer of Restoration England, John Ogilby, who got various Dutch books on geography translated and published in his name. See Schmidt (2002), p. 355.

[14] John Ogilby bought the copyright of *Aesop* which was repackaged by Thomas Roycroft and printed for "the author" Ogilby in 1665 and again in 1668. However, in the case of Valentijn, it is strongly suspected that he may have misappropriated Herber de Jager's manuscript on Persia and Coromandel, see Beekman (1996), pp. 130–31.

Taking an example from England, historian E.M. Beekman writes that Samuel Purchas' (1577–1626) monumental work can favourably be compared with Valentijn's *Oud en Nieuw Oost-Indiën*. According to him both are compilations primarily of other peoples' work and neither can be linked to the scholarly genealogies of their respective masters, Richard Hakluyt (1553–1616) and Eberhard Rumphius. However, both works succeeded in salvaging a great deal of material from being completely lost or forgotten (Beekman 1996, pp. 138–39). In terms of furnishing historical information, Valentijn's magnum opus can be seen as a repository of invaluable historical data even if he appropriated others' works.

PRODUCERS AND CONSUMERS OF KNOWLEDGE OF THE EAST

While such authors such as Abrahamus Rogerius, Philippus Baldaeus, and Daniel Havart dedicated their respective works to the Gentlemen of the VOC, Valentijn contravened this norm. He dedicated his *Oud en Nieuw Oost-Indiën* to a person named Egidius van den Bempden, praising him with high-sounding titles such as Wel-Edele, Groot-Achtbaare, Gestrenge Heer. Van den Bempden was wealthy and mighty, and Valentijn hoped to find favour and protection in times of hardship and difficulty (Valentijn 1724, Opdragt) Although he dedicated his work to the high and mighty, it seems that it was primarily intended for the general reading public in the Netherlands, which had developed an insatiable curiosity about the East.[15] As historian Markus Vink has recently shown, ever since the success of reports, journals, short stories and other accounts brought back by the Dutch "First Shipping" to Asia (1595–97), the subsequent travellers already had some understanding of the world they were visiting (Vink 2015, p. 145). They were also keenly aware of the demand and saleability of their accounts in the Dutch Republic. In order to differentiate his work from the other accounts, Valentijn emphasized in the Foreword how only someone who had travelled to the East and had mastered the language of a land could provide an authentic story. Furthermore, he claimed that his work could not be compared with any other earlier works on the East Indies because his volume dealt with a host of issues and had been presented in a neat

[15] Paul Hazard has discussed at length as how intellectual interests in the East has changed Europe's rather isolationist and self-obsessed world-view. See Hazard (1973), esp. Chapter 1, pp. 17–55.

order (Valentijn 1724).[16] Since Valentijn himself was a Predikant, he took a keen interest in describing the works produced on religious matters by other Predikants such as Rogerius and Baldaeus.

Since Valentijn himself had never been to the Coromandel Coast, his description entirely relies on the information gathered from other published and unpublished sources. While on the one hand the fact that Valentijn did not visit the Coromandel region could give rise to the criticism that his account is not a first-hand, eye-witness description, it may be also argued that his description is free from the shortcomings that a travelogue or an eye-witness account usually suffer. Valentijn relied on his personal collection of sources, and he applied his own critical faculties and used his own judgements to select and shift through the mass of data pertaining to the Coromandel Coast.

In the case of Rogerius, his situation was different than Valentijn's as his narrative is based on the accounts provided by the informants. In spite of Rogerius's slightly different objectives and the application of a different method in his work, the targeted audience for both his and Valentijn's the works were the Dutch or European readers interested in the East, particularly in the religion, faith in God, and other matters related to society and culture (Rogerius 1651, p. 2).[17] As the title of Rogerius' work *De Open-Deure tot het Verborgen Heydendom* suggests, he claimed to force-open the door to the hidden (knowledge) of heathendom. Therefore, a dialogue could be initiated with the Hindus for bringing at least some of them within the fold of the "true faith". Prejudiced as his accounts are, Rogerius was able to glean into the inner functioning of the Coromandel society. Also, he could avail of the help of some of the Portuguese-speaking Brahmans such as Padmanābha and others. Part of his work dealing with

[16] "Now moving to the book I have published, it is certain that all erudite and critical people will have to acknowledge that they have never seen before such an elaborate description of the East Indies, and also that in my work a lot of topics are available, which the reader has never seen in the books of other authors, let alone in good order." (Valentijn 1724, *Voorreden*, p. 2).

[17] See *Tot den Leser* where he begins by addressing to the "Benevolent reader, it is obvious that the East Indies have seen for a long time the flags of Christianity, and now for fifty years the flag of our Country; and that the nature and condition of those lands, even of China and Japan, have been made renowned by many European authors, so clear, as if they were original residents and natives of those lands; but none of those authors has been able to express clearly the fundamentals of their religion, and their own opinions about God, and divine issues."

religion and social organization can be taken as a compilation of a series of discussions with Brahmans.

VALENTIJN'S PLACE IN THE CONTEMPORARY ORIENTAL DISCOURSE

The seventeenth century discourse on the Eastern religion and society often refers to the "classical" writers who had already reflected on these matters. For example, when Valentijn discusses *sati* or the practice of widow immolating herself on the funeral pyre of her deceased husband, he refers to the classical authors who had dealt with similar themes. Rogerius also enumerates the names of earlier authors such as Cyprianus, Tertullianus, Hieronymus, Augustinus, Lactantius, Arnobius and others who had ever written on "heydendom". The renewed interest about the Eastern society, culture, religion and other forms of knowledge in early modern Europe often goes back to the history of such contentious and poorly understood issues. Yet, perhaps, it was the curiosity to know more about Indian/ Eastern religion and society and improve upon the already exiting body of knowledge through prevailing discourse that created a market in Europe for the books written on the aspects of religion and society.[18]

It was a period of intellectual churning in northwestern Europe where the process of Enlightenment was already under way, the long-established religious perceptions were being challenged, and new religious and political ideas were claiming space for themselves. Valentijn's work on religion and society on the Coromandel Coast seems to be intended to cater to the needs of this Dutch audience that was preoccupied with finding a solution to the social and religious problems within Europe. Thus, the practice of Orientalism in the Dutch Republic gained pace in order to form an understanding of European society's problems, and the body of ever-expanding Eastern knowledge further fuelled the process.[19]

---

[18] Robert Irwin while discussing European Orientalism in the Near East notes, "Libertine and Enlightenment authors were particularly fond of this sort of literary disguise. Voltaire wrote by turns in dispraise and praise of the Prophet, depending on what local political point he wished to make." (Irwin 2006, p. 117).

[19] Irwin seems to agree with Raymond Schwab's assertion that "the beginnings of true Orientalism [in India] are to be found in the late eighteenth century". However, the beginning of European intellectual interests in India can be dated back to the seventeenth century when the Dutch clergymen began to produce works on Hindu religion and society (Irwin 2006, p. 125).

This Orientalism had utilitarian importance for the Europeans' own self-assessment, and it was not necessarily related to the knowledge and power definition as formulated by Edward Said. To take an example from early colonial India, William Jones's interest in the Persian poetry was guided not by merchants' or administrative requirements of power and dominance; rather, he was keen on introducing Persian poets to a European audience (Irwin 2006, pp. 124–25).

There was a phenomenal growth in the publishing market in the Netherlands with Amsterdam taking a lead role. The Dutch Republic had emerged as one of the free-fields for the expression of new ideas in Europe. From the early seventeenth century Leiden University had become the centre of the Oriental studies and Orientalist's discourse, and the Huguenots (from the Dutch word *huisgenoot* or flat mate) were drawn from different parts of Europe to work together under one roof. Publication of the travel literature was particularly in vogue since such literature was sought after by the European "armchair travellers" as a source of new knowledge. Generally, the travellers who ventured to the East took it as their moral obligation to impart and bequeath whatever they saw worth reporting in the course of the journey even if the nature of their travel was primarily commercial. The publication of several studies in the Dutch Republic may be understood in terms of "the production and consumption of exotica", ranging from geography to myriad other matters (Schmidt 2002, pp. 349–50, 361). This followed on the heels of the chasm separating two different genres represented by Marco Polo's lay empiricism on the one hand and the more fantastic tales woven around the imaginary travel to Asia by John Mandeville on the other. However, as Jaś Elsner and Joan-Pau Rubiés note, eventually the pilgrimage literature of late medieval Europe had become a means for the empirical observations and credible research works that began to be produced from the late fourteenth century onwards (Elsner and Rubiés 1999, pp. 35–40). Valentijn's multi-volume work may be regarded as a substantial contribution to Europe's existing knowledge about the Eastern geography, trade, polity, society, religion, and so on. In contrast to the print culture and marketing of the cartographic renderings of the world in the Dutch Republic, the Portuguese pioneers seem to have lagged behind in taking advantage of this new technology. For example, Subrahmanyam (2002, p. 8) notes that though a considerable number of works on Asia were produced by the Portuguese in the sixteenth century, very little in fact went into print.

Valentijn's work on Coromandel's society and religion can be regarded as having been inspired first and foremost by a curiosity towards knowing and understanding the "heydendom" for a purely utilitarian point of view. For instance, it was meant to put the exalted Dutch Reformed Protestant religion on a higher pedestal vis-à-vis so-called heathendom's superstitious religion in the eyes of European readers. Such engagements with the heathendom also put the Reformed Protestant religion in a favourable light compared with the Catholics, who were often accused of idolatry—a heathenish practice in the eyes of the Protestants (Wielema 2003, p. 66). On a similar note, Valentijn wrote about social divisions and different castes within the Hindu society perhaps to compare and contrast it to the social structure within the Dutch Republic.[20] Thus, Valentijn could be counted amongst the early modern Orientalists whose interests in Eastern knowledge was driven primarily by a sociocultural, religious, or otherwise utilitarian agenda. Valentijn was not consciously drawing a scheme to represent the Other that would have been intended for the knowledge-power pursuit.[21] Moreover, Valentijn's work dealing with the social hierarchy can well be regarded as representing an insider's perspective even though it was laced with his own prejudice. The work of Rogerius, on which Valentijn has leaned too heavily for the information on Coromandel's society and religion, was successful in giving many insiders' views. As already noted, Rogerius had been a resident in the Coromandel region between 1632 and 1642, and he had closely collaborated with indigenous informants such as Padmanābha and other Brahmans. Here the process of knowledge production was the result of a dialectic between local and outside agents.[22] It can be suggested that the social hierarchy described by Rogerius and Valentijn broadly adheres to the Brahmanic textual point of view. Yet Rogerious decade-long stay on the Coromandel Coast must have allowed him to glean into the finer nuances of social organization. We can speculate that he would have certainly reported had he found some glaring anomaly between the textual description of the social hierarchy and the everyday observances of the social divisions.

---

[20] Edward Said (1979, p. 21) writes, "… I believe it needs to be made clear about cultural discourse and exchange within a culture that what is commonly circulated by it is not 'truth' but representations." However, Valentijn's representation of caste system was not his imagination and the caste system occupied European missionaries' discourse in India.

[21] Here in this context Said's representation of the Other linked to the knowledge and power relations do not quite fit the overall context. See Introduction in Said (1979). For further critique of Said's power question see, Clarke (1997) pp. 22–28.

[22] This may be compared with the later colonial knowledge production on the Tamil past where colonizers and colonized both became the co-participants. See Irschick (1994), p. 12.

READING VALENTIJN'S TEXT ALONG THE GRAIN

Below I will discuss Valentijn's text on the prevailing social hierarchy in the Coromandel region during the seventeenth and early eighteenth centuries. It is not surprising that in Valentijn's work one can see a systematic description of different social groups often referred to as castes, their functions in society, and the social ranks. Along with the seventeenth-century work of Rogerius, Valentijn's description can be regarded as an exposition of different caste groups and their activities in southeastern India. The information found in the Dutch sources clearly shows the functions of various caste groups. Valentijn has described different social groups in the five distinct categories of Brahmans (*Bramines*), Kṣatriyas (*Settreas*), Vaiśyas (*Weynjas*), Śūdras (*Soedras*) and the so-called outcastes or Pariyas (*Perrias*). Although this social division follows the textual Brahamanic social categories based on the fourfold *varṇa* (Sanskrit world literally meaning colour but often implied in the sense of order) hierarchy, the Dutch accounts prominently added a fifth category, i.e., the Pariyas or outcastes. Even though the outcastes were known as *chandāla*s in the Brahmanic textual sources, the addition of Pariyas shows that his description somewhat deviated from the normative textual scheme of the fourfold *varṇa* division. Such examples are not so unique, as branching out of the social category was an ongoing process. We will come across such instances in the following paragraphs.

Brahmans

According to Valentijn, and Rogerius before him, Brahmans were ranked at the top of the social order. As Valentijn writes:

All the heathens on this coast agree unanimously that God is well disposed, more than to any other human beings, towards the Brahmans, who stand in His utmost favour. Because of this, they also accord themselves higher social position and caste rank keeping above all the others (Valentijn 1726b, p. 73).[23]

---

[23] "Alle de Heydenen ter dezer Kust stemmen eenparig toe, dat God geen menschen zoo zeer bemind, dan de Bramines, die 't allerdiepst in zyne gunst staan, weshalven zy ook de rang aan hun stam en geslagt boven alle anderen geven". On the supreme position, even above the kings, accorded to the Brahmans in the Vedic and Brahmanic ritual texts and the hierarchy between the Brahmans and Purohita (Brahman chaplain), see Heesterman (1985), esp. pp. 35–38.

Already saddled in the highest social category, the Brahmans claimed other privileges and immunities for themselves. For example, killing a Brahman was considered to be one of the gravest sins according to the Brahmanic scriptures. Yet if someone inadvertently kills a Brahman either in haste or in rage, that person must go for a twelve-year penance pilgrimage, all the while begging with the skull of the killed Brahman and employ the same as a bowl for eating and drinking. He must put together all the alms begged during all these twelve years for building a temple dedicated to *Eswara* (that is, Lord Śiva). This description in Valentijn's work is a direct borrowing from the work of Rogerius.

Valentijn further writes that Brahmans claim that they have originated from the head of the God Brahmā. However, their religion is not formed around the cult of Brahmā; rather, one can find different sects within Brahmanism. These are, as I mentioned above, *Weistnoewa* or Vaiṣṇava, *Seivia* or Śaivas, *Smaerta* or Smārtas, *Schaerwaeka* or Cārvākas, *Pasenda* or Pāṣāṇḍas, and *Tschectea* or Śāktas. Valentijn tells us that these are the chief among their eighty-one or eighty-two sects (see also Bhattacharya 1968, p. 79).[24] He further goes on to describe that the Vaiṣṇavas are the followers of Viṣnu or Rām whom they consider their supreme God. The Vaiṣṇavas are subordinate to none other than their own God. Among the Vaiṣṇavas there are two types of Brahmans. The first is called the *Tadwadi Weistnoewa* or Tattvavādin Vaiṣṇava who possess *tattva* (or, an element of reality) on the knowledge of God. The second is the *Romaroeja Weistnoewa* or Rāmānuja Vaiṣṇava. The latter sect is named after its founder Rāmānuja (1017–1137, or, 1077–1157)—one of the greatest theologians of the Vedānta tradition, known especially for his *viśiṣṭādvaita* or qualified non-dualist philosophy.[25] Without elaborating further on their doctrinal differences, Valentijn sheds more light on their ritual practices. For example, the Tattvavādins put a mark of white line from the nose to the forehead. They also put markings on the shoulders and chest. Rāmānuja Vaiṣṇavas bear on their forehead a white mark, which resembles the Greek Epsilon. Going into

[24] Valentijn's information about numerous sects of Brahmans is largely true of even the modern period. The Brahmans of Telingana are subdivided in numerous distinct sections which can be broadly categorized in three sects which are Smartas, Sri Vaishnavas and Madhavas.

[25] For the biographical sketch as well as his activities in the Chola country and beyond, see Sydnor (2011), pp. 20–22.

further ethnographic details, Valentijn writes that the Rāmānuja Vaiṣṇavas consider themselves superior to other Brahmans primarily because they do not take to trading nor do they visit brothel. These qualities or attributes helped the Rāmānuja Vaiṣṇavas to define and distinguish themselves from other Brahmans.

The second sect of Brahmans is called Śaiva or *Aradh-Iha*. They behold their God *Eswara* or Īśvara as the supreme Lord to whom they believe even the God Viṣṇu bows. They put a three-stripe mark of cow-dung ash on their head. Some of them carry around their neck or in the hair an idol which is called *liṅgam* (a phallus symbolizing the divine regenerative energy). Their children, too, carry this *liṅgam* around their arm. The third sect, called the Smārtas, believe that there is no difference between Viṣṇu and Īśvara, who are not opposed to each other and are in fact the same.[26] Followers of the fourth sect are called the Cārvākas or materialists. They believe that this life is an end in itself and there is nothing to follow after the death, no punishment and no ordeal. Valentijn says that the Cārvākas do not believe in the doctrine of transmigration of soul subscribed to by nearly all other Hindu groups: they are like the Epicureans and have no religion (implying that they are atheist). The fifth sect is called the Pāṣāṇḍas, and many of their attributes overlap with the Cārvākas. They altogether reject the authority of the Vedas and hold that whatever is written in these scriptures is not true. Furthermore, according to Valentijn, the Pāṣāṇḍas live like animals and they entertain sexual relations even with their mothers and sisters.[27]

The mention of these despicable social practices of the Pāṣāṇḍas seems to be the condemnation of those who either drifted away from the dominant sects of Brahmanism or occupied a lowly position within the Brahmanic fold. These remarks can be imagined to be coming from Brahman Padmanābha—the foremost among the informants of Rogerius—who himself belonged to the Smārta Vaiṣṇava sect. However, the Cārvākas who were known to be atheists, did not attract much condemnation for their

[26] Smārta literally means the students of Smṛtis or the Hindu Law books. In southern India the followers of Śaṅkarācārya's monism are designated as Smārtas (Bhattacharya 1968, p. 483).

[27] "Zy leven als de beesten, maakende geen onderscheyd ter wereld 'er tusschen, of zy by hun moeder, dan of zy by hun suster, en, zoo over en weder ook, by hun vader, en broeder slapen" (Valentijn 1726b, p. 74).

beliefs. The sixth sect was that of the Śāktas who believed that Viṣṇu, Īśvara and Brahmā originated from the Śakti or the female source of existence. While the first three sects belonged to the orthodox Brahmanic fold, the last three sects were considered to be the heretical.

From the foregoing description, it appears that while Brahmans commanded the highest social position, there was considerable division within their ranks. The multiplicity of Brahmanic groups continues to persist even today and the claims for a superior status among the rival Brahman sects remain contested. The ethnographic information on Brahmans shows their regimented categories. Apart from the divisions, both Valentijn and Rogerius enunciate that since there was a large number of Brahmans in the realm, the king alone could not keep to the scriptural injunctions on his duty to ensure their welfare and upkeep. Therefore they engaged in occupations other than the study of the religious texts, namely conducting trade in commodities, dealing in medicine, etc. However, they were strictly forbidden to perform anything involving manual labour such as tilling the land, weaving, painting, or a similar servile duty. If any Brahman engaged in these lowly occupations, other Brahmans immediately ostracized him upon learning the breach of the practice (Rogerius 1651, pp. 29–30; Valentijn 1726b, p. 77).

Kṣatriyas and Vaiśyas

Keeping with the classical Brahmanic textual prescription on the *varṇa* hierarchy, Valentijn writes that the *Settreas* or Kṣatriyas are placed at the second highest position in society. He further writes that the aristocracy is primarily drawn from this social group and they constitute the ruling class. Members of this social group are known as Rajas (from Skt. *rājan*) whereas the kings are called the Rajas of Rajas (*Rajas' der Rajas'*). The king of Karnataka takes the *hoogmoediger* (haughtier) title calling himself God of the Rajas. According to Valentijn, from ancient times the Kṣatriyas are considered to belong to the two distinct lineages. The one is called *Soerwansjam* or Sūryavaṁśa—the Sun lineage and the other is known as *Somawansjam* or Somavaṁśa—the Moon lineage. Giving a clear sense of caste proliferation among the Kṣatriyas, Valentijn writes that beyond these two primary lineages, there are other lesser ones that have emerged resulting primarily from their intermarrying with those of the lesser aristocracy. About their duties, Valentijn (1726b, p. 87) writes, "This noble class governs and protects the country, they lead the war, and take care of Brahmans and strive to have a steady income for them (although that is impossible to do as completely as it is desired) and they also ensure that the justice is maintained appropriately."[28]

The *Weinsja*'s or Vaiśyas occupy the third social rank, and again this follows the classical Brahmanic normative textual prescription on social organization. Valentijn informs us that they have under them as *Comittis* (Komatis) and some other are called *Sitti Weapari*, i.e., Chetty Vyāpāri, meaning the Chetty traders:

> They keep themselves busy with trade which is the core activity from which they derive their subsistence, and they are obliged to run their business by fair means. Also, they should not make more than a reasonable profit. In their manners of living they follow the practices of Brahmans and they would not eat anything that has life. (Valentijn 1726b, p. 88).[29]

Valentijn further tells us that the Vaiśyas of Coromandel do not differ much in the observances of their religion from the *Benjaanen*, i.e., Banias (corrupted from Sanskrit *vaṇij* or *baṇij*, trader) of Gujarat. As regarding the practices of idol worship in the temples, these closely follow the norms of the Brahman priests. Furthermore, we are told that the Banias are divided in eighty-three castes, and there are four dominant sects among them, namely, the *Ceurawach*, the *Samaraet*, the *Jogi's* and the *Wistnoe's*. Valentijn says that under these sects, there are again twenty-seven different castes and they do not intermarry or socially mix among themselves. They generally practice endogamy. He observes that the Banias are very clever merchants, many functions as the agents or brokers, they are witty and very exact in arithmetic and they have precise knowledge of all jewelleries. He also remarks on some of the principal sects of the Banias.

[28] "Deze Edelen bestieren, en beschermen het land, zy voeren de oorlogen, dragen zorge voor de Bramines, dat zy hunne behoorlyke inkomsten hebben (hoewel dat ommogelyk zoo volkomen, als dat wel vereyscht werd, te doen is) en verzorgen ook, dat alomme de geregtigheyd werde gehandhaafd." (Valentijn 1726b, p. 87).

[29] "Deze houden sig besig in den Koophandel, waar van zy ook bestaan, ook zyn zy verplicht daar in regtveerdig te handelen, en mogen niet te veel winnen. In hunne levenswyze schikken zy zich meest na die der Bramines, en zullen niets, dat leven ontfangen heeft, eeten." (Valentijn 1726b, p. 88).

The *Ceurawach* sect of the Banias, for example, is ranked the highest and, as Valentijn tells us, the members of this sect do not kill any living beings—they do not even deprive an insect of its life. The priests of the sect cover their mouth with a piece of cloth and they are very careful while walking so as the insects should not get trampled. For this reason, they carry a broom and while walking they sweep the street in order to prevent the insects from coming under their feet. They only partly cover themselves with a small piece of cloth and other parts of their body are without any cloth. Valentijn notes that the priests do not cook themselves and they drink cold water because of the fear of killing any insect in the boiling process. Instead, the priests let other lay Banias cook for them because they do not allow fire or light in their house. They do not eat after sunset, nor do they take to the street in the dark for the same reason of harming or killing a living being (insects). These priests walk bare-footed and go out without covering their head. They take a white or black stick in their hand, and these colours serve to differentiate their ranks. They believe there is only one God, but they deny that He governs everything, attributing this to fortune. Their pious works include keeping fast and giving alms. The greatest holy seer of their faith is *Tel Thenker*, i.e., Tīrthaṅkara, who instituted their Holy laws. They say that the punishment and rewards, also governed by chance, are given after this life (Valentijn 1726b, pp. 89–90). Although Valentijn considers the *Ceurawach* sect as the sect of Banias, it is apparent from his description that the sect in question in fact resembled the Jain trading community.

Valentijn then talks of the second sect of the Banias, i.e., the *Samaraet*s. Just like the *Ceurawach* sect of Banias, the members of this sect would not follow a profession that entails harming a living being. Hence, they worked as smiths, carpenters, tailors, cleaners and similar other professions. He further says that among this sect there are soldiers (although this contradicts their abhorrence for killing), writers, and several others who organize their festivals, wedding parties, and marriages according to their own customs. Although accepting the supremacy of Parameśvara, this sect believes in three Gods. The first among these is *Bramma* or Brahmā, who controls the soul and also gives out the soul by the authority of *Permisceer* or Parameśvara. The second God is *Bussioena* or Viṣṇu who instructs the world and he is also worshipped as Parameśvara. The third God is called *Mais* or Maheśa. When someone dies the soul comes to this God who presents an account of the deceased person's deeds to Parameśvara. Thereafter it is decided as which animal should be the abode of the soul in the next life. They follow the funerary practice of burning their deceased. Many of their women with much courage voluntarily offer themselves up on the funeral pyre to be burnt along with their husbands. According to Valentijn, among this sect also come *Rasbuten* or Rājputs whose women also burn with their husband. Contrary to this, Valentjin writes, in fact in earlier times they would be forced to burn on the pyre believing that they will live then seven times longer (implying in the next seven lives) with their husband.

Valentijn further goes on to describe two other sects of Banias which are *Bisnoe* or Viṣṇu (probably Vaiṣṇavas) and the *Jogi's* or Yogins. He describes these sects' manners, customs, and festivals such as, for example, the marriage between the God Rām and the Goddess Sītā, on the occasion of which the idols of Rām and Sītā were adorned with pearls and expensive jewellery. The dietary pattern of the sect is simple. They eat mainly vegetables, unsalted butter, sweet curd, and *atsjaars* (Hin. *achārs* or pickles) made of different fruits. The Banias of this sect are mostly traders, agents or factors, and "tolkens", or interpreters, and are socially active mainly during their social or religious congregations and ceremonies. As Valentijn writes, the women of this sect are not allowed to become *sati* and burn themselves on the funeral pyre of their husbands. The widows were not allowed to marry or sleep with another man, although, Valentijn reports, in earlier times they could get married with their husband's brother (Valentijn 1726b, pp. 90–91).[30]

The *Jogi's* are the last of the four sects. They too are vegetarian, and they do not take to trading, or do any menial works; on the contrary, they live mostly outside the city or village. They worship their idol *Bruyn* and, next to it, the holy seer called *Medicis*, who is their law-giver.[31] They have their own temples but go mostly to the "Churches" of the *Samaraet*s not so much for the prayer but primarily for leisure and sleeping. Valentijn writes that people dislike these Yogins as they go around almost

[30] "... dog hunne vrouwen werd niet toegestaan zich met hunne mans te verbranden. Ook mogen zy niet hertrouwen, al waren zy niet beslapen. In vorige tyden egter trouwde 's mans broeder de weduwe, ..." (Valentijn 1726b, pp. 90–91).

[31] According to Andrea Acri (personal communication dated 13 May 2019), *Bruyn* may stand for Bhairon (from Skt. Bhairava, the demonic form of Śiva), while *Medicis* could be a heavily distorted form of Matsyendra(nātha)/Macchanda (or the unattested *Macchandeśa, where *īśa* = *nātha*?), a semi-legendary master venerated by the Nātha tradition of Haṭhayoga as well as by the Bhairava-worshiping tantrics of the Kaula stream.

naked, covering only their loins.[32] Instead of wearing clothes, they cover themselves by smearing with ashes, and they are considered holy by some other Banias.

Valentijn's description of the Banias or Vaiśya seems to be rather haphazard. He appears to have put together different sects of Hindus/Jains among the Vaiśya. In part the description follows the textual tradition of the *varṇa* division yet his portrayal of the Jains as Banias or trading castes seems to follow the logic of occupation-derived social identity. However, Valentijn's inclusion of the Rājputs, Vaiṣṇavas, Smārtas, Jains and Yogins among the Banias is intriguing. One may speculate that such inclusion under the generic term of Banias indicates that at least some people from other castes may have taken to trade and at the same time maintained their earlier caste identity. Also, possibly some of them may have associated with traders in one or the other ways. For example, the peripatetic Yogins were instrumental in information transfer, and traders would have much valued them for bringing the tidings about market conditions, commodity prices, and so on.

Śūdras

According to Valentijn, the fourth *geslacht* or social category is that of the *soedra's* or Śūdras. This comprises of the humble folks who are again divided in many different special categories (*zeer byzondre geslachten*), who always had to justify their social position by reference to certain cultural and social practices. As outside appearances can be misleading, one subtly finds out about their actual social rank by enquiring about their marriage relations, their burial practices, and demeanours (*pracht*) according to the perceptions of others. And, if these cannot be tolerated or endured (*verdragen*), then their social rank is immediately lowered.

All particular castes of the Śūdras have taken up different crafts for themselves, and they derive their caste identity from the specific work

[32] Germany-born Jesuit Fr. Athanasius Kircher (1602–80), when dealing with Chinese religion has compared aspects of cult and idolatry between China and India. He writes about the two classes of Brahmans: the wise ones lead a secular life while the Yogins, "live in isolated areas and go naked and are completely dedicated to divinations and other magical arts. If you examine their external life, you will find it austere and full of labors, but indeed inwardly they are hypocrites and criminals." (Kircher 1987, p. 147).

that they do. According to Valentijn, among all these castes those of the *Wellena* or Vellala(?) are the best. Among them are some farmers (Dutch *landbouwers*) and some managers or leaders. Next to the *Wellena* come the *Ambria's* or Ambrias who are mostly agriculturalists (Dutch *zaejers*, lit. sowers or cultivators), servants of the elites, and the masons (Dutch *metzelaars*). Valentijn also tells about another group called the *Cauwrea's*, which is one of the largest. The reason for this is, according to Valentijn, that all those who have forgotten (*vergeten*) their castes are put under the *Cauwrea's*. While some take part in governing or managing the community, others are textile or cloth painters and some among them even become soldiers (Valentijn 1726b, p. 88). Here once can see cases of caste mobility but such instances are mostly from the lower social scales, such as the Vaiśya and Śūdras.

Rather than give detailed descriptions of each of these groups, here I discuss only some of them in order to provide a general picture of their functions in society. For example, the *Sitti's* are traders and they also run errands. Those who deal with the sale and purchase of pigs and chickens are called *Palii*, and among them can also be found farmers (Dutch *zaejers*), painters (Dutch *schilders*) and soldiers (Dutch *soldaaten*). Valentijn also talks of the *Jenea's* who are weavers, and only few among them take to soldiery. Like the *Sitti's*, the *Cottewanten* are fruit sellers and the *Illewatien* sell fruits namely figs, coconuts and unrefined black sugar. According to Valentijn, the *Caikullen* are much scorned people and their wives are mostly prostitutes, and prostitution is not shameful for them as it is for the other groups. The male members are dancers, weavers, farmers, and some are soldiers. The *Sittikaram* are also traders but they deal in merchandises other than those traded by the *Sitti's*. The goldsmiths, blacksmiths, stone-cutters, carpenters, and bricklayers all come from the *Caltajas* caste. The *Carrean's*, the *Makkovars*, *Patnoewa's* and the *Callia's* are fishermen. A distinction is made among them based on their use of large or small nets. The *Conakapule's* who, according to Valentijn, are normally called *Kannekappels*, are the writers while the *Gurrea's* or *Bargeurra'es* are herders and the latters are considered as a relatively respectable caste among the Sūdras. Valentijn further talks about the *Riddi's*, the *Kanawaar's*, and the *Bergawillala* who are peasants (*landbouwers*), and there are also some soldiers from the first two groups. Also, that the *Tolowa's* have become extinct, and the *Palla's* are so few that they come next to the *Perrea's*.

Valentijn also talks of a social group, the *Correwa's* who belonged to the service caste and whose ways of life remind one of the Banjaras. Like the Banjaras, the *Correwa's* did not lead a sedentary life and kept on moving with their entire household. In terms of their calling, they mostly occupied themselves with making pot-covers, and they transported salt from the sea coast to the land by means of little donkeys. According to Valentijn, when they move landwards with the cargo of salt, they are not charged any tolls or duty (also, because they are very poor or, perhaps more importantly, they render indispensable services to the society). The women folk of this group are considered fortune-tellers and through this activity they earn a pretty few pennies every now and then (Valentijn 1726b, p. 88).

At the fifth or bottom rung of the social hierarchy, according to Valentijn, are the *Perrea's* (Pariahs or later derivative, such as Periyars) and *Siriperen*. Both of these sections appear to occupy the lowest of the lowly social status in southeastern Indian Hindu society. Valentijn talks about the hardships imposed on the Perreas by segregating or debarring them from entering the streets where Brahmans lived or from worshipping in the temples of Viṣṇu or Īśvara.[33]

In discussing all these social groups described in the seventeenth- and eighteenth-century Dutch sources, we find a number of hierarchically organized social categories or the so-called castes. We have already seen different factions within the Brahmans, and such multiplicity of subsets was a commonplace for the other social categories as well. Our sources are not very explicit as how society maintained or enforced the social status of these various groups of people, which in any case seem to have existed and functioned according to their respective position. While there appears to be some mobility at the lower rungs of social order, such instances seem to be fairly less common among the two dominant classes of the Brahmans and Kṣatriyas.

CONCLUSION

To see the precolonial Western interests in the Eastern knowledge as the inevitable prelude to imperial subjugation would represent a teleological view. Understanding this complex process entails an examination of the

[33] A parallel between Perrea caste of southern India and the Ragyappa of Tibet may be drawn here. Like the Perreas, the Ragyappas were also scavengers and were responsible for removing carcasses. The Ragyappas were also responsible for dismembering of deceased monks for feeding to the vultures, according to the Tibetan Buddhist tradition. Thus, the Ragyappas were compelled to live in the outskirts of Lhasa, they practised endogamy, and were held morally horrible and ritually dangerous. See Gould (1987), p. 83.

context that goes beyond the simple "knowledge and power" binaries. As I have discussed above, Renaissance Europe had attached great value to the empirical knowledge based on reason. The process of knowledge-production was shaped by, and inevitably led to, urgent needs of self-definition in contrast to the real or imagined Other. This process was also often characterized by unusual curiosity, learning, and relearning about the unexplored world's geographies, customs, mores, social organization, and so forth. The revolution in printing and publication greatly assisted this process in early modern Western Europe (Johns 1998).[34]

Valentijn's compilation of information on different social groups of the Coromandel Coast could be considered a simple enumeration of facts related to that society, or a repository of a significant quantity of historical data presented in an unpolished descriptive form. The data thus compiled serves the important purpose of reconstructing the social realities pertaining to the southeastern Indian society of his time. Whether plagiarized or not, information contained in Valentijn's work is certainly useful for the historian. The fact that he acknowledges the persons who provided him with manuscripts, maps, letters, and papers indeed contributes to enhance the authenticity and value of his work.

Nicholas Dirk criticizes early travel accounts and the missionary records because the information on social division in these sources is tainted with the views of the informants, mostly Brahmans (Dirks 2001, p. 31). On the other hand, he considers the Colin Mackenzie papers as the least mediated ones and as a result, they do not furnish any systematic information or a rounded picture of the castes or social groups.[35] Perhaps it would be a bit far-fetched to imagine that a lack of systematic information on social hierarchy or the caste system suggests the absence of any structural logic in the contexts where these social categories operated. The lack of comprehensive data could also be interpreted to mean that the existing caste hierarchy had become commonplace and this clearly obviated the need for documentation by the insiders in that society. For the foreign observers, such as Rogerius and Baldaeus, who mainly took an interest in

[34] Johns (1998) discusses how early modern Europeans put printing to use to create and maintain knowledge.

[35] According to Dirks (2001), the description of castes was found only in the drawings of Mackenzie, and the Mackenzie papers, produced and compiled by the Brahman local public officials, lacked any systematic description on this subject.

understanding the religion and social structure, social hierarchy or caste seems to have presented itself in multiple layered form. The detailed compilation of data in Valentijn's work on the Coromandel Coast shows a rather fairly systematized functioning of these social groups well before the British colonial authorities inventoried them through census in 1871–72.

Bibliography

Arasaratnam, Sinnappah. 1978. *Francois Valentijn's Description of Ceylon.* London: Hakluyt Society.

———. 1986. *Merchants, Companies and Commerce on the Coromandel Coast 1650–1740*. Delhi: Oxford University Press.

Baker, Christopher J., and David A. Washbrook. 1975. *South India: Political Institutions and Political Change 1880–1940*. Meerut: Macmillan.

Baldaeus, Philippus. 1672. *Afgoderye der Oost-Indische Heydenen zijnde Een Ware en naawkeurige verhandelinge van den Godtsdienst der Indostansche, Choromandelsche, Malabarsche en Ceylonsche Heydenen, hoe de Zelve afgebeelt en geëert werden.* Amsterdam: Johannes.

Beekman, E.M. 1996. *Troubled Pleasures: Dutch Colonial Literature from the East Indies, 1600–1950*. Oxford: Clarendon Press.

Bhattacharya, Jogendra Nath. 1968. *Hindu Castes and Sects: An Exposition of the Origin of the Hindu Caste System and the Bearing of the Sects towards Each Other and Towards Other Religious Systems*. Calcutta: Editions Indian.

Bouglé, Célestin. 1971. *Essays on the Caste System by Célestin Bouglé*. Translated by D.F. Pocock. Cambridge: Cambridge University Press.

Cary, Henry. 1848. *Herodotus: A New and Literal Version from the Text of Baehr with a Geographical and General Index*. London: Henry G. Bohn, York Street, Covent Garden.

Clarke, J.J. 1997. *Oriental Enlightenment: The Encounter between Asian and Western Thought*. London and New York: Routledge.

Dirks, Nicholas B. 2001. *Castes of Mind: Colonialism and the Making of Modern India*. Princeton: Princeton University Press.

Elsner, Jaś, and Joan-Pau Rubiés, eds. 1999. *Voyages and Visions: Towards a Cultural History of Travel*. Reaktion Books.

Gould, Harold A. 1987. *The Hindu Caste System: The Sacralization of a Social Order*. Vol. 1. Delhi: Chanakya Publications.

Guha, Sumit. 2013. *Beyond Caste: Identity and Power in South Asia, Past and Present*. Leiden, Boston: Brill.

Gupta, Dipankar, ed. 1992. *Social Stratification*. Delhi: Oxford University Press.

Havart, Daniël. 1693. *Op-en Ondergang van Cormandel in Zijn Binnenste Geheel Open, en ten Toon Gesteld. Waar in Nauwkeurig Verhandeld Word een Ware, en Duydelijke Beschrijving van Alles, Wat op Zuyder, en Noorder Cormandel, zo in Steden, Dorpen, Vlekken, Rivieren, Gebergtens, enz. Aanmerkens Waardig te Zien is* (t' Amsterdam: Jan ten Hoorn.

Hazard, Paul. 1973. *The European Mind 1680–1715*. Translated by J. Lewis May. London: Penguin Books.

Heeres, J.E., ed. 1907. *Corpus Diplomaticum Neerlando-Indicum: Verzameling van Politieke Contracten en verdere Verdragen door de Nederlanders in het Oosten gesloten, van Privilegebrieven, aan hen verleend*. Vol. 1, 1596–1650. 's-Gravenhage: Martinus Nijhoff.

Heesterman, Jan. 1985. "Brahamin, Ritual, and Renouncer". In *The Inner Conflict of Tradition: Essays in Indian Ritual, Kingship, and Society*, pp. 26–44. Chicago and London: University of Chicago Press.

Ingalls, Daniel H.H., trans. 1968. *Sanskrit Poetry from Vidyākara's "Treasury"*. Cambridge, MA: Harvard University Press.

Irschick, Eugene F. 1994. *Dialogue and History: Constructing South India, 1795–1895*. California: University of California Press.

Irwin, Robert. 2006. *For Lust of Knowing: The Orientalists and Their Enemies*. London: Allen Lane.

Johns, Adrian. 1998. *The Nature of the Book: Print and Knowledge in the Making*. Chicago and London: University of Chicago Press.

Kircher, Athanasius S.J. 1987. *China Illustrata: With Sacred and Secular Monuments, various Spectacles of Nature and Art and Other Memorabilia*, translated by Charles D. van Tuyl. Oklahoma: Indiana University Research Institute for Inner Asian Studies.

Lach, Donald F., and Edwin J. van Kley. 1993. *Asia in the Making of Europe* Chicago. Vol. 3, *A Century of Advance*, book 2: *South Asia*. London: University of Chicago Press.

Nationaal Archief, *Verenigde Oost-Indische Compagnië* (VOC), Inventaris Nummer 341.

O'Hanlon, Rosalind. 2017. "Caste and Its Histories in Colonial India: A Reappraisal". *Modern Asian Studies* 51, no. 2: 432–61.

Prakash, Om. 1998. *The New Cambridge History of India: European Commercial Enterprise in Pre-colonial India*. Cambridge: Cambridge University Press.

Raychaudhuri, Tapan. 1962. *Jan Company in Coromandel 1605–1690: A Study in the Interrelations of European Commerce and Traditional Economies*. 's-Gravenhage: Martinus Nijhoff.

Rogerius, D. Abrahamus. 1651. *De Open-Deure tot het Verborgen Heydendom: Ofte Waerachtigh vertoogh van het Leven ende Zeden, mitsgaders de Religie, ende Godsdienst der Bramines, op de Cust Chormandel, ende de Landen daar ontrent*. Leyden: Françoys Hackes.

Said, Edward W. 1979. *Orientalism*. New York: Vintage Books.

Schmidt, Benjamin. 2002. "Inventing Exoticism: The Project of Dutch Geography and the Marketing of the World, circa 1700". In *Merchants and Marvels:*

Commerce, Science, and Art in Early Modern Europe, edited by Pamela H. Smith and Paula Findlen. New York/London: Routledge.

Smith, Pamela H., and Paula Findlen, eds. 2002. *Merchants and Marvels: Commerce, Science, and Art in Early Modern Europe*. New York/London: Routledge.

Subrahmanyam, Sanjay. 2003. *Forcing the Doors of Heathendom: Ethnography, Violence and the Dutch East India Company*. The Wertheim Lecture 2002. Amsterdam: Centre for Asian Studies.

———. 2007. "Forcing the Doors of Heathendom: Ethnography, Violence, and the Dutch East India Company". In *Between the Middle Ages and Modernity: Individual and Community in the Early Modern World*, edited by Charles H. Parker and Jerry H. Bentley. Lanham: Rowman and Littlefield.

Sydnor, John Paul. 2011. *Ramanuja and Schleiermacher: Toward a Constructive Comparative Theology*. Eugene, Or.: Pickwick Publications.

Terpstra, Heert. 1911. *De Vestiging van de Nederlanders aan de Kust van Koromandel*. Groningen: M. De Wall.

Thomas, Max W. 2000. "Eschewing Credit: Heywood, Shakespeare, and Plagiarism before Copyright". *New Literary History* 31.

Toler, Pamela. n.d. "A Spy in the Spice Trade". *Wonder and Marvel*, http://www.wondersandmarvels.com/2015/11/a-spy-in-the-spice-trade.html (accessed 30 April 2019).

Valentijn, François. 1724. *Oud en Nieuw Oost-Indiën*. Deel I. Dordrecht/Amsterdam.

———. 1726a. *Oud en Nieuw Oost-Indiën*. Deel III. Boek 1: Keurlyke Beschryving van Choromandel, Pegu, Arrakan, Bengale, Mocha, van het Nederlandsch Comptoir in Persien, en eenige fraaje Zaken van Persopolis overblyzelen. Dordrecht/Amsterdam.

———. 1726b. Deel V, Boek 1. *Oud en Nieuw Oost-Indiën*. Dordrecht/Amsterdam.

Van Eerde, Katherine S. 1976. *John Ogilby and the Taste of His Times*. England: Dawson.

Vink, P.M. Markus. 2015. *Encounters on the Opposite Coast: The Dutch East India Company and the Nayaka State of Madurai in the Seventeenth Century*. Leiden, Boston: Brill.

van Linschoten, John Huyghen. 1885. *The Voyage of John Huyghen van Linschoten to the East Indies: From the Old English Translation of 1598*, edited by Arthur Coke Burnell, vol. 1. London: Hakluyt Society.

Wielema, Michiel. 2003. "Adriaan Koerbagh: Biblical Criticism and Enlightenment". In *The Early Enlightenment in the Dutch Republic, 1650–1750: Selected Papers of a Conference held at the Herzog August Bibliothek, Wolfenbuttel 22–23 March 2012*, edited by Wiep van Bunge. Leiden, Boston: Brill.

Wortham, Hale, trans. 1886. Śatakas of Brartṛihari. London: Trübner & Co.

Zinkin, Taya. 1962. *Caste Today*. London, New York: Oxford University Press.

5

British Romantic Poetics and the Idea of Asia

Anjana Sharma

European colonialism, embedded in the values of early capitalism, was, as we well know today, the fecund breeding ground of what was named as Orientalism, the obverse image of all that was then necessarily defined as the Occidental. This historical shift that began in the late seventeenth century gathered momentum in the eighteenth century and came to its fullness in the nineteenth century, forming a long and complex cultural, political, economic, and psychological narrative. This multilayered, multicultural, mixed race account still shapes the ways in which the new global order responds even in the twenty-first century. While initially it was the German and French orientalists who awoke to the "discovery" of new Asian civilizations with rich ancient cultures and traditions, ultimately it was the British colonialists with their army of erudite bureaucrats, lawmakers, and savants who were most successful in "translating" Asia and exporting it back to their mother country—a country soon to be named as Great Britain—from the Asian colonies. Among other modes they did this through lithographs and watercolours; poems, plays and novels; language, script, material objects, and ideas.

Eighteenth-century England, with its vast sweeping changes brought upon by the bloodless Glorious Revolution of 1688 altered forever the relationship between the British sovereign and the British people and became the natural breeding ground for this intercultural transfer. In consequence, in the "long eighteenth century" (thus named by literary critics), there were now present newly awakened republican subjects with a sense of their own individual worth. A populace living in hamlet, village, county, and increasingly in freshly industrialized towns, who were slowly discarding what the poet William Blake would famously describe as their "mind forg'd manacles." This spirit of libertarianism was fuelled by the increasing literacy that, in turn, led subjects to think about themselves in novel ways. The question "Who am I?" could no longer be answered in terms of the former Elizabethan "Great Chain of Being" where, for centuries, a person was cast in the smithy of an iron class demography, a system as old as the history of the founding of feudal Britain itself. The great shift came from the 1700s, when for the first time in British history, the question could be finally begun to be asked in terms of the particular individuated consciousness. With the growth of the coffee house culture in London in the first half of the 1700s, the widening base of the writers and their publics (no longer only dependent on aristocratic patrons), the increasing urbanization of the great city itself, changing patterns of migration and resettlement, and most of all the slow and steady growth of the middle class that aspired to be a *reading* class, England was a new world unto itself. Unsurprisingly then what emerged in its nascent state was the compelling and revolutionary idea of *a* person with not just a local habitation, a name and a length of service, but one with dreams and desires who sought and crafted an altered language to accommodate this new, early modern selfhood. Moreover, and what is central to the argument I am presenting in this chapter, a selfhood that was no longer derived from its socio-cultural-legal-political location in Britain alone was born. The colonial encounter became increasingly central to the ways in which home and not-home began to assume distinct identities.[1]

For a scholar engaged for decades with the study of the literary productions of eighteenth and nineteenth century Great Britain that is now grafted onto a newer interest in the study of intercivilizational dialogues, the shock of the encounter between what is oft still named as the Orient and the Occident is most effectively interrogated through the examination of what are the central texts of the British literary canon. Texts that are—to date—deeply familiar to all English-language educated students

[1] For a greater understanding of the idea of cultural contact and civilizational dialogue shaped by the forces of British colonialism, see Sharma (2018).

of the former colonies of the British Empire such as Samuel Johnson, William Jones, Samuel Taylor Coleridge, Lord Gordon Byron, Sir Percy Bysshe Shelley and, possibly, even a Robert Southey. Names and texts that bring back memories of sultry and warm schooldays where we read of unknown nightingales in dreaming musk rose-scented bowers, of Khans caught and killed in their ordered landscapes where "sinuous rills" burbled and sang, where the *Vanity of Human Wishes* and the great Johnsonian project of the writing of *the* definitive History of the English Language in the Dictionary were part of our colonially inflected school curricula in which we were taught, examined and, hopefully, declared proficient! For in this proficiency and in this success lay the dreaming seeds of our future greatness. Did they not?

And here lies the deep historical irony of our times. Freed one by one in the great wave of nationalism post the ruin of Britain after the Second World War when it lost its "great" tag quickly, Asian countries variously shrugged off, rose up, violently or pacifically overthrew the colonial yoke and became nations with their own constitutions, pledges, flags and systems of governance. Yet, this regime change did not, till much much later, really percolate into the educational ideology of the former subject nations. Hence, the emergence of the curious conundrum of freed citizens who in the same breath could inveigh against the evils of the British Empire and yet quote a line of verse from the pre-imperial Bard, the divine Shakespeare, and others of his ilk. This double bind between past and present continues to bedevil the ways in which the post-colonial imaginary and ways of seeing still work; we, can never quite escape the former masters' discourse of colonial power, prestige and inherent cultural superiority even as we rage against it. It is for now our immutable Other, without which we do not know how to define ourselves.

The opening up of this understanding, this cultural schizophrenia for many in the academy who taught, researched, wrote and guided students, especially in scores of English departments across postcolonial nations, occurred with the publication of the scintillating and original (if sometimes flawed and overstated) *Orientalism* by Edward Said in 1978. With Said's elaborate argumentation and multiple examples there emerged a ready-made methodology on how to opine and deconstruct the historical nightmare of being colonized. This, in turn, slowly crystallized into a fresh understanding of how the civilizational warfare had not ended with the penning back of the former masters into their own island nation. *Au contraire*, its ways of seeing, of naming, of value ascription are still very much embrasured in the Occidental vs. Oriental debate. A much-studied debate that is marked by hierarchy and discrimination that pits the values of a Classical, enlightened, rational and progressive Western consciousness against the eternal Other, the sensuous, slothful, regressive, hidebound Easterner, whose consciousness is best exemplified in literary figurations of its harems, its fanatics with fevered dreams, its Pashas, its Rajahs and its Khans. But sometimes, if only rarely, in the same historical time there is also a glimmer of an Asia that is held as a standard bearer of harmonious love, of a natural and civic-minded selfhood that is freed of tyranny and the inglorious spirit of insubordination and misrule.

So, what then is the point of origin of this epic narrative on the founding of nations, of empires, of British majesty and of a supervening aesthetic of racial and cultural hegemony? And what is the connection of all of this with the idea of Asia itself, which was, from the ancient past a space reflective of values, views, and anxieties of civilizational warfare and cultural and religious schisms? In fact, the history of its naming itself presages the later impossibility to fix its identifying characteristics. By most accounts it is the ancient Greek historian, Herodotus, who is identified as the possible person who first named Asia (even though the name seems to have had currency earlier) in about 440 BCE. Given that Herodotus was a historian who was writing the history that looked at the Homeric epics, particularly *The Iliad*, as a source of historic facts about the supremacy—cultural, martial and political—of the loose set of people called the Greek or the Pelops, he used the nomenclature Asia as a way to define those who were its immediate enemies, the Persian Empire, or Anatolia, the east bank of the Aegean Sea. However, as travel grew and maritime cultures flourished from the 1700s, the name Asia stretched progressively Eastwards to encompass regions, peoples, lands, lived traditions, faiths, races, ethnicities that were denied both their heterogeneity and their cultural syncretism. Rather, by and large, Asia was inscribed in a lexicon that swept away its multiplicity and replaced it with ideas that were patterned on the binary structures of thought that were the markers of the imperial enterprise globally.

Amitav Acharya's (2010) reworking of the famous clarion call for pan-Asian supremacy by Okakura—"Asia is One"—in the first decade of the twenty-first century, in an article titled "Asia Is Not One", is only one more signpost in the evolutionary nature of the Idea of Asia. As a someone who inhabits the disciplinary terrain of International Relations in U.S. Academia, Acharya comments on the concept of "region, regionalization, and regionalism" in the context of Asia in the following ways:

> There is a growing agreement in literature that (1) regions are not just material constructs but also ideational ones; (2) regions are not given or fixed, but are socially constructed—they are made and remade through political, economic, social and cultural interactions; and (3) just like nation states, regions may rise and wither. (Acharya 2010, p. 101).

In the imperial interregnum there was thus (in the light of Acharya's much later formulations) a concerted attempt by British pundits, punters, privateers, priests, Parliamentarians, publicans, poets, and prose writers to create an Asia that would be "remade" in their own image. This collective creation of a diverse yet limited formulation of "Asia" in the eighteenth century was inaugurated at home and by those in the colony with varying tonalities. My own account of Romantic poetics begins with the story of "Oriental" Jones, "Asiatic Jones", otherwise known as Sir William Jones. While Jones died in India, in Calcutta to be precise, almost at the dawn of British Romanticism in 1794, his immersion in and publication on all things East and Eastern became the rich underlying seam on which the idea of Asia flourished, not just in Britain, but in Germany and France too. The story of Jones and the setting up of the Asiatic society needs no replay here but certain salient contributions are still worthy of mention a bit later in this essay.

A close confidante of Samuel Johnson (who also shared his affinity for both the study of philology and the East), Jones was from his student days intrigued by the Orient, particularly its literary productions that were so far removed from the traditions derived either from the Greco-Roman Classical, Latinate heritage or from the Germanic, Norse, French, Spanish, and Italianate ones. Travel and trade brought back into the European world not just material objects related to consumption but also at first Persian, Arabic and Turkish poetics and later, Sanskrit drama and poetry of a kind that was beyond the domain of the expressive aesthetics enshrined in European poetics. From 1770 to 1825 there was a strong demand on the part of the reading public of the Republic of Letters in Britain for tales, accounts, travelogues, anything that let them encounter, explore, and inhabit worlds far removed from their own.

This shift in aesthetics and representations was premised—to say it with Benedict Anderson—upon the "philological-lexigraphic revolution" in the late eighteenth century that occurred not only in England but in many North European countries (Anderson 1983, p. 80). Elaborating on this phenomena, Aamir Mufti (2010) in his essay "Orientalism and the Institution of World Literatures" examines how

> the "discovery" of the classical languages of the East, the invention of the linguistic family tree whose basic form is still with us today, the translation and absorption into the Western languages of more and more works from Persian, Arabic, and the Indian languages, among other [is how] … non Western textual traditions made their first entry as literature, sacred and secular, into the international literary space that had emerged in early modern times in Europe as a structure of rivalries between the emerging vernacular traditions, transforming the scope and structure of that space forever. (Mufti 2010, p. 459)

This in turn created a revolution within the domain of print culture where there was now an economic imperative to orientalize. What was introduced as the new ingredient of good "taste" in Britain was the Oriental seasoning for a palate that demanded as its relish the exotic, the unexpected, the unknown i.e., the Eastern. John Bull and his wife Nancy drank, metaphorically speaking, their Anglo-Saxon ale along with the tea from China and read their Bible along with the new popular accounts of the Koran and the *Bhagvad Gītā*, the *Arabian Nights* and Kālidāsa's *Śakuntalā*, to name just a few. Consequently, beyond commodity that was ingested, worn or displayed there was the consumption of ideas that had their roots in the alien (and alienating?) culture of the East. Indeed, both the plebeian and the elite soon enthusiastically sought to explore all things Eastern. Oxford and Cambridge, both quick to recognize the value of study of Asian civilizations, began training a whole set of young, gifted enthusiasts in a curriculum that focused on the twin disciplines of linguistics and philological enquiry. Archaeology and the comparative mode of religious studies also received great financial support from the British Government.

So how did these representations, these imaginings, these visions travel across the breadth of low and high culture in late eighteenth and early nineteenth century Britain? They came via travelogues, missionary reports, administrative accounts, and also from scholarship done by Indologists and Orientalists. It was the latter in Britain who sowed the seeds for immense translation projects and consequently created a literature influenced by Eastern linguistic systems, by its culture, texts, archaeological findings, religious belief systems and practices.

The initial demand cohered around Persian poetry given that the first travels across the European landmass tended to sign off at that geographical median. Besides, the Persians were familiars from ancient times with their long history of clashes with the Greeks, moving on to the Crusades, and then to the threat and awe of the mighty Ottoman Empire. It was a threat that had Byron use up his immense wealth and die in a failed attempt to wrest Greek, Occidental pride from the Orientalized Ottomans in early nineteenth century.

Furthermore, the forays of the East India Company into India at the outset only served to increase the demand for the Persian language in Britain. Indeed, this interest in the Asian world led to a commercial boom in another form back "home". This was in the form of growing public demand for the "Persian tale", or, what was called in shorthand, the "Eastern tale", of romance and savagery. In a methodology that would become increasingly successful, simple concerns with filthy lucre based on a system of systematic exploitation and loot were, through the great industry of British writers, masked as cultural, scholarly, and fictive accounts of lands that were dark and in need of being saved by the enlightened rationalists who originated in Britain. The myth of the White Man's Burden was in wide circulation and became—for the credulous populace—both a means and an end to justify colonial enterprise. Long before Kipling's famous 1899 poem with the aforementioned title, "White Man's Burden", and its famous opening exhortation

Take up the White Man's burden—
Send forth the best ye breed—
Go bind your sons to exile
To serve your captives' need;

this task had been packaged, relayed and outfitted by a long list of colonialists. Men who clearly understood the vital need to disguise economic exploitation as cultural and intellectual advancement in the pure vein of the prevalent Enlightenment philosophy that spoke of equality, human sympathy and the endless capacity to improve the lot of the human race, especially if it was White.

In one of those curious ideological ironies with which history is replete, it was often those who were the champions of revolutionary liberty at "home" who were also the ones who reaped a rich financial harvest through tales, accounts, epics, and romances that insisted that the concept of liberty had a geographical boundary and thus did not apply to all peoples in all places, *ab initio*. For instance, many of the English Romantic poets, of both the first and second generation, wrote the most vivid and compelling poetic portraits of the evil, decadent East. This collaboration between State interests, publishing needs, and the financial position of many writers who were now devoid of a patronage system that sustained the life of the mind is most effectively analysed by Nigel Leask, in *British Romantic Writers and the East*. Published in 1992, Leask's work examines the history and politics of late eighteenth and early nineteenth century British Empire, and explores its anxieties, and its attempts to recreate an alternative narrative of ideological and intellectual dominance by encouraging the craving, for instance, of Persian tales: "The literary vogue for Persian is clearly linked with the fact that, as the official language of the Mughal Empire, Persian was the medium of official correspondence in British India until 1834, and the language in which British soldiers and bureaucrats were schooled" (Leask 1992, p. 18).

This training was embedded in the cultural practice and beliefs endorsed by a long list of scholars, intellectuals, poets, and government servants who lived in both the world of the Empire and the world that was the Empire. No figure better exemplifies the immense success of this revolutionary zeal to mine alien cultures than the founder member and first President of the Asiatic Society in Calcutta, Sir William Jones. Educated in a historical time where education and degrees were not bound by specialisms, Jones, even as a young man studying in Oxford in 1764, demonstrated a rare capacity to ceaselessly travel in realms that were not always akin—philology, Middle Eastern studies, "Oriental" literature, Greek and Hebrew scholarship among others. Moreover, he was a skilled jurist and noted legal scholar, a linguist trained in many tongues that traversed many worlds and continents far apart, a fellow of the Royal Society and a member of the select literary club lead by the redoubtable Dr Samuel Johnson. In this Johnsonian club of the enlightened elite he kept company with the likes of the famous Irish Parliamentarian, Edmund Burke, the renowned theatre owner and actor David Garrick, and the "natural scientist" Adam Smith among others.

As a youthful undergraduate William Jones had already begun dabbling in writing poems that moved away from the strictly British and Britain-focused themes and sought to go beyond into the subjects and sources that originated more in Britain's cultural encounters with an extensive Eastern world. While at Oxford he had begun writing works that had links with Persian literature. Nevertheless, it was not his immense literary and linguistic prowess that finally brought him to Calcutta on 25 September 1783; it was for his excellent command of a multicultural knowledge system coupled with his judicial expertise that he was sent off by the Crown to India.

What stumped the British in India despite their long sojourn in the country and their awareness of caste and religious systems was the nature of law and its administration within a multicultural society. A society, moreover, that ceaselessly jostled, for instances, Muslim and Hindu legal systems that imparted justice via laws that were not codified into a single document that could be parsed by all. British jurisprudence with its monologic narrative failed in supporting the British government servants who needed to increasingly govern colonial subjects who came from varying cultural and religious traditions that were the bedrock of personal law systems. It was this huge abyss in governance that made William Jones the best possible candidate at a crucial historical moment in the forward charge of British imperial policy in India.

Jones, however, was not the first Orientalist to arrive in India as a Company man; he was just the most gifted in a line of other Orientalists such as Charles Wilkins (1770), Nathanial Halhed (1772) and Jonathan Duncan (1772), who were the close coterie around Governor General Warren Hastings, who was still far away from the ignominy of a public impeachment in England in 1788 (lead by Jones' friend, Edmund Burke) over charges related to his misconduct, mismanagement, and fiscal corruption in India. Meanwhile, four years or so before Hastings' recall to England, he was instrumental in helping Jones realize his ambitions for India. The traveller Jones, ever the gentleman diarist true to the times he lived in, spoke of his voyage to India from Britain in his oft-quoted *First Anniversary Discourse* at the establishment of the Asiatic Society (with the blessings and patronage of Hastings) in 1784 in Calcutta:

> When I was at sea, last August, on my voyage to this country, which I had long and ardently desired to visit, I found one evening, on inspecting the observations of the day that *India* lay before us and *Persia* on our left, whist a breeze from *Arabia* blew nearly at our stern.... It gave me inexpressible pleasure to find myself in the midst of so noble an amphitheatre, almost encircled by the vast regions of *Asia,* which has ever been esteemed the nurse of the sciences, the inventerres of delightful arts, the scene of glorious actions, fertile in the productions of human genius, abounding in natural wonders, and infinitely diversified in the forms of religion and government, in the laws, manners, customs and languages, as well as in the features and complexions of men. (Jones 2010, p. 1).

This expansive sense of Asia coupled with the pioneering spirit of adventure and appreciation was not quite the note that was struck by others who, unlike Jones, never went beyond the traditional Gentleman's Tour of the classical and picturesque Europe, men whose minds were locked into the aesthetic notions of the sublime derived from Kant's and Burke's treatises on the subject. Neither was there, for the most part the panoptican Jonesian vision that found Sanskrit to be "more perfect than *Greek*, more copious than *Latin* and more exquisitely refined than either; yet bearing to both of them a stronger affinity, both in the roots of verbs, and in the forms of grammar, than could have been produced by accident…" (Jones 2010, p. 21).

Post Said, of course, such a generous reading of Jones would invite only brickbats from the academy, but it's a moment now in world history where it is possible for us to interrogate the Orientalist discourse in ways that both acknowledge the debt to Said and still make a departure from a reading that is defined by the same operative binary as was once used by the colonial masters against their subjects, so as to reprise novelist Thomas Hardy's evocative title, the Native is Returning, but to an altered territory. British response to the encounter with the multiple civilizations of Asia was—as post Saidian Javed Majeed very effectively argues in *Ungoverned Imaginings: James Mill's The History of British India and Orientalism* (1992)—on a variegated register. Majeed's thesis goes beyond Saidian formulations as he demonstrates how the views on the East, and particularly India, began to alter and harden in the nineteenth century: the "romantic" attitudes of Jones towards the riches of Asian traditions, heritage, texts, and languages, were steadily being effaced by the imperatives of an Evangelical and missionary imperial nation. It was a transformation that drew its historical legitimacy from the changeover in 1813 from India being a trading colony to becoming the veritable Jewel in the Imperial Crown.

It is the poetry and other writings of the British Poet Laureate, Robert Southey that best represent this transformation. Southey was a close companion of Coleridge, a fellow radical, and both espoused the cause of the French Revolution. Southey, who at the beginning of his career wrote extensively on England's slave trade, began, by 1798 to veer towards a cultural and political conservatism that soon congealed into a diatribe against all cultures that did not—for him—espouse the domain of Evangelical Christianity. In 1801, while still influenced by the celebratory views of Asia perpetuated by William Jones, Southey wrote an early long epic poem entitled *Thalaba the Destroyer*. With his creation of an enlightened and, virtuous Middle Eastern Muslim ruler, Thalaba, Southey critiqued home-grown forms of tyrannical authority in the revolutionary manner that is signature Romanticism.

But by 1810, with the strong British turn towards India as a source of securing wealth for its own people, Southey moved a great distance not only from the egalitarianism of a world citizen such as William Jones, but also totally rejected his own radical roots. Censorious of foreign cultures from as early as 1796 (when he went with his missionary uncle to Portugal), by 1810 Southey colluded with the aims of the British State to establish for the British public at large the necessity of the taking away of the freedom of other peoples and of other cultures. This rejection now went further geographically into Asia, as the world of Persian now gave way to the world of Sanskrit, namely India. This was most effectively done through the writing over ten years—from 1801 to 1810—of his last long epic poem, *The Curse of Kehama* (1810). Revealing the shift in taste, consequent in the shift in the engagement with Asia, the poem is not a "Persian tale" but a "Hindoo Romance". It would prove to be the most successful piece of poetry by Southey in a career distinguished by mediocre verse and low sales. Sited in an India that is not historically represented, it regales the British audience with an account of the monstrous religions and despotic, "orientalized" Reign of Terror unleashed by the Hindu King Kehama upon a hapless lower caste girl and her father as they are hounded by the cruel king across the three worlds. He is supported in his evil designs by the Brahmins and is finally only defeated by the direct intervention of the Hindu Gods themselves. Through its long length Southey provides a twisted ethno-religious account of Hinduisms and its monstrous ethos.

For a modern reader the poem lacks both intellectual coherence and poetic beauty; yet, that does not seem to have deterred the British reader who readily endorsed the vision propounded by Southey since the relationship between Crown and Colony had concretized. Despite his stated distaste for giving to his Christian, British readers images and behaviours embedded in "barbarous and licentious rites", he had "excellent political and cultural reasons" for publishing this poem (Bolton 2007, p. 120). Drawing upon the treasure trove of Indological and Eastern sources, Southey, now firmly an agent of British imperial policy, flatly derides Hindu culture, read as a high Brahmin and Kṣatriya culture, and excoriates its sensuality, power, lust, and sheer animality. *The Curse of Kehama* uses the works of early Orientalists to inscribe a narrative that creates a "nationalist aesthetic that relied on projecting British institutions and values against … less developed less moral norms", and provides a glimpse of the "new justifications of the imperial project and new anxieties on its depiction" (Bolton 2007, p. 3).

This anxiety and absolute rejection of Asian/Eastern aesthetics, religions, and systems of governance is most memorably found in a little, unfinished poem. In popular lore it is seen as an Eastern opium-induced fantasy and vision that most of us who have studied in English-language schools have known since childhood: Coleridge's *Kubla Khan*. For a little, seemingly fragmentary poem, the pithy account of the Khan Kubla has continued to bewilder and befuddle readers of English Romantic verse. Written either possibly around 1797 or 1798 by Coleridge, it was finally only published in 1816 under the patronage of the leader of the Romantic Brigade—Lord Byron. Coleridge's poem is a quintessential "Oriental" poem that melds Asian poppy and the "close association between dreaming and the setting of the Oriental tale" in popular imagination (Vallins, Oishi, and Perry 2013, p. 180).

Coleridge's version of the Mongolian, Asian bogey man, the powerful empire builder, Kublai Khan, obviously speaks to a huge cultural fear that existed in Britain with regard to Asian masculinity, Asian prowess, and Asian warrior culture being triumphant. The poem, of course, feeds off the British cultural fascination with China—given its recent encounters with the country—and is one of the rare instances where the image of an omnipotent Chinaman overlays portraits drawn from Muslim or Hindu sources. If ever a poem fits into the binary structure of the Orient versus the Occident it is *Kubla Khan*. In this little fragment of verse, the ordered, wealthy, controlled world of the Chinese garden that surrounds Kubla's palace in fabled Xanadu is ruptured by the sounds of first a "woman wailing for her demon lover", then threatened by the atavistic whispers "of ancient voices prophesying war", and finally destroyed by the "flashing eyes and floating hair" of the British poet with his lineage firmly anchored in Greco-Roman vatic traditions. The Chinese garden, "chinoserie", the "pleasure dome"—all a great rage in Britain in early nineteenth century—are totally displaced by Coleridge in a cultural shorthand that reinstates the superiority of the British over even the greatest threat to old Europe—the Mongolian marauders led by Kubla's ancestor, Chengiz Khan. It is, as we may agree even today, a memory of the fear of the Chinese dragon and its thunder and fire and power and might that still haunts the Western world.

So why did Byron resurrect the almost failed career of Coleridge through the judicious publication of an unfinished, hard-to-interpret poem that nevertheless scored high with the same British public which had earlier rejected the esoteric longer poems of Coleridge? Not, as literary critics would have us believe, because he was charitable towards an old genius whose work he sometimes admired. The reason for the choice of this poem lay in Byron's own success as a poet who was the most commercially and critically successful of all the Romantic poets.

Byron's spectacular partnership with the publisher John Murray—a partnership that endured even after Byron's exile from Britain—was based on their mutual recognition of the saleability of literary works related to the East. Murray urged him to cash in on the craze for the "Oriental Tale" and Byron was quick to agree. In the period from 1813 to 1816, Byron wrote no less than five highly successful long poems that had the East as their subject. In May 1813, Byron wrote to Irish poet Thomas Moore, urging him to: "Stick to the East … The North, the South, and West have been exhausted; but from the East we have only Southey's unsaleables… the public are orientalising and pave the path for you" (Byron 1813, p. 193). Commenting on this Nigel Leask says: "Byron speaks like a Levantine or East India merchant who has tapped a lucrative source of raw materials in a newly opened up Orient, which he feels will make a splash in the home markets." (Leask 1992, p. 13).

How very successful he was in becoming the primary exporter of Eastern manners and Eastern values is testified to by his presence in the scholarly pages of the *Asiatic Journal*, published in February 1830: "Of all the poets of this country, Lord Byron is preminently the poet of the East. He is the only real English poet who has painted Asiatic manners from personal observation" (*Asiatic Journal* 1830, p. 145). This endorsement derives not just from the many works with the loose Eastern setting that were in wide circulation, but more so on travel accounts of Byron as he travelled with his friend John Cam Hobhouse across the Mediterranean and then onto Albania and Turkey among others lands. Byron's version of the Gentleman's Tour—a vital centrepiece in the education of a true-blue British aristocrat—was a result of historical change and not of choice. Given that Napoleon Bonaparte's armies were cutting a huge swathe over large parts of Europe, Byron had no chance but to travel eastwards. It proved to be a boon since it gave him direct exposure to worlds that had only come to him textually so far. His stay in Albania particularly as the guest of the ruling Ali Pasha gave him an insider's view into Islamic culture and its customs, religious systems, and most significantly its treatment of women. While he appreciated the richness and architectural marvels of this world, most particularly Albanian dress, he also responds as an insular Britisher by castigating emblems of Oriental cruelty, tyranny, and deep-seated hierarchy. On his return to Britain he embarked on the task of writing *his* Occidental version of the Orient. Poem after poem is built on the clash of civilizations and the impossibility of reconciling the twain.

The Giaour, published in 1813 after Byron's returns from his travels, is the first of these long narrative poems. Inspired by the Greek War of

Independence against the mighty Ottoman Empire, the subtitle calls it "A Fragment of a Turkish Tale". It spins out in evocative verse the account of the battle between the Giaour (a pejorative term used by the Turks to denote a *kafir* or infidel) and his cultural *doppelganger*, Pasha Hassan. The crux of the tale is the clash between the unnamed Venetian, a reluctant Christian who does not espouse the faith, and the devout Muslim Pasha Hassan over a Christian slave girl, unsurprisingly called Layla, who falls in love with the Giaour and betrays the Pasha. Byron, uses the popular accounts brought by travellers to the East on how women are punished for infidelity by being killed to display the decadent cruelty of the misogynistic and chauvinistic Orient and crafts a narrative that is fast-paced and cinematic. Furthermore, the poem reveals in its lexicon how far the Persian vocabulary and religion has seeped into British culture by referring to Ramazan and the Feast of Bairam. The tale is complex and feeds into the great anxiety of the European male whose masculinity is under severe threat with the knowledge of the mighty sexual prowess of the Pashas and Sultans that is located in a specific material entity not found in Christian cultures—the harem.

The harem then, more than the mosque or the palace, becomes in British poetics the site and sign of the unbridgeable gap between Europe and Asia. It is the Venetian hero's ability to penetrate into this closed and secret world, the heart of Eastern pride and power, and steal away the "Circassian" slave Layla, that marks the poem as firmly embedded in European hegemony. Thus, for all the heroic valour and skill that Byron gives to the Pasha Hassan, it is ultimately the death blow given by the Venetian Giaour that provides the fitting dénouement on how the Occidental will absolutely defeat the Oriental, for that is the civilizational arc of the times that Byron is writing in and also that of those who are his committed readers. How widespread this ideology is across Europe can easily be seen through a single example I will share here. In the Louvre Museum in Paris hangs a famous painting by the Romantic French Painter, Eugene Delacroix, executed and displayed almost a decade and a half later in 1827. The painting is named thus: "Combat of the Giaour and the Pasha". There is no need for an explanatory gloss for the title which shows the fierce single combat of the two men from two cultures lodged in a death combat with each other. The spectacle is viewed by an audience well versed in the knowledge of the defeat of the Pasha by the Venetian, or, more aptly, of the victory of the Occidental civilizational values over the Oriental ones.

So, were the great contributions of a William Jones to propagate the values of Eastern culture as intellectually rich, religiously diverse, and of foundational importance to the construction of European cultures lost forever? Did no voice of the period speak out in the gathering clamour of racial and cultural superiority to endorse, celebrate, and glorify the syncretic heritage and deep textual traditions of the Eastern/Asiatic world?

There was one: Percy Bysshe Shelley. Literary and cultural studies today recognize that if there was any true inheritor of William Jones in the nineteenth century it was the truly radical and radicalized poet Shelley, whose later verse sang the Jonesian ode to the study and amalgamation of Oriental cultural, linguistic, and textual traditions. In the manner of Jones, Shelley too, sought through his writings to explore and examine the gaps and absences in the Occidental world, and fill them with not the material but the philosophical wealth of Eastern philosophy. Jones's publications on the comparative study of the gods of Greece, Italy, and India, his botanical and descriptive writing, his Sanskritic "*Hymn to Vishnu*" (1785), his writings on the Vedānta, the Upaniṣads, and yoga were all devoured by Shelley back home in Britain long after the demise of their charismatic author. Shelley's radical verse poems share Jones's admiration for Indian culture as the seed and fount of all that followed. While there are many poems I can turn to actualize this reading, for the purpose of this chapter, I will briefly look at one of the last poems of Shelley, composed before he tragically died in a freak storm while sailing in Lake Como.

It is the lyric (or psycho) drama *Prometheus Unbound* (1821) that is possibly the best example of his homage to Jones. Musical, mystical, and undeniably universalist in its treatment of ideas, cultures, and ideologies, *Prometheus Unbound* is a remarkable poetic and intellectual achievement. It combines Hellenic aesthetics, mythology, and politics of classical Greece as imagined and represented in the tragic dramatist, Aeschylus's play written in the fifth century BCE, *Prometheus Bound*, with an altered awareness of Eastern philosophy, Asian landscapes, and religious traditions. The classic Occidental story of the divine Prometheus who stole fire from the Gods and gave it to suffering humanity—a cultural shorthand for the Age of Enlightenment—was often used by Romantic writers who, in an overweening act of arrogance, cast themselves as the Promethean heroes of their own revolutionary times. For this violation Prometheus was imprisoned by the tyrant Jupiter, bound in the icy fastness of the Caucasian mountains, eternally doomed to have his heart and liver eaten by vultures every day into an endless future of torment, pain, and suffering. In the Aeschylian drama, the reprieve comes only when Prometheus bows down to the superior force of Jupiter and acknowledges his "crime".

In Shelley's hands though, the story of the unbinding of Prometheus takes on a whole different set of related meanings. *His* Prometheus is starkly different from the original Aeschylus' victim-hero, being embedded in a post-revolutionary dialectical thought world that flows both westwards and to the east seamlessly. The layered landscape of the poem accommodates multiple civilizations as Occidental and Oriental, Greek, Italian, and Indian are all intermixed and Shelley—in a significant bow in the direction of a peaceful and harmonious ancient Asia—recasts a myth central to Occidental imaginary. Thus, his own version of the hero of the world is bound not in the Russian Caucasus, but, in "a Ravine of Icy Rocks in the Indian Caucasus", i.e., in the Hindu Kush mountains of Asia, Kashmir to be precise. It is an alternative sacred geography that is rooted in and routed through Shelley's readings of Jones and other Orientalists who saw the Hindu Kush as the cradle of the human civilization from which all others originated. Through his short but productive poetic career Shelley read widely through works that had Indian locales or referents:

> In 1811, he wrote enthusiastically several times about *The Missionary, an Indian Tale*, by Lady Sydney Morgan, who had not been to India, but in 1812 he ordered Edward Moor's *Hindu Pantheon* and the works of Sir William Jones, both first hand observers ... In the spring of 1820, [the year in which *Prometheus Unbound* was being composed] writing to his cousin, Thomas Medwin, he showed his familiarity with the latter's *Sketches in Hindoostan*, which Ollier later published ... and when Medwin came to Pisa in that fall, Shelley not only began studying Arabic with him, but heard him read aloud portions of his journal in India. (Raben 1963, p. 99).

It is no surprise then that geography of a Classical text of ancient Greece no longer suffices in the nineteenth century for Shelley. In a revolutionary departure, in Shelley's version, it is not only the locale that changes but also the character of Prometheus that is recast: the transformation of the hatred filled Prometheus is a case in point. Unable, in the opening Act of the play, of forgiving Jupiter and his tyrannical power, and cursing him with rebellion and death, Shelley's psychodrama seems to be initially close to the original text. But then Shelley introduces—in a powerful interventionist move—the agent of liberation and of profound change in his rewriting of Promethean mythology. This figure is, perhaps on account of the increasingly masculinized world of early Victorian England not only a woman, but a woman named "Asia". It is her spirit of love and forgiveness that melts the metaphorical ice and ends and brings peace to the tortured heart of Prometheus, who then recants his curse upon Jupiter voluntarily. By his refusal to pursue vengeance and participate in a power struggle, Prometheus frees himself from the duality of love and hate, of freedom and its opposite, in effect from the Manichean world of Western culture which is, for Shelley, the ultimate psychic and spiritual prison of his times. This throwing off of the yoke of mental and spiritual enslavement happens in the play, as mentioned earlier, through the figure of Asia. Shelley's Asia is the living spirit of spring like resurrection and the character who unleashes the great, subterranean power residing in the universe to destroy oppression—Demogorgon—thus ensuring the downfall of Jupiter and the lyrical drama ends with her marriage to Prometheus.

Postcolonial readings of the play have yielded a rich harvest. Hence, the lyric drama, from being read for the longest time as a literary relic espousing elite values and too esoteric has now become the one Shelley poem one must read, at least in many English departments in India. Why is that? Because newer readings of the verse drama have adopted, adapted, and absorbed the Romantic aesthetics of Shelley by unravelling and embracing the universalist, unifying spirit of a Prometheus who is "redefined as a syncretic figure analogous to the Greek Dionysus, the Persian Zoroaster, the Jewish Noah and the Hindu God, Rama." (Khan 2008, p. 48). Accompanying him as his equal is the empowered and enlightened symbol of feminine energy, not an Occidental Europa, but an Indianized Asia, who is now often read as the principle of creative energy and fecundity, the Indian Goddess, Śakti. In this retelling of the Promethean tale Shelley slips the binding traditions of an Occidental world that is sterile and backwards and becomes the liberator of the Spirit of Asia that shines across the blue planet. For a brief, very brief moment then, the forward charge of Britannica is reversed by a lone voice, a British Poet of the imperial times whose poetic heart and practice is found in Asia.

In the words of Andrew Warren, what in effect occurs from the time of a Southey to a Shelley with regard to the "Orient" is a reversal of the values of conservatism and cultural myopia. Shelley's latter-day post-Revolutionary response reads at odds against the general arc of the narrative of the deepening of Britain's sense of its own racial and cultural superiority, and hence, is even more worthy of notice:

> The Orient hereby becomes a charged figure in the British ideological imaginary, one which reflects the internal politics of Regency England and shapes Britain's burgeoning colonial project. If Southey's

> Orient is an unchanging and timeless region that demands European interventions, then the Young Romantics present an Orient wherein change is not only possible, but inevitable and incalculable. (Warren 2014, p. 81)

I end anecdotally: given his great fascination for India, Shelley enquired late in his life if he could go to India as an East Indiaman. Tragically he died before he could fulfill that desire. But in his poetry and through his poetry he still lives in India, in Asia, and is at home in the world.

Bibliography

Acharya, Amitav. 2010. "Asia is Not One". *Journal of Asian Studies* 69, no. 4 (November): 1001–13.

Anderson, Benedict. 1983. *Imagined Communities: Reflections on the Origin and Spread of Nationalism*. London: Verso.

Asiatic Journal, The. 1830. January–April 1830. Vol. NS1 (February 1830), p. 145. London: Parbury, Allen and Co.

Bolton, Carol. 2007. *Writing the Empire: Robert Southey and the Romantic Colonialism*. London: Pickering and Chatto.

Byron, Lord Gordon. 1819. "Letter 134. To Mr. Moore. August 28, 1813". *Life, Letters and Journals of Lord Byron*. London: John Murray.

Drew, John. 1987. *India and the Romantic Imagination*. Delhi: Oxford University Press.

Franklin, Michael J. 2006. *Romantic Representations of British India*. London and New York: Routledge.

Hagerman, C.A. 2013. *Britain's Imperial Muse: The Classics, Imperialism, and the Indian Empire, 1784–1914*. New York: Palgrave Macmillan.

Jones, Sir William. 2010. *Man and Nature: Discourses of Sir William Jones*. Kolkata: The Asiatic Society.

Khan, Jala Uddin. 2008. "Shelley's Orientalia: Indian Elements in His Poetry". *ATLANTIS Journal of the Spanish Association of Anglo-American Studies* 30 (June): 35–51.

Leask, Nigel. 1992. *British Romantic Writers and the East: Anxieties of Empire*. Cambridge: Cambridge 1992. University Press.

Majeed, Javed. 1992. *Ungoverned Imaginings: James Mills' The History of British India and Orientalism*. Oxford: Clarendon Press, 1992.

Mufti, Aamir R. 2010. "Orientalism and the Institution of World Literatures". *Critical Inquiry* 36, no. 3 (Spring): 458–93.

Raben, Joseph. 1963. "Shelley's *Prometheus Unbound*: Why the Indian Caucasus?". *Keats-Shelley Journal* 12 (Winter): 95–106.

Said, Edward. 1978. *Orientalism*. New York: Pantheon Books.

Sharma, Anjana. 2018. "Records, Remnants and Inter-Asian Interconnections". In *Records, Remnants and Inter-Asian Interconnections: Decoding Cultural Heritage*, edited by Anjana Sharma. Singapore: ISEAS – Yusof Ishak Institute.

Vallins, David, Kaz Oishi, and Seamus Perry, eds. 2013. *Coleridge, Romanticism and the Orient*. London: Bloomsbury.

Warren, Andrew. 2014. *The Orient and the Young Romantics*. Cambridge: Cambridge University Press.

Part III

Networks of Knowledge Across the Indian Ocean

6

An Indian Ocean *Ribāṭ*: War and Religion in Sixteenth-Century Ponnāni, Malabar Coast

Mahmood Kooria

INTRODUCTION

"I encourage you for *ribāṭ*. [...] Two eyes will never be touched by the fire of Hell: an eye which weeps out of fear of the omnipotent God and an eye which spends the night in guarding in the Cause of God against the infidels," says Qāḍī Muḥammad al-Kālikūtī in a war-speech written around 1570 to incite his audience against the Portuguese intruders into the Malabar Coast in southwest India. This passage catches our attention for its use of the concept of *ribāṭ*—an unusual term in the socio-cultural context of the battles between the European and Asian powers in the waters of Indian Ocean.

This chapter is an attempt to examine the micro-level, socio-cultural setting of a region in the Malabar Coast in the sixteenth century (and its entanglements in the broader predicaments of the Indian Ocean world), at the time of wars between the Portuguese and the local rulers, the Zamorins, along with their Muslim supporters. The Muslim involvement in the anti-Portuguese wars was not inadvertent; rather, it was part of a larger web of commercial and religious interests, traditions, and histories. The Muslims in Malabar did have personal motivations to wage war, but so did the Zamorins, the Portuguese, the Mamlūks, and the Ottomans to collaborate with or counter one another in the maritime littoral. The existing conceptualizations of these battles have ignored the ways in which the local communities perceived and framed their military engagements in terms of a wider worldview and praxis. This chapter enquires such indigenous justifications and conceptualizations by looking at their own writings, and it suggests that the local Muslims ratiocinated their geo-political spheres in terms of *ribāṭ*, a concept of coastal guardianship rooted in Islamic vocabulary of war and peace.

In the last four decades, several historians have suggested various models to understand the political spectra in which the Muslims of Malabar or of broader South Asia had existed and operated. In a broader South Asian context, they have conceptualized the frontier zones in different ways (Eaton 1978; Gommans 2002; Green 2012; Hasan 2004; Ernst 2009). Although their studies inform my discussion, one should bear in mind that their analysis is grounded on a Delhi/Mughal-centrism, for they focus on the idea that a particular "space" becomes a frontier thanks to its being peripheral to an imperial centre. Only through that framework the "marginal" zones of the southern parts of the subcontinent get their due. As Malabar was never annexed to the empire of Delhi or Mughals, nor did it act as a periphery to the empire, such Delhi/Mughal-centric notions of frontier are of little help to analyse its historical nuances. The political and cultural specificities of Malabar, by way of not being a part of any major Islamic/Muslim kingdoms, and thanks to its marked religious diversity, have to be taken into due consideration when analysing the geo-cultural significance of a frontier. This point is all the more evident when one looks into other constructions of cartographical boundaries of the Muslim societies of South Asia. For example, the prime alternative geographical construction of *wilāya* or the spiritual jurisdiction of a Sufi-master (*shaykh*) in contrast to the political dominion of the rulers could not be clearly functional to Malabar, at least in the sixteenth century, during which we see very little references to the authority of Sufis or ʿulamāʾ over the community in its entirety.

In his study on the Māppiḷa Muslims, Stephen Dale (1980) identified Malabar as a "South Asian frontier". Taking the concept from the early Ottoman contexts, Dale suggested that the Māppiḷas formed a militarized frontier to fight against the Portuguese in the sixteenth century and against the British in the nineteenth and twentieth centuries. This suggestion is in several respects elusive as it does not encompass the peculiarities of the region and its history. Dale does not tell us what "South Asian" elements the Māppiḷas fought for or sought to protect, if Malabar was such a subcontinental frontier. The region and its Muslim community were hardly a part of the wider South Asian polity: it was never conquered by any mighty kingdom of northern India (Islamic or otherwise), and its communication with the rest of South Asia was a rarity rather than the norm in the premodern period. Malabar was a narrow strip of land along the Arabian Sea in the west and the untameable mountain ranges of the Western Ghats in the east blockading the region from the rest of South Asia overland. Notwithstanding minimal cultural and religious substrata, the region and its diverse communities belonged more to the socio-political and economic realms of the Indian Ocean, through which they communicated and interacted with the rest of the world. That was the frontier with which they were more concerned.

Bearing in mind that the mainland-centred conceptions of frontier do not help us evaluate the historical processes of a coastal belt like Malabar, here I suggest a very specific notion of frontier, namely *ribāṭ*, as conceptualized by the community in the period of encounters. This conception makes for a better tool to analyse the complexities of Malabar and its ʿulamāʾ networks in their circumstantial connections with the existing non-Islamic political structures and Islamic aristocracy. The concept of *ribāṭ* is sourced from Islamic classical texts, and it found elaborations as praxis in the Islamic heartlands as well as in several Muslim communities of the Mediterranean and Atlantic in times of war. As such, it provides a reasonable category to analyse the complex nature of the Muslim battles in the Indian Ocean coasts from South/East Africa to South/East Asia. It also helps us understand the ways in which Muslims from such distant lands as Malabar conceptualized their socio-political and religious struggles within the larger worldview of Islam.

In the following section, I will briefly describe the debates around the concept of *ribāṭ* among Islamicists and historians who have taken contrasting views on its origin, development and functions. Having highlighted the commonalities among their arguments, I will emphasize the centrality of religiosity, maritime conflicts, and defensive nature of *ribāṭ*s. On the basis of this framework and its potential to understand the Muslim engagements in wars in the Indian Ocean world, I will then zoom into one particular micro-region within Malabar: Ponnāni—which, with its port-town and equally important religious, educational, political, and military structures of the Muslims and the Zamorins, was the most important *ribāṭ* in the area. Having explored the formations and transformations in this *ribāṭ* in the course of battles between the Portuguese and local rulers in the sixteenth century, I will conclude with a reflection on the larger context of Indian Ocean Islamic networks of jihad (holy war) vis-à-vis European ventures and on the conceptual potentiality of *ribāṭ* to understand other conflict areas between the sixteenth and the nineteenth centuries.

RIBĀṬ AS A CONCEPT

The term *ribāṭ* is found in foundational and classical Islamic texts such as the Quran and the ḥadīths. Etymologically, it derives from the root *r.b.ṭ*. It refers to a link, relationship between two things or ideas, in which one is caused or affected by the other; or to a connection between a number of people, things, ideas, or places. Historically, there is a drastic shift from its early meanings and its usages in the scriptures to its new meanings associated with war-related contexts. Even so, historians have differing opinions on its connotation within the realm of war, for instance as to whether *ribāṭ* is simply an ideology of jihad associated with certain structures, whether it is an accumulation of actions and ideas into a particular place, or whether it implies any frontier fortifications. According to some, "it is impossible to present an unequivocal definition" of *ribāṭ* (Chabbi and Rabbat 1995).

In the early stages of Islamic expansion, the *ribāṭ*s functioned as watch-posts (precisely known as *miḥrā*s), as a detailed reference by the tenth-century Arab geographer al-Muqaddasī (947–990 CE) indicates (Muqaddasī 1897, p. 291, cited by Khalilieh 1999, pp. 213–14). At that time, the *ribāṭ* operated as an alarm system when the coastal frontiers were under attack. Whenever a threat appeared in the coastal lines, the watchtowers indicated the threat, via the signals of fire at night and smoke in daytime, to the adjacent post and then further inland until it reached the capital. In such contexts, Hassan Khalilieh argues that the *ribāṭ* indicated the safeguarding of frontiers of the Abode of Islam (*dār al-Islam*) by forces stationed at the harbours and frontier towns. He also emphasizes its role in the securing of maritime lane and in protecting commercial ships from enemies and pirate attacks (Khalilieh 1999).

Later on, the meanings and functions of the *ribāṭ*s expanded or changed, so much so that they ended up being perceived as fortifications to protect both overland and overseas commercial routes. They served as centres mostly for the isolated Muslim communities, situated nearby or within wider communities that had been established through particular settlement policies of free distribution of land and houses (Egar 2012, p. 435). They accommodated either military people only, or only pious Muslims, or an intermixture of army with Sufis and ʿulamāʾ. Many ʿulamāʾ and ḥadīth-specialists encouraged people to reside in *ribāṭ*s, stressing their religious significance and praising the volunteers to garrison in the coastal areas against the naval attacks. Asa Egar (2012) explores multiple possibilities in a *ribāṭ*'s functionality: it was mainly frontier forts, but it also acted as monasteries, convents for ascetic-warriors, trading posts, etc. In the eleventh and twelfth centuries, Sufis in the Maghrib frequently used *ribāṭ*s as their hospices to stand away from political authorities. They continued to do so even up until the nineteenth century (Kisaichi 1990). The famous Islamic scholar Ibn Taymiyya (1263–1328) wrote an interesting treatise on the *ribāṭ*s and the practices related to them, in which he argued that guarding the frontiers at *ribāṭ*s is far more virtuous than living and practising Islamic rituals in the holy cities of Mecca and Medina.[1]

Along these lines, Amikam El'Ad (1982) had regarded *ribāṭ*s as fortified coastal urban centres—of which the inhabitants and functionality changed from season to season from refugees to travellers and merchants—with living quarters, storage facilities, arms magazines, food, and signal tower. Chouki el Hamel (1999, pp. 64, 67–68) goes one step ahead and highlights their usage for educational purposes among the Almoravids of Western Sahara in the eleventh century: the first religious educational centre established by ʿAbdullāh bin Yāsīn was, indeed, in a *ribāṭ*, through which the introduction and spread of Arabic language, literacy, and authorship in the Arabic script were facilitated. All these scholars demonstrate the varied roles and identities of *ribāṭ* as it existed and functioned in the Islamic world. Thus, the concept of *ribāṭ* from the early centuries of Islamic expansion was differently adapted over time and place, but kept some foundational structures: a fortified wall, a masjid, and a bazaar inside. Even the notion of jihad, once central to *ribāṭ*s, was eventually expunged from their prime objectives.

*Ribāṭ*s were predominantly established in and around the Mediterranean and Atlantic coastal frontiers of Northern Africa (such as in Tunisia and Morocco) and the Syro-Palestinian regions (such as the seven cities named by al-Muqaddasī).[2] But they also spread to other parts of the Islamic world.

---

[1] Ibn Taymiyya (2002). I am grateful to Hassan Khalilieh for guiding me towards this treatise and sharing with me his translation-in-progress.

[2] In the North African context, the *ribāṭ*s had a standardized common plan: rooms around a courtyard built in two floors, a mosque in one of the rooms, and a minaret at the top (which acted as watch-tower and also beacon) (Egar 2012, p. 435). The Palestinian *ribāṭ*s also had a similar setting, but more complex and vast: four projecting circular towers at the corners and two semicircular towers, sixteen buttresses supporting walls (the number and size of towers and buttresses varied from place to place), a cistern, storehouses for provisions, magazines for arms, and a tower for signaling (Khalilieh 1999, p. 216).

In the eastern Islamic-Turkic frontier and Iran, they became popular under different names, such as *khanqah*, *tekke*, *manzil l'il marra*, and *khan*, where they also transformed from a fortification with prime military concerns into more of a specific social and cultural settlement. There they connoted "venerated shrines, hospices outside city gates for travellers, or caravanserais (rural inns) on internal desert routes", often named after their founders (Egar 2012, p. 435).

The idea and practice of *ribāṭ*s thus went through drastic changes chronologically and geographically, and many of those existed without a direct relation with war, sea, or fortification. However, at the core of this establishment was an expectation of war, and the residents were theoretically responsible to guard the place and its surroundings against external and internal attacks. The mystics and masters who occupied these places nurtured different interpretations in order to extend the notions of jihad, frontier, enemy, etc., towards more metaphysical and spiritual domains in which one should guard against evils and misdeeds that are internal and external to the soul and body. But the overall idea of *ribāṭ* as a place dedicated to the protection of borderlands and sea lanes prevailed, at least in the Islamic scholarship.

TO THE INDIAN OCEAN

Moving eastwards from the central Islamic lands to the Indian Ocean coasts in South and Southeast Asia, where Islam became a crucial factor in the later centuries, no one has so far discussed the existence of the *ribāṭs*, even in the context of coastal Islamic sultanates. This should be read along with the fact that the concept of *ribāṭ* stressing its military connotations was widely current only during the early Islamic expansions between the eighth and eleventh centuries, and we do not note many such references in the later period, even during the crusades. In the Indian Ocean context, in which Islam itself was only one among many different religions, Muslims began to articulate and reinterpret the ideas and practices of jihad from the sixteenth century onward in order to counter their enemies. In such articulations, the archetypal state of *ribāṭ* assumed a new meaning and relevance among these oceanic Muslims.

Since the *ribāṭ* as a concept and practice had undergone several transformations over time, it should be understood in the Indian Ocean context in a broader meaning, without limiting it to denote a single architectural complex or a simple watch-post. Rather, it denotes a broader coastal settlement in which multiple structures stood together within a fortified wall performing the foundational responsibilities of jihad and/or defence, according to its archetypal forms and functions. It also facilitated and catered for several means and prospects of Islamic mode of life while maintaining the notion of jihad and the attentiveness towards the maritime world. A quadrangle of maritime conflicts, defensive structures, coastal settlement, and Islamic community thus constitutes the *ribāṭ* of the Indian Ocean. It did not exclude other communities from being part of the venture as long as they stood together to fight against the maritime attacks. Such interconnected notions and praxis of *ribāṭ* provide an insightful framework to appreciate the Muslim understandings of their participation in wars of the oceanic littoral.

It is against this background that we should read the passage of Qāḍī Muḥammad al-Kālikūtī cited at the beginning of this chapter. Qāḍī Muḥammad accommodates the concept and practice of the *ribāṭ* with an urge for its immediate applicability in the upcoming Battle of Cāliyaṃ in 1571. In the context of the impending battle, he wanted to incite all the people to come forward in order to fight against the Portuguese with whatever resources, abilities, and supports each one could contribute. He dismissed the usual worries regarding family and poverty when one supports war physically or financially, and promised divine rewards in the material and metaphysical worlds. Following these assurances, he comes directly to the praxis of *ribāṭ*. He writes:

> You must spend, because one who equips a warrior has fought actually and one who looks after [the family of] a warrior has also, in fact, fought. You should not excuse being worried about the family and poverty. One who spends a fair amount, he has seven hundred rewards. One who spends for himself or his family, [he gains] ten times of it with merits. God will admit three persons to paradise for one arrow: the maker who aspires God's cause with it, the one who shoots it, and the one who hands it up for shooting.
>
> I encourage you for *ribāṭ*. To guard Muslims from infidels in God's cause for one day is better than the world and whatever is on its surface; a morning's or an evening's journey which a slave (person) travels in God's cause is better than the world and whatever is on its surface. Two eyes will never be touched by the fire of Hell: an eye which weeps out of fear of the omnipotent God and an eye which spends the night in guarding in the cause of Allah against the infidels. Both feet covered with dust in the cause of God will not be touched (by the Hellfire). The deeds of everyone who dies are sealed, except for the one who dies guarding the *ribāṭ*; for indeed, his actions are

> multiplied to him until the Day of Judgement, by the grace of God (al-Kālikūtī, *Khuṭbat al-jihādiyya*; for an annotated translation, see Kooria 2018, pp. 64–75).

The *ribāṭ* Qāḍī Muḥammad mentions in the passage was not his ratiocination in isolation; rather, it was part of a larger wartime practice and discourse with which he got familiarized at Ponnāni, and which could have been common across Malabar at that time. He was trained in an educational institution in Ponnāni, a sixteenth-century coastal hub of knowledge production and dissemination across religious and sectarian boundaries. It had a lively Islamic community in the period and had produced several jihad literature and Islamic sciences in general. The earliest text in this regard was the *Taḥrīḍ*, written in the 1510s by Zayn al-Dīn Sr. (d. 1522), the most towering figure among the Makhdūms of Ponnāni, who taught there until his death. In the *Taḥrīḍ*, the author also talks about the necessity of *ribāṭ*s and clearly states that "Engaging in ribat a day in God's service is better than the whole world and its riches" (Zayn al-Dīn Sr. 2013, verse 43).

The text must have been in circulation during the time when Qāḍī Muḥammad received his education. Also, the author of the famous *Tuḥfat al-mujāhidīn* was his contemporary and was living in Ponnāni after his return from Mecca, although the text may not yet have been released by then. After his education, Qāḍī Muḥammad returned to Calicut and was appointed as a judge. He also authored two more texts following the victory of the Battle of Cāliyaṃ: *Fatḥ al-mubīn li muḥibb al-Muslimīn al-Sāmirī ṣāḥib Kālikūt* ("Manifest Victory to the Zamorin of Calicut, Lover of Muslims"), which enumerates the incidents that led to and followed the battle, and *Qaṣīdat al-jihādiyya* ("Poem of War"), which proscribes the audience from piracy, for pirates are "warring enemies of God, the guide" and "spoilers of the earth" (al-Kālikūtī, *Khuṭbat al-jihādiyya*). All these writings and related historical developments indicate the primacy of Ponnāni in disseminating ideas related to jihad as much as it catalysed the actual naval attacks. The Muslim settlements in places like Cāliyaṃ and Iriṅṅal-Kōṭṭakkal and their participation in defending the Malabar Coast along with Ponnāni reflect either the fluctuating relevance of the *ribāṭ*s in the long run, or the changes in principal roles and/or the existence of a *ribāṭ*-network across the Malabar Coast.

PONNANI: THE SETTING

Thanks to its diplomatic, commercial, geo-physical, and societal significance, Ponnāni was the military capital of the Zamorins. Their arsenal and naval headquarters were established there by the fifteenth century, and the town was their stronghold in the south, bordering adjacent and rival kingdom of the Cochin Rajas. It was also their second political capital, after Calicut. Standing within such a crucial place under a non-Muslim ruler, a few Muslim ʿulamāʾ defined the geo-religious concepts of *dār al-Islam* and *dār al-ḥarb*, and called for rigorous jihad against the "cross- and image-worshipping" Christian Portuguese.[3] It might sound strange how this dichotomy of fidelity and infidelity worked at a time of war, but that is precisely what makes the case of Ponnāni interesting and appealing as a *ribāṭ* in the Indian Ocean rim.

The Zamorins were in their "golden stage" of political conquests and economic growth at the time of the Portuguese arrival. The ruling Zamorin Raja had a well-equipped army of 60,000 Nayars under his commanding officers (*Talaccannavars*), another 76,000 under his feudatories, and another big army under the Cochin contingent which he had subjugated. Furthermore, he also had a battalion of musketeers and corps of artillery primarily staffed by Muslims. Besides this military might, he also had a well-filled treasury and customary ships provided by the local merchants and the Arabs. But the situation got chaotic after the arrival of the Portuguese, who had interrupted his advancements as "the ruler of nearly half of Kerala" (Ayyar 1966, pp. 75–76).

The outcome of initial communications between the Portuguese and the Zamorin was not positive for either side; many studies have elaborated on this episode at length.[4] The Zamorin had his own reasons to reject the proposals of the Portuguese, especially when the Portuguese admiral Vasco da Gama asked him in 1502 to expel from Calicut all the Muslims who had come from Cairo and the Red Sea. The Zamorin rejected it, for he thought that they had contributed greatly to the growth of his kingdom and had been living there as locals (al-Malaybārī, *Tuḥfat al-mujāhidīn*; cf. Pearson 1979, p. 26). This negation by itself exasperated the Portuguese to engage in a hostile relation with him, which culminated in the bombarding of the Calicut port and the consequent approach of the Rajas of Cochin, who had been subjugated by the Zamorin, to commence trade with them. This not only affected the political ego of the Zamorin, but also caused

---

[3] For a recent overview of the jihadi treatises written in Malabar in the sixteenth century, see Amer (2016).

[4] For a detailed reading about the Portuguese-Zamorin relationship, see Subrahmanyam (1998); Pearson (2006); Mathew (1983).

him to anticipate the possible threat of loosening the economic power of Calicut against Cochin if the ties between the Portuguese and the Cochin Rajas strengthened.

In the first set of attacks between the Zamorin and the Portuguese commanded by Francisco de Almeida, the former was crushed severely. Though the Portuguese had encountered some reverses, they dominated the wars in the first decade of the century, except when they were destroyed in 1508 at Chaul and Dabul in a combined attack by the armies of Egyptian Mamlūks and the Gujarat Sultanate. This gave some relief to the Zamorin, but it did not last long, as the Portuguese quickly began to reassemble their army and power. This time the Zamorin Raja had to be more cautious, especially because the earlier defeat of the Portuguese was not caused by his ability or naval power. In such a context, he introduced campaigns and strategies in order to strengthen his army, requesting help from each and every individual and community he could depend on. That is how the Muslim military and religious elites come into the scenario, along with their suggestions of establishing a *ribāṭ* in the coast.

Along with all diplomatic attempts to seek support from the Mamlūks and Ottomans, the Zamorin tried to mobilize a good navy locally. He had a decent army for overland battles, but he did not have resources for naval attacks. The traditional army-men, the Nayars, were not trained in maritime battles, and many of them arguably were not ready to go to sea for religious restrictions—some Nayar men were taken by the Portuguese to be deployed in the navy as sailors, but this was mostly done by force. The Zamorin did not force them as he was well aware of the local customs. Just like the Nayars, the upper-caste Naṃpūtiris, who also played a role in the Zamorins' military, were incapable of engaging in naval battles. The only viable options for the Zamorin were the lower caste Hindus or caste-less people such as the fishermen community. He asked many of them to convert to Islam in order to join the overseas battles commanded by the Muslims (Innes and Evans 1915, p. 190). The most important force in the coast nevertheless was the Muslims who had been controlling the maritime trade across the Indian Ocean in general and the Malabar Coast in particular.

The local Muslims had their own reasons for teaming up with the Zamorin against the Portuguese. The Zamorin had always protected the Muslims in his kingdom, facilitating all their commercial needs. The Muslim merchants were major determinants of the Zamorin's economic and political moves by being quite influential in his decisions and actions (Bouchon 1989, pp. 2–4). A representative of the Muslim merchants was appointed by the Zamorin as the port-master (called *shāhbandar kōya*) of Calicut and Ponnāni, who also had the authority to collect taxes on imports and exports and to punish the troublemaking or law-breaking merchants on behalf of the ruler. Also, he had particular duties and responsibilities equal to the Rajas of Tirumanaśśēri and Veṭṭattu in the grand traditional festival of Māmāṅkaṃ that happened on the other side of Bhāratappuḻa of Ponnāni (Haridas 2016, pp. 30, 40, 174, 248–49). All these factors enabled a warm reciprocal relationship between the Zamorin and the Muslims, who had been serving him in his military expeditions much before the Portuguese arrival. In the wars against the Portuguese, the Muslims themselves wanted to oust the Portuguese from the Indian Ocean in order to maintain their existing prominence in the maritime trade. Their religious sentiments too were entangled in the struggle, as both sides perceived it as a war between Islamic and Christian forces. The war treatises ratified in the *ribāṭ*s of Malabar constantly invoked their audience to fight against the "cross-worshipping" Christians in retaliation to the attacks on Muslim institutions, settlements, traders, travellers, and pilgrims. Ponnāni stood at the forefront of these economic, political, and military stimuli by contributing a spiritual and physical outline rooted in an Islamic lexis.

Ponnāni had its opulence derived from a major settlement of Muslims there and it functioned as a centre of Islamic activities. By the second half of the fifteenth century, the Muslim population in Ponnāni included notable Muslim merchants and it also attracted a few affluent Muslim families from the Coromandel Coast and other parts of Malabar. Two families stood out among them: the Makhdūms and the Kuññāli Marakkārs. The Makhdūms are regarded to have arrived in Ponnāni in the late fifteenth century from Cochin, to where they had migrated earlier from the Coromandel Coast. They specialized in religious sciences and emerged as scholars through their education in Malabar and the Middle East. This family played a very important role in making the city a centre of Islamic learning, attracting several students from the subcontinent and the Indian Ocean littoral. The Kuññāli Marakkārs translocated to Ponnāni from Cochin in the early sixteenth century. They were a mercantile family active in Cochin until the arrival of the Portuguese, and after the hostile experiences they fled the port. In Ponnāni, both of these families joined hands against the Portuguese and the praxis of *ribāṭ*s stood as the connecting point between them with diverse nodes of interests.

The port-town also had a few geographical advantages: it was a crucial site in the coastal line, providing an immediate escape door to the hinterland via the mountain pass at the Palakkad Gap. In the sixteenth century, it was also located close to the borderline between the Zamorin's kingdom and Portuguese-dominated Cochin. These topographical elements, along with the religious, economic, and military components, added to the importance of Ponnāni as a significant settlement fitting into the conceptual requirement of *ribāṭ*. By the time the wars between the Portuguese and the Zamorins had resumed after a short break around the 1520s—when the former tried to assassinate the then king—Ponnāni had gained its central strategic role in the Malabar Coast. It had possessed the chief arsenal of the Zamorin; it had hosted his admirals, the Kuññāli Marakkārs, and a large chunk of the navy; and, most importantly it was constantly producing anti-Portuguese war treatises, addressing the Muslim population not only in Ponnāni but also throughout Malabar and beyond up to the Mamlūks, the Ottomans, and the Sultans of Bijapur. The production of such works was mainly initiated by the Islamic scholarly circle of Ponnāni, who displayed a strong religious sentiment in their writings against the Portuguese with calls for jihad. The Zamorin was supportive of those moves as he knew that all such incitements would ultimately benefit his cause, which had been hampered by the violent disruptions of the Portuguese.

If the volunteers of this anti-Portuguese jihad had religious and economic motivations to fortify the coasts and to secure the sea lanes, the Zamorin's own interest was more of a political and economic nature, as it was also the case with almost all the *ribāṭ*s in the Islamic world. In the Middle Eastern context, it has been argued that the political entities ensured that the maritime zones were secured through *ribāṭ*s so that favourable conditions for overseas trade could be created, which in turn would increase tax revenues and income of the proprietors of commercial vessels (Khalilieh 1999, pp. 218–19). The Zamorins procured a large wealth through maritime trade and taxes and they themselves had their own commercial enterprises through intermediaries and customary ships, all of which were attacked by the Portuguese. We come across references to the Zamorins ending their occasional truces with the Portuguese when the latter attacked the royal ships.[5] The economic motivations thus had a primary role in prompting the Zamorins to support the initiative of a Ponnāni *ribāṭ*. Buchon has

[5] For example, a Malayalam account *Kerala Varttamānam* copied at the dominion of the Zamorins mentions that a renewed friendship between the Zamorins and the Portuguese did not last long because "the Portuguese captured a royal ship at sea". British Library, OMS/MSS Malayalam 11*.

articulated how the *sambuk*s from Malabar heading to the Red Sea were escorted to the high seas by the *parao*s equipped with oarsmen, archers or harquebusiers, and artillery (Bouchon 1987, pp. 175–76). Throughout the *ribāṭ*s in the Middle Eastern and North African Islamic world, the same responsibilities were carried out by particular warships called *ḥarbīs* on a regular basis, and they indicate, as Khalilieh notes, "the government's interest and involvement in the shipping business" as well as in protecting and sustaining a *ribāṭ* (Khalilieh 1999, p. 218).

The location of frontier posts used to shift from time to time before and during the Portuguese interruptions, but the pronounced *ribāṭ*-characteristics were attached to these places only after the arrival of the Portuguese. Prior to the advent of the Portuguese, the Zamorins fought the Cochin Rajas keeping Koṭuṅṅallūr as a base. The chieftains of Koṭuṅṅallūr were in allegiance with the Zamorins and they facilitated many wars providing them with their military and logistical resources on the borders. While many Muslims partook in the wars, we do not have any evidences at this time to suggest that they had used any jihad-related frames to justify their battles under the banner of a non-Muslim kingdom against another non-Muslim kingdom. But in the early stages of the Portuguese wars, Ponnāni took over Koṭuṅṅallūr's position and thence references to the geopolitical conception of jihad and *ribāṭ* start to become detectable. By the end of the sixteenth century, the centre of battle moved to Iriṅṅal-Kōṭṭakkal, near Pantalāyani-Kollam in northern Malabar, where the same features of a *ribāṭ* were reinstated under the commanderships of the Kuññāli Marakkārs and the Makhdūms who both had relocated to the area. Later in the seventeenth century, however, we notice Ponnāni and Koṭuṅṅallūr regaining their diplomatic and military positions along with a new post at Cē<u>tt</u>uva. During the encounters of the Zamorins with the Dutch since the 1660s, Cē<u>tt</u>uva and Koṭuṅṅallūr once again became more significant. At that time, the Zamorin greatly depended on the Koṭuṅṅallūr chieftain as his most important ally: he was one of the few whom the Zamorin politically trusted outside his family. Gradually this relationship strengthened more and it led the Dutch governor Julius Stein van Gollenesse to note that the Koṭuṅṅallūr chief in 1743 was called "the father of the Zamorin's family" (Galletti and Groot 1911, p. 63). Further, the reigning Zamorin routinely had a third prince without a fixed head-quarter called Erānāṭṭu Mūnnāmkūr Nampiyātiri, whose primary duty was to act as governor to Neṭuṅṅanāṭ (around twenty miles away from Ponnāni) by staying at Cē<u>tt</u>uva or Koṭuṅṅallūr and by acting as a "warden of the southern marches". By staying at these places, "close to the storm centre", he always had to be "ready to take the offensive or assume the defensive against the Portuguese, afterwards the Dutch, and Cochin" (Ayyar 1929, pp. 16–17). Ponnāni was again reutilized by Tipu Sultan of Mysore (r. 1782–99) in the late eighteenth century during his attacks on the Zamorin.

The changes in the frontiers are significant in relation to the idea of a *ribāṭ*-network. In Middle Eastern contexts, there existed a network of *ribāṭ*s in which different frontier posts connected with each other depending on regional topography, strategic, and economic factors (Khalilieh 2008, pp. 166–67). In the coastal belt, the *ribāṭ*s were generally situated either on elevations or on flat areas allowing a visual command over the surroundings and facilitating quicker communications with adjacent station or *ribāṭ*. While we look at any of the aforementioned places from Koṭuṅṅallūr, Cēṯṯuva, Ponnāni, to Iriṅṅal-Kōṭṭakkal and the unmentioned areas of Parappanaṅṅāṭi and Cāliyaṃ—all which had fortified Muslim settlements—we see that they are situated in a line in the low lands of coastal belt uninterrupted by mountains that may have hindered frequent communication. Though we do not have clear evidence of the simultaneous existence of such a possible *ribāṭ* network in the context of Malabar, the shifts in the frontier posts lead me to speculate that a similar phenomenon might have occurred there, especially in view of the frequent battles that the Zamorins waged.

INTERNAL DYNAMICS

While the Zamorins had their political-economic motives to support the *ribāṭ*, its participants in Ponnāni had religious and economic aspirations to engage in wars and to protect the region. Besides the political authority of the Zamorins, there were three other functional groups associated with the conceptualization and materialization of jihad against the Portuguese in the region: the ʿulamāʾ (such as the Makhdūms), who ideologically incited their followers for jihad through sermons and writings; the warriors, like the Kuññāli Marakkārs, who physically went to the battlefield and led the fights; and the laypersons, who occasionally engaged in physical war, or otherwise supported it financially or psychologically.

The ʿulamāʾ of Ponnāni provided an ideological support to the conflict, contextualizing it in the tradition of anti-infidel wars that Muslims undertook since the early history of Islam. Due to the atrocities that the Portuguese were inflicting upon the Muslim settlements and institutions such as mosques and the pilgrims going for or returning from hajj, the scholars thought that it had become compulsory for the community to engage in jihad against whom they perceived as "cruel cross-worshipping Christian Portuguese". The first relevant source available to us on this matter is the *Taḥrīḍ ahl al-īmān ʿalā jihād ʿabadat al-ṣulbān* ("Exhortation to the believers to fight against the cross-worshippers") by Zayn al-Dīn Sr. This work is the earliest known local response to the Portuguese attacks on the Malabar Coast (Kooria 2013). Later on, many other scholars of Ponnāni contributed to this genre, which includes the widely translated *Tuḥfat al-mujāhidīn* of Zayn al-Dīn Jr. (d. 1583?). The aforesaid Qāḍī Muḥammad al-Kālikūtī has written in and around 1570 three analogous texts that have come down to us.[6]

The fact that all these texts were written in and around Ponnāni at different decades of the sixteenth century clearly demonstrates that there was a constant attempt to invoke the notion of jihad against the Portuguese, and that there was a demand for such genre of literature. Religious scholars continued to produce similar texts over the decades of the century, and those were a source of religious motivation for Muslim warriors, such as the Kuññāli Marakkārs. Sanjay Subrahmanyam (2012, p. 145) has written that Zayn al-Dīn Jr.'s vision of jihad between the Muslims and infidel Portuguese reflected more an ideal category than reality. This is, I have argued elsewhere, debatable, all the more so because he regards the *Tuḥfat al-mujāhidīn* as the only extant text of this sort from Malabar, whereas in fact it is only one among many analogous jihad-focused texts produced in the region since the beginning of the sixteenth century (Kooria 2016, p. 43). These texts were not idealistic and isolated; rather, they were part of similar writings and narratives against the Portuguese occupation of Islamic lands, more precisely in North and East Africa and South Arabia, in the fifteenth and sixteenth centuries. They stood as practical and even functional treatises in guiding the Muslim warriors to counter the European expansion. In Malabar, these texts contributed to the religious discourse of this period by interacting with the long-established textual genealogies of Islamic literatures on jihad, law, history, and culture. On the other hand, they also catered for their immediate socio-political contexts during the Portuguese attacks.

The ʿulamāʾ not only wrote war treatises; they also conducted lectures and gave sermons to popularize the notion of jihad in the local context. While the treatises were written in Arabic—which was mainly the language of religious elites in Malabar—the sermons and lectures facilitated direct

[6] I partly quoted above from his *Khuṭbat al-jihādiyya* ("Sermon of War").

interactions with the extended community through vernacular languages. The *Khuṭbat al-jihādiyya* indicates that the Friday sermon (*khuṭba*) at the congregational mosques had created a space for jihadi-incitements among the community. As much as the ʿulamāʾ tried to invoke local Muslims, they also tried to contact Muslim rulers from the Middle East and other parts of South Asia seeking military and material supports for jihad. Though the rulers responded occasionally to such calls, they were more concerned with their own benefits, especially when the Portuguese had interrupted their maritime interests in the Indian Ocean as it was the case with the Ottoman Empire.[7]

The second group, the warriors, were the actual undertakers of the jihad. While we do not get explicit historical evidence of the physical engagement of the ʿulamāʾ in the wars except in a particular case of the 1570s, warriors led by the Kuññāli Marakkārs operated as *mujāhidūn* ("holy warriors"). The Marakkārs were the connecting nodes between the diverse layers of religious, social, economic, and political establishments—of the ʿulamāʾ, the laypersons, the mercantile groups, and the Zamorins respectively. They are yet to attract serious academic studies that go beyond nationalistic glorifications, and we only have some partial descriptions and analyses on their characteristics and mode of functions.[8] Historians have described them differently according to their own predispositions or the sources they used, with terms varying from "corsarios", "corsairs", "pirates" and "privateers", "admirals" and "patriots"—labels that are a part and parcel of the cultural bias in historical writing (Pearson 1979, pp. 23–24).

The problem of labels aside, the name "Kuññāli" (a portmanteau word from the Malayalam name "Kuññu" and the Arabic name "ʿAlī") was a honorific title given by the Zamorin with right to wear silk turban, while "Marakkār" denoted the mercantile community that operated mainly in the Coromandel Coast, but with strong connections with Malabar. The leading warriors among them were four, who took commandership one after another; three of them were based in Ponnāni and the last one shifted his centre northwards. Their ancestors were settled in Cochin, and from there they moved to Ponnāni in the sixteenth century following Portuguese

[7] For a recent overview of the Ottoman interests in the Indian Ocean, see Casale (2010).

[8] See, for example, a work written more than a half century ago: Nambiar (1963), cf. Kurup (1997).

interruptions in their commercial enterprises in Cochin (Kunhali 1997, pp. 44–45).

The third group of laypersons was the common Māppiḷas, who were traders, brokers, and fishermen, or were actual army men already working for the Zamorins in overland expeditions. They did not always participate in the war, although they must have continuously supported it in many ways. They tried to make their livelihood through ordinary occupations, unless those were disrupted by the new monopolization attempts of the Portuguese, or if circumstances demanded that the Māppiḷas were forced or deeply motivated to sacrifice their lives. In general, they supported the Kuññālis' endeavours, even when the Zamorins broke with the Kuññālis after sensing a threat to their sovereignty and allied with the Portuguese in the late sixteenth century. In such contexts, the Zamorins supported the Portuguese to attack many settlements of the Māppiḷas. This was repeated in the 1630s too in a series of combined raids by the Portuguese and the Zamorins (Subrahmanyam 1990, p. 339).

Ponnāni was a centre of Islam in the whole coast, having become "the cultural and religious capital of Kerala Muslims" (Kanchana, 2012, fn 38). The township was thus organized in the typical way of the Muslim settlements, with the congregational mosque at the centre. It also hosted a religious educational centre. Apart from the main mosque, numerous minor mosques were also established, either at this time or later. The ʿulamāʾ concentrated in the main mosque but also dispersed in the other religious institutions or seminaries that functioned as the central catalysts in this *ribāṭ*.

As far as the social composition is concerned, apart from the scholars, there were influential merchants, militia, fishermen, and other occupational groups. At the township, the majority of the population was Muslims. In the early seventeenth century, the French navigator François Pyrard de Laval (1887, vol. 1, pp. 444–50) noticed the fortified Muslim settlements of Ponnāni and Tānūr, which were enclosed and built inside a wall. These fortifications must have been a continuation of their *ribāṭ* battlements in the sixteenth century. In such fortified settlements, we do not know how they controlled the entries and exits, how they put surveillance on land and sea, and how far they located from the crucial military spots like the Zamorin's palace, arsenal, and naval headquarter. I assume that the temples and churches of other communities were situated outside the fortification, if not the naval headquarter and arsenal—for they were controlled mainly by Muslims. This should be read along with the fact that the Hindu community in Malabar had followed a very strict tradition of caste system that influenced the settlement pattern with clear residential segregation and hierarchies. Viewed from a different perspective, the social organization within the fortified *ribāṭ*s of the Muslims resembled the Hindu caste hierarchy in which the non-Hindus, including Muslims and Christians, were kept at a social and physical distance from the upper-caste Hindus through residential segregation, distinct burial grounds, private worship places, and kinship contacts (al-Malaybārī, *Tuḥfat al-mujāhidīn*).

Regarding the social structures of other religionists, the practices of caste-system and the social hierarchy they maintained in the general context of Malabar, there is no reason to think that a radically different system existed in Ponnāni. Nonetheless, some observations made by Kunjan Pillai (1970, p. 196), a historian of premodern Kerala, are significant for the *ribāṭ*-structure of Ponnāni. While he talks about the gradual extinction of the Naṃpūtiri families in Malabar, he says that many of those were "destroyed during the period of the Portuguese". He does not elucidate why such attacks on the Naṃpūtiris had happened. But he points out that several Naṃpūtiris converted to Christianity and Islam, especially in areas adjacent to Ponnāni, such as as Pālayūr, Pāvaraṭṭy, and Tirunnāvāya, all of which were once important Naṃpūtiri centres, but has now become predominantly Christian.[9] The prominent Hindu temple-towns of Guruvāyūr and Mammiyūr had a noteworthy population of Naṃpūtiris and seventy-two families were in charge of the temple-trusteeship, but in mid-twentieth century there was only one family which itself faced extinction, he wrote in the 1970s (Kunjan Pillai 1970, p. 196). Thus, taking the case of Ponnāni, one may assume that numerous Naṃpūtiris too converted to Islam as part of this prevailing pattern of the time. The typical Hindu houses of *nālukeṭṭu*s and *eṭṭukeṭṭu*s still exist in the heart of Ponnāni, all of which are owned by elite Muslim families, and there is a popular belief among a few Muslim families of such house-complexes that their ancestors were Naṃpūtiris who converted to Islam. This conversion process, if it had happened at all, may have occurred during the fortification process of the township and during the Portuguese attacks, which may have motivated the Naṃpūtiris to seek protection under the warriors of the Kuññāli Marakkār.

[9] This observation should be taken with caution since we know from recent studies that the European missionaries found it very difficult, if not impossible, to convert the Brahmins in southern India. The arguable absence of earlier Brahmin families and the presence of a significant Christian population in the region warrant a better explanation (Županov 1999 and 2005).

The missionary activities of the 'ulamā' of the educational centres must also have contributed to this process.

Such gradual conversion process had left imprints on many cultural institutions and practices of the Māppiḷa Muslims of Ponnāni. It was reflected not merely in the housing complexes, but also in the mosque architectures, caste hierarchies, etc. Beyond Ponnāni, such architectural and cultural assimilations are visible throughout Malabar. We come across more instances of such frequent cultural cohesions in several other continuums of society, culture, and everyday life. These socio-cultural dynamics should be borne in mind when we look into the trajectories of Ponnāni *ribāṭ* in its defensive functionality against the Portuguese attacks within the wider context of its forms and characteristics as any *ribāṭ* in the war front.

RIBĀṬ AT WORK

Prior to and during the usage of Ponnāni as a military capital by the Kuññālis, the Portuguese had attacked the region more than once.[10] The first attack was conducted by Francisco de Almeida in 1507 against a large number of ships that were filled with cargos taken from the Ponnāni port and were about to leave for the Red Sea. In 1524, when the Zamorin's army encamped in Ponnāni after retreating from an unsuccessful war with the Raja of Cochin, the Portuguese attacked the town and stormed it with the help of the Raja of Purakkāṭu. However, in the same attack, the Portuguese captain Henry Menezes (or Dom Henrique de Maneses) suspected his local allies and ordered to attack them. This led the captain of Purakkāṭu to join the army of the Zamorins. This was followed by another attack in 1525 by Menezes. In the same year, the Portuguese managed to create a new base at Ponnāni. Basing themselves there, they attacked the Māppiḷa settlement and burnt a few ships anchored ashore. In retaliation to this Kuṭṭi 'Alī attacked the port of Cochin and set fire on the Portuguese ships. Another attack was in 1550, in which the Portuguese set fire to the Muslim establishments, including the congregational mosque.

The Portuguese attacks were not limited to Ponnāni, but also extended to other port-towns of Malabar which had been suspected to be supporters of the Zamorins or of the Kuññālis. The Kuññālis fought against the

[10] Since there are plenty of studies on the Portuguese conflicts in the Malabar Coast, I will limit myself to mention the incidents occurred in and around Ponnāni. Some of the important studies are Pearson (2006); Subrahmanyam (1990); Mathew (1983).

Portuguese even during the Zamorins' truce with them. In such contexts, the Portuguese used to retaliate by attacking the Muslim-majority settlements and killing all Muslims they were able to seize. The Kuññāli II is an exemplar in this regard, who was hardly perturbed by such attacks on his community at Tikkōṭi, Pantalāyani, Ponnāni, Cannanore, Dharmaṭam, and other places since 1550. With his help the Muslims retaliated against the Portuguese despite the treaty existing between them and the Zamorins since 1555. Kuññāli II destroyed the Portuguese fleets at Cannanore in 1563, at Putuppaṭṭaṇaṃ and Bhatkal in 1564, and at Diu in 1569. Consequently, the Portuguese aggregated their attacks on Muslim settlements at Tikkōṭi, Pantalāyani, Kāppāṭu, Tānūr, and Ponnāni (Bahauddin 1992, p. 53; Ayyar, 1966, p. 85; Koya 1997, p. 63).

The Raja of Tānūr, who ruled the other side of Bhāratappuḻa across Ponnāni, joined hands with the Portuguese as early as 1530. With his support, they built a fort at Cāliyaṃ, in the river-mouth of Beypore. This helped them control the coastal belt and maritime traffic between Calicut and Ponnāni. The Zamorin managed to destroy this fort in 1571 when he declared war and laid siege to Cāliyaṃ while the sultans of Ahmednagar and Bijapur attacked Diu and Goa respectively (al-Kālikūtī, "al-Fatḥ al-mubīn"). In response to their failure at Cāliyaṃ, the Portuguese raided Parappanaṅṅāṭi, Ponnāni, Calicut, and Tikkōṭi in 1572, and began to capture the rice-ships coming to Calicut. As a reward to the successful military commandership of Kuññāli III in the battle of Cāliyaṃ, the then Zamorin permitted him to build a fort in Putuppaṭṭaṇaṃ and held him as his vassal. This area and the fort came under the complete control of Kuññāli for quite some time, until his activities raised threats to the Zamorin's dominion towards the end of the sixteenth century.

In 1578, the Portuguese requested permission from the Zamorin to build a fort in Ponnāni, but their instance was refused. Even so, they headed to Ponnāni to execute the plan utilizing their friendship with the Raja of Tānūr. When the news about their presence in Tānūr reached the Zamorin's court, he asked the Raja to hand them over to him. Obviously he declined to obey given his strengthened friendship with the Portuguese. They went ahead with shiploads of construction materials like stones and mortar to Ponnāni to build the fort on the left bank of the river-mouth. But the convoy was completely destroyed in a heavy storm which dashed all the ships to the shore, except the "mast vessel". Some Portuguese were drowned and some were captured in Ponnāni, and the Zamorin took all the "big guns" from the Portuguese wreckages (Anonymous, "Kerala Varttamānam"; for its translation, see Kurup 1997, Appendix IV).

In the early 1580s, the Portuguese once again persuaded the Zamorin to give them permission to build a factory at Ponnāni. This time they succeeded, following a treaty in 1584. The main aim of the Portuguese was to construct the fort: they hoped that with the erection of a garrison at Ponnāni they could "destroy the fort of Kuññāli and would not permit its reconstruction" (Chauhan 1989, p. 32.). Though this truce did not last long, as the Portuguese attacked a royal ship of the Zamorin, Kuññāli did not like the decision of the Zamorin to allow the Portuguese to build a fort in Ponnāni. Therefore, while there was a truce between the Portuguese and the Zamorins, Kuññāli conducted two powerful naval attacks in 1586 and 1589, in which he defeated the Portuguese.

After some years of persuasion, the Zamorin revoked the permission to build the fort. Instead, in 1591 he allowed the Portuguese to settle in Calicut and offered his help to build a church there. Meanwhile, the Portuguese crown disapproved the erection of a fort at Ponnāni, and in its place he asked the viceroy "to utilize the funds for raising a fleet to combat the corsairs whose ships were still sailing to Mecca without Portuguese *cartazes*" (Subrahmanyam 1990, p. 270). In a crucial agreement between the Portuguese representative Alvaro de Abranches and the Zamorin in 1597, the latter agreed to free all the Portuguese prisoners including the priest D. Pedro Fernando Lobo and to generously allocate a place for the Portuguese to erect churches in Calicut and Ponnāni. In return, the Portuguese would help the Zamorin to crush all the powers of the Kuññālis, who now had become the Zamorin's enemy. Just before they jointly attacked the redoubt of Muhammad Kuññāli Marakkār at Ponnāni, a similar treaty was signed in 1599. As a consequence of this the Zamorin agreed to cease persecuting Christians, to allow the establishment of churches, and to support the Synod of Diamper on banishing the customs and practices of the local St. Thomas Christians.

This put the Kuññāli in a fix as his enemy became friends with his ruler. Thus, pushed to the brink, he was left with little choice and began attacking all ships of the Portuguese and the Zamorin. He cut the tail of an elephant and sent it to the court of the Zamorin—as a metaphorical insult and expression of his dissatisfaction with the Zamorin's finding common cause with the Portuguese. He also assumed the titles of "defender of the island, protector of the Muslims, and expeller of the Portuguese" (Chauhan 1989, p. 34). The king took all these as assaults on his sovereignty and declared war against him with the support of the Portuguese, killing him and his supporters in an overland attack by the Zamorin's army and a naval attack by the Portuguese.

The overall undercurrent of all these constant battles explicate the importance of Ponnāni as a maritime frontier town that helped the Kuññālis remain strong and aggressive, while the Portuguese sought ways to break the barrier and get access to its inside. Its Muslim settlement and congregational mosque often became targets for and instigators of the attacks. The ʿulamāʾ routinely asked the laypersons to fight against the Portuguese and to support the battles by all means by invoking the praxis of jihad and *ribāṭ* and the Kuññālis materialized those through their constant battles.

CONCLUSION

Ponnāni underwent several critical moments in its micro-history in the vast space of encounters between the indigenous and foreign powers. The Zamorins' acceptance of it as their second political capital and prime military capital or naval headquarters by the fifteenth–sixteenth centuries was crucial for Ponnāni's distinct identity. Its diplomatic, commercial, geophysical, and societal significance, as well as the Zamorins' tolerant and supportive attitude towards the Muslims, created a ground for the Muslim ʿulamāʾ and militia to engage in the ideologically charged wars against the Portuguese. The inhabitants of the Ponnāni *ribāṭ* were concerned about the increasing influence of the Portuguese with hostile attitudes towards their religion and enterprises. The characteristics of a *ribāṭ* frontier-space thus constituted a foundation for anti-Portuguese incitements. With an ideological back-up rooted in the long-established jihad tradition, the scholars of Ponnāni rearticulated the promises of a *ribāṭ* in their local contexts. The persuasive battles of the Kuññāli Marakkārs and the comforts of a fortified settlement provided them with the fundamental skeleton of the *ribāṭ*. This praxis in turn gives us a better framework to understand the spaces and practices in which the local Muslims understood their position in a wider tradition of their religion and its worldviews at the time of constant battles.

The Ponnāni *ribāṭ* leads us to rethink about the ways in which the battles of the indigenous communities in the Indian Ocean world at the wake of European expansion have been articulated in the existing scholarly literature. The generalized European ideas and categories like "frontiers" do not encompass the nuances of these coastal communities who hardly fought for any imperial centre in the interior, whether "South Asian", "Mughal", or "Delhi" kingdoms. Many of the Muslim communities in the Indian Ocean coastal belts were detached from or in constant conflicts with such hinterland empires, be they in East Africa, Southeast Asia, or

East Asia, and they attached themselves to the currents and undercurrents of larger maritime networks of politics, economy, and religion. At the wake of their conflicts with such European powers as the Portuguese, the concept and practice of *ribāṭ* provide us a framework to understand their struggles, settlements, and worldviews without superimposing analytical categories that are foreign to their specific context. Ponnāni is only one among several other such locales across the Indian Ocean rim where the institution of *ribāṭ* was practised since the sixteenth century.

Instances of other historical places and periods in which the praxis of *ribāṭ* found relevance need further research. One minor—yet significant—instance along these lines from this period comes from a connection point between Southeast Asia and the Middle East. One of the most famous and controversial Malay mystical poets, Hamzah Fansūrī from Sumatra, died and was buried in Mecca in 1527. Scholars have found and recently analysed the inscription in his tombstone which contains the term "*al-murābiṭ*" or the one who engaged in *ribāṭ*. Guillot and Kalus (2000) translate this term as "*combattant à la frontière*" and interpret it as indicative of Fansūrī's fights on the Islamic frontier in Barus. Braginsky (2001) questions the authenticity of the whole inscription for two reasons: first, neither the original stele nor a photograph is available, second, there are incongruences with other textual and contextual evidence. When analysing the term *al-murābiṭ*, Braginsky says that "this word—just like the very institution of frontier *ribāṭ* (a military-religious fortified settlement)—had lost such a meaning". While Braginsky may be right in questioning the authenticity of the epitaph, from the foregoing discussion it is obvious that his reasoning with respect to the institution of *ribāṭ* does not hold water.

The term, concept, and practice were common in the Indian Ocean littoral, from the 1510s throughout the century, when the authors of the *Taḥrīḍ* and *Khuṭbat al-jihādiyya* used and incited the praxis. This should be read along with the rise of fortified ports, towns and cities across the maritime littoral in the sixteenth century, a phenomenon that was uncommon before in the Bay of Bengal and Arabian Sea (Hall 2010, pp. 113–14; Prange 2018, pp. 44–58). Many of such new maritime fortifications were conceptualized and justified by the Muslim communities as *ribāṭ*s. Some of those must have been established in response to the increasing fortifications initiated by the European companies and traders in the littoral. Over the course of the time, its usage and connotations changed and we do see its usage in the nineteenth and twentieth centuries to connote exclusively educational and religious institutions in East Africa, the southern coast of

Arabia, etc., in the same way it was once used in the the eastern Islamic-Turkic frontiers.

Coming back to the *ribāṭ* of Ponnāni, it is worth noting that the port-town transformed into a diplomatic centre of great economic and political interest for both indigenous and foreign groups after the end of Kuññālis' influence over the region by the turn of the seventeenth century and the Portuguese decline a few decades thereafter. In the seventeenth and the eighteenth centuries it was a locus of diplomatic negotiations—of course along with its commercial dimension—for different groups. The religious institutions and networks functioned and transformed significantly in the sixteenth century by either confronting with the European structures or functioning in parallel to those. The Portuguese prominence in Malabar came to an end after the arrival of the Dutch East India Company, which defeated the Portuguese in a series of battles in and around Cochin in 1663. Although the Dutch allied with the Zamorins to fight against the Portuguese, their alliance did not last long. Often both parties fought against each other, as much as they frequently signed peace treaties. During such wars and treaties, Ponnāni was the only place in the kingdom of the Zamorin where the Dutch were allowed to trade (Kooria 2019). Oftentimes the Zamorin signed treaties or conflicted with the Dutch in this place whereas the Dutch tried to protect their factory and fort there at any cost, as it was their only stronghold to keep an eye on the developments in the Zamorin's kingdom. The arrival of the English and French traders in Malabar, particularly in Ponnāni, exacerbated Dutch anxieties and eventually the former would change the course of the *ribāṭ*'s history in the following two and half centuries.

References

Manuscripts

British Library, OMS/MSS Malayalam 11*, Anonymous. "Kerala Varttamānam".

British Library, IOR, MS. Islamic 2807e: al-Malaybārī, Zayn al-Dīn. "Tuḥfat al-mujāhidīn fī Baʿḍi Akhbār al-Burtuġāliyyīn".

British Library, IOR, MS. Islamic 2807f: al-Kālikūtī, Muḥammad. "al-Fatḥ al-mubīn".

al-Kālikūtī, Qādī Muḥammad. *Khuṭbat al-jihādiyya*. Ahmad Kōya Shāliyātī Kutub Khana, Malappuram, Kerala.

———. *Khuṭbat al-jihādiyya*. Collections of Pāññil Ahmad Kuṭṭi Musliyār, Malappuram, Kerala.

Published Sources

Abu-Lughod, Janet. 1987. "The Islamic City: Historic Myth, Islamic Essence, and Contemporary Relevance". *International Journal of Middle East Studies* 19, no. 2: 155–76.

Amer, Ayal. 2016. "The Rise of Jihādic Sentiments and the Writing of History in Sixteenth-Century Kerala". *Indian Economic & Social History Review* 53, no. 3: 297–319.

Ayyar, K.V. Krishna. 1929. *A History of the Zamorins of Calicut, part 1: From the Earliest Times to 1498 A.D.* Calicut: Publication Division, University of Calicut.

———. 1966. *A Short History of Kerala*. Eranakulam: Pai and Company.

Bahauddin, K.M. 1992. *Kerala Muslims: The Long Struggle*. Kottayam.

Bouchon, Geneviève. 1987. "Sixteenth Century Malabar and the Indian Ocean". In *India and the Indian Ocean, 1500–1800*, edited by M.N. Pearson and Ashin Das Gupta, pp. 168–82. Calcutta: Oxford University Press.

———. 1989. "Calicut at the Turn of the Sixteenth Century: The Portuguese Catalyst". *Indica* 49: 2–13.

Braginsky, Vladimir I. 2001. "On the Copy of Hamzah Fansuri's Epitaph". *Archipel* 62: 21–33.

Casale, Giancarlo. 2010. *The Ottoman Age of Exploration*. Oxford: Oxford University Press.

Chabbi, J., and Nasser Rabbat. 1995. "Ribāṭ". In *Encyclopaedia of Islam, Second Edition*, edited by P. Bearman, Th. Bianquis, C.E. Bosworth, E. van Donzel, W.P. Heinrichs. Consulted online on 28 April 2019.

Chauhan, R.R.S. 1989. "Kunjali's Naval Challenge to the Portuguese". In *Essays in Goan History*, edited by Teotonio R. De Souza. New Delhi: Concept Pubs. Co.

Dale, Stephen. 1980. *South Asian Frontier: A Study of Mappilas of Malabar*. Oxford: Clarendon Press.

de Laval, François Pyrard. 1887. *The Voyage of François Pyrard of Laval to the East Indies, the Maldives, the Moluccas and Brazil*, edited and translated by Albert Grey and H.C.P. Bell. London: The Hakluyt Society.

Eaton, Richard. 1978. *Sufis of Bijapur 1300–1700: Social Roles of Sufis in Medieval India*. Princeton: Princeton University Press.

Egar, Asa. 2012. "Ḥiṣn, Ribāṭ, Thaghr or Qaṣr? Semantics and Systems of Frontier Fortifications in the Early Islamic Period". In *The Lineaments of Islam: Studies in Honor of Fred McGraw Donner*, edited by Paul M. Cobb, pp. 427–56. Leiden: Brill.

El'Ad, Amikam. 1982. "The Coastal Cities of Palestine During the Early Middle Ages". *Jerusalem Cathedra* 2: 146–67.

Ernst, Carl. 2009. *Eternal Garden: Mysticism, History, and Politics at a South Asian Sufi Center*. New Delhi: Oxford University Press.

Galletti, A., and P. Groot. 1911. *The Dutch in Malabar being a Translation of Selections Nos. 1 and 2*. Madras: The Superintendent Government Press.

Gommans, Jos. 2002. *Mughal Warfare: Indian Frontiers and High Roads to Empire, 1500–1700*. London.

Green, Nile. 2012. *Making Space: Sufis and Settlers in Early Modern India*. New York/Oxford: Oxford University Press.

Guillot, Claude, and Ludvik Kalus. 2000. "La stèle funéraire de Hamzah Fansuri". *Archipel*: 3–24.

Hall, Kenneth R. 2010. "Ports-of-Trade, Maritime Diasporas, and Networks of Trade and Cultural Integration in the Bay of Bengal Region of the Indian Ocean: c. 1300-1500". *Journal of the Economic and Social History of the Orient* 53, no. 2: 109–45.

Hamel, Chouki el. 1999. "The Transmission of Islamic Knowledge in Moorish Society from the Rise of the Almoravids to the 19th Century". *Journal of Religion in Africa* 29, no. 1: 62–87.

Haridas, V.V. 2016. *Zamorins and the Political Culture of Medieval Kerala*. New Delhi: Orient Blackswan.

Hasan, Farhat. 2004. *State and Locality in Mughal India: Power Relations in Western India, c 1572–1730*. Cambridge: Cambridge University Press.

Hasan, Mohibbul. 2005. *History of Tipu Sultan*. Delhi: Aakar Books.

Ibn Taymiyya, Aḥmad. 2002. *Mas'ala fī al-Murābaṭa bil-Thughūr Afḍal am al-Mujāwara bi-Makkah Sharrafahā Allāh Ta'ālā*, edited by Ashraf ibn 'Abd al-Maqṣūd. Riyāḍ.

Innes, C.A., and F.B. Evans. 1915. *Madras District Gazetteer: Malabar and Anjengo*. Madras.

al-Kālikūtī, Qāḍī Muḥammad. 2012. *Fatḥ al-Mubīn: A Contemporary Account of the Portuguese Invasion on Malabar in Arabic Verse*. Calicut.

Kanchana, Radhika. 2012. "Kozhikode (Calicut)'s Kuttichira: Exclusivity Maintained Proudly". In *Muslims in Indian Cities: Trajectories of Marginalization*, edited by Christophe Jaffrelot and Laurent Gayer, pp. 263–86. London: Hurst.

Khalilieh, Hassan S. 1999. "The Ribāṭ System and its Role in Coastal Navigation". *Journal of the Economic and Social History of the Orient* 42, no. 2: 212–25.

———. 2008. "The Ribāṭ of Arsūf and the Coastal Defence System in Early Islamic Palestine". *Journal of Islamic Studies* 19, no. 2: 159–77.

Kisaichi, Masatoshi. 1990. "Sufi Saints in 12th Century Maghrib Society: Ribāṭ and Rābiṭa". *Journal of Sophia Asian Studies* 8: 5–33.

Kooria, Mahmood. 2013. "*Taḥrīḍ Ahl al-Imān*: An Indigenous Account against the Early European Interventions in Indian Ocean World". In *Tahrid Ahl al Iman*, edited and translated by KM Muhammad, pp. 19–45. Calicut.

———. 2016. " 'Killed the Hajj-pilgrims and Persecuted Them': Portuguese Estado da India's Encounters with Hajj Pilgrimage, 16th Century". In *Europe and Hajj in the Age of Empires*, edited by Umar Ryad, pp. 16–38. Leiden: Brill.

———. 2018. "*Khuṭbat al-jihādiyya*: A Sixteenth-Century Anti-Portuguese

Sermon". In *Malabar in the Indian Ocean: Cosmopolitanism in a Maritime Historical Region*, edited by Mahmood Kooria and Michael Pearson, pp. 64–72. New Delhi: Oxford University Press.

———. 2019. "Politics, Economy and Islam in 'Dutch Ponnāni', Malabar Coast". *Journal of the Economic and Social History of the Orient* 62, no. 1: 1–34.

Koya, S.M. Mohamed. 1997. "Arab Trade and the Zamorin's Political Power". In *India's Naval Traditions: The Role of Kunhali Marakkars*, edited by K.K.N. Kurup, pp. 60–65. New Delhi: Northern Book Centre.

Kunhali, V. 1997. "Origin of Kunhali Marakkars and Organization of Their Fighters". In *India's Naval Traditions: The Role of Kunhali Marakkars*, edited by K.K.N. Kurup, pp. 43–48. New Delhi: Northern Book Centre.

Kunjan Pillai, Elamkulam P.N. 1970. *Studies in Kerala History*. Kottayam.

Kurup, K.K.N., ed. 1997. *India's Naval Traditions: The Role of Kunhali Marakkars*. New Delhi: Northern Book Centre.

Kusuman, K.K. 1987. *A History of Trade & Commerce in Travancore, 1600–1805*. Delhi: Mittal Publications.

Mathew, K.S. 1983. *Portuguese Trade with India in the Sixteenth Century*. New Delhi: Manohar.

———. 1997. "Indian Naval Encounters with the Portuguese: Strengths and Weaknesses". In *India's Naval Traditions: The Role of Kunhali Marakkars*, edited by K.K.N. Kurup, pp. 6–25. New Delhi: Northern Book Centre.

Menon, Dilip M. 1999. "Houses by the Sea: State-Formation Experiments in Malabar, 1760–1800". *Economic and Political Weekly* 34, no. 29: 1995–2003.

Muqaddasī, Shams al-Dīn Abū ʿAbdallāh. 1897. *Aḥsan al-taqāsīm fī maʿrifat al-aqālīm*, translated and edited by G.S.A. Ranking and R.F. Azoo. Calcutta.

Nambiar, Odayamadath Kunjappa. 1963. *The Kunjalis: Admirals of Calicut*. London: Asia Publishing House.

Narayanan, M.G.S. 1972. *Cultural Symbiosis in Kerala*. Trivandrum: Kerala Historical Society.

Pearson, Michael. 1979. "Corruption and Corsairs in Sixteenth-Century Western India: A Functional Analysis". In *The Age of Partnership: Europeans in Asia before Dominion*, edited by Blair B. Kling and M.N. Pearson. Honolulu: The University Press of Hawaii.

———. 2006. *The Portuguese in India*. Cambridge: Cambridge University Press.

Prange, Sebastian. 2018. *Monsoon Islam: Trade and Faith on the Medieval Malabar Coast*. Cambridge: Cambridge University Press.

Raymond, André. 1994. "Islamic City, Arab City: Orientalist Myths and Recent Views". *British Journal of Middle Eastern Studies* 21, no. 1: 3–18.

Subrahmanyam, Sanjay. 1990. *The Political Economy of Commerce: Southern India 1500–1650*. Cambridge: Cambridge University Press.

———. 1998. *The Career and Legend of Vasco da Gama*. Cambridge: Cambridge University Press.

———. 2012. *The Portuguese Empire in Asia, 1500–1700: A Political and Economic History*. West Sussex: Wiley-Blackwell.
Zayn al-Dīn Sr., Shaykh. 2013. *Taḥrīḍ ahl al- īmān*, edited and translated by KM Muhammad. Calicut.
Županov, Ines G. 1999. *Disputed Mission: Jesuit Experiments and Brahmanical Knowledge in Seventeenth-Century India.* New Delhi: Oxford University Press.
———. 2005. *Missionary Tropics: The Catholic Frontier in India (16th–17th Centuries)*. Ann Arbor: The University of Michigan Press.

7

Travelling Spirits: Revisiting Melaka's *Keramat* from the Indian Ocean[1]

Fernando Rosa

> *διὰ τὸ θαυμάζειν οἱ ἄνθρωποι καὶ νῦν καὶ τὸ πρῶτον ἤρξαντο φιλοσοφεῖν.*
> Through wonder men began to philosophize, both now and in the beginning.
>
> *Aristotle, Metaphysics, Book 1, 982b*

[1] This contribution is based on a paper originally presented at the South African Contemporary History and Humanities Seminar, at the University of the Western Cape, on 17 September 2017, http://www.chrflagship.uwc.ac.za/seminar-fernando-rosa/. I am grateful to Aqbal Singh in Singapore, who first awakened my interest in the Sindhis and Balochis, as well as the Punjabis of his family's ancestral homeland, and also for having provided me over the years with much of the bibliography and a good deal of the ideas tentatively laid out in this essay; to Sumit Mandal from University of Nottingham Malaysia, for having discussed *keramat* and Indian Ocean histories with me; and to Andrea Acri at the École Pratique des Hautes Études in Paris, and the Nalanda-Sriwijaya Centre at ISEAS – Yusof Ishak Institute in Singapore, for having led me through the intricacies of the ancient histories of Monsoon Asia both in person and through his amazing work; and last but not least, to Sara Keller with the Laboratoire Orient & Méditerranée in Paris, for having shared with me a good deal of her immense store of knowledge of Gujarat's and India's history. In Melaka, I am particularly grateful to several members of the Chetty community in Gajah Berang, for having put up with my questions and my curiosity as well as my intrusion into their lives. Of course, any shortcomings here are my own.

धर्मक्षेत्रे कुरुक्षेत्रे
Dharmakṣetre, kurukṣetre
When in the field of virtue, in the field of Kuru [the battlefield][2]

I

In June 2017, Theresa May, in a first for a head of state, declared, after what was then the latest terrorist attack in London, that the military and security aspect was not the most important in the ongoing crisis, fundamental as it might seem under the circumstances: in the long run, the ideological aspect was the key, according to her.[3] It is interesting to note that she seemed to closely echo (unwittingly or not) similar concerns stated in a report by Ayaan Hirsi Ali in the United States a couple of months earlier, where Ali pointed out the importance of supporting reformist Muslims in the current predicament, and of seeing Islam as a political ideology (Ali 2017). In this way, both head of state and political activist seem to be calling for work with ideas. This chapter will try and probe what resources may be at our disposal for the task at hand, focusing on *keramat* in Melaka and expanding from there to wider oceanic histories related to religions and spirits, particularly those connecting the Middle East, South, and Southeast Asia.

In order to be effective in any ideological offensive (i.e., one based on countering or criticizing ideas), particularly one involving religion(s), we could do worse than adopting an attitude of Aristotelian-Platonic wonder or *thaumazein* (*θαυμάζειν*), through an engagement with enchantment. Joseph A. Josephson-Storm (2017) usefully historicizes the myth of disenchantment in his latest book of the same name, partly about the Frankfurt School and the Vienna Circle, besides the work of Freud and Max Weber, among other luminaries (including James Frazer and Edward B. Tylor). He accordingly proposes an explicit (re)enchantment of scholarship. Josephson-Storm shows how in Weber's and Bacon's work, for instance, disenchantment is actually powerfully predicated on the very enchantment which both Bacon and Weber supposedly reject (I say supposedly as Josephson-Storm cogently argues that neither Bacon

---

[2] First line, *The Bhagavad Gītā*, translated by Sargeant (2009).

[3] For instance, see http://www.independent.co.uk/news/uk/home-news/london-terror-attack-theresa-mays-statement-full-london-bridge-borough-market-a7771891.html (accessed 5 September 2017).

nor Weber were really scholars of disenchantment). Namely, according to Josephson-Storm, there never really is disenchantment, but just different, and often competing, forms of enchantment. In this way, what we might call here scholarly infatuation with contextualization and "randomness" is a form of self-conjured disenchantment-as-enchantment—what in fact Taussig openly calls "black magic" in scholarly writing (say, ethnographies), suggesting in turn the practice of an apotropaic writing to counter it (Taussig 2015).

Furthermore, Jeffrey Kripal proposes a perspective which allows us to engage with religions, though not theologically or in terms of discrete creed faiths (each with their own dogmas and orthodoxy), but instead in terms of an explicitly comparative perspective centred on human and spiritual agency. From this perspective, Kripal posits that "writing history is quite literally 'heretical', that is, a deeply personal choice (*hairesis*) or series of choices one makes out of one's own personal convictions, disciplined study, and still inarticulate intuitions, regardless of whether these conform to orthodoxy or religious authority" (Kripal 2007, p. 31). This injunction seems particularly apposite for my purposes here. Kripal, incidentally, not unlike Taussig, also emphasizes the enormous importance of writing in this process.

Besides Kripal and Josephson-Storm, I also take inspiration from the truly monumental oeuvre of Patricia Crone, a scholar who has reportedly done a good deal to reshape Islamic studies in the past half a century, until her untimely death in 2015. I have in mind in particular her broad comparative work *Nativist Prophets of Iran*, where she also invokes colonialism in Africa (Crone 2014). Crone's work is in fact not only on Medieval Islam; at the time of her death she was venturing out towards the early modern era in China, Central and South Asia, as well as, as mentioned above, both British and French colonialism in Africa in the past two centuries. Her wide-ranging, highly explorative, scholarly curiosity is thoroughly grounded moreover on a rigorous reading of various archives and specialized literature in an amazing array of languages, both European and Middle Eastern. Though I will not be quoting from her work below, her broad-ranging, comparative perspective has been a genuine source of inspiration for what follows.

In addition, I will also mention here the recent work of another philologist and historian of religions, namely, Andrea Acri, particularly his recent edited volume *Spirits and Ships* (Acri, Blench and Landmann 2017), where several contributors probe the deeper religious and material histories of the Indian Ocean and Monsoon Asia (stretching as far as East and Southern Africa, in fact, though only Madagascar is treated in the book—see my review, Rosa 2017). Both Crone and Acri are important specialists in deeply comparative historical methodologies—just as Kripal, who is a specialist in the comparative history of religions. In my attempt at creolizing different kinds of knowledge and perspectives from various domains and parts of the world, Josephson-Storm's injunction of bringing enchantment explicitly to the fore in scholarship will be a recurring concern. Below I discuss some theoretical aspects of religion in South and Southeast Asia, and later share some vignettes from my own research in Southeast Asia—specifically that concerning Malacca (also spelled Melaka, and henceforth so spelled here) in Malaysia.

II

> This study will show that in much of south India the shrines and divinities of the so-called convert groups were indispensable resources to the region's aspiring warrior lords. It did not matter that most of these rulers and their subjects observed forms of worship which we would now describe as Hindu; formal boundaries and orthodoxies were of little importance compared with the transforming sacred energy which was held to reside in these sites, and which could convey its powers of healing, destruction and sovereignty to all comers, regardless of affiliation or origin. This too is an important theme of the book. There are no fixed or "traditional" identities in south Asia. Neither caste nor religious and communal affiliations can be seen as static or immutable, as part of the established "ethnographic reality" of the subcontinent.
> …
> Indians have long perceived the power of divine beings as a particularly awesome form of the power which was claimed and exercised by kings and would-be rulers. The deity's shrines are seats of sovereign power; the reigning lord can not command his subjects unless he is able to control and expand his own network of sacred "kingly" shrines. (Bayly 1989, p. 2)

Bayly, a specialist in the historical anthropology of South India, has virtually no Indian Ocean or Monsoon Asia perspective in her work, as far as I can tell. Also, she does not go into any deeper histories beyond the period she is tackling: a period stretching from the early modern to the early colonial era, with forays into medieval histories of South India (including nods to North India). Her work is, moreover, marred by the seemingly opposed colonial (and ultimately monotheistic) construct of "village deities" versus "orthodox Brahmanism". Indians are therefore supposedly unable to carry out Thomistic-like theological thinking of any kind, being mired, one assumes, in various superstitions and myriad deities[4]—even though, of course, Bayly does not employ these categories.[5] Nonetheless, though not sufficiently critical of the religious and social categories that she tackles, Bayly's work retains valuable insights for my purposes here, one of which is exactly the complex historical processes of creolization at stake, which largely make labels such as "Hindu", "Muslim", "Buddhist", etc., at best somewhat questionable, if still undoubtedly powerful, and at worst positively misleading.

Ramey (2008) seems to confirm my suspicions. In this way, his study of present-day religious practices and beliefs of the Sindhi diaspora in both India and the United States is quite relevant here, as it provides a contrast to Bayly's perspective, also in what concerns his theoretical approach:

> Moreover, the varied emphases in these three movements did not exhaust the variety of choices made in other Sindhi Hindu movements that were not prominent in Lucknow. For example, in Chennai, the followers of the Sindhi spiritual leader Shahenshah maintained a religious site, Sufidar, that in both name and practice resembled Rochal Das's emphasis on Sufism while also incorporating an even wider array of elements. While the central room had a large image of Shahenshah, another room included elements focusing on Dastagir, a non-Sindhi Sufi Muslim to whom they regularly recited special prayers. Moreover, both rooms were filled with numerous additional two- and three-dimensional images, including a variety of deities (such as Ganesh, Lakshmi, and Jhule Lal) (see cover photo), Arabic calligraphy, images of *pirs* and their *dargahs*, Guru Nanak and his successors, the Guru Granth Sahib, Jesus, and more. (Ramey 2008, pp. 103–4)

[4] An analogous mindset in the ethnography and historiography of another Indian Ocean location, also related to Hinduism, i.e., Bali, has been critiqued by Acri (2011). He shows that Balinese Hindu practices are not only an orthopraxis—as ethnographers have posited—delinked from any sets of scriptural texts and theological discussions (say, Bali would supposedly be a kind of South India minus Brahmin theologians).

[5] In this regard, it is useful to mention here Josephson-Storm's critique of constructs on "superstition" in European social sciences and humanities, in the work of major luminaries of the West: see Josephson-Storm (2017), pp. 44–57.

Ramey's analysis is important, to my mind, because it indicates a shifting variety in practices and beliefs, but does not give in to an atomistic (his term) view of those as solely personal or community choices. Instead, Ramey emphasizes constantly changing processes of creolization (that he calls "syncretism") which require to be monitored, localized, and described in detail. In this regard, for instance, he invokes a powerful figure of the Sindhi pantheon: Jhule Lal (see Figure 7.1). This deity is also known by other names: Udero Lal, Zinda Pir, Amar Lal, and Darya Sahib, and, for many Muslims in Sindh, Khizir, a Qur'anic figure (Ramey 2008, p. 112). Of course, needless to say, not all stories and imaginings related to Jhule Lal are compatible or even congruent among themselves. This figure nonetheless epitomizes in many ways the issues under discussion here. Ramey says about Jhule Lal (his discussion on him starts on p. 107):

> On the other hand, a variety of elements in Jhule Lal's iconography diverge from typical images of Hindu deities. While most male Hindu deities are bare-chested, as was common among kings in India, Jhule Lal consistently wore an opulent tunic, which is more commonly associated with Persianate courts and rulers. The opulent tunic, therefore, identified Jhule Lal as a royal figure, just like the crown and other royal motifs in the images of Jhule Lal and many other deities. However, drawing on Persianate traditions of royal dress makes this aspect of Jhule Lal's iconography distinct among Hindu gods. Jhule Lal's full, white, neat beard also distinguished him from most Hindu deities who appeared clean- shaven and dark haired, with a few exceptions such as Visvakarman. The white hair and beard is common among images of Hindu ascetics, but most of these images emphasize their asceticism through elements such as unkempt hair and limited clothing that do not fit with the overall image of Jhule Lal.
>
> Most of these anomalous elements, however, fit with common imagery of Khwaja Khizr. As an immortal, wise being, he is often depicted as a white bearded man, and in typical Islamic fashion, Khwaja Khizr is fully clothed, usually in a green cloak (....). Furthermore, as images of Khwaja Khizr typically depict him standing on a fish, Jhule Lal's *vahana* contributes to the similarities, although his seated position on the fish pushes Jhule Lal's standard iconography toward [118] typical Hindu imagery and away from associations with Khwaja Khizr. (Ramey 2008, pp. 117–18)

Differently to Bayly, who is solely concerned with South India (mostly today's Kerala and Tamil Nadu), but not entirely unlike Ramey, I will take

FIGURE 7.1
Jhule Lal

Source: Pinterest, wallpaper.

a broader perspective, profiting in particular from Acri's recent, to my mind largely successful, attempt at probing into the very ancient histories largely shared within Monsoon Asia (i.e., a stretch of Asia and the Indian Ocean with vague boundaries in Madagascar in the east and Oceania in the west, besides Central Asia and China—see Acri, Blench, and Landmann 2017). This mosaic or network of cultures currently lacks a name, though the contributors in the volume in question often focus on its connections with Austroasiatic (i.e., largely pre-Austronesian) languages and "cultural packages". The label "Austroasiatic" is currently linguistically represented in today's Southeast Asia in languages such as Khmer or Mon, and in South Asia in the so-called "Munda" languages; yet, it has a descriptive scope which is much broader than that of linguistics.

To put a complex matter in a nutshell, people speaking Austroasiatic (and early Austronesian) languages would have fashioned a largely shared cultural matrix (which is, in a way, remindful of the old ethnological notion of the *Kulturkreis*). This matrix or "psychogeography" (Roger Blench's term in Acri, Blench, and Landmann 2017) would be common to both "civilizations" (say, as represented by, for instance, urban-based polities, large and small) and "tribal" peoples (for instance, the ones inhabiting today's Peninsular Malaysia, the Andaman Islands, Highland Southeast Asia, India's northeast and China's Yunnan, among other places).

What is no longer an open question is that, whatever the relevant—literally travelling—material cultures at stake here (for instance, buildings, ocean-going and other watercraft, pottery, and textiles), the matrix is, to employ now a more than mildly felicitous phrase coined by David White, and reclaimed by Acri in his own contribution (Acri 2017), a "demonological cosmopolis" (the term of course is no doubt intended to echo—as well as, perhaps, criticize—Pollock's famous "Sanskrit cosmopolis" focusing on Sanskrit vs. vernacular languages and literatures). This demonological cosmopolis includes the Indic notion of *śakti*, or a primordial divine force or power (also mentioned by Bayly in what concerns South India), which is largely of feminine origin, as well as the famous fierce goddesses and thunder gods of both South and Southeast Asia. Building on recent work debunking the idea that India somehow "civilized" Southeast Asia, Acri (2017, pp. 72–73) says:

> My main thesis is that phenomena that are perceived by current scholarship as being either "Indic" or "local"/"indigenous" in nature were in fact already shaped by multi-directional and supra-local circulatory dynamics; therefore, a perspective transcending the current paradigm is required to make sense of their genesis and transfer over a long period of time.

Various deities are evoked, such as Rudra (an ancient Vedic god) as well as Nkuu', a Semai (a "tribal" people in Peninsular Malaysia) deity. Both deities are related to thunder. Acri posits that religion, rather than merely yet another element in the picture, is actually the very basis of the unity of the region under scrutiny: namely, somehow the spirits are at the helm of the ships (sic). The equal centrality and importance of feminine power in both Semai and Indic religions is likewise brought to the fore. Besides, Acri persuasively indicates that there are far too many supposedly "peripheral" regions involved in Tantrism, for instance, for it to have such a narrow geographical cradle as today's or colonial India.[6] I will tackle below the issue of *kramat/keramat*, all the while keeping in mind the "Monsoon Asian psychogeography" briefly described above.

Cape Town aside, where *kramat* arrived with Dutch colonialism (which in turn brought to the Cape Muslim exiles from today's Indonesia—see Figure 7.10 below), and besides those in East Africa, the historically closer relatives of the *kramat* are undoubtedly the various South Asian *dargahs*, for instance, those of Sindh or Gujarat, besides those of South India.[7] In Peninsular Malaysia, Dentan (2017, p. 55) tells us that the Semai, a tribal people, go to grave "mounds" (*busut*) where spiritual powers (*keramat*) might linger. The community in question—in Bernam (meaning "mountain") —is of Khmer (i.e., Austroasiatic) origin. In Melaka's graves (officially called *makam*, but popularly known as *keramat*[8]), this association is somehow fuzzier, but is also there to my mind, especially as there was also a king, a fort and palace, and rich houses belonging to merchants, as well as religious and other diversity, even though less is known about pre-colonial Malacca—destroyed by the Portuguese invasion of 1511—than about, for instance, pre-colonial Gujarat port cities.[9]

Interestingly, there is a link between hill shrines and *keramat*. This link is in fact pre-Islamic, as Miksic points out. Malay royalty in one very famous narrative found in the *Sejarah Melayu* is in fact supposed to have started on a specific hill in eastern Sumatra, i.e., Seguntang, just across

[6] See also the contributions in his previous, path-breaking edited volume *Esoteric Buddhism in Mediaeval Maritime Asia* (Acri 2016).

[7] There are also, of course, the saintly graves of the East African coast. In Cape Town, *kramat* is used rather than *keramat* as in Malaysia and Indonesia.

[8] The Malaysian government religious authorities seem to strongly object to the use of the word *keramat*, insisting instead on the more neutral *maqam* (grave, tomb, mausoleum). Jawi (Malay in Perso-Arabic script) signs outside the entrance gates (as in the case of the *keramat* of Hang Jebat and Hang Kasturi in town—see Figures 7.3 and 7.10), as well as all official sign boards on site, accordingly mention *maqam* instead of *keramat*.

[9] See, for instance, the work of Thomaz (2000) and Pinto (2012), as well as Pires (2005, pp. 219–89) and my own book (Rosa 2015).

the straits from Melaka (Miksic 2007, pp. 190 and 334). That is where the first Malay sovereign would have alighted from heaven. The hill used to have Buddhist sanctuaries on it, according to Miksic. In fact, Miksic mentions that those sanctuaries were eventually replaced by *keramat*, which he describes as "pseudo-Islamic [sic] shrines". I find his seemingly disparaging description actually quite fascinating. The founder of Melaka, Parameswara (also an appellation to designate the paramount god Śiva, i.e., Parameśvara), is generally considered to be a Javanese prince who exiled himself from Palembang, which is where Seguntang is located. Śrīvijaya, the kingdom that had Palembang as its capital, in fact covered both sides of the Straits of Melaka (just as the later Malacca Sultanate, centuries later). Miksic also mentions that the site in question was a destination for royal pilgrimages.

Intriguingly, the first mention of *keramat* in a Malay text which I have come across is from the 1370s, and therefore towards the end of the period of Hindu-Buddhist ascendance in Sumatra and Java.[10] The text in question is the *Hikayat Bayan Budiman* (Winstedt 1966), which is considered to be the Malay translation or adaptation of a Persian translation or version of a Sanskrit text, namely, the *Śukasaptati*, "The Parrot's Seventy Tales". The word *keramat* appears five times in the text, in contexts and with a meaning which seem very close to those of today (in particular, a living or posthumously spiritually powerful figure). The tales in question are often very saucy, especially as they describe the ruses a wife employs in order to conceal her adultery. One of the stories involves incest, another (mock) zoophilia (Wortham 1911). Gaṇapati or Gaṇeśa—a deity also worshipped in Sumatra as well as Java—comes up in one of the saucy stories. Miksic tells us that Gaṇeśa in Southeast Asia acquired tantric traits, namely, skull motifs and snake bands, unknown in India proper. Also, a famous Sumatran text on Gaṇeśa migrated to Tibet in the eleventh century, where it is still read in translation. Of course, Tibet is famously a haven of Tantrism (Miksic 2007, p. 128). I will get back to Tantrism below.[11]

[10] See the Malay Concordance Project (http://mcp.anu.edu.au), consulted on 13 October 2017.

[11] For a brief but very useful discussion on the various meanings of the term, see Acri (2017, pp. 76–77). See also the relevant entry in Miksic, which makes a reference to Sumatra (2007, p. 381).

FIGURE 7.2
Keramat Hang Jebat in the Historic District of the Inner City, Melaka

Note: The *keramat* is on Jalan Kampung Kuli ("Coolie Village Street"—sic. The "coolies" in question were Chinese and are no longer around, as Melaka's old port is no longer in use). Its current compound is much smaller than that of the *keramat* Hang Tuah in Tanjung Keling, outside of town, though still considerably larger than the diminutive compound of *keramat* Hang Kasturi, located on Jonker Walk, perhaps the busiest street in town (see Figure 7.9 below).
Source: Author's photo, 2014.

III

Frankly, there is an impression among the public that the President spends more time visiting the tombs of old figures than living people.
—Nahdlatul Ulama (one of the largest and oldest Islamic organizations in Indonesia) cleric Attabik Ali, quoted in the *Jakarta Post*, 16 June 2001[12]

[12] Quoted in Chambert-Loir and Reid (2002, p. xv). The Indonesian president in question was the late Abdurrahman Wahid (likewise known as "Gus Dur"), also long-time president of Nahdlatul Ulama itself.

FIGURE 7.3
Offerings at Keramat (Officially a *Makam* or "Grave")
Datuk Manila, Gajah Berang, Melaka

Source: Author's photo, 2014.

According to Mandal,

> *Keramat* nicely offer a means of mapping syncretic practices across time, as well as within and beyond nation-state boundaries. That *keramat* constitute sites of reverence, if not worship, for people of different faiths and ethnic backgrounds is my point of departure. Furthermore, I propose that the culturally diverse population in question possesses a shared respect for, if not reverence of, *keramat* as sacred spaces. (Mandal 2012, p. 356)
>
> ...
>
> *Keramat* is the Malay word for popular sites of prayer that dot the social and physical landscapes of much of Muslim Southeast Asia. Typically, a *keramat* is the burial site of a person who in life gained the respect of their community through outstanding spiritual piety,

> learning, historical accomplishment or some other notable distinction. The word "*keramat*" is derived from the Arabic noun *karāmāt* which refers to the miracles performed by a *walī*, a revered spiritual figure or "saint" as it is often translated in English.[13] Chambert-Loir describes such a figure as "an individual who, by birth, by talent, through science or spiritual exercise, is endowed with supernatural powers". Almost without exception male, the gifted divine can assume the status of *keramat* not only after death but also in his lifetime. *Keramat hidup* (living *keramat*) nevertheless tend to be rare. (Mandal 2012, p. 357)[14]
>
> ...
>
> The multi-ethnic and hybrid practices of *keramat* build on the traditions of the Hindu-Buddhist—and perhaps an even more ancient—past in the region. This is the case not only terms of prayer and paying homage but in their physical location. *Keramat* are often built on pre-existing Hindu-Buddhist sites in Java. In Malaysia too *keramat* are found at sites of previous spiritual or otherworldly significance. A notable example is the Keramat Ujong Pasir in Negri Sembilan. The grave—reputedly of a Hadrami—lies adjacent to three megaliths attributed with supernatural powers. (Mandal 2012, p. 361)

I must say that I would much rather use "creolized" instead of "syncretic" or "hybrid", as Mandal does in the excerpts above, but otherwise I find his reflections very much to the point as concerns an understanding of the meaning and importance of *keramat*. Lowe (2003, p. 119) mentions that in the Togean (or Togian) Islands, in Central Sulawesi, the Sama (Bajau) people name the southern cape of Walea island as the Tanjung Keramat, that is, the Spirit Cape, where dangerous (sic) spirits are supposed to live (see Figure 7.11[15]). Locke (1954, p. 159) mentions a place called Keramat Dato' Paroi in Negeri Sembilan where a were-tiger of that name (sic) and tiger-king is believed to live, and where Malays, Indians, and Chinese go

[13] Ibn Khaldun, writing in the eleventh century, says of the Sufis: "Their experience of (supernatural activity) they call 'acts of divine grace' (*karâmah*)." (Ibn Khaldun 1958, p. 223). It is interesting to think that both the acts and their materialization (i.e. the "grave") are called by the same name.

[14] On *keramat hidup*, see Mohd Taib Osman (1972), p. 232.

[15] I am grateful to Andrea Acri for this photo and for having told me about his several extended visits to the islands in years past. According to Acri (p.c.), the islanders still visit the Cape—which they regard as being infested by spirits, especially at night—to pray and make offerings to the Genius Loci, in order to have their desires fulfilled.

FIGURE 7.4
Keramat Datuk Manila Compound, General View

Source: Author's photo, 2014.

FIGURE 7.5
Lamp Niche, Keramat Datuk Manila

Note: The lamp niche is supposed to be an Indian architectural trait.
Source: Author's photo, 2014.

to offer prayers and small offerings. Of course, *keramat* can also result from the grave of a known historical personage, as in the case of the eighteenth-century Raja Haji Fisabilillah in the Riau Islands (Barnard 1997, p. 518). Another Riau royal, Engkau Puteri, also has a *keramat* together with members of her family (Andaya 2003, p. 88). A tree can also be a *keramat*.

The online dictionary of the official Malaysian language body (Dewan Bahasa dan Pustaka), gives the following generic definitions (they are clearly inflected by official Islamic orthodoxy, though I have tried in my paraphrase to leave that out, and stress instead the more mundane meanings):[16] "glory" (god's gift to the faithful—sic); "the sacred" (*suci*); "place or thing that is sacred and is believed to bring wisdom"; "someone who is observant of religious obligations" (*warak*), and "pious" (*soleh*), a shade of meaning which is too orthodox to my mind, and is unlikely to be widely shared. Interestingly, the Dewan Bahasa dan Pustaka quotes—without saying so—a phrase directly out of *Sejarah Melayu* (perhaps the most famous classical Malay text), namely, *jikalau sungguh mati Chau Pandan, sungguhlah tuan keramat*, that is, "if Chaun Pandan dies, then you certainly possess *tuan keramat*—miraculous power" (*tuan* is a respectful term for a person of importance). Chaun Pandan is the son of the King of Siam who plans to invade Melaka. The phrase is uttered (*titah*)—ironically, one assumes—by Sultan Muzaffar Shah, in whose time the Malay heroes commemorated in the physical *keramat* in Melaka are supposed to have lived, and it is the only time the term is mentioned in *Sejarah Melayu*.[17] The Indonesian Pusat Bahasa's (an official language body) *Kamus Besar Bahasa Indonesia*, defines *keramat* in less lofty and less orthodox terms: "sacred/holy, because the sacredness in question can accomplish something miraculous or magic (*ajaib*), such as healing someone from a disease or bestow the blessings of safety or salvation. It is also defined as a place or something which is sacred or holy, and which can be something miraculous or magical such as a grave (sic); or else someone who is *suci* ("pious") (Sugono 2008, p. 742, entry "Keramat").

---

[16] The dictionary definition: http://ekamus.dbp.gov.my/Search.aspx?spec=false&type=1&cari=keramat — accessed 13 October 2017).

[17] The phrase is not in the Raffles recension (the most commonly used by scholars), however, but in the Shellabear one (Abdul Samad Ahmad 1979, pp. 95–96), as well as in the translation by Leyden and Raffles (1821, p. 133).

FIGURE 7.6
Keramat Datuk Manila, Kampung Chetty/Tengkera

Note: There is always an oil lamp at the head of the tomb, burning day and night (the keeper of the *keramat* is a Chetty man, who told me that his father kept it before him). Offerings of banana are quite common. Chinese neighbours will also on occasion cook their meals at home, and leave them here while they burn incense sticks and pray walking around the *keramat*. Afterwards, they take the pots home. In that way, it is believed that the food will transmit the power of the *keramat* to its eaters.
Source: Author's photo, 2014.

Mandal's perspective on *keramat* puts the stress on oceanic networks centred on Muslims not only as traders but, most importantly, as powerful spiritual figures. There are nonetheless quite varied communities that pray or worship at the *keramat*. In the case of Malaysia, those communities also included, until very recently, quite large numbers of Malays—in fact, all the way from Mindanao in the southern Philippines to Cape Town in South Africa, *keramat* are often associated with Malays, though even in Maritime Southeast Asia *keramat* have always had a broader ethno-religious referential, as Mandal himself notes, for instance (non-Muslim, Taoist, etc.) Chinese, or Javanese;[18] and they belong also in an ancient lineage of sacred sites and powers which is clearly not only pre-Islamic, but also pre-Hindu-Buddhist and even Neolithic (note the mention of the Negeri Sembilan megaliths in the quote above). An interesting point he makes is that *keramat* rise some time between 1500 and 1800, which gives us a very approximate timeframe for dating the structures at stake in Melaka (a port city originally founded in the early 1400s, and which became a colonial outpost as from 1511). However, as I mentioned above, *keramat* already appear as such in Malay literature in the 1370s. This is a very early date. There is one point that Mandal does not raise, and which has proved important in my own research: what we might call the partial coloniality of the *keramat*. My point is that the current structures in Melaka, even if they have ancient precolonial origins, are in fact probably Dutch period structures as they now are. This is also congruent with the character of *keramat* in general (and not only in Malaysia, but also those in, say, Java and Cape Town): namely, they change over time.[19]

Inside the Chetty community (a local community in Melaka of Creole, that is, Indian and Malay, origins), an (Hindu) informant told me that in the past there were sages coming from Arabia and Turkey (sic) who spread all over the region, together with their close followers. According to him, they spread their wisdom and spiritual power wherever they went, and one day they would eventually drop dead all over the place: the *keramat* are found exactly in the places where they dropped dead. Moreover, just as with the *keramat* Datuk Manila, their companions are also buried near them—in this particular case, in very modest graves—on the ground, in the same compound.[20] They were therefore what Joll (2012) called "Creole ambassadors" of knowledge and religion, or Pearson's cultural brokers (2010). The oceanic connections—and the Islamic character—are also pronounced in this story. Furthermore, it depicts the *keramat*

[18] The most famous *keramat* known today on Java are those of the renowned Wali Songo, or the nine saintly men from overseas, of varied origins, who brought Islam to the island as from the late fifteenth century. General saint worship and *keramat* pilgrimage (called *ziarah*) is an extremely important activity in today's Java, for which there are even specialized travel agencies which organize tours (see Chambert-Loir 2002; Hooker 2003, p. 64).

[19] This is a point that Mandal does, indeed, mention (Mandal 2012, pp. 356, 363, 370).

[20] The *keramat* associated with them is many times a compound, in the case of Datuk Manila also including a couple of fruit trees.

denizens as roving foreigners with a small retinue of followers that then somehow came to die and be worshipped locally (by all kinds of locals, that is). What always impresses me in all these narratives is that even in extremely prestigious *keramat*—the best examples are those of the Wali Songo in Java—the identity and personal history of the buried is quite often more than slightly fuzzy. Therefore, what the historiographical importance of the person in question might be, it seems, is a matter of relative indifference to worshippers. This of course leads us to suspect that the *keramat* attributed to the Malay heroes, namely, those of Hang Tuah, Hang Kasturi, and Hang Jebat, in Melaka[21] may also have been either constructed well after their lifetime or, say, perhaps reattributed to them at some point. The three heroes in question are supposed to have lived in the mid-fifteenth century, and therefore right before the approximate start of the age of *keramat* around 1500. That the chronology of the physical structures of the *keramat* and the biographies of their assumed occupants are at least vaguely congruent is in itself meaningful. Of course, though we cannot say so in Malaysia, the historicity of the Malay heroes itself is not a matter beyond dispute.

I will, however, adopt the point of view of many local Melakans, and consider that the historiographical discussion here cannot at all times necessarily upend the spiritual one. Federspiel (2008, p. 264), for instance, defines *keramat* as:

> Power; the godly presence or force found in Muslim shrines or in holy men, and that can be harnessed by devotees for use in personal action.

This generic definition might also underpin that of *śakti* in both South and Southeast Asia. In this way, here too the main difference would not be one related to demonic "village deities" versus "god-ridden" "Brahminical Hinduism" or "esoteric" versus "non-esoteric" Buddhism;[22] instead, it is one related to the fact that *śakti* is often a feminine spiritual force—as exemplified in the cult of the fierce goddesses of South and Southeast

[21] The last two are right inside the heart of the historic district, whereas the first is outside of town in Tanjung Keling or "(South) Indian Promontory" (sic). The name of the locale itself is significant here as it harks back to connections across the Bay of Bengal.

[22] In fact, this specific distinction is basically useless, as a great portion of mainstream Buddhism from the eighth century onwards was tantric and esoteric by definition; furthermore, "Hinduism" and "Buddhism" are entrenched categories that need interrogating.

FIGURE 7.7
Keramat (*Maqam*) Hang Tuah, Tanjung Keling, Melaka

Note: This is also a *keramat panjang*.
Source: Author's photo, 2013.

Asia—and Islamic *keramat* are supposed to be related to male saints only. This is virtually a historical deviation, therefore, from widespread and well-documented local pre-Islamic (sometimes still current) imaginings and practices, but one that is seemingly largely congruent with various orthodox and not so orthodox views of Islamic patriarchy, not to mention an apparent fear of female spiritual power (sic). Incidentally, both South India and Maritime Southeast Asia are regions where historically gender equality was far above the admittedly low level of contemporary European and other societies (including Dutch society, arguably one of the most gender-equal in early modern Europe), to the surprise of many a colonizer and Christian missionary. It is also a region which saw important tantric cults, as in the case of Sumatra—just across the Straits of Melaka from

Melaka proper, and in fact making up a unity with it during the time of the Melaka Sultanate—until very late in the fourteenth century (as related by Braginsky 2004 and 2017, for instance, and in my brief discussion below of Braginsky's work).

My assumption is, therefore, that the cosmopolitan character of early modern *keramat* may be traced further back to an earlier oceanic and land common cultural matrix or "psychogeography";[23] in particular, besides Tantrism, I am thinking here about Paul Mus' ideas about spiritually powerful (and spirits-ridden!) places that were the centres of "territory cults" across Monsoon Asia (Mus 2010 [1933]). This would also explain why the spiritual power of the denizens of *keramat* is what counts most, rather than their actual ethnic or religious affiliation, notwithstanding the obvious importance of the latter. That the personages associated with *keramat* often seem somewhat shadowy at best, or else have contested identities, or, still, do not seem to elicit much, if any, interest on the part of worshippers (as in the case of some of the *keramat* in Melaka), is in this way a sign that the *keramat* are first and foremost spiritually important. That is also clearly the fear and opinion of Malay religious authorities themselves, who are accordingly obviously uncomfortable with them—that the *keramat* are still nowadays as well as historically stamped as Islamic means of course that they cannot possibly disengage themselves from that issue under pain of, minimally, losing face. The religious authorities in Melaka in particular have shown themselves to be particularly concerned with the issue of *keramat* over the years.

IV

The issue posed by *keramat* and their spiritual power as understood at various Indian Ocean locations is interestingly quite central to any discussions involving Islam. It may seem an arcane and minor theological point, even a mere detail, but in fact it is not. As mentioned above, even the current "masculinized" version of spiritual power embodied in *keramat*—a notion that is of pre-Islamic origin—is clearly threatening

[23] To mention but a relatively minor issue (though certainly not minor to worshippers), in my experience in Melaka, for instance, offerings to *keramat* to this day are a complex mix of South Indian, Malay, and Chinese offerings—see figures above of Datuk Manila.

FIGURE 7.8
Official Signboard on the Site of Hang Tuah's Grave, Tanjung Keling ("(South) Indian Promontory"), Outside Melaka City Proper

Note: The signboard states: "It is forbidden to carry out activities that may result in *syirik* [*shirk* or intercession] and *khurafat* [superstitions]." See entry for *syirik* in Sugono (2008): praying to *tempat keramat* or "keramat places" (as well as graves and statues) is specifically mentioned as making up *syirik*, as is belief in the power of ancestors to influence one's life, or any belief in a power other than that of Allah being equal or similar to the latter (including the power of science).
Source: Author's photo.

to various religious authorities (in Malaysia, especially those connected to various state bodies devoted to Islam). The issue therefore deserves further scrutiny.

Van Bruinessen (2008, p. 218) tells us in what concerns Indonesia, that the

> Muhammadiyah, established in 1912, focused most of its energies on education and welfare, establishing hospitals and modern schools, both modelled on Christian missionary examples. In matters of religious belief and practice it was reformist and fiercely opposed to "syncretistic" practices such as those surrounding death and the visiting of graves and all other practises for which no precedent could be found in the Qur'an and *hadith*.

In Java, in fact, the *pesantren* tradition has held the visitation of graves in high esteem (ibid., p. 222). So-called "traditionalists" would favour such a visitation. The notion of *shirk* entails "associating anything with God, 'polytheism;' to puritan Muslims, the belief in the possibility of mediation between humans and God, for instance, by saints, or in the effectiveness of magical cures constitutes *shirk*" (Noor, Sikand and van Bruinessen 2008, p. 283). *Shirk* (literally, "association") is anything that breaks the unicity of God (*tawḥid*). As Lauzière (2016, p. 8) tells us:

> Allowing Muslims to build structures over tombs and declaring it permissible to seek divine favor through the auspices of a deceased patron are examples of legal opinions that, according to purist Salafis, endorse idolatry. This is one of the many reasons why they abhor Sufism, which they view as a hotbed for such innovations in deed and, ultimately, in creed.

The mention of Sufism is not incidental here. As Kahn (2016) indicates, Sufism is thriving in Java: Sufis there usually do not publicly confront Wahhabi imaginings and practices, nor do they necessarily subscribe to them, as Kahn stresses. There is an association in Maritime Southeast Asia and other places between Sufis and tombs, especially when Sufi masters and pious men are buried in them (needless to say, the same association often obtains in the Sahel and Sahara, as well as on the east coast of Africa). In Africa, places as far apart as Senegal and Somalia have most of their population apportioned among different Sufi brotherhoods exalting the charismatic power of various saints.[24] Of course, many Sufis also engage in ecstatic practices, which are also frowned upon. Interestingly, Indian pilgrims appear again, and once more are condemned, as they go

[24] Usually their respective founders. For Somalia—incidentally also an Indian Ocean location—see Lewis (2002), p. 63.

on pilgrimage to the tomb in Baghdad of the famous Sufi master Abd al-Qadir al-Jilani, and leave prohibited (sic) votive offerings there.[25] It seems that for over a hundred years now Indians (and others) have been criticized for their veneration of tombs. By the early 1900s, tomb visitation and asking the dead for help had become unacceptable,[26] though arguably not yet in wider circles of scholars. Shi'a scholars of course also joined the fray, though they had more lenient opinions: namely, tending and visiting shrines—the tombs of Shi'a imams—was acceptable, provided that these last did not become objects of worship (Lauzière 2016, p. 85). Nonetheless, the issue has remained highly contentious even much later into the twentieth century: once, while ranting against pilgrimages to tombs, an imam, al-Hilali, was reminded in Morocco that King Hassan II himself approved of saint worship (ibid., p. 181).

In reality, as Lauzière indicates, unsurprisingly, the grave of the Prophet in Mecca itself—as well as his home—became a matter of contention already in the 1920s (ibid., pp. 66ff.). By 1926 both his house and that where his first wife, Khadija, had lived, became the object of heated debate involving the famous Islamic reformist Rashid Rida from Syria, who wanted to establish schools in them, the King of the young state of Saudi Arabia (Abd al-Aziz), and the local 'ulama. Unsurprisingly, Rida's project was turned down by the latter (ibid., p. 68). Significantly, by then Indian pilgrims had turned both houses into objects of devotion. I wonder whether it is a coincidence that those pilgrims were Indians, if we take into consideration what we know of religion in India!

In a diatribe against Shi'as, Rida himself would later write:

> I invite all rational Muslims, especially those among the moderate Shi'is who are sincerely devoted to Islam, to join us in a courageous renaissance in order to revivify the pure monotheist creed (...), *condemn those who worship the dead*, be they from among the family of the Prophet or from the rest of the virtuous friends of God [*awliyā'*], and condemn [those who] cling to the teachings of the intellectually stagnant Shi'i jurists. (quoted in Lauzière 2016, p. 85; emphasis added)

---

[25] This condemnation appears in a source of 1907, mentioned by Lauzière (2016, p. 48). For Sufism in India, see Green (2006), and also Gilmartin and Lawrence (2000).

[26] Even though they were also common in the Maghreb, for instance, and in fact over large swathes of the Sahel and Sahara (Lauzière 2016, p. 52).

Getting their inspiration partly from Ibn Taymiyya (the same scholar who once had condemned Avicenna as heretic, and hailed by many, conservative and reformist alike, as a paragon of Sunni orthodoxy), Salafis considered the visiting of tombs as heretical:

> Hence, they argued that visiting tombs to seek favors from the dead was a heretical practice insofar as it contravened the unicity of God's lordship (*tawḥid al-rubūbiyya*) and the unicity of worship (*tawḥid al-'ibāda* or *tawhīd al-ulūhiyya*, meaning that worship is for God alone). Contravening the unicity of God, in turn, constituted a denial of one of His most central attributes. (ibid., p. 47)

In view of all this controversy, it is not at all surprising that Abdul A'la Maududi—a well-known Islamist thinker—should say:

> This, then, is the true meaning of "Jihad", a term about which you have heard much. If you ask me now where is that Islam, the Muslim Party and the "Jihad" whose ideology you have enunciated before us and why no trace of these may be discovered today among the Muslims of the world, I shall entreat you not to confront me with this question but ask it of those who have deflected the attention of the Muslims from their real mission to magical preparations like talismans, incantations, superstitious rites and supererogatory offerings. Ask it of those who prescribed short-cuts to salvation, reform and the attainment of the objective, so that all this may be obtained by no more striving or hard labour than is necessary for telling the beads or *propitiating a soul lying asleep in a grave*. (Maududi 1980, p. 32, emphasis added)

In Malaysia, you are officially entreated to pray for the soul of the dead at a *keramat*, but definitely *not to* his soul. Unless this may sound like some arcane theological shenanigan—say, a kind of merely internal debate among various factions of mullahs—let us explore Maududi's thought through the text I quoted above, seemingly delivered as a talk in Lahore, British India (today in Pakistan), in 1938. I am not claiming here that either its author or the talk in question are necessarily representative of any specific current of Islamic thought or policy—say, that followed by the current Malay government in Malaysia. Nonetheless, I do propose that both Maududi and his speech are relevant for my purposes here (also because I happen to have come across Maududi's work, and this particular text, through my local connections in Maritime Southeast Asia. As I said above, Maududi is clearly locally read). Maududi is quite interesting because he also presents a diametrically opposed view to that of most forms of Tantrism and esoteric Buddhism/Hinduism, where feminine power is not only explicitly disowned, but in fact, in my opinion, very much feared.

First, however, a parenthesis, as well as a contrast. Ibn Khaldun, writing about a thousand years ago, states that jurists believe that adepts of mysticism cannot possibly have attained any mystical station, since "sainthood can be obtained only through divine worship". Ibn Khaldun states unequivocally that the jurists' position is an "error". He quotes from the Qur'an: "God bestows His grace upon whomever He wants to". And goes on to comment that the attainment of sainthood is not restricted to (the correct performance of) divine worship, or anything else. "When the human soul is firmly established as existent, God may single it out for whatever gifts of His He wants to give it" (Ibn Khaldûn 1958, pp. 224–25). This position is seemingly greatly at variance with Maududi's: the latter seems in fact close to that of the jurists whom Ibn Khaldun criticizes.

Interestingly, to Maududi, Islam is not really a religion (sic). He is also emphatic that Muslims are not a kind of nation, nor really, except fleetingly, contextually, and superficially, members of any nation as such (including, it is interesting to note, purportedly Islamic nation-states). Instead of a mere religion, Maududi (1980, p. 5) states that Islam is in fact a:

> revolutionary ideology and programme which seeks to alter the social order of the whole world and rebuild it in conformity with its own tenets and ideals. "Muslim" is the title of that International Revolutionary Party organized by Islam to carry into effect its revolutionary programme. And "Jihād" refers to that revolutionary struggle and utmost exertion which the Islamic Party brings into play to achieve this objective.

Of course, by "International Revolutionary Party" Maududi does not really mean any specific, then extant party (remember this is late colonial India). He does suggest a few party denominations, however (see below). If Maududi often sounds like a Marxist revolutionary—and he does[27]—it is because Western politics, including Marxist ones, are clearly a vital

[27] In fact, I personally hear echoes of Frantz Fanon in his work, and definitely echoes of Trotsky.

inspirational source for him. I cannot go into the matter here, but in spite of its Qur'anic and Hadith garb, Maududi's thought is actually deeply rooted in twentieth century political and social trends of the West. However, he also arguably takes his distance from the latter, at least in its secular forms, by grounding his perspective firmly in a divinely ordained order: namely, though he even goes as far as trumpeting the fundamental religious tolerance (sic) of Islam, he is clearly not proposing a secular-style political order. But allow me to let him talk for himself:

> Islam is not merely a religious creed or compound name for a few forms of worship, but a comprehensive system which envisages to annihilate all tyrannical and evil systems in the world and enforces its own programme of reform which it deems best for the well-being of mankind. Islam addresses its call for effecting this programme of destruction and reconstruction, revolution and reform not just to one nation or a group of people, but to all humanity. Islam itself calls upon all the classes which oppress and exploit the people unlawfully, its call is addressed even to the kings and the noblemen to affirm faith in Islam and bind themselves to remain within the lawful limits enjoined upon them by their Lord (Maududi 1980, pp. 16–18).

This quote is from a subsection on "The Need and Objective of Jihad". Note that Islam here is clearly proposed as divinely mandated existential (i.e., both bodily and mental) as well as political philosophy. Emphatically for Maududi, it is *not* "just" a religion. In this way, capturing political power is not only desirable, it is actually an imperative and an injunction for every believer, wherever they may find themselves. This is how Maududi clinches his totalizing argumentation:

> If you suffer the authority of an inimical doctrine in the State, it is a proof positive that your faith is false and the natural result of this is, and can only be this, that your nominal devotion to the doctrine of Islam will also finally wear off. (ibid. 1980, p. 21)

The scope of Islam is therefore truly universal, and virtually knows no borders. The revolutionary Islamic Party therefore aims for the liberation of the whole of humanity and the world. The role of the *dhimmis* (i.e., practitioners of another monotheistic religion or "non-believers") in an Islamic-controlled state is nonetheless quite significant here. Maududi insists that Islam is fundamentally tolerant and does not enforce conversion. Nonetheless, there are important caveats here. In fact, the status of *dhimmis*, rather than peripheral, is quite central to Maududi's thought.

> Islamic "Jihad" does not seek to interfere with the faith, ideology, rituals of worship or social customs of the people. It allows them perfect freedom of religious belief and permits them to act according to their creed. However, Islamic "Jihad" does not recognize their right to administer state affairs according to a system which, in the view of Islam, is evil. Furthermore, Islamic "Jihad" also refuses to admit their right to continue with such practices under an Islamic government which fatally affect the public interest from the viewpoint of Islam. For instance, as soon as the Ummah of Islam captures state power it will ban all forms of business prosecuted on the basis of usury or interest; it will not permit the practice of gambling; it will curb all forms of business and financial dealings which are forbidden by Islamic law; it will close down all dens of prostitution and other vices and for all; it will make it obligatory for non-Muslim women to observe the minimum standards of modesty in dress as required by Islamic law and will forbid them to go about displaying their beauty like the days of ignorance [he means the *Jahiliyya* or the pre-Islamic era in Arabia]; the Muslim Party will clamp censorship on the Cinema. The Islamic government with a view to securing general welfare of the public and for reasons of self-defence will not permit such cultural activities as may be permissible in non-Muslim creeds, but which, from the viewpoint of Islam are corrosive of moral fibres and fatal (ibid., pp. 27–28).

Maududi revealingly also makes a point of disabusing us of any notion of an easy divide here between "us" and "them". In his text, he is clearly addressing *dhimmis* as well as those inside the house of Islam who are not pious enough, besides his own followers. The existential and political philosophy he puts forth implies in fact a severe, and explicitly joyless, kind of strict and masculinist asceticism. At no point are even the *houris* in paradise bandied around in his text. Significantly, the only women mentioned in his text (besides those in a Qur'anic quote), are *dhimmi* ones who are sources of moral turpitude, as in the quote above. Note also the word "fatal", with which Maududi concludes his reflection. The matter of pleasure is not a small moral issue: it threatens in fact to upset his whole edifice. His thinking is in fact at the antipodes of any variety of Tantrism, or any creolized cultural and religious phenomenon across the Indian Ocean. He explicitly inveighs against "carnal pleasures":

> The "Jihad" of Islam is a dry labour, devoid of pleasure. It is nothing but a sacrifice of life, wealth and carnal desires (....) This God-conscious head of state cannot occupy a magnificent palace, nor can

> he live with pomp and glory nor can he procure means of pleasure and merriment. At all hours, he is seized with the fear that one day he will be severely called to account for every deed he commits in this world and if it is found that he received a single penny as illicit gains, or snatched away the smallest patch of land from any one by force, or displayed the slightest measure of pride or haughtiness, or practised tyranny or injustice in a single instance or succumbed even for one moment before carnal pleasures, he would be condemned to endure the most dreadful torture. The world has not seen a greater fool than the man who truly loves to gain the world and yet is willing to carry the burden of state responsibility under Islamic law. (ibid., pp. 29–30)

I do not think, in the light of the quotes above, that official Malaysian government discomfiture with *keramat* is merely a side story or a shenanigan. *Keramat* are Islamic, and, concurrently, clearly pre-Islamic and also para-Islamic, and even un-Islamic. Namely, there are far too many characteristics to them which make people like Maududi uncomfortable, to say the least. Also, they cannot really be easily sanitized, so to speak: hence Saudi Arabia's renowned, truly extensive destruction of historical grave sites (a destruction which Melaka has also experienced in the past, for instance, in Pulau Besar, where there is a great concentration of *keramat*).[28] I know this will sound unlikely, and perhaps even preposterous, but in such a tightly controlling, totalizing dispensation as Maududi's, a single *keramat* may have the potential not only to destabilize, but, who knows,

[28] Years ago, quite a few *keramat* on the island were destroyed, until the local Jawi Peranakan (Creole Indian Muslim) community negotiated with the government not only the cessation of the destruction, but also the reconstruction of a few of the destroyed shrines. Specific groups within that community are said to be the keepers of the *keramat* along the western coast of Peninsular Malaysia (personal communication, Chris Joll, an anthropologist with Thammasat University, Bangkok). However, the government keeps the Pulau Besar *keramat* under lock, and only opens them for public visitation on Sundays. The island is a site of pilgrimage, nowadays seemingly almost only for local Hindus and Chinese, usually in search of spiritual intercession for some earthly cause (for instance, a friend's father would reportedly go there just before a gambling spree). It is averred that one should not sleep on the island lest one have nightmares, incur bad luck or the wrath of the *keramat* (however, the government has built a hotel on it, though it is, perhaps unsurprisingly enough, reportedly commercially unsuccessful); one should moreover abstain from pork and sexual relations just before a visit. The last time I visited the Keramat Datuk Manila on the mainland in 2014, it was also under lock (usually *keramat* in town only have unlocked iron gates which are however dutifully kept closed, in my experience).

even undermine the entire system at stake. No wonder the Malaysian government seems to be constantly vigilant here.

It is glaringly obvious here that any notion of feminine power seems to be highly threatening, and concurrently sexuality and eroticism are also entirely noxious. I cannot emphasize often enough how that view is hugely at variance with the social worlds of both South and Southeast Asia, not to mention the Sahel and Sahara and East Africa, including the traditional social worlds of many local Muslims themselves. In fact, what Maududi is proposing is nothing other than a frontal, all-out attack on those worlds, one that, to my mind, is already taking place in various ways and diverse war theatres in the region (just think about Rakhine State in Myanmar; south Thailand; and Mindanao in the Philippines).

My point here is that invoking the legacy of Tantrism, the Monsoon Asian cultural matrix or "psychogeography", and Mus' idea of "territory cults"—largely set against a background of varying degrees of Islamization, and the presence, as in India historically, of Islamicate polities (to use now Hodgson's classic notion: Hodgson 1974)—is not only an academic exercise, but potentially one that has important consequences for our current predicament. In this sense, extending the notion of colonialism, for instance, to historical Islamic polities (as Crone does for the non-African Middle East)[29] is potentially path-breaking. I consider the heritages of Tantrism and of the Monsoon Asian cultural matrix as important cultural and even political resources at our disposal in the current confrontation with jihadism, especially as they have historically engaged in important ways with Islam from various perspectives, both in South and Southeast Asia.

To sum up, the course of action based on the Monsoon Asian *kulturkreis* in question is one in which the cultural, the religious, the artistic, the mystical, and the political domains, are all tied together. Nonetheless, they are brought together as so many creolized perspectives, not as distinct creed faiths or varied political ideologies as such. If anything religious and mystical is to be key here—as I believe it has to be—then I think the only perspective we can take is that of Jeffrey Kripal.[30] That is, religiosity,

[29] See Crone (2014). Intriguingly, Crone was also interested in polyandry and historical accounts of communal sex and wife-sharing.

[30] See also Kahn (2016), who is inspired by Kripal's work.

FIGURE 7.9
Keramat Hang Kasturi

Note: It is located on Jonker Walk, where a famous, busy *pasar malam* (night market) is held over the weekend. Typically, the entrance gate is then blocked by a vendor's stall. It is squeezed between a late nineteenth century Chinese temple in a shop house and a parking lot. It is a very small structure and compound. It is so cramped that it is impossible not to suspect that its compound was in fact much larger in earlier times, almost certainly encompassing part or all of the parking lot next door. It is a mere stone throw's away from Keramat Hang Jebat (see Figure 7.2 above).
Source: Author's photo, 2014.

the mystical, etc., can only be considered *comparatively* (sic) and in their historical multifarious mutual enmeshment too. Namely, they only make sense as so many historical (and current) processes of creolization. The sense of connected histories (Subrahmanyam 1997) is quite important here, but so is that of processes of creolization affecting cosmological perspectives with deep roots in the past.

I end this paper with a speculation, but one that is actually quite fundamental, I believe: if we are to act cogently in today's world, we have to learn to relate our thought and forms of political practice to the tantric legacy briefly discussed above, incredibly exotic as this notion may seem. Braginsky (2004) has shown that in Sumatra Malay luminaries such as Hamzah Fansuri and Syamsuddin Al-Sumatrani (whose *keramat* incidentally is located in Melaka's historic district) were fully cognizant of tantric practices, though they were also condemnatory of them. More recently Braginsky (2017) has discussed in detail a whole treasure trove of Sufi-Tantric (sic) texts in Classical Malay, especially that related to *ilm al-nisa* or the Sufi-Tantric "science of women". Instead of only a marginal genre, such texts are actually much more important than previously thought. They indicate two things: well into the nineteenth century, there was a long period of creolization of Sufism and Tantrism of which we are only now becoming fully aware. The other thing is that, especially in the case of the Straits of Melaka, i.e., Sumatra and Peninsular Malaysia,[31] that past can now only be brought back to life with great difficulty. We have therefore to create—or perhaps rediscover—a connected history here, inspired by the wondrous findings and work of the scholars from various fields contributing to the volumes edited by Acri (2016) and Acri, Blench and Landmann (2017).[32]

A revolutionary political ideology that goes for the jugular, so to speak, such as the one exemplified by Maududi's thought, cannot be successfully countered by a secular state—and academia—which is not cognizant in some way or on some level, of the cosmological, ordering power of religion and the mystical, whether in its own territory or in another's (of course, needless to add, I am not proposing here that we should take leave of the secular state); nor by any academic imaginings and theorizations that do not take account of the same power *qua* itself, instead of a phenomenon standing for something else that would be somehow truer (say, political interests, cultural clashes, colonialism, etc.). Kripal (2007, 2014) showed his mettle, when he proposed that religion has to be taken as its own domain, and that, furthermore, the only heuristically satisfying way of accomplishing this is both comparative and "heretical" (in Kripal's sense discussed above). We could do worse than taking our inspiration from him,

[31] Java, whose tantric past seems to go deeper and be much more vibrant than that described by Braginsky, even today, is seemingly another story.

[32] There are of course ways of tracing connections here, via Neoplatonism and Vedāntism, for instance, as scholars of religion and philosophy have long noticed (see for instance Harris 1981; Conze 1967; Staal 1961; and the introduction in Uždavinys 2009).

FIGURE 7.10
Keramat/Dargah Shaykh Yusuf, in Macassar, Cape Town, South Africa

Note: I am grateful to Shaun Viljoen for having taken me to this *keramat*. The site is reportedly from the late seventeenth century, but the current structure and compound are from nearly a hundred years ago (1918–25 is the time frame provided by the explanatory boards on the site). It is located by the Eerste River, not far from the sea (there is also a Macassar beach nearby), but originally it was a very desolate and remote location. Shaykh Yusuf was a famous exile under the Dutch East India Company. His companions are also buried in the same site. Macassar (sic), the neighbourhood, is an apartheid-era urban creation. Shaykh Yusuf was of course from Makassar in today's Indonesia. In signboards on site, this compound—popularly known as a *keramat*—nonetheless is indicated as a *dargah* (a term traditionally used in India). In this place, seemingly, both the Indian and the Maritime South East Asian traditions have appositely come together.
Source: Author's photo, 2017.

as well as from Josephson-Storm (2017) and his injunction to explicitly acknowledge and practise an enchanted form of scholarly writing—what Taussig (2015) has called, in the context of ethnographic writing, an apotropaic writing. It is my hope that my weaving in and out of various Indian Ocean histories related to *keramat* has made a small contribution to this collective effort.

FIGURE 7.11
***Keramat* Structure on the Togean (Togian) Islands, Gulf of Tomini, off the Coast of Central Sulawesi, Indonesia**

Source: Andrea Acri, 2004.

References

Abdul Samad Ahmad. 1979. *Sulalatus Salatin (Sejarah Melayu)*. Kuala Lumpur: Dewan Bahasa dan Pustaka.

Acri, Andrea. 2011. "A New Perspective for 'Balinese Hinduism' in the Light of the Pre-Modern Religious Discourse: A Textual-Historical Approach". In *The Politics of Religion in Indonesia: Syncretism, Orthodoxy, and Religious Contention in Java and Bali*, edited by Michel Picard and Rémy Madinier, pp. 142–66. Routledge.

———, ed. 2016. *Esoteric Buddhism in Mediaeval Maritime Asia. Networks of Masters, Texts, Icons*. Singapore: ISEAS – Yusof Ishak Institute.

———. 2017. "Trantrism 'Seen from the East'". In *Spirits and Ships. Cultural Transfers in Early Monsoon Asia*, edited by Andrea Acri, Roger Blench, and Alexandra Landmann, pp. 71–144. Singapore: ISEAS – Yusof Ishak Institute.

———, Roger Blench, and Alexandra Landmann, eds. 2017. In *Spirits and Ships. Cultural Transfers in Early Monsoon Asia*. Singapore: ISEAS – Yusof Ishak Institute.

Ali, Ayaan Hirsi. 2017. *The Challenge of Dawa. Political Islam as Ideology and Movement and How to Counter It*. Stanford: Hoover Institution Press.

Andaya, Barbara Watson. 2003. "Gender, Islam and the Bugis Diaspora in Nineteenth and Twentieth Century Riau". *Sari* 21: 77–108.

Barnard, Timothy P. 1997. "Local Heroes and National Consciousness: The Politics of Historiography in Riau". *Bijdragen Tot De Taal-, Land- En Volkenkunde* 153, no. 4: 509–26.

Bayly, Susan. 1989. *Saints, Goddesses and Kings: Muslims and Christians in South Indian Society, 1700–1900*. Cambridge: Cambridge University Press.

Braginsky, Vladimir. 2004. "The Science of Women and the Jewel: The Synthesis of Tantrism and Sufism in a Corpus of Mystical Texts from Aceh". *Indonesia and the Malay World* 32, no. 93: 141–75.

———. 2017. "The Manner of the Prophet—Concealed, Found and Regained. Revisiting the Science of Women". *Indonesia and the Malay World* 45, no. 132: 250–91.

Burgat, François. 2008. *Islamism in the Shadow of Al-Qaeda*. Translated by Patrick Hutchinson. Austin: University of Texas Press.

Chambert-Loir, Henri. 2002. "Saints and Ancestors: The Cult of Muslim Saints in Java". In *The Potent Dead. Ancestors, Saints and Heroes in Contemporary Indonesia*, by Henri Chambert-Loir and Anthony Reid, pp. 132–40. Honolulu and London: Allen & Unwin and University of Hawai'i Press.

Conze, Edward J.D. 1967. *Thirty Years of Buddhist Studies: Selected Essays by Edward Conze*. Oxford: Cassirer.

Crone, Patricia. 2012. *The Nativist Prophets of Early Islamic Iran Rural Revolt and Local Zoroastrianism*. New Yor: Cambridge University Press.

Dentan, Robert K. 2017. "Fearsome Bleeding, Boogeyman Gods and Chaos Victorious: A Conjectural History of Insular South Asian Religious Tropes". In *Spirits and Ships. Cultural Transfers in Early Monsoon Asia*, edited by Andrea Acri, Roger Blench, and Alexandra Landmann, pp. 38–70. Singapore: ISEAS – Yusof Ishak Institute.

Federspiel, Howard M. 2008. *Sultans, Shamans, and Saints: Islam and Muslims in Southeast Asia*. Chiang Mai: Silkworm Books.

Gilmartin, David, and Bruce B. Lawrence. 2000. *Beyond Turk and Hindu: Rethinking Religious Identities in Islamicate South Asia*. Gainesville, FL: University Press of Florida.

Green, Nile. 2006. *Indian Sufism since the Seventeenth Century: Saints, Books and Empires in the Muslim Deccan*. London: Routledge.

Harris, R. Baine. 1981. *Neoplatonism and Indian Thought*. Albany: State University of New York Press.

Hodgson, Marshall G.S. 1974. *The Venture of Islam: Conscience and History in a World Civilization*. 3 vols. Chicago: University of Chicago Press.

Hooker, M.B. 2003. *Indonesian Islam: Social Change through Contemporary*

Fatawa. Asian Studies Association of Australia in association with Allen & Unwin and University of Hawaii Press Honolulu.

Ibn Khaldûn. 1958. *The Muqaddimah. An Introduction to History*. Vol. 1. Translated by Franz Rosenthal. New York: Bollingen Foundation and Pantheon Books.

Joll, Christopher. 2012. "Islam's Creole Ambassadors". In *The Ghosts of the Past in Southern Thailand: Essays on the History and Historiography of Patan*, edited by P. Jory, pp. 129–46. Singapore: NUS Press.

Josephson-Storm, Jason Ānanda. 2017. *The Myth of Disenchantment: Magic, Modernity, and the Birth of the Human Sciences*. Chicago, London: University of Chicago Press.

Kahn, Joel S. 2016. *Asia, Modernity, and the Pursuit of the Sacred: Gnostics, Scholars, Mystics and Reformers*. New York: Palgrave Macmillan.

Kripal, Jeffrey J. 1998. *Kali's Child: The Mystical and the Erotic in the Life and Teachings of Ramakrishna*. 2nd ed. Chicago: University of Chicago Press.

———. 2004. "Comparative Mystics. Scholars as Gnostic Diplomats". *Common Knowledge* 10, no. 3: 485–517.

———. 2007. *The Serpent's Gift: Gnostic Reflections on the Study of Religion*. Chicago: University of Chicago Press.

———. 2014. *Comparing Religions*. Oxford: Wiley Blackwell.

Lauzière, Henri. 2016. *The Making of Salafism. Islamic Reform in the Twentieth Century*. New York: Columbia University Press.

Lewis, I.M. 2002. *A Modern History of the Somali. Revised, Updated & Expanded*. Oxford and Athens: James Currey and Ohio University Press.

Leyden, John, and Thomas Stamford Raffles. 1821. *Malay Annals*. London: Longman.

Locke, A. 1954. *Tigers of Trengganu*. London: Museum Press.

Lowe, Celia. 2003. "The Magic of Place; Sama at Sea and on Land in Sulawesi, Indonesia". *Bijdragen tot de Taal-, Land- en Volkenkunde* 159, no. 1: 109–33.

Mandal, Sumit K. 2012. "Popular Sites of Prayer, Transoceanic Migration, and Cultural Diversity: Exploring the Significance of *Keramat* in Southeast Asia". *Modern Asian Studies* 46, no. 2: 355–72.

Mandelslo, J.A.V., and A. Olearius. 1658. *Des Hoch Edelgebornen Johann Albrechts von Mandelslo Morgenländische Reyse-Beschreibung; ... herausgegeben durch A. Olearium; mit desselben notis, oder Anmerckungen, wie auch vielen Kupffer Platen gezieret*. Schlesswig.

Maududi, Abdul A'la. 1980. *Jihad in Islam*. Beirut: The Holy Quran Publishing House. Non-dated.

Miksic, John N. 2007. *Historical Dictionary of Ancient Southeast Asia*. Lanham, MD: Scarecrow Press.

Mohd. Taib Osman. 1972. "Patterns of supernatural premises underlying the institution of the Bomoh in Malay culture". *Bijdragen tot de taal-, land- en volkenkunde/Journal of the Humanities and Social Sciences of Southeast Asia* 128, Issue 2: 219–34.

Mus, Paul. 2010. *India Seen from the East: Indian and Indigenous Cults in Champa*, revised edition translated by Iain Mabbett and edited by David Chandler. Caulfield: Monash University Press.

Noor, Farish A., Yoginder Sikand, and Martin van Bruinessen, eds. 2008. *The Madrasa in Asia Political Activism and Transnational Linkages*. Amsterdam: ISIM/Amsterdam University Press.

Pearson, Michael N. 2010. "Connecting the Littorals: Cultural Brokers in the Early Modern Indian Ocean". In *Eyes Across the Water: Navigating the Indian Ocean*, edited by P. Gupta, I. Hofmeyr, and M. Pearson, pp. 32–47. Pretoria: UNISA Press.

Pinto, Paulo Jorge de Sousa, and Roopanjali Roy, trans. 2012. *The Portuguese and the Straits of Melaka, 1575–1619: Power, Trade, and Diplomacy*. Singapore: NUS Press.

Pires, Tomé, Armando Cortesão, and Francisco Rodrigues. 2005. *The Suma Oriental of Tome Pires: An Account of the East, from the Red Sea to China, Written in Malacca and India in 1512–1515; and, the Book of Francisco Rodrigues*. Vol. II. New Delhi: Asian Educational Services.

Ramey, Steven Wesley. 2008. *Hindu, Sufi, or Sikh: Contested Practices and Identifications of Sindhi Hindus in India and Beyond*. New York: Palgrave Macmillan.

Rangan, Haripriya, Judith Carney, and Tim Denham. 2012. "Environmental History of Plant Exchanges in the Indian Ocean". *Environment and History* 18: 311–42.

Rangan, Haripriya, Edward A. Alpers, Tim Denham, Christian A. Kull, and Judith Carney. 2015. "Food Traditions and Landscape Histories of the Indian Ocean World: Theoretical and Methodological Reflections". *Environment and History* 21: 135–57.

Rosa, Fernando. 2015. *The Portuguese and the Creole Indian Ocean: Essays in Historical Cosmopolitanism*. New York: Palgrave Macmillan.

———. 2017. "Review of *Spirits and Ships: Cultural Transfers in Early Monsoon Asia*, edited by Andrea Acri, Roger Blench, and Alexandra Landmann". *Suvannabhumi* 9, no. 2: 167–73.

Sargeant, Winthrop, trans. 2009. *The Bhagavad Gita*. Albany: State University of New York Press.

Staal, Frits. 1961. *Advaita and Neoplatonism: A Critical Study in Comparative Philosophy*. Madras: University of Madras.

Subrahmanyam, Sanjay. 1997. "Connected Histories: Notes towards a Reconfiguration of Early Modern Eurasia". *Modern Asian Studies* 31, no. 3: 735–62.

Sugono, Dendy, ed. 2008. *Kamus Besar Bahasa Indonesia*. Jakarta: Pusat Bahasa.

Taussig, Michael. 1991. *Mimesis and Alterity. A History of the Senses*. New York: Random House.

———. 2015. *The Corn Wolf.* Chicago: University of Chicago Press.

Thomaz, Luís Filipe F.R., and Manuel Joaquim Pintado, trans. 2000. *Early Portuguese Malacca.* Macau: CTMCDP/IPM.

Uždavinys, Algis, and Porphyry. 2009. *The Heart of Plotinus: The Essential Enneads.* Bloomington: World Wisdom.

Van Bruinessen, Martin. 2008. "Traditionalist and Reformist Pesantrens in Contemporary Indonesia". In *The Madrasa in Asia Political Activism and Transnational Linkages*, edited by Farish A. Noor, Yoginder Sikand and Martin van Bruinessen, pp. 217–46. Amsterdam: ISIM/Amsterdam University Press.

Winstedt, Richard O., ed. 1966. *Hikayat Bayan Budiman.* Kuala Lumpur: Oxford University Press.

Wortham, B. Hale. 1911. *The Enchanted Parrot.* London: Luzac.

Part IV

Histories and Geographies of Pilgrimage in Asia

8

Transmissions, Translations, Reconstitutions: Revisiting Geographies of Buddha Relics in the Southern Asian Worlds

Sraman Mukherjee

OWNERSHIP AND VALUES

In his note of 1909, the ethnologist Herbert Hope Risley, a member of the Legislative Department of the British Indian Government, argued on a rather irate note that "… Buddhist bones *belong to nobody and have no value*!".[1] The occasion was the proposed presentation of Buddhist relics, discovered from the site of Shah-ji-ki-Dehri near Peshawar (now in Pakistan), to the Buddhists of Burma. The situation was already complicated by competing demands of various communities and associations over the custody of these relics. To make matters worse for the government, the Afghan Muslim landowners of the site, the two brothers Sayed Amir Badshah and Sayed Ahmed Shah, claimed a share in the finds. They supported these claims

[1] Note dated 28 August 1909, from Sir H.H. Risley, Home Secretary, Simla Records 2, 1909, Government of India, Home Department, Archaeology and Epigraphy – A, Proceedings nos. 13–16, December 1909: "Petition from Sayed Amir Badshah and Sayed Ahmed Shah, owners of land from which Buddhist relics were recently found at Peshawar claiming a share of the relics." National Archives of India, New Delhi (henceforth, NAI), italics mine.

by citing a prior agreement they had entered with the excavator, Dr David Brainerd Spooner, the Superintending Archaeologist of the Frontier Circle of the Archaeological Survey of India (henceforth, ASI). This agreement, the owners claimed, promised them an equal share in the finds and financial compensation for any loss to cultivation incurred during excavations. Asserting their landowner's rights, the Sayed brothers now claimed half the share of the total finds unearthed from the Dehri or its equivalent financial value from the Buddhists claiming a share of the relics.

The finds from the excavations included four bits of bones, a crystal reliquary, a clay seal intended to encase the bone fragments in the crystal reliquary, an inscribed metal reliquary housing all these objects, and an old coin.[2] The decoding of inscriptions on the metal casket identified the bone fragments as authentic corporeal relics of the Gautama Buddha. For the antiquarians and archaeologists, the inscriptions, more importantly, attested the reliquary and the remains of the ancient *stūpa* (Buddhist funerary and/or commemorative mound) at the site of Shah-ji-ki-Dehri as the gift of the second-century monarch of the Kushan Dynasty, Kanishka (Asher 2012) (see Figures 8.1 and 8.2).

The situation created by such demand was entirely new for the colonial state. The problem of determining the price of centuries-old Buddhist bones unprecedented, and the Afghan Muslims were never seen to take any keen interest in Buddhist remains that abound throughout this region. In fact, beginning with the nineteenth century, Muslims in general, and especially Pathan Muslims of the Northwest Frontier region, were stereotypically represented in the colonial archives as ignorant native vandals, mischievous troublemakers, religious fanatics, and zealous iconoclasts. Their only interest in the Buddhist remains unearthed during chance diggings was seen to lie in sporadic acts of "Islamic iconoclasm"—i.e., destroying and defiling ancient Buddhist sculptures in the name of religion. The specter of the "unruly" and "tribal" Muslims on the Northwestern Frontier of the British Indian Empire informed subsequent deliberations on the possible destination of the Shah-ji-ki-Dehri relics and continued to haunt the colonial archaeological records. It legitimized (and still does) the carting away of

[2] Petition from Sayed Amir Badshah and Sayed Ahmed Shah, Mahulla Basate Gul Hassan, Peshawar City, to the Agent to the Governor General and Chief Commissioner, North-West Frontier Province. Simla Records 2, 1909, Government of India, Home Department, Archaeology and Epigraphy – A, Proceedings no. 13, December 1909, NAI.

FIGURE 8.1
Undated Photograph of the Inscribed "Kanishka" Reliquary

Source: Photographer unknown. Courtesy of Archaeological Survey of India.

antiquities from archaeological sites, especially in these regions, to the safe custody of museums.

The narrative of Islamic iconoclasm and destruction of India's pre-Islamic past emerged as a recurring theme in most colonial and early nationalist histories of India. As a discipline of distinctly colonial origins, archaeology in India inherited the theme of medieval and contemporary Islamic vandalism of India's ancient (Buddhist) civilization. It was against these narratives of uninformed vandalism that disciplines and institutions

FIGURE 8.2
Photograph of the Replica of the Inscribed "Kanishka" Reliquary in the British Museum

Source: Author, 2016.

like archaeology and museums would posit themselves as the legitimate protectors of the material traces of India's ancient past.[3] The specter of Islamic iconoclasm and the associated stereotypical representations of Muslims, especially in parts of Pakistan and Afghanistan, as religious

[3] On the politics of "protection" of Gandhara Buddhist sculptures from the supposedly "zealous iconoclasm" of Frontier Pathan Muslims, see Guha-Thakurta (2004) and Asher (2012).

fanatics stranded in a world of "medieval vandalism" have returned to haunt our contemporary world with the destruction of the Bamiyan Buddha sculptures by the erstwhile Taliban Government of Afghanistan in 2001.[4]

In an effort to ease out the complications, in 1909–10, government officials tried to negotiate a deal to determine a one-time pay-off price for the transfer and acquisition of the relics. Very few officers of the colonial establishment, including Risley himself, actually believed that the relics were devoid of any financial value. Sir Harold Stuart, Home Secretary to the Government of India, contended that the market value of the relics was considerable and that the "... Buddhists of Japan, Siam or Burma or Ceylon would probably give lakhs of rupees for them."[5] John Hubert Marshall, the Director General of the ASI, argued that while the relics had very little "intrinsic" value, the owners of the site might be allotted a small gratuity of about 200 rupees since they have "behaved very well about the digging operations".[6] Almost all officers involved with the Shah-ji-ki-Dehri relics agreed that they were extremely valuable from antiquarian, archaeological, historical, aesthetic, diplomatic, and religious points of view. Though the intrinsic or the sheer constituent materials' value of the bones, reliquaries, the seal, and the coin did not amount to much, it was a range of these competing values that made the relics highly prized commodities with potentials for fetching very high market price. However, great confusion raged about exactly which value was to be considered in acquiring the relics. There was little consensus

[4] Though informed by different politics of material engagement with images in the world of electronic media and worldwide web, and targeted primarily for an audience of museum and art connoisseurs in Europe and North America, and not for practising Buddhist communities in Asia, the destruction of the Bamiyan Buddhas continues to be commonly perceived, in our present world of post-9/11 Islamophobia, only and essentially as an act of "Islamic iconoclasm". Such a reading, as Finbarr Barry Flood (2002) argues, completely overlooks the political contingencies in which the destruction was staged as a politically symbolic act and denies any active agency to the actors by freezing them in temporal and civilization registers.

[5] Response to the petition seeking a share of the relics dated 27 August 1909, Simla Records 2, 1909, Government of India, Home Department, Archaeology and Epigraphy – A, Proceedings, December 1909, Nos. 13–16, NAI.

[6] Letter from Sir John H. Marshall to Sir Harold Stuart, no. 1211, dated 25 August 1909, Simla Records 2, 1909, Government of India, Home Department, Archaeology and Epigraphy – A, Proceedings, December 1909, Nos. 13–16, NAI.

among the government officers and the provisions of the Treasure Trove Act, the Act that these officers would increasingly fall back on to legitimize the proposed state acquisition of the relics, did not provide any definite clues.

Passed by the colonial state in 1878, the Indian Treasure Trove Act (Act No. VI of 1878) was primarily designed to consolidate the compulsory acquisition powers of the state over moveable antiquities and bullion buried under the soil. Read as a text of power produced under conditions of colonialism (and subsequently enforced by the postcolonial nation states), the Treasure Trove Act along with a host of other related acts passed in the closing years of the nineteenth and opening years of the twentieth century—namely, the Land Acquisition Act (1894) and the Ancient Monuments Preservation Act (1904)—was drafted to consolidate, enhance, and legitimize state power to an unprecedented scale. All these acts granted the state compulsory acquisition powers over economic, political, and cultural resources of the colony. Objects of acquisition for most of these acts, moveable treasure, land itself, ancient monuments and material traces of the past, were selected solely by the discretion of the government officers and acquired as state/public property in the name of "public good" and "utility". Most of these acts came with heavy penalty clauses for "offenders".

In the Treasure Trove Act, treasure implied "anything of value hidden in the soil, or anything affixed thereto".[7] Anything exceeding in amount or value of ten rupees, was to be reported by the finder of the treasure to the Collector, a revenue officer in independent charge of a district. The written notice from the "finder" to the Collector was to contain a detailed description of the nature, amount, and approximate value of the treasure, and the place and date of its discovery. The finder was then required to submit the "treasure" to the nearest government treasury or produce the treasure at a time and place as notified by the Collector. In case the "finder" and the "owner" of the site of the discovery of the treasure happened to be different parties, as was the case with the Shah-ji-ki-Dehri relics, the Collector issued notices for both to appear before him for claiming their share. Where there was no prior formal agreement in force between the owner and the finder over the distribution of such treasure, the Collector was empowered to allot three-fourths of the treasure to the finder and

[7] Indian Treasure Trove Act, 1878 (Act No. VI 1878), 12 February 1878.

the residue to the owner. The Collector could also sell such "treasure" in public auction and distribute the money to both parties. The Act enlisted details of heavy penalties, ranging from conviction before Magistrate, imprisonment from six months to a year, fine and all the above, for both the finder and the owner if they failed to notify the finds, or deposit such treasure, or failed to provide adequate security, or tried to alter or conceal its identity.[8]

The most important sections of the Act, however, related to compulsory acquisition powers of the government. First, there were lengthy provisions on declaring the treasure "ownerless"—either when the concerned person(s) did not appear before the Collector to lay claims or did not institute a suit in a Civil Court to establish his right within a time limit decided by the Collector, or where such suit was instituted and the plaintiff's claim was finally rejected.[9] Sections 16 and 17 of the Act empowered the Collector to acquire the treasure on behalf of the government "by payment to the persons entitled ... a sum equal to *the value of the materials of such treasure*... together with one-fifth of such value...".[10] No decisions taken by the Collector under the provisions of this Act could be called into question by any Civil Court, and no suit or other proceedings could be initiated against him "for anything done ... in exercise of ... powers" conferred by the Act.[11]

The Act, however, remained extremely vague about the different kinds of value that could be taken into consideration during acquisition. As H.H. Risley pointed out in his note, value in section 4 of the Act, implied "market value" and in section 16 implied "intrinsic" or simply the value of the constituent materials of the treasure.[12] This imprecision on the question of value was a deliberate manoeuvre on part of the government to widen the scope of state's compulsory acquisitions. Under section 4 of the Act, a penal section, value was deliberately used in the sense of "market value" to widen the obligation of a finder to give notice of his finds over and above a paltry sum of 10 rupees. If simply intrinsic/

[8] Ibid.

[9] Ibid.

[10] Ibid., section 16, italics mine.

[11] Ibid., section 17.

[12] Note dated 28 August 1909, from Sir H.H. Risley.

constituent materials' value was used in this section, then several objects of antiquarian interest without any great intrinsic value would have escaped notification and subsequent state acquisition and "protection". Again, in section 16, the section laying out the details of price to be paid by the government, value was deliberately used in the sense of intrinsic value only to mitigate the financial obligations of the state in acquiring objects of antiquarian interest.[13]

While the intrinsic value of the metal and crystal reliquaries could be ascertained, Risley pointed out the difficulty of driving home the point with the Sayed brothers, bent on making a fortune out of the relics, that ancient Buddhist bones have no (intrinsic) value, that they cannot be claimed as personal property, and therefore these bones were by default the property of the state.[14] What frustrated him and others was this lack of precision on the question of value in the Treasure Trove Act that now opened the doors to the "crafty" Afghan landowners of the Shah-ji-ki-Dehri to lay claims on the market value of the relics, a value determined at the intersection of competing religious, historical, antiquarian, aesthetic, and political values. For Risley and several other officials, the best bait in this case appeared compulsory acquisition under the Treasure Trove Act. However, a continuous thorn on the Government's side remained the agreement between Spooner and the owners of the Dehri that the Sayed brothers were now calling into evidence in support of their claims. The challenge for the government was now to avoid litigations at all cost. However, the government ran out of luck. The news of the discovery spread rapidly in the printed press and along with it the news of claims and counterclaims of various countries, communities, and associations across South and Southeast Asia over a share of these relics. As the state was weighing the relative merits of these competing demands, negotiations with the landowners of the Dehri took a turn unanticipated by the government.

The lawyer of the Sayed brothers now sent a notice arguing that the government's plans to gift these seemingly "valueless" pieces of bones to the Buddhists betrayed that "the Relics are priceless on account of their religious association and antiquarian interest..." In appraising the importance of the relics, the lawyer asserted that "the only value which can be taken into consideration ... is their religious and antiquarian value

[13] Ibid.

[14] Ibid.

..." and that his clients be compensated accordingly.[15] Threatened with the possibility of legal action the government decided to act quickly. All speculations on antiquarian, artistic, and religious values of the relics were brushed aside and the Collector of Peshawar was instructed to acquire the relics and reliquaries under the provisions of the Treasure Trove Act.

D.B. Spooner, who had been routinely reprimanded by various offices of the state for entering into an agreement that stood in the path of compulsory state acquisition, now gave in under pressure. He denied any prior agreement on the terms which the owners of the Dehri were now claiming. The verbal agreement entered with the owners before excavations, Spooner contended, had laid out that they would relinquish all claims over stone sculptures unearthed, and in return would be entitled to only half the share of the price of precious stones, bullion, or gold and silver statues.[16] Since the finds in question—the bones and the reliquaries—did not fit the criterion of bullion with high intrinsic value, the verbal agreement, Spooner argued, did not cover these objects. D.B. Blakeway, the Collector of Peshawar, contended that no prior agreement could override the provisions of section 16 of the Treasure Trove Act and deprive the government the "right of acquiring the whole treasure".[17]

To initiate the process of acquisition, Blakeway now moved quickly to access the intrinsic value of the finds. After a survey of local markets of metal smiths and stone cutters, he proposed a sum of 5 rupees as the intrinsic value of the inscribed metal reliquary and 40 rupees for the polished crystal reliquary. The bones and clay seal, he repeated, had no intrinsic value at all and contrary to the owners' claims, the Treasure Trove Act did not permit any price for these objects. The total intrinsic value of the finds was fixed at 45 rupees and according to sections 12 and 16 of the Treasure Trove Act the owners were jointly entitled to

[15] Attachment to copy of an order, dated 18 February 1910, passed by the Collector, Peshawar District. File No. 204, 1909–1910, Files from the Office of the Director General of the Archaeological Survey of India (DGASI).

[16] Order of the Collector of Peshawar, dated 18 February 1910, attached to Letter No. 523G, dated 2 March 1910, from Mr W.R.H. Merk, Agent to the Governor General and Chief Commissioner, North-West Frontier Province, to the Secretary to the Government of India, Home Department. Government of India, Home Department, Archaeology and Epigraphy – A, Proceedings No. 69, May 1910, NAI.

[17] Ibid.

one-fourth of one and one-fifth of this total sum. The owners' total share was calculated at 13.8 rupees. On 18 February 1910, by the order of the Collector, the four bits of bones assumed to be the corporeal relics of the Buddha, the ancient crystal reliquary and clay seal, the inscribed metal reliquary, and the coin of Kushana antiquity all became the property of the state.[18] Colonial archives do not record whether the Sayed brothers bothered to accept this paltry sum assigned by the state in lieu of the high fortunes they had been pitching for. There are also no records to indicate whether they instituted legal suit or appeals against such shoddy treatment. However, this entry in the colonial archives establish that by early twentieth century Buddhist corporeal relics had come to be valued by actors with different interests in these objects—scholarly, religious, political, or even purely financial.

At this point the individual presence of the Sayed brothers of Shah-ji-ki-Dehri vanishes from the archives. They only return from time to time as part of a nameless collective threat—as iconoclast Muslim vandals on the Northwest Frontier of the British Indian Empire, menacing the historic sanctity of ancient Buddhist archaeological sites and necessitating objects like the Shah-ji-ki-Dehri relics to travel out of open sites to the "safe custody" of museums and to practising Buddhist temples. The Shah-ji-ki-Dehri relics took this precise route. The inscribed metal reliquary, the clay seal, and the coin were sent off to the Peshawar Museum and after much deliberations the four bone fragments in the crystal reliquary were presented to the Buddhists of Burma to be enshrined in a new relic temple in the erstwhile royal capital city, Mandalay.

This was not the first instance, nor indeed the last, where ancient Buddhist corporeal relics discovered in the course of archaeological excavations in colonial South Asia were presented to Buddhist communities. Over the nineteenth and early decades of the twentieth century, archaeologists identified and excavated a number of ancient *stūpa* sites, where they unearthed Buddhist corporeal relics deposited in ancient reliquaries. The inscriptions on the reliquaries were decoded by scholars identifying the relics as corporeal remains of either the historical Buddha or of prominent ancient Buddhist monks. On each occasion the British Indian state distributed these relics to various Buddhist countries, communities, and Buddhist associations across South and mainland Southeast Asia. In every case, the old inscribed reliquaries which housed the corporeal

[18] Ibid.

remains at the moments of their discovery were retained in museums as objects of art, history, and antiquity. The bare bones were classified as purely sacred objects, having no historic value, and were given away for ritual enshrinements in new relic caskets especially designed for these occasions by the colonial state and its archaeological department.

Having discussed narratives of competing values and custodianship over the Shah-ji-ki-Dehri relics, this chapter will now turn to explore why and how this trajectory of classification of bones as essentially sacred, and of the ancient reliquaries housing them as objects of art and history, was produced. Cultural apparatuses of British colonialism in South Asia, such as institutions of archaeology and museums, were by no means the sole determinants of meanings and values of ancient Buddhist corporeal remains. However, colonial interventions produced new values, visibility, and created different objects out of these Buddhist relics. Circulation of Buddhist relics predated both European colonialism and rise of modern nation states in South and Southeast Asia. But colonial (and postcolonial nation) states produced new networks and protocols of exchange and circulation that lent to the production of different and competing values and meanings around these objects across the Southern Asian worlds and beyond. Mapping the different journeys and destinations of these relics and their reliquaries, we will return to the questions of new and diverse values that accrued around them.

THE NEW VISIBILITY: BUDDHIST RELICS CONNECTING TRANSNATIONAL RELIGION AND HISTORY

The separation of corporeal remains from their reliquaries that ensued from the late nineteenth and early twentieth century state-mediated relic presentations stood in sharp contrast to early colonial archaeological encounters with Buddhist relics. In the 1850s Alexander Cunningham and F.C. Maisey had ferreted out several Buddhist funerary caskets with charred pieces of bones, etc., from Sanchi and the neighbouring sites of Sonari and Satdhara, in the territory of the Begum of Bhopal (in central India), which eventually found their way to the British Museum and the India House Museum (now the Victoria and Albert Museum) in London.[19]

[19] On the modern biographies of the Sanchi, Sonari, and Satdhara relics, see Brekke (2007), Mathur (2008), and Guha-Thakurta (2013).

Till the mid-nineteenth century Buddhist corporeal relics along with their reliquaries continued to travel from sites in the colony to museums in Britain. There was no established code which could prevent Buddhist relics, both corporeal remains and reliquaries, from being treated as unsuitable objects of specialized scholarly analysis, scientific preservation, and public display. The religious sacrality of the bones and historicist sanctity of the reliquaries did not remain fixed and permanently coded over time. The new visibility and classifications produced around Buddhist relics were forged by concurrent refashioning of Theravāda Buddhism at the intersection of worlds of scholarship and devotion, and by colonial state's politics of relic diplomacy.

The nineteenth-century critical editing and reprinting of precolonial Pali, Sinhalese, and Chinese Buddhist manuscripts led to the discursive emergence of a textual "pure" Buddhism as a humanist, rational, and quasi-spiritual creed (Almond 1988). The dominant trope of European "discovery" of Buddhism, as Philip C. Almond (1988) had argued, was predicated on a discourse about the sheer absence of the survival of the religion as a practising faith for most of South Asia. Surviving traces of "living" Buddhism in parts of South and mainland Southeast Asia—i.e., Nepal, Ceylon, Burma, and Siam—were often labelled as corruption and fall from the "authentic" cannons of "pure" Buddhism. This nineteenth-century Western fascination with Buddhism, with its scriptures and doctrines of faith, as well as the persona of its founder, had specifically British and Victorian origins. Critical religious studies scholarship has argued that by the mid-nineteenth century, the essence of an authentic Buddhist faith came to be discovered not in the physical landscape of the colonies in the East, but in the major metropolitan libraries and archives in Europe and through the European scholarly control over Buddhism's own textual past. Such narratives of a purely "Orientalist discovery" of Buddhism involving only European Orientalist scholars and with its prime location in metropolitan libraries and archives, almost paraphrasing the modular form set by Edward Said, has been later countered by scholars like Anne Blackburn (2010a), who argue for a geographically dispersed and far more nuanced account of realignment of colonial power relations in the process. These domains of scholarship and practice had diverse locations involving different actors, European scholars of Buddhism, Buddhist monastic leaders, lay elites, political activists, religious reformers, and Buddhist sovereigns. Modern worlds of Therāvada scholarship and practice were configured across different "locations" of discursive mediations and material transactions across the Southern Asian worlds and beyond (ibid.). Antiquarian and archaeological scholarship remained an integral part of this field.

By the mid-nineteenth century, colonial archaeology in British India was largely focused on Buddhism, giving rise to text-aided archaeological surveys, excavations, and subsequent discoveries of Buddhist sites and objects. Archaeology inherited the Orientalist assumption that the authentic history of Buddhism could only be recovered by specialists, who until then were predominantly Western scholars. It, however, sought to move the study of Buddhism beyond textual archives in Europe to the physical landscape of the colony, where discoveries of artefacts and structures led to the emergence of distinct cognitive categories such as historical monuments and objects of antiquity (Guha-Thakurta 2004).

Shah-ji-ki-Dehri's identification as the site of Kanishka's *stūpa* was the product of this particular Orientalist framing, of colonial archaeology's reading of selective Buddhist histories into sites and movable antiquities. Two nineteenth-century Orientalist texts on Buddhism, the translations of Faxian's and Xuanzang's accounts by Stanislas Julien and Samuel Beal, attained a Biblical status in the colonial archaeological project (Julien 1857–58; Beal 1884a, 1884b). In the age of nineteenth-century empirical positivism, ancient pilgrimage itineraries began to be read as physical maps and geographical pointers often overlooking the context and intended audience of these textual narratives. Xuanzang's *Xiyuji*, for instance, was written from memory after his return to China from India and was not a modern survey field-note taken on the spot (Deeg 2012; Asher 2012). Following these nineteenth century translations of Chinese pilgrimage itineraries, colonial archaeologists like Alexander Cunningham and John Marshall began to identify the ruins of ancient Buddhist sites by translating ancient Chinese units of distance to Roman and British miles, and translating the Chinese toponyms first to Sanskrit and then to current place names in use. The process involved several slippages. However, in following Xuanzang on the outskirts of Peshawar, Spooner participated in an established code of disciplinary practice in the colony. He had his precedents in H.A. Deane (1896) and Alfred Foucher (1901), who had indicated the site of Shah-ji-ki-Dehri as the possible location of Kanishka's monument. Following their lead, Spooner began excavations in 1908 and discovered the relics in the chamber of the Shah-ji-ki-Dehri stupa in 1909.[20]

[20] For a detailed account of the archeological discovery of Kanishka's *stūpa* at Shah-ji-ki-Dehri, see Letter No. 1038 dated 31 July 1909, from J.H. Marshall, Director General of Archaeology in India to the Secretary to the Government of India, Home Department. Government of India, Home Department, Archaeology and Epigraphy – A, Proceedings No. 33, May 1910, NAI; Spooner (1907–08), pp. 17–24; Spooner (1908–09), pp. 38–59; Spooner (1909–10), pp. 135–41. For recent critical studies on the discovery of the site, see Asher (2012) and Ray (2014).

The making of antiquity through archaeological practices was central to the production of history and heritage in colonial South Asia. Because of the alleged absence of scientific textual records of the colony's past, a predominant trope in early colonial archaeological discourse, the material remains were consecrated as the signifiers of the colony's lost history and heritage which had to be protected and conserved against the ravages of time and "native" misappropriation. The state investment in the protection and conservation of these remains asserted the proprietary rights of the colonial state over the history and heritage of the colony. The drive for state protection and conservation of the material traces of the colony's past found its legal embodiment in the Ancient Monuments Preservation Act passed by the British Indian state in 1904.

The Act encoded the policy of preservation of structural remains and moveable antiquities as the central concern of the newly reorganized archaeological department. Like the Treasure Trove Act, this Act endowed the colonial state compulsory acquisition powers over historic structures and objects of antiquarian interest. However, it was strictly guaranteed that the Government's powers of compulsory purchase would not be exercised in the case of any building, structure, or objects currently in use for religious worship.[21] The Act thus envisaged a greater state control over antiquities than ever before. At the same time, there was a conscious steering away from granting protected status to the buildings or objects still in "religious" use. This was in line with the official commitment of the colonial state, from the middle decades of the nineteenth century onwards, to maintain a policy of non-intervention in matters of religion of the colonized population.

Within a colonial archaeological ethos, Buddhist relics unearthed during archaeological excavations could and did emerge as important material signifiers of the colony's ancient Buddhist civilization and came to be collected, preserved, and exhibited for their historic, antiquarian, and aesthetic values. However, it is precisely at this juncture that these corporeal remains emerged as sites of religious reclamations and reconsecrations. The context was the consolidation of transnational Theravāda Buddhist reform and revival movements across South and mainland Southeast Asia.

[21] A Bill to provide for the preservation of monuments and objects of historical or artistic interest, Draft, in Accompaniments to the Letter to the Government of India, No. 689, dated 5 February 1902, File No. 89, April 1902, DGASI.

The emergence of reformist Buddhism first in Colombo and then in other major port cities on the Bay of Bengal network is attributed to a complex fashioning of "Buddhist modernism". Initiated as a reaction of Buddhist elites to the challenges posed by colonialism, Christian missionary proselytizing, and modernization, consolidation of a reformist Therāvada practice was marked by the rise of new Buddhist associations, schools, and colleges. Institutions like the Young Men's Buddhist Association, the Maha Bodhi Society, were characteristic of colonial modernity and intrinsically tied to the imperial network of print capitalism, transport networks of steamship and railways, the spread of Western education, the development of English as the lingua franca of empire, the rise of a Western-educated class of elites, and a complex fashioning of nationalist consciousness.[22] Limited in its appeal to the bilingual intelligentsia in the major urban centres, these new media and networks of communication allowed new Buddhist associations and leaders to connect not only to the Theravāda Buddhist world of South and Southeast Asia but also to a wider network of spiritualists like the Theosophists, and couch their aspirations in a new language of internationalism (Frost 2002). These institutions sought to create an ideal Buddhist citizen halfway between the status of a monk and a lay man by returning to an ancient "pure" Buddhism, now fashioned in Orientalist textual and archaeological scholarship as a rational, humanitarian faith.

One prominent transnational Buddhist association, the Maha Bodhi Society, with its offices across Ceylon, India, and Burma, moved the language of reformism to a different direction. Under the direction of Anagarika Dharmapala the Society shifted its focus from texts and the canonical Buddhist scriptures to the physical site and space of Buddhist pilgrimage in Ceylon and India. Its agenda moved beyond the search for scriptural purity to demands for recovery and restitution of ancient Buddhist sites in South Asia. This brought the world of practising Buddhism into intimate encounters both with the historicist vision of archaeological conservation of ancient monuments and with rights of other religious communities as it happened at the site of Bodh Gaya in eastern India.[23] This

[22] Literature on the complex histories of Theravāda reform and revival and "Buddhist Modernism" is vast: see, for example, Malagoda (1976), Obeyeskere (1984), Gombrich and Obeyesekere (1988), Bond (1988), and Blackburn (2010a).

[23] Recent historical and anthropological scholarship on Bodh Gaya Temple (marking the site of Buddha's enlightenment) has argued that the archaeological identification of the site as

process drew on the same authenticating tactics of colonial archaeology which sought to discover an essentially Buddhist past for ancient India by reading into objects and structures *a priori* histories of Buddhism. The Society carried it one step further. Now that archaeology had established beyond doubt the original Buddhist character of objects and monuments, they were to be returned to their original sacral meanings and associations, to the communities of the reformed practising Buddhists of which the Society claimed to be the sole spokesman. The "scientific" authenticating practices of archaeology opened up monuments and antiquities to a new set of resacralization claims. A whole range of religious revivalist politics consolidated around sites and objects which reclaimed them as sacred objects of belief and practice. It is within this changed context that Buddhist corporeal relics unearthed during archaeological excavations emerged as potential objects of Buddhist reconsecrations. Deemed unsuitable for a complete state "protection" as historical remains, Buddhist corporeal relics now entered into a new life in their careers as objects of colonial diplomatic presentations.

THE EMPIRE OF RELICS: CONTENDERS AND DESTINATIONS

Using Buddhist relics for political purposes was not an invention of European colonialism. Recent works on Buddhist relics have demonstrated that literary and inscriptional evidence from Sri Lanka and mainland Southeast Asia point to the centrality of relics in the formation of new Buddhist polities and dynasties, and in the legitimization of state authority both in times of military crisis and restoration of power (Blackburn 2010b; Strong 2004). Early interface of British colonialism with Buddhist relics unfolded at Sri Lanka around the Tooth Relic of Buddha. In sharp contrast to early modern narratives of the Portuguese capture, subsequent destruction, and contending narratives of resurrection of the Tooth Relic

essentially Buddhist and its contentious restoration paved the way for Maha Bodhi Society and Dharmapala to reclaim it for solely for the Buddhists, a claim that ran counter to and later led to an elaborate legal case with the Śaiva Hindu Giri Mahant proprietors of the site who had till then exercised a customary ownership over the Temple and the adjoining site. On the complex history of Buddhist reclamations of Bodh Gaya, see Guha-Thakurta (2004) and Trevithick (2006). See also, on Bodh Gaya and global religious networks in the later part of the twentieth century, Geary (2017).

of the Buddha in the mid-sixteenth century, the nineteenth-century British colonial involvement with the Temple of Tooth Relic (Dalada Maligawa in Kandy) was marked by the rhetoric of political and legal custodianship, deemed to be a necessary prerequisite of legitimizing sovereign authority over the island.

The British engagement with Dalada Maligawa unfolded as early colonial state's participation in "native" rituals of precolonial sovereignty. In face of mounting criticism from the Church of England and the missionaries in the colonies, the British colonial state had to finally give up on these ritual participations. In 1847 the colonial state in Sri Lanka handed over the administration of the Temple to a committee of elders constituted by representatives of prominent Buddhist monasteries (Strong 2010). From the late 1850s onwards the colonial state, now officially committed to religious non-intervention in the colony, had to devise other ways of forging connections with the colonized communities. By the late nineteenth century Buddhist corporeal relics discovered during archaeological digs and loaded with potentials for religious reclamations, appealed to the diplomatic instincts of the colonial state in a revived Theravada Buddhist world.

In 1898 William Caxton Peppe excavated a brick mound in his estate at Piprahwa Kot (on the border of Nepal) which led to the unearthing of Buddhist corporeal remains. The finds from the excavations included two stucco slabs, three steatite urns, a crystal bowl, small gems and pieces of stamped gold leaf, and a handful of charred bones and ashes all deposited in a large stone coffer. One of the steatite urns bore an inscription which G. Buhler decoded as a relic shrine of the Buddha built by his Śākya clansmen (Peppe and Smith 1898; Buhler 1898). While the Piprahwa relics would later be shrouded in the specter of being a forged antiquity, for the moment, it aroused great interest within a revived Buddhist world (Allen 2010).

Jinavaravansa, a high priest and cousin of King Rama V (Chulalongkorn) of Siam (Thailand), was in the neighbourhood for pilgrimage and he sent a memorandum requesting Peppe the relics for a formal presentation to the King of Siam as the head of the orthodox Theravada Buddhist community and as "the only reigning Buddhist sovereign" in the late nineteenth century.[24] Dr W. Hoey, the Officiating Commissioner of Gorakhpur Division,

[24] Presentation to the King of Siam of certain Buddhist relics discovered near Piprahwa in the Basti district. Visit of Phya Sukhum to India to receive the relics. April 1899, Pro. No. 115 (of 92–117), Foreign Department, External A, Proceedings, 1899, NAI.

lent his support to the claims of Siam arguing that the presentation of the relics would provide a great opportunity to the British Indian State to reconnect with its Buddhist subjects and neighbouring Buddhist countries in a situation where the issue of Buddhist propriety of the Maha Bodhi Temple at Bodh Gaya remained a sore point, especially at a time when the state had to maintain a formal commitment of religious non-intervention.

As the only independent buffer state between British Burma on one side and French Indochina on the other, Siam assumed a special importance in colonial frontier diplomacy. The ultimate decision to present the Piprahwa relics to King Rama V (Chulalongkorn) of Siam reflected British anxieties to increase their political influence over Siam.[25] In an elaborately orchestrated ceremony through which the British Indian state drew on an image of premodern imperial benefactors of the Buddhists, the Piprahwa relics were presented to Phya Sukhum, the Royal Commissioner of the Lingor Circle, who had come down to India as a representative of Chulalongkorn. Portions of the relics were distributed by Chulalongkorn to Buddhists from Rangoon and Mandalay (in Burma), to Anuradhapura, Kandy, and Colombo (in Sri Lanka), and to Japan. Siam's portion of the relics was enshrined in the royal capital city of Bangkok in a newly built *stūpa* at Wat Saket (Ray 2014; Mukherjee 2018). Reinvented as an artifact of frontier and foreign diplomacy of the colonial government, Buddhist corporeal relics now emerged as highly prized objects and their contenders did not, as we will see in the case of the Shah-ji-ki-Dehri relics, remain restricted among Buddhist communities.

In 1909, by the time the Shah-ji-ki-Dehri relics came up for distribution John Marshall proposed a different course action. He argued that as subjects of the British Empire, the Buddhists of Burma and Ceylon had special claims on a share of these relics. Marshall prescribed that the relics should be divided into four portions and presented to Buddhists of Ceylon, Burma, the King of Siam, and to Japan. As before, relic presentations were designed to secure the loyalty of Buddhist subjects at the frontiers of the British Indian Empire—in Ceylon, in Burma, and in the independent Kingdom of Siam. The late nineteenth and early

[25] Letter No. 4366 – VII-32, dated 13 April 1898, from Dr W. Hoey, Officiating Commissioner, Gorakhpur Division, to the Chief Secretary to the Government of the North-Western Frontier Provinces and Oudh. Pro. No. 94 (of 92–117), Foreign Department, External A, Proceedings, 1899, NAI.

twentieth century also witnessed Japan's rise as a colonial contender in the Western Pacific and in the East Asia region, a zone of control and influence that would later extend to Southeast Asia during the Second World War under the guise of Greater East Asia Co-Prosperity Sphere. With strong colonial investments in South and Southeast Asia, British Empire's foreign policy in the early twentieth century had to factor in Japan. Donning the robe of imperial benefactors of the Buddhists of Asia, Marshall assumed, would appeal to Japan's Buddhist sensibilities and presentation of a portion of the Shah-ji-ki-Dehri relics would seal the deal. Relic presentations, Marshall argued, were important rituals of the Empire, too important to be left to the mediation of Chulalongkorn though he remained the formal figure heading the Theravāda Buddhist world. Marshall prescribed that this time round, the presentations should be made directly by the office of the Viceroy of India.[26] While including Siam in the foreign policy of the Empire, Marshall sought to contain Chulalongkorn from becoming the sole moral arbitrator in the Theravāda Buddhist world. Direct state involvement in the relic presentations was designed to connect the British Empire to its Buddhist subjects, to its geopolitical buffer in mainland Southeast Asia, and to diplomatically counteract its fierce colonial competitor in the East.

Marshall also hoped that while the contested issue of Buddhist proprietorship of the Maha Bodhi Temple at Bodh Gaya was still sore, with the legal case between Anagarika Dharmapala of the Maha Bodhi Society and the Śaiva Giri Mahants of Bodh Gaya Math quite unsettled, the presentation of the relics would compensate for the failure of the colonial state to help the Buddhists "regain possession of their most sacred shrine at Bodh Gaya".[27] Relics as compensation for Bodh Gaya would feature time and again in course of the Piprahwa, Shah-ji-ki-Dehri, and other subsequent relic presentations. On the occasion of Shah-ji-ki-Dehri relic distribution some government officials hoped that the relics' enshrinement in a new shrine at Bodh Gaya would settle the dispute between the Maha Bodhi Society and the Giri Mahants. Others, including the Home Secretary Harold Stuart, and Marshall himself, vetoed this proposal arguing that

[26] Letter No. 1038, dated 31 July 1909, from J.H. Marshall, Director General of Archaeology in India to the Secretary to the Government of India, Home Department. Government of India, Home Department, Archaeology and Epigraphy – A, Proceedings No. 33, May 1910, NAI.

[27] Ibid.

the housing of the relics at Bodh Gaya might actually accentuate and not mitigate the already terse relations between the Giris and the Buddhists at the site (Asher 2012).

Contrary to the government's expectations the Buddhists did not present themselves as a monolithic community nor did they fit in easily within the neat boundaries of frontier provinces and foreign territories as colonial officials had hoped for. First there were a number of requests from other Buddhist frontier provinces and territories, including Darjeeling, Sikkim, Tibet, and Ladakh for a portion of these relics.[28] Then a number of requests came in from different monastic establishments in Burma and Ceylon. New Buddhist associations like the Maha Bodhi Society, the Bengal Buddhist Association, and the Buddhist Association of Chittagong (now in Bangladesh) claimed that the relics should be enshrined in India and not given away to "foreign" countries. The Maha Bodhi Society had in fact proposed the building of a new relic temple in Sarnath (near Benares in north India) to house the relics.[29]

New Hindu revivalist organizations like the Hindu Sabha and the Sanatan Dharma Pravardhini Sabha also claimed a share in the relics arguing for Buddha as one of the ten *avatarās* of the god Viṣṇu.[30] Hindu revivalist journals like the *Brahmavadin* (1895–1914) warned against the involvement of secular officers of the state in the distribution of the relics

[28] Letter No. 904, dated 17 February 1910, from Lieutenant-Colonel J. Ramsay, Officiating Resident in Kashmir, to Mr S.H. Butler, Secretary to the Government of India, Foreign Department; Letter No. 237-T, dated 7 September 1909, from C.A. Bell, Political Officer in Sikkim, to the Secretary to the Government of India, Foreign Department. Home Department, Archaeology and Epigraphy – A, Proceedings Nos. 13–16, September 1909, and Proceedings Nos. 31–80, May 1910, NAI.

[29] Telegram dated 26 July 1909, from the Secretary, Bengal Buddhist Association, Calcutta, to the Private Secretary to the Viceroy (Pro. No. 21); Translation of petition, dated 25 August 1909, from the nine Trustees of the Shwe Dagon Pagoda, Rangoon, to the Lieutenant-Governor of Burma (Pro. No. 35); Letter No. 013001, dated 26 August 1909, from H.L. Crawford, Acting Colonial Secretary, Colombo, to the Secretary to the Government of India, Home Department (Pro. No. 36); Letters dated 7 December 1909 and 3 February 1910, from the General Secretary, Maha Bodhi Society. Home Department, Archaeology and Epigraphy – A, Proceedings Nos. 31–80, May 1910, NAI.

[30] Telegram, dated September 10, 1909, and October 4, 1909, from the President, Punjab Hindu Sabha, Lahore, and to the President, Sanatan Dharma Pravardhini Sabha, Cawnpore to the Private Secretary to the Viceroy, Government of India. Home Department, Archaeology and Epigraphy – A, Proceedings Nos. 31-80, May 1910, NAI.

and similar "sacrosanct treasures of the nation and religion" (Ray 2014, pp. 98–99, 111–12). Even new literary and antiquarian societies, without any overt religious associations, like the *Bangiya-Sahityaanusilani Sabha* of Guahati (in Assam), demanded that the relics be enshrined within British India's territorial limits.[31] The wide spectrum of claims and counterclaims on the Buddhist relics overwhelmed the government. Most officers agreed that in face of congealing "nationalist sentiments" around the Shah-ji-ki-Dehri relics, it would be unwise to alienate the Indian subjects of the Empire to ingratiate the colonial state to "foreign Buddhists" in Siam and Japan.[32] However, the question on the exact location of housing the relics in India still remained uncertain.

Bodh Gaya had already been discarded as a possible destination and Mian Muhammad Shafi, a barrister, warned the government of pilgrims from the Far East coming down to India in great numbers to visit the relic and accentuating the dangers of the "Yellow Peril" in their interactions with the local Hindu population. He suggested that the relics should ideally be sent off to London to be housed in the British Museum.[33] While Mr Shafi's suggestions would be soon discarded as "Anglo-Mohammedan" hyperbole, others like Sir Louis Dane, Lieutenant-Governor of Punjab, suggested the Lahore Museum as a safe repository for the relics, while the Viceroy, Lord Minto, was in favour of preserving the relics at the site of Shah-ji-ki-Dehri itself.[34] In the changed context of Buddhist (and Hindu) religious reclamations of the relics, their visibility within the space of any museum was thought inadvisable. Spooner, Marshall, and other

[31] Letter dated 13 October 1909, from H. Le Mesurier, Chief Secretary to the Government of Eastern Bengal and Assam, to the Secretary to the Government of India. Pro. No. 52. Home Department, Archaeology and Epigraphy – A, Proceedings Nos. 31–80, May 1910, NAI.

[32] Letter No. 1251, dated 30 August 1909, from J.H. Marshall to Sir H.A. Stuart. Home Department, Archaeology and Epigraphy – A, Proceedings Nos. 13–16, September 1909, NAI.

[33] Extract of a letter dated 26 July 1909, from Mr Mian Muhammad Shafi, Bar-at-Law, to Private Secretary to the Viceroy. Home Department, Archaeology and Epigraphy – A, Proceedings Nos. 13–16, September 1909, NAI.

[34] Letter dated 3 September 1909, from Captain A. Ramsay, Private Secretary to the Lieutenant-Governor of Punjab, to J.H. Marshall; Extract of a letter, dated 22 September 1909, from the Viceroy, to Sir H. Thirkell White, Lieutenant-Governor of Burma. Home Department, Archaeology and Epigraphy – A, Proceedings Nos. 13–16, September 1909, NAI.

higher officials contended that the preservation of the relics at the site of Shah-ji-ki-Dehri was quite out of the question. It would expose the historic and religious sanctity of the relics and the site, and the lives of "hapless Buddhist pilgrims" to the "homicidal", iconoclastic raids of the Frontier Pathan Muslims.[35] However, the relics still needed to be housed within the territorial limits of the British Indian Empire, not only to satisfy the popular "religious" and "nationalist" upsurge around them but also to meet the expectations of prominent European Buddhologists like Thomas Rhys Davids, who favoured the preservation of the relics in the "Land of Birth" of the historical Buddha and Buddhism.[36] At this crucial juncture Burma now presented itself as an ideal destination.

Burma's candidacy for the Shah-ji-ki-Dehri relics had its most vocal exponent in Sir Herbert Thirkell White, Lieutenant-Governor of Burma. The claimants from Burma for a share of these relics included the Trustees of the Shwe Dagon Pagoda, Saw Hke, Chief of Hsipaw, one of the Shan States, prominent residents of Mandalay, and above all Kyimyin Mibaya, one of the queens of the late King of Burma, Mindon Min. The last petitioner offered to contribute 1 lakh rupees to build a temple after the model of the Maha Bodhi Temple at Bodh Gaya or Ananda Pagoda of Pagan (present Bagan) at the site of the burnt-down Atumashi Kyaung at Mandalay for enshrining the relics.[37] Based on the strengths of these petitions Herbert White now began to push the case of Burma arguing first and foremost that Burma was an integral part of the British Indian Empire and the only "Buddhist majority province" where Buddhism as a practising religion was still to be found in its "purest" form.

[35] Letter No. 326, dated 30 August 1909, to J.H. Marshall. Home Department, Archaeology and Epigraphy – A, Proceedings Nos. 13–16, September 1909, NAI.

[36] Note dated 29 August 1909, by H.H. Risley. Home Department, Archaeology and Epigraphy – A, Proceedings Nos. 13–16, September 1909, NAI.

[37] Translation of petition, dated 25 August 1909, from the nine trustees of the Shwe Dagon Pagoda, Rangoon, to the Lieutenant-Governor of Burma (Pro. No. 35); Translation of letter, No. 1310, dated 8 September 1909, from Saw Hke, Sawbwa of Hsipaw, to Sir H.T. White, Lieutenant-Governor of Burma (Pro. No. 44); Translation of memorial, dated 10 September 1909, from U. Kyaw Tan and other residents of Mandalay to Lieutenant-Governor of Burma (Pro. No. 45); Translation of letter, dated 27 August1909, to Taw Sien Ko, Superintendent, Archaeological Survey, Burma (Pro. No. 37). Home Department, Archaeology and Epigraphy – A, Proceedings Nos. 31–80, May 1910, NAI.

For White, the "Hindu" claims on the Buddhist relics were completely unfounded and entirely fictitious. Having given up on the teachings of the Buddha in the past, they had no moral authority over objects of Buddhist ritual worship and their claims were purely motivated by "anti-government" political (nationalist) moves. Compared to the Buddhists of Burma, integral part of British Indian subjects, the claims of "foreign" Buddhists (of Siam, Ceylon, and Japan) seemed to fade away. In 1886 Burma had been finally annexed to the British India after three bloody Anglo-Burmese wars. Exiling the last Burmese King Thibaw and his family to India, the British had taken over the country, imposed heavy economic and political sanctions that ran the resources dry, and shifted the capital from a plague and fire-ravaged royal capital city of Mandalay to Rangoon (present Yangon) in lower Burma. Around the same time Burmese restoration mission to Bodh Gaya had been thwarted by the intervention of the colonial state and its archaeological department. Despite a long history of Burmese pilgrimage and restoration at the site, the archaeologists argued that in their zeal of religiously inspired restorations the Burmese were hasting the ruination of an important "historical monument", the Maha Bodhi Temple (see Myint-U 2001; Trevithick 2006; Asher 2012). The presentation of the relics to Burma was consciously designed both as a compensation to Bodh Gaya and as tool for legitimizing the new-found British authority over Burma and integrating its "loyal Burmese Buddhist" subjects to the heart of British India. The opportunity for diplomacy closer home appealed to the government who reiterated Burma's status as an integral province of British India. After some deliberations over Rangoon and Mandalay as the possible destination of the relics, Mandalay, "the centre of the Burmese Buddhist life" in contrast to Rangoon, "hardly a Burmese or a Buddhist city", was chosen as the ultimate home of the Shah-ji-ki-Dehri relics[38] (Figure 8.3).

On 19 March 1910, in an elaborately crafted presentation ceremony at Calcutta presided over by the Viceroy, Lord Minto, and with speeches by the Viceroy and John Marshall on the archaeological discovery and the historic "authenticity" of the Shah-ji-ki-Dehri relics, the relics were presented to a Burmese deputation headed by the Lieutenant-Governor

[38] Letter dated 12 September 1909, from Sir H. Thirkell White to the Viceroy; Letter, No. 209, dated 12 November 1909, from H. Thirkell White to Sir Harold Stuart. Home Department, Archaeology and Epigraphy – A, Proceedings Nos. 31–80, May 1910, NAI.

FIGURE 8.3
Undated Photograph of the *Dattaw*, Mandalay Hill, the Pagoda Designed to Enshrine the Buddha Relics

Source: Photographer unknown. Reproduced from Enriquez (1914).

Herbert White, Taw Sein Ko, the Superintendent Archaeologist, Burma Circle, and chosen members of the erstwhile Burmese royal family, ministry, and prominent Buddhist residents of Mandalay.[39] Reinvented as objects of colonial diplomatic presentations, Buddhist relics reflected a cautious positioning of the colonial state vis-à-vis these corporeal remains. In their stark materiality, for colonial archaeologists the relics attested, even if not the actual physical presence of a historical Buddha, an important material index to map the spread and extent of an ancient Buddhist civilization in South Asia. They also provided the government the means to enter the world of modern transnational Buddhism even while remaining ritually

[39] Final draft dated 18 March 1910, of the Program of Presentation of the Buddha Relics. Home Department, Archaeology and Epigraphy – A, Proceedings Nos. 31–80, May 1910, NAI.

unconnected to religious overtones of the cult of relics. As new rituals of state in British India, the relic presentations to Buddhist territories and countries on the frontiers of the British Empire, to Siam and Burma, provided the British state in South Asia with an opportunity to fashion themselves in the image of premodern ancient imperial benefactors of the Buddhists. Scholars of colonial Buddhism have noted a concomitant rise of scholarly interest in the role of Aśoka, the ancient Mauryan emperor, in the spread of Buddhism and empire through presentation of Buddhist relics. By the early twentieth century British India was playing Aśoka on the frontiers of its empire in mainland Southeast Asia (Ray 2014). It now remained for the state to try it on in the imperial heartland.[40]

ALTERED MATERIALITY: OLD BONES, NEW RELIQUARIES

The occasion of the presentations of Piprahwa and Shah-ji-ki-Dehri relics set in motion a new trend of separation of ancient reliquaries from the corporeal remains, a practice that would be followed and tried with varying degrees of success in subsequent relic presentations. As the Piprahwa relics came up for presentation to the King of Siam, Vincent A. Smith, a renowned Indologist and the then Chief Secretary, contended that the stone coffer, ancient reliquaries, and associated objects were of immense value from the historical, antiquarian, and archaeological points of view, and that as such they should be conserved and exhibited in the space of museums. The bone fragments and ashes were deemed fit for presentation to Siam as purely sacred objects with little antiquarian or aesthetic value. Accordingly, after William Peppe had claimed his "finder's share" of the Piprahwa jewels, the reliquaries were sent off to the Indian Museum in Calcutta (the then capital of British India). On 16 February 1899, the bone fragments were placed in gold-plated small pagodas, which the representative from Siam carried with him, and presented in the formal ceremony at Gorakhpur.[41]

[40] For a history of subsequent relic presentations and their housing in new relic temples in India, see Ray (2014), and Mukherjee (2014).

[41] Presentation to the King of Siam of certain Buddhist relics discovered near Piprahwa in the Basti district. Visit of Phya Sukhum to India to receive the relics. April 1899, Pro. Nos. 92–117, Foreign Department, External A, Proceedings, 1899, NAI.

Following the precedent of the Piprahwa relics, it was suggested by various archaeologists and officers of the state, including John Marshall himself, that while the "four bits of bones" were treasured by the Buddhists from a religious perspective, the reliquaries, especially the inscribed metal reliquary should be preserved at a museum in India, either in the local museum at Peshawar (then called Victoria Hall) or in the Indian Museum in Calcutta. Marshall actually now suggested making a copy of the original metal reliquary with a small gold receptacle inside to house the relics inside the old crystal casket. The gold receptacle was to be inscribed with an account of the archaeological discovery of the relics, a summary translation of the ancient Kharoṣṭhī inscriptions on the metal reliquary, and finally a statement of generous gift of the British King to the Burmese subjects of the empire.[42] From the various communications that followed it now appears that the sheer lack of time leading up to the ultimate presentation of the relics prevented Marshall from going ahead with the plans for making an exact replica of the ancient metal reliquary. On instructions from the government the noted jewellery firm Messrs Hamilton and Company ultimately prepared a new reliquary in gold following the designs supplied by Marshall himself. Designed in the shape of an ancient stupa with a sacred *hti* (ritual umbrella) on the top and railing around the middle, the dome of the new reliquary was adorned with lotus leaves and inlaid with nine precious stones held sacred by the Buddhists, including diamond on the top of the *hti* and ruby, emerald, sapphire, topaz, amethyst, crystal, coral, and pearl interspersed between and below the leaves of the lotus[43] (Figures 8.4 and 8.5). The engraving on the new reliquary read as follows:

> The bones enclosed within this casket are believed to be the relics of the Buddha Sakyamuni, deposited by the great Kushana Emperor Kanishka in a once magnificent and famous *stupa* near the city of Peshawar. Beneath the ruins of that *stupa* they were found enclosed in the crystal reliquary in which they still repose, and within a casket of bronze bearing the effigy of the Emperor Kanishka. They are entrusted

[42] Letter No. 1038 dated 31 July 1909, from J.H. Marshall, Director General of Archaeology in India to the Secretary to the Government of India, Home Department. Government of India, Home Department, Archaeology and Epigraphy – A, Proceedings No. 33, May 1910, NAI.

[43] Letter dated 18 February 1910, from John Marshall to Harold Stuart. Government of India, Home Department, Archaeology and Epigraphy – A, Proceedings Nos. 31–80, May 1910, NAI.

FIGURE 8.4
Photograph of the New Reliquary Now in *Dattaw*, Mandalay Hill, Designed for the Presentation of the Shah-Ji-Ki-Dehri Relics by the Archaeological Survey of India with the New Engraving Certifying the Imperial Gift from the British Government to the "Buddhists of the Indian Empire"

Source: Author, 2013.

> by His Excellency the Earl of Minto, Viceroy and Governor General of India, to the Buddhists of the Indian Empire, to be enshrined by them at the city of Mandalay in Burma.
>
> In the tenth year of the reign of His Majesty King Edward VII, Emperor of India.[44]

[44] Letter dated 1 March 1910, from P.W. Monie, Under Secretary to the Government of India, Home Department, to Messrs Hamilton & Co., Jewellers& Silversmiths, Calcutta. Government of India, Home Department, Archaeology and Epigraphy – A, Proceeding No. 58 (of 31–80), May 1910, NAI.

FIGURE 8.5
Photograph of the Relic Cask Encrusted with Rubies Now in *Dattaw*, Mandalay Hill, Housing a Portion of the Corporeal Remains of the Shah-ji-ki-Dehri Relics Presented the British Government to the "Buddhists of the Indian Empire"

Source: Author, 2013.

The new reliquary cost the government around 150 pounds. Along with the relics in the new casket the original metal casket was given on a loan of two months to convince the Burmese of the "authentic antiquarian" value of the relics.[45] Post presentations in Calcutta the relics in their new

[45] Letter dated 7 May 1910, from P.W. Monie, Under Secretary to the Government of India, Home Department, to the Agent to the Governor General and the Chief Commissioner, North-West Frontier Province. Government of India, Home Department, Archaeology and Epigraphy – A, Proceeding No. 80 (of 31–80), May 1910, NAI.

casket travelled through various cities in Burma and ultimately came to be housed in the Arakan Pagoda in Mandalay awaiting the completion of the new relic shrine, the *Dattaw*, at the foot of the Mandalay Hill where they rest within a locked vault at the moment (Enriquez 1914). The metal reliquary went back to the Peshawar Museum only to travel once to the British Museum in the 1960s for specialist cleaning and restoration (Asher 2012). But why did the government incur such expenses and take such pains in designing a new reliquary for the Shah-ji-ki-Dehri relics, a precedent that would be followed repeatedly during subsequent relic presentations in the colony? For it is here that our clue to the dual fashioning of reliquaries as aesthetic and historical objects and corporeal remains as purely sacred objects with no antiquarian value lies.

Frederick Asher argues that the corporeal remains, "even if they were actual bones of the Buddha, did little to unveil a shrouded past" to colonial archaeologists (ibid., p. 150). The reliquary, in its turn, because of its inscription and stylistically assumed to be part of the Gandhāra school of ancient Buddhist art, which in the colonial context was read as an evidence of an prior history of ancient Greek colonization of India, legitimizing the nineteenth–twentieth century British civilizing mission, attracted the attention of archaeologists, historians, art historians, epigraphists, and museum curators (see Asher 2012; Abe 1995). This focus on the ancient reliquary as a historical object reflected a deeply colonialist understanding of notions of India's ancient pasts, a programme of scientific historical practice where objects of religion and superstition like the supposed bone fragments of the Buddha had little or no place. Discussing the different context of repatriation of Buddhist relics from the Victoria and the Albert Museum to India during the 1950s, Torkel Brekke (2007) had argued that the idea of hanging on to the original reliquaries or at the most making copies of reliquaries for relic-repatriation by the museum authorities reveal that they did not believe in the sacrality of these objects, not primarily because they belonged to an alien religion, but because of their modern secular worldview. Keeping in mind Brekke's (2007) and Asher's (2012) arguments about different epistemologies of knowledge and belief at work around Buddhist relics, I conclude by arguing that the commitment to the making of duplicate reliquaries can be explained further by the material particularity of the objects in question—the corporeal remains and relations to their reliquaries in general and in the specific context of Buddhist relics in colonial and postcolonial South Asia.

At the most fundamental level, "relic" usually denotes the body or fragment of the body of a deceased person revered as holy. Alongside corporeal relics are non-corporeal items that were possessed by, or came into direct contact with, the individual in question (Walsham 2010). Unlike other material objects, a corporeal relic requires a physical frame in space and time that explicitly signals its status as sacred object. The symbolic potentials of such relics are constructed in the ways they are physically and ritually framed. In sharp contrast to icons and images, the relic's absence of representational features and its recognition as a moment of unmitigated corporeality is construed by the denotative work done by its frame, its reliquary. A relic without its reliquary loses its identity, becoming a hallowed object (Sharf 1999).

In the context of colonial South Asia, the heightened importance of the reliquaries also relates to new practices of identification and authentication of ancient Buddhist corporeal relics. In pre and early modern polities across South and Southeast Asia the test of authenticity of Buddhist relics lay in their magical ritual powers woven around narratives of their durability, resistance to decay, indestructibility, healing powers, and miraculous mobility. In sharp contrast to these attributes, the primary identification of Buddhist corporeal relics, especially those unearthed during archaeological excavations across colonial South Asia, lay in the decoding of ancient inscriptions on the reliquaries. This was a world of modern specialist scholarly expertise, a new domain of archaeological/epigraphic research that was introduced in South Asia under the aegis of the colonial state.

For all concerned parties the separation of bones from reliquaries threatened to turn Buddhist corporeal relics into meaningless scraps. To prevent this, the colonial state took upon itself the onus to get fresh relic caskets made, and would often even dispense with, as in the case of the Shah-ji-ki-Dehri relics, the uninscribed crystal reliquary or any associated objects without inscriptions. Despite its ancient crafting, the crystal reliquary did not bear any ancient script that could be decoded by epigraphists to provide definite clues on the colony's uncharted pasts. The new reliquary now inscribed with a brief statement of the discovery of the relic and a translation of the original inscription sought to attest the enshrined bones' identity as an authentic Buddhist. In the absence of the ancient inscribed metal reliquary, it became the new authenticating register, a new material certificate stamped with the "scientific" and diplomatic approval of the colonial state. This divorcing of the reliquaries from the corporeal remains led the production of a new order of Buddhist relics centred only on the symbolic sacrality of the bones. It would require more than the demands of religious reconsecrations to reclaim relics and reliquaries from the custody of museums and archaeology. In context of South and mainland Southeast

Asia, it would be the politics of postcolonial nationalist repatriations that would drag bones and ancient reliquaries from museums in Europe to the sanctums of new Buddhist temples.

Bibliography

Abe, Stanley K. 1995. "Inside the Wonder House: Buddhist Art and the West". In *Curators of the Buddha: The Study of Buddhism under Colonialism*, edited by Donald Lopez Jr., pp. 63–95 Chicago: University of Chicago Press.

Allen, Charles. 2010. *The Buddha and Dr. Fuhrer: An Archaeological Scandal.* New Delhi: Penguin Books.

Almond, Philip C. 1988. *The British Discovery of Buddhism.* Cambridge: Cambridge University Press.

Asher, Frederick M. 2012. "Travels of a Reliquary, Its Contents Separated at Birth". *South Asian Studies* 28, no. 2: 147–56.

Beal, Samuel. 1884a. *Si-Yu-Ki: Buddhist Records of the Western World: Translated from the Chinese of Hiuen Tsiang A.D. 629.* London: K. Paul, Trench, Trubner & Co.

———. 1884b. *Buddhism in China.* London: S.P.C.K.

Blackburn, Anne M. 2010a. *Locations of Buddhism: Colonialism and Modernity in Sri Lanka.* Chicago and London: University of Chicago Press.

———. 2010b. "Buddha-Relics in the Lives of Southern Asian Polities". *Numen* 57: 318–40.

Bond, G.D. 1988. *The Buddhist Revival in Sri Lanka.* New Delhi: Motilal Banarasidass.

Brekke, Torkel. 2007. "Bones of Contention: Buddhist Relics, Nationalism and the Politics of Archaeology". *Numen* 54, no. 3: 270–303.

Buhler, G. 1898. "Preliminary Note on a Recently Discovered Sakya Inscription". *Journal of the Asiatic Society of Great Britain and Ireland*, New Series, 30, no. 2 (April).

Deane, H.A. 1896. "Notes on Udyāna and Gandhāra". *Journal of the Royal Asiatic Society of Great Britain and Ireland* (October): 655–75.

Deeg, Max. 2012. "'Show Me the Land Where the Buddha Dwelled ...' Xuanzang's 'Record of the Western Regions' (Xiyuji): A Misunderstood Text?". *China Report* 48, nos. 1&2: 89–113.

Enriquez, Captain C.M. 1914. "The History of the Relics of the Exalted One (Found at Peshawur)". *Burma Research Society's Journal* 4, no. 3 (December): 161–70.

Flood, Finbarr Barry. 2002. "Between Cult and Culture: Bamiyan, Islamic Iconoclasm, and the Museum". *The Art Bulletin* 84, no. 4: 641–59.

Foucher, Alfred. 1901. "Notes sur la géographieancienne du Gandhâra (Commentaire à unchapitre de Hiuen-Tsang)". *Bulletin de l'Ecole française d'Extrême-Orient* 1, no. 4 (October): 322–69.

Frost, Mark. 2002. "'Wider Opportunities': Religious Revival, Nationalist Awakening and Global Dimension in Colombo, 1870–1920". *Modern Asian Studies* 36, no. 4: 937–67.

Geary, David. 2017. *The Rebirth of Bodh Gaya: Buddhism and the Making of a World Heritage Site* Seattle and London: University of Washington Press.

Gombrich, Richard F., and Gananath Obeyesekere. 1988. *Buddhism Transformed: Religious Change in Sri Lanka*. Princeton, NJ: Princeton University Press.

Guha-Thakurta, Tapati. 2004. *Monuments, Objects, Histories: Institutions of Art in Colonial and Postcolonial India*. New Delhi: Permanent Black.

———. 2013. "The Production and Reproduction of a Monument: The Many Lives of the Sanchi Stupa". *South Asian Studies* 29, no. 1: 77–109.

Julien, Stanislas. 1857–58. *Mémoires sur les Contrées Occidentales traduits du Sanscrit en Chinois, enl'an 648, par Hiouen-Thsang, et du Chinois en Francais*. Vols. 1 and 2. Paris: L'Imprimerie Imperial.

Malagoda, Kitsiri. 1976. *Buddhism in Sinhalese Society, 1750–1900*. Berkeley: University of California Press.

Mathur, Saloni. 2008. "A Parable of Postcolonial Return". In *India by Design: Colonial History and Cultural Display*, by Saloni Mathur, pp. 133–64. Berkeley: University of California Press.

Mukherjee, Sraman. 2014. "From Sites and Museums to Temples: Relics, Ruins, and New Buddhist Viharas in Colonial India". *Archive Series*, Centre for Studies in Social Sciences, Calcutta, No. 5 (January).

———. 2018. "Relics in Transition: Material Mediations in Changing Worlds". *Ars Orientalis* 48: 20–42.

Myint-U, Thant. 2001. *The Making of Modern Burma*. Cambridge: Cambridge University Press.

Obeyeskere, Ranjini. 1984. "The Bilingual Intelligentsia: Their Contribution to the Intellectual Life of Sri Lanka in the Twentieth Century". In *Honouring E.F.C. Ludowyk: Felicitation Essays*, edited by P. Colin-Thome and A. Halpe, pp. 71–91. Colombo: Tisara Prakasakayo.

Peppe, William Caxton, and Vincent A. Smith. 1898 "The Piprahwa Stupa, Containing the Relics of the Buddha". *Journal of the Asiatic Society of Great Britain and Ireland*, New Series, 30, no. 3 (July): 573–88.

Ray, Himanshu Prabha. 2014. *The Return of the Buddha: Ancient Symbols for a New Nation*. New Delhi: Routledge.

Sharf, Robert H. 1999. "On the Allure of Buddhist Relics". *Representations* 66 (Spring): 75–99.

Strong, John S. 2004. *Relics of the Buddha*. Princeton: Princeton University Press.

———. 2010. "'The Devil was in that Little Bone': The Portuguese Capture and Destruction of the Buddha's Tooth-Relic, Goa, 1561". *Past and Present* 206, supplement 5:184–98.

Trevithick, Alan. 2006. *The Revival of Buddhist Pilgrimage at Bodh Gaya*

(1811–1949): Anagarika Dharmapala and the Mahabodhi Temple. New Delhi: Motilal Banarasidass.

Walsham, Alexandra. 2010. "Introduction: Relics and Remains". *Past and Present* 206, supplement 5: 9–36.

Unpublished Literature Accessed at the Archaeological Survey of India, New Delhi

Spooner, D.B. 1907–08. "Excavations at Shah-ji-ki-Dheri". *Annual Report, Archaeological Survey of India, Frontier Circle*, pp. 17–24. Not published.

———. 1908–09. *Archaeological Survey of India Annual Report*, pp. 38–59. Not published.

———. 1909–10. "The Kanishka Casket Inscription". *Archaeological Survey of India Annual Report*, pp. 135–41. Not published.

List of Unpublished Filed Correspondences Accessed at the Office of the Director General, Archaeological Survey of India, New Delhi

1. Attachment to copy of an order, dated 18 February 1910, passed by the Collector, Peshawar District. File No. 204, 1909–1910, Files from the Office of the Director General of the Archaeological Survey of India (henceforth, DGASI)
2. A Bill to provide for the preservation of monuments and objects of historical or artistic interest, Draft, in Accompaniments to the Letter to the Government of India, No. 689, dated 5 February 1902, File No. 89, April 1902, DGASI.

List of Unpublished Filed Correspondences Accessed at the National Archives of India, New Delhi

1. Note dated 28 August 1909, from Sir H.H. Risley, Home Secretary, Simla Records 2, 1909, Government of India, Home Department, Archaeology and Epigraphy – A, Proceedings nos. 13–16, December 1909: "Petition from Sayed Amir Badshah and Sayed Ahmed Shah, owners of land from which Buddhist relics were recently found at Peshawar claiming a share of the relics." National Archives of India, New Delhi (NAI).
2. Petition from Sayed Amir Badshah and Sayed Ahmed Shah, Mahulla Basate Gul Hassan, Peshawar City, to the Agent to the Governor General and Chief Commissioner, North-West Frontier Province. Simla Records 2, 1909, Government of India, Home Department, Archaeology and Epigraphy – A, Proceedings no. 13, December 1909, NAI.
3. Response to the petition seeking a share of the relics dated 27 August 1909, Simla Records 2, 1909, Government of India, Home Department, Archaeology and Epigraphy – A, Proceedings, December 1909, Nos. 13–16, NAI
4. Letter from Sir John H. Marshall to Sir Harold Stuart, no. 1211, dated 25 August 1909, Simla Records 2, 1909, Government of India, Home

Department, Archaeology and Epigraphy – A, Proceedings, December 1909, Nos. 13–16, NAI.

5. Order of the Collector of Peshawar, dated 18 February 1910, attached to Letter No. 523G, dated 2 March 1910, from Mr W.R.H. Merk, Agent to the Governor General and Chief Commissioner, North-West Frontier Province, to the Secretary to the Government of India, Home Department. Government of India, Home Department, Archaeology and Epigraphy – A, Proceedings No. 69, May 1910, NAI.
6. Letter No. 1038, dated 31 July 1909, from J.H. Marshall, Director General of Archaeology in India to the Secretary to the Government of India, Home Department. Government of India, Home Department, Archaeology and Epigraphy – A, Proceedings No. 33, May 1910, NAI.
7. Presentation to the King of Siam of certain Buddhist relics discovered near Piprahwa in the Basti district. Visit of Phya Sukhum to India to receive the relics. April 1899, Pro. No. 115 (of 92–117), Foreign Department, External A, Proceedings, 1899, NAI.
8. Letter No. 4366 – VII-32, dated 13 April 1898, from Dr W. Hoey, Officiating Commissioner, Gorakhpur Division, to the Chief Secretary to the Government of the North-Western Frontier Provinces and Oudh. Pro. No. 94 (of 92–117), Foreign Department, External A, Proceedings, 1899, NAI.
9. Letter No. 904, dated 17 February 1910, from Lieutenant-Colonel J. Ramsay, Officiating Resident in Kashmir, to Mr S.H. Butler, Secretary to the Government of India, Foreign Department; Letter No. 237-T, dated 7 September 1909, from C.A. Bell, Political Officer in Sikkim, to the Secretary to the Government of India, Foreign Department. Home Department, Archaeology and Epigraphy – A, Proceedings Nos. 13–16, September 1909, and Proceedings Nos. 31–80, May 1910, NAI.
10. Telegram dated 26 July 1909, from the Secretary, Bengal Buddhist Association, Calcutta, to the Private Secretary to the Viceroy (Pro. No. 21); Translation of petition, dated 25 August 1909, from the nine Trustees of the Shwe Dagon Pagoda, Rangoon, to the Lieutenant-Governor of Burma (Pro. No. 35); Letter No. 013001, dated 26 August 1909, from H.L. Crawford, Acting Colonial Secretary, Colombo, to the Secretary to the Government of India, Home Department (Pro. No. 36); Letters dated 7 December 1909, and 3 February 1910, from the General Secretary, Maha Bodhi Society. Home Department, Archaeology and Epigraphy – A, Proceedings Nos. 31–80, May 1910, NAI.
11. Telegram dated 10 September 1909 and 4 October 1909, from the President, Punjab Hindu Sabha, Lahore, and to the President, Sanatan Dharma Pravardhini Sabha, Cawnpore to the Private Secretary to the Viceroy, Government of India. Home Department, Archaeology and Epigraphy – A, Proceedings Nos. 31–80, May 1910, NAI.
12. Letter dated 13 October 1909, from H. Le Mesurier, Chief Secretary to the Government of Eastern Bengal and Assam, to the Secretary to the Government

of India. Pro. No. 52. Home Department, Archaeology and Epigraphy – A, Proceedings Nos. 31–80, May 1910, NAI.

13. Letter No. 1251, dated 30 August 1909, from J.H. Marshall to Sir H.A. Stuart. Home Department, Archaeology and Epigraphy – A, Proceedings Nos. 13–16, September 1909, NAI.
14. Extract of a letter, dated 26 July 1909, from Mr Mian Muhammad Shafi, Bar-at-Law, to Private Secretary to the Viceroy. Home Department, Archaeology and Epigraphy – A, Proceedings Nos. 13–16, September 1909, NAI.
15. Letter dated 3 September 1909, from Captain A. Ramsay, Private Secretary to the Lieutenant-Governor of Punjab, to J.H. Marshall; Extract of a letter, dated 22 September 1909, from the Viceroy, to Sir H. Thirkell White, Lieutenant-Governor of Burma. Home Department, Archaeology and Epigraphy – A, Proceedings Nos. 13–16, September 1909, NAI.
16. Letter No. 326, dated 30 August 1909, to J.H. Marshall. Home Department, Archaeology and Epigraphy – A, Proceedings Nos. 13–16, September 1909, NAI.
17. Note dated 29 August 1909, by H.H. Risley. Home Department, Archaeology and Epigraphy – A, Proceedings Nos. 13–16, September 1909, NAI.
18. Translation of petition, dated 25 August 1909, from the nine trustees of the Shwe Dagon Pagoda, Rangoon, to the Lieutenant-Governor of Burma (Pro. No. 35); Translation of letter, No. 1310, dated 8 September 1909, from Saw Hke, Sawbwa of Hsipaw, to Sir H.T. White, Lieutenant-Governor of Burma (Pro. No. 44); Translation of memorial, dated 10 September 1909, from U. Kyaw Tan and other residents of Mandalay to Lieutenant-Governor of Burma (Pro. No. 45); Translation of letter dated 27 August1909, to Taw Sien Ko, Superintendent, Archaeological Survey, Burma (Pro. No. 37). Home Department, Archaeology and Epigraphy – A, Proceedings Nos. 31–80, May 1910, NAI.
19. Letter, dated 12 September 1909, from Sir H. Thirkell White to the Viceroy; Letter, No. 209, dated 12 November 1909, from H. Thirkell White to Sir Harold Stuart. Home Department, Archaeology and Epigraphy – A, Proceedings Nos. 31–80, May 1910, NAI.
20. Final draft dated 18 March 1910, of the Program of Presentation of the Buddha Relics. Home Department, Archaeology and Epigraphy – A, Proceedings Nos. 31–80, May 1910, NAI.
21. Presentation to the King of Siam of certain Buddhist relics discovered near Piprahwa in the Basti district. Visit of Phya Sukhum to India to receive the relics. April 1899, Pro. Nos. 92–117, Foreign Department, External A, Proceedings, 1899, NAI.
22. Letter No. 1038 dated 31 July 1909, from J.H. Marshall, Director General of Archaeology in India to the Secretary to the Government of India, Home Department. Government of India, Home Department, Archaeology and Epigraphy – A, Proceedings No. 33, May 1910, NAI.

23. Letter, dated 18 February 1910, from John Marshall to Harold Stuart. Government of India, Home Department, Archaeology and Epigraphy – A, Proceedings Nos. 31–80, May 1910, NAI.
24. Letter dated 1 March 1910, from P.W. Monie, Under Secretary to the Government of India, Home Department, to Messrs Hamilton & Co., Jewellers & Silversmiths, Calcutta. Government of India, Home Department, Archaeology and Epigraphy – A, Proceeding No. 58 (of 31–80), May 1910, NAI.
25. Letter dated 7 May 1910, from P.W. Monie, Under Secretary to the Government of India, Home Department, to the Agent to the Governor General and the Chief Commissioner, North-West Frontier Province. Government of India, Home Department, Archaeology and Epigraphy – A, Proceeding No. 80 (of 31–80), May 1910, NAI.

9

The Politics of Pilgrimage: Reception of Hajj among South Asian Muslims

Kashshaf Ghani

INTRODUCTION

The rise of British colonialism in the eighteenth century witnessed a simultaneous decline in the political fortunes among Muslims in South Asia. The loss of authority—both political and social—following the dissolution of the Mughal Empire came as a rude shock to the community from which it struggled to recover throughout the nineteenth century. It was from the late nineteenth and early twentieth century that Muslims across South Asia started manifesting signs of political and social awareness as a community. One of the contributing factors was the rise of print culture in the 1870s, which, in spite of its delayed reception by South Asian Muslims, was a major turning point shaping their socio-political attitude. Print provided them with the technological tool with which the community could aspire to connect with Muslim societies beyond their immediate homeland, and in turn express themselves as an integral part of the global Muslim *ummah* (Robinson 1993).

This idea of self-consciousness not only manifested itself within the educated Muslim elite of north India, led by individuals like Syed Ahmed Khan, but almost equally among Muslims in Bengal. The region proved to be the bridgehead to British presence in South Asia after the fall of the Bengal Nawabs in 1757. Bengali Muslims, now concentrated largely in Bangladesh and the Indian state of West Bengal, constitute one of the largest ethnic communities of Muslims after the Arabs (Ahmed 1996; Eaton 1993). In the run up to the First World War in the early twentieth century, Muslims worldwide, particularly across South Asia, failed to hide their anxiety over a weakening Ottoman Turkish Empire facing the European onslaught. The consequences of this weakness would be dual. First, it pushed into uncertainty the fate of the Islamic Caliphate whose seat was the Ottoman capital at Ankara. Second, growing British presence in a conflict-ridden Hejaz made Turkey's position precarious as the *Khadim ul Haramayn ul Sharifayn* (Servitor/Protector of the Two Holy Sanctuaries of Mecca and Medina).

In the following discussion I will explore how Bengali periodicals, particularly two—*Sultan* and *Ahl-i Hadith*—served as important mediums in keeping Bengali Muslims informed on the course of events around Turkey and the Hejaz. These periodicals, along with other media carrying news on the volatile situation in West Asia, made it possible for Bengali Muslims to overcome their limitation to access printed news in Urdu and English. The proliferation of Bengali periodicals in the early twentieth century successfully competed with their Urdu and English counterparts from north India reporting on the Hejaz—particularly the uncertain conditions around hajj resulting from the political strife between Husayn, an Ottoman ally and the Grand Sharif of Mecca, and Abdul Aziz Al Saud, the ruler of Najd, aspiring for an Arab Empire.

OTTOMANS IN THE HEJAZ

The survival of Ottoman authority in the Arab peninsula depended on a network of alliances which the Sultanate could work out with local ruling houses whose *amir*s were recognized as representing the authority of the Ottoman Sultan. These alliances were cemented with extensive subsidies and gifts from the Ottoman court, primarily to ensure the safety of pilgrimage caravans and Ottoman garrisons, particularly in the Hejaz. The Meccan elite (*ashraf*) who had established, and gradually strengthened, their authority over the city from 961 onwards traced their descent from the family of the Prophet Muhammad—his daughter Fatima and grandsons Hasan and Husayn. The latter are the fountainhead of two main genealogical lines of the Sharifian, the Hasanids and Husaynids, respectively. While the former controlled Mecca, the latter held power in Medina. The tribal descent of the Sharifs can be traced to Hashim ibn Abd Monaf, who established the Banu Hashim clan of the Quraysh tribe—the most dominant tribe during the Prophet's lifetime in Mecca (Yamani 2006, pp. 2–3).

The Ottoman conquest of Mamluk territories in 1516–17 brought the area of Hejaz under their control, and together with it the two holy cities of Mecca and Medina. In 1517 Sharif Barakat of Mecca recognized the authority of the Ottoman Sultan not only as a political sovereign but also as the Caliph of the Islamic world. This resulted in the appointment of an Ottoman pasha in Jeddah, as well as the stationing of Ottoman garrisons in Jeddah, Mecca, Medina, and other towns of the Hejaz. In reality, however, the Sharif had a free hand in the administration of the land. The Grand Sharif earned money as the head of the entire hajj pilgrimage, ensuring its occurrence every year for Muslims all over the globe. His prestige was secured by his lineage from the house of the Prophet, which accorded him a high status not only in the eyes of Muslims worldwide but also of the Ottoman Sultan.

The Ottoman Sultans, on the contrary, could never claim a lineage from the family of the Prophet. Hence their authority came to be exercised through a model commonly found in large Islamic empires across the early modern world—combination of political power and religious piety. This was executed especially in the form of welfare projects and subsidies in favour of Hejazi residents, along with their exemption from taxation and military conscription (ibid.). In the eve of the First World War matters began to turn against the Ottomans when their control over the Hejaz began to weaken. Losing no opportunity, their most trusted ally in the region, Sharif Husayn Ibn Ali (who had been appointed Grand Sharif of Mecca in 1908), openly revolted with support from the British in 1916. Lord Kitchener, the British agent in Egypt, assured Sharif Husayn of all possible support against external aggression, together with the promise to make him the "King of the Arab Lands" after the war. Though, in the oasis of Hail, Ibn Rashid declared his allegiance to the Ottoman Sultan, he did not offer the Sultan any military support. On the other hand, Al Saud continued to be supported by the British (Al Rasheed 2002, Introduction).

THE PERIODICAL *SULTAN*

The First World War ended in 1918, and with it ended any semblance of Ottoman control over the Hejaz and Central Arabia. Through the Anglo-Saudi Treaty of 1915 the British recognized Al Saud's authority over Najd, Hasa, Qatif, and Jubayl, supporting him with 1,000 rifles, a bonus of 20,000 sterling pounds, a monthly subsidy of 5,000 sterling pounds, and a continuous supply of machine guns and rifles, thanks to which the Amir from Najd was all set to break loose in his ambition to unite the Arab peninsula (ibid., p. 42). With the decline of the Ottoman Empire after the World War the political authority of the pro-Ottoman Rashidis in Central Arabia was considerably weakened. Ibn Rashid failed to stop the Saudi army from entering his territories in the 1920s. Hail was captured in 1921 with people from the oasis swearing allegiance to Abdul Aziz Al Saud on 4 November. The victory stretched Saudi frontiers further north up to the British-occupied Trans-Jordan regions (ibid., pp. 43–44).

Al Saud could now set his eyes on the Hejaz, the jewel in the Arabian Peninsula that until the early 1920s adorned the crown of Husayn, the Grand Sharif of Hejaz. In May 1920, under the leadership of his son Faisal, Al Saud wrested the capital town of Abha in northern Asir from the control of Muhammad al Idrisi. By 1923 the Saudis had successfully consolidated their position in Asir, thereby preparing for an offensive in the heart of the Hejaz through entry from the south. In 1923 the periodical *Sultan* collated information from multiple sources, informing its readers in Bengal on the "real" picture of the Hejaz, precisely on the degree of British control over the region.[1]

Britain's interference in the peninsula began in the pre-War years, encouraged by Al Saud's aggressive military activities from Central Arabia towards the eastern and northern regions, with only nominal acknowledgement to the Ottoman Sultan. Britain recognized Al Saud as an Ottoman subordinate but stopped short of antagonizing him to ensure the safety of their possessions stretching from Kuwait to Muscat along with the Trans-Jordan territories. However, with the approaching First World War, Britain began to support Al Saud in his campaigns in the Arab peninsula against Ottoman Turkish allies, particularly the Rashidis. Again, when Husayn aspired to become the "King of the Arabs" (*malik al diyar al arabiya*), Britain supported him against Ottoman Turkey in 1916, recognizing him as the independent ruler of the Hejaz (Al Rasheed 2002, Introduction; Kostiner 1993, Introduction).

Finding himself isolated in the face of Saudi hostilities, in 1923 Sharif Husayn entered into an agreement with the British which limited his territorial jurisdiction and nipped any chances of an alliance with foreign

[1] *Sultan*, vol. 16, Bhadra 1330 (1923), p. 7.

powers other than Britain. This not only made Husayn vulnerable in the Hejaz but at the same time deprived him of any chances to secure help from Muslim powers in the region, like Turkey or Egypt. Reports in the *Sultan* expressed concern over the sanctity of the holy cities of Mecca and Medina being at risk, and at the same time criticized Sharif Husayn for his lack of far-sightedness in allying with the British.[2]

In other reports published in the *Sultan* it was argued as to how an individual can expect support of Muslims worldwide when his own claim to power rested on rebellion against the authority of the Caliph—the head of the Muslim world. Sharif Husayn had acted against the traditions of Islam, and was in a way forced to seek support from the British, who granted him an annual pension of few thousand pounds, which was gradually reduced and finally abolished in 1920 (Kostiner 1993, p. 61).[3]

Another series of reports, besides continuing to assess the political situation, also made readers take note of the inhuman conditions and the degree of harassment pilgrims were subjected to in the period after the independence of the Hejaz, under Sharif Husayn. To begin with, hajjis (pilgrims) were held for twenty-four hours in the quarantine at Jeddah, with bare minimum provisions for water and food—for which they were even charged. Furthermore, an entry fee was levied on those who wished to collect water from the holy Zamzam well.[4] Exorbitant rates were demanded from hajjis who wanted to hire camels for travelling, not without getting fleeced on the way by tribes who forcefully extracted money from them. Those who chose to walk still had to pay money to the administration, who harassed those refusing to pay such duties (Kostiner 1993, pp. 65–66).[5]

In September 1924 the *Sultan* published a report on the first-hand experience of a certain Haji Mohammad Tayeb, who claimed that the situation in the Hejaz was turning from bad to worse. Almost 10,000 pilgrims lost their lives to the carelessness and indifferent attitude of the

[2] *Sultan*, vol. 16, Bhadra 1330 (1923), p. 8.

[3] Ibid., p. 7.

[4] The Zamzam well located within the Masjid-ul Haram in Mecca lies to the east of the Kaaba, the direction of prayer for Muslims. The origin of the well is connected to a miracle when Prophet Abraham's infant son Ismail cried in thirst and started scraping the ground with his feet. The well is supposed to have originated in that very place. Visiting the well and collecting water from it forms an integral part of the hajj pilgrimage.

[5] *Sultan*, vol. 16, Bhadra 1330 (1923), p. 8.

Sharif administration, which did not ensure the basic standards of care. No arrangements whatsoever were made for their proper burial. Under such deteriorating conditions it was worth considering whether Muslims should at all risk their lives at the hands of such an oppressive and inept regime in their quest for piety.[6]

Interesting reports were carried regarding hajjis from Karachi and Sind who refused to yield to such unjust extortions and were taken to the court of Husayn, who remarked,

> If you are unable to pay these taxes then go back to your own country. To your religious leaders. You belong to the Khilafat group, don't you? Then with what purpose have you come to this place?[7]

Such hostile attitude was not limited towards South Asians alone. Pilgrims from Egypt too were denied permission to arrive for the hajj. Anticipating resentment among other hajjis and also in the larger Islamic world, Husayn attempted a justification on the ground that the annual pilgrim caravan (*kafela*) from Egypt carrying the *Mahmal*, or the ceremonial palanquin, was refused entry into Mecca since they had an English doctor in their group. Of course, none were ready to buy the logic of Sharif Husayn at a time when he was being openly supported by British presence in the Hejaz (Kostiner 1993, p. 66).[8]

Under such circumstances it was repeatedly harped upon that Muslims should consider it their pious duty to save the holy land from the evil intentions of the British and at the same time from the atrocities and oppression of the Sharif regime. And the first step towards this design was seen in the temporary suspension of the holy pilgrimage:

> The Alims of Egypt have unanimously issued a fatwa supporting the suspension of Hajj for all Muslims under the regime of the Sharif. Hajj is not mandatory (*farz*) in a situation where the roads are unsafe. Even after being aware of this if someone undertakes Hajj, he is voluntarily becoming a sinner.[9]

---

[6] *Sultan*, vol. 17, Bhadra 1331 (1924), p. 4.

[7] *Sultan*, vol. 16, Bhadra 1330 (1923), p. 9.

[8] Ibid.

[9] Ibid.

It was argued that the Sharif administration used the revenue generated from hajj to fund their immoral activities with support from Britain. Under such circumstances, by performing hajj, Muslims in a way funded the unjust and oppressive agendas of the Sharif together with providing sustenance to a foreign power in the holy land of Islam. Therefore, the immediate solution was to suspend hajj for two to three years in order to dry up the resources of the Sharif administration. In the aftermath of the suspension of annual donations from Egypt and the subsidy from Britain, the financial backbone of the Sharif administration depended on the revenue generated from the annual pilgrimage. If this source of revenue, it was argued, dried up, then the administrative machinery of the Hejaz would collapse and tribes would revolt against the Sharif. This would provide an opportunity to the Najdis and Yemenis to overthrow this corrupt regime.[10]

Thus, it was proposed that a *fatwa* suspending hajj should be issued with support from the religious leaders of India, Afghanistan, Turkey, Iran, Egypt, and Tunis. If possible, support must also be enlisted from China and Sumatra.[11] Till this proposal could be turned to reality, the *Jamaat-i Ulama-i Bengal* made every effort to make the passage of hajj pilgrims from Bengal as comfortable as possible. Volunteers were posted in all rail stations to help hajjis with their tickets and passports, and arrangements were made for the allotment of resting places. The *Jamaat* considered it their pious duty to help their brothers in their journey to the holy land of Islam.

If later reports of the *Sultan* are to be believed then, in spite of such widely circulated news regarding the mismanagement of hajjis and growing discontent against his regime in the Muslim world, the Sharif left no stone unturned to ensure his position and authority in the Hejaz. It was reported that in the aftermath of the abolition of the Caliphate in early 1924 a strong demand was raised from the Muslim world, especially India, through the Khilafat Movement, for its restoration. Furthering his own interests, Sharif Husayn sent a deputation to meet Mahatma Gandhi with the hope that Gandhi would be in a position to influence Indian Muslims to support the candidature of the Sharif as the next Caliph of the Islamic world. It was further remarked in the reports that Muslims have great respect for Gandhi. But they are extremely doubtful as to whether an individual of the stature

[10] Ibid., p. 10.

[11] Ibid.

of Gandhi would come forward to appeal to the Muslims in support of a person who, under the influence of the British, did not for once hesitate to take up arms against the then Caliph of the Islamic world, and is now lobbying for the same position.[12]

THE PERIODICAL *AHL-I HADIS*

While the *Sultan* enlightened Muslims in Bengal on the atrocities of the Sharif administration and the subsequent hazards faced by hajjis on their holy journey, another periodical, the *Ahl-i Hadis*, focussed on the position of Al Saud, addressing him with high-sounding titles like Sultan and Ghazi, at a time when both Sharif Husayn and Al Saud were locked in a bitter struggle for control over the holy sites of the Hejaz.

In early 1923 the newly established Middle East Department of the Colonial Office decided to relieve the British exchequer by cutting down on the total expenditure on subsidies from 33.5 million pounds per annum to 4 million pounds per annum. The goal was to be achieved in the next one year (Kostiner 1993, pp. 61–62). Al Saud received a setback when Britain stopped its monthly subsidy of 5,000 sterling pounds in early 1924. Contented that their agenda had been fulfilled with the defeat of Ottoman Turkey in the First World War by weakening its Arab allies, the British could now afford to dispense with Al Saud, leaving him alone with his expansionist ambitions. Al Saud, suddenly finding himself cash strapped to fund his military expeditions deeper into the Hejaz, had no other option but securing revenues from pilgrimage taxes and custom duties in Jeddah to supplement his meagre income from Najd and Ahsa (Al Rasheed 2002, pp. 45–48).

At the same time, Sharif Husayn sought to position himself in the seat of the Caliphate which was abolished by the Turkish assembly in March 1924, but Al Saud refused to recognize Husayn in that position of global authority. In a matter of six months, in September 1924, Saudi troops appeared at the doors of Taif, a mountainous resort near Mecca. The town was plundered for three days at the end of which Husayn abdicated in favour of his son Ali on 6 October 1924. Ali along with his troops retreated to Mecca. Husayn was sent to the port-city of Jeddah from where he was temporarily shifted to Aqaba before being moved to Cyprus. The abdication

[12] *Sultan*, vol. 17, Shraban 1331 (1924), p. 12.

of Husayn left the field open for Al Saud who marched to Mecca in October 1924, with the intention to "guarantee the liberty of pilgrimage and to settle the destiny of the Holy Land in a manner satisfactory to the Islamic world" (ibid.). He entered the holy city on 5 December 1924 wearing an *ihram*, the attire of any Muslim pilgrim to hajj and *umrah*.

On 5 January 1925 the army of Al Saud reached the gates of Jeddah, where Ali had taken refuge with his troops after leaving Mecca, beginning a siege that lasted for almost a year till December, when Sharif Ali finally left the city for Baghdad, thereby ending the millennium-long Hashemite rule over the Hejaz. Medina had already surrendered in December 1924, leaving no hindrance in the way of Al Saud, who declared himself the "King of Hejaz, Sultan of Najd and its Dependencies". Residents of the Hejaz were already familiar with the idea of kingship from the time of Sharif Husayn, and therefore had little issues to accept Al Saud with a similar title. By January 1926 the rout was complete with Najd, Hasa, Hejaz, and Asir being united under the authority of a single ruler for the first time since the eighteenth century. Though Britain did not openly intervene in the struggle for supremacy between Sharif Husayn and Al Saud, it takes no great insight to understand that not only did Britain fail to restrain Al Saud, but it also left the Sharif to his own fate after supporting him towards securing authority over the Hejaz (ibid., p. 64).

As the struggle for control over the Hejaz intensified, in late 1925, the *Ahl-i Hadis* carried reports on the interaction between Al Saud and representatives of the Khilafat Committee and the Jamaat-i Ulama-i Hind who had gone to the Hejaz to lend their support to Al Saud in his fight against Sharif Husayn. The report was centred on a long statement of Al Saud where he thanked the representatives from India for their support and stressed on the fact that repeated atrocities of the Sharif administration on his men, residents of Mecca and Medina, and innocent hajj pilgrims forced him to take up arms to free his motherland.[13]

The *Ahl-i Hadis* reported that by the grace of the Almighty, Al Saud hoped to free his country from the clutches of the Sharif administration and towards that end focused on three aims: firstly, reinforce the truth of Islam throughout the Hejaz and at the same time call Muslims to the "true" path of God—for it is through one's firm faith in religion and the creator that a Muslim can earn a life of respect in this world and the

[13] *Ahl-i Hadis*, vol. 1, Ashwin 1332 (1925), pp. 10–11.

after; secondly, he intended to do away with the schools of jurisprudence (*mazhab*) in Islam in an attempt to bring all believers to follow the words of God, and the path of the Prophet and his Companions, rather than the canons of the four schools—Hanafi, Shafi, Maliki, and Hanbali; thirdly, Al Saud refused to compromise on the sovereign integrity of his country, by allowing a foreign power like Britain to take control of affairs in his motherland. This statement can be read as a direct retort to the policies of Sharif Husayn who enlisted British support in his revolt against the Caliph and subsequently to maintain his power in the Hejaz. Al Saud went on to state that, keeping with the tradition of the Caliphs of Islam, he only aimed to maintain diplomatic relations with foreign powers rather than make them partners in his administration. To gain control over his motherland, he relied more on the blessings of the Almighty and the power of his sword.[14] In his initial interactions with the residents of Mecca, Al Saud reiterated the fact that an individual's worth lies in his honest deeds rather than in his family lineage, even if that were of the Syeds. He further emphasized that his primary duty would be to protect the faith of Islam, its followers, and the Shariah.[15]

Al Saud's claims of non-interference by Western powers in affairs of the Hejaz reads much in contradiction to the course of events which propelled him to the throne of the Hejaz, actively supported by the British. Even a cursory reading of Al Saud's gradual rise in the Hejaz, elaborated above, clear doubts with regard to the support he received from the British from time to time. By the early 1920s, Al Saud's relation with the British had become cordial to an extent that the latter did not oppose his expansionist agendas, so long as it did not infringe on British interests in the Trans-Jordan territories. Al Saud was intent on expanding his territories into the heart of the Hejaz by marshalling his tribes at any given opportunity. A pragmatic approach, coupled with British support, secured for him a large territory comprising Najd, Hasa, Qasim, and Hail (Kostiner 1993, p. 54). In June 1921 Al Saud declared himself "Sultan over the whole of Najd and its dependencies". Religious authorities recognized the title, and so did the British, who confirmed Al Saud's position as the Sultan in August 1921 (Al Rasheed 2002, pp. 63–64). British attitude towards Al Saud can

[14] Ibid., p. 12.

[15] Ibid., pp. 13–14.

be gleaned through the words of Arthur Balfour, former Foreign Secretary, who in June 1922 remarked: "Ibn Saud has on the whole behaved very well and has shown loyalty to His Majesty's government. Moreover, of all the chieftains of Arabia, he alone has shown signs of statesmanship." (Kostiner 1993, p. 54).

In a separate address Al Saud shared his dislike for war and hostility, and that he preferred peace, compromise, and internal solidarity. However, as he would argue, his political opponents compelled him to pull out his sword involving him in a series of battles. His only reason for jihad was to liberate the holy sites of Islam from the evil grip of a dynasty which did not hesitate to commit repeated acts of sin in those sacred places. Al Saud further proposed that a representative be elected from the Muslim world who would take charge of affairs in the Hejaz, working as per the suggestions of the global *ummah*. As part of his agenda, Al Saud emphasized that the Hejaz will be for all Muslims across the world. Opinion would be sought from Muslims worldwide through the World Muslim Conference to decide, through consensus, on an individual who would be the ruler of the Hejaz. He would be responsible for protecting the frontiers of the region, securing the economy, law and order, the judicial system, and financial affairs. Such a rule has to be based on the principles of the Shariah, which would ensure complete autonomy for the region. On political matters the Hejaz government could not enter into alliances with foreign Western powers. On economic issues it would have the right to forge alliances only with Muslim powers.[16]

In an attempt to valourize the struggle of Al Saud, the *Ahl-i Hadis* also carried detailed reports of the ills of the Sharif administration corroborated through letters and reports from the Hejaz. On the basis of one such letter from Maulana Muhammad Irfan, the Secretary of the Jamaat i-Ulama i-Hind, the periodical reported that thousands of refugees from Medina took shelter in Rabigh, an ancient town on the western coast of Arabia along the Red Sea, which reduced the population of Medina from 20,000 to just 250.[17] Those who chose to stay back faced severe hardship due to lack of food and amenities. All the grain stores were emptied to feed the army of the Sharif, which forced Al Saud to arrange open kitchens for

[16] *Ahl-i Hadis,* vol. 3, Agrahayan 1332 (1925), pp. 110–13.

[17] Ibid., p. 113.

the destitute. Reports carried information on how the army of the Sharif looted grain convoys meant for the refugees, and saluted the efforts of Al Saud who opened a market in Rabigh where food and other amenities were made available at a cheaper price than Medina.[18]

People who wished to flee Medina were allowed to do so on the condition that they would not take any belongings with them. To ensure this the Sharif administration recruited guards with the duty to frisk every individual leaving the gates of Medina. Even women were not spared and frisked by male soldiers who cared little for their modesty. All this was done to ensure that they could not carry anything with them apart from their garments.[19]

Based on letters from residents of Medina it was further reported that all their properties were seized by the Sharif administration.

> Many houses in Medina have been destroyed. The army of the Sharif plans to empty the treasury of its gold and silver deposits. We pray the attention of the Muslim world in this hour of crisis. We are thankful to the army of Al Saud since they have helped us and treated us well. We pray to our Muslim brothers to save us from this tyranny and restore the glory of Islam in this holy land.[20]

As reports of misconduct by the Sharifian army started coming to light, a counter-propaganda was started by the Sharif administration against the army of Al Saud. The focus of this propaganda revolved around the issue that the army of Al Saud had destroyed the minaret and dome of Prophet Muhammad's tomb complex along with the tombs of other eminent individuals of the Prophet's time.[21] In a telegram to the President of the Central Khilafat Committee, Maulana Muhammad Shaukat Ali, on 7 September 1925, Al Saud clarified that his army laid siege on the holy city of Medina but stopped short of initiating hostilities. This was done so as not to damage the structures of the city and harm its inhabitants. Therefore, the rumour spread by the Sharif administration regarding the

---

[18] Ibid., p. 114.

[19] Ibid.

[20] Ibid., p. 115.

[21] *Ahl-i Hadis*, vol. 1, Ashwin 1332 (1925), p. 14.

destruction of the tomb of the Prophet was false. Al Saud ended the letter by reiterating the importance of the holy sites of Mecca and Medina and ensuring that his army would do no harm to them and would try their best to ensure the safety of these structures.[22]

The *Ahl-i Hadis* also carried telegrams sent from Cairo and Karachi in early September, which confirmed that news of the Prophet's tomb having been destroyed by cannon fire were untrue. Sir Denys Bray, Secretary of the Foreign Department, Government of India, assured Indian Muslims that the British Consul in Jeddah would be asked to provide first-hand information on this issue. Similar telegrams from Al Saud's political agent in Cairo to Maulana Shaukat Ali confirmed that cannon fire was unleashed only at the army of the Sharif, while the historic sites and mausoleums were duly respected by the Saudi forces.[23] The periodical argued that it was a propaganda spread by Sharif Ali to malign Al Saud in the Muslim world to accuse him of being incapable of handling affairs of the Hejaz, thereby allowing for British control over the region.[24]

The claim of Al Saud was corroborated a few days later when the Secretary of the Syrian Khilafat Committee, Janab Taufiq Sharif, arrived in Bombay on 23 September 1925 and in an interview reiterated that the rumour of the Prophet's tomb being destroyed from cannon fire by the Saudi army was false. Taufiq Sharif further elaborated that the aim of the Sharif administration behind such propaganda was to create panic in the Muslim world, which then would have recourse to soliciting help from foreign powers against Al Saud. Rather, Al Saud issued strict orders to his army not to use firearms in order not to harm the holy structures in the city. As a result, his army camped 5 miles away from the city and placed it under siege by severing all supply lines.[25]

On 1 October 1925, Sulaiman Ali, the agent of Al Saud in Damascus, gave a press release where he stated that the Najd army did not open

---

[22] Ibid., pp. 19–20.

[23] Ibid., p. 18. Al Saud has assured members of the Khilafat Committee that the mausoleum of the Prophet together with other holy sites will be protected. He has further pledged that if any of the holy and historical sites get damaged by Nejdis or their army then it will be renovated completely by Al Saud.

[24] *Ahl-i Hadis*, vol. 1, Ashwin 1332 (1925), pp. 14–17.

[25] Ibid., pp. 19–20.

fire on the inhabitants or the holy structures in Medina. Such audacity was unthinkable on part of any Muslim. He further stressed that Muslim countries and organizations were most welcome to send deputations to check the veracity of Al Saud's claims on protecting the holy city of Medina and its tombs. The cost of the deputation will be borne by the Najdi Council in Damascus. This would help Muslims across the world to ascertain the truth behind the false propaganda made by the Sharif administration.[26]

Soon after, the Central Khilafat Committee received report from the agent of Al Saud in Cairo that the army of Al Saud had entered the holy city without any bloodshed, with the support of the residents of Medina. The army of Najd successfully captured the Hejaz railway from Mecca to Tabuk, thereby securing supply and telegraph lines. The army of Saud was spontaneously welcomed by the celebratory mood of the residents of Medina, who along with the army prayed at the mosque of the Prophet and offered their gratitude for the success.[27] As a reply to this a message was send on 3 October 1925 on behalf of the staff, teachers and students of Dar ul Uloom at Deoband, congratulating Al Saud on his peaceful entry to the city of Medina and also for protecting the sanctity and lives of the residents.[28]

Representatives of the Central Khilafat Committee in a telegram from Port Sudan on 4 December 1925 confirmed that the holy structures of the city, like mosques, graves, and minarets, remained unharmed except for slight damages on the exterior. Quoting these telegrams, the *Ahl-i Hadith* reported that immediately after gaining control of the city orders were issued by Al Saud entrusting his son with the responsibility for renovating all the holy structures of the city which had remained uncared for under the Sharif regime or suffered damage from gunfire during the battle between Saudi and Sharifi forces. Sufficient funds, around 10,000 pounds, were released towards this purpose.[29]

Another report later in the month on 23 December 1925 carried news from Indian representatives of the Khilafat Committee in Medina on the surrender of the city, which led to the confiscation of a large number of

---

[26] Ibid., pp. 20–21.

[27] Ibid., p. 22.

[28] Ibid., p. 23.

[29] *Ahl-i Hadis*, vol. 2, Kartik 1332 (1925), pp. 93–95.

weapons and war equipment by the Najdi forces. Though rumours regarding extensive damage of the dome of the Prophet's mosque were dispelled, the report nonetheless mentioned the presence of bullet marks on the main dome. Superficial damage was also noticed on the exterior of other graves in the vicinity. All other historical sites were reported to be safe. It was reported on the authority of Abdul Majid, the commander of the victorious forces, that the army of Husayn carried away expensive carpets and other valuable items of decoration from the Prophet's mosque. Though the army and Saudi officials showed great concern for the residents of Medina, the report commented on the deplorable conditions of the residents under the impact of war. The representatives took active measures to arrange for basic necessities for the residents, which included starting a free kitchen, with support from the local municipality, at a cost of 4,000 rupees.[30]

Such reports captured headlines in the *Ahl-i Hadis*, which lost no opportunity to eulogize Al Saud for his humane attitude towards the vanquished residents of Medina and Mecca. At the same time his efforts at championing the cause of Islam in the holy land, protecting the holy structures and restoring peace in the birthplace of Islam were equally lauded. When Al Saud was declared King of Hejaz and Mecca by eminent individuals of the land the *Ahl-i Hadis* saluted this move on the ground that the honour bestowed befitted an individual who risked his life for the cause of Islam and the motherland.[31]

From early 1926 the *Ahl-i Hadis* carried regular reports highlighting the benevolent administration of Al Saud. It emphasized how hajj pilgrims visiting the Hejaz immediately after the transition were satisfied with the easy availability of transport, safer roads, better security measures, and other arrangements made to facilitate their visit to the holy sites. The *Ahl-i Hadis* went to the extent of comparing the Saud regime with that of the first four Caliphs of Islam, when theft, armed robbery, murder, and other misdeeds were supposedly unheard of.[32] Individuals without any work under the Sharif regime were given employment in the police force by Al Saud in an attempt to ensure that local elements did not harass hajj pilgrims.[33]

[30] *Ahl-i Hadis*, vol. 3, Agrahayan 1332 (1925), pp. 116–17.

[31] *Ahl-i Hadis*, vol. 4, Pous 1332 (1926), pp. 169–70.

[32] *Ahl-i Hadis*, vol. 10, Ashar 1333 (1926), p. 424.

[33] *Ahl-i Hadis*, vol. 7, Chaitra 1332 (1926), p. 291.

Building on the above, the *Ahl-i Hadis* also carried a conversation between Maulana Muhammad Maula Baksh, a representative of the *Anjuman Ahl-i Hadis i-Bangala* to the Hejaz, and Muhammad bin Yahya bin Aquil and Muhammad Aquil bin Muhammad al Fataf—both residents of the Hejaz. According to them, the tyranny of Sharif Ali had reached its extreme, and Al Saud appeared as mercy from the Almighty to save the people of the Hejaz.[34] The degree of peace and prosperity witnessed under the new rule was something unheard of earlier. Under such circumstances the condition was perfect to resume the holy pilgrimage. It was further stressed that since the Hejaz was not suitable for agriculture, it was the duty of the Muslim world to come forward and undertake the pilgrimage in large numbers so that Hejazis may earn their living by serving hajjis. In this regard the *Ahl-i Hadis* even appealed to Bengali Muslims to come forward in unity, send material help to the Hejaz, and undertake the holy pilgrimage to support the residents while gaining spiritual benefits at the same time.[35]

Even in the midst of such praises heaped on Al Saud for saving the holy land of Islam from the clutches of a rebel and despot, criticisms began to be heard from corners which were wary of Al Saud's inclinations towards a conservative brand of Islam that came to be identified as Wahhabism. Reports began to appear in some newspapers about the attitude of the new administration towards graves and funerary memorials. Many of such constructions were razed to the ground as a conscious policy to eliminate any possibility of such sites turning into places of worship. Even tombstones were not spared.

It is to be noted here that the roots of such a conservative ideology go deep into the origins of the Saudi state. The latter emerged from an alliance between Muhammad bin Abdul Wahhab (1703–92), a preacher and theologian from Najd, and Muhammad bin Saud, the ruler of Southern Najd. Wahhabism as a reformist ideology advocated the unity of almighty God and through it a singular belief system beyond all innovation (*bida*) in an attempt to return to an "imagined" pure past of Islam. Any idea that challenges this sense of purity is defined by the Wahhabis as idolatry (*shirk*) leading to disbelief (*kufr*). In this context Wahhabism views, many

[34] *Ahl-i Hadis*, vol. 1, Ashwin 1332 (1925), p. 47.

[35] Ibid., p. 48.

of the rituals and customs within the Islamic world as superstitious, like rituals honouring the Prophet and his companions, the celebration of the Prophet's birthday, visiting Sufi shrines, and paying respect at graves and tombs (Yamani 2006, p. 4).

The rise of the Saudi political power and authority coupled with the implementation of their religious beliefs resulted in large-scale destruction of holy tombs and burial grounds, as well as any, allegedly un-Islamic, site that could turn into a potential place of worship. At an ideological level this purification meant doing away with the Islamic schools of jurisprudence/thought (*madhahib*), together with the material remains from the historic past of Islam. Foremost among those were the houses of the Prophet, his wives and close companions, on the premise that they could turn into sites of prayer for the lay Muslim devotees, pushing them into the folds of sin and heresy. However, the destruction of architectural and material remains brought international Muslim pressure on the Saudi government, which had to rein its puritanical agendas and assure that no further harm would be done to the holy shrines (ibid., p. 10).

The *Ahl-i Hadis* consciously chose to remain silent on this questionable aspect of the Saudi administration. Rather, it channelled its resources to directly attack the Ali brothers—Maulana Muhammad Ali and Maulana Shaukat Ali, who were critical of the conservative attitude of the new ruler of Hejaz. They accused Al Saud of destroying the sites which carried the earthly remains of the Prophet's family, his near and dear ones, his companions, and other noteworthy individuals in the history of Islam.[36] Believers in the Hanafi *madhab*, millions of Muslims in Bengal and India, were severely hurt by this destructive act of Al Saud.

The *Ahl-i Hadis* in its reports considered it extremely unjust on the part of the Ali brothers to move accusations against an individual who had taken the onus to relieve the Hejaz from the tyranny of the Sharif administration. The periodical further argued that at a time when the entire Muslim world remained a silent spectator to the atrocities of Sharif Hussein, it was Al Saud who took on his shoulders the responsibility of reinstating the holy land of Islam to its pristine glory. In comparison, in spite of all their attempts, the Ali brothers failed to ensure the continuity of the Caliphate. Hence, as the *Ahl-i Hadis* stressed, they should remain

[36] *Ahl-i Hadis*, vol. 12, Bhadra 1333 (1926), pp. 539–46.

grateful to Al Saud for protecting the honour of Islam rather than being unduly critical of his actions. It further stated that the actions of Al Saud were completely justified in the eyes of the Shariah, which regards as blasphemy the worship of any object other than the One Almighty, even if it be the last physical remains of the Prophet or his family. Hence the Ali brothers should look closer to their turf and consider securing the fate of Indian Muslims from the clutches of British rule, instead of being judgemental on the activities of Al Saud, who was by then unconditionally accepted as the King of Hejaz by all Muslim nations.[37]

Hajjis like Munshi Amir Ahmed Alawi in his *Safar i-Saadat* (Propitious Journey)—written as a daily diary after his return from the holy pilgrimage of hajj in 1929—recollects with great pathos the destruction of tombs and gravesites carried by the Saud administration in the name of restraining the spread of *shirk* or deification through grave worship (Alawi 2009, Introduction; Ghani 2016). For individuals like the Ali brothers and Alawi, along with millions of Muslims from South Asia, these sites were places that helped them to physically connect with and pray for the great souls of Islam, the Prophet's family, his companions, and other significant individuals. Destroying the last remaining traces of such sites was for many Muslims a grave loss of heritage and an act of destruction and pillage which lacked any moral or religious justification.

POLITICAL AGENDA OF BENGALI PERIODICALS

Reports published by the two periodicals discussed above, focusing on issues of geo-politics and pilgrimage in the region of the Hejaz, reflect different positions. Apparently, the periodicals sought to work on their respective agendas primarily through an engagement with the activities of two individuals—Sharif Husayn of Hejaz and Al Saud of Najd. The *Sultan* wrote critically on the administration of Sharif Husayn in the Hejaz and the harassment of pilgrims visiting the holy cities of Mecca and Medina. The mismanagement of facilities for pilgrims on part of the Sharif administration went to such an extent that voices were raised calling for suspension of hajj visits as long as Sharif Husayn remained in control of the Hejaz.

[37] Ibid.

On the other hand, reports in the *Ahl-i Hadis* were all praise for Al Saud and his efforts towards freeing the Hejaz from the political control of Sharif Husayn and his successors. The success of Al Saud, as the *Ahl-i Hadis* would want its readers to believe, would result in a subsequent improvement in the overall condition of the Hejaz. This in turn would provide better conditions for hajj pilgrims arriving in the Hejaz from all parts of the world. His efforts towards public welfare after the capture of the holy cities and surrounding areas also received much attention through the *Ahl-i Hadis*, which carried a number of reports from eyewitnesses attesting Al Saud's attempts at restoring law and order in the Hejaz, while bringing it back to an Islamic way of life.

It can be argued that the adoption of certain positions by these periodicals were not arbitrarily done. Rather, the reasons behind their respective agendas can be sought in the origins and background of these periodicals, and in the particular historical context within which they were established. The *Sultan* was started by Maulana Maniruzzaman Islamabadi, supported by intellectuals like Syed Ismail Hossain Siraji. Islamabadi can be considered a pioneer in the field of Muslim journalism in Bengal and a number of fortnightly and monthly periodicals in Bengali were published under his editorship. Of these the weekly *Sultan*, remodelled and improved from 1923, was of primary importance and reflected Islamabadi's strong inclination towards Ottoman affairs (Rahman 1966, p. 11).

This was the time when the Khilafat Movement was gaining ground in India not only as an isolated endeavour among South Asian Muslims, but also carried a national resonance. With Gandhi's encouraging participation, the Khilafat Movement was also seen as a stage for addressing Hindu-Muslim relations in South Asia. The demand for the reinstatement of the Ottoman Sultan as the Caliph gathered momentum not only among the Muslims but was accepted even at the national level. In such a situation it is understandable that the *Sultan*, named so out of respect for the Ottoman Sultan, would spare no criticisms for any political authority, particularly the person of Sharif Husayn, aspiring for the position of the Caliph in the Muslim world. All the more so since Husayn himself was a subordinate ally of the Ottoman Empire in the Hejaz. His friendly overtures with the British leading to political alliances and financial support, which the Amir later utilized to rebel against the Ottoman Caliph, did not go particularly well with Muslims in South and West Asia.

On the other hand, the Ahl-i Hadis movement had its roots in the All India Ahl-i Hadis Conference in 1906. The Ahl-i Hadis, in much similarity with the Deobandis, were committed to revival of Islamic law by reform and custom. With these agendas in mind, and drawing their name as "people of the Hadith tradition", they advocated a strict adherence towards the textual sources of religion—the Quran and the Hadith. Their approach to these fundamental texts of Islam remained strictly literal and extremely narrow. At the same time, they vehemently refused to recognize Sufi institutions and practices that had anything to do with veneration of Sufis, saints, mystics, pilgrimages to their tombs and paying respect at their mausoleums, and indulging with any related practices and rituals, especially when those involved music and poetry (Metcalf 1982, pp. 264–65; Lemah 2012, p. 5). Needless to say, the ideological inspiration for the Ahl-i Hadis was drawn from the reformist Wahhabi ideas preached by Muhammad ibn Abdul Wahhab (1703–92). Wahhabism became Saudi Arabia's only Islamic tradition endorsed by Muhammad Al Saud (d. 1765) through the establishment of the Saudi-Wahhabi Emirate (1744–1818).

In 1914 the *Anjuman-i Ahl-i Hadis i-Bangala and Assam* was founded in Calcutta, followed by their monthly mouthpiece in Bengali called the *Ahl-i Hadis* from 1915. Its first editor was Muhammad Babar Ali. In this context it hardly comes as a surprise that the Ahl-i Hadis would frame their reports in strong support of the Saudi establishment particularly the Amir from Najd, and later the Sultan Al Saud. Leaving aside the Central Khilafat Committee, a large chunk of reports originated from representatives of the *Jamaat-i Ulama-i Hind* and the *Anjuman-i Ahl-i Hadis i-Bangala*, who left no stone unturned to valourize the activities of Al Saud, elevating him to a position alongside the Righteous Caliphs of Islam.

CONCLUSION

The career of Islam in Asia has given rise to multiple narratives across various socio-political contexts. These narratives concern themselves with Islam being an integral element in the formation of large political structures, as much as with its localized instantiations across geographically distant regions like Bengal and the Hejaz. Generalized notions of religion and faith do not help towards approaching these societies as homogeneous entities. Rather, the multiplicity of actors involved in the formation of certain networks between diverse societies like Bengal and Arabia, along common parameters of hajj, brings into sharper focus the centrality of practices in Islamic societies. And at the same time the historical position of Arabia within the Islamic world, as the site of the holiest shrines of Islam, towards which millions of Muslims turn their faces for prayer (Al Rasheed

2002, p. 5). In the Islamic tradition, practices like hajj resonate beyond the geographical confines of the Arab peninsula, successfully bringing together millions of Muslims worldwide, from diverse socio-cultural and ethnic backgrounds, thereby contributing towards an understanding of Muslim societies across multiple sites even if they be mediated through Western-derived technology and medias.

South Asian historiography focusing on Bengal, while recognizing the trend among Bengali Muslims to connect with Muslim societies beyond their homeland, individuates different reasons behind such a development. Some scholars regard the coming of Syed Jamaluddin Afghani in Calcutta in the late nineteenth century to be the starting point of a pan-Islamic outlook among Bengali Muslims who were influenced by the idea of building up a larger Islamic brotherhood beyond geographical, racial, and national limits in order to fight British imperialism (Wasti 2006; Ozcan 1997; Keddie 1972). Thus, the emerging middle-class Bengal Muslim intelligentsia increasingly began to accommodate various aspects of Islamic societies in their literary and academic pursuits. These ranged from biographical accounts to writing histories and novels to composing poetry. On many occasions this endeavour went beyond the limits of intellectual pursuit, as reflected by their journalistic activities.

Rather than adding to the list of reasons mentioned above, the main intention of this chapter was to explore diverse trends within this larger transregional attitude among Bengal Muslims, from the late nineteenth to the mid-twentieth century—thus well beyond the Khilafat period—by analysing the various mediums through which Muslims in both Bengal and North India connected to the tumultuous fortunes of Muslim societies in the Hejaz—through individual experiences, pilgrimage, and writing. The development of print culture among the Bengali Muslim society helped its members familiarize themselves with Muslim societies within and beyond South Asia through newspapers, periodicals, books, and pamphlets, and in turn connect to these societies without undertaking the exercise of physical relocation.

Acknowledgement

The current chapter is the outcome of the author's ongoing postdoctoral research on transcultural and transregional connections among Muslim societies in South and West Asia, initiated at the Zentrum Moderner Orient, Berlin, and supported by the Maulana Abul Kalam Azad Institute for Asian Studies, Kolkata.

Bibliography

Ahmed, Rafiuddin. 1996. *The Bengal Muslims 1871–1906: A Quest for Identity*. Delhi and New York: Oxford University Press.

Al Rasheed, Madawi. 2002. *A History of Saudi Arabia*. London: Cambridge University Press.

Alawi, Amir Ahmad. 2009. "Safar i-Saadat". In *Journey to the Holy Land: A Pilgrim's Diary*, translated by Mushirul Hasan and Rakhshanda Jalil. Delhi: Oxford University Press.

Eaton, Richard. 1997. *The Rise of Islam and the Bengal Frontier 1204–1760*. Delhi and New York: Oxford University Press.

Ghani, Kashshaf. 2016. "United in Faith, Divided in Practice: South Asian Muslims and their World(s) of Islam". Paper presented at the International Conference on "Global Muslim Encounters: Homogenization and Diversity Across Time and Space", University of Cambridge, 9–10 December 2016.

Keddie, Nikki R. 1972. *Sayyid Jamal Ad-Din "Al-Afghani": A Political Biography*. Berkeley: University of California Press.

Kostiner, Joseph. 1993. *The Making of Saudi Arabia 1916–1936: From Chieftaincy to Monarchical State*. Oxford: Oxford University Press.

Lemah, Ibn Sa. 2012. *Jamiati Tatparatar Samkhiptasar* [Short Account of Jamiati Activities]. Calcutta.

Metcalf, Barbara. 1982. *Islamic Revival in British India: Deoband 1860–1900*. Princeton: Princeton University Press.

Ozcan, Azmi. 1997. *Pan Islamism: Indian Muslims, the Ottoman and Britain 1877–1924*. Leiden: E.J. Brill.

Rahman, Chaudhury Shamsur. 1966. "Muslim Bangla Samayik Patra". In *Muslim Bangla Samayik Patra*, edited by Talim Hossain. Dacca: Pakistan Publications.

Robinson, Francis. 1993. "Technology and Religious Change: Islam and the Impact of Print". *Modern Asian Studies* 27, no. 1 (February): 229–51.

Wasti, Syed Tanvir. 2006. "The Political Aspirations of Indian Muslims and the Ottoman Nexus". *Middle Eastern Studies* 42, no. 5: 709–22.

Yamani, Mai. 2006. *Cradle of Islam: The Hijaz and the Quest for an Arabian Identity*. New York: I.B. Tauris.

Periodicals

Ahl i-Hadis. Vol. 1, Ashwin 1332 (1925).

———. Vol. 2, Kartik 1332 (1925).

———. Vol. 3, Agrahayan 1332 (1925).

———. Vol. 4, Pous 1332 (1926).

———. Vol. 7, Chaitra 1332 (1926).

———. Vol. 10, Ashar 1333 (1926).

———. Vol. 12, Bhadra 1333 (1926).

Sultan. Vol. 16, Bhadra 1330 (1923).

———. Vol. 17, Shraban 1331 (1924).

———. Vol. 17, Bhadra 1331 (1924).

Part V

Trans-Local Dynamics and Intra-Asian Connections across Space and Time

10

Sanskritic Buddhism as an Asian Universalism

Iain Sinclair

The concept of Sanskritic Buddhism is discussed here in connection with the problem of a standard, common or universal form of the Buddhist religion. Buddhism has a heterogeneous appearance, manifesting in a variety of sects and ethnic or national types, and whatever homogeneity it possesses has been hard to articulate, both for those within the religion as well as for those outside it. The question of how much of Buddhism is universal, that is, especially prevalent and accepted, cannot be answered solely with citations of canonical scripture, as every sect has its own canonical language and iteration of the canon. What will be discussed in this chapter is the notion of commonality, and in particular the applications of a common discursive or metadiscursive protocol. The focus will be on the use of Sanskrit, the only canonical language of Buddhism that was also a sacred language for non-Buddhists within its native territory.

Some of the factors that led Buddhists to take up Sanskrit—originally the preserve of Brahmins, an exclusive "language of the gods"—have most

---

This chapter expands on an introductory section of my doctoral thesis, Sinclair (2016), pp. 33–35ff. I thank Andrea Acri, Achim Bayer, Gudrun Bühnemann, Alexander von Rospatt, and my fellow participants at the "Imagining Asia" workshop for their feedback on parts of this chapter at various stages of its development. Its shortcomings are solely my responsibility.

recently been examined by Johannes Bronkhorst, Vincent Eltschinger, Jan Houben and others. As the rationales for adoption are now receiving due scholarly attention, this chapter will examine the ways in which Sanskrit and Buddhism work together in practice, and the extent to which this combination displays a degree of universality that is not found in either the language or the religion on its own. To this end, both the classical and the modern situation will be looked at, as they complement each other and demonstrate different kinds of universality. Many other aspects of Sanskritic Buddhism, such as its associated canons, genres, institutions, social systems, writing systems, and constructions of sacred space, are yet to be studied systematically and can be mentioned only in passing here.

THE SANSKRIT LANGUAGE IN COMBINATION WITH THE BUDDHIST RELIGION

Sanskritic Buddhism is the form of the Buddhist religion that propagates some or all of its discourses in a variety of Sanskrit. A Sanskritic environment is one in which other languages can be used together with Sanskrit, or where a non-standard variety of Sanskrit can be used. The expression "Sanskritic Buddhism" was probably first used in a 1906 review referring to "Northern (Sanskritic) Buddhism".[1] While Buddhists in the north did prefer to use Sanskrit, they also used it in and beyond the rest of the subcontinent. In a 1929 article by Niharranjan Ray, "Sanskritic Buddhism" referred to a typical situation: the coexistence, outside India, of a Buddhist community—not identified with a more particular sect or type—together with Brahmanism. The term implies a contrast with what might be called Prakritic Buddhism, which today is mainly represented in Pali scripture and its associated monastic order, the so-called Theravāda. Whereas the Pali canon enshrines the immutable religion of one monastic order, Sanskritic Buddhism is not confined to a particular sect, body of teaching or subcontinental region. It is a metacategory with no direct emic counterpart, which "simply means the Buddhism in which Sanskritic elements are found".[2]

Some senses of the term "Sanskritic" should be fleshed out here. Buddhism demonstrates a relatively flexible and pragmatic attitude to

[1] Grierson (1906).

[2] Junghare (1999), p. 67.

the use of Sanskrit. As is well known, the teaching of the Buddha has been conveyed in various languages, each redaction being authoritative for a particular monastic order (*nikāya*). This teaching has never been bound to a single mode of expression, but it is transmitted with an oft-stated preference for speaking in ways that are easily understood by the listener. Some statements of the vernacular tradition have been interpreted as rejections of the archaic, intoned speech of the Vedas, sacred to Brahmins.[3] This teaching, attributed to the Buddha, is believed to deprecate "artificial", "perfected" speech, that is, *saṃskṛta* language in general.[4] Whatever the import of these statements, it is evident that Buddhism has been in competition with Sanskrit-speaking Brahmins from the start,[5] while remaining open to accepting Brahmins as converts. As such, the use of Sanskrit could hardly be precluded in all situations. The innovation of Buddhist Hybrid Sanskrit and other such "Mixed" dialects[6] can be seen as part of an effort to imbue teaching in the vernacular with Sanskritic formalism and prestige. A Sanskritized patois appears to be recognized internally by expressions such as "intermediate redaction" (*madhyoddeśika*),[7] as might be spoken "on the fly" by an "interpolation preacher" (**madhyamabhāṇaka*).[8] Along with the canonical Prakrits, Hybrid Sanskrit and, eventually, Sanskrit itself were widely accepted as languages of the *buddhavacana*.[9]

Monastic law permits Sanskrit to be used in conjunction with a second language, and this has most likely contributed to its overall

[3] Pollock (2006), p. 54; Bahulkar and Deokar (2012), pp. 41–43; Eltschinger (2017), pp. 313–15; Houben (2018), pp. 11–12.

[4] Pollock (2006), p. 55; Eltschinger (2017), p. 315, n. 22.

[5] See, for instance, among a large literature, Yamazaki (2005), pp. 21ff, on Buddhist criticisms of Brahmins; on "philosophical" differences, Bronkhorst (2011) et al.

[6] See, respectively, Edgerton (1953) and Lamotte (1988), pp. 574–91. Most likely new conceptions of the non-standard Sanskrits will be needed in the light of new discoveries; such a need was already anticipated by Brough (1954).

[7] A *vinaya* canon of the Mahāsaṃghika order identifies itself as such a redaction (Karashima 2014, p. 80).

[8] The term *madhyimabhāṇaka*, as found in a manuscript fragment from Gandhara, would be unusually specialized if it meant, as Matsuda (2014), p. 166, translates, "a reciter of the *Madhyama*[-*āgama*]."

[9] Lamotte (1988), p. 593.

acceptability and currency within Buddhism. In general, a monastic order has to practise the religion as it is taught in the language of its scriptural canon. The explanation, paraphrase, or translation of the Buddha's formal teaching—all classed as *nirukti*—is supposed to be allowed only in exceptional circumstances.[10] However, the use of "one's own mode of expression" appears to have been condoned in principle,[11] such that Sanskrit would be in the background rather than the foreground in many situations where it was accepted as the language of canon. In practice, translation was normal. A massive translation enterprise, taking place across several centuries and countries, transported the teaching of the Buddha far outside the native range of Indic languages. The existence of this highly linguistically diversified *buddhavacana* was, in turn, acknowledged back in the heartland, albeit at a late stage and without affecting the established language-bound sectarian structures there. It was recognized within the Sanskritic tradition that comprehensive Buddhist teaching (pertaining to all three "vehicles", the *yānatraya*) was also put into writing in Chinese, Tibetan and other languages, such as Farsi, much of which now seems to be lost.[12] There was then a clear awareness that mature Buddhist teaching had spread, through translation, to the limits of the known world. This awareness most likely grounds the contemporaneous characterization of Sanskrit as a "parochial" (*prādeśika*) language, in contrast to the universal discourse of the Buddha, who speaks "the speech of all-knowledge having as essence the speech-sounds [made by] all [kinds of] beings".[13] Sanskrit is, in this understanding, just another linguistic conveyance of an omniscient awareness, and has no special qualities or applications.

---

[10] The monastic law in question, summarized in Guṇaprabha's *Vinayasūtra* 2, relates to monks who do not break their vows by inadvertently misspeaking in other languages. It was studied by Schopen (2013), pp. 171–75. Schopen understands *nirukti* to mean "language" (presumably following Lamotte 1988, p. 553) and to be synonymous with *bhāṣā*.

[11] Houben (2018), p. 12.

[12] The enumeration of languages of the *yānatraya* such as Farsi (*pārasikabhāṣā*), Tibetan (*bhoṭabhāṣā*), Chinese (*mahācīnabhāṣā*), *suvarṇākhyaviṣayabhāṣā campakaviṣayabhāṣā* et al.—the referents of which still remain obscure—is given in Puṇḍarīka's *Vimalaprabhā* 1.4, ed. Upadhyaya (1986), p. $41_{18\text{–}23}$, trans. Newman (1987), p. 362.

[13] I.e., *anena prādeśikasaṃskṛtavacanena buddho 'pi prādeśiko bhavati | sarvasattvarutasvabhāvinyā sarvajñabhāṣayā vinā* (Puṇḍarīka's *Vimalaprabhā* 1.4, ed. Upadhyaya 1986, p. $34_{11\text{–}12}$), also quoted in Bahulkar and Deokar (2012), p. 49.

Sanskrit has further occupied a critical position as an auxiliary or bridge language between the various orders. Since a large part of the monastic community, if not the "majoritarian" part,[14] had over time codified their canon in some variety of Sanskrit, the language would have been a practical choice for trans-sectarian communications. There are a number of situations in which a common language is desirable, such as when different orders are in regular contact with each other, are operating outside their usual bases, or are dealing with an outside party as a single entity. The notion of a translocal monastic community, dispersed throughout the "four quarters" (*cāturdiśa*), was already present in Prakritic Buddhism[15] and the conservative canon.[16] However, this particular idea of translocality does not necessarily recognize the existence of multiple orders and linguistic spheres.[17] It is in Sanskrit texts that the *saṅgha* first becomes clearly defined as a corporate body made up of several sects, usually enumerated as eighteen orders (*aṣṭādaśa nikāya*) or four superorders (*cātur mahānikāya*). This definition of the multisectarian *saṅgha* emerges out of necessity in the metadiscourse of Buddhism—in the donative literature, the exegetical literature and so on[18]—because each canon-bound sectarian entity exists independently, without any obligation to acknowledge other orders.

As Sanskrit assumes the role of a bridge language only informally, and in ways that are yet to be examined in depth, a few examples of how it fulfils this role will be given here. Vajrāsana (Bodhgaya), the nominal

---

[14] Early references to the *mahāsāṃghika* faction, later recognized as particular order or superorder, are in Hybrid Sanskrit. On the relevant Mathurā inscriptions, see, e.g., Skinner (2017), pp. 266, 268, 280, 288, 294 etc., appearing from about 95 CE onwards (cf. Tsukamoto 1996, p. 685, Math 116). See also Karashima (2015).

[15] See Tsukamoto (1996), Prakrit inscriptions Kanh 25, 28, 34, 38, 43, 78, 84, Karl 26, 33 and Nasi 6, 7, 10, 12, 16, 19, 25, etc., all clustered around present-day Mumbaī. In addition, Skinner (2017), p. 341, notices a bowl dedicated in Gāndhārī to the monks of the four quarters (*saṃghe caüdiśami*, Skt. **cāturdiśe*).

[16] Expressions meaning "congregation of the four quarters" occur in some recensions of the *Kūṭatāṇḍyasūtra* of the *Dīrghāgama*; see Meisig (2011), p. 82 n. 227 (I thank Marcus Bingenheimer for this reference).

[17] See, e.g., Senart (1902–03), pp. 59–60.

[18] The *aṣṭādaśa nikāya* is nominated as one of the *śrāvakatattva* in Bhāviveka's *Madhymakahṛdaya* 4.8 (cf. ed. Lindtner 2001, p. 50). The eighteen schools are also mentioned in a Vallabhī inscription of king Guhasena, c. *circa* 565–7 CE (Tsukamoto 1996, pp. 530–33, Wala 5_8).

seat of Buddhism, preserves many Sanskrit epigraphs written by monks from non-Sanskritic orders, who had journeyed there from places such as Sri Lanka[19] and Sindh.[20] At nearby Kurkihar, dozens of bronze statuettes were dedicated in Sanskrit by monks from Kanchipuram in present-day Tamil Nadu. It is highly likely that these monks also belonged to a Prakritic rather than a Sanskritic order.[21]

Nālandā monastery provides a paradigmatic case of a catholic, cosmopolitan community, where the teachings of the four superorders were studied.[22] The fact that nearly all of Nālandā's inscriptions are in Sanskrit indicates that it was an important bridge language for the various monastic orders there. However, this Sanskrit-mediated ecumenism evidently had its limits. The Prakritic Sāṃmatīya order is said to have been made to make its base outside Nālandā.[23] One late Theravāda work from Sri Lanka sees the ecumenism of Nālandā as an oppressive project, going so far as to describe the seventeen non-Thera orders residing at Nālandā as non-Buddhist (*tīrthaka*).[24] Nonetheless, in Sri Lanka there was at least one multisectarian monastery that accepted Sanskrit as its auxiliary language. An inscription at the Jētavanārāma monastery, Anurādhapura, explains how the *saṅgha* there is to be constituted from among the monks of the four superorders.[25] This *saṅgha* included at least one faction made up of the Prakritic Sthavira order, which features in all enumerations of the four

---

[19] Tsukamoto (1996), pp. 143, 147–8, BoGa 21, 31.

[20] Tsukamoto (1996), pp. 140, 144, BoGa 15, 24.

[21] The tenth-century Kurkihar bronzes were engraved by monks self-professedly coming from Kāñcideśa, etc. (Tsukamoto 1996, pp. 179ff, Kurk 2, etc.). Prasad (2014), pp. 125–29, understands that some of the bronzes' donors were Tamils or in any case did not have Sanskritic names. On the canonical languages of Tamil Buddhists, see Schalk (2002), pp. 52, 54, 384, etc.

[22] Yijing 義淨 (635–713) gives information on the four orders (**cātur nikāya* 四種尼迦耶) and their distribution relative to Nālandā 那爛陀 in his *Nanhai jigui neifa zhuan* 南海寄歸內法傳, Taishō Tripiṭaka No. 2125, p. 205 b_{3-4}; trans. Takakusu (1896), p. 8.

[23] In particular, the Sāṃmatīya *sthavira*s had to found their own monastery not far from Nālandā, namely Uddaṇḍapura at Bihar Sharif (Dimitrov 2010, p. 48). Even there, however, they followed Sanskrit epigraphic conventions (cf., e.g., Shastri 1942, pp. 105–6; Tsukamoto 1996, p. 146, BoGa 29).

[24] Shastri (1942), p. 13, here quotes the late fourteenth century Sinhalese *Nikāyasaṅgrahaya*.

[25] Wickremasinghe (1912), p. 533.

mahānikāyas.[26] The Sthaviras at Jētavanārāma, while observing behavioural norms codified in a Prakrit canon, would also have been bound to follow the local monastic regulations in Sanskrit.[27] Sanskrit most likely served as the default language in monasteries that housed multiple orders under one roof. Such situations are especially representative of Sanskritic Buddhism, in that the language itself expresses an authority potentially greater than the classical sectarian structure.

The Superseding of Conservative Canon (*Śrāvakapiṭaka*) by Comprehensive Soteriology (*Yānatraya*)

Although Sanskrit has been used to convey the full range of Buddhist teaching disseminated in the heartland—and it seems to have been the only native language to have had such wide application within Buddhism—the use of Sanskrit is generally associated more with the expanded, developed religion than its conservative canon. By convention, the teaching of the Buddha is apportioned into three categories: general preaching (*sūtra*), rules for monastic life (*vinaya*) and systematic doctrine (*abhidharma*). The mature corpus of Buddhist teaching additionally includes scripture that diverges from the conservative canon, i.e. the *śrāvakapiṭaka*, in its soteriological content and modes of expression. Much of this broader teaching affiliates itself to the Mahāyāna, generally understood as the "great vehicle" of soteriology, but which probably meant "great gnosis" in its incipient stages.[28] Mahāyāna scripture has a more visionary, experimental and yogic orientation than the teaching for the rote learners, the *śrāvakas*. It is characteristically concerned with the figure of the Buddha-to-be, the bodhisattva, whose defining practice is selfless altruism. Whereas the *śrāvakapiṭaka* caters above all to renunciants, and is redacted in various Indic dialects ranging from Prakrit to Sanskrit, the *bodhisattvapiṭaka* teaches

---

[26] See, e.g., Takakusu (1896), p. 8.

[27] The local ordinance *nikāyabhedaṃ vināpi gṛhītaniśrayāḥ* (Wickremasinghe 1912, p. 4) enforces nondenominationalism. Wickremasinghe takes *niśraya* to mean a novice, as in Pali Buddhism, but following Edgerton (1953) II, p. 307a, it may mean that "supplies received" are not split up among each sect.

[28] Early occurrences of the Sanskrit term *mahāyāna* are forced disambiguations of the polysemic Prakrit word *mahājāna*, which can also mean *mahājñāna* ("great gnosis"), according to Karashima (2015).

an aspirational Buddhism that is more amenable to non-monks, and ended up being propagated mainly in the Sanskrit language.

Early Buddhist adopters of Sanskrit were also proponents of the Mahāyāna. The imagery of the Mahāyāna, certainly, appears alongside the first Sanskritic Buddhist inscriptions, found at Mathurā.[29] Nonetheless, the ideology of the Mahāyāna may not be inherently related to the Buddhists' acceptance of Sanskritic discourse. The earliest manuscript witnesses for the Mahāyānasūtras and Buddhist *mantrapada*—a parallel development—are written in vernaculars such as Gāndhārī, and in non-Brahmic writing systems.[30] From the start, there was a Prakritic Mahāyāna, although its primary sources and all memory of them[31] were lost and have only recently been rediscovered in the old region of Gandhara. In time, at least one order or faction is said to have accepted both a Prakritic *śrāvakapiṭaka* and a Mahāyāna scriptural collection—probably including tantras—in Sanskrit.[32] Still, the Mahāyānasūtras' use of highly language-specific discourse, such as versified teaching (*gāthā*), etymological explanations (*nirukti*), mnemonics (*dhāraṇī*) and so on, definitely knows of, encourages and entrenches Sanskritic norms.

Just as the canon was expanded in tandem with the adoption of Sanskrit, so too was the scope of Buddhist interpretive culture. The essentialization of the teaching in fixed lists of scripture and doctrinal categories—fundamental to the conception of vernacular *śrāvakapiṭaka*s and the Abhidharma

[29] A statue of the Mahāyānic Buddha Amitābha, unearthed near Mathurā, was inscribed in Sanskrit in the 26th regnal year of Huviṣka, reckoned to be 104 CE (Tsukamoto 1996, p. 666, Math 791). See also Skinner (2017), pp. 105–6.

[30] On the now "proven hypothesis" that certain "Early Mahāyāna scriptures were originally in Prakrit not in Sanskrit", see Karashima (2015), pp. 113–14. The earliest document of *buddhavacana* magic is written in Kharoṣṭhī script (Strauch 2014).

[31] In the aforementioned *Vimalaprabhā*, it is said, evidently without knowledge of Gandharan origins, that the (Mahāyāna) Sūtrānta was put into writing (*pustake likhitam*) in Sanskrit (*saṃskṛtabhāṣayā*); cf. ed. Upadhyaya (1986), p. 41_{16}.

[32] Karashima (2018), p. 188, refers to Xuanzang's 玄奘 brief notice of the *Mahāyāna-Sthaviravāda at Abhayagiri in Sri Lanka, 646 CE (cf. Taishō Tripiṭaka No. 2087, p. $934a_{14–18}$). The deliberate acceptance of Mahāyāna or tantric scripture by a Sthavira order, as documented by Xuanzang, would, however, have to be differentiated from "Tantric Theravāda," which McGovern 2017 uses to describe the presence of elements resembling tantric Buddhism (if not tantric Hinduism) among Theravādin Buddhists in Thailand and Cambodia.

interpretations associated with them—is deprecated by the *Prajñāpāramitās* and Nāgārjuna. For Nāgārjuna, who writes in Sanskrit at an early stage of its adoption in Buddhism,[33] the teaching of the Buddha is defined not by an essence but the lack of it, and in this regard, it is synonymous with emptiness (*śūnyatā*). Nāgārjuna thereby abstracts Buddhist teaching in a way that transcends the hard-coded and divisive internal doxography of the language-bound conservative canons. What Nāgārjuna is understood to have been arguing for in his Madhyamaka interpretative project is, likewise, the canonization of (Sanskrit) Mahāyānasūtras that teach an inessentialist worldview.[34] At the same time, the identification of *buddhavacana* with the *dharma* of emptiness turns out to have provided the most lasting point of distinction from Brahmanism and other religions that used Sanskrit.[35] Similarly, the complementary interpretive position, that the reality taught by the Buddha reduces to "nothing but consciousness" (*vijñaptimātra*)—that is, the position of the Yogācāra, the "yoga practitioner"—is set out only in Sanskrit and without especial reliance on the conservative canon.

The doctrinal content of Sanskritic Buddhism is then inclusive of the Mahāyāna by default, since talking with authority about the Buddha's word in Sanskrit entails some knowledge of Madhyamaka and Yogācāra schools of thought, not only the Abhidharma. As the *śrāvakapiṭaka* and *bodhisattvapiṭaka* of Sanskritic Buddhism share a common language, the Sanskrit-speaking community as a whole could hardly claim to be unaware of the Mahāyānasūtras. Accordingly, the conservative canon is not in any practical sense "mainstream"[36] in the developed Sanskritic tradition, if "mainstream" means having prime authority for everyone. Rather, the Bodhisattvayāna is routinely distinguished from and given higher value than

[33] The dating of Nāgārjuna is discussed by Mabbett (1998), in part with reference to a Prakrit inscription at Amarāvatī purportedly engraved in about 100 CE (Tsukamoto 1996, p. 248, Amar 70).

[34] Walser (1997), p. 26, is among the few scholars to understand the Madhyamaka as concerned primarily with conservative Buddhism, aiming to "reopen the quasi-closure of the canon which was the practice of the mainstream Śrāvakayānists". On the "emptiness of dharmas" as characteristic of early Mahāyānasūtras, see, e.g., Bronkhorst (2013).

[35] Sferra (2001), p. 74.

[36] Harrison and Hartmann (2014), p. xii, contend that the vast Sanskrit Buddhist corpus of Nepal (on which see note 124 below) is not "mainstream".

the Śrāvakayāna and Pratyekabuddhayāna[37] in the soteriological triad, the *yānatraya*.[38] The chief interpreters of Sanskritic Buddhism made much of *śrāvaka* scripture obsolete. They wrote epitomes of doctrine that substituted for its scriptural sources, in the case of the Abhidharma and Abhivinaya genres, or they bypassed scripture altogether in Madhyamaka–Yogācāra theoretical discussions. To use Sanskrit in the developed tradition is then to admit at least an awareness of ideas and beliefs that exist outside the sectarian *tripiṭaka*.

The Technical and Literary Discourses (*Śāstra* and *Kāvya*)

By taking up Sanskrit, Buddhists gained access to *śāstra* and *kāvya*, the technical and literary discourses of the Sanskritic world.[39] These two types of discourse rest on religious revelation, but they are also capable of self-contained functioning, and in this sense, they can express secular and universalist qualities. Sanskrit was the preferred medium of expression in fields that were not intrinsically religious, since many of them had developed as ancillaries to Vedic studies (*vedāṅga*): grammar, etymology, phonology, prosody, ritual and astronomy.[40] It was common to describe learned Brahmins as "versed in the Vedas and the Vedic ancillaries", not just one or the other.[41] In order to be erudite in worldly settings, Sanskrit often had to be used, owing to the combined gravitas of the Sanskrit knowledge systems and their pre-existing religious foundations. Of course, the theoretical writings produced in the Prakrits are heavily indebted to Sanskritic conventions,[42] yet they have rarely carried the same weight as Sanskrit treatises in the wider scholarly arena.

---

[37] Karashima (2015), pp. 181, 185–90.

[38] The three *yāna*s are usually enumerated as Śrāvaka-, Pratyekabuddha- and Mahāyāna (e.g., *Bodhisattvabhūmi* 18, ed. Dutt 1978, pp. 1999–11). Tantric Buddhism ("Vajrayāna") can be subsumed under Mahāyāna.

[39] Pollock (2006), p. 3, characterizes the two genres as a "dichotomy", whereas Lienhard (1984), pp. 2–3, sees them as two ends of a continuum.

[40] *vede vyākaraṇe nirukte śikṣāyāṃ chandasvinyāṃ yajñakalpe jyotiṣe* (*Lalitavistara* 12.33+, ed. Hokazono 1994, p. 592_{10}). The names and sequential order of the *vedāṅga*s vary across various sources.

[41] *dvijānām ālayo ramyo vedavedāṅgavedinā* is a typical expression, used in the present case as late as the early tenth century, i.e. Rājyapāladeva regnal year 28 (Tsukamoto 1996 p. 187, Kurk 52_{1-2}; cf. Prasad 2014, p. 129).

[42] For instance, regarding the reliance of Pali grammars on their Sanskrit forerunners, see Scharfe (1977), pp. 194–95.

The format and specialist language of *śāstra* have made it possible, and desirable, to speak about the teaching of the Buddha in relatively abstract terms and among people who were not receptive to this teaching being presented in sectarian, vernacular packages. Nāgārjuna, again, provides an ideal example: he treats the whole teaching of the Buddha and none of it in particular in his *Mūlamādhyamikakārikā*s, without having quoted a single line of *āgama*. Using *śāstra* norms, Nāgārjuna's foundational work is also able address topics of "philosophy" in general, such as existence, causation and motion. One consequence of the shift towards a common idiom is that non-Buddhist theorists ended up having to address the Madhyamaka and Yogācāra in their own universalist ("six-system," *ṣaḍdarśana*[43]) doxographies.

Followers of the path of the bodhisattva were expected to learn not only the in-house "spirituality" (*adhyātmavidyā*) rooted in a particular canon[44] but also the technical skills for carrying them into the wider world. To this end, the education of the bodhisattva also includes the trivia of logic, language and medicine (*hetu-*, *śabda-*, *cikitsā-vidyā*), as well as craftsmanship—altogether five fields of knowledge (*pañca vidyā*).[45] The study of language, and of Sanskrit in particular, was in this way undertaken for the advancement of self and others, but also for engaging in public contests for prestige. It helped the student "to speak the truth, or at least to cause others to believe so", and to "defeat the allodox", as Vincent Eltschinger has explained.[46] On the whole, it was more profitable for Buddhists to respond to the "language of the gods" with critique and appropriation than to simply ignore it. Buddhist linguistic analyses sidestepped the customary Brahmanical authority over the language, and omitted aspects of the language particular to the Vedas—a controversial move.[47] They have helped pave the way for Sanskrit to be studied with

---

[43] Pahlajrai (2004).

[44] Eltschinger (2017), p. 322, n. 54, notes that *adhyātmavidyā* is said to be synonymous with *buddhavacana.*

[45] *adhyātmavidyā hetuvidyā śabdavidyā vyādhicikitsāvidyā śilpakarmasthānavidyā ca | itīmāni pañca vidyāsthānāni yāni bodhisattvaḥ paryeṣate* (*Bodhisattvabhūmi* 8, ed. Dutt 1978, p. $68_{7\text{–}9}$, trans. Engle 2016, p. 174). See also Eltschinger (2017), p. 322.

[46] Eltschinger (2017), p. 319.

[47] The Buddhist grammarian Puruṣottamadeva's omission of Pāṇini's rules relating to the Vedas was, for instance, called "sacrilege" by Chakravarti (1918), p. 7. Another scholar, Abhyankar (1961), p. 272, explains this omission with reference to a (doubtful) legend that Puruṣottamadeva's sponsor "was not qualified to understand Vedic Language". See also Pollock (2006), p. 62.

fewer of its customary socio-religious trappings and to be made more fit for multireligious or nonreligious uses.

That Buddhist *śāstrin*s were part of a universalist enterprise is evident in the fact that their works were used by many non-Buddhists, and in the persistence of these works long after the devastation of the religion itself. In general, the religious underpinnings of certain technical treatises were often imperceptible to readers of other religions, and these were often also the most widely circulated treatises. A portion of the Sanskrit medical literature seems to have been written by people familiar with Buddhism, but much of this literature is hard to locate in a particular religious milieu.[48] The Buddhist orientation of a *śāstra* could be slight enough for scribes to change it easily to suit their own religious leanings.[49] Treatises of more obviously Buddhist affiliation could also be made acceptable to the broad *śāstra* readership by applying strategies of interpretation. The *Amarakośa*, the widely used Sanskrit dictionary, gives synonyms for the Buddha in its opening section, and there are indications that it originated in a Buddhist environment;[50] however, the commentarial literature varies greatly in how far it acknowledges the Buddhist character of the text, if at all.[51]

While the religious orientation of a "secular" Sanskrit treatise is in many cases incidental to the content, in some *śāstra* genres it is integral and unalterable. Inessentialism is a major theoretical concern in the literature on epistemology (*pramāṇa*), for instance. Similarly, the discourses surrounding the tantras are animated by exchanges between Hinduism and Buddhism, which often take place without acknowledgement of origin. Tantric masters concern themselves with *yoga*, the *guru*, the bodily *cakra*s and other terms of praxis shared across religious boundaries (and also now current in English), stressing their universality. Sanskritic thought in this way develops a continuum of expression related to ontology and consciousness, articulated with reference to universalist ideas, in which

---

[48] This subject is yet to be studied comprehensively. On the Buddhist content of Vāgbhaṭa's *aṣṭāṅgika* medical treatises, see most recently Klebanov (2010), pp. 43–50.

[49] For instance, one copy of Subhūticandra's *Subantaratnākara* has omitted the explicitly Buddhist opening verse (referring to *śākyo muniḥ*), which commentaries discuss. For the text of the verse, see Deokar (2017), pp. 667ff (though the significance of its absence from some witnesses is not remarked upon).

[50] Braarvig et al. (2018), p. 313.

[51] Deokar (2012), pp. 133–34.

the sectarian origins of these ideas can be contested or obscured in order to claim a higher reality.[52] Nonetheless, in some fields the traces left by Buddhism are ineradicable,[53] as in the theories of the Pratyabhijñā and other streams of Śaivism.[54] Such deep impacts on the thinking of the other are universalist effects, which could probably only have been created by using a common learned language. The Madhyamaka and Yogācāra were still being discussed in Sanskrit by Indian pundits centuries after the Buddha's word and its proponents had disappeared from view—as late as the early colonial era, in one case.[55] The primary legacy of Buddhist thought in its homeland is therefore an ideology expressed in Sanskritic and abstract terms—not a *buddhavacana* canon, nor a sect-marked "religion" as such.

The epic literary artform, the *kāvya*, is another fixture of non- or semi-religious culture expressed primarily in Sanskrit. In contrast with *śāstra*, which tends towards the dry and scientific, *kāvya* embodies sensuality and celebrity—so much so that Buddhist teaching that sounded like it was initially dismissed as spurious.[56] However, *kāvya*'s special aesthetic appeal eventually complemented and amplified the plain-spoken messaging of the Buddha. The ornate, mannered style was the preferred literary mode for epigraphs, dance-dramas, and so on, which in turn affected the common culture of devotion. Certain themes and literary forms originating in the Sanskrit epic were taken into Mahāyāna scripture, as for example in the

---

[52] Sferra (2001), pp. 69ff, gives several examples of tantrists who quote the "other side" without attribution in support of their own agenda.

[53] For instance, Hindu commentators had to explain the presence of the Buddha Akṣobhya on the crown of the Hinduized Tārā (i.e., her *mahāvidyā* incarnation); see Bühnemann (1996), p. 475.

[54] Regarding Pratyabhijñā responses to Buddhism, see Torella (2013) and Nemec (2017), among others. Much remains to be done on Śaiva borrowings from Buddhism. Uses of the characteristically Buddhist terms *śūnyatā* and *nirvāṇa* in the Vīraśaiva context are noticed in brief by Nandimath (1942), pp. 108–9, 172–73.

[55] The Madhyamaka, Yogācāra and Sautrāntika are discussed in a Mīmāṃsā treatise written for Mānaveda, king of Kozhikode, Kerala (r. 1655–58), namely Nārāyaṇa Paṇḍita's half of the *Mānameyodaya* (ed. & trans. Raja & Sastri 1975, pp. 302–10); see also Verpoorten (1987), p. 49.

[56] Karashima (2015), pp. 115, 134–35 n. 64, in this regard highlights critical passages of the *Saddharmapuṇḍarīka* (presumably vv. 12.7–8) and *Aṣṭasāhasrikā Prajñāpāramitā*. On *kīrti*, *prīti*, etc. as goals of *kāvya* writers, see Lienhard (1984), p. 4.

Laṅkāvatāra and the *Lalitavistara*.[57] Buddhists also composed exemplary specimens of *kāvya* proper, such as Āryaśūra's *Jātakamālā* and Aśvaghoṣa's *Buddhacarita*. These and other kavified, Sanskritic reworkings of tales of the Buddha's past lives—the birth story (*jātaka*) and karmic adventure (*avadāna*)—became popular enough to overshadow their canonical sources.[58] They also had some success as "missionary" works, though their effect on the wider literary world was indirect, for the most part.[59] Again, Buddhists not only worked within a multireligious medium, but managed to contribute to shaping it. Aśvaghoṣa is regarded as a pioneer of the *mahākāvya*, while the genre of *campū*, which alternates between prose and verse, is regarded as a Buddhist innovation.[60]

The universality of *kāvya*, like that of *śāstra*, lies in its capacity for compelling acceptance and exerting authority without committing—at the level of form, rather than content—to a particular religious standpoint. In the Sanskrit epic it is at least possible to find non-Buddhists presenting Buddhism in a neutral if not positive light, and vice versa. Anthologies of "well-said" verse (*subhāṣita*) bring together poets with a variety of religious sympathies, and at the same time make some of their sympathies explicit.[61] A few *subhāṣita* authors have been identified as "Buddhist–Śaiva" in the secondary literature.[62] This designation has no formal religious counterpart; it conveys a receptiveness to the plurality of high Sanskritic civilization, as personified in the Hindu-Buddhist ruler.

Insofar as *śāstra–kāvya* expresses transcendent qualities in a language-bound manner, its universalist flavour is not necessarily replicated when its conventions are transposed into another language. Practitioners of Prakritic

[57] See, He (2011) and Guruge (2003), respectively.

[58] Tubb (2014), p. 76. The elevation of *kāvya* and like texts such as the *Lalitavistara* into the mini-canon (i.e., for tantric "beginners", *ādikarmika*) is discussed in Sinclair (2016), pp. 92ff.

[59] For instance, nearly all of the external citations of Aśvaghoṣa noted by Bhattacharya (1976), pp. 30–31, 42–46 are made by authors who are either Buddhist or who seem to be unaware of the religious identity of their source.

[60] Hahn (2010), p. 466.

[61] At least seventeen poets in the major *subhāṣita* anthologies have the title *bhadanta* (Sternbach 1980, pp. 119–20), which generally means (Buddhist) mendicant.

[62] Sternbach 1978, pp. 26, 441 and 1980, pp. 194, 399, 533, 575, identifies certain *subhāṣita* poets as "Buddhist–Śaiva", but does not define this label (or the label "Śaiva–Vaiṣṇava").

Buddhism who accepted canonical teaching in the vernacular, and who in many cases are known to have written in the vernaculars, have had to turn to Sanskrit in order to speak in an especially prestigious literary register.[63]

Ultimately, the adoption of poetic *kāvya* and prosaic *śāstra* has conveyed the Buddhist worldview into the civic arena to a much greater degree than would have been possible by remaining confined to canons of scripture that had no currency outside their own dialect. Sanskrit's cachet extends into social and religious culture alike, which the shapeshifting (*kāmarūpin*) bodhisattva Avalokiteśvara, in a seventh-century revealed text, claims to pervade:

> I will be involved with buying, selling, speaking [and] conversing among the great masses. I am involved with grammar, logic, *sūtra*s, dance-drama, song, [and] orchestral music related to *śāstra*, *kāvya*, [and] Vedic mantra amid the public sphere. I will create oral teaching on the path, on [monastic] discipline, Mahāyāna, [and] Abhidharma in the discourse on awakening. For Brahmins I teach the Purāṇas, the Vedas, fire sacrifice, the [*Mahā*]*bhārata*, the *Rāmāyaṇa*. By speaking mantra I create oral teaching on mantra muttering, maṇḍalas, hand gestures, rituals, *dhāraṇī* muttering, the fire rituals [of] pacification, enriching, exorcism and so on.[64]

This passage specifies much of the universalist substance that differentiates Sanskritic Buddhism from its Prakritic counterpart. Not only do the languages of Prakritic Buddhism lack the currency of Sanskrit in the worldly domain, they are unable to challenge Hinduism on its own terms.

---

[63] For instance, Ratnaśrījñāna (fl. 944–52, according to Dimitrov 2016), who wrote in Pali and Sinhala, also wrote extensively in Sanskrit, including works on grammar and poetics (*alaṃkāraśāstra*).

[64] *mahājanamadhye krayavikraya-ālāpasaṃlāpa saṃvyavahariṣyāmi | sabhāmadhye śāstrakāvyavedamantrayuktavyākaraṇasūtranāṭakagītigāndharvva[ṃ] saṃvyavaharāmi | bodhiprakaraṇe nayavinayamahāyānābhidharmopadeśaṃ*[†] *kariṣyāmi | brāhmaṇānāṃ purāṇavedāgnihotrabhāratarāmāyaṇam*[‡] *upadiśāmi | mantravādinā mantrajāpamaṇḍalamudrākalpadhāraṇījāpahomaśāntikāpauṣṭikābhicārukādīny upadeśaṃ*[§] *karomi*... (*Amoghapāśakalparāja* Laukikasādhanavidhi, ed. Otsuka 2004, p. 137); [†]ed. *-ādhidharmopadeśaṃ*; [‡]ed. *-rāmāyaṇopadiśāmi*; [§]ed. *-ābhicārukādīnyopadeśaṃ*, read: *-ābhicārukādīn'opadeśaṃ*. The parallel translations into Chinese (Taishō Tripiṭaka No. 1092, p. $290b_{27}$–c_8) and into Tibetan seem to be based on different recensions. This previously unstudied passage may counterpose the idea that Śiva is present in *śāstra*, on which see, e.g., Torella (2013), p. 471.

Although the Buddha is said to have preferred to speak in languages spoken widely in his lifetime, the canonical Prakrits such as Pali have since come to be spoken only by monks and only in connection with the conservative canon. Due to this acquired narrowness, no Prakritic tradition could be called, as Ananda W.P. Guruge (2009) does, "Universal Buddhism". The eventual spread of Pali Buddhism into the Southeast Asian mainland is not necessarily a reflection of its linguistic or doctrinal capabilities, just as mere internationalism is not in itself universalism.

The Geographic Extent of Sanskritic Buddhism

The Sanskritic tradition, viewed empirically, is the most widespread form of native Buddhism, extending far beyond the bounds of India and of any other single country or polity. The Buddhist religion and the Sanskrit language co-occur throughout an area that has its northernwestern limit in present-day upper Pakistan, reaches southwards to Sri Lanka and the Maldives,[65] and stretches in the east to the Sunda Shelf and the Philippines.[66] This macroregion has been given various names: Greater India, the East Indies, the Indianized States, the Indo-Pacific.[67] However, insofar as these toponyms imply the definite centrality of India, they obscure the outsized activity on the "periphery". Much of what belongs to Sanskritic Buddhism has been concentrated outside the present-day Republic of India in Kashmir, Bangladesh, Nepal, Sri Lanka and Southeast Asia. In such places, the cultural and linguistic norms of the superregion can be at least as strongly present as they are supposed to be in the "centre."

As the combination of Buddhism and Sanskrit has always been transnationally distributed, it may be more fruitful to identify its natural counterparts than to describe it with reference to a patchwork of nations. It can be assigned to a native habitat insofar as it corresponds to premodern

[65] Gippert 2013–14 studies a mantra of the ferocious Yamāntaka inscribed in coral in the Maldives. Another possible source for this mantra, besides the two nominated by Gippert (*Guhyasamāja* 14.8+ and the *Mañjuśrīmūlakalpa*), is *Māyājālamahātantra* 5 (Chinese trans. Taishō Tripiṭaka No. 890, p. 569a_{19}–b_{14}).

[66] Orlina 2012 discusses a Buddhist inscription in Sanskrit recovered from the Philippines, namely the Aparājitāhṛdaya of Mahāpratisarā (I thank Andrea Acri for this reference). In parts of Indonesia not on the Sunda Shelf, such as South Sulawesi, "high Indic culture [...] would appear absent" (Bulbeck 2000, p. 12).

[67] On these terms see Acri (2017b).

circulations of people, flora, fauna. The tropospheric winds that carried maritime traffic within Monsoon Asia[68] extend to the findspot of the westernmost Sanskritic Buddhist inscriptions at Socotra, near Yemen.[69] There is a still closer correlation with the Indomalayan bioregion,[70] the range of which—in one demarcation[71]—is similar to that of Sanskritic civilization as a whole (Figure 10.1). The diffusion of Sanskrit language proficiency, in particular, largely follows the spread of the Brahmin settlements up to the arc of the Himalayas and the Wallace Line.[72] However, rudimentary and formulaic Sanskrit usage, common in tantric Buddhism, is much more widely encountered, as will be explained below.

The overall prevalence of Sanskritic Buddhism can be gauged from the epigraphic record of Greater India. Inscriptions provide direct linguistic testimony that can be localized in place and time with confidence. Buddhist inscriptions occur in Sanskrit across a contiguous transnational field, which has only rarely, however, been treated as a contiguous area.[73] Inscriptional data relating to Buddhism have been aggregated for present-day India and Pakistan in surveys published by Keisho Tsukamoto in 1996 and 2003, respectively. In these surveys, India yielded 394 Sanskrit inscriptions and 194 in Hybrid Sanskrit; fewer inscriptions in the vernaculars were found.[74] Just six inscriptions in India have been classified as Pali, among which three repeat a stock phrase that is most likely not in the Pali language.[75]

While the extension of the epigraphic corpus to Greater India would increase the proportion of data in the Prakrits, especially in Pali, the

[68] Acri (2017a), pp. 3–9, describes the conceptual history of the Monsoon Asia region.

[69] Strauch and Bukharin (2004), pp. 133–34.

[70] The name "Indo-Malaya" was first associated with a bioregion by Wallace (1876).

[71] The closest correlation exists with the Oriental subset of Indomalaya, demarcated by removing its adjacent "transitional zones" (Kreft and Jetz 2013).

[72] Bronkhorst (2011), p. 265.

[73] The collection of "Inscriptions bearing on Indian History and Civilization" of Sircar (1983) is among the few to have included Nepalese and Southeast Asian epigraphs.

[74] These figures were not supplied in Tsukamoto (1996); they have been manually counted using the volume's index entries, ibid., pp. 1057–58.

[75] The three Bihar inscriptions of the *pratītyasamutpādagāthā* classified as Pali by Tsukamoto (1996), pp. 216–17, were most likely written in what is now called Saindhavī (Dimitrov 2016), being inscribed in the "house script" of the Sāṃmatīya order, Bhaikṣukī (Hanisch 2008, pp. 198–99).

FIGURE 10.1
Approximate Premodern Distribution of Sanskritic (Yellow) and Semi-Sanskritic (Blue) Buddhist Epigraphs in Asia, Overlaid on the Oriental Bioregion of Indomalaya (Green)

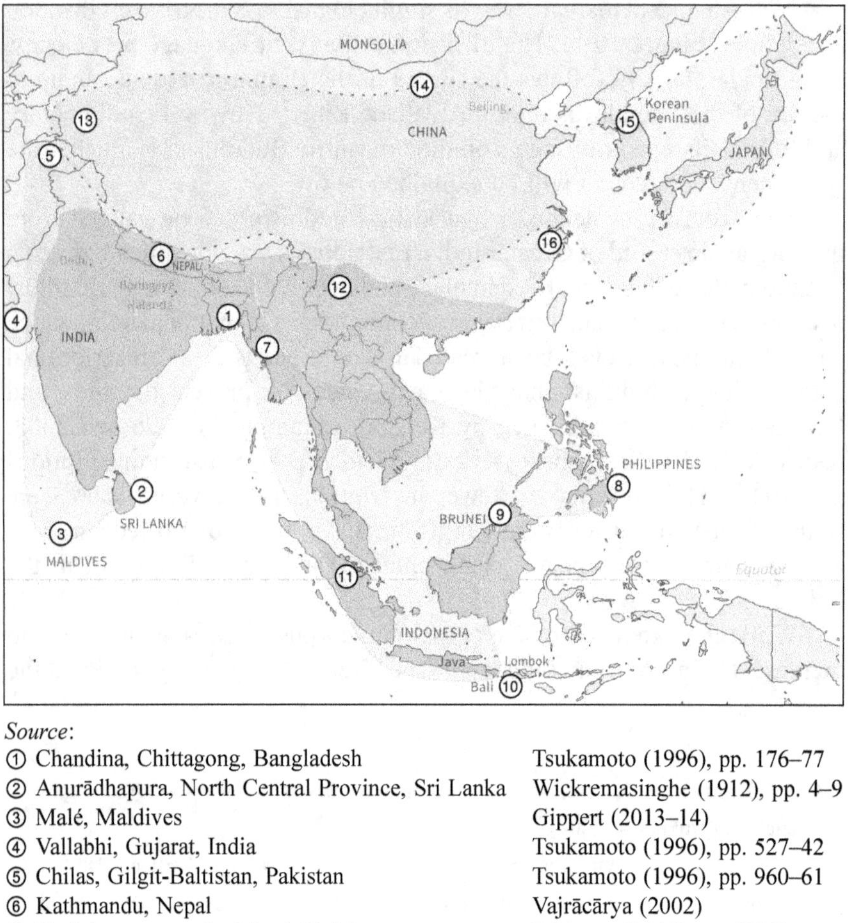

Source:

① Chandina, Chittagong, Bangladesh	Tsukamoto (1996), pp. 176–77
② Anurādhapura, North Central Province, Sri Lanka	Wickremasinghe (1912), pp. 4–9
③ Malé, Maldives	Gippert (2013–14)
④ Vallabhi, Gujarat, India	Tsukamoto (1996), pp. 527–42
⑤ Chilas, Gilgit-Baltistan, Pakistan	Tsukamoto (1996), pp. 960–61
⑥ Kathmandu, Nepal	Vajrācārya (2002)
⑦ Shai-thaung pagoda, Mrauk U, Myanmar	Johnston (1944), pp. 359ff
⑧ Esperanza, Mindanao, Philippines	Orlina (2012), p. 94
⑨ Makam Dagang, Bandar Seri Begawan, Brunei	Skilling (2015), pp. 38–39
⑩ Pejeng, Bali, Indonesia	Warshall (2012), pp. 48ff
⑪ Pagaruyung, Sumatra, Indonesia	Kern (1917)
⑫ Dali, Yunnan, China	Liebenthal (1947), p. 5
⑬ Mnga' ris, Tibet Autonomous Region, China	Liao (2016), p. 5
⑭ Arjai Caves, Ordos, Inner Mongolia, China	Editorial Board et al. (2010)
⑮ Yeonbok Bell, Kaesong Namdaemun, North Korea	Yuyama (1985)
⑯ Feilai Feng, Hangzhou, China	Ye (2014)

Pali inscriptions are concentrated in just a small fraction of this region, most of which became Theravāda majority areas after than the medieval period. The Sanskritic Buddhist epigraphic corpus outside India and Pakistan, in places such as Nepal, is yet to be inventoried and studied in a transnational context.[76] Furthermore, Tsukamoto's survey of Sanskrit inscriptional material in India was not comprehensive. It can be asked whether the corpus should have included Hindu-Buddhist epigraphs that refer to Buddhism from the perspectives of outsiders, which provide a more rounded picture of the religion.[77] To summarize: Buddhism-related inscriptions occur predominantly in Sanskrit throughout the Greater Indian region, though their distribution is not temporally or geographically uniform. Wherever precolonial epigraphs in Pali are found, Sanskrit epigraphs are almost always found in the same general area, but the reverse is not true. Throughout the whole of the Sanskrit *sprachraum*, canonical Prakrits such as Pali are attested only sparsely.[78]

Buddhist Sanskrit epigraphs in Sanskrit also occur in East and Central Asia, far outside the Indo-Aryan language space. Here Sanskrit is used in superficial and stereotyped ways, due to the lack of native Indic language competence. This semi-Sanskritic variety of Buddhism is represented by traditions that use mantras in the regular religion and as such have an ongoing need to produce Sanskrit sounds and letterforms. Most of these traditions have Chinese or Tibetan as their language of scripture, and convey mantras as phonetic transcriptions in their native writing systems. In all language environments it was understood that mantras have to be spoken in their original pronunciation, as far as possible, in order to be effective.[79] Although the recitation of phrases hardcoded in Sanskrit (e.g.,

[76] A total of 270 Nepalese inscriptions earlier than the fourteenth century, most in Sanskrit, are inventoried by Dhanavajra Vajrācārya (2002, 2011).

[77] A few non-Buddhist inscriptions were already included in the survey, e.g., Tsukamoto (1996), p. 149, BoGa 32. An example of a Buddhism-related inscription of non-Buddhist origin not referenced by Tsukamoto is the Śravaṇa Beḷagoḷa inscription of 1129 CE, which recalls the debate won by the Jain "pious saint Akalaṅka, by whom […] Târâ […] was overcome together with the Bauddhas" (*tārā yena vinirjjitā* […] *baudhdhaiyyo* […] *devākaḷaṃkaḥ* [*sic*]; ed. and trans. Hultzsch (1895), pp. 148–51, 200.

[78] The few inscriptions in Pali from the classical period are confined mainly to present-day Sri Lanka and Myanmar, while nearly all of those occuring elsewhere, in Cambodia and Thailand, are of post-fourteenth century vintage. The general priority of Sanskrit in the region is stressed by Lammerts and Griffiths (2015).

[79] Bahulkar and Deokar (2012), p. 48; Eltschinger (2017), p. 321.

dhāraṇī) is optional within the Mahāyāna as a whole, it is mandatory wherever tantric lineages are transmitted, as tantric processes generally involve the speaking of mantras. Consequently, the Sanskrit language has diffused well into the north and east of Asia along with the spread of tantric Buddhism. The language continues to be encountered—albeit in only monosyllabic form in many cases—across Sinophone territory and the Tibetan and Mongolian Plateaus. In some areas, such as Yunnan and the Korean Peninsula,[80] Sanskrit writing has ceased to be an integral part of religious practice, but it is still being produced in much of the rest of this extended region.

The universality of the combination of Sanskrit and Buddhism is then evident in the scale of its pan-Asian diffusion. It permeates not only the Indosphere—defined as the set of languages in or in contact with the Indo-Aryan language family—but also, to a lesser degree, the Sinosphere. The dispersal of Sanskritic Buddhism has not been confined to the vicinity of Brahmin "native speakers"; its memes do not just follow genes, to express the situation in Dennettian terms.[81] They have jumped major boundaries of biogeography, spanning three or more linguistic crossroads or *sprachbünde*.[82] These are grounds for appraising Sanskritic Buddhism as a major cultural undercurrent in Asia and the world. Its premodern extent is currently inhabited by over half of the world's population.[83] Nonetheless, the number of people who practise Buddhism in its Sanskritic mode is now relatively low.

[80] Yunnan has an extensive corpus of premodern Sanskrit writing (see, e.g., Liebenthal 1947), which does not seem to be propagated in the (semi-Sanskritic) local religions, though little information is available; see, e.g., Li (2009). Temple bells cast with Sanskrit mantras (*beomja*) are extant across the Korean Peninsula, of which the Yeonbok Bell, Kaesong Namdaemun, North Korea, cast in 1346 (Yuyama 1985), is among the earliest.

[81] Whether or not the spread of Sanskritic Buddhism can be considered "mimesis", in the sense of memetic transmission described by Dennett (2017), it does not appear to be strongly correlated with a single genetic flow.

[82] The areal-linguistic demarcation of South Asia, Mainland Southeast Asia and Northeast Asia as *sprachbünde* depends on how a linguistic area or league is defined, on which see, e.g., Urban (2007).

[83] The current estimated combined population of Eastern Asia, Southern Asia and Southeastern Asia (excluding countries where Sanskrit is not traditionally used, such as Timor-Leste) is 4,192,688,926 out of the world total of 7,632,819,325 persons, i.e., 54.9 per cent (United Nations Population Division data, 2017, https://esa.un.org/).

THE LIVING TRADITIONS OF SANSKRITIC BUDDHISM

An indicator of universality is persistence over time, as demonstrated in the ability to withstand dynastic change, war, natural disasters, and major intellectual and social shifts. The fact that Buddhism practised in the Sanskrit language has persisted in living traditions for almost two millennia is a measure of its staying power, and the contents of living traditions, likewise, provide the most vital foil for the historical record. By examining the Sanskritic Buddhism of the present along with that of the past, its unitary character can be seen more clearly, and its corpus analysed from a long-term perspective. The living traditions keep up key universalist properties of the premodern religion. They coexist in a common social and discursive space articulated in Sanskrit; their scriptural corpus is broader than the conservative canon; and they manifest diglossia, with Sanskrit as the formal language and local languages being used for informal, everyday communication.

The common factor in the classical and the living traditions is the use of Sanskrit together with Buddhist self-identification. In other respects, the various contemporary Sanskritic Buddhisms share a few of their predecessors' particulars. Today there are no institutions of lifelong celibate monasticism—the driving concern of the *śrāvakapiṭaka*. There is no enthusiasm for intricate interpretive projects of the sort that academic bystanders in the West deem to be important. Doctrinal disputes are rare, and almost all ground on social issues is ceded to Hinduism or to whatever modality prevails in the sociopolitical sphere. Competence in Sanskrit is not regarded as necessary for the routine practice of the religion, and many aspects of religious behaviour, even quite crucial ones, are not codified. In short, contemporary Sanskritic Buddhism does not look much like what it might be expected it to look like, if expectations are formed solely on the basis of the limited antiquarian data.

Certainly, the living Sanskritic traditions tend to be overlooked in universalist presentations of Buddhism created by modern observers. The religion of the Sanskrit texts is treated as a museum piece. The belief that Buddhism disappeared from its Indian homeland for good back in the thirteenth century (the ostensible date of disappearance is yet to be agreed upon[84]) exerts a powerful hold on the Western imagination. It suits

[84] The last Buddhist epigraph of classical India is dated 1308 CE (Tsukamoto 1996, p. 147, is BoGa 30). The question of how much Buddhism survived beyond this date is discussed by McKeown (2010). On the Mahāsāṃghika monks of India who resided at Thamel, Nepal up to 1499, see Sinclair (2016), p. 166. A state-supported monastery in Baghelkhand is mentioned in a letter sent to Tibet as late as 1601 (Templeman 2008, pp. 218–21).

both colonial and postcolonial prerogatives for the Sanskritic tradition of Buddhism to be "safely idealised by virtue of its distance in time", and to exist chiefly "in a state of non-existence", as David Templeman has put it.[85] As a step towards forming a more realistic picture, the living traditions will be introduced here with a view to identifying their common Sanskritic properties.

Remnant Buddhists of East India and Bangladesh

Small enclaves of self-identified Buddhists, which had apparently survived from the precolonial era and had no known connection with either the Pali or Tibetan traditions, re-emerged in the late nineteenth century in British Indian census data.[86] These enclaves are scattered across the eastern fringes of the subcontinent, and their populations have been consistently identified as Buddhist over decades of census taking. Insofar as they have survived as a distinct religion, the question arises as to how this religion has been differentiated from the broad category of Hinduism, if not through some verbal or textual representation of their beliefs. Where Sanskrit continues to be used, a degree of continuity or discontinuity with the preexisting tradition is discernible; where it has fallen out of use, prior links with Sanskritic civilization have been obscured. Various non-Brahmanical Bengali cults carried on solely in the vernacular are yet to yield any definite indications of Buddhist origin.[87]

The Chakmas, the easternmost indigenous Buddhists of the subcontinent,[88] have preserved just a few traces of their Sanskritic tradition. Formerly concentrated in the Chittagong Hill Tracts, over the past century the Chakmas have spread throughout Bangladesh and a wider diaspora after undergoing a nineteenth-century conversion to the Theravāda, which was led

[85] Templeman (2008), p. 26.

[86] Gait (1902); Tallents (1923); Porter (1933).

[87] The "modern" and "revival" "Buddhisms" of East India, so called by Shastri (1897), Vasu (1911) et al., have not been found to contain any definitely Buddhist content and are in effect an indistinguishable part of ambient Hinduism. On the non-Buddhist character of the Bengali cult of Dharma Ṭhākur, see Sen (1945).

[88] The Chakmas are distinct from the other major Buddhist population of the region (apparently Theravādin from the start), the Baruas; see Chaudhuri (1982), pp. 45–57. The Chakmas' demonym is said to be both Sanskritic and Buddhist; an etymology given (without sources) by Bhikkhu (2010), pp. 275–76, derives it from **śākya-ma*[*nuṣya*].

by missionaries from neighbouring Arakan.[89] Artefacts of the preconversion religion include statues of bodhisattvas such as Khasarpaṇa, Mañjuśrī and Tārā stored in converted monasteries in Chittagong and inscribed with Sanskrit donative formulas. The latest of these inscriptions is dated 1386,[90] though the local Sanskritic tradition doubtless continued well past this date.[91] A worship culture associated with images such as these is said to have survived into the twentieth century, and to have included "tantric" practice.[92] With the loss of their Sanskritic religion, the Chakmas have also lost a means for maintaining their traditional religious identity within an accepted regional idiom. While current practices of *pūjā*, *saṃskāra* and so on of Bangladeshi Theravādins mimic the common Indic devotional culture in Sanskrit,[93] they are at the same time kept firmly apart from it by their use of the Pali language.

One Sanskritic Buddhist community persists in India itself among the Saraks of the Cuttack district of Odisha, today numbering perhaps a few thousand people.[94] Traditionally the Saraks have been handloom weavers (*tānti*) by trade, though their demonym, cognate with the word *śrāvaka*, points to a professional religious identity. They are distinct from other remnant quasi- and crypto-Buddhist populations of Odisha, about whom less is known.[95] The Saraks claim to be the descendants of monks brought from Bengal to officiate at the Jagannātha temple at Puri, and to

---

[89] From Lianchhinga (1996), p. 83, it seems that the process was somewhat coercive.

[90] Law (1932), p. 334, adds that "they are productions of local artists", not imports.

[91] Late Chakma (Tibetan *lcag ma*) monks such as Śāriputra and Vanaratna are discussed by McKeown (2010), pp. 188, 411ff.

[92] The attenuated Buddhist tantrism in the Chittagong area is discussed in Dge 'dun chos 'phel's *Gtam rgyud gser gyi thang ma* (tr. Jinpa and Lopez 2014, pp. 412–13), completed in 1939.

[93] In Bangladesh, Theravādin Buddhist offerings of flowers, food, oil lamps and so on are accompanied by statements in verse using expressions such as *pūjayāmi* (Barua 2001, pp. 17, 19), which, though allowable in the Prakritic Śrāvakayāna, are more appropriate in Mahāyāna and Sanskritic religiosity. On the use of Pali in Bangladeshi Barua wedding and funeral *saṃskāra*s, see Barua (2002, 2003).

[94] Barik (2012) reports some current population figures.

[95] Vasu (1911), pp. 15ff, for instance, discusses the Bāthuri a.k.a. Bathudi, now a scheduled tribe, and others. The Rangani, a "service caste" of dyers associated with the Saraks, "claim Buddhist origins" but have adopted Vaiṣṇavism and now "are classified as Hindus" (Dash 2002, pp. 40, 43).

have been later removed from this position.[96] They currently have a role at the temple as makers of its ceremonial cloths.[97] They otherwise follow no canon of scripture or institutional religion. Instead, the Sanskritic tradition of the Saraks is articulated for the most part[98] in ritual, which characteristically does not involve Brahmin priests, and begins by uttering the creed "non-harm is the highest religion" (**ahiṃsā paramo dharmaḥ*[99]). The essentialization of the religion as harmlessness or nonviolence—a tenet more emblematic of Jainism[100]—is unusual in Sanskrit Buddhist works, though some precedent for it exists.[101] The primary source for the Saraks' ritual is the *Śiśuveda*, a short collection of utterances of local origin, which includes Sanskrit verses. No *buddhavacana* has been identified in the *Śiśuveda* so far.[102] It also admits Brahmanism[103] to a degree seen rarely if at all in pan-Asian Buddhist works. Nonetheless, the orientation of the *Śiśuveda* is made clear in its various praises to the Buddha and his manifestation as the famous icon Jagannātha:

> Homage, homage to the resident of Nīlācala [Puri], who is Buddhist by nature.[104]

---

[96] The banishment is said to have occurred either in the late twelfth century or in 1518. There may have been more than one such incident (Dash 2002, pp. 16, 37).

[97] Hacker (2004), p. 115.

[98] For instance, the salutation *namo buddhāya* is written over the doors of some Sarak houses, as seen in photographs in a recent report (Misra 2017).

[99] Gait (1902), pp. 429–30 and Dash (2002), pp. 31–35, give the form *paramadharma*.

[100] While nonviolence is of course central in Buddhist ethics, *ahiṃsā paramo dharmaḥ* is "an often-heard slogan among the Jainas" (Zydenbos 1999, p. 184).

[101] Vāgīśvarakīrti's Buddhist *Mṛtyuvañcanopadeśa* 3.11ab (ed. Schneider 2010, p. 144) asserts that this creed "agrees with all systems of thought" (*sarvasiddhāntasaṃmataḥ*). The phrase also occurs in the non-tantric but most likely late *Dvāviṃśatyavadāna* 8.68a (ed. Okada 1993, p. 79).

[102] The *Śiśuveda* is at present accessible only through a partial diacritics-free transcript in Dash (2002), pp. 46–49; it is also said to have been published "in a town near Puri" (Kimiaki Tanaka, email, 31 March 2017). According to Dash, "the language [...] seems to be a mixture of Sanskrit, Pali, Bengali, and Oriya". In any case, the text—the extent of variation is not known—begins with recognizable Sanskrit *ślokas*.

[103] The praise of **jīvātmā*, *parā*[*mā*†]*tmā* and *kevalabrahmā* in *Śiśuveda* v.[2] (conjecturally restored after Dash *ibid.*; †conj. Gudrun Bühnemann) is an example.

[104] **nīlācalanivāsāya bauddharūpī namo namaḥ* (*Śiśuveda* v.[3]cd; Dash *ibid.*).

In the twentieth century the Saraks managed to be recognized as Buddhists by representatives of the global traditions from across Asia.[105] Although this recognition owed little to their use of a universal language, the Saraks' connection to the pan-Asian religion could not have been sustained through informal or nonverbal practice alone—by venerating Buddhist images, for instance. Many such images remaining in Odisha from the premodern era are now worshipped in entirely Hindu settings, their original identities and communities of worship long gone.[106] As such, the retention of Sanskrit, however vestigially, has managed to strengthen the translocal thread in an otherwise localized religious fabric.

Postcolonial Buddhist *Śāstra* and *Kāvya*

The production of learned treatises and literature in Sanskrit has continued throughout the colonial era and into the present day, though the ways in which Buddhism is articulated in Sanskrit have changed along with the general state of the religion. The British Indian study of the past revealed the widespread disappearance of Buddhism to local intellectuals. The recovery of a plethora of Buddhist Sanskrit texts from the margins of colonial South Asia provided the first impetus for contemporary composition, as the printing of old scripture necessitated the writing of new introductions, summaries and other formalities of modern scholarship. This colonial scholastic output, most of it produced by native pundits, forms a large part of the sum of Sanskrit writings on Buddhism. It is generally ignored in the West.[107] Buddhist studies specialists have shown little interest in contemporary South Asian reactions to the word of the Buddha, and have rather maintained the colonial-era focus on antiquity and the competitive discovery of *verbum dei*. Speaking in Sanskrit is no longer enough, in itself, to compel the attention of the powers that be.

---

[105] The Saraks have enjoyed occasional support from the Mahabodhi Society, Nichidatsu Fujii (1885–1985) and the Dalai Lama XIV (Dash 2002, pp. 53–56).

[106] Donaldson (2001) records numerous Buddhist icons being worshipped in Śaiva *maṭha*s and the like in Odisha. They include unambiguous Buddha depictions such as Ratnasambhava (ibid., fig. 48) and Māravijaya (fig. 91), as well as a variety of tantric goddesses: Vajratārā (figs. 320–321), Prajñāpāramitā (figs. 327–329) et al.

[107] For instance, e-text archives such as the University of Göttingen's GRETIL (http://gretil.sub.uni-goettingen.de/) routinely do not reproduce any front or back matter in Sanskrit from their source publications.

Since the late nineteenth century, much of the new information about Buddhism in India has been funnelled into nostalgic and nationalist sentiment, which modern Sanskritists have often developed through the studying and writing of *kāvya*. At least five Sanskrit commentaries and other works on Aśvaghoṣa's poems have been published, for instance; this level of interest in a non-Hindu *kavi* is unusual. The *Uttarabuddhacarita*, a 1963 back-translation into Sanskrit of the lost second half of Aśvaghoṣa's *Buddhacarita* from a chain of translations in other languages,[108] is a typically enthusiastic if unimaginative modern project. Original *kāvya* expressing some sympathy for Buddhism have also been created, among which the works of Satyavrata Śāstrī (b. 1930) stand out.[109]

The authors of contemporary Sanskrit writing in India are almost never Buddhist in a formal or institutional sense. Their output on Buddhist subjects demonstrates the continuing capacity of the literary form for engaging with religion without "believing in" it, all the more so now that there is no Sanskrit-speaking *saṅgha* in India to disagree with them. If Buddhist-oriented *śāstra* and *kāvya* were once produced to support the aims of the Sanskritic *saṅgha*, what purpose could they serve today? The remnants of the old religion, with no religious community able to claim them, are easily assimilated into a homogeneous national discourse; they join the ranks of the heritageized. Latter-day Sanskrit writers are free to reimagine Buddhism as the emblem of a harmonious, timeless Brahminized order, as in one recently published poem:

> Again I hail India, illuminated all round [by] the masterful glow of [the sages] Vaśiṣṭha, Gādhi's son and Agastya, [and] Buddhists, Jains.[110]

The figure of Śākyamuni, while being invoked in support of nationalism, at the same time embodies the unity of Greater India.[111] As Satyavrata Śāstri describes Thailand to his South and Southeast Asian readers:

---

[108] The *Uttarabuddhacarite Dhātuvibhājana nāma* of Rāmchandra Dās Śāstrī draws on a Hindi translation of Johnston's 1937 English translation of the Tibetan and Chinese translations of the complete original *Buddhacarita* (Śāstrī 1963, p. 1).

[109] Satyavrata Śāstrī's *Śrībodhisattvacarita* (1962), *Thāideśavilāsa* (1979) and *Rāmakīrtimahākāvya* (1990) refer to Buddhism to varying extents. On the latter two works, see in brief Anand 2003.

[110] *vaśiṣṭhagādhisūnvagastyajainabauddhasādhanātapaḥ prabhāprapūritaṃ punar namāmi bhāratam* (Premanārāyaṇa Dvivedī's *Punar namāmi Bhāratam* v. 8cd, 2012, ed. Dvivedī, Tripaṭhī & Ṛṣanbhāradvāja 2012, p. 54).

[111] Favourable depictions of the region by modern Sanskritists, including Satyavrata Śāstrī, are discussed by Anand *ibid.*, pp. 443ff.

> On the one [hand] there is worship of the Sugata, fervent; on the other, [devotion] to Brahmā is apparent.[112]

Poetry provides one of the few remaining uses for Sanskrit following the gradual entrenchment of English, Hindi, and the vernaculars as languages of science, administration and literature. Sanskrit is also again primarily a language of religion, but even in this area its currency is limited in the nominally secular Republic of India. The most prevalent form of Buddhism introduced into India in the modern era has Pali as its sacred language, and wants little or nothing to do with contemporary Sanskrit discourse. The figurehead of this movement, the anti-caste lawyer, activist and Theravādin convert Bhimrao Ambedkar (1891–1956), was himself influential enough to have been the subject of three Sanskrit *kāvya*s to date. One *kavi* found it appropriate to describe Ambedkar in terms that can best be described as inclusivist:

> Bhim, [impressed] by the power of nationalism, was adorned now [with] the nonviolent Buddhist religion, a faction of the Hindus.[113]

On this point, the Hindu kavified biographies of Ambedkar[114] contrast markedly with the *Bhīmāmbedkaraśataka* of the Sinhalese *sugatakaviratna* Śāntibhikṣu Śāstrī (1912–91), who refers to "the hate-inciting deed [of caste discrimination] which was done to him [Ambedkar] by Hindus".[115] As Ambedkar remains a highly respected figure for many people, it is striking to see such dissonant views of his life—more examples could be given—expressed in Sanskrit, the linguistic medium that traditionally embodied authority and universality. In this respect, the Ambedkarite Buddhists may be justified in seeing Sanskrit to be a

---

[112] *ekatra pūjā sugatasya bhaktyā 'paratra brahmaṇa āvir asti* (*Thāideśavilāsa* v. 12cd, Shastri 1979, p. 3; cf. also trans. *ibid.*, p. 66). Here *ekatra* and *aparatra* can also suggest that two sites of worship are in close proximity to each other.

[113] *rāṣṭravādasya bhāvena bhīmena samalaṃkṛtaḥ | hindūnāṃ bhāgarūpo 'yaṃ bauddhadharmo*[ ]*nv ahiṃsakaḥ* (*Bhīmaśataka* v. 86, Semavāl 1991, p. 29). This repeats much the same sentiment of v. 83, *ibid.*, p. 28.

[114] A third Sanskrit biography, Prabhākara Śaṅkara Jośī's *Bhīmāyana*, opens with an *īśāvatārasya pārśvabhūmi* and is dedicated to Pārvatī (Jośī 2011, p. 1).

[115] *hindubhir yā kṛtā tatrāvamānajananī kriyā* (Śāntibhikṣu Śāstrī's *Bhīmāmbedkaraśataka*, v. 84ab, ed. Singh 2012, p. 84).

more partisan than universal medium. As Śāntibhikṣu Śāstrī asks in his *Bhīmāmbedkaraśataka*:

> How could a casteless person of low birth have the opportunity of speaking [Sanskrit]?[116]

Most contemporary Sanskrit writing, likewise, is "about" Buddhists, not "by" or "for" them. Since Indian treatments of Buddhist philosophy are usually published in Hindi within the educational system, discussions of *buddhavacana* are obliged to focus on Pali, as Sanskrit *sūtra*s hold no authority for Ambedkarite and Theravādin Buddhists, who now comprise the majority of the *saṅgha* in South Asia.

The relation between language choice and content, as well as the range of modern writing in this area, is illustrated by the work of the nationalist *śāstrin* Rāhula Sāṅkṛtyāyana (1893–1963), a polyglot who published in several languages. Sāṅkṛtyāyana's writings in Sanskrit include a back-translation from Chinese of an otherwise lost *sūtra*, a report on the uses of the Sanskrit language in Sri Lanka, a comparison of Marxism with Buddhism,[117] and various introductions to classical works. Sāṅkṛtyāyana's work, though impressive in its range and volume, exemplifies the aridity of recent Sanskrit writing on religion. It is written not on the basis of personal familiarity with Buddhist praxis, but precisely for those who lack it. Such scholarship represents another deep break with premodern literary production, in that it is never "experiential" (*jñānin*), even though it may have something of the "learned" (*paṇḍita*), to make use of a Sanskritic distinction.[118]

Sanskrit is still being used by conservative Buddhists outside India in certain limited contexts. In Sri Lanka, Theravādin monks continue their premodern practice of turning to Sanskrit to reach beyond the confines of sect and locality, though it is no longer necessarily the preferred language for this purpose. The writings of Theravādin Sanskritists remain confined

---

[116] *avarṇo hīnajātis tat kathaṃ syād avakāśabhāk* (Śāntibhikṣu Śāstrī's *Bhīmāmbedkaraśātakam*, v.27cd). The accompanying Hindi and English translations here supply "Sanskrit", which is specified by name (*saṃskṛtādhyetā*) in the next verse.

[117] Sāṅkṛtyāyana (1954, 1960, 1985), respectively.

[118] Aklujkar (2001), p. 24.

to traditional topics: *pañcavidyā* treatises, original poetry, and commentary on non-canonical Sanskrit texts.[119]

The local Lankan subjects that have been deemed worthy of *kāvya* treatment and translocal attention are exemplified by the works of two prolific Theravādin scholars. Śīlaskandha (1848–1924) wrote a verse history of the *śrāvakayāna* highlighting events such as the early Buddhist councils, which are immaterial in the extant Sanskrit corpus. A more contemporary focus is evident in the poetry of Jñāneśvara Sthavira (1915–2017), which includes a poem on the Sri Lankan Civil War.[120] For these writers, the choice of Sanskrit, while narrowing the potential audience, continues to lend a compelling voice, as evidenced by precise, hard-won linguistic skills. Although literature patterned after the *kāvya* form has been produced in Pali and Sinhalese,[121] it is known to be imitative of high Sanskrit style and lacks cachet. The allure of *kāvya* in its original linguistic idiom is such that one Sri Lankan academic was moved to publish a series of fabricated Sanskrit verse and prose inscriptions, trying to fill gaps in the history of the region with his whimsical classicist narrative.[122] Again, it is clear that Sanskrit continues to embody prestige for Buddhists in Sri Lanka, even though it is not their scriptural, "sacred" language. For that matter, Sanskrit may be preferable for some kinds of new writing precisely because it is inconsequential for religious practice and the workings of the local *saṅgha*, and in this respect, its power is limited by design, as in postcolonial India.

Newar Buddhism as Paradigmatic Sanskritic Buddhism

The most substantial living instance of Sanskritic Buddhism is practised by the Newars of the Kathmandu Valley. Around a hundred thousand

---

[119] Sinhalese Buddhist literary writings in Sanskrit are discussed by Bechert (2005), pp. 68ff. A few works not noticed by Bechert, e.g., a *Kalpalatāvyākhyā* on Aśvaghoṣa's *Saundarananda*, a *Samantakūṭakāvya* of *Jñānasiṃha Sthavira, etc., are mentioned in Piyaratana (2013).

[120] See, respectively, *Saddharmamakaraṇḍa* 20-2 (Śīlaskandha 1911, pp. 230–79), and regarding Jñāneśvara's *Yatidūta* (1987), Piyaratana 2013, pp. [81–3], [149–55].

[121] Bechert (2008) discusses Sri Lankan vernacular *kāvya*.

[122] Guruge (1996) revisits the Sanskrit "interlinear inscriptions" and "text preserved in the archives of Śrī Vijaya" published by Senarat Paranavitana (1896–1972) after retiring from the University of Sri Lanka. One confection of this type not noticed by Guruge (and Bechert 2005, p. 34) is Paranavitana (1974), posthumously published in a prestigious American journal.

Newars follow a Buddhism solemnized in Sanskrit utterances.[123] The locally transmitted Sanskrit corpus, comprising well over eleven thousand Buddhist manuscripts distributed among private and public collections,[124] provides the largest primary resource for the understanding of Buddhism as a mature system. The Nepalese corpus does not transmit the conservative canon, the *śrāvakapiṭaka*, apart from a few fragments from the premedieval period, and its exclusion from the corpus appears to be more deliberate than accidental.[125] Likewise, the religion espoused in these abandoned texts, that of lifelong celibate monasticism, has not been practised within the Newar tradition in recent memory. Monks and monasteries are still an integral part of Newar Buddhism, but their functions are rarely explained with reference to the standard Sanskritic categories—*saṅgha*, *vinaya*, *nikāya* and so on. The usual approach in the secondary literature is to emphasize localism and the "religion of the place" that lacks the qualities of a "great tradition".[126] For this reason, it will hardly be possible to identify the properties of Sanskritic civilization in Nepal, of its common *saṃskṛti*,[127] by relying on the received view. For the present purposes, the localized operation of two aspects of the universalist tradition, namely diglossia and nondenominationalism, will be briefly examined here, as they are most often mistaken for parochialism.

In Newar Buddhism, the convention of dual language use established in the classical Sanskritic tradition persists. Sanskrit is formal speech: it is the language of canon,[128] canonical liturgy, and of communicating with higher powers—which included, until recently, the king or the king's

---

[123] In the 2011 Nepal census, 141,982 persons out of a total of 1,321,933 identified as Buddhist Newars (Dahal 2014, p. 42). The proportion of this number that follows the native Sanskritic tradition is unrecorded, but is most likely a large majority.

[124] The largest single inventory, assembled by the Nepal-German Manuscript Preservation Project (2003), categorizes over eleven thousand manuscripts as "Buddhist".

[125] Sinclair (2016), pp. 93–96.

[126] Such characterizations are briefly reviewed in Sinclair (2016), pp. 69–70.

[127] Gellner (2018) examines the concept of *saṃskṛti* with reference to "culture" or "civilization" in Nepal.

[128] It has been contended that Newar Buddhism "looks to three canonical languages: Sanskrit, Tibetan and Pali, and utilizes two vernaculars, Newari and Nepali" (Tuladhar-Douglas 2004, p. 7). Nonetheless, only Sanskrit has institutional validity as a sacred language in Newar Buddhism, and only Newar, so far, has been customarily accepted as the vernacular in these institutions.

representatives. In nearly all Buddhist contexts, this formal register is used in conjunction with informal, conversational speech, namely, the Newar language.[129] There is no requirement for those who speak Sanskrit in connection with Buddhism to understand it in any depth,[130] but there is some expectation that the gist (*artha*) of Sanskrit speech will be able to be conveyed in the vernacular, where desired. This expectation has become more pronounced as followers of the Newar tradition become better acquainted with the operation of different kinds of Buddhism,[131] in the same way that the tradition progressed in contact with other parts of the Indosphere in the precolonial era.

A general understanding that scripture (*āgama*) should be conveyable in comprehensible speech (*bhāṣā*) is expressed in various ways. Translation "on the fly" is documented, by the fourteenth century at the latest, in annotations to manuscripts that record them being recited in Sanskrit and simultaneously paraphrased in Newar.[132] The practice of reciting Sanskrit teaching and at the same time recommunicating it in everyday language has continued into the present day, though it is rarely noticed.[133] Public proclamations—especially those that address the sovereign, the *deva*—are often formulated with a prologue in Sanskrit followed by explanations in *deśabhāṣā* or *nepālabhāṣā*, terms that are explicitly used in such contexts (Figure 10.2). Diglossia of this kind was of course once a widespread convention, also seen in Sanskritic Southeast Asia, and its continuation shows an ongoing awareness of the distinction of formal and informal speech. There are many examples of diglossia in everyday religious life, such as the common practice of giving monasteries both Sanskrit and Newar names.[134] In the early nineteenth century, when

---

[129] Gellner (2016), p. 20, however points out that Newar (a.k.a. "Newari") is now being rapidly displaced by the Parbatīya ("Nepali") language among the Newars.

[130] For instance, the largest *saṅgha* in Bhaktapur, Nepal, reportedly has no Sanskrit-literate monks (Andrea Wollein, email, 23 September 2016).

[131] von Rospatt (2012), pp. 225–26.

[132] On the names and dates of a *pāṭhaka* and *ṭīkāpāṭhaka* mentioned in a colophon of the *Aṣṭasāhasrikā Prajñāpāramitā* manuscript Cambridge Add.1544, see Sinclair (2016), p. 41, n. 85.

[133] Lewis (1984), p. 229, gives one report of this practice.

[134] For some lists of these Sanskrit and Newar *vihāra* names in Sanskrit sources, see Sinclair (2010, 2017).

the Newar scholar Amṛtānanda surveyed the Buddhist *saṅgha* of Lalitpur (a.k.a. Patan), he began by acknowledging its language dualism:

> Many monasteries gleam in Lalit Patan, girt by the glorious Nepal mandala. I will write down their names which are in the Sanskrit language, which are in the Prakrit [Newar] language.[135]

Amṛtānanda's statement, and the remainder of the account that follows it, is typical of his time and place in that it completely lacks interest in, and awareness of, classical sectarian structure. The *saṅgha* of the Kathmandu Valley has operated without self-conscious *nikāya* affiliation for several centuries. The use of Sanskrit has shifted from the bridge language used between different orders to the sole, default, standard language of a nondenominational monastic community. For a long time, all Newar procedures for monastic ordination (*pravrajyā*) have followed the norms of the Mūlasarvāstivāda order, as specified in one of the order's old handbooks, the **Ekottarakarmaśataka*. Naturally, the contents of this sectarian handbook have long since been transmitted outside a sectarian context; after being incorporated into the *Kriyāsaṃgrahapañjikā*, a manual of monastery construction compiled in mid-eleventh century Nepal,[136] it ceased to circulate as an independent work. All current sources for the Newars' ordination procedure derive from the *Kriyāsaṃgrahapañjikā*, and do not involve as much as the idea of a sectarian canon.[137] Only the names of the four superorders are preserved in the *Kriyāsaṃgrahapañjikā*, in its specification of the monastic gong[138]—which itself sounds like part of a *cāturnikāya* establishment. In a like manner, the Nepalese story anthologies, the *avadānamālā*s, while drawing much of their material from

[135] *śrīmannepālamaṇḍalāntarvarti-lalitapattane bahavo vihārā vilasanti | teṣāṃ saṃskṛtabhāṣī yāni nāmāni prākṛtabhāṣī yāni 'valikhyate* (India Office Library Hodgson Collection, British Library, vol. 27, fol. 114).

[136] The reconstructed title **Ekottarakarmaśataka* (Chinese translation: *Bai yi jiemo* 百一羯磨, Taishō Tripiṭaka No. 1453, pp. 455c$_{25}$ff) is ventured by Kishino (2013), p. 17 n. 48. Its partial incorporation into the eleventh-century *Kriyāsaṃgrahapañjikā* was first noticed by Tanemura (1994). The date and place of the *Kriyāsaṃgrahapañjikā*'s compilation is discussed by Sinclair (2016), pp. 203–4.

[137] Over twenty Nepalese handbooks for the *pravrajyāvidhi* have been surveyed in preliminary research summarized in Sinclair (2016), p. 245.

[138] Tanemura (1993), p. 40.

FIGURE 10.2
Diglossia in Nepalese Buddhist Epigraphs

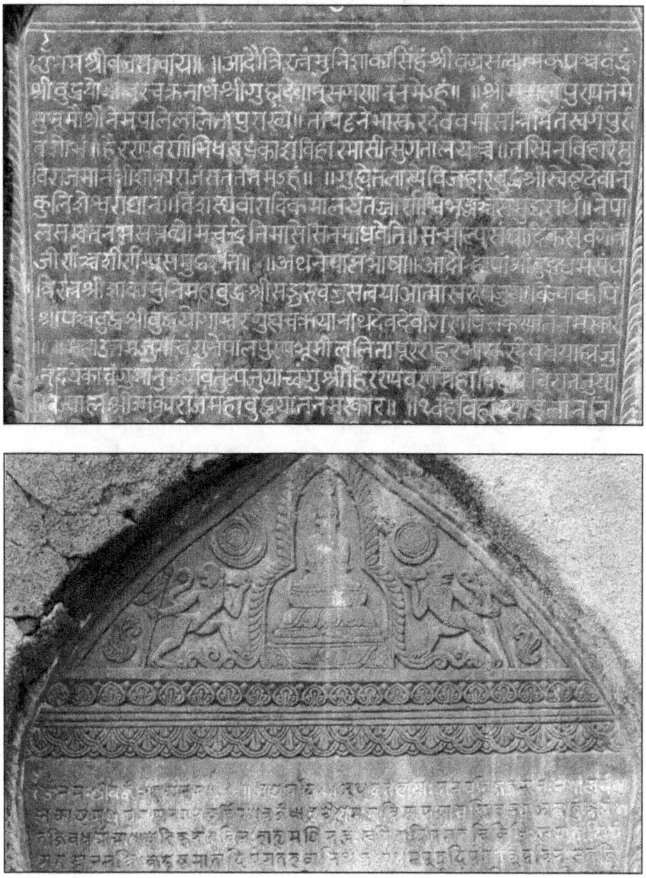

a.

b.

Notes:

a: Upper half of a bilingual Sanskrit-Newar Buddhist inscription at the tantric shrine (*digi*) in Īlā Nani, Lalitpur, Nepal. The Sanskrit portion is followed by a portion with a loose Newar translation beginning in line 8 with the words *atha nepālabhāṣā*. It is dated in a chronogram (*nabha-sapta-vyoma-candre*) in the Sanskrit portion and with numerals in the Nepalese era (*śrīnepālasamvat* 1070 *vaiśākha* — not shown) in the Newar portion, both corresponding to 1950 CE.

b: Upper third of a Buddhist inscription, Kathmandu, Nepal, dated Nepalese era 1017 (1897 CE). This inscription displays "in-principle" diglossia. The text begins with a token Sanskrit phrase (*athetyādi*×). The inscription continues in Newar after the phrase *atha desabhāṣāḥ*. The monkeys in the cartouche are iconographically ambiguous, displaying attributes of both the Hindu Hanumān (*dhvaja*) and the Buddhist Jñānākara (*panasaphala*).

Source: Author's photos.

the canons of certain *nikāyas*, have circulated apart from these canons, and have in effect replaced them.[139] In this way, through anthologizing and recontextualization, various elements of Buddhist sectarian culture have been propagated without reliance on sectarian institutions, and have been subsumed into a generic, non-sectarian, Sanskritic religion.

Javano-Balinese Sanskritic Buddhism in Bali

The Buddhism natively practised on Bali, Indonesia, represents the farthest limit of the native Sanskritic tradition, both in terms of its minimalism and its position at the eastern edge of the Indomalayan region. As a successor of the former Majapahit empire, and the Old Javanese literary tradition, it is an instance of a wider Javano-Balinese cultural complex. Further vestiges still exist in the islands adjoining Bali, including Java itself[140] and Lombok.[141] However, the culture of the Balinese is distinct from other remnant Hindu and Buddhist populations of Java, whose formal religion is attenuated to the point that it is no longer readily identified, as in the case of the Javanese Tengger people.[142] The Sanskritic heritage of the Archipelago, preserved most extensively in Bali, should also be distinguished from the global religions imported into Indonesia after Independence.

Indigenous Buddhism in Bali displays universalist traits: it has a minimal *buddhavacana* corpus, recognizable as such by others; its tenets are expressed in ways rooted in universalist forms; it is linguistically compatible with other native religions and the expectations of the civic arena. The

---

139 Lévi (1907), pp. 107–9, noticed that the Mūlasarvāstivāda *vinaya* is a source for the *Divyāvadāna*, which in turn informs later Nepalese retellings of *avadānas* (see also Sinclair 2016, pp. 120–21). The Nepalese *Bhadrakalpāvadāna* is an adaptation of the Mahāvastu (Tatelman 1996, p. vi) of the Mahāsāṃghika-Lokottaravāda order.

140 In the central Javanese district of Temanggung, for instance, Buddhist ideas have been transmitted wholly informally in the idiom of *kejawen*. Published Sanskrit texts are now studied in a small community there (Tanto 2003, pp. 122, 126).

141 Hooykaas (1973), p. 251, documents dozens of Buddhist officiants in Lombok.

142 The Tenggerese religion is often said to include Buddhism (of the "Mahāyāna" variety, i.e., non-Theravāda), but according to Hefner (1993), p. 4 n. 1, no definitely Buddhist elements have been identified. For instance, it is not known how long the Tengger village of Ngadas, "the highest village in Java" on the slopes of Mount Bromo, has had its *wihara* and *agama buddha* population, counted as 49.4 per cent of the village in 2011, clearly differentiated from *agama hindu* (Haryanto 2014, p. 206).

Balinese sense of belonging to a universal civilization or cosmopolis is strong, while the sense of affiliation to a discrete translocal religion is slight. In Bali the notion of the Hindu–Buddhist polity, going back to the old formulation of the **śaiva-saugata* polity (often also formulated so as to include non-specific *ṛṣi*s),[143] has continued as an everyday reality. The faithspace occupied by Śiva and/or the Buddha is a compelling realization of universality, all the more so as it does "not constitute a merger or synthesis", in the considered view of Acri and others.[144] Its practical manifestations include the rituals performed by officiants of both religions sitting side by side.[145]

Native Buddhism is personified in Bali by the *pedanda buda* (also spelled *budha*, *boda*, *bauddha*, etc.) class of officiant. Today she or he is a Brahmin by caste,[146] although in the past non-Brahmins were also able to perform Javano-Balinese *bauddha* ritual. The Buddhist *pedanda* has a Śaiva counterpart, the *pedanda siwa*. These two *pedanda* classes have large overlaps in their ritual repertoire,[147] which in part reflect the need to perform the same kinds of ritual for different clients, or to perform separately in common settings. Before Independence the two were considered to comprise a single religion; more recently the *pedanda buda*s have had to be disambiguated as Hindus for the sake of getting recognized by the government.[148]

---

[143] Vernacular equivalents of the term **śaivasaugata* are used in the inscribed copper plates of the Balinese villages of Babahan (one dated 917 CE) and Sembiran (dated 951–1183 CE), on which see most recently Prihatmoko (2017) and Hauser-Schäublin and Ardika (2008), pp. 278–94, respectively.

[144] Acri (2015), p. 268. Against "syncretism" in this particular context, see further Hornbacher (2013), p. 213, and Gottowik (2016), p. 205.

[145] Jointly officiated rituals have long been noticed (Eerde 1910, pp. 7ff; Lévi 1933, p. xiv), but are yet to be studied as a distinct type. For some recent information see Hornbacher (2013), pp. 219–20, on the annual festival at Samuan Tiga, Blahbatuh, and Gottowik (2016) on the rituals performed on pilgrimage to Gunung Rinjani on Lombok.

[146] Goudriaan and Hooykaas (1971), p. 17. Women *pedanda*s outnumbered men a century ago (Eerde *ibid.*). Apparently, the Brahmin *pedanda* monopoly on performing ritual for others is being challenged (Picard 2011, pp. 487–88 n. 9; Maretha 2017).

[147] Of the 124 *stuti*s "known to the Padanda Bauddha", just 39 (31.4 per cent) "have Buddhist contents"; cf. Goudriaan and Hooykaas (1971), p. 573, Appendix 3.

[148] On native Buddhism as perceived as part of *agama bali*, see Picard (2011), pp. 487–88, 496; as part of premodern *agama tirtha*, see Eerde, *ibid.*

In Bali, the old complementarity of religions is not a partnership of equals, as others have observed.[149] Buddhists have comprised a small, inconspicuous fraction of the population since the colonial era.[150] There is no native *saṅgha* to speak of; the *pedanda*s reside in households, not monasteries;[151] iconic objects of worship, such as Buddha statues, are rarely seen.[152] The sophisticated literary culture inherited from Java, which is understood to have been shaped by Buddhist *kāvya* at various points,[153] remains one of the few milieux in which the religion of the bodhisattva is kept alive in the public consciousness.[154] The absence of overt and unambiguous markers of identity is so widespread that there can be no doubt that it is deliberate; other living Sanskritic Buddhisms, especially Nepal's, have a similarly muted outward presentation. While the Buddhism of Bali in this way coexists comfortably with Hinduism,[155] it is also overlooked by its globalized coreligionists in the Archipelago, who possess their own, often quite different ideas about the normative religion. The question of how much of the Javano-Balinese heritage can be discerned as Sanskritic Buddhism, or for that matter as any universal religion,[156] therefore has ongoing implications for its position in the global religious landscape.

[149] Acri (2015), pp. 268ff.

[150] Buddhists number less than 1 per cent of the Balinese population, among which the *pedanda*s form just one subgroup. An incomplete survey of Buddhist households (*geria*, **gṛha*) by Hooykaas (1973) counted 165 inhabitants, including 121 on West Lombok; 19 were counted on Lombok by Eerde (1910).

[151] Some *pura*s in Bali appear to be former *vihāra* sites (Hornbacher *ibid.*).

[152] The relatively aniconic character of Balinese religion has been mentioned by many including Lévi (1933), p. xiv. To give two counterexamples, both probably recent but nonetheless accepted within the tradition: The *pura puseh* at Batubulan features two Buddha images on its frontage (Yamaguchi 2003, p. 17 fig. 1); and a set of *cetiya*s is worshipped as the *triratna* at Budakeling (Tanto 2012, p. 206).

[153] Hunter (2014a, 2014b) finds that the *Lalitavistara* and *Buddhacarita*, respectively, have provided models for (non-Buddhist and Buddhist) Kakawin prosody and style.

[154] The *Sutasoma* Kakawin (a.k.a. *Poruṣādaśānta*) has been most emblematic of Buddhism for the local public (cf. e.g. Eerde 1910, p. 14). Besides numerous depictions of the *Sutasoma* in art, the story is now also brought to life through *wayang kulit* and *topeng* performance.

[155] See, e.g., Lévi (1933), p. xiii.

[156] On the professed doubts about whether the Balinese have "religion", see Acri (2011) and Picard (2011).

Again, it is the use of universal language that allows Buddhism to exist as a distinct entity in a milieu that has inclined towards homogeneity over time. The *pedanda buda*s' utterances contain unambiguous Buddhist vocabulary—*triratna*, *bodhicitta*, *tathāgata*, and so on.[157] Their textual corpus, although far from exhaustively studied, has long been known to preserve Sanskrit mantras, phrases and other textual elements of the pan-Asian Mahāyāna.[158] An apt example is a verse of Balinese daily ritual that occurs in other varieties of Buddhism, including the Yogācāra and the *vinaya*s of at least three orders:

> Abstaining from all sin, nurturing the wholesome, taming one's mind completely: this is the Buddha's teaching.[159]

An especially compelling representative of the Javano-Balinese Sanskritic tradition is the *Sang Hyang Kamahāyānikan*, a work of yogic instruction accompanied by Old Javanese glosses that is still used by Balinese Buddhists.[160] Its Sanskrit portions derive entirely from Buddhist tantras and tantric commentaries that were circulating across Asia by about the late eighth century.[161] The Buddhist orientation of these and other *pedanda*

---

[157] Goudriaan and Hooykaas (1971), pp. 435, 442, etc.

[158] The Balinese corpus has been collated with parallels in the transnational Sanskrit corpus by Goudriaan and Hooykaas (1971), pp. 600–3. On the transregional relevance of Sanskritic Balinese texts in general, see Acri (2006).

[159] *sarvapāpasyākaraṇaṃ kuśalasyopasaṃpadā* | *svacittaparidāmanam*† *etad buddhānuśāsanam* (*Triratnasaṃbodhana*, ed. Goudriaan and Hooykaas 1971, p. 307); †*-dāmanam* in some parallels; *dharmanam* in editors' MSS. Apart from the *Udānavarga* (identified by Goudriaan and Hooykaas *ibid.*), the verse is found in works such as the Prātimokṣasūtras of the Sarvāstivāda, Mūlasarvāstivāda and Mahāsāṃghika-Lokottaravāda *nikāya*s, the Mahāvastu of the latter, the *Yogācārabhūmi*, etc.

[160] Pedanda Gede Wayan Demung, personal communication, 2 November 2004.

[161] All forty-two verses of the *Sang Hyang Kamahāyānikan* ultimately derive from either the *Mahāvairocanābhisaṃbodhi*, the *Adhyardhaśatikā Prajñāpāramitā* or the commentarial literature on the *Guhyasamāja* (Kandahjaya 2016, pp. 70, 72). Note that the twenty-fifth verse (ed. Speyer 1913, p. 358), on dealing with initiates who spurn tantric Buddhism (**samaye dviṣṭāḥ*, Tib. *dam tshig la sdang*), and for which no Sanskrit parallel has yet been identified, is certainly not from the Buddha-spoken, non-tantric *Ratnamegha* (as proposed *op. cit.*), but from the tantric commentarial literature, being cited in at least four works in Tibetan translation, including a **Guhyasamājatantraṭīkā* attributed to Nāgārjuna (cf. Ui et al. 1934 No. 1784 237b$_7$).

buda Sanskritic texts is unmistakable. However, today Sanskrit is of strictly limited use in differentiating the various actors of the Balinese faithscape. Only a few specialists comprehend the language well, and its relative unintelligibility may have helped to obscure rather than settle hard differences between the Sanskritic religions.[162] This is not itself a new situation, and the Sanskritic elements of the Balinese Buddhist corpus continue to disclose universalist meanings to those who can grasp them, as in the past.

Contemporary Semi-Sanskritic Buddhism in the Sinosphere

The wide diffusion of Sanskrit in combination with Buddhism outside its native *sprachraum* has continued into the modern era, where it is now represented by two main streams, Sino-Japanese and Tibetan. These two streams realize only a little of Sanskrit's universalism; having developed apart from each other, they remain incompatible at the practical and institutional levels, and are unable to use Sanskrit as an auxiliary language. For example, the credentials and expertise of (say) a Tibetan Dge lugs pa monk are not automatically compatible with those of the Japanese Shingon school, and vice versa, even though they may accept the same Buddhist tantras as authorities. Practitioners are expected to use Sanskrit primarily for the repetition of clichéd phrases, and the language is not taught within traditional institutions for any other religious purpose.[163] Such limitations on the use of the language derive from the defining condition of semi-Sanskritic Buddhism, namely, lack of proximity to the Indo-Aryan language space.[164]

Where Sanskrit is accepted as a language of mantras but not of the scripture in everyday use, it expresses a more specialized kind of

---

[162] For instance, the resanskritization of Hindu daily ritual in the 1950s and 1960s was accompanied by non-literal vernacular translations (Lanus 2014).

[163] In this respect the condition of Sanskritic Buddhism outside the Indosphere differs from that of Pali Buddhism as practised in countries such as Myanmar and Thailand, where Pali can be used as an auxlang among practitioners of different backgrounds.

[164] The vernaculars in places where Sanskritic Buddhism lasted longest have close proximity to Sanskrit—i.e., Bengali (37 per cent separation), Oriya (40.9 per cent), Bihari (41.1 per cent), and Sinhalese (53.5 per cent)—or have major inflows from Sanskrit, as Newar, Javanese, Balinese, et al. do (figures from http://elinguistics.net, 2018).

universality, associated with suprarational communication. Both inside and outside the Indosphere, it was widely accepted that a mantra is meant to be heard and comprehended on a "supersensible" level.[165] Some mantric language was conventionally intelligible in the places where it originated, but much of this residual intelligibility is lost as it travels into other *sprachraums*. The obscurity of semi-Sanskritic Buddhism is conveyed with terms that emphasize secret or occult (*guhya*) workings: the "secret teaching" (*mikkyō* 密教, **guhyaśāsana*), the "secret sect" (*mizong* 密宗, **guhyamata*) and of course "secret mantra" (*gsang sngags*, *guhyamantra*). These sorts of characterizations have had little currency in the Sanskritic heartland, because these mantras are still able to signify without the obscuration of language barriers, and the workings of mantras are not always expected to involve secrecy. Yet mantric speech that is not understood on the literal level is not bound to be a "mystical" discourse, dependent on an uncomprehended "meme complex".[166] Rather, paralinguistic understandings are encouraged in semi-Sanskritic settings. What a mantra connotes (e.g., a call to action) is considered to be as significant as what it denotes (e.g., the semantic content of the request). In this way, Sanskrit mantras function outside the Indosphere as non-discursive "extraordinary language",[167] albeit still with the aid of local-language *nirukti*, which is most developed in Japan.

As Sanskrit in the Sinosphere is mostly connotative in its function, its role is more prominent in visual and performative culture than in literature. The language has come to manifest "talismanic power"[168] due to being habitually encountered in esotericist settings. Its arcane quality is accentuated by the fact that it is written in scripts that are no longer in use in the subcontinent. The continuing use of these scripts is a kind of iconophilia, in which the shapes of letterforms embody special significances, and have to retain the precise form in which they were first transmitted. Writing systems formerly common in South Asia now persist only in ethnoregional isolates: the Siddhamātṛkā script is confined to Sino-Japanese Buddhism, while the user community of Rañjanā is chiefly

---

165 Eltschinger (2017), p. 311.

166 Dennett (2017), pp. 218ff, discusses the transmission of memes that are not comprehended by their transmitters.

167 Payne (2017).

168 Dine (2012), p. 91.

Tibeto-Himalayan.[169] So far it seems to have been unimaginable to replace these scripts with Devanāgarī—the de facto standard for writing Sanskrit on the subcontinent—in the talismanic practices of semi-Sanskritic Buddhism. As a result, the mantra syllables written on sculptures, textiles, buildings, and other sacra are now decipherable only by the local cognoscenti. A typical example of usage can be seen at the Qing-era Yonghe Gong in Beijing, where Sanskrit writing is a prominent feature of the architecture (Figure 10.3), but has no place on the quadrilingual signage displayed at the temple. Throughout East Asia, mantra phonemes have come to connote the act of transcendent signification, whatever their particular phonic values or semantic referents. The charm of these phonemes is such that their use has extended beyond Buddhism proper and into Shintō, Daoism and other native religions.[170]

The lack of native comprehensibility of Sanskrit in the Sinosphere, together with a persistent demand for grasping the language in the context of local religious practice, has generated a body of scholarship oriented towards the needs of semi-Sanskritic Buddhists. Many alphasyllabaries (*varṇamālā*) and lexicographical works (*kośa*) were produced in the premodern era and are still useful tools for Sanskritists. In the modern era, there has also been renewed interest in Sanskrit as a source of denotation, that is, of literal meaning. Over the past century Japan, in particular, has produced hundreds of editions and translations of Mahāyāna works using manuscript sources. The ability to practise "Indology" from first principles has been regarded as a hallmark of modern learning in Japan. When the teaching of Sanskrit was introduced to Japan in the colonial era, it set universities apart from their sectarian academic counterparts, which remained focused on Chinese-language exegesis;[171] it still distinguishes Japan as a whole from most of the rest of the East Asian academy.

Studies of Buddhist scriptures in their original languages are funded in Japan under the banner of scientific research,[172] as in most of the West. Their findings are naturally of more interest for Buddhists than for the public

---

[169] For examples of these scripts in use in the Sinosphere, see Dine (2012) and Ye (2014), respectively. Both scripts are in use throughout Asia's Chinese communities.

[170] See, respectively, Dine (2012) and Capitanio (2018). In Bön the Tibetan script seems to be preferred for writing mantric phonemes.

[171] Hayashi (2014), p. 21.

[172] The Database of Grants-in-Aid for Scientific Research (Kagaku Kenkyūhi josei jigyō 科学研究費助成事業, https://kaken.nii.ac.jp/index/) lists over 350 projects tagged with *sanskritto* サンスクリット dating back to 1972, of which 12 are ongoing at the time of writing.

FIGURE 10.3
Ornamental Uses of Sanskrit Mantra Syllables in the Sinosphere

a.

b.

Notes:
a: Yonghe Gong, Beijing, China. From top to bottom — Eave rafter ends: *oṃ āḥ hūṃ* (repeated); eave-purlin: *o*[*m̊*] *vajrapāṇi hūṃ phaṭ*; recesses: *oṃ āḥ hūṃ* (repeated), *shou* 寿 (repeated); beam above lintel: *hkṣmlvryam̊*; lintel: *oṃ maṇipadme hūṃ hrī*[*ḥ*].
b: Amitabha Buddhist Centre, Geylang, Singapore. Wall: *oṃ āḥ hūṃ*| *oṃ maṇipadme hūṃ*; prayer wheels: *oṃ maṇipadme hūṃ*.
Source: Author's photos.

at large, yet these studies are also largely irrelevant for the institutional practice of Buddhism in Japan. This has begun to be remarked on by scholars there.[173] Sanskrit scholarship is valued solely in the context of this "despiritualized" discourse,[174] just as it is in India and the rest of the non-Buddhist world. Japan's Sanskrit scholarship may be relevant to a wide international audience, showcasing its high educational standards, but the fact of its extremely limited reach has not escaped notice.[175] On the other hand, the academic study of *bukkyō* 仏教—which by default means locally transmitted, sectarian, Sinitic Buddhism—is increasingly seen within Japan as difficult to support.[176]

Sanskrit has a more vital presence in Tibetan Buddhism, as all Tibetan denominations have sought from time to time to emphasize their affinity with the ambiance of the subcontinent. The Sanskrit language, in addition to being used in the aforementioned talismanic contexts, is sometimes used in new composition, unlike in East Asia. Tibetan treatises are often given artificial titles in Sanskrit to endow them with the look and feel of a canonical *śāstra*. Likewise, newly composed verses written in ornate scripts impart the desired "Indianness" to locally produced works.[177] This originality has extended in a few cases to the creation of complete multilingual treatises, such as the *Tuṣitarāja*.[178]

Competence in Sanskrit has persisted as a mark of distinction among the Tibetan intelligentsia, providing access to the rejuvenating wellsprings of Indian universalism. Apart from its use in the established semi-Sanskritic practices of translation, consecration, and ornamentation, the language has

---

[173] See, e.g., Saito (2014), p. 252.

[174] Aklujkar *ibid.* uses this term in describing one modern fate of the *paṇḍita*.

[175] "… if Japanese scholars do not publish their research and academic findings in English, their research findings may end up being completely overlooked" (Tanaka 2017, p. 151). Publishing some findings in Sanskrit would also enlarge the potential readership at least a little. Tanaka himself provides abstracts translated into Tibetan (e.g. ibid., p. 5).

[176] Aspects of the decline of Buddhist universities in Japan are reported by Reader (2011), pp. 243–44, including the internal debate on "whether to jettison the term 'Buddhism' (*bukkyō*) from their titles."

[177] On "Indianness" as a source of legitimacy in Tibet, see Templeman (2008), pp. 207–11.

[178] The *Tuṣitarājo nāma gurūpacārakrama* (Tib. *Bla ma'i rnal 'byor*, a.k.a. *Shangshi xiangying* 上師相應) is a blockprinted Sanskrit-Tibetan ritual manual composed in the Qing era, first noticed by von Staël-Holstein (1932). A similar, previously unnoticed work engraved by the same calligrapher (*citrakara*, Tib. *lha bris*), Dam pa, is Buddhist Digital Resource Centre W1EE70.

occasionally been used to communicate with living South Asians. In his biography of the wandering yogin Buddhaguptanātha, for example, Kun dga' snying po Tāranātha (1575–1634) records a nonreligious verse on the delights of Sri Lanka:

> Pearls in the water, gems on the ground, elephants in the lush forests,
> a lotuslike woman in every house — O Sinhala, land of plenty.[179]

The *śloka* quoted to display worldly as well as religious knowledge occasionally features in the writings of Tibetan Sanskritists, such as the travelogues of Si tu paṇ chen chos kyi 'byung gnas (c. 1699–1774).[180] A more recent example is the work of Dge 'dun chos 'phel (1903–51), whose papers contain such *ślokas* alongside inscriptions copied out in their original scripts, together with transliterations, translations and quotations from modern editions of Sanskrit Buddhist texts.[181]

The new access to the Sanskrit sources of Tibetan religion that has been opened up in the modern era has not, however, led to a religious renaissance among the people of the Land of Snows. Instead, modern Tibetan Buddhist interest in Sanskrit texts conforms to the despiritualized, heritageized paradigm established in the colonial era, with only a few exceptions. Within the Tibetan diaspora, the Central University of Tibetan Studies at Sarnath has published hundreds of Sanskrit Buddhist texts using modern scholarly techniques. At the same time, a department of the University focusing on "restoration" (back-translation) of canonical texts has been rendering into Sanskrit the writings of Dge lugs pa hierarchs[182] and other figures who are

---

[179] **jale muktī*[s] *tale māṇikā raṇe vane kuñjarā*[*ḥ*] | *ghare ghare padminī nārī bharadeśa siṃhala* (Tib.: *dza lī mukti ta lī ma ṇi ka ra ne ba ne ku nydza ra / gha ri gha re pa dma nī nā ri bha lā de śa siṅgga la*; *Grub chen Buddha gupta'i rnam thar, Tā ra nā tha'i gsung 'bum*, Dpe bsdur ma ed., vol. 34 p. 105, via http://tbrc.org). For a transcription from another witness and a translation of Tāranātha's Tibetan translation, see Templeman (2008), p. 261. It is unclear how much the verse conformed to Sanskrit grammar at the point at which it was transmitted to Tāranātha. Its reconstitution as a *śloka* here serves a mainly heuristic purpose.

[180] Verhagen (2013).

[181] Lopez (2013), esp. pp. 76, 85, 90.

[182] Several works of Jo bo rje "Atiśa" and Tsong kha pa (1357–1419) have been translated from Tibetan into various languages at Sarnath. Of note are the University's back-translations into Sanskrit of Atiśa's **Bodhipathapradīpa* and *Vimalaratnalekhā*; back-translations of both texts had already been attempted earlier in the twentieth century. See also the University's website, http://www.cuts.ac.in.

respected in the religiosity of the diaspora. The production of such arcana deviates from modernist orthodoxy by furthering religious objectives of making merit and spreading the dharma. These works, unlike the ersatz Sanskrit compositions of premodern Tibet,[183] are today expected to find an actual, live Sanskrit-literate audience.

The modern dissemination of Tibetan writings in Sanskrit also assists the soft-power projection aims of the diaspora, in that it provides an uncontroversial medium for spreading Tibetan religious ideas in the exile environment. The *Śraddhātrayaprakāśana*, an homage in verse to the great pundits of Nālandā,[184] composed by the Dalai Lama XIV in 2001 and published in five languages including Sanskrit, is a non-trivial project. It is required reading for attendees of talks at the diaspora's base in Dharamsala, India.[185] The pragmatic attitude of this work might be seen in its being dedicated to the "god of the gods" (*devadeva*) rather than the Buddha as such.[186] For that matter, the diaspora's mere use of Sanskrit shows it is serious about accommodating itself to South Asian conditions. To this end, the natural kinship that is said to exist between Sanskritic and Tibetic civilizations is also played up. As the Dalai Lama XIV told the 2014 World Hindu Congress:

> Buddhism became so rich because of the intellectual challenge posed by Hindu thought. [...] I often tell Indians: We are the chelas [**ceṭāḥ*] of ancient Indians, not the modern ones.[187]

Interest is also growing in the Sanskritic heritage of the Tibetan Autonomous Region of the People's Republic of China.[188] From 2006 to 2011, over a

---

[183] An unusual premodern attempt at codifying Dge lugs pa liturgy in Sanskrit is the abovementioned *Tuṣitarāja*. On the calibre of its Sanskrit, see Bhattacharya (1935).

[184] *śraddhātrayaprakāśanam ity abhidhānā śrīnālandāmahāvihārasya saptadaśānāṃ mahāpaṇḍitānām iyam adhyeṣaṇā* (Bstan 'dzin rgya mtsho 2006, p. 25). The seventeen great pundits named in the poem may not have been active at Nālandā itself; rather, they embody the Mādhyamika-Yogācāra tradition of the author.

[185] So it is officially reported at http://www.dalailama.com/news/2016/third-day-of-teachings-requested-by-the-nalanda-shiksha. For the text see Bstan 'dzin rgya mtsho 2006.

[186] Tib. *lha yi lha* (*Śraddhātrayaprakāśana* v.1b, Bstan 'dzin rgya mtsho 2006, p. 1) is, however, a common epithet of the Buddha.

[187] Sreedathan (2014).

[188] Steinkellner (2003) summarizes the situation up to the beginning of this century.

thousand manuscripts kept there were sought out, photographed, rehoused and reproduced in facsimile in sixty-one portfolio volumes as part of a state-sponsored survey.[189] These manuscripts are understood to contain a high proportion of unique, rare or previously unstudied material.[190] They and other documents from the "Western regions" are studied in at least two institutes, one at Beijing University and one established in Lhasa in 2014.[191] However, the publication of findings on these texts has so far had to rely heavily on international cooperation. The Sanskrit Texts from the Tibetan Autonomous Region publication series, cofounded with the Austrian Academy of Sciences, has contributed more than twenty volumes to the current "great leap forward in the recovery of Buddhist literature", as Ernst Steinkellner calls it.[192]

China's investment in the study of Sanskrit is presented as beneficial for the country's global research profile,[193] and the exclusive focus on "scientific" outputs is of course understandable, both in the context of China's secular culture and in terms of what other global players value. There are now few other possibilities for exploiting a "prestige" language that has lost its connections to temporal power. Due to this very situation, the main reason for studying Sanskrit today is in order to understand or practise religion, and this may be hard to justify in the absence of a large, traditionalist religious constituency. A glimmer of interest in the wider potential of China's Sanskrit resources is detectable in recent musings

[189] Xinhua.net (2018). The facsimile volumes are titled *Bod rang skyong ljongs su nyar tshags byas pa'i ta la'i lo ma'i dpe cha kun btus par ma* (*Xizang zizhiqu zhencang beiye jing yingyin daquan* 西藏自治区珍藏贝叶经影印大全); cf. Pu (2017).

[190] See, e.g., Hahn (2010). Work on a previously unreported Sanskrit manuscript of Nāgārjuna's *Suhṛllekha* (**Qinyou shu* 亲友书) is reported to be underway (Xinhua.net 2018).

[191] Beijing University's Research Institute of Sanskrit Manuscripts & Buddhist Literature 梵文贝叶经与佛教文献研究所 publishes an eponymous Series (Fojiao wencian xilie congshu 梵文贝叶经与佛教文献系列丛书). The Lhasa palmleaf manuscript research institute is formally titled Xizang Zizhiqu Kexueyuan Beiyejing Yanjiusuo 西藏自治区社会科学院贝叶经研究所, abbreviated as Tib. Ta la'i lo ma'i dpe cha zhib 'jug khang.

[192] Steinkellner (2016), p. 3. The phrase "great leap forward" is not conveyed literally (i.e. as a *da yuejin* 大跃进) in the Chinese translation appended to Prof. Steinkellner's remarks.

[193] It has been remarked that "few foreign palmleaf manuscript researchers have quite as much material at their disposal [as in Tibet]" (外国贝叶经研究者很少有这么多一手资料), and that studies in this area are read in "Austrian, Japanese etc. Tibetology institutes" (奥地利、日本等藏学研究机构); see Xinhua.net (2018).

that India, and Nālandā University in particular, ought to work on them.[194] It will certainly take a good deal of imagination to develop a discourse that can compete with the mantras of modern cosmopolitanism and the hegemony of Western thought.

CONCLUSIONS

It is through the use of Sanskrit that Buddhism has been able to attain its widest spatial and temporal footprint, to codify the full range of its teaching, to make its deepest impacts upon the thinking of others, and to endure adverse socioreligious conditions in its native habitat. These universalist properties do not occur to a comparable degree, or without reliance on Sanskritic norms, in any other natively practised form of Buddhism.

To define Sanskritic Buddhism in its own terms, it is the metatradition in which the canon (*tripiṭaka*) optionally includes some or all of the conservative canon (*śrāvakapiṭaka*); which gives technical and literary discourse (*śāstra-kāvya*) an authority comparable to that of scripture (*āgama*); which provides the auxiliary language for all three soteriological vehicles (*yānatraya*) and all eighteen orders (*aṣṭādaśanikāya*); which condones translation (*nirukti*) and diglossia; which can be dissociated from sectarian identity (*nikāyabheda*); and which manifests across a pan-Asian scope (*digvijaya*) overlapping with but extending beyond that of *vaidika*, *paurāṇika* and *tāntrika* Hinduism.

Finally, it should be said that the identification of universalist properties does not necessarily entail a favourable value judgement or a foretelling of future viability. Now that there are no Sanskritic polities left to flourish in, Sanskritic Buddhists' millennia-long efforts to accommodate their Hindu rivals are finally at an impasse. The living Sanskritic traditions have miniscule populations, diminishing bases of support, low profiles, and no allies or ambitions. Their universalist inheritance is not bringing them much benefit at present, nor has it facilitated a much-needed reorientation to the contemporary world.[195] The modern disengagement of Sanskritic learning from its traditional environment has helped to freeze Sanskritic traditions in their premodern states rather than reinvigorate them.

---

[194] Krishnan (2017).

[195] See, e.g., von Rospatt (2012), pp. 225ff, with regard to Newar Buddhism.

On the other hand, there are no real rivals for the universalism of Sanskrit in the pan-Asian purview. Although Pali Buddhism is increasingly put forward by its adherents as universal and as normative for other Buddhists, the Pali language remains intrinsically tied to one denomination and one type of praxis. Pali Buddhism represents a linguistic and religious monoverse, not a universe. Furthermore, in spite of the wide currency of English in Asia, and its centrality in ambitious ongoing *tripiṭaka* translation projects,[196] English does not exert standard or institutional force as a canonical language of Buddhism, nor will it be able to in the absence of a ground-up reimagining of the religion. Consequently, the teaching of the Buddha in Sanskrit, as transmitted and understood by its traditional custodians, will continue to express singular authority in the search for transcendence *sans frontières*.

Bibliography

Abhyankar, Kashinath Vasudev. 1961. *A Dictionary of Sanskrit Grammar*. Baroda: Oriental Institute. 2nd. ed., 1977.

Acri, Andrea. 2006. "The Sanskrit-Old Javanese Tutur Literature from Bali. The Textual Basis of Śaivism in Ancient Indonesia". *Rivista di Studi Sudasiatici* I: 107–37.

———. 2011. "A new perspective for 'Balinese Hinduism' in the light of the pre-modern religious discourse. A textual-historical approach". In *The Politics of Religion in Indonesia. Syncretism, Orthodoxy, and Religious Contention in Java and Bali*, edited by Michael Picard and Rémy Madinier. Oxon: Routledge.

———. 2015. "Revisiting the Cult of 'Śiva-Buddha' in Java and Bali". In *Buddhist Dynamics in Premodern and Early Modern Southeast Asia*, edited by D. Christian Lammerts, pp. 261–82. Singapore: Institute of Southeast Asian Studies.

———. 2017a. "Introduction: Re-connecting Histories across the Indo-Pacific". In *Spirits and Ships: Cultural Transfers in Early Monsoon Asia*, edited by Andrea Acri, Roger Blench and Alexandra Landmann, pp. 1–37. Singapore: ISEAS – Yusof Ishak Institute.

———. 2017b. " 'Local' vs. 'Cosmopolitan' in the Study of Premodern Southeast Asia". *Suvannabhumi* 9, no. 1: 7–52.

[196] These include, chiefly, 84000: Translating The Words Of The Buddha (https://84000.co) and the Bukkyō Dendō Kyōkai Tripiṭaka (https://bdkamerica.org). Both have utilized Sanskrit texts (often informally) in the translation process.

Aklujkar, Ashok. 2001. "*Paṇḍita* and Pandits in History". In *The Paṇḍit: Traditional Scholarship in India*, edited by Axel Michaels. New Delhi: Manohar.

Anand, Kamal. 2003. "Cultural Heritage in Modern Sanskrit Literature on Southeast Asia". In *Pramodasindhu: Professor Pramod Ganesh Lalye's 75th Birthday Felicitation Volume*, edited by Kalyan Kale, N.B. Marathe, and Shreenand L. Bapat, pp. 443–62. Pune: Mansanman Prakashan.

Bahulkar, Shrikant S., and Mahesh Deokar. 2012. "Ideology and Language Identity: A Buddhist Perspective". In *Sāṁskṛta-sādhutā: Goodness of Sanskrit. Essays in Honour of Ashok Aklujkar*, edited by Chikafumi Watanabe, Michele Desmarais, and Yoshichika Honda, pp. 37–53. New Delhi: DK Print World.

Barik, Bibhuti. 2012. "A tour down Buddhist lane—Visit Maniabandha in Cuttack for its weaving activities and temples". *The Telegraph India*, 17 September. http://www.telegraphindia.com/1120918/jsp/odisha/.

Barua, Dilip Kumar. 2001. "Ritualistic Buddhism and Folk Belief in Bangladesh—A Case Study". *Journal of Pali and Buddhist Studies* 15, no. 2: 15–26.

———. 2002. "Marriage Ceremony of Barua Buddhist in Bangladesh—A Study on Popular Rites and Rituals". *Journal of Pali and Buddhist Studies* 16: 43–57.

———. 2003. "Funeral Rituals of Buddhist in Bangladesh: A Study on Barua Community". *Journal of Indian and Buddhist Studies* 51, no. 2: 12–16.

Bechert, Heinz. 2005. *Eine regionale hochsprachliche Tradition in Südasien: Sanskrit-literatur bei den Buddhistischen Singhalesen*. Wien: Verlag der Österreichischen Akademie der Wissenschaften.

———. 2008. "Kāvya-Literatur in der frühen und mittelalterlichen Tradition der Singhalesen in Sri Lanka". In *Sauddhasāhityastabakāvalī. Essays and Studies in Buddhist Sanskrit Literature*, edited by Dragomir Dimitrov, Michael Hahn, and Roland Steiner, pp. 1–15. Marburg: Indica et Tibetica Verlag.

Bhattacharya, Vidhushekhara. 1935. "A Sanskrit treatise by a Tibetan author". *Journal of the Greater India Society* 2: 47–54.

Bhattacharya, Biswanath. 1976. *Aśvaghoṣa: A Critical Study*. Santiniketan: Bidyut Ranjan Basu.

Bhikkhu, Prajnalankar. 2010. "Buddhism in Chittagong Hill Tracts: Past and Present". In *Buddhist Culture in Asia: Unity in Diversity*, edited by Kalpakam Sankarnarayanan, pp. 263–83. Mumbai: Somaiya Publications.

Braarvig, Jens, Jaehee Han, Hyebin Lee, and Weerachai Leuritthikul. 2018. "A synonym lexicon similar to the *Amarakośa*". *Annual Report of the International Research Institute for Advanced Buddhology at Soka University* 21: 309–13.

Bronkhorst, Johannes. 2011. "The spread of Sanskrit in Southeast Asia". In *Early Interactions between South and Southeast Asia: Reflections on Cross-Cultural Exchange*, edited by Pierre-Yves Manguin, Geoff Wade, and A. Mani, pp. 264–75. Singapore: Institute of Southeast Asian Studies.

———. 2013. "Reflections on the origins of the Mahāyāna". *Estudios Filológicos* 337: 489–502.

Brough, John. 1954. “The Language of the Buddhist Sanskrit Texts”. *Bulletin of the School of Oriental and African Studies* 16, no. 2: 351–75.

Bstan ’dzin rgya mtsho, Dalai Lama XIV and Kendrīya-Tibbatī-Ucca-Śikṣā-Saṃsthānam. 2006. *Dpal Nālanda’i paṇ chen bcu bdun gyi gsol ’debs dad gsum gsal byed ces bya ba bzhugs so*. Sarnath: Central Institute of Higher Tibetan Studies.

Bühnemann, Gudrun. 1996. “The Goddess Mahācīnakrama-Tārā (Ugra-Tārā) in Buddhist and Hindu Tantrism”. *Bulletin of the School of Oriental and African Studies* 59, no. 3: 472–93. https://doi.org/10.1017/S0041977X00030603.

Bulbeck, F. David. 2000. “Economy, Military and Ideology in Pre-Islamic Luwu, South Sulawesi, Indonesia”. *Australasian Historical Archaeology* 18: 3–16.

Capitanio, Joshua. 2018. “Sanskrit and Pseudo-Sanskrit Incantations in Daoist Ritual Texts”. *History of Religions* 57, no. 4: 348–405. https://doi.org/10.1086/696568.

Chakravarti, Srish Chandra, ed. 1918. *The Bhasha vritti*. Rajshahi: Varendra Research Society.

Chaudhuri, Sukomal. 1982. *Contemporary Buddhism in Bangladesh*. Calcutta: Atisha Memorial Publishing Society.

Dahal, Dilli Ram. 2014. *Social Composition of the Population: Caste/Ethnicity and Religion in Nepal. Population Monograph of Nepal*. Volume II: Social Demography. Kathmandu: Central Bureau of Statistics.

Dash, Sarita. 2002. *The Bauddhatantis of Orissa*. Birahakrushnapur: Society for Environment Action and Restoration of Cultural Heritage.

Dennett, D.C. 2017. *From bacteria to Bach and back: The evolution of minds*. New York: W.W. Norton & Co.

Deokar, Lata M. 2012. “Some Observations on Buddhism and Lexicography”. In *Sāṁskṛta-sādhutā: Goodness of Sanskrit. Essays in Honour of Ashok Aklujkar*, edited by Chikafumi Watanabe, Michele Desmarais, and Yoshichika Honda, pp. 126–49. New Delhi: DK Print World.

———. 2017. “Subantaratnākara: An Unknown Text of Subhūticandra”. In *Indic Manuscript Cultures through the Ages: Material, Textual, and Historical Investigations*, edited by Vincenzo Vergiani, Daniele Cuneo, and Camillo Alessio Formigatti, pp. 655–93. Berlin, Boston: De Gruyter. https://doi.org/10.1515/9783110543100-020.

Dimitrov, Dragomir. 2010. *The Bhaikṣukī Manuscript of the Candrālaṃkāra*. Cambridge, Mass.: Harvard Oriental Series.

———. 2016. *The Legacy of the Jewel Mind: On the Sanskrit, Pali, and Sinhalese Works by Ratnamati*. Napoli: Departimento Asia Africa e Mediterraneo Università degli studi di Napoli “L’Orientale”.

Dine, Susan. 2012. “Sanskrit Beyond Text: The Use of Bonji (Siddham) in Mandala and Other Imagery in Ancient and Medieval Japan”. MA thesis, University of Washington.

Donaldson, Thomas Eugene. 2001. *Iconography of the Buddhist Sculpture of Orissa*. 2 vols. New Delhi: Indira Gandhi National Centre for the Arts.
Dutt, Nalinaksha. 1978. *Bodhisattvabhūmīḥ*. Patna: K.P. Jayaswal Research Institute.
Dvivedī, Premanārāyaṇa, Rādhāvallabha Tripaṭhī, and Ṛṣanbhāradvāja, eds. 2012. *Paṃ. Premanārāyaṇadvivediracanāvaliḥ. Prathamo bhāgah: Kāvyasaṅgrahaḥ*. Navadehalī, Rāṣṭriyasaṃskṛtasaṃsthānam.
Editorial Board of Murals in Ar-er-zhai Grottoes (鄂托克旗文化广播电视电影局). 2010. *A'erzhai shiku bihua* 阿尔寨石窟壁画 (*Ar-er-zhai grotto murals*). Hohhot: Nei Menggu renmin chubanshe 内蒙古人民出版社.
Edgerton, Franklin. 1953. *Buddhist Hybrid Sanskrit Grammar and Dictionary*. 2 vols. New Haven: Yale University Press.
Eerde, J.C. van. 1910. "Hindu-Javānsche en Balische Eeredienst". *Bijdragen tot de Taal-, Land- en Volkenkunde van Nederlandsch-Indie* 64: 1–39.
Eltschinger, Vincent. 2017. "Why Did the Buddhists Adopt Sanskrit?". *Open Linguistics* 3 (Topical Issue on Historical Sociolinguistic Philology, edited by Chiara Barbati and Christian Gastgeber): 308–26. https://doi.org/10.1515/opli-2017-0015.
Engle, Artemus B, trans. 2016. *The Bodhisattva path to unsurpassed enlightenment: A complete translation of the Bodhisattvabhūmi*. Boulder: Snow Lion.
Gait, E.A. 1902. *Census of India, 1901. Volume VI: The Lower Provinces of Bengal and their Feudatories. Part I: The Report*. Calcutta: Bengal Secretariat Press.
Gellner, David N. 2016. *The Idea of Nepal*. Kathmandu: Social Science Baha.
———. 2018. "Civilization as a Key Guiding Idea in South Asia". In *Anthropological and Civilizational Analysis: Eurasian Explorations*, edited by Johann P. Arnason and Chris Hann, pp. 99–120. Albany: State University of New York Press.
Gippert, Jost. 2013–14. "A Glimpse into the Buddhist Past of the Maldives: II. Two Sanskrit Inscriptions". *Wiener Zeitschrift für die Kunde Südasiens* 55: 111–44.
Gottowik, Volker. 2016. "In Search of Holy Water: Hindu Pilgrimage to Gunung Rinjani on Lombok, Indonesia, as a Multi-religious Site". In *Religion, Place and Modernity. Spatial Articulations in Southeast Asia and East Asia*, edited by Andrea Lauser and Michael Dickhardt, pp. 205–43. Leiden: Brill.
Goudriaan, Teun, and Christian Hooykaas. 1971. *Stuti and Stava (Bauddha, Śaiva and Vaiṣṇava) of Balinese Brahman priests*. Amsterdam, London: North-Holland Publishing Company.
Grierson, George A. 1906. "Review of *The Thirty-seven Nats, a phase of Spirit-Worship prevailing in Burma*, by R.C. Temple". *Journal of The Royal Asiatic Society of Great Britain and Ireland for 1907*: 237–42.
Guruge, Ananda W.P. 1996. "Senarat Paranavitana as a writer of historical fiction in Sanskrit". *Vidyodaya Journal of Social Science* 7, nos. 1 & 2: 157–79.
———. 2003. "Allusions to the *Rāmāyaṇa* in Buddhist Sanskrit literature". *Indologica Taurinensia* 29: 171–88.

———. 2009. “Does the Theravāda Tradition of Buddhism Exist Today?” In *Buddhist and Pali studies in honour of the Venerable Professor Kakkapalliye Anuruddha*, edited by Kuala Lumpur Dhammajoti and Y. Karunadasa, pp. 97–118. Hong Kong: University of Hong Kong.

Hacker, Katherine. 2004. “Dressing Lord Jagannatha in Silk: Cloth, Clothes, and Status”. *Journal of Social Science* 8, no. 2: 113–27.

Hahn, Michael. 2010. “The Buddhist Contribution the Indian *belles letteres*”. *Acta Orientalia* 63, no. 4: 455–71. https://doi.org/10.1556/AOrient.63.2010.4.4.

Hanisch, Albrecht. 2008. “Sarvarakṣita’s *Maṇicūḍajātaka*. Reproduction of the Codex Unicus with Diplomatic Transcript and Palaeographic Introdution to the Bhakṣukī Script”. In *Sanskrit Texts from Giuseppe Tucci’s Collection Part I*, edited by Francesco Sferra, pp. 195–342. Rome: IsIAO.

Harrison, Paul, and Jens-Uwe Hartmann. 2014. “Introduction”. In *From Birch Bark to Digital Data: Recent Advances in Buddhist Manuscript Research*, edited by Paul Harrison and Jens-Uwe Hartmann, pp. vii–xxii. Wien: Verlag der Österreichen Akademie der Wissenschaften.

Haryanto, Joko Tri. 2014. “Kearifan lokal pendukung kerukunan beragama pada komunitas Tengger Malang jatim (Local Wisdom Supporting Religious Harmony in Tengger Community, Malang, East Java, Indonesia)”. *Jurnal “Analisa”* 21, no. 2: 201–13.

Hauser-Schäublin, Brigitta, and I Wayan Ardika. 2008. *Burials, Texts and Rituals: Ethnoarchaeological Investigations in North Bali, Indonesia*. Göttingen: Universitätsverlag Göttingen.

Hayashi, Makoto. 2014. “The Birth of Buddhist Universities”. *Japanese Religions* 39, nos. 1 & 2: 11–29.

He, Xi. 2011. “The Prose *Varṇaka* in the *Lalitavistara*”. In *South Asian Texts in History: Critical Engagements with Sheldon Pollock*, edited by Yigal Bronner, Whitney Cox, and Lawrence McCrea, pp. 83–101. Ann Arbor: Association for Asian Studies, Inc. (Reprinted, Delhi: Primus, 2016).

Hefner, Robert W. 1993. *The Political Economy of Mountain Java: An Interpretive History*. Berkeley: University of California Press.

Hokazono, Kōichi (外薗幸一). 1994. *Raritavisutara no kenkyū* ラリタヴィスタラの研究. Tokyo: Daitō Shuppansha 大東出版社.

Hooykaas, Christian. 1973. *Balinese Bauddha brahmans*. Amsterdam: North-Holland Publishing Company.

Hornbacher, Annette. 2013. “The ‘Unforced Force’ of Religious Identification: Indonesian Hindu-Buddhism between Ritual Integration, National Control and Nativist Tendencies”. In *Challenging Paradigms: Buddhism and Nativism. Framing Identity Discourse in Buddhist Environments*, edited by Henk Blezer and Mark Teeuwen. Leiden: Brill.

Houben, Jan E.M. 2018. “Linguistic Paradox and Diglossia: the emergence of Sanskrit and Sanskritic language in Ancient India”. *Open Linguistics* 4: 1–18. https://doi.org/10.1515/opli-2018-0001.

Hultzsch, E. 1895. "No. 26.—Sravana-Belgola Epitaph of Mallishena; after Saka-Samvat 1050". *Epigraphia Indica* 3: 184–207.

Hunter, Thomas M. 2014a. "A Constant Flow of Pilgrims: *Kāvya* and the Early History of the *Kakawin*". In *Innovations and Turning Points: Toward a History of* Kāvya *Literature*, edited by Yigal Bronner, David Shulman, and Gary Tubb, pp. 195–232. Delhi: Oxford.

———. 2014b. "A Distant Mirror: Innovation and Change in the East Javanese *Kakawin*". In *Innovations and Turning Points: Toward a History of* Kāvya *Literature*, edited by Yigal Bronner, David Shulman, and Gary Tubb, pp. 739–86. Delhi: Oxford.

Jinpa, Thupten, and Donald S. Lopez, trans. 2014. *Grains of gold: Tales of a cosmopolitan traveler*. Chicago: University of Chicago Press.

Johnston, E.H. 1944. "Some Sanskrit inscriptions of Arakan". *Bulletin of the School of Oriental and African Studies* 11, no. 2: 357–85.

Jośī, Prabhākara Śaṅkara. [2011.] *Bhīmāyanam*. Śāradā-gaurava-grantha-mālā 11. [Pune:] Vasanta Ananta Gāḍagīḷa.

Junghare, Indira Y. 1999. "Sanskritic Buddhism in South-East Asia". In *Tantric Buddhism*, edited by N.N. Bhattacharyya, pp. 65–80. Delhi: Manohar Publishers.

Kandahjaya, Hudaya. 2016. "*Saṅ Hyaṅ Kamahāyānikan*, Borobudur, and the Origins of Esoteric Buddhism in Indonesia". In *Esoteric Buddhism in Mediaeval Maritime Asia: Networks of Masters, Texts, Icons*, edited by Andrea Acri, pp. 67–112. Singapore: ISEAS – Yusof Ishak Institute.

Karashima, Seishi. 2014. "The Language of the *Abhisamācārikā Dharmāḥ*: The Oldest Buddhist Hybrid Sanskrit Text". *Annual Report of The International Research Institute for Advanced Buddhology at Soka University* 17: 77–88.

———. 2015. "Who Composed the Mahāyāna Scriptures? The Mahāsāṃghikas and Vaitulya Scriptures". *Annual Report of The International Research Institute for Advanced Buddhology at Soka University* 18: 113–62.

———. 2018. "Ajita and Maitreya: More evidence of the early Mahāyāna scriptures' origins from the Mahāsāṃghikas and a clue as to the school-affiliation of the Kanaganahalli-*stūpa*". *Annual Report of The International Research Institute for Advanced Buddhology at Soka University* 21: 181–96.

Kern, Hendrik. 1907. "Concerning some old Sanskrit Inscriptions in the Malay Peninsula". *Journal of the Straits Branch of the Royal Asiatic Society*, No. 49 (December): 95–101.

Kishino IV, Ryoji. 2013. "A Study of the *Nidāna*: An Underrated Canonical Text of the Mūlasarvāstivāda-vinaya". PhD dissertation, University of California, Los Angeles.

Klebanov, Andrey. 2010. "The Nepalese Version of the *Suśrutasaṃhitā* and its Interrelation with Buddhism and the Buddhists". MA thesis, Universität Hamburg.

Kreft, Holger, and Walter Jetz. 2013. "Comment on 'An Update of Wallace's Zoogeographic Regions of the World'". *Science* 341 (no. 6144), 25 July 2013, p. 343. https://doi.org/10.1126/science.1237471.

Krishnan, Ananth. 2017. "The lost Sanskrit treasures of Tibet". *India Today*, 3 June 2017. https://www.indiatoday.in/magazine/neighbours/story/20170612-sanskrit-tibet-chinese-scholars-buddhism-986510-2017-06-03.

Lammerts, Christian, and Arlo Griffiths. 2015. "Epigraphy: Southeast Asia". In *Brill's Encyclopedia of Buddhism*, edited by Jonathan A. Silk, pp. 988–1009. Leiden: Brill.

Lamotte, Etienne, and Sara Webb-Boin, trans. 1988. *History of Indian Buddhism: From the Origins to the Śaka Era*. Louvain-la-Neuve: Université catholique de Louvain, Institut orientaliste.

Lanus, Sugi. 2014. "Puja Tri Sandhyā: Indian Mantras Recomposed and Standardised in Bali". *Journal of Hindu Studies* 7, pp. 243–72. https://doi.org/10.1093/jhs/hiu021.

Law, Narendra Nath. 1932. "Some Images and Traces of Mahāyāna Buddhism in Chittagong". *Indian Historical Quarterly* 8: 332–41.

Lévi, Sylvain. 1907. "Les éléments de formation du Divyāvadāna". *T'oung Pao (Second Series)* 8, no. 1: 105–22.

———. 1933. *Sanskrit Texts from Bali*. Baroda: Oriental Institute.

Lewis, Todd. 1984. "The Tuladhars of Kathmandu: A study of Buddhist tradition in a Newar merchant community". PhD dissertation, Columbia University.

Lianchhinga, Fanai. 1996. "The Chakmas and their religious beliefs and practices (with special reference to the Chakmas of Mizoram)". PhD dissertation, Gauhati University.

Li, Dong Hong, and Steven Laurits Watkins, trans. 2009. "The influence of Indian Buddhism on Bai identification and understanding of their origins as a people: A research note". *Asian Ethnicity* 10: 19–23.

Liao, Yang. 2016. "Xizang xibu caca mingwen tansuo 西藏西部擦擦銘文探索" [A brief survey of inscriptions on tsha tshas found in Western Tibet]. In *Xizang Guge caca yishu* 西藏古格擦擦艺术 [Art of Tsha tshas from Guge, Tibet], edited by Wenbin Xiong and Yizhi Li, pp. 14–56. Beijing: Zhongguo Zangxue chubanshe.

Liebenthal, Walter. 1947. "Sanskrit inscriptions from Yunnan I". *Monumenta Serica* 12: 1–40.

Lienhard, Siegfried. 1984. *A history of classical poetry: Sanskrit-Pali-Prakrit*. Wiesbaden: Harrassowitz.

Lindtner, Chr. 2001. Madhyamakahṛdayam *of Bhavya*. Chennai: The Adyar Library and Research Centre.

Lopez, Donald S. 2013. *Gendun Chopel: Tibet's First Modern Artist*. New York: Trace Foundation's Latse Library; Chicago, Illinois: in association with Serindia Publications, Inc.

Mabbett, Ian. 1998. "The Problem of the Historical Nāgārjuna Revisited".

Journal of the American Oriental Society 118, no. 3: 332–46. https://doi.org/10.2307/606062.

Maretha, Ni Ketut Windhi. 2017. "Pandita Mpu Sebagai representasi simbol kepanditaan pada Masyarakat Hindu di Kota Mataram". *Ganeç Swara* 11, no. 2: 1–6.

Matsuda, Kazunobu. 2014. "Japanese Collections of Buddhist Manuscript Fragments from the Same Region as the Schoyen Collection". In *From Birch Bark to Digital Data: Recent Advances in Buddhist Manuscript Research*, edited by Paul M. Harrison and Jens-Uwe Hartmann. Wien: Verlag der Österreichischen Akademie der Wissenschaften.

McGovern, Nathan. 2017. "Esoteric Buddhism in Southeast Asia". *Oxford Research Encyclopedia of Religion*. https://doi.org/10.1093/acrefore/9780199340378.013.617.

McKeown, Arthur Philip. 2010. "From Bodhgayā to Lhasa to Beijing: The Life and Times of Śāriputra (c.1335–1426), Last Abbot of Bodhgayā". PhD dissertation, Harvard University.

Meisig, Konrad. 2011. *Beginnings of Buddhist Ethics: The Chinese Parallel to the Kūṭadantasutta*. Wiesbaden: Harrassowitz.

Mishra, Jitu. 2017. "Buddhist Weavers of Maniabandha: A Confluence of Ideas". *Virasat E Hind Blog*, 24 February 2017. https://blogvirasatehind.com/2017/02/24/buddhist-weavers-of-maniabandh-nuapatna-a-confluence-of-ideas/.

Nemec, John. 2017. "On the contributions of the Śivadṛṣṭi of Somānanda to the Intellectual History of the Pratyabhijñā". *Annuaire de l'École pratique des hautes études (EPHE), Section des sciences religieuses* [En ligne] 124. http://journals.openedition.org/asr/1679.

Nepal-German Manuscript Preservation Project. 2003. *Preliminary list of manuscripts, blockprints, and historical documents microfilmed by NGMPP*. CD-ROM. Hamburg: University of Hamburg, Asia-Africa Institute, Dept of Indian and Tibetan Studies.

Newman, John. 1987. "The Outer Wheel of Time: Vajrayāna Buddhist Cosmology in the Kālacakra Tantra". PhD dissertation, University of Wisconsin-Madison.

Okada, Mamiko. 1993. *Dvāviṃśatyavadānakathā. Ein mittelalterlicher buddhistische Text zur Spendenfrömmigkeit*. Bonn: Indica et Tibetica Verlag.

Orlina, Roderick. 2012. "Epigraphical evidence for the cult of Mahāpratisarā in the Philippines". *Journal of the International Association of Buddhist Studies* 35, no. 1–2: 91–101.

Otsuka, Nobuo. 2004. "*Fukū kenjaku shinpen shingon kyō* Bonbun shahon tensha tekisuto (5) 『不空羂索神変真言経』梵文写本転写テキスト(5)". *Annual of the Institute for Comprehensive Studies of Buddhism* (Taisho University) 26: 120–83.

Pahlajrai, Prem. 2004. "Doxographies: Why *six darśanas*? Which six?", Paper presented at the 2004 Asian Studies Graduate Student Colloquium". https://faculty.washington.edu/prem/Colloquium04-Doxographies.pdf.

Paranavitana, Senarat. 1974. "The *Dhvanikārikās* in fifteenth century Ceylon". *Journal of the American Oriental Society* 94, no. 1: 131–33.

Payne, Richard K. 2017. "On Not Understanding Extraordinary Language in the Buddhist Tantra of Japan". *Religions* 8, no. 10: 223. https://doi.org/10.3390/rel8100223.

Picard, Michel. 2011. "Balinese Religion in Search of Recognition: From Agama Hindu Bali to Agama Hindu (1945–1965)". *Bijdragen tot de Taal-, Land- en Volkenkunde* 167, no. 4: 482–510.

Piyaratana, Hingulwala. 2013. "Modern Sanskrit literature in Sri Lanka and the status of Sanskrit in contemporary Sri Lanka, a study". PhD dissertation, Andhra University.

Pollock, Sheldon. 2006. *The Language of the Gods in the World of Men*. Berkeley and Los Angeles: University of California Press.

Porter, A.E. 1933. *Census of India, 1931, Volume V: Bengal & Sikkim. Part I: Report*. Calcutta: Central Publication Branch.

Prasad, Birendra Nath. 2014. "The Socio-Religious Dimensions of Dedicatory Inscriptions on Sculptures Donated to a Buddhist Establishment in Early Medieval Magadha: Kurkihar, c.800–1200 CE". *Journal of the Oxford Centre for Buddhist Studies* 7: 116–52.

Prihatmoko, Hedwi. 2016. "Kajian Epigrafis Prasasti Babahan (Epigraphy Study of Babahan Inscriptions)". *Forum Arkeologi* 29, no. 3: 117–36. https://doi.org/10.24832/fa.v29i3.100.

Pu, Cang (普仓). 2017. "Xizang xin faxian de Longshu *Bao man lun song* Fanwen xieben 西藏新发现的龙树《宝鬘论颂》梵文写本". *Fanfoyan* 梵佛研, 14 March 2017. http://www.fanfoyan.com/new.htm (accessed 17 July 2018).

Raja, C. Kunha, and S.S. Suryanarayana Sastri. 1975. *Manameyodaya of Nārāyaṇa (An Elementary Treatise on the Mīmāṃsā)*. Madras: The Adyar Library and Research Centre.

Ray, Niharranjan. 1929. "Brahmanical Gods in Buddhist Burma". *The Visva-bharati Quarterly* 7, no. 1–2: 60–71.

Reader, Ian. 2011. "Buddhism in Crisis? Institutional Decline in Modern Japan". *Buddhist Studies Review* 28, no. 2: 233–63. https://doi.org/10.1558/bsrv.v28i2.233.

Saito, Akira. 2014. "How Can Buddhist Thought Be Brought Back to Life? Buddhist Scriptures, Terms, and Translation in Present-day Japan". *Kokusai Tetsugaku Kenkyū* 3: 249–55.

Sāṅkṛtyāyana, Rāhula. 1954. *Mahā Pari Nirvāṇa Sūtra*. Udayapura: Rājasthāna Viśva Vidyāpīṭha, Sāhitya-saṃsthāna.

———. 1960. "Simhaleṣu Saṃskṛtam". *Samskrita Pratibha* 2, no. 1: 59–68.

———. 1985. "Buddha-Mārksayor vādasāmyam". In *Bauddhadarśana aura Mārksavāda*, edited by Rameśa Kumāra Dvivedī, pp. 3–8. Vārāṇasī: Saṃpūrṇānanda-Saṃskṛta-Viśvavidyālaya (Bauddhadarśanavibhāga).

Śāstrī, Mahanta Śrī Rāmacandradāsa. 1963. *Mahākaviśrīmadaśvaghoṣaviracitaṃ Buddhacaritam. 'Prakāśa' Hindīvyākhyopetam (dvitīyo bhagaḥ)*. Vārāṇasī: Caukhambā Vidyābhavana.

Schalk, Peter, ed. Āḷvāppiḷḷai Vēluppiḷḷai, co-ed. 2002. *Buddhism among Tamils in Pre-Colonial Tamiḻakam and Īḻam*. 2 vols. Uppsala: Uppsala Universitet.

Scharfe, Hartmut. 1977. *Grammatical Literature*. Wiesbaden: Otto Harrassowitz.

Schneider, Johannes. 2010. *Vāgīśvarakīrtis* Mṛtyuvañcanopadeśa, *eine buddhistische Lehrschrift zur Abwehr des Todes*. Wien: Verlag der Österreichischen Akademie der Wissenschaften.

Schopen, Gregory. 2013. "Regional Languages and the Law in Some Early North Indian Buddhist Monasteries and Convents". *Bulletin of the Asia Institute* 23: 171–79.

Semavāl, Śrīkṛṣṇa. 1991. *Bhīmaśatakam*. Dillī: Dillī Saṃskrta Akādamī.

Sen, Sukumar. 1945. "Is the cult of Dharma a living relic of Buddhism in Bengal?". In *B.C. Law Volume. Part I*, edited by D.R. Bhandarkar et al., pp. 669–74. Calcutta: The Indian Research Institute.

Senart, Émile. 1902–03. "The inscriptions in the caves at Karle". *Epigraphia Indica* 7: 47–74.

Sferra, Francesco. 2001. "Some Considerations on the Relationship between Hindu and Buddhist Tantras." In *Buddhist Asia 1: Papers from the First Conference of Buddhist Studies Held in Naples in May 2001*, edited by Giovanni Verardi and Silvio Vita, pp. 57–84. Kyoto: Italian School of East Asian Studies.

Shastri, Haraprasad. 1897. *Discovery of Living Buddhism in Bèngal*. Calcutta: Sanskrit Press Depository.

Shastri, Hirananda. 1942. *Nalanda and its epigraphic material*. Delhi: Manager of publications.

Shastri, Satya Vrat. 1979. *Thāideśavilāsam*. Delhi: Eastern Book Linkers.

Śīlaskandha. 1911. *Saddharmamakarandaḥ: Dīpaṅkarādīnāṃ caturviṃśatisambuddhānāṃ sakāśeṣu vyākaraṇalābhādipūrvvakam bhagavataḥ Śrīśakyamuneḥ sajjivanacaritam*. Sri Lanka: S.T. Guṇavardhana.

Sinclair, Iain. 2010. "Hymns and Mantras used in a Buddhist procession of Lalitpur". *Paleswan* 26: 19–47.

———. 2016. "The appearance of tantric monasticism in Nepal: A history of the public image and fasting ritual of Newar Buddhism, 980–1380". PhD dissertation. Monash University. https://doi.org/10.4225/03/58ab8cadcf152.

———, and Caroline Riberaigua, trans. 2017. "*Nepālamaṇḍalābhyantaragata-buddhavihāra-nāmāni* = Noms des monastères bouddhiques de la région du Népal". Paris: Salamandre, Collège de France. http://salamandre.college-de-france.fr.

Singh, Priya Sen, ed. 2012. *Bhīmāmbedkaraśatakam. Sugatakaviratnasya Śāntibhikṣuśāstriṇaḥ*. New Delhi: Rāṣṭriya Saṃskṛta Saṃsthānam.

Sircar, D.C. 1983. *Select Inscriptions bearing on Indian History and Civilization. From the Sixth to the Eighteenth Century A.D.* 2 vols. Delhi: Motilal Banarsidass.

Skilling, Peter. 2015. "An Untraced Buddhist verse inscription from Peninsular Southeast Asia". In *Buddhist Dynamics in Premodern and Early Modern Southeast Asia*, edited by D. Christian Lammerts, pp. 18–77. Singapore: Institute of Southeast Asian Studies.

Skinner, Michael C. 2017. "Marks of Empire: Extracting a Narrative from the Corpus of Kuṣāṇa Inscriptions". PhD dissertation, University of Washington.

Speyer, Jacob S. 1913. "Ein altjavanischer mahāyānistischer Katechismus". *Zeitschrift der Deutschen Morgenländischen Gesellschaft* 67: 347–62.

Sreedathan, G. 2014. "800 yrs on, Hindus have reclaimed Delhi: VHP". *Business Standard*, 22 November. http://www.business-standard.com/article/politics/800-yrs-on-hindus-have-reclaimed-delhi-vhp-114112200037_1.html.

Steinkellner, Ernst. 2003. *A Tale of Leaves: Sanskrit Manuscripts in Tibet, their Past and their Future*. Amsterdam: Royal Netherlands Academy of Arts and Sciences.

———. 2016. "Sanskrit manuscripts on palm-leaves, paper and birch-bark in the TAR: What now?". Keynote, 6th Beijing International Seminar on Tibetan Studies, 2 August.

Sternbach, Ludwik. 1978. *A Descriptive Catalogue of Poets quoted in Sanskrit Anthologies and Inscriptions. Volume 1: Aṁśudhara - Dhoyi*. Wiesbaden: Otto Harrassowitz.

———. 1980. *A Descriptive Catalogue of Poets quoted in Sanskrit Anthologies and Inscriptions. Volume 2: Nakula - Hevidhanesora*. Wiesbaden: Otto Harrassowitz.

Strauch, Ingo, and Michael D. Bukharin. 2004. "Indian Inscriptions from the Cave Ḥoq on Suquṭrā (Yemen)". *Annali dell'Università degli Studi di Napoli "L'Orientale"* 74, no. 1–4: 121–36.

Taishō Tripiṭaka: The SAT Daizōkyō Text Database Committee. 2012. *The SAT Daizōkyō Text Database 大蔵経テキストデータベース*. Tokyo: University of Tokyo. http://21dzk.l.u-tokyo.ac.jp/SAT/.

Takakusu, Juniro, trans.; I-Tsing. 1896. *A Record of the Buddhist religion as practised in India and the Malay Archipelago (A.D. 671–695)*. Oxford: The Clarendon Press.

Tallents, P.C. 1923. *Census of India 1921. Volume VII: Bihar and Orissa. Part I. Report*. Patna: Government Printing, Bihar and Orissa.

Tanaka, Kimiaki. 2017. *The Sanskrit commentary on the* Samantabhadra nāma sādhana-ṭīkā *of Buddhajñānapāda*. Tokyo: Watanabe Publishing Co., Ltd.

Tanemura, Ryugen. 1993. "The Four *nikāya*s Mentioned in the *Gaṇḍīlakṣaṇa* Chapter of the *Kriyāsaṃgraha*". *Journal of Indian and Buddhist Studies* 41(2): 40–42.

———. 1994. "*Kriyāsaṃgraha* no shukke sahō (Kriyāsaṃgraha の出家作法)". *Studies of Indian philosophy and Buddhism* 2: 53–67.

Tanto, Sugeng. 2003. "Syncretistic Beliefs in Javanese Buddhism: A Case Study Focusing on Kalimanggis Village". *Journal of Pali and Buddhist Studies* 17: 121–27.

———. 2012. "Indoneshia, Bari-jima ni okeru daijo bukkyō". In *Ajia no bukkyō to kamigami* アジアの仏教と神々, edited by Musashi Tachikawa, pp. 194–207. Kyoto: Hōzōkan 法藏館.

Tatelman, Joel. 1996. "The Trials of Yaśodharā: A Critical Edition, Annotated Translation and Study of *Bhadrakalpāvadāna* II–V". PhD dissertation, University of Oxford.

Templeman, David. 2008. "Becoming Indian: A Study of the Life of the 16–17th Century Tibetan Lama, Tāranātha". PhD dissertation, Monash University.

Torella, Raffaele. 2013. "Inherited cognitions: *Prasiddhi, āgama, pratibhā, śabdana* – Bhartṛhari, Utpaladeva, Abhinavagupta, Kumārila and Dharmakīrti in dialogue". In *Scriptural authority, reason and action. Proceedings of a panel at the 14th World Sanskrit Conference, Kyoto, Sept. 1–5, 2009*, edited by Vincent Eltschinger and Helmut Krasser, pp. 455–80. Wien: Verlag der Österreichischen Akademie der Wissenschaften.

Tsukamoto, Keisho (塚本 啓祥). 1996. *Indo bukkyō himei no kenkyū* インド仏教碑銘の研究 [A comprehensive study of Indian Buddhist inscriptions]. Volume I: Text, notes and Japanese translation. Kyoto: The Heirakuji-shoten.

Tubb, Gary. 2014. "Baking Umā". In *Innovations and Turning Points: Toward a History of Kāvya Literature*, edited by Yigal Bronner, David Shulman, and Gary Tubb, pp. 71–85. Delhi: Oxford.

Tuladhar-Douglas, Will. 2004. "From One to Many: Canonical language(s), Newar Buddhism and Eclectic Buddhism". Unpublished manuscript.

Ui, Hakuju, Munetada Suzuki, and Enshō Kanakura. 1934. *A complete catalogue of the Tibetan Buddhist Canons (Bkaḥ-ḥgyur and Bstan-ḥgyur)*. Sendai: Tōhoku Imperial University.

Upadhyaya, Jagannatha, ed. 1986. *Vimalaprabhāṭīkā of Kalki Śrī Puṇḍarīka on Śrī Laghukālacakratantrarāja*. Sarnath: Central Institute of Higher Tibetan Studies.

Urban, Mateusz. 2007. "Defining the linguistic area/league: An invitation to discussion". *Studia Linguistica* 124: 137–59.

Vajrācārya, Dhanavajra. [1973]. *Licchavikālakā abhilekha (anuvāda, aitihāsika vyākhyāsahita)*. Kathmandu: Nepāla ra Eśiyālī Adhyayana Saṃsthāna, Tribhuvana Viśvavidyālaya (repr. 2002).

———. [2011]. *Pūrvamadhyakālakā abhilekha*. Kathmandu: Nepāla ra Eśiyālī Anusandhāna Kendra, Tribhuvana Viśvavidyālaya.

Vasu, Nagendra Náth. 1911. *The modern Buddhism and its followers in Orissa.* Calcutta: [s.p.].

Verhagen, Peter. 2013. "Notes Apropos to the Oeuvre of Si tu paṇ chen chos kyi 'byung gnas (1699?–1774) (4): A Tibetan Sanskritist in Nepal". *Journal of the International Association of Tibetan Studies* 7: 316–39.

Verpoorten, Jean-Marie. 1987. *Mīmāṃsā Literature*. Wiesbaden: Otto Harrassowitz.

von Rospatt, Alexander. 2012. "Past continuity and recent changes in the ritual practice of Newar Buddhism: Reflections on the impact of Tibetan Buddhism and the advent of modernity". In *Revisiting Rituals in a Changing Tibetan World*, edited by Katie Buffetrille. Leiden/Boston: Brill.

von Staël-Holstein, Baron A. 1932. *On a Tibetan text translated into Sanskrit under Ch'ien Lung (XVIII cent.) and into Chinese under Tao Kuang (XIX cent.)*. Peiping: National Library of Peiping.

Wallace, Alfred Russel. 1876. *The geographical distribution of animals*. 2 vols. London: Macmillan and Co.

Warshall, Sophia van Zyle. 2012. "The Sanskrit Inscriptions of Pedjeng: A case study of the utility of Sanskrit epigraphy in the study of Bali's socio-religious history". MA thesis, Concordia University.

Wickremasinghe, Don Martino de Zilva. 1912. *Epigraphica Zeylanica*. Volume I. London: Oxford University Press.

Xinhua.net (中国新闻网). 2018. "Xizang beiyejing yanjiu chu xian 'guoji fan' 西藏贝叶经研究初显"国际范" [Tibetan palmleaf manuscript study's prominent beginning, the 'international model']". 28 April. xinhuanet.com/xz/2018-04/28/c_137143250.htm.

Yamaguchi, Shinobu (山口 しのぶ). 2003. "Bari-Hindū jiin no shinzō ni tsuite バリ・ヒンドゥー寺院の神像について：バドゥブラン・プサ寺院の事例報告" [On the images of Hindu Deities in a Balinese Temple]. *The Mikkyō Zuzō* 22: 15–27.

Yamazaki, Gen'ichi. 2005. *The Structure of Ancient Indian Society: Theory and Reality of the Varṇa System*. Toyo Bunko Research Library 6. Tokyo: The Toyo Bunko.

Ye, Shaoyong (葉少勇). 2014. "Feilaifeng shi ke Fanwen tuoluoni de Lanzha ziti 飞来峰石刻梵文陀罗尼的兰札字体". In *Jiang nan Zang chuan fojiao yishu* 江南藏传佛教艺术, edited by Jisheng Xie, pp. 178–84. Beijing: Zhongguo Zangxue chubanshe.

Yuyama, Akira (湯山 明). 1985. "Enfukuji no Bongo meibun oboekagi: Kono shōron wo Suematsu Yasuzaku kyōju ni sasagu 演福寺銅鐘の梵語銘文覚書：この小論を末松保和教授に捧ぐ" [The Sanskrit Inscription Cast on a Bell at the Yeon-bog-jeol Temple in Korea]. *Toyo Gakuho* 東洋学報 66, no. 1–4: 319–24.

Zydenbos, Robert J. 1999. "Jainism as the religion of non-violence". In *Violence Denied: Violence, Non-Violence and the Rationalization of Violence in South Asian Cultural History*, edited by Jan E.M. Houben and Karel R. Van Kooij, pp. 184–210. Brill: Leiden.

11

Interconnectedness and Mobility in the Middle Ages/Nowadays: From Baghdad to Chang'an and from Istanbul to Tokyo

Federica A. Broilo

Here is the Tigris with nothing between us and China,
and on it arrives everything that the sea can bring.
Al-Tabarī, *History*, vol. XXVIII

INTRODUCTION

The mapping of the active networks of circulation and exchange in Eurasia during the Middle Ages would make easier the comparison between cultural systems which, although different among them, were not kept in sealed boxes. This is certainly the case of the Abbasid Caliphate of Baghdad and Tang China. Chang'an and Baghdad were at that time two of the largest cities in the world, marked by strong rule, successful diplomatic relationships, economic expansion, and a cultural efflorescence characterized by a cosmopolitan style. A comparative methodology allows to effectively describe both entanglements and contacts among artistic and architectural practices belonging to different cultural systems that appear distant on the geographic chart, but are actually much closer than originally thought. The case of Tang China is particularly evident through the adoption of Central Asian fashion and customs at the court of Chang'an. Similarly relevant is the appreciation for Chinese porcelains at the Abbassid court, which would eventually lead to the production of local imitations and adoptions of new patterns and shapes. The adoption of models moving within the broad borders of Asia is very relevant to our days. If trade is what unites the modern global system and Asia is the focal point of the new century, this phenomenon cannot be understood without searching in the past for a similar phenomenon of interconnectedness and mobility of objects, workers, written texts, and ideas. Bentley (1996, p. 752) maintains that in the discourse of cross-cultural interactions in premodern times there are three kinds of processes which had significant repercussions across the boundaries of societies and cultural regions: mass migrations, campaign of imperial expansions, and long-distance trade. Different interactions between the Mediterranean and Asia are here presented following a chronological order, focusing in particular on how trade and trade diaspora communities played an important role to facilitate the transportation and exchange of commodities and at the same time served as avenues of diffusion of technology and also religious beliefs in both premodern and modern societies. In fact the selected case studies show how long-distance trade has contributed to the diffusion of Islam to China under the Tang dynasty (618–907) and in Japan under the Taishō (1912–26) and early Shōwa (1926–89) eras.[1] A final thought is dedicated to the growing relations, both economic and cultural, of Turkey and Japan, culminating with the reconstruction of the Tokyo Mosque in the year 2000.

CHINA AND ISLAM

The Tang dynasty ruled China from 618 to 907 CE, a period regarded as one of the most successful and creative of all Chinese history (Curtin 1984, p. 104). The Tang capital at Chang'an became the greatest urban centre in the world, with nearly two million people in the urban area and a million within the city walls (ibid., p. 105). Both Chang'an and Luoyang, the second most important city of the Tang, were charmed by exotic goods. Foreign embassies into the Tang capital brought into

[1] Ali Merthan Dündar's book (Dündar 2008) on the history of Turks in Japan and Manchuria and the cultural heritage of the twentieth century built Tatar mosques in Japan in Turkish language is probably the most updated publication on this topic together with Larisa Usmanova's (Usmanova 2007), *The Türk-Tatar Diaspora in Northeast Asia. Transformation of Consciousness: A Historical and Sociological Account between 1898 and the 1950s.*

its walls people and sought-after luxury goods from all over Asia. The fashion, food, and lifestyles of the courts were often dictated by new trends imported from abroad.[2] Eventually during the seventh century the taste for all sort of foreign luxuries and wonders began to spread from the court outward, leading in the eighth century to foster oversea trade by securing and improving existing waterways and highways that would be used to bring in luxury items such as ivory, frankincense, camphor, and copper ingots from faraway countries to the cities in the north. There were in fact two ways to China: overland by caravan and oversea through the South China Sea and the Indian Ocean. The two most important trading cities were Guangzhou[3] in the south and Yangzhou in the north. The latter was considered the jewel of China until the eighth century but would be later eclipsed by Quanzhou. Nevertheless, in the early period of trade between the Arabs and Persian merchants and China, the Chinese Emperor would send his envoys to the coastal city of Guangzhou to purchase the goods imported from West Asia. Persians and Arabs are usually called *da-shi* and not differentiated in Chinese historical documents. It is widely agreed upon that *da-shi* stood for the Umayyad Arab Caliphate (661–750) and its successor, the Abbasid Caliphate (750–1258). However, in many instances this name was a general term for the Muslim world, regardless of the separate political units or ethnic groups. Sometimes Muslim merchants were also designed simply as "foreign merchants" (*shang-hu*) or "guests" (*fan-ke*). Abū Zayd al-Sīrāfī[4] mentions the city of Guangzhou as the main destination of the Arabs merchants:

> This city [Khānfū] is the destination of Arab merchants and lays a few days' journey from the sea on a great river where the waters flow fresh. […] One of the prominent foreign merchants, a man whose reports are beyond doubt, related that he went to meet an eunuch official whom the Great King had sent to the city in Khānfū to take the pick of certain goods of Arab provenience that were needed. (al-Sīrāfī 2014, p. 77)

---

[2] For a detailed account of the taste for exotic at the Tang court of Chang'an, see Schafer (1985).

[3] Canton.

[4] Abū Zayd al-Sīrāfī is believed to be the author of a ninth century work entitled *Akhbār al-Ṣīn wa'l-Hind,* which designates two narratives concerning travelling to China and India.

But what exactly was traded between West and East? Again al-Sīrāfī comes to our rescue with some passages from the *Akhbār al-Ṣīn wa'l-Hind*:

> An example of this is the story of a certain man from Khurasan who came to Iraq, brought a large quantity of goods, and took them to China. He was of a miserly and exceedingly avaricious nature, and a dispute arose between him and one of the Great King's eunuchs, who had been sent by his master in Khānfū (the city to where the Arab merchants go) to get various items the King required from among the goods imported on Arab ships [ivory and other goods]. (al-Sīrāfī, 2014, p. 99).

Among the imports to China he also mentions frankincense, copper ingots, turtle's shells, and rhinoceros' horns that were turned into belts, while the Chinese used the maritime route to export the musk to the Arab lands (al-Sīrāfī 2014, p. 105). Unfortunately, written sources like the *Akhbār al-Ṣīn wa'l-Hind* are rare and not sufficiently detailed to permit much speculation on the matter of trade between China and West Asia. However, over the past decade significant new research has been undertaken on the topic of long-distance trade between the Abbasid caliphate and Tang China in the wake of the recent shipwreck's discoveries in the Java Sea, Indonesia (George 2015, p. 579). It was the wreck of an Arabian *dhow* which had sailed from East Africa to China around the year 830. The ship had completed the outward journey, but had sunk on the return journey off the coast of Belitung Island in Sumatra. The wreck has allowed archaeologists to make two major discoveries: the biggest single collection of Tang dynasty artefacts found in one location—the so-called "Tang Treasure" now part of a permanent exhibition at the Asian Civilisation Museum of Singapore; and the Arabian *dhow*, which gives a new insight into the trade routes between China and West Asia during that period.

TRADE AND EXCHANGE OF KNOWLEDGE

By the ninth century, China and West Asia were actively trading spices, glass, textiles, and ceramics. Du Huan, the eighth century author of the *Jingxing*, describes the market of Kufa, the first Abbasid capital, as: "full of beautiful textiles, pearls and shells. Glassware and metal vases and jugs became common." (Ling Ying-Yu Yusen 2012, p. 315). Glassware and metalwork from West Asia found their ways to China, where they were highly regarded as prized possessions. For instance, a number of glasswork from Iran and Syria has been retrieved from the crypt, otherwise known as "the underground palace", of the Famen Temple in the Shaanxi province. The crypt had been sealed in 874 after the ceremony ordered by Emperor Yizong for the worship of the Buddhist relics (Sen 2014, p. 47). Among the precious donations given to the temple in this occasion were twenty pieces of glasswork, nineteen of which were intact and of proved Middle Eastern origin (probably Nishapur, Iran and Syria) Islamic glass kept being imported to China also after the end of the Tang Dynasty. In fact, more glasswork of Iranian origin has been found in multiple locations, such as the Tomb of Princess Changuo and her husband in Naiman, Inner Mongolia, the stūpa of the Dule Temple in Jixian, Tianjing, and the Northern Pagoda in Chaoyong, Liaoning province (Jiayao 1991, p. 123). Of six shallow plates of Iranian dark blue glass found at the Famen Temple, one presents crescent shapes embellishing the rim. The dish has a floral motif in the centre with a precise parallel in a blue on-white dish of Basran origin. This indicates not only the close relationship between Islamic glass and ceramics at this time but also the potential of both media to have exerted influence on Chinese ceramic production (Hallett 2011, p. 78). Indeed, one thing is certain: the influence from one side of Asia to the other had been mutual during the Tang-Abbasid period. The findings from the Belitung shipwreck provide the best example of the interconnectedness and mobility of ideas and technologies in the Middle Ages.

Trade was not the only way for exotic commodities to travel from one side of Asia to the other. Tang's court annals mention that between the mid-seventh and late ninth century, numerous *dashi* embassies stemming from caliphal circles had left the capital, Chang'an, carrying luxury presents. A later Persian source, the historian Bayhaqī (995–1077) recalls that the governor of Khurasan, 'Ali ibn 'Isa, had sent as a present to the Abbasid Caliph Hārūn al-Rashīd (786–809): "twenty pieces of imperial China-ware, including bowls, cups and half-cups, the like of which had never been seen at a Caliph's court before, in addition to two thousands other pieces of porcelain." (See Figure 11.1.) Chinese ceramic were so highly prized that the Arabic word *sīnīyya* (the adjective meaning "Chinese") would eventually be used to generally address good-quality ceramic. Abū Zayd al-Sīrāfī does not fail to praise the beauty of these exotic items: "They [the Chinese] have a fine type of clay that is made into cups as delicate as glass: when held up to the light, any liquid in them can be seen through the body of the cup even though it is of clay." The wonder towards Chinese imports must have been real because all the Middle Eastern pottery of the period was made of yellow earthenware

FIGURE 11.1
Bowl Rim Fragment. Chinese Green Splash Ware on White Ground. Excavated in Samarra, Iraq.

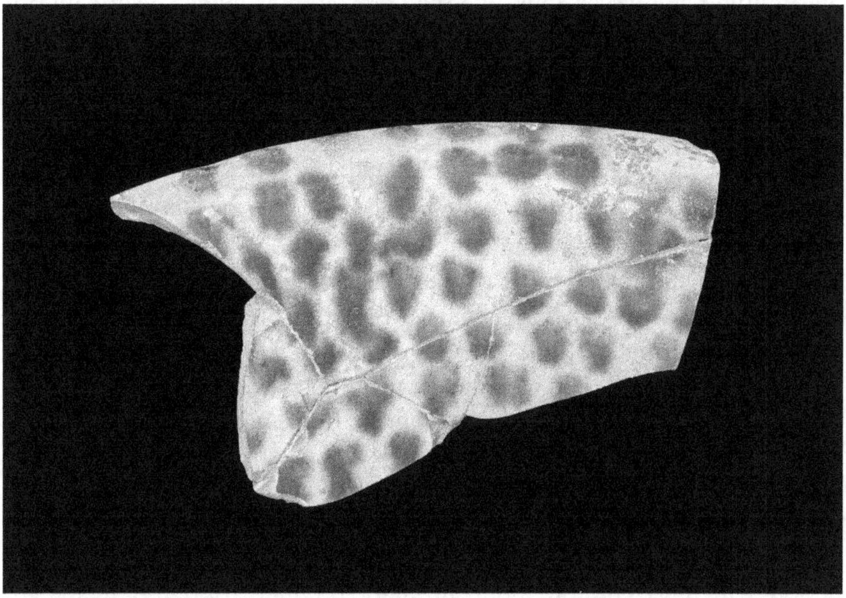

Source: British Museum, London.

fired at a relatively low temperature. Therefore, when cargoes of ceramics from East Asia started to be unloaded in the port cities of the Persian Gulf, the local potters tried to imitate the white stone wares from the Gonxian kiln in northern China. Because they neither possessed the raw material nor the technology to produce the high-fired Chinese stone wares they had to settle with a mere imitation of the outer appearance of their ceramics through the application of an opaque white glaze over the yellow body. After achieving the desired whiteness, the potters of Basra (and probably Samarra) started to experiment with colours to appeal the taste of the local market for a more elaborate decoration. The potters at Basra applied cobalt onto their new white glazes most effectively in the forms of palmettes, garlands, palm trees, and some Arabic writing, mostly blessings (Krahl 2011, p. 209). Among the ceramics retrieved from the Belitung shipwreck there are three white dishes painted with a blue design. These are among the earliest known intact pieces of Chinese blue-and-white ware. Cobalt blue had been employed by the Gonxian potters in polychrome or monochrome glazes and, most rarely, on white wares in combination with yellow (on pieces meant not for daily use but for funerary contexts) at least since the eighth century. But the pieces from the Belitung shipwreck look like they are samples made specifically for the West Asian market since their decoration made of one or two lozenges surrounded by sprigs of foliage was definitely not in the Tang repertoire, and was also most probably inspired by Basran samples that at that point were well known to the Gonxian potters (see Hallett 2011, p. 80, Figs. 64–65). West Asian influence on Chinese art is not limited to the use of underglaze cobalt blue on white ground, which later will become the epitome of Chinese ceramic production in the Yuan and Ming period, but includes the adoption of shapes originated by Islamic metalwork, such as the case of the magnificent ewer from the Belitung shipwreck. The elaborated shape of this object is clearly taken from metalwork even though the medium is ceramic and the technique is entirely Chinese Tang. Green-splashed ceramics certainly appealed to foreign markets and have been found in Iraq, at the Abbasid city of Samarra, and in Iran, at the port of Siraf, at Susa, and at Nishapur, far inland to the north, among many other sites in West Asia. These more colourful products, like those featuring cobalt blue, did not accord with the general Chinese taste of the period, which prized more monochromatic products for daily life and left the coloured ones for either export or funerary contexts. Three Islamic turquoise glazed storage jars with relief decorations were found in the burial of a Chinese princess (Hallett 2011, p. 78). Fragments belonging to this typology have been found on Chinese coastal sites since they were widely used to transport from West Asia goods such as fresh, wine, dates, and date syrup, the latter highly praised in Chinese medicine for its healing property.

Another example of interconnectedness and exchange of ideas is to be found again in the realm of ceramics. After experimenting with the cobalt blue, the Basran potters introduced an innovation in glazing technology that resulted in the making of lustrewares. Those pieces are characterized by a decoration which, by depositing an infinitesimally thin layer of metallic particles in the upper surface of a glaze, reflects and transforms light in near-miraculous ways (Watson 2015, p. 159*)*. Lustre decoration was applied to different shapes of wares. What appears to be worth mentioning is a small cup in quatrefoil shape now in the David Collection, in Copenhagen. The cup, which belongs to tenth century Iraq, is decorated with lustre over white glaze and stamped at the base, and bears the signature of the potter who made it ("made by Ibn Hani"). It reflects Chinese influence during the Tang period, when gold and silver bowls, as well as cheaper variants in the era's porcelain-like stoneware, were made in this particular shape (Figure 11.2). Fragments of Chinese stoneware bowls of this kind have been excavated in the Abbasid capital of Samarra. Chinese imports provided the technical and, in some cases, also aesthetic ideals that local potters tried to imitate in different ways. It is known by some *hadiths* that drinking from gold or silver vessels should be avoided by Muslims if they desire to be able to use this kind of precious materials in the afterlife. The reproductions of those quatrefoil cups with the lustre decoration might have been an attempt to elude this taboo but at the same time to stay true to the shape and material of the more luxurious Chinese bowls like the ones

FIGURE 11.2
Small Lobed, Oval Bowl, Reddish Earthenware Body Similar to the One Currently in the David Collection, Copenhagen. The Shape Derives from T'ang Chinese Silver and Golden Prototypes. 9th Century.

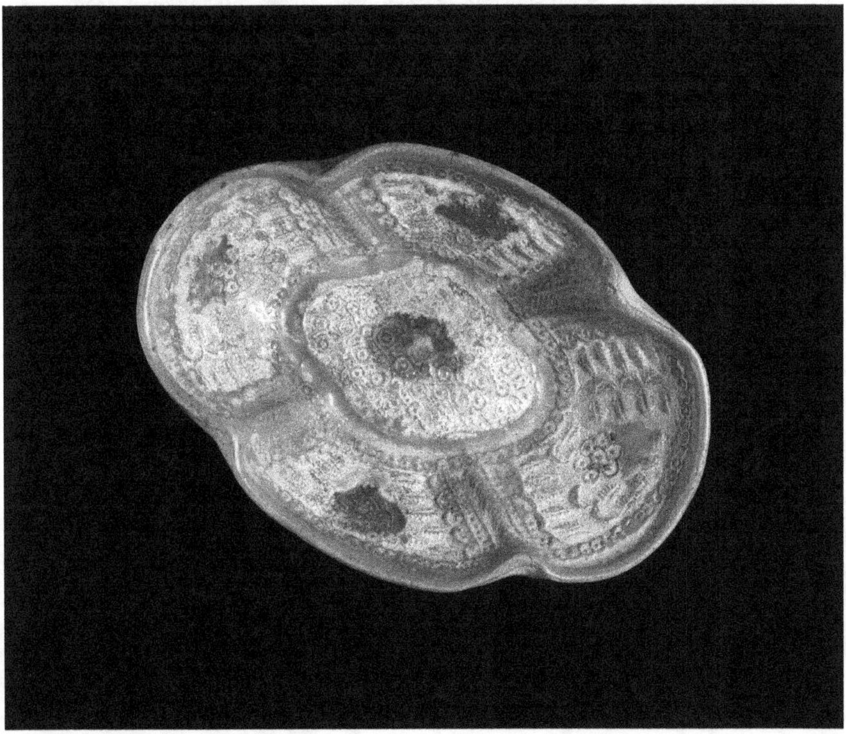

Source: British Museum, London.

found in the Belitung shipwreck, which would have been available only to a much more restricted pool of owners. While the taste for Chinese wares was probably popularized by the Abbasid court at Baghdad or Samarra, it seems likely that it was the merchants who set out from Basra on the long voyage to China who provided the real impetus for these innovations in ceramic technology. Those voyages would suddenly get a halt because of Huang Chao's sacking of Guangzhou in 879:

> Among their major cities is Khānfū, the port for shipping, which has twenty lesser cities under it. (al-Sīrāfī 2014, p. 45)
>
> ...
>
> The reason for the deterioration of law and order in China, and for the end of the China trading voyages from Sīraf, was an uprising led by a rebel from outside the ruling dynasty known as Huang Chao.... In time, when his fighting capacity, the size of his forces, and his lust for power had grown strong enough, he marched on the great cities of China, among them Khānfū: this city is the destination of Arab merchants and lies a few days' journey from the sea on a great river where the water flows fresh. At first, the citizen of Khānfū held out against him, but he subjected them to a long siege (this was the year 264 [877–78]) until, at last, he took the city and put its people to the sword. Experts on Chinese affairs reported that the number of Muslims, Jews, Christians, and Zoroastrian massacred by him, quite apart from the native Chinese, was 120,000; all of them had gone to settle in this city and become merchants there. (ibid., pp. 67–69)

But the trade from West Asia would reprise soon under the Song (960–1279) and Yuan (1279–1368). The Maghreb-born traveller Ibn Battūta writing about China under the Yuan dynasty recalls that:

> Chinese pottery is made only in the city of Zaitūn and in Sīn Kalān. It is made from an earth from mountains there which burns like charcoal, as we shall explain. They add to it a stone which is found there and burn it for three days. Then they pour water on it and it becomes powdery again. Then they ferment it. The best is that which has fermented for a whole month, but no more. What has fermented for ten days is inferior. The price is that of pottery in our country, or less. It is exported to India and other parts of the world till it reaches our country in the Maghrib. It is the most superb kind of pottery. (Ibn Battūta 1994, p. 889).

EARLY ISLAMIC SETTLEMENTS IN THE COASTAL CITIES OF CHINA

Even with the multicultural presence in Chang'an and records of relations between the Chinese court and the Arab Muslim merchants, there is no archeological evidence of a mosque built in the Tang capital.[5] This can be reasonably attributed to the fact that most Arab merchants came to China in the Tang period by sea and entered at the southeastern coastal cities (Steinhardt 2008, p. 331), thus forming their first settlement there. The period of immigration was predominantly during the Tang (618–907) and Song dynasties (907–1279). There were two routes for them to enter China—one by the South China Sea to Canton and another by the Silk Road. During that period, Persians, Arabs, and Turkic peoples came to China to trade and later a number of them became permanent residents of such coastal cities as Guangzhou, Quanzhou, Hangzhou, Yangzhou, and then of Chang'an, the capital located further inland (Lei 2010, p. 137). According to Al-Sīrāfī, Guangzhou was the hub where the Muslim merchants settled before Huang Chao's rebellion (874–884) which eventually led to the end of the Tang dynasty and temporary halted the trading voyages from and towards West Asia. The Muslim communities that developed in the ports of southeastern China were part of a trade diaspora that played a central role in the commercial life of maritime Asia. In the very early period of the Song dynasty, trade and merchants were concentrated in Guangzhou (Chaffer 2006). According to Ibn Battūta:

> In every city of China is a quarter where the Muslims live separately and have mosques for their Friday prayers and other assemblies. They are highly regarded and treated with respect. (Ibn Battūta 1994, p. 890)
>
> [At Quanzhou] The Muslims live in a separate city. (ibid. 1994, p. 894)

[5] Like the Great Mosques at Guangzhou, Quanzhou, Hangzhou, and Yangzhou, the Great Mosque of Xian (the modern name for Chang'an) is thought to have existed as early as the seventh century. The mosque that stands today, however, was begun in 1392 in the twenty-fifth year of the Ming Dynasty and the well-known "Tang" stele, which dates the mosque to 742, appears to be a fabrication from no earlier than the fifteenth century (Cowen 1983, p. 138).

> [Guangzhou] In one part of this city is the town of the Muslims who have there the congregational mosque, a *zāwiya*,[6] and the bazaar. (ibid 1994, p. 896)
>
> [Hang Chou] On the third day we entered the third city which is inhabited by Muslims. It is a fine city and the bazaars are laid out as in Muslim countries. There are mosques and muezzins, whom we heard giving the call to the noon prayer as we entered [...]. They have a hospice called the ʿOthmānīya, handsomely built and well endowed. There is a band of Sufis there. The said ʿOthmān built the congregational mosque in this city and bestowed on it and on the hospice vast endowments. The number of Muslims here is great. (ibid. 1994, pp. 901–902)

It is reasonable to assume that mosques were already built under the Tang period, maybe even in Chang'an, but no physical traces of those structures have come down to us.[7] That could be strictly related to the destruction brought upon Chinese cities like Chang'an and Guangzhou following the passage of Huang Chao and his army. It is also safe to assume that the reprise of the commercial activities under the Song and Yuan had seen the necessity of building newer and larger mosques for the growing Muslim community. Donald Leslie has suggested that the mosques were "built for the needs of the local community rather than for the glory of Allah or the spreading of the faith" (Leslie 1986, p. 41). Nowadays, the Huaishengsi in Guangzhou is regarded as China's oldest mosque; its imposing round minaret/lighthouse is called Guangta or Shining Pagoda. The next four oldest mosques are in the other important economical hubs of the period: two in Quanzhou (the Shengyousi and the Qingzhensi), the Fenghuangsi[8]

---

[6] Sufi convent.

[7] According to the *Zhongguo Qingzhensi Zonglan* (Compendium of Mosques in China) compiled during the 1990s by teams of Chinese scholars working from archival sources in each province of China and edited by Jianwei Wu, the first recorded mosques in China were established in Kunming and Taiyuan in 632 and 635 CE, during the Tang dynasty (Ryavec and Henderson 2015, p. 106). Those dates seem to fall into the realm of the legend together with the foundation date of the Huaishengsi in Guangzhou said to have been originally built by Muhammad's uncle in 627 (Steinhardt 2008, p. 335).

[8] First built during the Tang dynasty, then destroyed in the Song, and rebuilt again in the period 1314–20 and later in 1451 (Steinhardt 2008, p. 342).

in Hangzhou, and finally Yangzhou Xianhesi (Steinhardt 2008, p. 331). All those mosques present a successful blend of Chinese traditional building techniques together with the requirements for the Muslim worship (ablution hall, prayer hall, *qibla* wall, *mihrab* and minaret). Only the Shengyousi at Quanzhou bears a close resemblance with a Western Islamic mosque with its stone pointed arch at its entry that looks like an *iwan*; it also has a hypostyle prayer hall that closely resembles the one of the eleventh century Friday mosque at the Qal'a of the Banu Hammad in Algeria. It is not impossible to assume that those traits were inspired by Islamic architecture by way of a West Asian builder or patron that according to a stone inscription could have been originally from Shiraz, in Iran (Steinhardt 2008, p. 339). Since the reconstruction of the Shengyousi seems to have followed the eleventh century original it is also safe to assume that maybe the mosques of the early period in China might have had a closer resemblance with their Western Asian counterpart than the Song, Yuan, and Ming buildings that are known today. Ibn Battūta, despite mentioning the mosques of several Chinese cities like Guangzhou, Quanzhou, and Hangzhou, fails to describe them giving the impression that the buildings were nothing out of the ordinary. Islam came to China through the trade diaspora described above. Muslim merchants would travel all the way from the harbour cities of the Persian Gulf to the coastal cities of China and from there to inner China and would settle there, building their own facilities, like mosques, *zawiya*, and markets. Geographical knowledge improved massively over time. Some encounters would be fruitful right away and result in the immediate adoption of foreign customs and technologies;[9] others would have to wait some centuries before being understood, appreciated,[10] and accepted.[11] But in China this period of interconnectedness and mobility

[9] An interesting example is the adoption of the game of *polo* that originated in Persia and became very popular in China under the Tang dynasty. Many emperors of the Tang Dynasty were fans of the game, not only playing themselves, but encouraging officials, soldiers, civilians even maids-in-waiting to join in.

[10] Tea makes a good example of later adoption into West Asia. Teas produced in this period were mainly tea bricks which were often used as currency, especially further from the centre of the empire where coins lost their value. In this period, tea leaves were steamed, then pounded and shaped into cake or brick forms. Initially it was not appreciated by foreigner merchants.

[11] A very hilarious case is told by the Arab side and involves toilet paper. A horrified al-Sīrāfī describes the Chinese as unhygienic for their use of toilet paper, not water, to clean their backside after defecating.

from one side of Asia to the other would sign the beginning of the Hui culture: a combination of two great traditions, the Chinese and the Islamic.[12]

JAPAN AND ISLAM

At the same time when the exchanges described above were happening, a limited selection of exotic goods from West Asia also reached Japan. This fact may be evinced from a collection of objects originally belonging to emperor Shōmu (701–756) found in the Shosoin repository located within the grounds of the temple Todaiji in the city of Nara, which includes several pieces of glasswork whose exact attribution is still a controversial subject of dispute among scholars (see Fathil and Fathil 2011, p. 132; George 2015, p. 605). In fact, the first substantial contact of Japan with Islam had to wait until late nineteenth century with the establishment of diplomatic relations between the Meiji emperor and the Ottoman sultan. After several visits by Japanese dignitaries, the Ottoman Sultan Abdülhamid II decided to send the frigate Ertuğrul to Japan in 1889. On a stormy day,[13] after a three-month stay, the Ertuğrul sunk four days after leaving Yokohama's harbour due to the adverse weather conditions, claiming over five hundred lives. The shipwreck is said to have been the starting point of the friendship between both countries, which would carry long-term consequences (Misawa 2009, p. 36). At the time it ignited several solidarity initiatives by the Japanese government and Japanese people. A memorial for the victims of the tragedy was built near the lighthouse in the town of Kushimoto, Wakayama, and opened on 15 September 1891—one year after the shipwreck took place. Japanese individuals were sent to Istanbul to hand over donations collected for the families of the victims of the shipwreck, and in one of those journeys in 1891 Noda Shōtarō converted to Islam, becoming the first Japanese Muslim recorded in official documents (Misawa and Akçadağ 2007). But the interest of Japan towards Islam and the Turkic world was actually driven by a double-headed strategic agenda. After the proclamation of the *Dai Nippon Teikoku* (大日本帝國) in 1868 as a result of its impending imperialistic plans of expansion towards

[12] To learn more about the role of Hui community in Guangzhou, see Jian-Zhao (1996).

[13] 18 September 1890 around midnight (Jian-Zhao 1996).

China and Southeast Asia, where many Muslim communities lived, Japan became gradually interested in learning about Islam.[14] The country pursued the diplomatic route with the Turkic communities from Central Asia, giving asylum to several hundred Tatar Turks escaping the Bolshevik revolution, and supporting the edification of the first mosques on Japanese soil. In 1931, the first mosque was built in Nagoya, central Japan.[15] After Nagoya, two other mosques were built in Kobe in 1935 and in Tokyo in 1938. After the dismemberment of the Ottoman Empire and the subsequent foundation of the Republic of Turkey in 1922, Japan would again keep strong diplomatic ties with the newly founded state, officially recognizing Turkey in 1924 and opening an embassy in Ankara the following year. On 4 April 1934 both countries would sign a bilateral treaty related to commerce and navigation. The relationship with Turkey would remain stable until January 1945, when Turkey severed relations with Japan and declared war on Japan and Germany the following month. The persecution against the Hui communities in China could have been one of the reasons that might have contributed to compromise the otherwise prosperous relationship between Turkey and Japan.[16] During the Second Sino-Japanese war from 1937 to 1945 Japan adopted a repressive policy towards the Hui communities of China that ended up with the destruction of more than 200 mosques and countless lives (Lei 2010). Thus, it is in this context of duplicity that the mosques of Kobe and Tokyo were conceptualized. When Muslim communities immigrated to Japan started to build their own worship places, they faced the same dilemma their predecessors in China had probably faced themselves centuries before: since there was no pre-existent Islamic architecture on site, what to build? And, how to build it? The very first

[14] See Krämer (2014).

[15] The mosque in Nagoya burned down during World War II.

[16] Because of the intensive activity of false propaganda actuated by the Japanese government, the China Huimin National Salvation Federation decided to send delegates to Saudi Arabia, India, Egypt, Turkey, and other Muslim countries to explain the painful situation suffered by Muslim minority of China. So, in 1938 the delegation led by Wang Zengshan, who had graduated from Istanbul University, left China and despite some difficulties managed to reach Turkey successfully (Lei 2010). The educational background of some of the members of the delegation sent to West Asia clearly shows the extent of the contacts between the Hui communities in China and the most important educational centres of Muslim West Asia at the time, notably Istanbul (Istanbul University) and Cairo (Al-Ahzar University).

mosque was built in Nagoya by the Tatar Turkic community who had migrated there from Russia during the early 1920s. The plain wooden building occupied a surface of 40 square metres and had the outer appearance of a regular two-storeyed house. The only indication that it was a Muslim space of worship was the *alem*[17] with the crescent on the top of a domed oriel window on the first floor.[18] Muslim traders from India specialized in the textile trade had long been established in Japan,[19] but it was only during and after World War I that their numbers in Kobe increased to such an extent that they deemed it appropriate to have a place of worship of their own in Kobe. No definite move towards this end appears to have been made until the arrival in 1928 of Muhammad Abdul Karim Bochia, who with the assistance of other members of the Indian Muslim community of Kobe started collecting funds for the project which ultimately reached the sum of 76,000 yen. The largest donation for the construction of the mosque was given by Mr Ferozzudin, a Muslim businessman from Calcutta resident in Kobe. Members of the community were also dispatched to travel and collect funds in India. At the same time a large number of Tatar Turks arrived from Russia and immediately joined forces with the Indian Muslims on the project. The design of the mosque itself was commissioned to Czech architect Jan Josef Švagr (1885–1969) who was also known for having built several other religious buildings in Japan. The mosque consists of a three-storeyed building characterized by a high entrance portal flanked by two minarets. Overall, the style chosen for this mosque is not immediately identifiable.[20] Sometimes its style is compared to nineteenth

---

[17] The *alem* is a metal finial, usually in the shape of the crescent that traditionally tops the minarets and the domes of the mosques.

[18] For a photograph of the original mosque of Nagoya before its destruction by an American air raid in 1945, see Dündar (2008), p. 239.

[19] According to Green (2015) by 1930 there were over thirty Indian businesses operating in Yokoama. In Kobe there were around 130 Indian companies, usually run by one or two Indian official residents.

[20] Kobe's Mayor Ginjiro Katsuda's words in his congratulating message to the committee for the opening of the mosque in 1935 were very appreciative of the new building in town to the point of comparing Kobe to Mecca: "It is the first Muslim Mosque built in Japan, and Kobe may well be proud of it. The appearance of the New Mosque is quite befitting such a Cosmopolitan city as Kobe, and it adds new attraction to the already numerous places of interest in the city. The new Mosque affords a place of worship for Muslim people not only in Kobe, but for those living in other places of Japan, making Kobe the Mecca of Japan" (Dündar 2008, p. 168).

century Indian Islamic architecture but more often is described as having been built in "Turkish-style" (see Figure 11.3). Švagr had studied engineering at the University of Prague and then had been hired to work in the construction of the Trans-Siberian railway in China and Mongolia. Only after 1923 he would move to live and work in Japan until 1941, when he was forced to leave the country for good and eventually moved to South America. Now the fact he had worked on the Trans-Siberian line might be very relevant in understanding the architecture of those early mosques in Japan. In fact, it is highly possible that during his stay in China and Mongolia, Švagr had the chance to witness first-hand some examples of Turkic-Tatar architecture. Nowadays unfortunately there are not many buildings left in those regions that can be compared with the Kobe Mosque and the first Tokyo Mosque, but the Urumqui Tatar Mosque (塔塔尔寺) in the Xinjiang Uygur Autonomous Region is one of them. The mosque was built in 1897 with the funds raised by the local Tatar diaspora (of Kazak origin). The building bears a resemblance with the Kobe Mosque

FIGURE 11.3
The Façade of the Kobe Mosque Designed by Czech Architect Jan Josef Švagr (1885–1969) Who Was Also Known for Having Built Several Other Religious Buildings in Japan

in the spatial arrangement of the two minarets and the central dome. On the other hand, the first Tokyo Mosque had only one minaret at the entrance like the Congressional Mosque in Tver, Russia. Permission was granted to build the mosque in 1905 and the construction was completed in 1905. It comprises a cube building with a minaret and the whole structure is decorated with pink and red stripes. Similar to that spatial arrangement with a central minaret at the entrance and a dome but on a smaller scale are the Black Mosque erected by Bukhara merchants in 1816 and the Red Mosque also from the nineteenth century in Astrakhan. Several other examples could be added to this list, like the Siberian Tatar Mosque at Irkutsk on the Baykal Lake built on the initiative of the brothers Zaiduilla and Shaykhulla Shafigullin in 1897. In short, it looks like early Japanese mosques were inspired by the mosques built by the Tatar diaspora in Russia, Mongolia, and China since the first half of the nineteenth century. The fact that the very first monumental mosque of Japan was built in one of Japan's port city like Kobe reminds us of dynamics that are somehow comparable to those affecting mosque-building in the port cities of Guangzhou, Quanzhou, Hangzhou, and Yangzhou in the Tang and Song period. The first mosque was not built in the capital cities of Chang'an or Tokyo but in portal cities which were, and still are, the most important terrain of cultural exchanges.[21] In both cases, mercantile communities of Muslim immigrants were responsible for the foundation of mosques and other social institutions. Kobe in fact, like Guangzhou under the Tang dynasty, was one of the several ports opened to foreign trade by the treaties signed with the United States and various European powers in the 1850s and 60s (Green 2015, p. 243).

JAPAN AND TURKEY NOWADAYS

Nowadays, Islam in Japan is mostly represented by small immigrant communities from other parts of Asia.[22] A study from 2008 (Sakurai 2008)

---

[21] Curry is one of the products introduced to Japan thanks to the Indian merchants. It would become later the ingredient for a number of much appreciated *yōshoku* dishes such as curry *udon*, curry bread, and "katsu-curry", *tonkatsu* served with curry sauce.

[22] For a detailed chronological account of the different phases of Muslim immigration to Japan, see Hosaka (2011).

estimated that 80–90 per cent of the Muslims in Japan were foreign-born migrants primarily from Indonesia, Pakistan, Bangladesh, and Iran. It has been estimated that the Muslim immigrant population amounts to 70,000–100,000 people, while the "estimated number of Japanese Muslims ranges from thousands to tens of thousands" (Sakurai 2008, pp. 69–70). In the numbers shown in this study, the Turkish community is not even mentioned but according to the data given by the Ministry of Foreign Affairs of Japan, as of December 2015, there are 4,723 Turkish residents living in Japan and 2,049 Japanese residents in Turkey (as of October 2014). As we have seen above, diplomatic and economic relationships between those two countries have always been very prolific for over a century with a hiatus of almost a decade starting from 1945 after the declaration of war from Turkey to Japan and Germany. But in 1952 Turkey reopened its embassy in Japan, followed one year later by the reopening of the Japanese embassy in Ankara. Since then there has been a long history of bilateral treaties and agreements, the most recent of those being about the co-operation in the use of nuclear energy for peaceful purposes (2014) and the co-operation for development of a nuclear power industry in the Republic of Turkey (2015). At the beginning of 2015, 193 Japanese companies were operating in Turkey, while only two Turkish companies worked in Japan. The 23rd Meeting of Turkish-Japan Business Council was held in Tokyo, with the organization of Foreign Economic Relations Board (DEİK) and Japan Business Federation (KEIDANREN) in November 2015. For the period 2002–2015/January the Japanese foreign direct investment (FDI) in Turkey was a little more than US$1.52 billion. With the loans provided by Japanese International Cooperation Agency, important engineering projects had been financed such as: the Marmaray, the Bridge of Haliç, the Hasan Uğurlu Barrage, the Altınkaya Barrage, and the Second Bosporus Bridge. The past two decades have seen a surge in the "Neo-Ottomanization" of Japan that has no precedents. This phenomenon started in 1998 with the reconstruction of the Tokyo mosque. We have previously seen that the first monumental mosque in Tokyo had been built in 1938 by the Turkic Tatar community, three years after the opening of the one in Kobe. The original building from the 1930s was also following the Tatar diaspora style introduced by Jan Josef Švagr in Kobe but it was demolished in 1986 due to its damaged structure. Under the direction and support of Turkey's Diyanet İşleri Başkanlığı a new building was begun in 1998 and the new Tokyo mosque opened to the public in 2000 (Figure 11.4). The Turkish government provided comprehensive support for the construction work and covered most of the

FIGURE 11.4
Interior of the New Tokyo Mosque in Neo-Ottoman Style. It Was Built Under the Direction and Support of Turkey's Diyanet İşleri Başkanlığı and Opened to the Public in 2000

1.2 billion yen construction cost.[23] The project of the mosque, modelled after sixteenth-century Ottoman mosque architecture, was assigned to the Turkish architectural firm Hassa Architecture, founded in Istanbul in 1983 by Muharrem Hilmi Şenalp. To ensure conformance with Japanese building codes, Kajima Corp., one of Japan's Big Four general contractors, was given the task of handling the main construction work while Turkish craftsmen were responsible for the interior and exterior facings and furnishings characterized by any religious significance. Approximately seventy Turkish craftsmen were dispatched to perform the finishing details, which entailed also the use of a considerable quantity of imported marble from Turkey. Probably on the wave of this newly found interested for all thing Turkish, the Kashiwazaki Turkish Culture Village in Nigata prefecture

[23] The overall project cost is estimated to have been considerably more than 3.0 billion yen.

opened in July 1996. Kajima subsidiary Kajima Design was responsible for the improbable aesthetics of the Kashiwazaki Turkish Culture Village, while Kajima Corp. itself was responsible for its construction. This ill-projected theme park did not last long, and in fact it closed its door in 2003, revealing to be a total failure despite several attempts to revive it. It is not surprising considering the odd mix of Neo-Ottomanism (with the help of a secularized interpretation of an Ottoman mosque, with minarets but no *mihrab* or *minbar*) and pre-Islamic Anatolian heritage (a wooden Trojan horse, a variety of classical ruins, and a stranded Noah's Ark housing a cattery of cats from the Lake Van in Southeastern Turkey). And a four-metre-high bronze statue of Mustafa Kemal Ataturk on horseback especially commissioned by the Turkish Ministry of Culture and Tourism from sculptor Metin Yurdanur. After the closure of the park in 2003 this statue caused a small diplomatic crisis that was eventually solved in 2010 by transporting the statue to Kushimoto and placing it in the plaza in front of the lighthouse, a spot chosen by the Turkish Embassy, to be formally unveiled on 3 June 2010, the 120th anniversary of the wreck of the Ertuğrul frigate. In 2010, on the occasion of the 120th year of the disaster, 186 cultural events took place under the framework of "the Japan Year 2010 in Turkey". The Japanese-Turkish film production "Kainan 1890" was produced and showed in both countries in 2015 on the 125th year anniversary of the shipwreck. At the same time of the construction of the Tokyo mosque and the Kashiwazaki Turkish Culture Village, a Turkish-Japanese foundation culture centre was opened in Ankara by Suleyman Demirel, President of the Republic of Turkey and Prince and Princess Tomohito of Mikasa. As of 2017, Tripadvisor gives approximately 1,700 results about Turkish food available all over Japan including a surprising number of Turkish restaurants in the main cities such Tokyo and Osaka. The names are meant to be evocative for the general Japanese public such as: Etuğrul, Istanbul Saray, Pamukkale, Izmir, Darvish and Ayasofya. In fact, according to the Association of Turkish Travel agencies (TÜRSAB) in 2015 the number of tourists travelling from Japan to Turkey was around 170,000. They would favour Istanbul, Cappadocia, and Pamukkale (Denizli). The same site gives about 730 results about Japanese food all around Turkey, with most restaurants being located in the main cities of Istanbul, Izmir, and Ankara. Japanese food is a quite recent phenomenon in Turkey, but in the past decade an astonishing number of sushi-style restaurants have been opening their doors throughout the country. At the same time, in Japan, the number of Muslim tourists has risen, so have *halal* facilities and services.

CONCLUSION

In the light of all the events taken into consideration so far, "globalization seems to be a very old story that has yet to be remembered" (Euben 2008, p. 175). The mobility of objects, workers, texts, knowledge, and ideas circulating within the broad borders of Asia is not just a recent phenomenon but it is common to both premodern and modern societies. For instance, it is said that the remarkable knowledge of world geography of the Chinese geographer Chia-tan (785–805) was derived from personal interviews with the foreign diplomats at the Tang court when he was appointed Head of the Departments of Arms. Trade and trade diasporas have been also the medium for the diffusion of knowledge. Arabic writing, for example. In one particular ceramic bowl made in the Changsha kilns specifically for export and found in the Belitung shipwreck the treatment of the Arabic calligraphy as visual form is translated in the word "الله" (Allāh) in place of the traditional Chinese repertoire. Also in later examples of Chinese porcelain from the Ming and Qing Dynasties, Arabic calligraphy is part of the repertoire for the pieces meant for the Muslim market abroad. In Japan, the first Quran in Arabic was printed in 1934 by Kurban Galiev (1892–1972), a Tatar activist who had established the Islamic Printing House in Tokyo in 1930 thanks to a second-hand Arabic printing machine bought from newly founded Turkey at a very low price (Misawa 2009, p. 39). Nowadays new media are emerging to spread knowledge within Asia. This is the case, for instance, of a recent online project called *muslimmanga.org* aiming at using the power of the medium of Japanese *manga* to portray Islam and Muslims in a positive light. Luxury items have been always carefully traded or exchanged in both premodern and modern societies. Ceramics, golden ware, silverware, and glasswork, have been all mentioned in the first half of this article. Silk is another example. Textiles were one of the greatest developments of the Abbasid period and it seems that some *tiraz* silks even found their way to China, most probably as a tribute gift. Despite the fact that there are several *hadith* that warns against the use of silk garments for both men and women, high-quality silk was admired and highly sought after. But Chinese silks were of a higher quality and they were rarely used for trade and, given their very expensive nature, were usually bestowed as gifts. They were the most exquisite textiles as al-Sīrāfī recalls in several occasions:

> The Chinese, whether young or old, wear silk in both winter and summer. Their ruling classes wear the finest silk; other classes wear

> whatever quality they can afford.... These slave official of theirs, and their prominent military commanders, dress in silk of exquisite quality, the like of which is never exported to Arab lands because the Chinese themselves pay such inflated price for it.... The merchant ... found that he [the Chinese eunuch] was wearing five tunics, one on the top of the other; the mole could be seen through them all. Furthermore, the silk described here was of the raw, unbleached sort; the kind worn by their rulers is even more extraordinarily fine. (al-Sīrāfī 2014, p. 77)

It is almost ironic how nowadays Chinese textiles are to be found in every European and West Asia marketplace and are sadly renowned for their mediocre quality.

Bibliography

Primary Sources

Abu Zayd al-Sīrāfī. 2014. *Two Arabic Travel Books: Accounts of China and India and Mission to the Volga*, edited and translated by Tim Mackintosh-Smith. New York University Press.

Ibn Battūta. 1994. *The travels of Ibn Battūta A.D. 1325–1354, Vol. IV*, translated with revisions and notes from the Arabic by C. Defrémery and B.R. Sanguinetti by H.A.R. Gibb. London: The Hakluyt Society.

Secondary Literature

Bentley, J.H. 1996. "Cross-cultural Interaction and Periodization in World History". *American Historical Review* 101, no. 3: 749–70.

Chaffee, J. 2006. "Diasporic Identities in the Historical Development of the Maritime Muslim Communities of Song-yuan China". *Journal of the Economic and Social History of the Orient* 49: 395–420.

Cowen, J.S. 1983. "Dongdasi of Xian: A Mosque in the Guise of a Buddhist Temple". *Oriental Art Richmond-Surrey* 29, no. 2: 134–47.

Curtin, P.D. 1984. *Cross-Cultural Trade in World History*. Cambridge: Cambridge University Press.

Dündar, A.M. 2008. *Japonya'da Türk izleri: bir kültür mirası olarak Mançurya ve Japonya Türk-Tatar camileri*. Vol. 15. Vadi Yayınları.

Esenbel, S., and I. Chiharu. 2003. *The Rising Sun and the Turkish Crescent: New Perspectives on the History of Japanese Turkish Relations*. Boğaziçi University Press.

Euben, R.L. 2008. *Journeys to the Other Shore: Muslim and Western Travelers in Search of Knowledge*. Princeton: Princeton University Press.

Fathil, F., and F. Fathil. 2011. "Islam in Minority Muslim Countries: A Case Study on Japan and Korea". *World Journal of Islamic History and Civilization* 1, no. 2: 130–41.

George, A. 2015. "Direct Sea Trade between Early Islamic Iraq and Tang China: from the Exchange of Goods to the Transmission of Ideas". *Journal of the Royal Asiatic Society (Third Series)* 25: 579–624.

Green, N. 2015. *Terrains of Exchange: Religious Economies of Global Islam*. Oxford University Press.

Hallett, J. 2011. "Pearl Cups Like the Moon: The Abbasid Reception of Chinese Ceramics". In *Shipwrecked: Tang Treasures and Monsoon Winds*, pp. 75–81. Singapore: Arthur M. Sackler Gallery, Smithsonian Institution, the National Heritage Board, Singapore, and the Singapore Tourism Board.

Hosaka, S. 2011. "Japan and the Gulf: A Historical Perspective of Pre-Oil Relations". *Kyoto Bulletin of Islamic Area Studies* 4, nos. 1–2 (March 2011): 3–24.

Jian-Zhao, M. 1996. "The Role of Islam in the Formation of the Culture and Economy of the Hui Community in Guangzhou". *Journal of Muslim Minority Affairs* 16, no. 1: 31–39.

Jiayao, A. 1991. "Dated Islamic Glass in China". *Bulletin of the Asia Institute* 5 (new series): 123–37.

Krahl, R. 2011. "Tang Blue-and-White". In *Shipwrecked: Tang Treasures and Monsoon Winds*, pp. 209–11. Singapore: Arthur M. Sackler Gallery, Smithsonian Institution, the National Heritage Board, Singapore, and the Singapore Tourism Board.

Krämer, H.M. 2014. "Pan-Asianism's Religious Undercurrents: The Reception of Islam and Translation of the Qur'ān in Twentieth-Century Japan". *Journal of Asian Studies* 73, no. 3: 619–40.

Lei, W. 2010. "The Chinese Islamic 'Goodwill Mission to the Middle East' During the Anti-Japanese War". *Dîvân Disiplinlerarasi Çalişmalar Dergisi* Vol. 15, no. 29 (2): 133–70.

Leslie, D.D. 1986. *Islam in Traditional China*. Canberra: Canberra College of Advanced Education.

Li, Q. 2006. *Maritime Silk Road*. 五洲传播出版社.

Lin Ying-Yu Yusen. 2012. "The Arab Empire in Chinese Sources from the 8th Century to the 10th Century". In *Arabia, Greece and Byzantium: Cultural Contacts in Ancient and Medieval Times*, edited by Abdulaziz Al-Helabi, Dimitrios Letsios, Moshalleh Al-Moraekhi, Abdullah Al-Abduljabbar, Part II, pp. 311–20. Riyadh.

Misawa, N. 2009. "The Influence of the Ottoman Print Media in Japan: The Linkage of Intellectuals in the Eurasian World". *Kyoto Bulletin of Islamic Area Studies* 2, no. 2 (March): 36–42.

——— and Göknur Akçadağ. 2007. *The First Japanese Muslim, Shôtarô NODA (1868–1904)*. *AJAMES* 23-1.

Ryavec. K.E., and M. Henderson. 2015. "A Core-Periphery GIS Model of the Historical Growth and Spread of Islam in China". *Historical Methods* 48, no. 2 (April–June): 103–11.

Sakurai, K. 2008. "Muslims in Contemporary Japan". *Asia Policy* 5, no. 1: 69–87.

Schafer, E.H. 1985. *The Golden Peaches of Samarkand: A Study of T'ang Exotics*. Berkeley and Los Angeles: University of California Press.

Schottenhammer, A. 2015. "China's Gate to the South: Iranian and Arab Merchant Networks in Guangzhou during the Tang-Song Transition (c. 750–1050), PART II: 900–c. 1050". *AAS Working Papers in Social Anthropology. Öaw Arbeitspapiere Zur Sozialanthropologie* 29: 1–30.

Sen, T. 2014. "Relic Worship at the Famen Temple and the Buddhist World of the Tang Dynasty". In *Secrets of the Fallen Pagoda: Treasures from Famen Temple and the Tang Court*, edited by Alan Chong, pp. 24–49. Singapore: Asian Civilizations Museum.

Steinhardt, N.S. 2008. "China's Earliest Mosques". *Journal of the Society of Architectural Historians* 67, no. 3: 330–61.

Usmanova, L. 2007. *The Türk-Tatar Diaspora in Northeast Asia. Transformation of Consciousness: A Historical and Sociological Account Between 1898 and the 1950s*. Tokyo: Rakudasha.

Watson, O. 2015. "Pottery and Light". In *God is the Light of the Heavens and the Earth: Light in Islamic Art and Culture (The Biennial Hamad Bin Khalifa Symposium on Islamic Art)*, pp. 156–75. Yale University Press.

12

Connecting Networks and Orienting Space: Relocating Nguyen Cochinchina between East and Southeast Asia in the Sixteenth and Eighteenth Centuries

Vu Duc Liem[1]

"For the western direction, there is no road to reach it
For the northern direction, it is so difficult to go there.
For the southern direction, it is visible.
The only fear is the Da Vach [highlanders]."

Nguyen Cu Trinh (1750, p. 56)

INTRODUCTION: PROBLEMS OF SPATIAL ORIENTATION IN VIETNAMESE HISTORY

History was born when some specific times and places were connected. While the spatial frame defines historical experience, the agents who act

[1] The author would like to thank Dr Andrea Acri, Dr Kashshaf Ghani, Dr Murari Jha, and Dr Sraman Mukherjee for the invitation to the "Imagining Asia(s)" conference at the ISEAS – Yusof Ishak Institute, Singapore in October 2016, where this paper was first presented. He also offers sincere thanks to the participants in that conference, Professor Hue Tam Ho Tai, and Professor Victor Lieberman for their encouragement, criticism, and valuable suggestions.

in time and space give meaning to history. Approaches to the evolution of Vietnamese geography mostly concentrate on the internal structure of the historically mobile spaces in which the relationship between movement and imagination constructs the recognizable configuration of Vietnam. Keith Taylor's pattern of regional conflict and Li Tana's new way of conceptualizing Vietnam target the "Southeast Asian character" of Cochinchina, in contrast to the Sinicized Tonkin (Taylor 1998; Li 1998a). Victor Lieberman borrows Pierre Gourou's terminology to describe the Vietnamese coast as "the least coherent territory in the world" (Gourou 1936, p. 8; Lieberman 2003, p. 338). Nola Cooke (1991, 1995) and Choi Byung Wook (2004) recommend the process of political centralization and Confucianization under which modern Vietnamese states recognized the territorial status of the lower Mekong. The above-mentioned scholars aim to demonstrate the "Southeast Asian" cultural factors in the making of Vietnam, and in so doing, they challenge the conventional monotonous narrative of national unification offered by twentieth century nationalist historiography. This historiography has played down, for the interest of nationalism, Cochinchinese autonomy while defining the Sinicized North as a touchstone of historical evolution through the mythic discourse of *nam tien* or "marching to the south" as a territorial "manifest destiny".

Another side of the coin, however, are the scholars who conceptualize Cochinchina as an "East Asian style" political project that settled in "Southeast Asian" landscape. One particular aspect of the Nguyen Cochinchina that has been tackled recently is Confucianism. Historian Liam Kelley challenges previous assumptions suggesting that the Nguyen "differentiated themselves from their own ancestral people in the north in order to secure their own political survival" because the Confucian repertoire was inappropriate for the southern political project (Li 1998b, p. 101). In contrast, he argues that although

> the Nguyen found themselves ruling within and over a novel human environment, they continued to operate primarily through recourse to practices that had been established in the north, from appropriating spirits and patronizing Buddhist establishments to justifying their political position by reference to ideas from the Confucian repertoire, such as the mandate of Heaven. (Kelley 2006, p. 346)

Neither historians of both sides nor contemporary area analysts dedicate adequate interests in constructing Cochinchina as a space of multiple geographical imaginations, historical experiences, and sociopolitical projections. This chapter will not take side on the debate of Cochinchina's cultural characters, whether "Southeast Asian" or "East Asian"—both of which in fact are modern labels of geo-cultural configuration. Instead, it examines how the inhabitants of Cochinchina spatially oriented themselves and expressed geographical interests on their own terms. Thus, the region is regarded as a stage of interaction, a field of interconnecting human flows, and a theatre for a wide range of economic, social, and political phenomena which have been recently conceptualized in such multifarious ways as "Chinese century" (Reid 1997; Wang and Ng 2004), "Chinese circulation" (Tagliacozzo and Chang 2011), "civilizing process" (Faure and Siu 1995), "civilizing mission" (Ang 2012), Eurasian *Strange Parallels* (Lieberman 2003; 2009), and "Southeast Asian porous borders" (Tagliacozzo 2005). This approach conceptualizes the sites of Cochinchina beyond any rigid, self-contained, and unified connotation of being either "Southeast Asian" or "Sinicized", and investigates their historical experiences within a new spatial perspective framed by human mobility and imagination. This chapter not only aims to connect times and places in telling alternative (hi)stories of Asia (Tagliacozzo, Siu, and Perdue 2015b, 2015a), but pays considerable attention to the actors' dynamic mobility in view of the fact that these movements shape the contours of the historical theatre. In this framework, a wide range of Cochinchinese phenomena can be taken into consideration, including political orientation, religious transmission, commercial exchange, and migratory diffusion, especially among the Vietnamese and expatriate Chinese communities.

Constructing new imagined geographies leads to unconventional knowledge production and new interpretations of historical experience (van Schendel 2002, pp. 647–68; Kratoska, Raben, and Nordholt 2005, p. 3). The spatial contours of Cochinchina temporally shifted with various historical and geographical articulations following the Nguyen state projection, and through incorporation of mobile peoples along its elastic frontier. Between the sixteenth and eighteenth centuries the landscape was, therefore, perceived by diverse spatial imaginations and geographical configurations mapped by interconnected networks, circulation of peoples, technology, religious ideas, commercial linkage, and piracy in the South China Sea (Antony 2013; Cooke and Li 2004). The South China Sea, long regarded as a mini-Mediterranean, allows surrounding societies to benefit from vibrant human contact in the *longue durée* (Ptak 2008, pp. 53–72; Guillot, Lombard, and Ptak 1998). Cochinchina's long coast, miscellaneous terrain, and complex ethnic mosaic are exemplary of an Asian society where identity was fashioned through trajectories of migratory diffusion and flow of commodities, particularly during the so-called "commercial age" (Reid

1988, 1993; Antony 2007). Such imagined spatial configuration framed by the interaction of networks, actors, and sites, will be made object of a structural investigation to define Cochinchinese history as a pattern of inter-Asian connections.

Before colonial empires dominated geopolitical and economic interest in Southeast Asia, people in the region mapped their own economic and political networks. Their spatial conception produced the distinctive worldview that divided the region into different geographical spaces within which certain networks and interests were at play. By the sixteenth century, a group of Vietnamese left behind their traditional base in the Red river delta, moving southward to the areas of present-day central and southern Vietnam. They established an autonomous domain called the Inner Region (Dang Trong), or known to the West as Nguyen Cochinchina. Growing prosperously for two centuries, this region was able not only to defend itself from northern rivals in Hanoi, but also to expand dramatically into the lower Mekong and the Khmer frontier along the present-day Vietnamese-Cambodian border (Vũ 2016). Its rulers presented a unique geographical consciousness in order to position themselves in the world of Asia Pacific. There is no place in the early modern age that better reveal the idea of connecting geographies and orienting spaces between East and Southeast Asia than the Nguyen realm.

This chapter examines early modern Vietnam's geographical configuration through connecting economic networks and orienting political landscapes. It argues that the Nguyen Cochinchina had developed a distinctive perspective of geographical orientation along the frontier between East and Southeast Asia. The Cochinchinese were directed economically and territorially southward to the lower Mekong and other Southeast Asian neighbours, but culturally and politically northward to the Sino-world. As such, they provide historians with a fascinating example of those standing at the crossroad of Asian networks, between the geopolitical and cultural entities that are now labeled as East Asia and Southeast Asia. Anthony Reid (2015) recognizes Southeast Asia as a space of "not China, not India", but is unable to precisely define what is in the between. By tracing networks and identifying the spatial aspects of socio-political acclimatization, this chapter reveals the players in the between and how they defined identity in their own perspective of geographical self-consciousness. It also suggests how alternative geographies determine historical interpretations that reach beyond colonial and national configurations of space. These paradigms of capturing landscape have dominated the academic scene by modelling our expectations about the realities of experiences Asia. This investigation, therefore, aims to conjoin, and make sense of, interrelation between people, places, and identity that are often glossed over in historical debate. In fact, Cochinchina was a society that operated "in motion": its social and political movement did not coincide with any conventionally defined modern geographical configurations (Figure 12.1).

SITES OF COCHINCHINA AS GEOGRAPHICAL IMAGINATIONS

> *As for their ports, it is wonderful that in a coast little more than a hundred leagues in length, there should be above sixty most convenient landing-places, which is so, because there are many large arms of the seas.*
>
> Christoforo Borri 1621 (Dror and Taylor 2006, p. 133)

Winter 1558: thousands of soldiers and clan members of the Nguyen family headed south to Thuan Hoa. Their leader was Nguyen Hoang (1525–1613), the second son of the powerful Nguyen Kim, who helped to restore Le King back to the throne. Nguyen Kim was unfortunately poisoned in 1545 and was replaced by his son-in-law of the Trinh family, who started targeting the Nguyen competitors in order to achieve supremacy. Living with the sword of Damocles, Hoang found a chance for his life to be away from the Le-Trinh court. According to Nguyen dynastic chronicles, he dispatched an emissary to consult the great scholar Nguyen Binh Khiem (1491–1585), and was advised that "in the region of Hoanh mountain is space to stand for thousands of years" (*The Veritable Records of Dai Nam*, hereafter: DNTL), 1, p. 20; Taylor 1993).[2] This statement marked the beginning of Nguyen Cochinchina, and in fact, the starting point of modern Vietnam. In other words, the "national" configuration was triggered and designed by a geopolitical initiative.

Unlike the Red River delta, surrounded by large, and densely populated flatlands, Cochinchina was built upon an enormous geographical complexity.

[2] Although this story was mentioned in various nineteenth-century sources, the narrative should be read with critical eyes. Virtually no sixteenth-century source informs us about the Trinh-Nguyen antagonism. Nguyen Hoang himself returned to the north between 1592 and 1600 for military service under the Le-Trinh court. The emergence of Cochinchina thus can be dated back to 1600, when Nguyen Hoang withdrew his army from Tonkin and gradually declared regional autonomy. My thanks go to Professor Hue Tam Ho Tai for her insights concerning these events.

FIGURE 12.1
Regional Division in Early Modern Vietnam

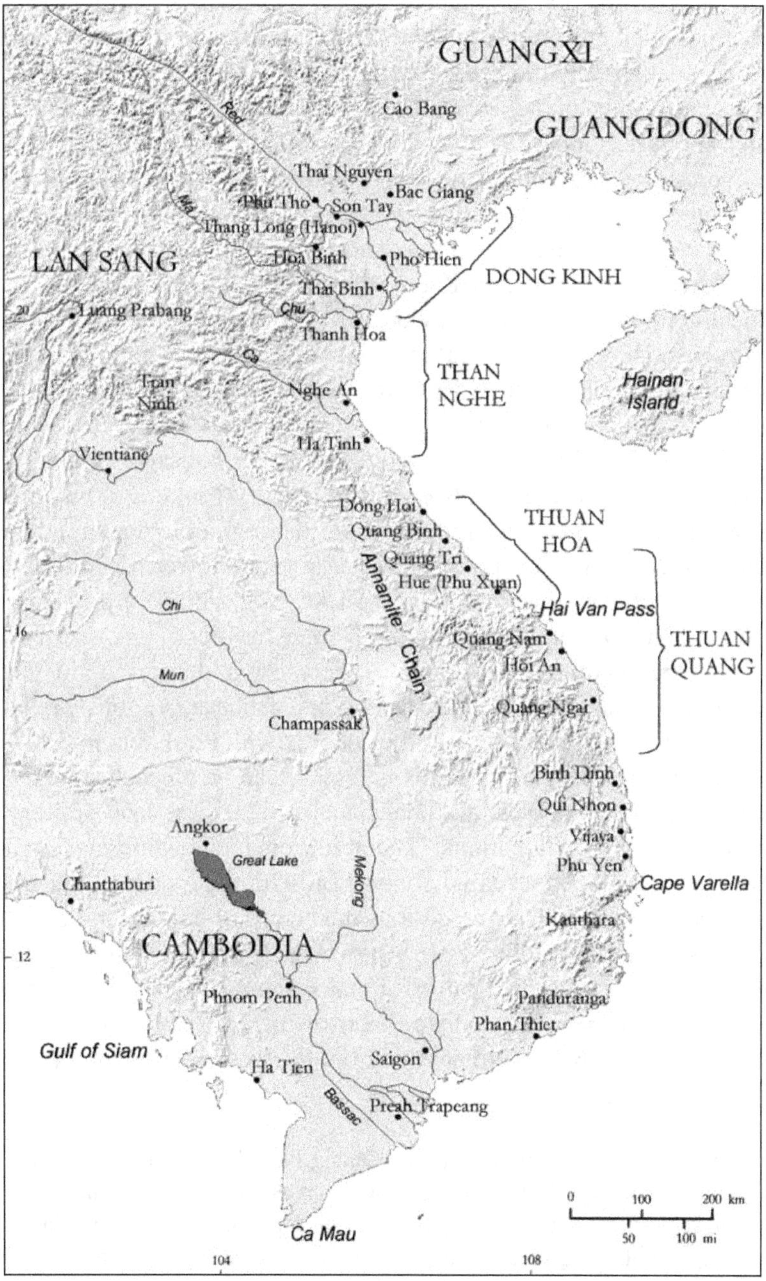

Source: Lieberman (2003), p. 339.

Most of its topography was fashioned by the extremely narrow coastal strip, wedged between sea and mountains, forming the "s"-curved section of Vietnamese territory. Mountain passes, river estuaries, narrow east-west basins, and deep gulfs constitute the 800-mile corridor of central Vietnam. Land-ocean interfaces created a multifaceted social ecology that influenced human agents and their network in establishing a hybrid sociopolitical entity. A thousand mile south of Nguyen Hoang's first base was another world of water, forests, and swamps of the lower Mekong. Travel and communication between the two were extremely challenging. No overland-connected route existed until the eighteenth century. Southwest Indochina was inhabited by the lower Khmer (Khmer Krom), but their linkage to upper Khmer's political centres was fragile (Taylor 2014). A thirteenth-century Chinese Yuan record shows the areas along Mekong river as generally empty of people and filled with extensive tracts of swampy forests and water buffaloes (Chen 1975, p. 57). Some vast areas downstream (such as the Plain of Reeds/Dong Thap Muoi) were abandoned for a thousand of years after the Khmer retreated there in the seventh century (Sakurai 2004, pp. 38, 40). When the Khmer land suffered from demographic decline after the collapse of Angkor (1431), power vacancy in the lower Mekong invited a flood of intruders and immigrants. These events marked the departure of Cochinchina in approaching to the Khmer frontier.

The Cochinchinese geographical perception mirrors a fluctuation between terrestrial and maritime orientations, which are variously reflected during its 200-year history. Its frame accords with fluid human flows and constant territorial expansion. This trajectory can be gleaned from a wide range of temporal and spatial dimensions in which the land appeared to capture different imaginations. The traditional Vietnamese geomantic world view developed a spatial connection with the North, in the area of what is now China, and regarded it as the centre of culture, morality, and political superiority (Kelley 2016); however, Nguyen Hoang segregated his domain at the far-flung frontier of that system, while expressed a great deal of concern to the immediate threat of the Le-Trinh. His last words on the deathbed (1613) were anything but the vision for his heir to locate this state project:

> To its north, the region of Thuan-Quang has Mount Hoanh and the Linh River, which serve as [protective] barriers, while to the south lies the security provided by the Hai Van pass and the Da Bia mountains. The mountains give us gold and iron, and the seas give us fish and salt. Truly, this is a favorable land for heroes. If one knows how to

> teach the people to train as soldiers in order to resist the Trinh clan, this will be sufficient to establish a legacy that will endure for myriad generations. If it turns out that their powerful force cannot be overcome, then you must strive to guard and protect our territories and await a suitable opportunity. Do not forget these, my commands. (DNTL 1, p. 29; Dutton, Werner, and Whitmore 2012, p. 155)

Cochinchina in Hoang's imagination was defensive and self-isolated. It was intended to preserve itself through topographical complexity and the reliance on local resources. Indeed, before his successors could think of expanding southward, Cochinchina witnessed seven military campaigns launched by the Le-Trinh between 1627 and 1672. Such northern challenge caused the Nguyen to realize their limitations with respect to resources and space for operation, and led them to embrace a new spatial recognition, both in a literal sense as their political project expanded, and in a conceptual sense as their increasingly intricate institutionalization demanded new ideological foundations of legitimization. In other words, Nguyen expansion to the Lower Mekong is a story of how the Vietnamese positioned themselves within new spatial, temporal, and cultural-political geographies. The convergence between internal demand for expansion and the human movements brought about a transformation of social and ethnic groups, of the landscape in which they were situated, and of the dislocating frontier with shifting geographical connection.

Lord Nguyen Phuc Khoat (1714–65) was the key figure in this novel identity-making process. Finding his domain free from northern intimidation, he channelled Cochinchinese spatial discourse to the south. In 1743, the ruler declared that he had already controlled half of the Vietnamese empire and planned to gain the rest. Proclaiming himself as "king" (Viet. *vuong*, C. *wang*) and conducting an administrative reform, he viewed Cochinchina as a source of empire-making (DNTL 1, pp. 136–37). Khoat, however, was not alone in pursuing this discourse of political orientation. His most faithful companion, Nguyen Cu Trinh, was also the chief architect of Cochinchinese territorial expansion. In a literary work compiled in 1750, that is five years before leading an army into the Khmer frontier, the official wrote:

> For the western direction, there is no road to reach it
> For the northern direction, it is so difficult to go there.
> For the southern direction, it is visible.
> The only fear is the Da Vach [highlanders]. (Nguyễn 1750, pp. 56–57)

This piece of writing reveals some intriguing aspects about the realm's shifting geographical perception. In the first place, spatial consciousness clearly became an essential notion of political design that captured the imagination of the intellectual elite. Secondly, the lower Mekong was undoubtedly the landscape of choice to realize the eighteenth-century Vietnamese *manifest destiny*, as Trinh declared with no ambiguity in his 1756-campaign along the Mekong river: "from the ancient, the employment of army mostly aims to remove ringleaders and annex land" (DNTL 1, p. 147). In doing this, the general offered the strategy of *tam thuc*, or gradual territorial annexation—like silkworms eating mulberry leaves. By recognizing the significance of commandeering territory, Trinh's approach was shared by none among his contemporary Southeast Asian counterparts, who regarded peripheral land as nothing but sites of "forests and mosquitoes" (Lieberman 2003, p. 27). Instead, their ultimate target in conducting warfare was to capture people and depopulate enemy's lands (Pawakapan 2014, p. 1; Scott 2009, pp. 4, 64–72). Nguyen Cu Trinh orchestrated a dissimilar territorial practice, which resulted from the awareness shared by Nguyen bureaucracy on the power of geography in which natural richness and labors are both associated with. Trinh himself got involved in pacifying highland plunders (Da Vach) in the present-day Quang Ngai before constructing a state-governing topography along the Cochinchinese western frontier (Nguyen 1750, pp. 57–58). His subsequent campaigns in the late 1750s brought Vietnamese settlements and military garrisons to the areas which gradually emerged as the Vietnamese-Cambodian border (Vũ 2016). The expansion of Cochinchina between 1600 and 1760 is not only significant in its physical aspects, but also with respect to the transformation of the concept of space and the appreciation of those inhabited the land, especially as the known physical world was enlarged to include a vast rage of unfamiliar places, terrains, peoples, and cultures.

In 1693, the remnants of the Champa kingdom were placed under Nguyen's direct control by Lord Phuc Chu (1675–1725), although a small Cham court managed to survive until 1834. In the south, despite the uncertainty governing the event of the marriage between a Nguyen princess and the Cambodia king in 1620, which did not get recorded in both Vietnamese and Khmer chronicles, early seventeenth century marked the watershed of Vietnamese unprecedented southward migration (Vickery 2011; Phan 1969). Following this demographic movement, in 1679, Nguyen lords allowed thousands of Ming loyalists to settle along the Mekong riverbanks where new economic centres emerged, namely My Tho, Dong Nai, and Bien Hoa. The landscape of thin Khmer dwellings added new pieces to the mosaic of ethnicities, economic activities, and social networks in the region. The Nguyen intended to colour the geography with a new political identity too. Their first administrative headquarter appeared in Gia Dinh in 1698, marking the beginning of what is known today as Ho Chi Minh City. A decade later, Hatien entered Vietnamese vassalage. The control of Gia Dinh and Hatien provided the Nguyen with a strategic corridor that divided the Khmer world into upper and lower parts, and permitted Vietnamese and Chinese to penetrate deeper into the Mekong plain (Vũ 1818, pp. 3a–b; Nguyễn 1970, pp. 3–24). The dominance of Cochinchina and its Chinese vassals reframed the previously power-vacuum geography with new spatial imaginations and a political occupation.

In fact, the spatially extended and ethnically incorporated Cochinchina opened new boundaries for socio-political constructions. The interaction between physical expansion and human incorporation favoured the establishment of social structures that allowed the emergence of complex and dynamic forms of human organizations. By opening the frontier for further exploration, the Mekong Delta became a source of attraction to actors from the areas now defined as Southeast and East Asia. Here, the movements of human beings were not framed by national boundaries but by human flows, topography, and political and economic factors. Such movements shaped the contours of Cochinchina across multiple geographies, and initiated new spatial perceptions. Human influxes being continuously mobile, so were the boundaries of Cochinchina. By the seventeenth century, the Nguyen domain already became a stage of intermediation and a regional hub of commerce, religion, and political asylum. The welcoming land hosted Japanese merchants of the Red-sealed Ship age, European factories, Chinese asylum seekers, merchants, pirates, and Buddhist pilgrims, just to name a few. It might be said with no exaggeration that such degree of diverse human interaction is second to none in early modern Southeast Asia.

Different spatial recognitions captured by both outsiders and Cochinchinese resulted in the representation of multiple geographical imaginations and terrestrial identities. Nguyen Lords named their realm as Dai Viet ("Great Viet") and continued to use Le king's reign title in official documents (Dashan 1987, p. 1). The interesting fact is that Dai Viet is the term used by dynasties in Tonkin between eleventh and eighteenth centuries with reference to their domain. Cochinchinese rulers, by this appellation, not only claimed equal to the Le-Trinh realm, but also stated a legitimate Vietnamese identity despite of the shifting geography. In letters sent to the Dutch VOC in 1626, however, the Nguyen presented themselves as An Nam (Kleinen et al. 2008, p. 23). Literarily meaning "the Pacified South", this term recalls the Red River delta under the Tang Chinese domination. We observe in this lexical choice a strong sentiment of historical continuity and a profound linkage to the North and the Sinitic heritage. A close examination of Nguyen's diplomatic exchanges with Japan Tokugawa supply us with even more intriguing geopolitical identifications constructed by Cochinchinese rulers. A 1601 document declared their domain as *An Nam Quoc*, or the "Kingdom of Pacified South", and in 1606, *Thien Nam Quoc*, or "the Kingdom of Heavenly South". Two other letters in 1688 reverted the label to *An Nam* (Võ 2013). This trajectory of appellation clearly unearths the struggle of naming, self-presentation, and identity-construction of the Nguyen. These Vietnamese had already moved away from Viet's traditionally identified space. In spite of establishing themselves in a strange landscape surrounded by largely non-Viet inhabitants, which gave rise to a new social and political enterprise, the North was always perceived as the source of legitimacy.

The Cochinchinese political status associated with Le-Trinh court was even more obscure. While declaring Cochinchina an independent kingdom (Viet. *Quoc*, C. *guo*), the Nguyen still recognized the Le emperor. By the late eighteenth century, however, when facing a Trinh assault, the Nguyen Lord responded in a letter, announcing his dynasty's status as *Thuan Hoa Quang Nam dang xu bien than* ("Frontier officials of Thuan Hoa and Quang Nam"), which accepted their dependence to Tonkin. Moreover, in diplomatic letters sent to Qing China to request conferred titles and vassal status, Cochinchinese officials presented their domain as *Hai ngoai Viet Quoc* ("Oversea Viet Kingdom") (Lê II: pp. 170a, 175-56a). By stressing on shifting geography, the term allowed the Nguyen to both differentiate themselves from Tonkin and at the same time trace their cultural and civilizational lineage back to the Viet. It is obvious that Cochinchina was struggling in defining its geopolitical identity, especially with respect to the one to present to outsiders. The challenge was anything but to connect Viet identity and the new geographical and cultural landscape where a hybrid social organization was on the ascendancy. The Nguyen's endeavours did not limit to manoeuvre the political linkage with Tonkin and create an alternative geographical perspective of their own land by constructing a "southern" lineage parallels to the north. In a broader conceptual (and even sentimental) way, it was also a search to make sense of themselves and to have their realm make sense to others.

Outside perceptions of the Nguyen domain are also greatly diverse. Chinese and Japanese responding letters usually utilized terms such as Giao Chi, Dai Viet, and Quang Nam (the most important province) to designate Cochinchina.[3] In 1694, a Chinese Buddhist abbot in Guangzhou, Shilian Dashan, paid a visit to the Nguyen's capital and as many of his time, came to be aware of the two Viet domains, An Nam in the Red River Delta, and Dai Viet Cochinchina (Dashan 1987, pp. 1–2). Japanese merchants also labeled Cochinchina as Quang Nam or Giao Chi, while recognized Tonkin as Dong Kinh (Ishii 1998, p. 154; Nöel 1923, pp. 3–4, 30).[4] Northern Vietnamese intellectuals, however, denied Cochinchinese legitimate territorial claim. The prominent eighteenth-century scholar Le Quy Don in his work, *Phu Bien Tap Luc* ("Chronicles of the Prefectural Borders", 1776) rejected an independent history of Cochinchina, insisting that it was just part of the Tonkin's past and that its political identity was nothing but a northern frontier prefecture (Lê II: pp. 169b–170a; Dương 2009, pp. 1b–2a).

Geographical images of Cochinchina were also presented to suit a different European spatial awareness. The popular appellation "Cochinchina" features differently in various European accounts, including *Quachymchyna, Concamchina, Cauchimchyna, Cachenchina, Cauchenchina, Cauchinchina, Coccincina* (Léonard 1924, pp. 563–79). Although French scholars have discussed the issue extensively, none of their conclusions is definitive. Some suggest that the Cochin term originated from "Ke Cho" (which referred to Hanoi), and then were distortedly pronounced in Japanese or Chinese (Nöel 1923, p. 5). Others pursued the idea that Cochin might perhaps derive from Co Chiem or Co Cham, which denote the previous ancient Cham kingdom. Paul Pelliot believed it was "Giao Chi" that had been transcribed by Portuguese through Japanese and Chinese pronunciation (1903, p. 299). Although the last view is widely accepted, recent scholarship has pointed to the fact that there is a Malay term—Kuchi, probably itself derived from

[3] Giao Chi is the term employed by Han China to refer to their colony in northern Vietnam.

[4] Dong Kinh (Eastern capital) refers to Thang Long (present-day Ha Noi).

Chinese *jiaozhi*[5]—that is linguistically related to the Portuguese term of Cochinchina (Pires 1967, p. 104; Reid 1993, p. 211; Dror and Taylor 2006, p. 17).

The diversity of geographical characters characterizing Cochinchina partly fashioned a criss-crossed identity shaped by accumulating spatial orientations of networks and agents in the southern Chinese maritime frontier, Mainland Southeast Asia, and the theatre of European operations in the South China Sea. The emergence of the Nguyen domain stretching from central Vietnam to the Gulf of Thailand resulted from dynamic local responses to the global factors of trade, migration, and territorial expansion. Cochinchinese were highly aware, to their advantage, of the international flows of peoples and commodities channelled through their space; and were able to orient themselves along those networks for the sake of furthering their interests, security, patronage, and prosperity. By doing this, the Cochinchinese were able to engage with global factors by connecting their local systems to the translocal ones. The result was that the realm became a member of the "Pacific world" through physical and imagined linkages with other parts of Asia. The world in which Cochinchinese found themselves presented both a geographical dimension, characterized by networks of exchanges, and a cultural and political structure, featuring a hierarchy of civility and morality. Within this domain, those premodern actors operated in multiple geographies, whether political, physical, temporal, and cultural. What is intriguing about the trajectory of remapping Cochinchina is the fact that new lines were being drawn and superimposed upon existing administrative, cultural, and ethnic demarcations. Very often, these lines extended beyond the boundary of Viet (intended as an ethnic, cultural, and political entity), and therefore opened up new imaginings and favoured the construction of alternative identities. This state of affairs suggests the profound significance of geography for shaping the direction in which human beings create their field of action, and for labelling the identity that they associate with the landscape.

AGENTS

> The government of Cochin-China, in general, is a medium of betwixt those of China and Japan: for whereas the Japanese make less account

[5] Jiaozhi (V. Giao Chi) was the centre of the Chinese colony in northern Vietnam, established since the Han dynasty. See Taylor (1983), p. 30.

> of learning than military knowledge: and on the contrary, the Chinese attribute all to learning, taking little notice of warlike affairs. The Cochin-Chinses following the example of neither equally encourage learning, and skill in war, according as occasion offers; sometimes preferring the soldier, and sometimes the scholars, and so repulsing them as appears most convenient.
>
> Christoforo Borri 1621 (Dror and Taylor 2006, p. 122)

This section examines the patterns of hybrid social and political structure that emerged in Cochinchina between the sixteenth and the eighteenth centuries, suggesting that they were the direct result of the social enterprises facilitated by Nguyen patronage. To illustrate this point, it positions Cochinchinese actors in the fluid landscape with porous frontiers where the agents' background, motivation, and spatial orientation were tremendously wide-ranging.

It is beyond doubt that the people of Cochinchina had experienced an extraordinary journey to transform a Vietnamese "low-civilized frontier", a declining "Indianized kingdom" (Champa), and an amphibious landscape characterized by a power vacuum into a dynamic playfield for actors from all around the South China Sea. Such achievement could only have been acquired through an energetic social engagement and a political negotiation where status, network, and opportunity were offered to those who entered the circuit. Both Italian missionary Borri (1621) and Tonkinese scholar Le Quy Don (1776) observed the same trait of Cochinchinese pragmatism in which institutional complexity, such as systematic administration and mass civil service examination, were rejected (Dror and Taylor 2006, p. 122; Lê 1973, 2: p. 142b).

Cochinchinese demographic structure was characterized by mutual interaction between physical expansion and population enlargement, which became the hallmark of the realm's chronological evolution. The entrance of new actors into the sociopolitical circle can be translated in geographical terms: new physical networks were incorporated, new boundary lines were drawn on the existing ones, and new spatial orientations prevailed to compete the existing ones. In other words, the Cochinchinese frontier was constructed not only through a power contest, but also through competing geographical imaginations. Frederick Turner in his thesis on the American frontier introduced an Anglo American-centric definition, the "meeting point between savagery and civilization" (Turner 1994, p. 32). Cochinchina's demographic paradigm, however, positioned the region in a highly complex spatial intermingling. Neither the "meeting point" nor the representation of "savagery" (*di*) and "civility" (*hoa*) were clearly situated. Many Vietnamese and Chinese settlements existed as "civilized" oases among the barbarian "otherness". For the sake of survival, however, it was essential for the "civilized" not to emphasize the discourse of cultural differentiation, but rather to join the networks and take part in the economic chain, social hierarchy, and political patronage.[6]

The trajectory of demographic integration is an enduring and sophisticated process. It reveals the mechanism under which different Vietnamese, Chinese, Cham, Malay, Khmer, and Europeans came to establish themselves in Cochinchina; constructed new identities that associated to the site; and conceptualized the region through their own recognitions. The Vietnamese, for instance, did not come to Cochinchina as a single group, but through different waves across time and space. The first wave reportedly advanced into the central Vietnam in the fourteenth and fifteenth centuries following a set of military campaigns (Cadière 1902, pp. 55–73; Cadière 1903, pp. 164–205). Hoang's journey in 1558 added a significant event to this chronology, but before that, a half-century warfare between Le-Trinh in Thanh Hoa and Mac in Tonkin (until 1593) paved the way for a sizeable number of northerners to move south. Even members of the Mac family of Tonkin could find their way to Quang Nam, at the centre of Nguyen domain (Huỳnh 1997, pp. 22–30; Zottoli 2011, pp. 107–16). A considerable supplement to Cochinchina's population came from Tonkinese war captives during the fifty-year Trinh-Nguyen war (1627–72), who were resettled in the southernmost Cochinchinese areas (*Kham dinh Viet su thong giam cuong muc*, 1884, pp. 22a–b; Quách and Quách 1988, pp. 20–23). Other essential demographic elements were involved in the incorporation of Cham and Khmer peoples, especially when the last Cham kingdom lost their independence to the Nguyen in 1693 and the Vietnamese dramatically expanded in the Khmer landscape. Although nationalist historical scholarship seems to "forget" these actors, in fact, they hold a critical role, particularly because their nautical knowledge, technology, and long-established trade networks were inherited by Viet, Chinese, and others (Piétri 1949; Li Tana 1998, pp. 32, 132; Wheeler 2001, pp. 72–130).

[6] After establishing control of the lower Mekong in early nineteenth century, the Nguyen dynasty will speak otherwise, focusing on the binary rhetoric of civility-barbarism and Vietnamese *mission civilisatrice* (Vũ 2016, pp. 537–43).

Chinese sojourners and diaspora were active agents in the expansion of the Cochinchinese theatre in various geographical dimensions. They created new imaginations in the realm that resulted in multiple boundaries, not necessarily physical, but also cultural, civilizational, intellectual, and religious. Emile Gaspardone (1952), Tran Kinh Hoa (1964), Li Tana (1998), Lombard-Salmon (2003), Li and Cooke (2004), Choi Byung Wook (2004), Yumio Sakurai (2004), Truong Minh Dat (2008), and Claudine Ang (2012) have conducted extensive investigations about different Chinese groups who became Cochinchinese at different chronological points. The first wave of their penetration was in 1679, when some 3,000 Ming loyalists were allowed to settle along riverbanks of Bien Hoa and My Tho. The project of territorializing the lower Mekong was indeed a joint endeavor between the Nguyen and those Chinese corps. Their networks were vital to foster the inter- and intra- Cochinchinese connections that generated a social highway to integrate the intellectual elite into the political upper structure, as well as to link the realm to different maritime communities in the South China Sea. The submission of Ha Tien in 1707 expanded the Cochinchinese domain westwards to the Gulf of Thailand, where it now bordered the Tai world, Malay polities, and peninsular Chinese settlements (Lombard-Salmon 2003, pp. 177–227). The event was not only territorially significant, but widened Cochinchina's spatial linkages by relocating the polity among broader regional connections. Sino-civilizational projects such as those going on in the Hatien and Nguyen realm and their extended intellectual networks not only provide a geographical frame of "civilized" Cochinchina but also construct an imagined cultural space reaching beyond the realm to include Guangdong in the southern Chinese coast (Ang 2012, pp. 1–9).

The mosaic of Cochinchinese actors, however, was highly diverse. Intruders such as Chinese and Malay pirates and Vietnamese vagrants reportedly penetrated into the region through its open frontiers. The topographical landscape unlocked to all directions welcomed settlers of varied backgrounds, including pirates, smugglers, merchants, and military corps. They joined all altogether into a vibrant social structure based on a multitude of ethnicities (Lê 1811, book 3; Anderson 2001, pp. 82–105; Antony 2003). The result was a rapid demographic growth in a scale that doubled that of Tonkin. In Thuan Quang, for instance, the population increased from 378,000 in 1555 to 900,000 in the 1770s (Li 1998b, pp. 29–30, 171; Lieberman 2003, p. 410).

Europeans (Viet. *nguoi phuong Tay*: "Westerners") should have their voice in our story of imagining Cochinchina insofar that it allows us to position the place in the geography of global connections. Their appearance not only added vibrancy to the demographic landscape but also introduced new geographies to the Cochinchinese. Economically, they established linkages among Chinese and regional networks, as well as European global empires. Moreover, through the agency of Westerners, the Nguyen domain became part of the early modern imperial world fashioned by movements of merchants, missionaries, astronomers, physicians, mercenaries, and gun-makers. Cochinchinese elites found themselves in favour of this world because it reinforced their political projection and expanded their concept of space beyond a Sino-centric moral and civilizational geography (Cooke 2008; Volkov 2013). Although there were short clashes between the Nguyen, the Dutch VOC (1643), and the British (1705), the rulers came up with an encouraging perspective toward Europeans (Wong Tze-Ken 2012). Nola Cooke argues that the prohibition of Christianity in 1690 was an exceptional political practice in early modern Vietnam, where no persecution of believers was ever conducted (Cooke 2008). This stands in sharp contrast to other East Asian polities, such as Japan, Qing China, and Tonkin, which reserved tougher treatments for the same religious movements (De Rhodes 1966). In fact, it is reported that 10 per cent of Cochinchinese or ca. 60,000 people were converted to Christianity in the 1660s (Rochon 1793, p. 390; Guennou 1986, p. 137). French traveller Alexis Marie de Rochon wrote in his late eighteenth century account: "the king, above all, is very fond of them [the missionaries]; and encourages them to frequent his ports for the sake of carrying on commerce with them" (Rochon 1793, p. 388).

This panorama of agents evidently depicts Cochinchina as a theatre of regional interaction. Those actors introduced to the realm their social organizations, political patterns, economic networks, religious institutions, and cultural distinctiveness, and linked Cochinchina to different geographies. The spatial evolution of Cochinchina in fact resulted from competing geographies and the Vietnamese skillful manoeuvre to enlarge their territory. French scholar Paul Mus represents this geopolitical expansion through the imagery of a flood. In his words, the Vietnamese "flowed across Indochina like a flood carrying off other peoples wherever they occupied lowland rice field[s] or where it could be put under rice" (Mus 1952, p. 17). Besides water-rice cultivation, the Viet carried along with them village-structure and centralized political institutions that they had practised in the Red River plains for millennia. In fact, those immigrants had little choice but to adapt to an entirely unfamiliar natural landscape. Short and sloping rivers, small and divided plains are hallmark features central Vietnam, where people were economically less dependent on agriculture. Instead, commercial exchange was facilitated through networks that linked the highlands to downstream communities and littoral centres (see Bronson's model of the Malay riverine exchange network, Bronson 1977, pp. 39–54; cf. Hall 2011, p. 32; Hardy 2008, pp. 55–65). Cham and other indigenous actors in central Vietnam had already been part of the Asian maritime system for millennia through linkages reaching out to the Malay world and Chinese seaports (Reid 1999, pp. 40–55). Their nautical knowledge and navigational skills were undoubtedly necessary for the economic and military emergence of the Nguyen. The Cochinchinese navy was responsible for not only a successful deterrence against the North, but also a dramatic southward expansion through maritime expeditions and commercial activities. It is by no accident that economic and political centres such as Hoi An, Thanh Ha, Thi Nai, and Sai Gon were sea- or river-linked, and stood at the crossroads of networks that connected East to Southeast Asia and beyond.

In the lower Mekong, geography offers an alternative landscape for human imagination. Topographical intricacy determines the perception of space and the patterns of institutions designed to control moving people. Every time the terrain shifts, so does the human scheme of spatial management. The swamps, thick forests, rich natural resources, and open frontiers offered an alternative scenery for the Vietnamese power project, under which the establishment of dense villages and construction of steady sociopolitical institutions was not ideal because of insufficient state knowledge and its poor capacity of governance.[7] In fact, the pattern of human-geographical interaction shaped a flexible economic and social systems that followed waxed and waned seasonal floods. The society was constituted by different communities and networks where each of these actors, whether Viet, Khmer, Malay, Chinese, or Cham had a distinctive role to perform. The Vietnamese state entered the region in 1669 via such administrative activities as measuring rice-fields, standardizing taxation, and promoting the claim of virgin lands (DNTL I, pp. 72–73). The infrastructures of statecraft were then added following military

[7] Such endeavours to transform landscape into an administratively more convenient format required huge amount of manpower and investment, as witnessed during the imperial and colonial periods, from the 1820s to the 1930s: see Scott (1998), p. 3; Biggs (2010).

campaigns. Newly established military corridors between Gia Dinh and Hatien drew new boundaries and governing lines over the intermingling demographic landscape, and that marked the opaque topography with new identifiable visuality (Nguyễn 1970). The Nguyen attempted to construct a governmental groundwork at their frontiers using a keen intelligence in spatial design and the capability to organize and incorporate the various agents into an effervescent sociopolitical construct. Thus, the newly occupied landscape became geographically, demographically, and politically "Cochinchinese".

The Nguyen realm is a striking case in point to illustrate the ability of mastering spatial design and geopolitical orientation in early modern Southeast Asia. By locating its economic, social, and power networks among the multitude of cultural zones and overlapping political influence, its rulers were able to take advantage of the interconnected position of the region situated between the southern Chinese maritime frontier, the Malay world, and the worlds of Khmer, Tai, Vietnamese, and Cham. Contributing to this historical sustainability and dynamism is the capacity of adaptation and the flexibility of integration to maintain a durable social enterprise. The society did not function through uncompromising and complex institutions, but through practical and flexible ones. Because of that, the land was regarded by foreigners as incredibly attractive:

> His [the Nguyen lord's] territory soon became the country of every industrious men, who wished to settle there. His harbor was free to everyone. The woods were cleared, the grounds wisely cultivated, and sown with rice, their fields were watered by canals, cut from the river and plentiful harvests, after supplying them with subsistence, furnished an object of extensive trade. (Poivre 1769, p. 89).

FOLLOWING NETWORKS

> … Yet they are very ready to admit of strangers, and were very well pleased that should come not only from the neighboring countries, but from the remotest parts to trade with them.…
>
> Christoforo Borri (1621)

In this section, I trace the networks that shaped the contours, and maintained the structure, of Cochinchinese geography. These networks were constructed by varied actors along an expanding linkage that would allow the remapping of the Nguyen realm beyond the bounded twentieth-century configurations of Asian subregions. As a matter of fact, the concepts of "East Asia" and

"Southeast Asia" are products of the geographical perception of outsiders, and ultimately serve their own interests (Tagliacozzo, Siu, and Perdue 2015a, p. 3). Those formations have very little, if any, relevance for Cochinchinese historical movements, particularly the multitude of translocal networks and social miscellany that overlapped and interconnected. Drawing a legible boundary among those networks is a daunting task, since they were characterized by undecipherable interactions ranging from economic exchange and political patronage, to religious propagation and marital alliance. Each network participated in shaping the spatial frame and social structure of Cochinchina. Here one finds the tie between geography, construction of social space, and identity—a matter that deserves a detailed investigation.

China's southern maritime frontier deserved utmost consideration as a channel for the Nguyen realm to seek economic prosperity, legitimate political authority, and territorial expansion. Through exchanges with the Sino-world, the Nguyen also acquired their political ideology and a model to run their state. Their ties with the Buddhist network along the South Chinese coasts (Guangdong in particular) were crucial because they facilitated multifaceted exchanges, not only religious but also commercial, intellectual, and political, which extended Cochinchinese communication to Southern China, Taiwan, and Japan. Some of these linkages bore further implications, allowing the Nguyen to submit a proposal of vassalage to Qing China (Lê 1776). Chinese Buddhist abbots such as Dashan were frequently hosted in Cochinchina following royal invitations. There, apart from Buddhist doctrine, the art of administration and governance was extensively and enthusiastically discussed (Chen 1960, pp. 17–25). The Nguyen state was also added into the geography of intellectual exchange during the Ming-Qing transition, when a considerable number of southern Chinese scholars made the land the destination of frequent visits (Chu 1657; Wheeler 2015).

Cochinchina was located along the dynamic channel of maritime trade that involved movements of commodities and peoples from all walks of life. Qing military suppression in southern China forced numerous Han Chinese to flee south, but other migratory and economic dynamics were also at play. By the 1640s, Japan limited foreign trading ships to Nagasaki, and the immediate result was the rechanneling of Junks from Canton and Hong Kong to the south seas, a large quantity of which anchored in Cochinchinese waters (Chen 1957, p. 7). As a result, expanding Chinese business had commercial associations organized in complex guilds, such as the Thirteen Hongs of Canton (Tang 2001). Moreover, increasing rice demand from south China soon elevated the lower Mekong as a regional major rice producer (Li 1998, p. 69; Lieberman 2003, p. 409; Reid 2004, p. 23). A record of 1695 suggested that ten to twelve Chinese ships traded with Hoi An annually (Lamb 1970, p. 52; Cadière and Mir 1920, pp. 183–240). In the same year, Lord Nguyen Phuc Chu wrote that the number of Junks that traded with his realm increased from six/seven to sixteen/seventeen annually (Dashan 1695, p. 63). Chinese and Japanese sources also revealed that one-fourth of the Japanese Red-Sealed Ships conducted commercial exchange with Cochinchina, while 30 per cent of the Chinese Junks that arrived at Nagasaki between 1642 and 1720 set sails from the regional coasts (Li 1998, pp. 68–69).

Religious and intellectual exchanges were critical catalysts for facilitating a burgeoning flow of human agents and ideas into the Nguyen domain. Phu Xuan (the capital) and other centres, such as Hoi An, Hatien, and Gia Dinh, were intellectually attached to a larger network of circulation of knowledge that included South China and Japan (Chu 1657; Wheeler 2015). The Cochinchinese elites actively sought to position themselves within this intellectual web, and demonstrated an active engagement with the East Asian World. Twenty-five out of thirty-two members of the Hatien's poetic association (*Tao dan Chieu Anh Cac*) were from southeast China (Lê 1973, II, p. 149b). These Chinese scholars contributed to create a new configuration for the land—both geographical and civilizational.

The Chinese factor was an indispensable component of the Nguyen political project. In 1677, the Chinese monk Yuanshao was invited at the court and appointed as *Quoc Si* (Ch., *guoshi*), "Master of the Realm" (Wheeler 2015, p. 138). Shilian Dashan's political discussions with Lord Nguyen Phuc Chu (1695) were no less significant than his Buddhist doctrinal mission. The abbot presented a libel called "brief politics of state-formation" (*lap quoc chinh uoc*) offering essential techniques of good governance. In response, the Lord acknowledged that "our political system (*phap do*) is likely improper. Because of the Aged Abbot's appreciation for us, he presents eighteen points [about the politics of state-formation]. [These principles] Should be written on boards and exhibited outside official buildings to educate military, civilian officials, and people" (Chen 1960, pp. 23–24). The Chinese monk also encouraged the Nguyen to inaugurate a relationship of vassalage with Qing China to legitimize the Cochinchinese territorial and political status quo (Chen 1960, p. 25). Nearly a decade later, an envoy was dispatched to Guangdong to seek for vassalage recognition. The diplomatic letter clearly recalled the connection between Nguyen court, Chinese Buddhist monks, and intellectual figures as a source of civilizational and political catalysis:

> I [Lord Phuc Chu] have inherited my ancestral legacy [the Cochinchinese lordship] for many years and opened my land beyond the sea. Together with other southern states, [I] have never depended upon anyone. The road is far, the land is small, yet [I] dare to correspond with the Superior Dynasty (i.e. the Chinese Qing). My ancestors faithfully believed in Buddha from generation to generation. My master is the Aged Abbot Shilian [Dashan] of Changshou Temple in Guangdong, who, apart from teaching Buddhist canons, always praises your Majesty's great military and civilian virtue as a Heavenly Saint. Guangdong's assembled regular students (*jiangsheng*) such as Huangzhang and Buddhist monk Xingche, [and they] all praised the Celestial Court's civility that spreads to all corners of the world. The imperial grace is splendid as moon and sun light. [I] Wish to be a dependent state [of the Qing], and by that, [I] can glorify the succession of my ancestors and distribute benevolence to my people (DNTL, I, p. 106; Lê 1776, II, p. 176a).

This is an intriguing example reflecting the way in which Cochinchina was set amidst a multitude of geographies—physical, civilizational, political, and temporal. A selective spatial orientation however was made to present an intended artificial identity, in this case, to enter the Qing geography of moral and cultural order. By doing so, the Nguyen stressed on their relocation from the Vietnamese heartland of the Red River to the southern frontier, where they established an independent kingdom of their own. Although this physical displacement profoundly transformed terrains, cultures, and the local ethnic mosaic into new realities of social and political enterprise, it did not prevent Cochinchina from returning to the traditional geographical order of East Asia. Experiencing dislocation, in fact, was an occasion to diversify their geographical worldview, that is to say, not only the way in which Cochinchinese repositioned themselves in the region, but also the way they reconceptualized the world surrounding them. Entering Qing vassalage was an attempt to occupy the geography with which, among other configurations, the Nguyen saw themselves connected. Here we observe the profound interaction between space and identity in shaping the position of the Nguyen in a civilizational hierarchical world that allowed the emergence of new identities, legitimization strategies, recognition, and the adaptation to the prevalent political theories and governing models.

Connecting to the external world required the construction of an identity, as well as the integration of internal geographies grounded on competing and negotiating distinct individualities and interests. Each Cochinchinese group acted within its own environment of culture, terrain, network, and tradition. By "inviting" them to the state projection, the Nguyen not only located these groups within the administrative landscape but also manipulated their spatial orientation and network-building capacities. As a result, the inclusive and loose geographical entity known as "Cochinchina" emerged through a wide range of strategies, going from marital alliance, military campaign, cultural assimilation, and negotiation, to exchange of economic interests. Shifting geographical identities became the Nguyen's main approach in controlling space by making opaque topography legible. In return, Cochinchinese rulers offered the ability of integrating different geographical realities shaped by varied sociopolitical and economic axes into a constructed common spatial identity, and provided it with a guaranteed hierarchical status.

Multiple actors and networks entered the Cochinchinese sociopolitical enterprise and created a new frame—both physical and imagined—for the Nguyen realm. At the peak of the age of Japanese Red Sealed Ships, Lord Phuc Nguyen married his daughter to Japanese merchant Araki Sotaro (1619) as an effort to link the realm to the East Asian maritime system (Matsuda 2012, p. 89). The move was also a strategy to deal with increasing Japanese piracy along the Chinese coast, particularly during the late Ming and early Qing period (Antony 2003; Chin 2014, pp. 93–112; Dardess 2013, pp. 89–138). As a young prince, Nguyen Phuc Nguyen himself had defeated such sea raids by Japanese fleet of Shirahama Kenchi in 1585, just offshore of Cochinchina (DNTL 1, p. 24). There were at least two other marriages arranged by that ruler, including one to the Cambodian King Chey Chetta II (1620) as mentioned above, an event that was believed by many historians to mark the beginning of Vietnamese penetration into lower Mekong; and the other to Po Rome, the King of Champa (*c.*1627–51) (Wong Tze-Ken 2011, p. 246). Although a more careful consideration of existing historical sources is required in both cases, these marriages reveal the clear intention of the Nguyen ruler to expand his political domain and sphere of influence.

While the Sinitic model and ideology inspired Cochinchinese administrative design, land, labours, and resources were widely available in the Mekong delta, opening up to a wide range of Southeast Asian and European interactions. The region not only occupied the connecting space of the Chinese frontier, but also lied at the intersection of the northern

Malay world, Southeast Asian mining zones, and the contact zone between the mainland and the outlying islands (Trocki 2009; Reid 2004, p. 24). Its seaports and river ports featured coordinating sites between Chinese north, the Malay south, the Mainland west and the Island east. Historian Barbara Andaya in her investigation of early modern Sumatran history stresses upon the significant role of intermediaries occupied by places like Cochinchina and Hatien with respect to their function as trading partners with the Indonesian Archipelago, particularly in exchanging pepper and tin from Sumatra, Bangka, Riau, and Malay Peninsula (Andaya 1993, pp. 123, 191, 218, 219). Nguyen vessels were also reported to have shipped rice to Batavia in Java, while other sources suggest that by the mid-seventeenth century four Cochinchinese ships traded with Manila in the Philippines annually (Chaunu Pierre 1960, pp. 60–62, Li 1998b, p. 76).

Charlotte Pham (2016, pp. 101–2) argues that Cochinchinese waters offered the safest sea-lane for the Inter-Asia shipping traffic between the Strait of Melaka and the southeastern coasts of China. Such geographical advantage favoured the Lower Mekong during its last phrase of autonomous standing at the intersection of different centralized states. The combination of topographical and political attractiveness allowed Cochinchina to enter the major regional currents of peoples and commodities that shaped early modern Asia-Pacific. The Nguyen realm is a compelling case in point to illustrate the power of geography in the early modern global world, where international engagement not only provided resources, technology, and an expanding imagined worldview, but also knowledge that allowed people to conceptualize and claim their position in that growing world. Italian missionary Christoforo Borri (1621) highlighted the Cochinchinese enthusiastic endeavours in engaging with outside world as follows:

> … Nor do they need to use any art for this purpose; strangers being sufficiently allured by the fruitfulness of the country, and the great wealth, which abounds there; and therefore they resort thither not only from Tonkin, Cambogia, Chincheos (Canton), and other neighboring places, but from the remotest, as China, Macao, Japan, Manila, and Malacca. All of them carrying silver to Cochinchina to carry away the commodities of the country… the king of Cochinchina gave free admittance to all nations whatsoever, the Dutch resorted thither with all sorts of commodities… He pretended to be afraid of no nation in the world; quite contrary to the king of China, who being afraid of everybody, forbids all strangers trading in his kingdoms… (Dror and Taylor 2006, pp. 132–33, 135).

Fascinated by those harbours, wealthy littoral centres, and local resources, Europeans earned tremendous benefits through their factories' bustling trade with Cochinchinese, Chinese, and Japanese. Realizing the strategic location of the land, the British negotiated for the establishment of a factory in Hoi An, where in 1643 a Dutch settlement stood. Their representative, Thomas Bowyear (1695), was able to acquire permission to set up a factory, but the choice of Hoi An was rejected. Con Dao Island (Pulo Condore) subsequently became the alternative location where the British run a factory between 1702 and 1705 (Wong Tze-Ken 2012, pp. 1103–8). Such connection was essential for the advent of Nguyen Cochinchina, in particular for shaping its territorial orientation and for providing resources to implement the political project—including military technology, cannon-making, and ship-building (Mantienne 2003; Vũ 2017). Cochinchinese dependence upon Western supply of technology was more vital than that of Tonkin, and the reliance was maintained well beyond the period of Vietnamese unification (1802). European exchanges profoundly contributed to determine the destiny of early modern Vietnamese history through the engagement of the West in the game of geopolitical competition among regional centres, such as Tonkin, Cochinchina, and Tayson. One significant consequence of this was the influence on the paradigm of power and territory trajectory under which modern Vietnam emerged: territory expanded southward while the power of unification headed northward.

None of the other East Asian polities, such as China, Japan, and Tonkin, had the same approach towards the West as the Nguyen's. By the 1640s, Japan limited trading with Europeans and prosecuted Christians. Tonkin ended its honeymoon with the Dutch after realizing that the alliance bore no promising impact on the defeat of Cochinchina (Hoàng 2007, pp. 115–23). In spite of a short conflict with the Dutch (1643), the raid on the British factory (1705), and a brief Christian ban (1690), European merchants, gun-makers, doctors, and astronomers were always welcome to the Nguyen realm. There was a strong tradition of association with Westerners in Cochinchinese social, military, and scientific missions. Many missionaries served as royal physicians, comprising Bartolomeu da Costa (or d'Acosta, 1629?–1695?), Giambattista Sanna (1682–1726), Johann Siebert (1708–45), Karl Slamenski (1708?–46), Johann Koffler (1711–85), and João de Loureiro (1710–91). Others practiced as astronomers, namely Juan Antonio Arnedo (1660–1715), Francisco de Lima (1688–1726), Josef Neügebauer (1706–59), Francisco Xavier de Monteiro (?–1776), and Bento

Ferreira (1750s). The list in fact can extend till the end of the eighteenth century with a very prominent figure, Pierre-Joseph Pigneaux de Béhaine (1741–99), who played multiple roles as Nguyen lord's advisor, supplying network organizer, ambassador, and representative in negotiating with Europeans (Duteil 1998, pp. 283–97; John 1806, p. 273; Crawfurd 1967, pp. 504–5).

Western weapons, military supplies, and mercenaries were increasingly involved in warfare in Cochinchina. Borri reported that confiscated Portuguese and Dutch shipwrecks contributed at least sixty large cannons to protect the realm's capital (Dror and Taylor 2006, p. 127). A major source of artillery in the early eighteenth century however were the Portuguese, who had arrived as early as 1584 and directly participated in the state gun foundry (Manguin 1972, p. 3). João da Cruz (1610?–82), who served under Lord Nguyen Phuc Tan, was one of the most famous Portuguese experts. Two of his cannons are now exhibited in front of Thai Ministry of Defence in Bangkok. Although it is unknown how they ended up there, both were made in 1667 and 1670, and bear inscriptions that read: "For King and Great Lord of Cochinchina, of Champa, and of Cambodia, João da Crus made it [i.e. the cannon]" (Volkov 2013, p. 62). Historian Charles Boxer also revealed the Nguyen ambition of acquiring more guns made by the Europeans. Their primary source of acquisition was the Portuguese cannon foundry Bocarro of Macau (1627–80), which was famous for producing the finest bronze guns in the East (Boxer 1985, p. 167). Those efforts resulted in a dramatic increase of cannons in Cochinchina to 1,200 in 1750, most of which were casted in a state factory in Hue using Portuguese technology (Li and Reid 1993, p. 70). Undoubtedly, Nguyen military power heavily relied upon those weapons to defend its northern frontier and expand it into the Mekong delta. Such weaponry, technology, and knowledge absorbed into Cochinchina were part of the global-local interaction of the early modern age. Like Japan, where European handguns contributed to territorial unification in 1600, Cochinchina witnessed an identical geopolitical impact. As a result, the Nguyen realm was introduced into a new geography shaped by European imagination of global empires, where the "global" stands both as a configuration and an approach to modernity. At the local level, advanced military power permitted the realm to extend in the scale of regional influence, which resulted in the transformation of opaque physical and human landscape into a legible and manipulable geography.

READING COCHINCHINA IN SPACE: GEOGRAPHY, NETWORK, AND IDENTITY

Human beings divide the surface of the earth into regions for the interest of labelling landscape, marking geographical identity, and managing space (more precisely, administering the inhabitants of the identifiable space). The division of East and Southeast Asia addresses a peculiar twentieth-century human intention that developed in the strategic mindsets of colonialism, Cold War, and global geopolitics. None of those reflects the regions' determinations of constructing their own spatial identity. In fact, colonial and imperial geographical configurations blurred local conceptions of space and undermined their terrestrial dynamism. The Cochinchinese project of state-formation shows the way of self-imagining a sociopolitical space that frames the theatre of their own history. This configuration was constructed by vibrant networks, including elastic socio-economic and political structures that none of the modern conventional topographical entities is able to represent. The Cochinchinese case of local spatial orientation reveals a vivid example in which modern historians are required to envision a field of study extending beyond any fixed, bounded, and conventional geographical body. By tracking down agents, following networks, and connecting sites, the newly constructed space allows alternative historical interpretation and knowledge production.

Recent scholarship has formulated new ways of framing landscape that transcend national boundaries, for example, by individuating alternative geographical contours that contain flows of peoples and commodities. Charles Wheeler, for instance, examines the pattern of Hoi An history through what has been conceptualized as cross-cultural trade and transregional networks (2001). This chapter has offered an alternative approach to historical Cochinchina that follow its moving landscape, sites, events, and agents. In doing so, it has suggested that new imagined configurations and dynamics of place-making were at play during the most vibrant period of its regional history. By following the spatial structure of the networks and human flows, the geographical imagination of Cochinchina was expanded along linkages that stretched from the waters of southeast China to Island Southeast Asia. Cochinchina has revealed to be a field of interaction and exchange containing encompassing cultural repertoires. Such approach is indeed needed to form a new narrative of Vietnamese history from a broader regional perspective. The framing of a geographical entity is essential in knowledge production. Some of these historical spaces and actors had long been neglected in academic circles, or had their voice silenced because of their intersecting or blurry nature, or because they overlapped with modern geographical demarcations. One of such alternative spaces has been described recently by Willem van Schendel and James Scott, namely *Zomia*, the highland areas stretching from the Vietnamese Central Highlands to Southwest China, Northeastern India, Pakistan, and Afghanistan, whose inhabitants chose to stand outside of state-building until very recently (Van Schendel 2002; Scott 2009). This research has been inspired by such geographical reconstructions. It has highlighted Cochinchina's geographical experiences by relocating the historical makers between the two modern entities of East and Southeast Asia. Corresponding to their mobility, human movements need to be accounted for to describe the spatial imaginings of Cochinchina, where radical phenomena of terrestrial displacement had a profound impact upon individual and collective identities. The ensuing new geographies represented a kind of dislocation and overlapping visualizations in which human agents captured multiple spatial realities and confronted themselves with the need of self-repositioning and reconceptualizing the world surround them.

Nguyen Cochinchina is neither a civilizational margin, as described by contemporary Tonkinese scholars, nor a civilizational frontier where Sinicized East Asian Tonkin faced "Indianized Southeast Asian" Champa, as conceptualized by colonial historiography (Lê 1973; Cœdès 1944). In contrast, Cochinchinese geographical perception arose from its own topography and maritime communication lanes that shaped the political and cultural identity of the region by establishing sites, inviting actors, and constructing networks. The power of geography was to create a theatre for historical agency that expanded transregionally from East Asian water to Southeast Asian seas. Cochinchina was a society framed by networks of human movement in which landscape and imagined configurations—including an expanding territory, porous boundaries, and open frontiers—profoundly determined the construction of identity. The result of such elastic geography was the incorporation of diverse agents into the vibrant sociopolitical structure that formed a node of the inter-Asian connection network. This phenomenon is a compelling case in point for illustrating the interrelation between geography and spatial orientation of human societies. On the one hand, geography determines the directional expansion of human flows and their social organization, but on the other, human beings give meaning to geography and design landscape through their imagination and conceptualization of space.

Bibliography

Andaya, Barbara Watson. 1993. *To Live as Brothers: Southeast Sumatra in the Seventeenth and Eighteenth Centuries*. Honolulu: University of Hawaii Press.

Anderson, John L. 2001. "Piracy and World History: An Economic Perspective on Maritime Predation". In *Bandits at Sea: A Pirates Reader*, edited by C.R. Pennell, pp. 82–105. New York: New York University Press.

Ang, Claudine. 2012. "Statecraft on the Margins: Drama, Poetry, and the Civilizing Mission in Eighteenth-Century Southern Vietnam". PhD dissertation, Ithaca, NY: Cornell University.

Antony, Robert J. 2003. *Like Froth Floating on the Sea: The World of Pirates and Seafarers in Late Imperial South China*. Berkeley: University of California Press.

———. 2007. *Pirates in the Age of Sail*. New York: W.W. Norton & Company.

———. 2013. "Turbulent Waters: Sea Raiding in Early Modern South East Asia". *The Mariner's Mirror* 99, no. 1: 23–38.

Barrow, John. 1806. *A Voyage to Cochinchina, in the Years 1792 and 1793: To Which Is Annexed an Account of a Journey Made in the Years 1801 and 1802, to the Residence of the Chief of the Booshuana Nation*. London: T. Cadell and W. Davies.

Biggs, David. 2010. *Quagmire: Nation-Building and Nature in the Mekong Delta*. Seattle: University of Washington Press.

Boxer, Charles R. 1985. *Portuguese Conquest and Commerce in Southern Asia, 1500–1750*. London: Variorum Reprints.

Bronson, Bennet. 1977. "Exchange at the Upstream and Downstream Ends: Notes toward a Functional Model of the Coastal State in Southeast Asia". In *Economic Exchange and Social Interaction in Southeast Asia: Perspectives from Prehistory, History, and Ethnography*, edited by Karl Hutterer, pp. 39–54. Center for South and Southeast Asian Studies, University of Michigan.

Cadière, Leopold. 1902. "Géographie historique du Quảng Bình d'apres les annales impériales". *Bulletin de l'École française d'Extrême-Orient* 2: 55–73.

———. 1903. "Les lieux historiques du Quảng Bình". *Bulletin de l'École française d'Extrême-Orient* 3, no. 1: 164–205.

———. 1920. "Les européens qui ont vu le vieux Hué: Thomas Bowyear 1695–1696". *Bulletin des amis du vieux Hue* 2: 183–240.

Chaunu, Pierre. 1960. *Les Philippines et le Pacifique des ibériques: XVIe, XVIIe, XVIIIe siècles*. Paris: S.E.V.P.E.N.

Chen, Jinghe 陳荊和. 1957. "清初華舶之長崎貿易及日南貿易 [*Qing chu Huabo Zhi Changqi Maoyi ji Rinan maoyi*—The Role of Chinese Junks in Nagasaki-South Trade and Navigation during the Early Qing]". 南洋學報 13, no. 1: 1–52.

———. 1960. 十七世紀廣南之新史料 [*Shiqi shiji Guangnan zhi xan shiliao—*

New Historical Material of the Seventeenth Century Quang Nam]. Hongkong: *Zhonghua congshu* 中華叢書.
———. 1964. 承天明鄉社陳氏正譜 [*Chengtian Mingxiang she Chenshi zhengpu*—Geneaology of Tran Family of the Ming Chinese Town of Thua Thien]. Hongkong: Southeast Asia Studies Section, New Asia Research Institute, Chinese University of Hong Kong.
Chen, Zhengxiang 陳正祥. 1975. 真臘風土記研究 [*Zhenla fentuji yanjiu*—Study of the Customs of Cambodia]. Hongkong: *Xianggang zhongwen daxue* 香港中文大學.
Chin, James K. 2014. "A Hokkien Maritime Empire in the East and South China Seas, 1620–83". In *Persistent Piracy-Maritime Violence and State-Formation in Global Historical Perspective*, edited by Stefan Eklöf Amirell and Leos Müller, pp. 93–112. Basingstoke: Palgrave Macmillan.
Choi, Byung Wook. 2004. *Southern Vietnam under the Reign of Minh Mạng (1820–1841): Central Policies and Local Response*. Ithaca, NY: Cornell University Southeast Asia Program Publications.
Chu, Thuấn Thủy. 1657. 安南供役紀事 *[An Nam Cung Dịch Kỷ Sự] Memoir of Service in Vietnam*. Hà Nội: Hội khoa học Lịch sử Việt Nam, 1999.
Cooke, Nola. 2008. "Strange Brew: Global, Regional and Local Factors behind the 1690 Prohibition of Christian Practice in Nguyễn Cochinchina". *Journal of Southeast Asian Studies* 39, no. 3: 383–409.
Cooke, Nola, and Li Tana, eds. 2004. *Water Frontier: Commerce and the Chinese in the Lower Mekong Region, 1750–1880*. Boulder: Rowman & Littlefield Publishers.
Crawfurd, John. 1967. *Journal of an Embassy to the Courts of Siam and Cochinchina*. Kuala Lumpur: Oxford University Press.
大南實錄 *[Đại Nam Thực Lục] The Veritable Records of Dai Nam* [DNTL]. 20 vols. Tokyo: Institute of Cultural and Linguistic Studies, Keio University, 1977.
Dardess, John W. 2013. *A Political Life in Ming China: A Grand Secretary and His Times*. Lanham: Rowman & Littlefield Publishers, Inc.
Dashan. 1695. 海外紀事 *[Haiwai Jishi] Record of Travel Overseas*. Beijing: *Zhonghua shiju* 中華書局, 1987.
De Rhodes, Alexander. 1966. *Rhodes of Vietnam: The Travels and Missions of Father Alexander de Rhodes in China and Other Kingdoms of the Orient*. Westminster, Maryland: Newman Press.
Dror, Olga, and K.W. Taylor, eds. 2006. *Views of Seventeenth-Century Vietnam: Christorforo Borri on Cochinchina and Samuel Baron on Tonkin*. Ithaca, NY: Cornell Southeast Asia Program.
Dương, Văn An. 1555. 烏州近錄 *[Ô Châu Cận Lục]* A Recent Record of O Chau. Hà Nội: Nxb Giáo Dục [2009].
Duteil, Jean-Pierre. 1998. "Entre deux états en révolution: Pierre-Joseph Pigneaux de Béhaine, la France et le Dai-Viêt". *Revue d'histoire de l'église de France* 84 (213): 283–97.

Dutton, George E., Jayne S. Werner, and John K. Whitmore. 2012. *Sources of Vietnamese Tradition*. New York: Columbia University Press.

Faure, David., and Helen F. Siu, eds. 1995. *Down to Earth: The Territorial Bond in South China*. Stanford: Stanford University Press.

Gaspardone, Émile. 1952. "Un Chinois des mers du Sud, le fondateur de Hà Tiên". *Journal Asiatique* 240, no. 3: 363–85.

Gourou, Pierre. 1936. *Les paysans du Delta tonkinois*. Paris: Publications de l'École française d'Extrême-Orient.

Guennou, Jean. 1986. *Missions Etrangeres de Paris*. Paris: Le Sarment Fayard.

Guillot, C., Denys Lombard, and Roderich Ptak, eds. 1998. *From the Mediterranean to the China Sea: Miscellaneous Notes*. Wiesbaden: Harrassowitz.

Hall, Kenneth R. 2011. *A History of Early South East Asia*. Boulder: Rowman & Littlefield Publishers.

Hardy, Andrew. 2008. " 'Nguồn' Trong Kinh Tế Hàng Hóa Ở Đàng Trong [Sources in Nguyen Cochinchinese Economy]". In UBND Tỉnh Thanh Hóa - Hội Khoa Học Lịch Sử Việt Nam, *Chúa Nguyễn và Vương Triều Nguyễn Trong Lịch Sử Việt Nam Từ Thế Kỷ XVI Đến Thế Kỷ XIX [Proceedings of the Conference on Nguyen Lords and Nguyen Dynaty of Vietnam]*, pp. 55–65. Hà Nội: Thế Giới.

———, and Nguyễn Tiến Đông. 2013. "Đá Vách: Nguyễn Cochinchina's Eighteenth-Century Political Crisis and the Origins of Conflict in Quảng Ngãi". Paper presented at the workshop "Nguyễn Vietnam, 1558–1885: Domestic Issues", Harvard University, 11–12 May 2013.

Hoàng, Anh Tuấn. 2007. *Silk for Silver: Dutch-Vietnamese Relations, 1637–1700*. Leiden: Brill.

Huỳnh, Công Bá. 1997. "Về Quyển Gia Phả Của Hậu Duệ Nhà Mạc Ở Trà Kiệu (Duy Xuyên – Quảng Nam) [A Later Mạc Geneaology in Trà Kiệu (Duy Xuyên – Quảng Nam)]". In *Thông Báo Hán Nôm Học*, pp. 22–30.

Ishii, Yoneo, ed. 1998. *The Junk Trade from Southeast Asia, Translations from the Tôsen Fusetsu-Gaki, 1674–1723*. Singapore: Institute of Southeast Asian Studies.

欽定越史通鑑綱目 [*Khâm Định Việt Sử Thông Giám Cương Mục – The Imperially Ordered Mirror and Commentary on the History of the Viet*]. 1884. National Library, book 44, R.524.

Kelley, Liam C. 2006. "Confucianism" in Vietnam: A State of the Field Essay". *Journal of Vietnamese Studies* 1, nos. 1–2: 314–70.

———. 2016. "From a Reliant Land to a Kingdom in Asia: Premodern Geographic Knowledge and the Emergence of the Geo-Body in Late Imperial Vietnam". *Cross-Currents: East Asian History and Culture Review* 20 (September): 7–39.

Kleinen, John, Bert van der Zwan, Hans Moors, and Ton van Zeeland, eds. 2008. *Sư Tử và Rồng: Bốn Thế Kỷ Quan Hệ Việt Nam Hà Lan [Lion and*

Dragon: Four Centuries of Dutch and Vietnamese Relations]. Hà Nội: Thế Giới.

Kratoska, Paul H., Remco Raben, and Henk Schulte Nordholt, eds. 2005. *Locating Southeast Asia: Geographies of Knowledge and Politics of Space*. Singapore: Singapore University Press.

Lamb, Alastair. 1970. *Mandarin Road to Old Hue: Narratives of Anglo-Vietnamese Diplomacy from the 17th Century to the Eve of the French Conquest*. Hamden, Conn.: Archon Books.

Lê, Đản. 1811. "南河捷錄 [Nam Hà Tiệp Lục – Record of the Achievements of Nam Ha]". *Nghiên Cứu và Phát Triển* 3–4 (2012).

Lê, Đôn Quý. 1776. 撫邊雜錄 *[Phủ Biên Tạp Lục – Miscellaneous Chronicles of the Pacified Frontier]*. 2 vols. Sài Gòn: Tủ sách cổ văn, Ủy ban dịch thuật, 1973.

Léonard, Aurousseau. 1924. "Sur le nom de Cochinchine". *Bulletin de l'École française d'Extrême-Orient* 24, no. 1: 563–79.

Li, Tana. 1998a. "An Alternative Vietnam? The Nguyen Kingdom in the Seventeenth and Eighteenth Centuries". *Journal of Southeast Asian Studies* 29, no. 1: 111–21.

———. 1998b. *Nguyen Cochinchina, Southern Vietnam in the Seventeenth and Eighteenth Centuries*. Ithaca, NY: Cornell University Press.

———, and Anthony Reid, eds. 1993. *Southern Vietnam under the Nguyễn: Documents on the Economic History of Cochinchina (Đàng Trong), 1602–1777*. Singapore: Institute of Southeast Asian Studies.

Lieberman, Victor B. 2003. *Strange Parallels: Volume 1, Integration on the Mainland: Southeast Asia in Global Context, c.800–1830*. Cambridge: Cambridge University Press.

———. 2009. *Strange Parallels: Volume 2, Mainland Mirrors: Europe, Japan, China, South Asia, and the Islands: Southeast Asia in Global Context, C.800–1830*. Cambridge: Cambridge University Press.

Lombard-Salmon, Claudine. 2003. "Réfugiés Ming dans les Mers du Sud vus à travers diverses inscriptions (Ca. 1650–Ca. 1730)". *Bulletin de l'École française d'Extrême-Orient* 90–91: 177–227.

Manguin, Pierre-Yves. 1972. *Les Portugais sur les côtes du Viet-Nam et du Campa*. Paris: Paris: École française d'Extrême-Orient.

Mantienne, Frédéric. 2003. "The Transfer of Western Military Technology to Vietnam in the Late Eighteenth and Early Nineteenth Centuries: The Case of the Nguyên". *Journal of Southeast Asian Studies* 34, no. 3: 519–34.

Matsuda, Matt. 2012. *Pacific Worlds: A History of Seas, Peoples, and Cultures*. Cambridge: Cambridge University Press.

Mus, Paul. 1952. *Sociologie d'une guerre*. Paris: Éditions du Seuil.

Nguyễn, Cư Trinh. 1750. *Sãi Vãi [Monk and Nun]*. Unpublished, Yale University Library, AB.383.

Nguyễn, Văn Hầu. 1970. "Sự Thôn Thuộc và Khai Thác Đất Tầm Phong Long"

[The Annexation and Exploitation of Tầm Phong Long]. *Sử Địa* 19–20: 3–24.

Nöel, Péri. 1923. "Essai sur les relations du Japon et de l'Indochine aux XVIe et XVIIe siècles". *Bulletin de l'École française d'Extrême-Orient* 23, no. 1: 1–104.

Pawakapan, Puangthong R. 2014. "Warfare and Depopulation of the Trans-Mekong Basin and the Revival of Siam's Economy", Southeast Asia Research Centre (City University of Hong Kong), *Working Paper Series*, no. 156, 2014: 1–25. www.cityu.edu.hk/searc/Resources/Paper/156%20-%20WP%20-%20Dr%20 Puangthong.pdf (accessed 30 April 2019).

Pelliot, Paul. 1903. "Le Fou-Nan". *Bulletin de l'École française d'Extrême-Orient* 3, no. 1: 248–303.

Phan, Khoang. 1969. *Việt Sử: Xứ Đàng Trong 1558–1777 (Cuộc Nam Tiến Của Dân Tộc Việtnam)* [A Vietnamese History of the Cochinchina 1558–1777: Marching to the South of the Vietnamese Nation]. Saigon: Khai Trí.

Piétri, J.B. 1949. *Voiliers d'Indochine*. Saigon: Société des Imprimeries et Librairies Indochinoises.

Pires, Tome. 1967. *The Suma Oriental of Tome Pires*. London: The Hakluyt Society.

Poivre, Pierre. 1769. *Travels of a Philosopher, or, Observations on the Manners and Arts of Various Nations in Africa and Asia*. London: T. Becket.

Ptak, Roderich. 2008. "The Gulf of Tongking: A Mini-Mediterranean?". In *The East Asian Mediterranean: Maritime Crossroads of Culture, Commerce and Human Migration*, edited by Angela Schottenhammer, pp. 53–72. Wiesbaden: Harrassowitz Verlag.

Quách, Tấn, and Giao Quách. 1988. *Nhà Tây Sơn [The Tayson Dynasy]*. Quy Nhơn: Sở văn hóa và thông tin Nghĩa Bình.

Reid, Anthony. 1988. *Southeast Asia in the Age of Commerce, 1450–1680. Vol. 1: The Lands below the Winds*. New Haven: Yale University Press.

———. 1993. *Southeast Asia in the Age of Commerce, 1450–1680. Vol. 2: Expansion and Crisis*. New Haven: Yale University Press.

———, ed. 1997. *The Last Stand of Asian Autonomies: Responses to Modernity in the Diverse States of Southeast Asia and Korea, 1750–1900*. New York: St. Martin's Press.

———. 1999. *Charting the Shape of Early Modern Southeast Asia*. Chiangmai: Silkworm Books.

———. 2004. "Chinese Trade and Southeast Asian Economic Expansion in the Later Eighteenth and Early Nineteenth Centuries: An Overview". In *Water Frontier: Commerce and the Chinese in the Lower Mekong Region, 1750–1880*, edited by Nola Cooke and Tana Li, pp. 21–34. Boulder: Rowman & Littlefield.

———. 2015. *A History of Southeast Asia: Critical Crossroads*. Chichester: Wiley Blackwell.

Rochon, Alexis Marie de. 1793. *A Voyage to Madagascar and the East Indies*. London: E. Jeffery.

Sakurai, Yumio. 2004. "Eighteenth-Century Chinese Pioneers on the Water Frontier of Indochina". In *Water Frontier: Commerce and the Chinese in the Lower Mekong Region, 1750–1880*, edited by Nola Cooke and Tana Li, pp. 32–52. Boulder: Rowman & Littlefield Publishers.

Scott, James C. 1998. *Seeing Like a State: How Certain Schemes to Improve the Human Condition Have Failed*. New Haven, Conn.: Yale University Press.

———. 2009. *The Art of Not Being Governed: An Anarchist History of Upland Southeast Asia*. Yale University Press.

Tagliacozzo, Eric. 2005. *Secret Trades, Porous Borders: Smuggling and States Along a Southeast Asian Frontier, 1865–1915*. New Haven: Yale University Press.

———, and Wen-Chin Chang, eds. 2011. *Chinese Circulations: Capital, Commodities, and Networks in Southeast Asia*. Durham, NC: Duke University Press.

———, Helen F. Siu, and Peter C. Perdue, eds. 2015a. *Asia Inside Out: Changing Times*. Cambridge, MA: Harvard University Press.

———, Helen F. Siu, and Peter C. Perdue, eds. 2015b. *Asia Inside Out: Connected Places*. Cambridge, MA: Harvard University Press.

Tang, Wenya 唐文雅, ed. 2001. 广州十三行沧桑 *Guangzhou shisan xing cangsang* [The Thirteen Commercial Guilds of Guangzhou]. Guangzhou: Guangdong sheng ditu chubanshe 广东省地图出版社.

Taylor, Keith Weller. 1983. *The Birth of Vietnam*. Berkeley: University of California Press.

———. 1993. "Nguyễn Hoàng and the Beginning of Việt Nam's Southward Expansion". In *Southeast Asia in the Early Modern Era: Trade, Power, and Belief*, edited by Anthony Reid, pp. 42–85. Ithaca, NY: Cornell University Press.

———. 1998. "Surface Orientations in Vietnam: Beyond Histories of Nation and Region". *Journal of Asian Studies* 57, no. 4: 949–78.

Taylor, Philip. 2014. *The Khmer Lands of Vietnam: Environment, Cosmology, and Sovereignty*. Singapore: NUS Press.

Trocki, Carl A. 2009. "Chinese Revenue Farms and Borders in Southeast Asia". *Modern Asian Studies* 43, no. 1: 335–62.

Trương, Minh Đạt. 2008. *Nghiên Cứu Hà Tiên* [Study of Hatien]. Thành Phố Hồ Chí Minh: Nxb Trẻ.

Turner, Frederick Jackson. 1994. "The Significance of the Frontier in American History". In *Rereading Frederick Jackson Turner: "The Significance of the Frontier in American History" and Other Essays*, edited by John Mack Faragher, pp. 31–60. New Haven: Yale University Press.

Van Schendel, Willem. 2002. "Geographies of Knowing, Geographies of Ignorance:

Jumping Scale in Southeast Asia". *Environment and Planning D: Society and Space* 20, no. 6: 647–68.

Vickery, Michael. 2011. "1620, A Cautionary Tale". In *New Perspectives on the History and Historiography of Southeast Asia, Continuing Explorations*, edited by Michael Arthur Aung-Thwin and Kenneth R. Hall, pp. 157–66. London: Routledge.

Võ, Vinh Quang. 2013. "Lược Khảo Văn Bản 'An Nam Quốc Thư'" [A Brief Study of the Document of Ăn Nam Quoc Thu"]. *Tạp Chí Nghiên Cứu và Phát Triển* 9, no. 107: 61–71.

Volkov, Alexei. 2013. "Evangelization, Politics, and Technology Transfer in 17th-Century Cochin-China: The Case of João Da Cruz". In *Europe and China: Science and Arts in the 17th and 18th Centuries*, edited by Luís Saraiva, pp. 31–67. Singapore: World Scientific Publishing.

Vũ, Đức Liêm. 2016. "Vietnam at the Khmer Frontier: Boundary Politics, 1802–1847". *Cross-Currents: East Asian History and Culture Review* 5, no. 2: 534–64.

———. 2017. "The Age of Sea Falcons: Naval Warfare in Vietnam, 1771–1802". In *Warring Societies of Pre-Colonial Southeast Asia: Local Cultures of Conflict Within a Regional Context*, edited by Kathryn Wellen and Michael Charney, pp. 103–29. Copenhagen: Nordic Institute of Asian Studies.

Vũ, Thế Dinh. 1818. "河仙鎮叶鎮鄚氏家譜 [Hà Tiên Trấn Hiệp Trấn Mạc Thị Gia Phả – Mac Geneaology of Ha Tien]". Unpublished manuscript, Viện Hán Nôm, A.1321.

Wang, Gungwu, and Ng Chin-Keong, eds. 2004. *Maritime China in Transition 1750–1850*. Wiesbaden: Harrassowitz.

Wheeler, Charles James. 2001. "Cross-Cultural Trade and Trans-Regional Networks in the Port of Hoi An: Maritime Vietnam in the Early Modern Era". PhD dissertation, Yale University.

———. 2015. "1683: An Off Shore Perspective on Vietnamese Zen". In *Asia Inside Out: Changing Times*, edited by Eric Tagliacozzo, Helen F. Siu, and Peter C. Perdue, pp. 136–62. Cambridge, MA: Harvard University Press.

Wong Tze-Ken, Danny. 2011. "Vietnam–Champa Relations during the Seventeenth and Eighteenth Centuries". In *The Cham of Vietnam*, edited by Bruce Lokchart and Ky Phuong Tran, pp. 238–62. Singapore: NUS Press.

———. 2012. "The Destruction of the English East India Company Factory on Condore Island, 1702–1705". *Modern Asian Studies* 46, no. 5: 1097–115.

Zottoli, Brian A. 2011. "Reconceptualizing Southern Vietnamese History from the 15th to 18th Centuries: Competition along the Coasts from Guangdong to Cambodia". PhD dissertation, University of Michigan.

13

The Highlands of West Sumatra and Their Maritime Trading Connections

Mai Lin Tjoa-Bonatz

INTRODUCTION

Not much is known about the settlement processes that have contributed to create the unique ethnic and cultural diversity in the highlands of Sumatra. Archaeological fieldwork since 2003 in the upland regions—in Kerinci, the highlands of Jambi (Bonatz et al. 2009; Bonatz 2012; Tjoa-Bonatz 2009, 2015a), and in Tanah Datar, West Sumatra—point to commercial interactions between the highland and maritime regions since the first millennium CE. From 2010 to 2014, an interdisciplinary team under the direction of Dominik Bonatz has undertaken field research in Tanah Datar (literally "flat land"), a valley in West Sumatra in the core area of the Minangkabau community (Figures 13.1 and 13.2). The Institute of Ancient Near Eastern Archaeology at Freie Universität Berlin (FU Berlin) sponsored by the German Research Foundation has pursued excavations and surveys in cooperation with international institutions. Meanwhile, Arlo Griffiths (École française d'Extrême-Orient Jakarta) directed an epigraphic research project. The focus of the project is the reign of King Ādityavarman (c.1347–75), who established the centre of his polity in the highlands of Tanah Datar and issued twenty-two inscriptions from the middle of the fourteenth century. These dated inscriptions (Figure 13.3) provide the

FIGURE 13.1
The county Tanah Datar in West Sumatra, Indonesia

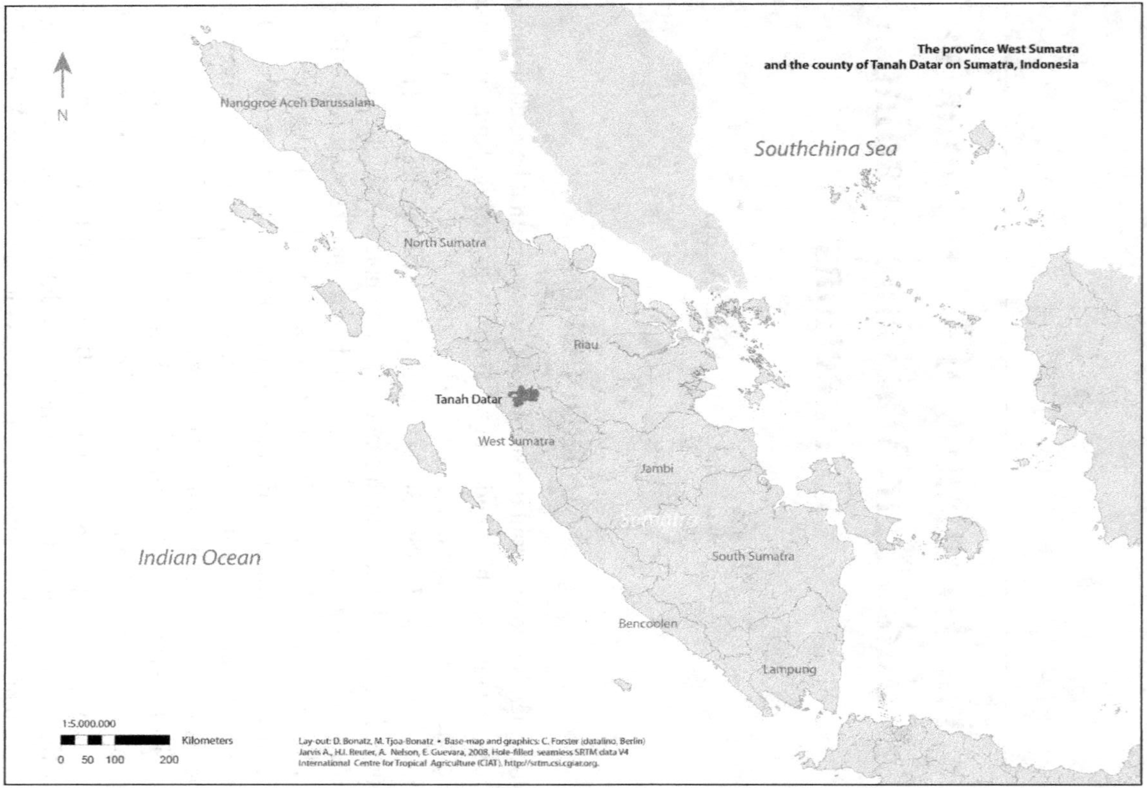

Source: Layout by D. Bonatz, M.L. Tjoa-Bonatz; base map and graphics by C. Förster.

FIGURE 13.2
Panoramic view from Bukit Gombak towards Mount Merapi, taken from the octocopter. Today, wet rice fields dominate the landscape of the fertile valley of Tanah Datar

Source: Photo by M. Tonch, D. Bonatz.

FIGURE 13.3
The Ādityavarman-inscription at Pagaruyung ($260 \times 133 \times 38$ cm) dated to 1356 written in Sanskrit

Source: Photo by J. Greger, D. Bonatz.

chronological anchor and fulcrum of the research project, which deals with the archaeological remains and the reconstruction of regional settlement processes before and after this period (Tjoa-Bonatz forthcoming).

Many fundamental changes can be identified in the societies of Southeast Asia when a new global economy emerged in the fifteenth century, a period characterized by Reid (1993) as the “Age of Commerce”. Scholars have emphasized the importance of the fifteenth century as the starting point for the modern period of Southeast Asian history (see, e.g., Wade and Laichen 2010). When archaeological materials are brought into account, a key question that arises when this shift appeared, probably not as a sudden event, a sharp discontinuity with the former times, but as a gradual change towards new economic modes that were already in existence before 1400 (Miksic 2010, p. 385). The archaeological material at hand to test this hypothesis in island Southeast Asia is rather limited. In the Indonesian Archipelago only a few settlement sites in North Sumatra, Western and Eastern Java, Riau as well as Singapore, Brunei, Sarawak, in the central Philippines of the fourteenth and fifteenth centuries, have been published in archaeological reports (Junker 1999; Edwards McKinnon 2006; Miksic 2006, pp. 148–50; 2010, pp. 392–96, fn. 11; Edwards McKinnon et al. 2012; Damanik and Edwards McKinnon 2012). Most sites for which data are available on the distribution of imported sherds are located in coastal areas, where the frequency of ceramics is generally higher than in the uplands.

During the middle Ming dynasty of the fourteenth and early fifteenth century, the shortage of Chinese ware was filled by exports of mainland Southeast Asian trade ceramics. The evidence for this phenomenon from various shipwreck cargoes is persuasive but has not yet been examined enough at land sites (Brown 2009). Therefore, finds of imported ceramics deserve primary attention, including the rare middle Ming blue-and-white ware dating from between 1465 or 1487 to 1522 which were found at the excavation in Tanah Datar. These are best explored in the context of an early commercial boom connected to expanding maritime trade which has also reached the highlands.

NEW DOCUMENTATION TECHNIQUES

In the cadre of our project, new aerial documentation and remote sensing techniques methods were introduced for the first time in the highlands of Indonesia. The geophysical surveys conducted by Benjamin Vining included a gradient magnetometer to cover 9,300 m^2 of the northern and central portion of the mound (Figure 13.4). This coincided with the initial

FIGURE 13.4
Geomagnetic surveys pursued on Bukit Gombak

Source: Photo by J. Greger, D. Bonatz.

weeks of the excavation during the 2011 field season at Bukit Gombak in order to locate potential features of archaeological interest. Despite the difficulty in assessing archaeological targets, and disregarding anomalies created by recent disturbances such as plowing in modern days which has moved the topsoil into furrows, archaeological anomalies of high- and low-magnitude were found.

During fieldwork in 2012 a remote-controlled and autonomous flying system, an octocopter, was tested in order to provide large-scale maps such as numeric maps and orthophotos as well as digital surface models (DSMs). An unmanned aerial vehicle (UAV) was equipped with a digital camera, which allowed the team to take aerial photos at a combined temporal and spatial resolution and from a height up to 100 m (Figure 13.2). Each flight took pictures from a height of 60 m with an exact spatial resolution of about 2 cm. This new promising acquisition technique for aerial imagery allowed for the development of large-scale mapping, supporting the documentation of the archaeological fieldwork and our understanding of the larger spatial context of the excavation sites, as well as the geoarchaeological environment of the region.

LONG-DISTANCE TRADE TO BOTH COASTLINES

The Barisan Mountains of Sumatra stretch from Lampung in the south to Aceh in the north. This mountain range is the watershed between the wide plains of the east coast and the narrow strip of the west coast of Sumatra (Figure 13.1). From early times, settlement cores of rather diverse cultural identity developed in fertile valleys in the mountainous region and along the river systems (Bonatz et al. 2009). The Minangkabau represent one of the best-known highland communities on this island due to its rich material culture and the matrifocal lineage system (e.g., Summerfield and Summerfield 1999). But historical processes have never been deduced from the archaeological evidence, all the more so because there have been no previous excavations. The precolonial history of the Minangkabau is, therefore, still poorly understood. Most historians only elaborate on the period after the seventeenth century, for which European sources and indigenous literature are available (Dobbin 1983; Drakard 1999). There are brief inventories of archaeological remains of the region (Krom 1912, pp. 27–36; Bronson, Basoeki and Wisseman 1973, pp. 13–14), but the first archaeological surveys were conducted only in the late 1980s (Miksic 1986, 1987, 2004). We have followed Miksic's initial footsteps into this region and have received invaluable assistance from him during our work.

Since the second half of the fourteenth century, land routes from Tanah Datar to the west and to the east coast were well established. The trading routes shifted according to the best available commercial opportunities, and the rivers were the connecting routes between the highlands and the ports at the coast. The majority of Ādityavarman's inscription stones are located in Tanah Datar (Figure 13.3). Six inscriptions are still found *in situ*. Considering the regional topography, they marked the route towards the west, and represent visual signs of the extension of his empire in that direction (Figure 13.5). Established within a close network of aligned settlements, these stones evidently covered the function of benchmarks, located in the vicinity of places for rest or trading nodes along the footpath from one settlement to another. From Bukit Gombak the trading route went to the southwest, passing Ponggongan, Kubarajo, Rambatan up to Ombilin on the shore of Lake Singkarak, via Paninggahan down to Pariaman. The inscription at Paninggahan is the most westerly one, found *in situ* in the district of Solok. The port of Pariaman, along with Barus and Tiku, was known as a west coast gold-trading harbour of the Minangkabau from the sixteenth to the early seventeenth centuries (Pires 1967 [1512–15], p. 161;

van der Meulen 1974, p. 13). Maritime routes passing Sumatra's west coast were well in use since the late first millennium CE (Tjoa-Bonatz 2015b). The *in situ* inscription at Saruaso at the Selo River represents the easternmost one in Tanah Datar. It drains into the River Indragiri which flows to the east coast, where another main port for the Minangkabau was maintained in the early sixteenth century. Apart from the connection along the Kampar River, the route to Jambi via the Batang Hari River seems to represent the most important link to the coast. Here two monuments are connected to Ādityavarman: the Amoghapāśa statue from Rambahan and the monumental "Bhairava" statue of Padang Roco (now identified as Mahākāla by Bautze-Picron 2014, pp. 113–14). Both artefacts were found at the Batang Hari site in Dharmasraya, which denotes a kingdom or court in the thirteenth and fourteenth century (Reichle 2007; Miksic 2015). After the founding of Melaka as a colonial port in 1511, the international maritime trade intensified along the straits and included Sumatra's east coast. Melaka became the main trading partner for the Minangkabau during the sixteenth century (cf. Dalboquerque 1963 [1518], vol. III, pp. 142, 161; van der Meulen 1974, p. 13, fn. 45 citing João de Barros 1560).

ĀDITYAVARMAN AND THE MINANGKABAU

The term *manangkabwa* appears first in the *Deśavarṇana* (or *Nāgarakṛtāgama*) of 1365, mentioned as the only highland area of Sumatra at the time when the East Javanese kingdom of Majapahit became aware of the importance of this region (Canto 13, verse 1; Robson 1995, p. 133). The area is listed among the overseas vassals of Majapahit, but this claim is likely to be a wishful thought of the court rather than reflect a political reality (Miksic 2015, p. 31). During the fourteenth century the identity of the ethnic group of the Minangkabau has been formulated and framed into a political entity. In the early fifteenth century the Minangkabau acquired an international reputation as a thriving indigenous polity, a fact reflected in European and Chinese sources. Chinese envoys sent imperial proclamations to the "country" of "Mi-nang-ge-bu" in 1405 (Wade n.d.).

In the middle of the fourteenth century Ādityavarman became the progenitor of the Minangkabau monarchy and, as some historians contend, also represented the ruler of Melayu-Jambi (Andaya 2001, pp. 323, 328; Wolters 1970, pp. 37–38). Controversies exist about Ādityavarman's lineage, but most authors agree on his descent from a Sumatran princess and his connection to the East Javanese court (de Casparis 1989; Suhadi 1990, p. 231; Miksic 2001, p. 104; Reichle 2007, pp. 195–201; Kulke

2009, p. 232; Kozok and Reijn 2010, pp. 135–36; Miksic 2015, pp. 32–34). In the traditional Minangkabau chronicles (*tambo*) he is acknowledged as a king who came as an outsider to Sumatra, where a long-established system of leadership by clan organization and local government by lineage elders already existed. There were two political traditions, an autocratic *Bodi Caniago* and more democratic *Koto Piliang* system (Abdullah 1972, pp. 183–87; Drakard 1999, p. 23, fn. 33). When the founders of these two traditions quarrelled about the leadership, one of them recognized the royal status of the newcomer Ādityavarman. According to one account Ādityavarman was given investiture by marrying into the ruling family. In another story narrated by the chronicle Alexander the Great is mentioned (just like in many other regions influenced by Islam), and China and Turkey are said to be the countries of origin of the Minangkabau ancestors. This account also alludes to international maritime trading connections.

By the early sixteenth century various European writers had identified the Minangkabau region as the place where the Sumatran gold originated from (Hess 1930–32 [1602–1797], p. 76; Dobbin 1983, p. 61; Drakard 1999, pp. 25–29). A source from 1601 specifies that most important to the rise of the Minangkabau highland kingdom was their craft of weapons, and the export of pepper and gold (Kroeskamp 1919, pp. 14–16). Ādityavarman's claim in five of his inscriptions that he is the sovereign of the gold land or earth puts a special emphasis on his economically motivated aim to take control of the gold-exporting region. For example, in the Kubarajo inscription Kanakamedinī, "the Golden Earth" is synonymous for Suvarṇadvīpa, i.e., Sumatra (Kern 1917, p. 219; Suleiman 2008 [1977], p. 66; Kulke 2009). The archaeological evidence of processing gold in Tanah Datar is provided by a recent find at the excavation at Ponggongan in 2010/2011 by Budi Istiawan, formerly a member of the local heritage office (Balai Pelestarian Cagar Budaya Batusangkar, or BPCP Batusangkar): a crucible of rather coarse earthenware (6.5 cm diameter) was used to melt the gold. Gold was mainly retrieved by mining, although some was panned in the rivers. Gold mines in Bukit Gombak and Saruaso are mentioned in the seventeenth century (Kroeskamp 1919, p. 56). From the late eighteenth century supplies of gold in Tanah Datar diminished (Dobbin 1983, p. 66).

After the time of Ādityavarman the supremacy of the royal family was constantly contested and frequent conflicts arose among competing lineages in the vast Minangkabau region. Because of these conflicts, trade declined severely from the 1580s until 1619 (Andaya 1993, p. 49). The 1670s and 1680s appear to have been a time of change in the organization of the Minangkabau kingdom, when the lineage of Pagaryung—the leading royal family until today—seized power. This lineage is already mentioned in Dutch records in 1641 but in connection with the Buo-Kumanis region at the eastern fringe of Tanah Datar from where, according to a local legend, the family is said to have moved to central Tanah Datar (Drakard 1999, pp. 33, 103). These historical references can be matched with our archaeological evidence, which clearly points to the fact that Bukit Gombak fell into oblivion in the last decades of the seventeenth century.

THE SETTLEMENT ON BUKIT GOMBAK

The possible centre of the polity during the reign of Ādityavarman lies on Bukit Gombak south of Batusangkar, as already suggested by Miksic (1987, p. 21; 2004, p. 204). In the area of Bukit Gombak, artefacts associated with this king and four of his inscriptions—though their exact location is not known—were found, two of which are dated to 1347 and 1356. They mention the existence of religious architecture, monumental gates, and other structures. The large mound of 5.13 ha and 428 m asl at its maximum height overlooks the fertile plain of the valley of Tanah Datar which stretches south of the volcano Merapi at the rivers Silaki and Selo (Figure 13.2). Here it controls the transition zone which gives access to the lowlands towards the east, and channels the way to the west, along the River Selo to the southwest. Apart from these geostrategic features, the direct view of the volcano, regarded as a feared but power-filled sacred mountain, and the connection to the waterways, characterize this place as the most prominent settlement site in central Tanah Datar. The veneration of the mountains, in particular Mount Merapi, is a topic in Ādityavarman's inscriptions. In the local accounts this mountain is also described as the nucleus of the Minangkabau heartland (Abdullah 1972, p. 184). Physical elevation, in our case the position of his presumed royal seat on a hilltop, is seen as a key element in the exercise of authority and the enhancement of status all over Sumatra (Andaya 1993, pp. 30, 34).

At Bukit Gombak eleven areas were excavated, totalling 1,159.5 m^2 (Table 13.1; Figure 13.6). Accumulated settlement deposits were not found. Agricultural ploughing in recent decades and the shallow depth (max. *c.*20 cm) of the cultural layers are the greatest cause of modern disturbance of the topsoil. The residential area covers the whole hilltop from the northwest to the southeast, totalling 51,301 m^2. The settlement density is most concentrated at the northern slope and central plateau, based on ceramic recovery per square metre (trenches B–D, K).

FIGURE 13.5
Central Tanah Datar provides a high density of heritage places: burial sites, stone alignments of meeting places. In Kubarajo, Ponggonan, Rambatan and Ombilin the inscription stones of Ādityavarman are still preserved *in situ*

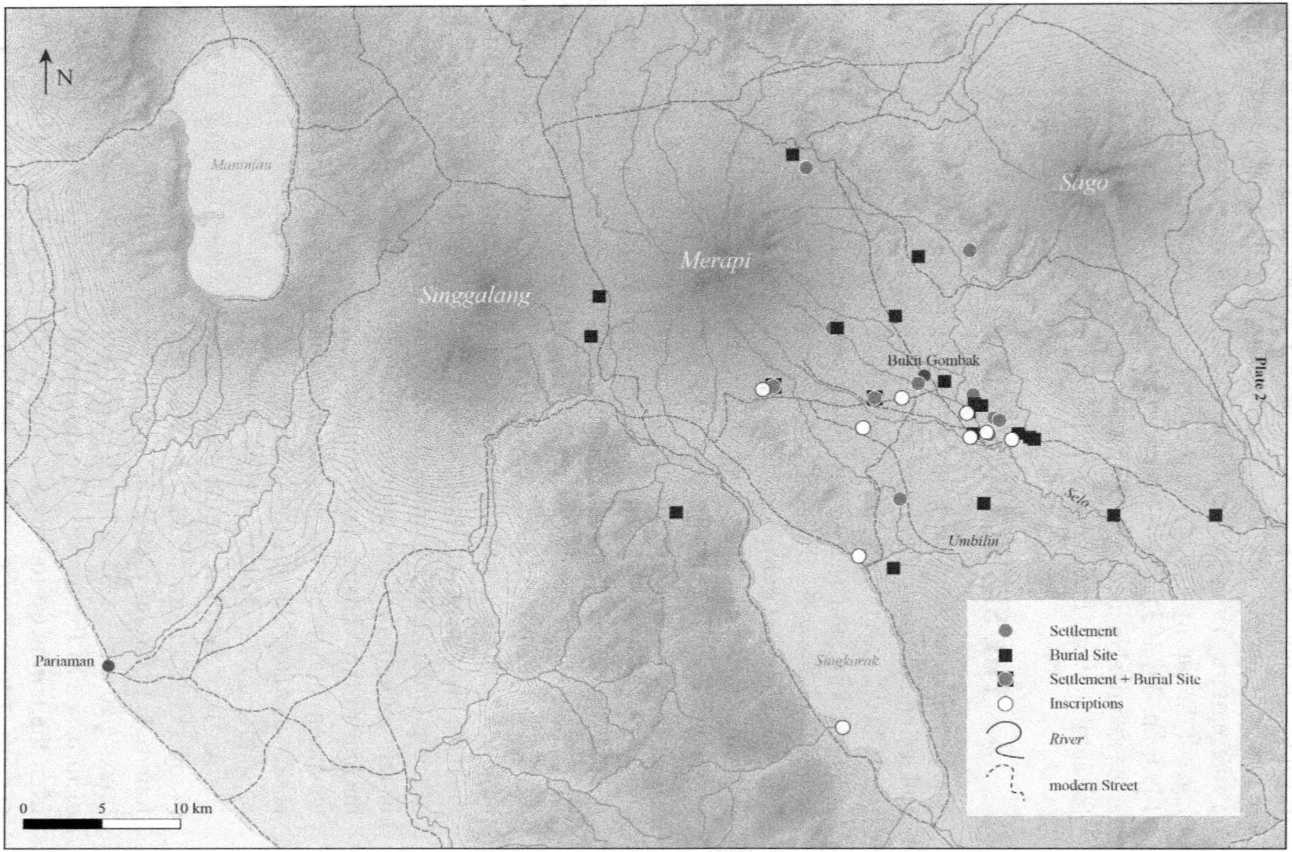

Source: Layout by M.L. Tjoa-Bonatz; base map and graphics by C. Förster.

In most trenches (A–D, F, M, T) postholes of various diameters (19–34 cm) were found, but mostly without any obvious alignment. On the eastern plateau twenty-four postholes (15–20 cm in diameter) were visible, most of which were discovered in 2011 (Figure 13.6). Twenty were aligned, suggesting a pile building with a rectangular ground plan of at least 7.72 × 2.62 m which is three spans wide from west to east and seven to eight spans long from north to south (found in trenches F, M, T). I assume that the ridgepole of the dwelling stretched along the longitudinal north–south axis (4–7 bays with 90–100 cm intervals) parallel to smaller bays (two bays with 70–80 cm intervals), so that the long side of the house—and probably the entrance—faced Mount Merapi to the northwest. This house plan provides the earliest material evidence of the points of reference of traditional Minangkabau houses, which is still a disputed topic among anthropologists. Lai (1993, p. 60) has argued that houses are oriented to cardinal points north–south. Rather, our data support the assumption of Nakamura (1999) and Vellinga (2004, pp. 268–71, fn. 20) that mountains and streams are the spatial nodes for orientation.

A striking feature is the extremely small interval between a post and another, and their limited diameter. If the number of house posts reflects socio-economic status, then the building—raised on many narrow piles—could have constituted a prestigious house. Another unclear issue is whether the double posts in the centre of the shorter sides of the building represent replacements or rather denote a certain architectural style. I assume the latter due to close comparisons with traditional Minangkabau houses of the Bodi Caniago tradition. It is also not known whether the discoloured layer of round diameter (the material is full of stony, orange-yellow inclusions and charcoal) which only goes down to 15–20 cm marks the actual post-pits or just the location where the house posts were raised on foundation stones. Traditional houses of this region are stilted on stones to better preserve the wooden structure, but there is evidence that Sumatran houses of the twelfth to fourteenth centuries were directly sunk into the ground (Lai Chee Kien 1993, p. 60; Tjoa-Bonatz 2012). One circular flat stone found *in situ* at the western side of the house may represent a foundation stone.

Human activities identified by occupation debris, e.g., earthenware, stoneware, porcelain, and stone tools, are relegated to the western and northern parts of the house (cf. Tjoa-Bonatz 2015a, Fig. 9). Two outdoor hearths of ovoid shape (0.48 × 0.77 m) were recognized from their fills with compact burnt clay and charcoal chunks. A stone close to each of the hearts was surrounded by smaller postholes and a wood ash layer

TABLE 13.1
Distribution and density of sherds retrieved at Bukit Gombak

Trench	*Size (m)*	*Volume excavated (m^3)*	*Weight of sherds (g)*	*Number of all sherds*	*Density sherds/m^3*	*Number of imported sherds*
A	9 × 9	49.06	915	311	6.34	27
B	2 × (9 × 9)	65.41	16,589	2,416	36.94	92
C	2 × (9 × 9)	84.09	26,766	6,280	74.68	121
D	2 × (9 × 9)	44.79	14,800	4,163	92.95	150
E	9 × 9	36.76	890	259	7.05	5
F	9 × 9	9.2	600	146	15.87	17
K	4.5 × 9	11.42	4,105	918	80.39	25
M	9 × 9	36.93	905	246	6.66	30
N	9 × 4	5.74	4,415	871	151.74	19
S	6 × 6, 30 m^2	2.41	390	140	58.09	4
T	9 × 9	16.31	280	58	3.56	8
Survey/surface				25		11
Total		362.12	70,655	15,833	534.27	509

Notes: Joints of the same vessel were counted once. Different to earthenware sherds imported ware sherds of less than 2 cm size were included in the count.

FIGURE 13.6
Excavation sites in Tanah Datar: Bukit Gombak, the burial site, Bukit Kincir, fourteenth to seventeenth centuries and the prehistoric Tanah Luah site

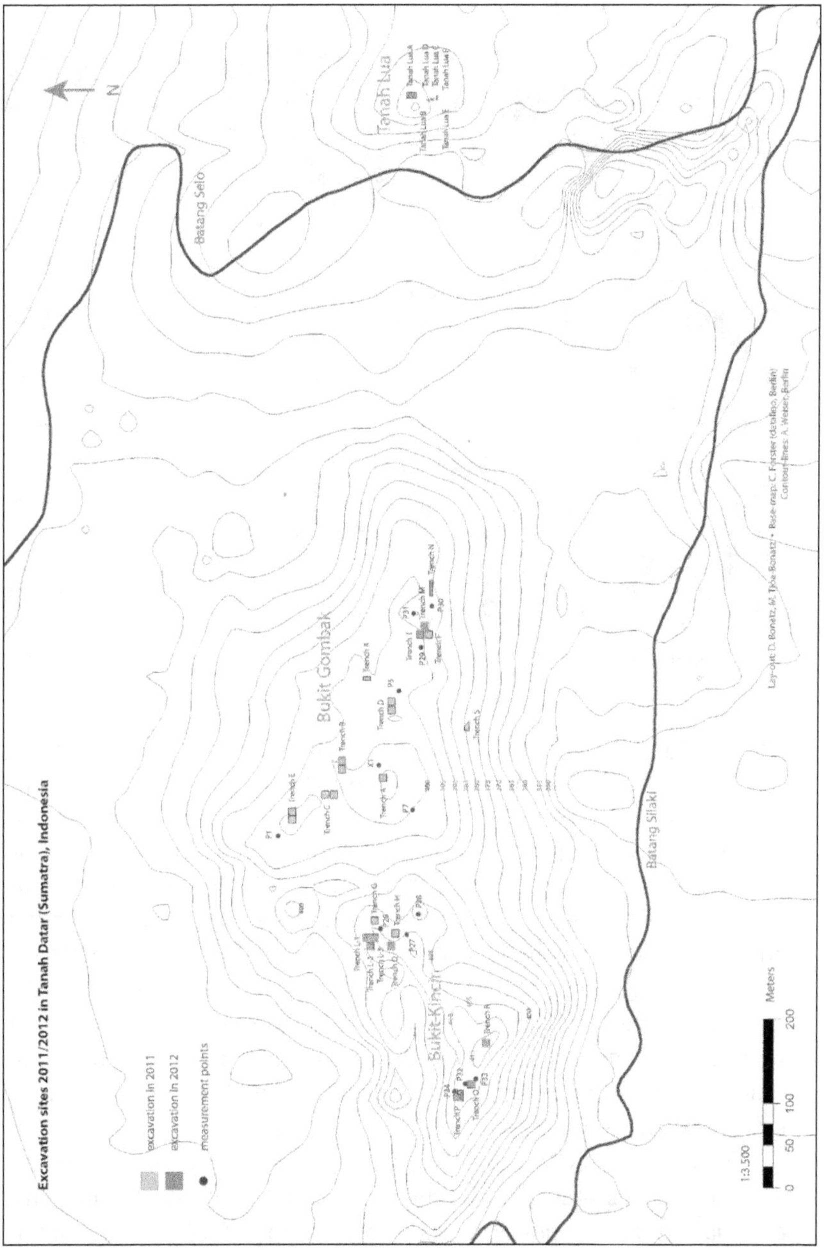

Source: Layout by D. Bonatz, M.L. Tjoa-Bonatz; base map and graphics by C. Förster.

FIGURE 13.7
In 2011, eighteen postholes of a pile building were excavated in the eastern part of Bukit Gombak, trench F

Source: Photo by K. Teuwsen, D. Bonatz.

that clearly point to cooking or burning activities. Similar anthropogenic features were detected by geophysical surveys. Anomalies of low magnitude were more diffuse and may represent anthropogenic sediments such as changes in the compaction or composition of soils due to archaeological occupation. Anomalies of high magnitude include pieces of eroded burnt clay, andesite river cobbles that were transported to the site for building purposes, anthropogenically modified soils, and artefacts. These features may reflect both residential and potentially industrial activities. Similar features at Pulau Majapahit in North Sumatra (Kota Rentang, Sumatra) were excavated, and found to correspond to living floors of compacted sandy sediments that contrasted magnetically with the surrounding natural soil (Edwards McKinnon et al. 2012, pp. 72–74).

Excavations in trench C verified the results of the remote sensing, uncovering features (burnt clay, charcoal, postholes) and retrieving occupation finds (pottery, glass beads, metal objects, stone tools). Sediments which were discoloured and compacted, apparently constituting anthropogenic vitrified concretions, were widely distributed on Bukit

Gombak (concentrated in trenches B–F, M). The residential area also included small-scale craft production such as metalworking, as seen from the recoveries of iron slag (in trenches B–D, N). This is the first archaeological evidence for iron production in the area, which became a local specialization of the Minangkabau as documented in ethnographic literature.

Around 30 m down the plateau at the southern slope of Bukit Gombak (trench S) an ancient water source was discovered in an artificially terraced wall of rock (Tjoa-Bonatz 2013a, Fig. 8). The flow of water was blocked by a piece of petrified wood, and water basins were carved into the first terrace to create a bathing place of 5 × 6 m. This spring, along with one at the eastern slope of the hill, provided water supply for the settlement but may also have served for ritual purposes as artefacts such as sherds of a Javanese(?) *kendi* or a stone adze found in the vicinity may tentatively suggest. A stone statue of a Bodhisattva probably 700–900 from the Central Javanese Period and a crude water fountain was said to come from Bukit Gombak (Krom 1912, pp. 42–43, nos. 23–26). The female torso which holds her breasts reflects an East Javanese iconography, e.g., a statue found at the site of Belahan (Miksic 1987, Fig. 12–3).

THE BURIAL SITE AT BUKIT KINCIR

A burial site (totalling around 8,500 m^2) can be directly linked to the habitation area, located in a depression between the slopes of Bukit Gombak and Bukit Kincir (Figure 13.6). In an excavation area covering 486 m^2, a total of 124 mostly upstanding river stones of slightly rectangular shape were found (Figure 13.8; cf. Tjoa-Bonatz 2013b, Fig. 7). The excavators assume that all these stones mark burials, although bone material did not survive due to acidic soil conditions. Roughly rectangular pits (up to 2 m long and 1.13 m deep in trench L1) denote whole body burials. This fact would lead to the assumption that the local population did not convert to cremation practices as expected within the realm of Ādityavarman, a follower of a Hindu-Buddhist religious and ritual paradigm as it is clear from his inscriptions.

Layers of fired clay and charcoal relate to the burials, and local earthenware was used in burial rituals. The differences seen in the grave structures—full-body burials next to cremation—and rarely found foreign vessels among the burial goods may indicate social strata, different burial practices due to religious belief or distinctions between the individuals. Five stone formations (in trenches G, H, L3) were exposed and most of

FIGURE 13.8
A total of 124 erected stones mark burial places on Bukit Kincir; most face Mount Merapi. Five stone formations in the foreground of the photo are exposed, partly enhanced by imported ceramics

Source: Photo by J. Greger, D. Bonatz.

them include imported ceramics. An L-shape (1.1 × 2.3 m) formed by eighteen stones was found further up the slope (trench L3), where a black-glazed sherd of a Khmer jar was discovered. Two alignments consist of, respectively, five and seven stones, together with an ovoid shape of eight stones. At the latter (in trench H), a fourteenth century Longquan plate with a fluted cavetto and a diameter of 36 cm, together with a Ming dynasty blue-and-white sherd, may indicate the distinctive social position of the deceased. Two Celadon sherds were retrieved near to an ovoid shape of 3.10 × 1.9 m made up by nineteen pebbles (trench G). Among the imported finds from this burial place, five out of the seven sherds found are green-glazed. Due to these ceramic finds and two thermoluminescent dates (TL) found in trench L, the burial place was used from the fourteenth century to at least the seventeenth century (Table 13.2).

SETTLEMENT HISTORY

The site of Bukit Gombak included both habitation and economic functions. The settlement existed without fortification, but with a clear

TABLE 13.2
^{14}C-dating and TL-dating for Bukit Gombak (BG; trenches A–D, M), and settlement (trenches O, P, R) and burial sites (trenches G, L) on Bukit Kincir (BK)

Lab no. (MAMS-)	*Site*	*Trench*	*^{14}C-sample*	*TL-sample*	*Age*
13928	BG	A	A-26, BG-0010	—	Cal CE 1418–34/1410–40
13919	BG	A	A-31, BG-0013	—	Cal BCE 748–428/753–415
13917	BG	B	B-6, BG-0512	—	Cal CE 1451–1608/1446–1617
113208	BG	B	—	B-4 BG-0526	930 ± 110/350 BP
13927	BG	C	C-17, BG-1023	—	Cal CE 1413–29/1405–38
13922	BG	C	D-25, BG-0093	—	Cal CE 1665–1950/1662–1951
13923	BG	C	D-22, BG-0067	—	Cal CE 1407–25/1330–1436
13924	BG	C	D-10, BG-0069	—	Cal CE 1643–61/1529–1795
13925	BG	C	D-19, BG-0078	—	Cal CE 1643–61/1529–1796
15657	BG	M	M-5, BG-0305	—	Cal CE 1416–33/1408–40
15666	BK	O	O-4, BG-0738	—	Cal CE 1662–1950/1653–1951
122967	BK	O	—	O-4, BG-0732	1090 ± 600 BP
15656	BK	P	P-4, BG-0658	—	Cal CE 1452–1613/1446–1620
15655	BK	R	R-11, BG-1360	—	Cal CE 1650–1793/1644–1950
13918	BK	G	G-6, BG-1209	—	Cal BCE 1876–1741/1883–1693
15654	BK	L	L2-30, BG-0222	—	Cal CE 1190–1252/1170–1258
122965	BK	L	—	L3-24, BG-0265	200 ± 65 BP
122971	BK	L	—	L3-29, BG-0269	470 ± 200/460 ± 70 BP

Notes: The early ^{14}C-dates seem not applicable. BP means before 1950.

division between the residential area uphill and the agricultural land scattered down the hill in the plain. Probably since the fourteenth century this valley formed the agricultural core of the region. It is assumed that irrigated rice cultivation was spreading in Tanah Datar by that time, under Ādityavarman. In the Batu Papahat inscription of 135? the installation of an irrigation channel is mentioned, enabling the development of a wet rice (*sawah*)-based kingdom (Krom 1912, no. 39; Bambang Budi Utomo 2007, p. 56). From the water source the channel can be followed to where it still directs water to the level of the fields towards the east before it drains to the River Selo.

The assumption that the highlands, in particular West Sumatra, were one of the most densely populated areas of the island in pre-colonial times as suggested by Miksic (1989, pp. 16, 21) can be supported by our archaeological evidence. More sites, such as Tanah Lua at the water source of Batu Papahat and one at the hilltop of Bukit Kincir, were identified in close vicinity to Bukit Gombak (Figure 13.6). The excavation trenches at Tanah Lua, covering 116 m^2, yielded earthenware, cooking supports, and obsidian tools, but no imported ceramics were retrieved.

The small settlement site of 9,859 m^2 on the plateau of Bukit Kincir of 444 m asl was bordered on its eastern side by a ditch where bamboo was planted at some undetermined time in the past. The sherd density is higher on the western part of this mound where metal slag, compact burnt clay, obsidian tools, and river stones indicate household and craft production. This was a metalworking site. The small number of only three imported kinds of vessel types include one or two brown-glazed storage jar(s), a fine two-lug Celadon jarlet (Figure 13.9, P_BG-0701-11), and a single blue-and-white rim sherd of a Ming bowl. Dupoizet and Harkantiningsih (2007, p. 37) suggest that two-lug jarlets of the Song (960–1279) or Yuan (1279–1368) dynasty were specially "linked to Southeast Asian needs" and were therefore produced for a long time. Considering the possible time span of the ceramics and two ^{14}C-dates the habitation period at this site from at least the middle of the fifteenth century was contemporaneous with Bukit Gombak (see Table 13.2). But the population structure of Bukit Kincir seems different. The limited amount of tradeware suggests that they did not have the same access to imported goods as did the inhabitants of Bukit Gombak.

Other sites in the region attest to trading contacts. At four sites where Ādityavarman's inscriptions are located, survey finds range from the Yuan dynasty to Swatow sherds of the seventeenth century at Rambatan; from Longquan ware of the thirteenth or fourteenth centuries (cf. Dupoizat 2009, pl. 9, no. 6), early Ming dynasty, to Dutch ware of the nineteenth century at Padang Roco; from late Ming to Ching period porcelain at a goldworking workshop at Ponggongan, which may date from at least the seventeenth to the nineteenth century, along with andesite and brick structures; and from Wan Li (1573–1619) and Swatow dishes to Dutch nineteenth century stoneware at Saruaso. This last dating was kindly proposed by Edwards McKinnon (personal communication 22 January 2013). The survey material found at the two last sites does not conclusively mean that the sites were not occupied during the time of Āditvavarman but the investigated surface finds did not include earlier material.

The findings from the excavations in the region of Tanah Datar fit into a scheme revealing that in the fourteenth century, a complex and probably more permanent settlement pattern began to be established in this fertile highland plain. Sites which were important in the time of Ādityavarman, as shown by inscriptions, statues, and surface finds of foreign ceramics and earthenware, reveal settlement remains from at least the fourteenth century.

CERAMICS

The total quantity of ceramic material recovered from the 2011–12 excavations amounts to 15,833 sherds, weighing nearly 72 kg, including 509 foreign ceramic sherds (see Table 13.1). A full publication on the finds is in preparation, but my preliminary analysis allows for the following observations (Tjoa-Bonatz forthcoming). Pottery is the most abundant type of artefact found at our excavations. Three ware types can be distinguished on the basis of the texture, temper and colour. The earthenware of Bukit Gombak mostly consists of vessels of daily consumption, water containers, cooking or storage pots, some of which were covered by lids. Restricted vessels outnumber unrestricted ones by far. The decoration is extremely limited and simple—mostly paddle-and-anvil patterns which start on the shoulder and cover the body of the vessel. While local pottery continued to fulfil domestic and utilitarian roles, porcelain and stoneware from abroad were imported as rare items of prestige.

The ceramics can be divided into several types according to their place of manufacture and their characteristics, such as decoration or glaze (Table 13.3). In the inventory of imported ware, Chinese ceramics outnumber those from Southeast Asia. These mainly consist of blue-and-white ware from the Jingdezhen kilns, Jiangxi (nearly half of the total amount), followed by greenwares which comprise Zhejian Celadons from the Longquan kilns or from kilns in Fujian. Coarse stoneware jars

TABLE 13.3
Imported wares from Bukit Gombak
(including 11 sherds from survey finds)

Imported ceramics	*Number of sherds*
Chinese blue-and-white ware	238
Vietnamese blue-and-white	2
Chinese whiteware	17
Chinese greenware	110
Thai (Sawankhalok)	33
Storage jars (Chinese/mainland Southeast Asian)	89
Persian ceramics	8
Southeast Asian ceramics	6
Other (European ware, Chinese red-overglazed ware)	6
Total	509

probably originating from China or Mainland Southeast Asia constitute a distinct group. White-bodied wares from Jiangxi or Fujian kilns appear in smaller amounts together with a single over-glazed copper-red sherd. Most Southeast Asian ceramics were Sawankhalok ceramics produced in Thailand. Shards of earthenware *kendi* probably from Java, blue-and-white ware from Vietnam, fragments of a lead-glazed jar from Burma, and Persian stoneware pots add to the picture that Bukit Gombak obtained a relatively wide range of foreign vessels.

Thirteenth to sixteenth century Chinese monochromes constitute the second largest class of wares in the excavated imported material (if counting all Chinese white- and greenware). They mostly consist of green-glazed ceramics starting from lotus-peddled or plain Song dynasty bowls either with unglazed foot which expose their reddish-brown body material or similar to those found at Kota Cina as suggested by Miksic (personal communication, 27 March 2012), to Yuan and middle Ming vessels such as a dish with a floral moulded relief. A green-glazed dish with a fish in relief which came to light close to the posthole structure mentioned above (see Figure 13.7) dates to the late thirteenth to fourteenth centuries. This type of Longquan dish is found extensively in places connected with the maritime trade of Southeast Asia, in general at coastal sites of the archipelago (cf. Locsin and Locsin 1967, no. 53; Gompertz 1980, Fig. 83B; Tregear 1982, Fig. 245; Adhyatman 1990, no. 215; Edwards McKinnon 1992, p. 67; Dupoizet and Harkantiningsih 1994, III. 78, nos. 1–2; He Li

1996, no. 355; Dupoizat and Harkantiningsih 2007, p. 36, no. 4; Dupoizat 2009, pl. 7, nos. 1–2; Miksic 2011, 21.22). The brittle ware jars may well date to the thirteenth to fourteenth centuries and are unglazed, of brown or black color.

The majority of the underglazed blue dishes are Chinese trade ware regarded by Brown (2009, pp. 29–30) as commonly exported everyday ceramics from Jingdezhen during the reigns of Chenghua (1465–87) or Hongzhi (1488–1505). This ware group includes bowls decorated with a trellis border (Figure 13.9: P_BG-0003-7), chrysanthemum or light lotus scrolls above sketchily drawn lotus panels (Figure 13.9: P_BG 1000-104), and small bowls with flaring rim and a honey-comb pattern at the outside (Figure 13.9: P_BG-0003-5 and Figure 13.10). This eye-catching motif of a hexagon which includes a mutilated Sanskrit letter has also been recorded on a shipwreck directed to Brunei, as well as at harbour sites of Sumatra and Singapore (cf. Goddio and Casal 2002, nos. 219, 228–30; Dupoizet 2009, pl. 17 nos. 4a, 5; Brown 2009, p. 49, no. 16, pl. 63 no. 5). Similarly, tentative comparisons are given by shipwreck finds of the same time period for a bowl with a double ring and a leaf spray at the center (Figure 13.9, P_BG-0063-1; cf. Brown 2009, pl. 54, no. 24) and a dish with a border of trefoils and floral motifs set in reserve against a background of waves (Figure 13.9, P_BG-0050-66; cf. Goddio and Casal 2002, nos. 109–10). A bowl with cloud design in spirals tentatively originates from Jingdezhen in the late Hongwu reign (1368–98) (Figure 13.9, P_BG-0003-19; cf. Gotuaco, Tan, and Diem 1997, p. 111).

Restrictions on foreign trade implemented by Ming government policies caused a severe shortage of Chinese ceramics in the first half of the fifteenth century and also a second moderate decline from 1520 to 1567. As attested by archaeological finds of shipwreck cargoes, sufficient Chinese blue-and-whites were only exported in the second half of the fifteenth century, and an increase of imports of mainland Southeast Asian ceramics can be discerned (Brown 2009). This is seen by a Vietnamese blue-and-white bowl with a band of scrolls (Figure 13.9, P_BG-1006-160; cf. Dupoizet 2009, p. 92, Fig. 28) and Sawankhalok celadon dishes with an undulating vine at the upper cavetto, both ware types of the fifteenth century found on Bukit Gombak. Burmese exports to Indonesia are documented only for a short period from 1470 to 1505, giving a tentative date for our brown-glazed sherd (Brown 2004, pp. 7–8). The latest recoveries from China on Bukit Gombak are Swatow dishes with a heavy and sandy ring foot, manufactured at the Zhangzhou kilns of south Fujian in the early seventeenth century.

FIGURE 13.9
Imported blue-and-white ceramics of the Ming dynasty from Bukit Gombak of the fifteenth or sixteenth century and a small, two-lug jarlet of the Song or Yuan dynasties from Bukit Kincir, thirteenth of fourteenth centuries

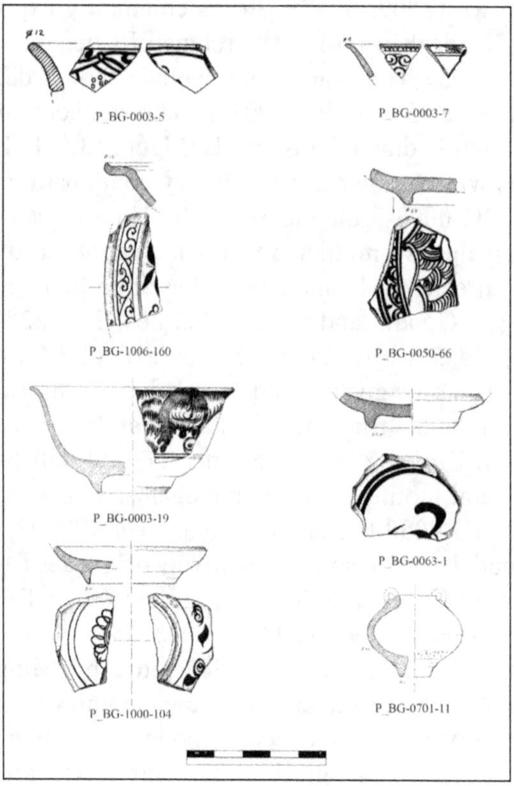

Source: Drawings by Dayat Hidayat, lay-out: M.L. Tjoa-Bonatz.

The assemblage of imported ware ranges between the thirteenth to the early seventeenth centuries. The late fifteenth century indicates an increase in imported porcelain. This as well as the historical and epigraphic evidence may point to occupation of the site as early as the fourteenth century. The hill was probably left abandoned after the seventeenth century. The Dutch or British sherds of the nineteenth century were all found in one trench at the outer border (trench N) of the settlement hill where a street during the colonial period was built. This time frame corresponds to the results of ^{14}C-analysis. Eight dates point to a habitation period between the early

FIGURE 13.10
The blue-and-white sherd of a bowl from Bukit Gombak with a flaring rim and a honey-comb pattern at the outside and beaded designs on the interior walls, tentatively dated to the late fifteenth or early sixteenth century

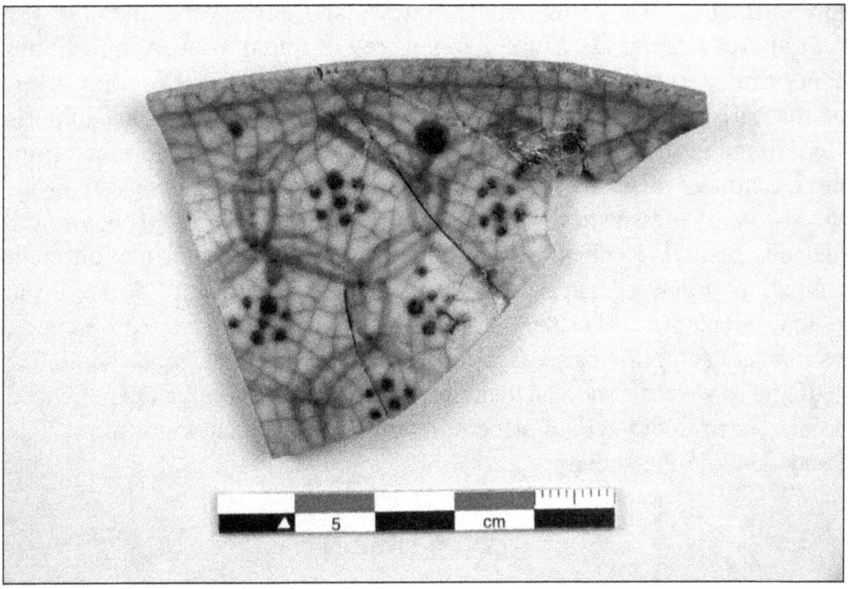

Source: Photo by J. Greger.

decades of the fifteenth century until the second half of the seventeenth century (Table 13.2).

The diversity of the trade ware indicates that a sophisticated society lived at Bukit Gombak, whose economic surplus was invested in trade and the conspicuous consumption of foreign luxuries. Only a limited range of forms reached the highlands—jars, bowls or cups, a few plates—in general smaller vessels which could be more easily transported hundreds of kilometers into the uplands. The quality varies, ranging from very rare fine examples to rather sketchy painted ones of modest decoration and uneven glaze. The market for foreign goods was maintained in the highlands either via an integrated market system or directly by Minangkabau and Chinese tradesmen. A letter of 1636 found in colonial records emphasizes the existence of well-established direct trade, so much so that the Minangkabau did not come down to Jambi because they were "now so spoiled having Chinese bring the goods to them" (Reid 1993, p. 312).

The imported material is spread all over the site, so I assume that ceramics were available to several households living on Bukit Gombak (Figure 13.11). All excavation areas yielded blue-and-white porcelain. Having a closer look at each ware group, the distribution pattern of imported goods within the settlement reveals spatial differences. The few special rarities from Persia, Burma, and Java were found in the central area (trench D). Storage jars were not found in every trench, but concentrated in the northern and central part (trenches C–D), where most of the early white- and greenwares were retrieved. Most Thai imports were found in the northern trench (B). The discovery of trade wares from three centuries raises an element of uncertainty: due to the consistency of the absolute dates from different locations (trenches A–C, M) across the plateau of Bukit Gombak, no obvious chronological sequence of different habitation structures can be discerned. Although we cannot decide if the spatial imbalance of certain ceramics types alludes to status differences, varying consumption patterns, or different access to trade goods within the settlement, we can conclude that the society of Bukit Gombak experienced an increasing socio-economic complexity when different kinds of prestige goods entered the society.

CONCLUSION

Since the fourteenth century a relatively dense settlement pattern and a sophisticated trading society has evolved at the highland valley of Tanah Datar in West Sumatra. Trading activities went to both coastlines, bringing foreign commodities to the upland regions in exchange for gold, forest products and, since the sixteenth century, pepper and weapons. Bukit Gombak became a place of some importance from the fourteenth to seventeenth centuries, most possibly the centre of Ādityavarman's kingdom. Most remains from his reign have been collected around Bukit Gombak, and its topography and the density of habitation remains in comparison to other sites in Tanah Datar make it the most prominent site excavated in this region so far. Essential to its development into a trading centre were three main economic factors: control of the trading network of this subregion and access to gold resources; a surplus obtained by wet rice cultivation; and specialized crafts like metalworking. The finding of occupation debris and features, as well as evidence for local handicraft production (pottery, metalworking including gold smelting), underline a sufficiently differentiated habitation pattern. It was possible to identify a pile dwelling with outdoor hearths and pits probably of the fourteenth century.

FIGURE 13.11
Find distribution of the imported ware groups in the excavation trenches on Bukit Gombak, the burial site and Bukit Kincir as percent of total

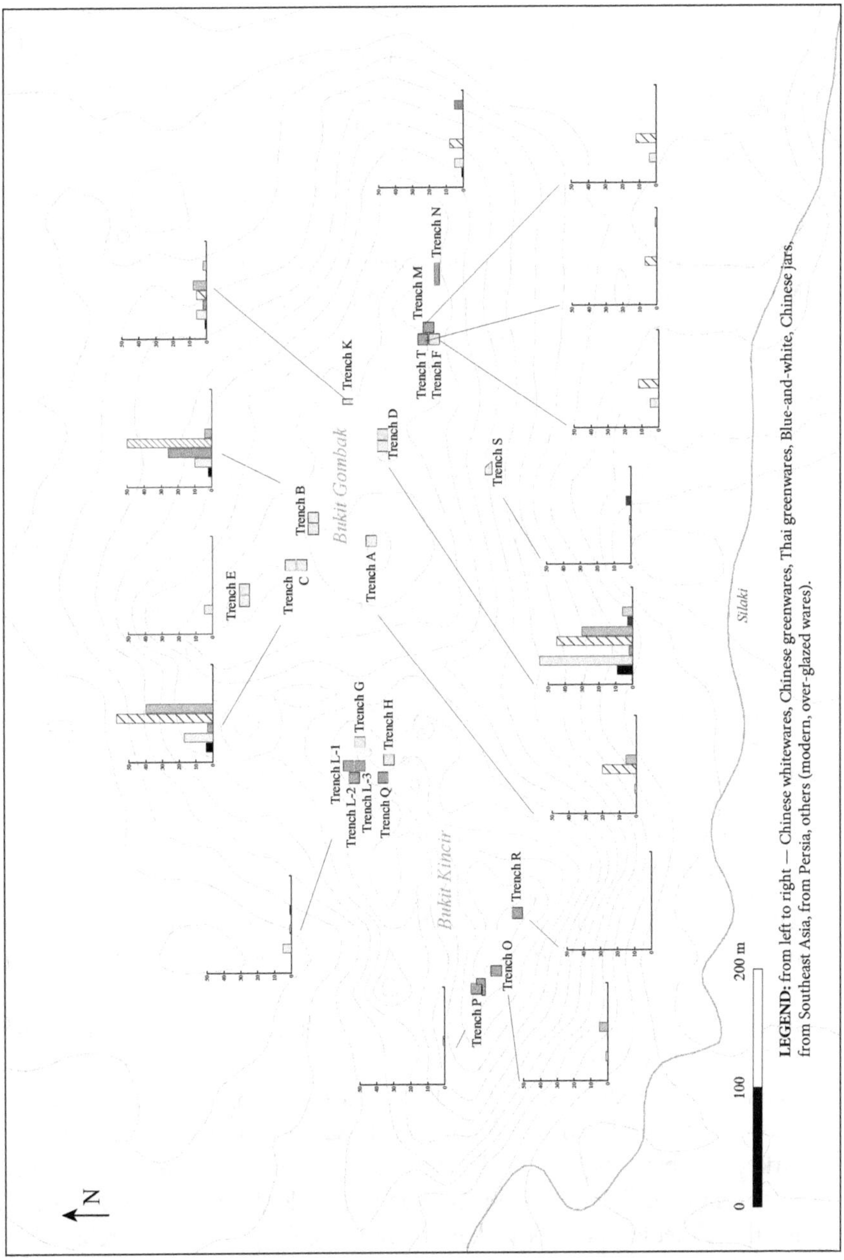

Source: Layout by M.L. Tjoa-Bonatz; base map and graphics by M. Tonch.

The imported material, if compared with the much greater amount of trade wares found at other fifteenth or sixteenth century coastal sites of the archipelago, seems to represent scant proof of a volume of long-distance trade capable of causing cultural change. But even these relatively few imported objects are enough to allow us to hypothesize that a gradual change occurred in the highland of Sumatra over the period taken into account in this discussion. The increase in imported porcelain at Bukit Gombak during the fifteenth century alludes to the rising significance of foreign trade in this society. Only a few porcelain sherds are connected to a specific area of the burial site. These commodities came from afar: the Middle East, Java (?), mainland Southeast Asia, and mostly from China.

Returning to my initial research question of whether the fifteenth century was a turning point for highland Sumatra, I conclude that international trade networks were already well established during the second half of the fourteenth century. The commercial boom in Tanah Datar was related to territorial consolidation—indicated by the stone structures and inscriptions—and made possible changes in trade patterns and material culture. In the subsequent centuries these changes were stabilized, and an economically complex society was created, which could use surplus wealth to obtain foreign trade commodities such as porcelain, glass beads and stoneware to a much greater extent than previously. The polity of the Minangkabau was not only a forgotten "Kingdom of Words", as described after the eighteenth century by Drakard (1993), but also of the very few internationally recognized highland communities of early island Southeast Asia and well connected to the maritime-based trade network.

Acknowledgements

This project would not have been possible without the substantial assistance of a large team, including researchers and students from the following institutions: FU Berlin, Universitas Indonesia, University of Adelaide, Hochschule für Technik und Wirtschaft Berlin, École française d'Extrême-Orient Jakarta, Boston University, National Museum of Cambodia Phnom Penh, Balai Medan, Balai Bandung and BPCP Batusangkar. The project was undertaken in co-operation with Pusat Penelitian dan Pengembangan Arkeologi Nasional (PUSLIT ARKENAS) and with the research permit from RISTEK (Kementerian Riset dan Teknologi Republik Indonesia). The local archaeological body (BPCP Batusangkar) collected archaeological material and sources from the region, gratefully supported by Budi Istiawan. Geoarchaeological research and area mapping were investigated by the

Institute of Geographical Sciences of the FU Berlin and Benjamin Vining from the University of Boston. My thanks go to Uli Kozok who kindly introduced me to the region in 2008, to Hermann Kulke and John Miksic who came to visit the excavations and my ceramic lab. I am most grateful for John Miksic's enduring guidance and evaluation of the ceramics, and the valuable comments of Johannes Moser and Edmund Edwards McKinnon on the excavated material. The excellent drawings of Dayat Hidayat were most helpful to understand the artefacts. Arlo Griffiths and Véronique Degroot have kindly read an earlier version of the paper. Dating studies were pursued by the Curt-Engelhorn-Zentrum Archäometrie in Mannheim (MAMS).

References

Abdullah, T. 1972. "Modernization in the Minangkabau World: West Sumatra in the Early Decades of the Twentieth Century". In *Culture and Politics in Indonesia*, edited by C. Holt, pp. 179–245. Ithaca and London: Equinox.

Adhyatman, S. 1990. *Antique Ceramics Found in Indonesia*. Jakarta: Ceramic Society of Indonesia.

Andaya, B.W. 1993. *To Live as Brothers: Southeast Sumatra in the Seventeenth and Eighteenth Centuries*. Honolulu: University of Hawai'i Press.

Andaya, L. 2001. "The Search for the 'Origins' of Melayu". *Journal of Southeast Asian Studies* 32, no. 3: 315–30.

Bambang Budi Utomo 2007. *Prasasti-Prasasti Sumatra*. Jakarta: PUSLIT.

Bautze-Picron, P. 2014. "Buddhist Images from Padang Lawas Region and the South Asian Connection". In *History of Padang Lawas, North Sumatra; II: Societies of Padang Lawas (Mid-Ninth–Thirteenth century CE)*, edited by D. Perret, pp. 107–28. Paris: Cahiers d'Archipel.

Bonatz, D. 2012. "A Highland Perspective on the Archaeology and Settlement History of Sumatra". *Archipel* 84: 35–81.

Bonatz, D., J. Miksic, J.D. Neidel, and M.L. Tjoa-Bonatz, eds. 2009. *From Distant Tales. Ethnohistory and Archaeology in Highland Sumatra*. Newcastle-upon-Tyne: Cambridge Scholars Publication.

Bronson, B., Machi Suhadi Basoeki, and J. Wisseman. 1973. "Laporan Penelitian Arkeologi di Sumatera, 20 Mei–8 Jul, 1973" [Archaeological research report of Sumatra, 20 May–8 July 1973]. Unpublished manuscript. Jakarta/ Philadelphia: Lembaga Purbakala dan Peninggalan Nasional/The University of Pennsylvania Museum.

Brown, R.M. 2009. *The Ming Gap and Shipwreck Ceramics in Southeast Asia. Towards a Chronology of Thai Trade Ware*. Bangkok: Siam Society under Royal Patronage.

Dalboquerque, A. 1963 [reprint]. *The Commentaries of the Great Afonso*

Dalboquerque/Trasl. from the Portuguese edition of 1774 (4 vol.). New York: Franklin.

Damanik, L. Erond and E. Edwards McKinnon. 2012. "Traces of Early Chinese and Southeast Asian Trade at Benteng Puteri Hijau, Namu Rambe, Northeast Sumatra". In *Proceedings of the 13th International Conference of the European Association of Southeast Asian Archaeologists*, edited by M.L. Tjoa-Bonatz, A. Reinecke and D. Bonatz, pp. 53–66. Singapore: NUS Press.

de Casparis, J.G. 1989. "Peranan Adityawarman, Putera Melayu di Asia Tenggara". In *Tamadun Melayu* (3), edited by I. Hussein, A. Deraman and A. Rahman al-Ahmadi, pp. 918–43. Kuala Lumpur: Dewan Bahasa dan Pustaka, Kementerian Pendidikan Malaysia.

Dobbin, C. 1983. *Islamic Revivalism in a Changing Peasant Economy: Central Sumatra, 1784–1847*. London and Malmö: Scandinavian Institute of Asian Studies.

Drakard, J. 1999. *A Kingdom of Words: Language and Power in Sumatra*. Oxford University Press.

Dupoizat, M.-F. 2009. "Grès et porcelaines des sites de Barus postérieurs à Lobu Tua". In *Histoire de Barus, Vol. III: Regards sur une place marchande de l'océan Indien (XIIe-milieu du XVIIe s.)*, edited by D. Perret and Heddy Surachman, pp. 81–152. Paris: Association Archipel.

Dupoizet, M.-F. and Naniek Harkantiningsih. 1994. "La céramique importee". In *Banten avant l'Islam. Étude archéologique de Banten Girang (Java-Indonésie) 932?–1526*, edited by C. Guillot, Lukman Nurhakim and Sonny Wibisono, pp. 137–68. Paris: École Française d'Extrême-Orient.

Dupoizet, M.-F. and Naniek Harkantiningsih. 2007. *Catalogue of the Chinese Style Ceramics of Majapahit: Tentative Inventory*. Paris: Association Archipel.

Edwards McKinnon, E. 1992. "Ceramic Recoveries (Surface Finds) at Lambaro, Aceh". *Journal of East-West Maritime Relations* 2: 63–73.

———. 2006. "Mediaeval Landfall Sites in Aceh, North Sumatra". In *Uncovering Southeast Asia's Past. Selected Papers from the 10th International Conference of the European Association of Southeast Asian Archaeologists, The British Museum London 14th–17th September 2004*, edited by E. Bacus, I.C. Glover and V.C. Pigott, pp. 325–34. Singapore: NUS Press.

———, Naniek Harkantiningsih Wibisono, Heddy Surachman, Sarjiyanto, Stanov Purnawibowo, Lim Chen Sian and B. Vining. 2012. "The Kota Rentang Excavations". In *Proceedings of the 13th International Conference of the European Association of Southeast Asian Archaeologists*, edited by M.L. Tjoa-Bonatz, A. Reinecke and D. Bonatz, pp. 67–81. Singapore: NUS Press.

Goddio, F., and G.S. Casal. 2002. *Lost at Sea: The Strange Route of the Lena Shoal Junk*. London: Periplus.

Gompertz, G.S.G.M. 1980. *Chinese Celadon Wares*. London: Faber and Faber.

Gotuaco, L., R.C. Tan, and A.I. Diem. 1997. *Chinese and Vietnamese Blue and White Wares Found in the Philippines*. Makati City: Bookmark.

He Li. 1996. *Chinese Ceramics: The New Standard Guide*. London: Thames and Hudson.

Hess, E. 1930–32 [1602–1797]. *Reisebeschreibungen von deutschen Beamten und Kriegsleuten im Dienst der Niederländischen West- und Ost-Indischen Kompagnien 1602–1797*. The Hague: Nijhoff.

Junker, L.L. 1999. *Raiding, Trading, and Feasting: The Political Economy of Philippine Chiefdoms*. Honolulu: University of Hawai'i Press.

Kern, H. 1917. "Het sanskrit-inschrift op den grafsteen van vorst Ādityavarman te Kubur Raja (Mēnangkabau; ± 1300 Çāka)". *Verspreide Geschriften* 7 (1917 [1913]): 215–21.

Kozok, U. and E. van Reijn. 2010. "Ādityawarman: Three Inscriptions of the Sumatran 'King of all Supreme Kings' translated and annotated from H. Kern and F.D.K. Bosch". *Indonesia and the Malay World* 38, no. 110: 135–58.

Kroeskamp, H. 1919. "De Westkust en Minangkabau 1665–1668". PhD Thesis, Universiteit Leiden. Utrecht: Schotanus & Jens.

Krom, N.J. 1912. "Inventaris der oudheden in de Padangsche bowenlanden". *Oudheidkundige Verslag* G: 33–50.

Kulke, H. 2009. "Adityavarman's Highland Kingdom". In *Distant Tales. Ethnohistory and Archaeology in the Highland of Sumatra, Indonesia*, edited by D. Bonatz, J. Miksic, J.D. Neidel and M.L. Tjoa-Bonatz, pp. 229–62. Newcastle-upon-Tyne: Cambridge Scholars Publication.

Lai Chee Kien. 1993. "Deducing from Balimbing: Measuring a Minangkabau House". *Architecture Journal*: 59–69.

Locsin, L., and C. Locsin. 1967. *Oriental Ceramics Discovered in the Philippines*. Tokyo: Tuttle.

Miksic, J.N. 1986. "A Valley of Megaliths in West Sumatra. Mahat (Schnitger's Aoer Doeri) Revisited". *Journal of the Malaysian Branch of the Royal Asiatic Society* 59: 27–32.

———. 1987. "From Seri Vijaya to Melaka: 'Batu Tagak' in Historical and Cultural Context". *Journal of the Malayan Branch of the Royal Asiatic Society* 60, no. 2: 1–42.

———. 1989. "Urbanization and Social Change. The Case of Sumatra". *Archipel 'Villes d'Insulinde II'* 37: 3–29.

———. 2001 [1996]. "Sumatran Kingdoms after Sriwijaya". In *Ancient History*, edited by J. Miksic, pp. 104–5. Singapore: Periplus.

———. 2004. "From Megaliths to Tombstones: The Transition from Prehistory to the Early Islamic Period in Highland West Sumatra". *Indonesia and the Malay World* 32: 191–210.

———. 2006. "Chinese Ceramics and the Economics of Early Southeast Asian Urbanisation, 14th to 16th centuries". *Bulletin of the Indo-Pacific Prehistory Association* 26: 147–53.

———. 2010. “Before and after Zheng He: Comparing Some Southeast Asian Archaeological Sites of the 14th and 15th Centuries”. In *Southeast Asia in the Fifteenth Century. The Ming Factor*, edited by G. Wade and Sun Laichen, pp. 384–408. Singapore: NUS Press.
———. 2011. *Sherd Library. From the Archaeological Collection of Dr. John Miksic*. Singapore: National University of Singapore Museum.
———. 2015. “Kerinci and the Ancient History of Jambi”. In *A 14th Century Malay Code of Laws: The Nītisārasamucaya*, edited by U. Kozok, pp. 17–49. Singapore: Institute of Southeast Asian Studies.
Nakamura, S. 1998. “Spatial Organization in an Indonesian Village in West Sumatra (Meanings of the Minangkabau Ethnical Group)”. *Architectural Institute of Japan* 38, no. 6004: 369–72.
Pires, T. 1967 [1512–15]. *The Suma Oriental of Tomé Pires and The Book of Francisco Rodrigues*, translated by A. Cortesão. Wiesbaden: Lessing.
Reichle, N. 2007. *Violence and Serenity. Late Buddhist Sculpture from Indonesia*. Honolulu: University of Hawai’i Press.
Reid, A. 1993. *Southeast Asia in the Age of Commerce, 1450–1680, Vol. 2: Expansion and Crisis*. New Haven: Yale University Press.
Robson, S., trans. 1995. *Deśawarṇana (Nāgarakṛtāgama)*, by Mpu Prapañca. Leiden: KITLV Press.
Suhadi, M. 1990. “Silsilah Adityawarman”. *Kalpataru Majalah Arkeologi* 9: 219–39.
Suleiman, S. 2008 [1977]. “The Archaeology and History of West Sumatra”. In *Capita Selecta Bulletin of the National Research Centre of Archaeology of Indonesia*, edited by Pusat Penelitian dan Pengembangan Arkeologi Nasional, pp. 57–82. Jakarta: PUSLIT.
Summerfield, A., and J. Summerfield, eds. 1999. *Walk in Splendor. Ceremonial Dress and the Minangkabau*. Los Angeles: University of California.
Tjoa-Bonatz, M.L. 2009. “The Megaliths and the Pottery. Studying the Early Material Culture of Highland Jambi”. In *From Distant Tales. Ethnohistory and Archaeology in Highland Sumatra*, edited by D. Bonatz, J. Miksic, J.D. Neidel and M.L. Tjoa-Bonatz, pp. 196–228. Newcastle-upon-Tyne: Cambridge Scholars Publication.
———. 2012. “3400 Years of Earthenware Traditions in Highland Jambi, Indonesia”. In *Proceedings of the 13th International Conference of the European Association of Southeast Asian Archaeologists*, edited by M.L. Tjoa-Bonatz, A. Reinecke and D. Bonatz, pp. 16–31. Singapore: NUS Press.
———. 2012. “The Earliest Archaeological Sources of Vernacular Architecture on Sumatra”. In *Insular Diversity: Architecture – Culture – Identity in Indonesia*, edited by Technische Universität Wien and Gadjah Mada Universitas Yogyakarta, pp. 67–80. Vienna: IVA-ICRA.
———. 2013a. “Das Entstehen komplexer Siedlungsstrukturen im zentralen

Hochland von Sumatra, Indonesien". *Mitteilungen der Berliner Gesellschaft für Anthropologie, Ethnologie und Urgeschichte* 34: 147–56.
———. 2013b. "Im Goldland der Minangkabau. Auf der Suche nach dem letzten hindu-buddhistischen Königreich". *Antike Welt* 5, no. 13: 14–20.
———. 2015a. "Über 3000 Jahre alte Siedlungsspuren: Das Hochland von Sumatra (Indonesien)". In *Im Schatten von Angkor. Archäologie und Geschichte von Südostasien*, edited by M.L. Tjoa-Bonatz and A. Reinecke, pp. 56–65. Darmstadt: von Zabern.
——— and J. Hämmerle. 2015b. "Siedler, Sklaven und Seefahrer. Zum Ursprung der Megalithkultur auf Nias (Indonesien)". In *Im Schatten von Angkor. Archäologie und Geschichte von Südostasien*, edited by M.L. Tjoa-Bonatz and A. Reinecke, pp. 66–75. Darmstadt: von Zabern.
———. Forthcoming. *Tanah Datar. Early Settlement Archaeology and History of the Minangkabau Highlands on Sumatra, Indonesia*. Singapore: ISEAS – Yusof Ishak Institute.
Tregear, M. 1982. *Die Keramik der Song-Zeit*. Munich: Hirmer.
van der Meulen, W.J. 1974. Suvarṇadvîpa and the Chrysê Chersonêsos. *Indonesia* 18: 1–40.
Vellinga, M. 2004. *Constituting Unity and Differences. Vernacular Architecture in a Minangkabau Village*. Leiden: KITLV Press.
Wade, G., translator. (n.d.). "Southeast Asia in the Ming Shi-lu: An Open Access Resource". Singapore: Asia Research Institute and the Singapore E-Press, National University of Singapore. http://epress.nus.edu.sg/msl/entry/513 (accessed 13 August 2012).
——— and Sun Laichen. 2010. *Southeast Asia in the Fifteenth Century. The Ming Factor*. Singapore: NUS Press.
Wolters, O.W. 1970. *The Fall of Srivijaya in Malay History*. Ithaca: Cornell University Press.

INDEX

Note: Page numbers followed by "n" refer to notes.

A

Abbasid Caliph Hārūn al-Rashīd, 338
Abbasid Caliphate, 9, 334, 336, 337
Abode of Islam, 155
Abu-Lughod, Janet, 48n26
Abu Talib Ahmad, 19, 19n3
Acharya, Amitav, 81, 88, 128
Acri, Andrea, 117n31, 187n15, 205, 358n1
  Balinese Hinduism, 179n4
  Monsoon Asian religious matrix, 46, 181–82
  Spirits and Ships, 177–78
  syncretism, 309n144
Ādityavarman, 393
  Bukit Gombak, 10
  inscription at Pagaruyung, 395
  inscription stones of, 398, 402, 410
  and Minangkabau, 399–401
Adloff, Richard, 80, 81
Age of Explorations, 94
agents, 370–76
Ahl-i Hadis
  movement, 269–70
  periodical, 258–68
Ahmed Khan, Syed, 251
Ahmed Shah, Sayed, 215
al-Kālikūtī, Qāḍī Muḥammad, 147, 153, 154
Al Saud, Abdul Aziz, 254, 258–64, 268
Al Saud, Muhammad, 270
al-Sīrāfī, Abū Zayd, 336, 336n4, 338
Al-Sumatrani, Syamsuddin, 205
Alawi, Amir Ahmad, 268
Ali, Ayaan Hirsi, 176
Ali, Maulana Muhammad, 267
Ali, Maulana Shaukat, 267
Ali Pasha, 137
Ali, Sulaiman, 263
All India Muslim League, 61–62
All-India Radio, 61, 70, 72
Allied Powers, 75
Almond, Philip C., 226
altered materiality, 239–45
Ambedkar, Bhimrao, 301–2
Amir Badshah, Sayed, 215
An Nam, 368, 369
Ancient Monuments Preservation Act, 220, 228
Andaya, Barbara Watson, 40, 44, 381
Anderson, John, 27, 28
Ang, Claudine, 373
Anglo-Saudi Treaty of 1915, 253
Antony, Robert, 39, 40n13
Arab-Jew issue, 83
Arab League, 74, 82
Arabic calligraphy, 179, 354
Arasaratnam, Sinnappah, 97, 98

Aristotelian-Platonic wonder, 176
armchair travellers, 109
Asher, Frederick, 243
Asia. *See also* Maritime Asia
  act of violence, 21–29
  area studies scholarship, 1–4
  arresting gaze, 17–21
  geographical construct of, 3
  political boundaries, 18
  post-empire imperial epistemologies, 29–34
Asia in the Modern World (Venkatasubbiah), 68, 84
"Asia is One", 128
Asia-Pacific Economic Cooperation (APEC), 87
Asia-Pacific Journal/Japan Focus, 40n14
"Asian Century", 3
Asian Relations Conference 1947
  Arab-Jew issue, 83
  Arab League, 82
  Asian Relations Organization, 84
  Association of Southeast Asia, 87
  in China, 81
  Dawn newspaper, *see Dawn* newspaper
  Gandhi, 71–72, 79
  gunboat epistemology, 88
  Hindustan Times, 63, 63n8
  inauguration of, 83
  Indian Council of World Affairs, 64–65
  Indian Planning Committee, 80
  Inter-Asian Migration, 77
  interim government in India, 61, 73, 75
  issues, 66
  language, 65–66, 68
  Muslim League, 61–62, 82, 83
  newspapers, 60–61, 69–70
  participating countries and organizations, 67–68
  racial problems, 77
  round-table sessions, 69, 74–76
  Steering Committee, 78
Asian Relations Organization (ARO), 81, 82, 84, 85
Asiatic Journal, 137
Association of Southeast Asia (ASA), 87
Association of Southeast Asian Nations (ASEAN), 82, 87
Aston, Edward, 23n7
Azzam, Abdul Ahab, 74

B

Baghdad
  Abbasid Caliphate of, 334
  Abbasid court at, 342
  Sharif Ali, 259
Baldaeus, Philippus, 93, 95, 99, 100–4, 106, 121
Bali, Javano-Balinese Sanskritic Buddhism in, 308–12
Bamiyan Buddha sculptures, 219, 219n4
Bangiya-Sahityaanusilani Sabha, 235
Bangladesh, remnant Buddhists, 296–99
Banu Hashim clan, 252–53
Batang Hari, 399
Bauman, Zygmunt, 21, 21n6
Bayhaqī, 338
Bayly, Susan, 178–80
Beal, Samuel, 227
Beekman, E.M., 106
Belitung shipwreck, 338–42
Bellina, Bérénice, 45
Bengali Muslims, 8, 251–52, 271
Bentley, J.H., 335
Bergman, Hugo, 74
Bien Hoa, 367, 373
Birla, 64n9
Black Mosque, 350
Blackburn, Anne M., 226

Blake, William, 126
Blakeway, D.B., 223
Blench, Robert, 46, 205
Bocarro of Macau (1627–80), 383
Bochia, Muhammad Abdul Karim, 348
Bodh Gaya
  Buddhism, 229
  Burmese restoration mission to, 237
  historical and anthropological scholarship on, 229n23
  Maha Bodhi Temple at, 232–36
Boemus, Johannes, 23–24, 23n7
Bonatz, D., 393
Borri, Christoforo, 371, 381, 383
Bose, Sugata, 3
Bowl Rim Fragment, 339
Bowyear, Thomas, 382
Boxer, Charles R., 383
Braginsky, Vladimir, 169, 205
Brahmans, 111–14, 276, 283
Brahmavādin, 234
Bray, Denys, 263
Brekke, Torkel, 243
British Museum, 218, 225, 235, 243
British romantic poetics
  Byron, Gordon, 127, 136–37
  Coleridge, Samuel Taylor, 127, 136
  Jones, William, 127, 129, 132–35, 138–40
  Shelley, Percy Bysshe, 127, 139–42
  Southey, Robert, 127, 134–35
British Romantic Writers and the East (Leask), 132
Broilo, Federica, 9
Bronkhorst, Johannes, 276
Brouwer, Hendrik, 98
Brown, R.M., 413
Buddhacarita, 288, 300
buddhavacana, 277, 278, 283, 298
Buddhism
  Bodh Gaya, 229
  Javano-Balinese Sanskritic, 308–12
  land-based approach to the spread of, 48n25
  Newar, 303–8
  Pali, 290, 321
  Prakritic, 276, 279
  Sanskritic, 47–51
  semi-Sanskritic, 312–20
  Sino-Japanese, 313
  Tibetan, 316
  Universal, 290
Buddhist Hybrid Sanskrit, 277
Buddhist modernism, 229, 229n22
Buddhist relics
  connecting transnational religion and history, 225–30
  empire of, 230–39
  repatriation, 243
  test of authenticity, 244
  worship of, 338
Bühler, G., 231
Bukit Gombak
  blue-and-white ceramics, 414, 415
  ^{14}C-dating, 409
  commercial interactions, 393
  distribution and density of sherds, 404
  excavation sites in Tanah Datar, 405
  excavation trenches on, 417
  geomagnetic surveys pursued on, 397
  gold mines in, 400
  households living on, 416
  imported wares from, 412
  pile building, 406
  settlement on, 401–7
  southern slope of, 407
  TL-dating, 409
  2011 field season at, 397

Bukit Kincir, burial site at, 405, 407–9, 417
Burke, Edmund, 132
Burns, Peter M., 18
Byron, Gordon, 127, 136–37

C

Cāliyaṃ, battle of, 153, 154, 166
Cape Muslim, 183
capitalism, 125
  colonial, 18, 27, 28
  industrial, 18
ceramic material, 411–16
Ceurawach, 115, 116
Chakmas, 296–97, 296n88
Chatham House, 64
Chaudhuri, K.N., 3, 31n11, 33, 37n4, 43–44
Chaun Pandan, 189
Chey Chetta II, 380
China
  early Islamic settlements, 343–46
  exchange of knowledge, 337–42
  Green Splash Ware, 339
  and Islam, 335–37
  Oval Bowl, 341
  trade, 337–42
Choi, Byung Wook, 359, 373
Chola empire, 30
Co Chiem/Cham, 369
Cochinchina, 359–61, 380
  agents, 370–76
  demographic structure, 371
  as geographical imaginations, 362–70
  geography, 384–85
  historical movements, 377
  identity, 384–85
  networks, 376–85
  spatial evolution of, 374
Cohn, Bernard S., 18
Coleridge, Samuel Taylor, 127, 136
colonial capitalism, 18, 27, 28
colonial power, 27, 75, 127, 226
colonialism, 29, 75, 84, 125, 177
commercial age, 360
Confessions of an Opium-Eater (de Quincey), 26
Confucianism, 359
Congressional Mosque, 350
"connected histories", 37, 51, 204
Conquest of America, The (Todorov), 21, 22
convert groups, 178
Cooke, Nola, 359, 373, 374
Coromandel Coast, 98–100, 105
Cosmographia (Munster), 24
Crawfurd, John, 27, 28
creolization, 179, 180, 204, 205
Crone, Patricia, 177
cultural expansion, 31n11
cultural matrix, 8, 45, 182, 194, 203
Cunningham, Alexander, 225, 227
Curse of Kehama, The (Southey), 135

D

da Cruz, João, 383
da Gama, Vasco, 155
Dai Nippon Teikoku, 346
Dai Viet, 367–69
Dalai Lama XIV, 318
Dale, Stephen, 148
dār al-ḥarb, 155
dār al-Islam, 150, 155
Dargah Shaykh Yusuf, in Macassar, 206
da-shi, 336
Das, Rochal, 179
Dattaw, 243
  new reliquary in, 241
  relic cask encrusted with rubies, 242
  undated photograph of, 238
Datuk Manila, 186, 188, 190, 191
Dawn newspaper
  Arab-Jew issue, 83

Asian Relations Conference, 62n6, 62n7, 64, 64n9, 66–67, 86
Hindu Congress, 82
Muslim League as Pakistan Day, 83
sensational headlines, 79
de Bry, Theodorus, 24–25, 28
de Laval, François Pyrard, 163
De Open-Deure tot het Verborgen Heydendom (Rogerius), 101, 107
de Quincey, Thomas, 26–27
Deane, H.A., 227
decentralization, in Indonesia, 20n4
Degroot, Véronique, 419
Delacroix, Eugene, 138
Delhi empire, 148, 168
Demirel, Suleyman, 353
Dentan, Robert K., 46, 183
dhimmis, 200, 201
digital surface models (DSMs), 397
Dirks, Nicholas B., 95, 121, 121n35
Diyanet İşleri Başkanlığı, 351, 352
Donaldson, Thomas Eugene, 299n106
Dong Nai, 367
Drakard, J., 418
Duara, Prasenjit, 2, 37n2, 40n13
Duncan, Jonathan, 133
Dündar, A.M., 335n1
Dupoizet, M.-F., 410

E

Earl of Minto, 241
early Islamic settlements, 343–46
East Asia Summit (EAS), 87
East India, remnant Buddhists, 296–99
Edward VII, King, 241
Edwards McKinnon, E., 411, 419
Egar, Asa, 151
El'Ad, Amikam, 151
Elsner, Jas, 109
Eltschinger, Vincent, 276, 285
empiricism, 109
epistemology, 22, 65
gunboat, 88
imperial, 29–34
Erānāṭṭu Mūnnāmkūr Nampiyātiri, 159
ethnographic reality, 178
Eurasia, 84
conceptualization of premodern, 42
landmass, 48
in mainstream historical scholarship, 39
networks of circulation and exchange in, 334
political-economic unity, 53
excavation sites
blue-and-white porcelain, 416
on Bukit Gombak, 417
in South Asia, 244
in Tanah Datar, 405
trenches, 406, 410
exchange of knowledge, 337–42

F

Fardle of Facions, The (Waterman), 23n7
Favereau, Aude, 45
Federspiel, Howard M., 192
Ferozzudin, 348
First Anniversary Discourse, 133
Flood, Finbarr Barry, 219n4
Foucher, Alfred, 227
Frank, Andre G., 44

G

Galiev, Kurban, 354
Gandhi, Mahatma, 71–72, 79, 87, 257
Garrick, David, 132
Gaspardone, Emile, 373
Gautama Buddha, 216

Gellner, David N., 304n127
Geographia (Munster), 24
Ghani, Kashshaf, 8, 358n1
Gia Dinh, 367, 378
Giaour, The (Byron), 137–38
Ginjiro Katsuda, 348
Global Asias, 3
Glorious Revolution of 1688, 125
Gommans, Jos, 93n1
Goody, Jack, 40n13
Gourou, Pierre, 359
Green, N., 348n19
Griffiths, Arlo, 393, 419
Guangzhou, 336, 343
Guha, Sumit, 95
Guillot, Claude, 38, 169
gunboat epistemology, 88
Gupta, Sunil, 46
Guruge, Ananda W.P., 290, 303n122

H

Hakluyt, Richard, 106
Halhed, Nathanial, 133
Hamel, Chouki el, 151
Hamzah Fansuri, 205
Hang Tuah, 193, 195–97
Hann, Chris, 39, 53
Hardy, Thomas, 134
Harkantiningsih, Naniek, 410
Harmsen, Antonius, 93n1
Hastings, Warren, 133
Havart, Daniel, 99, 106
Hazard, Paul, 106n15
Hejaz, Ottomans in, 252–53
Heldt, Gustav, 48n26
Herodotus, 94, 128
heydendom, 94–95, 110
Heydensche Godsdienst, 100
Hikayat Bayan Budiman, 184
Hindu Congress, 62, 63, 82, 318
Hindu Imperialism, 64n9
Hindu Pantheon (Moor), 140
Hindu Sabha, 234
Hindu, The, 64
Hinduism, 9, 135, 286, 289
Hindustan Times (HT), 63, 63n8
History of Java (Raffles), 33
Ho, Engseng, 52
Hobhouse, John Cam, 137
Hoey, W., 231
Hoi An, 375, 378, 382
Holmes, Catherine, 47
Hoogervorst, Tom, 46
Houben, Jan, 276
Huang Chao, 342–44
Hymn to Vishnu (Jones), 139

I

ibn Abdul Wahhab, Muhammad, 266, 270
Ibn Ali, Sharif Husayn, 253–56, 258–60, 268
Ibn Battūta, 343
Ibn Khaldun, 187n13, 199
Ibn Rashid, 253, 254
Ibn Taymiyya, 151, 151n1, 198
Iliad, The, 128
imperial epistemology, 29–34
In Search of Southeast Asia: A Modern History (Steinberg), 31–32
"indeterminate equilibrium", 100
India
  Asian Relations Conference, of 1947. *See* Asian Relations Conference 1947
  interim government in, 61, 73, 75
  "Look East" policy, 30n11
  Ministry of Culture, 53
  Muslims of, 61
  Sanskrit, 135, 291
Indian Council of World Affairs (ICWA), 64–65
"Indian Ocean system", 44
Indian Planning Committee, 80
Indianization, 31n11, 46

Indo-Aryan language, 293, 294, 312
Indology, 314
Indomalaya Ecozone, 41, 291–92
Indonesia
  Archipelago, 49
  Burmese exports to, 413
  decentralization in, 20n4
  keramat structure, 207
  Tanah Datar, 394
industrial capitalism, 18
interim government in India, 61, 73, 75
International Relations and Political Theory, 32
International Revolutionary Party, 199
Irschick, Eugene F., 100n4
Irwin, Robert, 108n18, 108n19
Islam, 200
  China and, 335–37
  in Japan, 346, 350–53
  settlements, 343–46
  in Turkey, 350–53
Islamabadi, Maulana Maniruzzaman, 269
Islamic Caliphate, 252
Islamic iconoclasm, 216
Islamic Printing House, 354
Ismail Hossain Siraji, Syed, 269

J

Jainism, 298
Jamaat-i Ulama-i Bengal, 257
Jameson, Fredric, 18
Japan
  Islam in, 346, 350–53
  Muslim, 346, 347, 351
  Neo-Ottomanization, 351
Javano-Balinese Sanskritic Buddhism, 308–12
Jha, Murari K., 6, 358n1
Jhule Lal, 180–81
jiaozhi, 370, 370n5
Jinavaravansa, 231
Jinnah, Mohammad Ali, 61, 62, 62n6, 82
Jitao, Dai, 73
Johns, Adrian, 121n34
Johnson, Samuel, 127, 129, 132
Joll, Chris, 191, 202n28
Jones, William, 109, 127, 129, 132–35, 138–40
Jorisson, Jacob, 105
Josephson-Storm, Joseph A., 176, 178, 179n5, 206
Julien, Stanislas, 227

K

Kahn, Joel S., 196
"Kainan 1890", 353
Kalus, Ludvik, 169
Kanishka reliquary, 217, 218
Karashima, Seishi, 282
Kauz, Ralph, 43
Kāvya, 284–90, 299–303
Kazakhstan, 78
Keitumetse, Susan, 19n2
Keller, Sara, 175n1
Kelley, Liam, 359
Kerala Muslims, 163
Kerala Varttamānam, 158n5
keramat
  cosmopolitan character, 194
  Hang Jebat, 185
  Hang Kasturi, 204
  Hang Tuah, 193
  hill shrines and, 183
  Indonesia, 207
  on Java, 191n18
  in Makassar, 206
  in Melaka, 185–6, 191–2
  Mandal's perspective on, 190
  multiethnic and hybrid practices of, 187
  oceanic histories, 176
  offerings at, 186

sanctuaries replaced by, 184
structure on the Togean Islands, 187, 207
keramat Datuk Manila, 191, 202n28
compound, 188
Kampung Chetty/Tengkera, 190
lamp niche, 188
Khalilieh, Hassan S., 150
Khilafat Committee, 264–65
Khilafat Movement, 257, 269
Khuṭbat al-jihādiyya, 162
Khwaja Khizr, 180
Kircher, Athanasius, 118n32
Kitchener, Lord, 253
knowledge exchange, 337–42
Kobe Mosque, 349
Koning, Paula, 93n1
Kooria, Mahmood, 7
Kozok, Uli, 419
kramat, 183, 183n7
Kripal, Jeffrey, 177, 203, 205
Kṣatriyas, 114–18
Kubla Khan (Coleridge), 136
Kuli, Mohammad, 98
Kulke, Hermann, 419
Kuññāli Marakkārs, 158, 160, 162, 164–68

L

Lahore Museum, 235
Lai Chee Kien, 403
Land Acquisition Act, 220
Lauzière, Henri, 196, 197
Le King, 362, 367
Le Quy Don, 371
Leask, Nigel, 132, 137
Leslie, D.D., 344
Lewis, Martin W., 42
Leydekker, Henrik, 96
Li, Tana, 359, 373
libertarianism, 126
Lieberman, Victor B., 42, 359
Lingor Circle, 232
Locke, A., 187
Lombard, Denys, 38
Lombard-Salmon, Claudine, 373
long-distance trade, 398–99
longue durée, 2, 4, 37n3, 51
"Look East" policy, 30n11
Louvre Museum, 138
low-civilized frontier, 371
Lowe, Celia, 187

M

MacArthur, General, 66
Mackenzie, Colin, 121
madhyimabhāṇaka, 277, 277n8
Maha Bodhi Temple, 229, 232–37
Mahāyāna, 282
Mahmal, 256
Maisey, F.C., 225
Majeed, Javed, 134
Majid, Abdul, 265
Malabar Coast
complexities of, 149
internal dynamics, 160–65
Muslims of, 147–48, 158
Portuguese intruders into, 147
sambuks from, 159
socio-cultural setting, 147
Malay Bible, 96
manangkabwa, 399
Manchester Guardian, 64
Mandal, Sumit K., 175n1, 186, 190
Mandeville, John, 109
Manners, Lawes and Customs of all Nations, The (Aston), 23n7
Mansergh, Nicholas, 81
Māppiḷa Muslims, 148, 163, 165
Marco Polo, 109
Maritime Asia
archaeological contexts, 47
boats and navigation techniques, 44
cultural matrix, 45
Eurasia, 39, 41–42, 51, 53
geographical construct of, 41

heuristic category of, 51–54
Indianization, 46
"Indian Ocean system," 44
Indomalaya Ecozone, 41
interconnected network, 37, 38
macro-region, 37
Sanskritic Buddhism, 47–51
transocean, 41
transport surface, 44
"Maritime Silk Roads", 39, 39n10, 45, 50
maritime trade
Ādityavarman and Minangkabau, 399–401
Bukit Gombak, 401–7
Bukit Kincir, 407–8
West Sumatra, 396, 398–99
Marshall, John, 227, 240
Maududi, Abdul A'la, 198–200
Mausam Project, 44n20, 53
May, Theresa, 176
Meccan elite, 252
Mediaeval Maritime Asia, 47–51
medieval vandalism, 219
Mekong Delta, 367
Mekong plain, 367
Menezes, Henry, 165
Miksic, John, 410, 419
Minangkabau, 399–401
Minto, Lord, 237
Missionary, an Indian Tale, The (Morgan), 140
modernity, 17, 27, 29, 33
Momen, Mustafa, 82
monastic law, 277–78, 278n10
Monsoon Islam (Prange), 52
Moor, Edward, 140
Moser, Johannes, 419
mosques, 344–45, 352
Black Mosque, 350
Congressional Mosque, 350
Kobe Mosque, 349
Ottoman mosque, 352, 353
Red Mosque, 350
Siberian Tatar Mosque, 350
Tokyo Mosque, 349, 350, 352
Urumqui Tatar Mosque, 349
Mountbatten, Lord, 61, 72
Mufti, Aamir, 129
Mughal kingdom, 148, 168
Mukherjee, Sraman, 8, 44n20, 358n1
Mamluks, 147, 156, 158
Munda languages, 182
Munster, Sebastian, 24
Murphey, Rhoads, 41
Murray, John, 137
Mus, Paul, 374
Muslim League, 61–64, 82, 83
muslimmanga.org, 354
Muslims
Arab-Jew issue, 83
Bengali, 8, 251–52, 271
Cape Muslim, 183
drinking from gold/silver vessels, 341
immigrants, 350
of India, 61, 348
Japanese, 346, 347, 351
Kerala, 163
in Malabar, 147–49, 158
merchants, 336, 343, 345
Pathan, 216
South Asian, 251
worship, 348
Mutual Broadcasting System of New York, 70
My Tho, 367, 373

N

Nāgārjuna, 283, 283n33, 285
Naidu, Sarojini, 63n7, 70, 72, 79, 83, 86–87
Nakamura, S., 403
Nālandā monastery, 280
Naṃpūtiris, 156, 164
Napoleon, 137

national identities, 18, 20
native identity, 18
Nehru, Jawaharlal, 71–75
  colonial rule, 61
  External Affairs, charge of, 75
  Interim Government, 70
  Japan's Absence in Asian Relations Conference, 66, 67n15
  "One World", 86
Neo-Ottomanism, 351–53
networks, 49–50, 49n28, 376–83
Newar Buddhism, 303–8
Nguyen Binh Khiem, 362
Nguyen Cochinchina, 359–61, 380
  agents, 370–76
  demographic structure, 371
  as geographical imaginations, 362–70
  geography, 384–85
  historical movements, 377
  identity, 384–85
  networks, 376–85
  political project, 378
  realm, 376, 381
  spatial evolution of, 374
Nguyen Cu Trinh, 365, 366
Nguyen Hoang, 362, 364–65
Nguyen Kim, 362
Nguyen Phuc Chu, Lord, 378
Nguyen Phuc Khoat, Lord, 365
Nguyen Phuc Tan, Lord, 383
Nieuhof, Johan, 27
nirukti, 278, 313
nominal construct, 22, 26, 27, 33
Noor, Farish, 5, 65
Novelli, Marina, 18

O

Ogilby, John, 105n13, 105n14
O'Hanlon, Rosalind, 95
Okakura, 128
Olympic Council of Asia, 88
Omnium Gentium Mores, Leges et Ritus (Boemus), 23
"One World", 86
Orientalism, 100, 108–9, 125
Orientalism (Said), 127
"Oriental Tale", 137
Ottoman Empire, 131, 162
Ottoman mosque, 352, 353
Ottoman Sultan, 252–54, 269, 346
Ottomans, 156, 158
  in Hejaz, 252–53
Oud en Nieuw Oost-Indiën (Valentijn), 96, 97

P

paganism, 101
Palakollu village, 98
Palembang, 184
Pali Buddhism, 290, 321
Pali Cosmopolis, 4, 43, 52
Pali language, 291, 293
Pali scripture, 276
pan-Asian diffusion of Sanskrit and Buddhism, 294
Pannikar, K.M., 83
Paranavitana, Senarat, 303n122
Pasha Hassan, 138
Pathan Muslims, 216, 236
Pearson, Michael, 3, 43, 44
Pelliot, Paul, 369
Peppe, William, 231, 239
periodicals
  Ahl-i Hadis, 258–68
  Bengali, 268–70
  Sultan, 253–58
periodization of Asian history, mediaeval, 48n26
Persian poetry, 130–31
Peshawar Museum, 224, 243
Pham, Charlotte, 381
Philippine islands, 49
philological-lexigraphic revolution, 129

Phu Bien Tap Luc, 369
Phu Xuan, 378
Phya Sukhum, 232
Pietersz, Jacob, 98
Pigneaux de Béhaine, Pierre-Joseph, 383
pilgrimage
  Bengali periodicals, 268–70
  Ottomans in Hejaz, 252–53
  periodical *Ahl-i Hadis*, 258–68
  periodical *Sultan*, 253–58
Pillai, Kunjan, 164
Pollock, Sheldon, 48n26
Ponggongan, goldworking workshop at, 411
Ponnāni, 7, 149, 154–60
  educational institution in, 154
  internal dynamics, 160–65
  Kerala Muslims, 163
  Māppiḷa Muslims of, 165
  as military capital of Zamorins, 154–60
  Naṃpūtiris, 164
  ribāṭ at work, 165–68
Portuguese
  decline in Malabar, 170
  invasion of Malacca, 183
  wars in Malabar, 147–68
postcolonial Buddhist, 299–303
post-empire imperial epistemologies, 29–34
post-Gupta period, 48n26
postmodernity, 18
Prakritic Buddhism, 276, 279
Prange, Sebastian, 52
Prometheus, 140–41
Prometheus Unbound (Jones), 139
Provisional Council, 81
psychogeography, 182, 194, 203
Ptak, Roderich, 38, 38n7, 38n8, 40
Pulau Besar, 202, 202n28
Purana Qila grounds, 70
Purchas, Samuel, 106

Q
Qing China, 368, 374, 377, 378
Qing military suppression, 377
Quang Nam, 369, 372
Quang Ngai, 366
Quanzhou, 345

R
Raffles, Thomas Stamford, 27, 28, 33
Ragyappas, 120n33
Raleigh, Walter, 25, 26, 28
Ramey, Steven Wesley, 179, 180
Ray, Niharranjan, 43, 276
Red Mosque, 350
Reid, Anthony, 361, 396
relic caskets, 225, 242
remnant Buddhists, 296–99
resanskritization, 312n162
revivalism, 20n4
ribāṭ, 7, 148
  defensive nature of, 149
  as fortified coastal urban centres, 151
  idea and practice of, 152
  to the Indian Ocean, 152–54
  internal dynamics, 160–65
  meanings and functions, 150
  Palestinian, 151n2
  Ponnāni, 154–60
  usages, 150
  at work, 165–68
  Zamorins, 147, 149, 155–63
Ricci, Ronit, 52
Richter, Linda K., 18, 18n1
Rida, Rashid, 197
Risley, H.H., 215, 215n1, 221, 222
Rochon, Alexis Marie de, 374
Rogerius, Abrahamus, 93, 95, 99
  Brahmans, 111
  De Open-Deure tot het Verborgen Heydendom, 101–2
  interest in religion and social structure, 121–22

Valentijn's work, 100, 104, 107, 110, 112
Verenigde Oost-Indische Compagnië, 106
Rosa, Fernando, 7–8
Roycroft, Thomas, 105n14
Rubiés, Joan-Pau, 109
Rumphius, Georg Eberhard, 97, 106

S
Sabharwal, Gopa, 5
Safar i-Saadat, 268
Said, Edward, 100n4, 109, 110n20, 127, 134
Sakurai, Yumio, 373
Salafis, 198
Sanatan Dharma Pravardhini Sabha, 234
saṅgha, 279, 280
Sāṅkṛtyāyana, Rāhula, 302
Sanskrit Cosmopolis, 43, 88
Sanskritic Buddhism, 47–51, 275
Buddhist Hybrid Sanskrit, 277
comprehensive soteriology, 281–84
conservative canon, 281–84
epigraphs, 307
geographic extent of, 290–94
living traditions of, 295–96
mainstream, 283
monastic law, 277–78, 278n10
Nālandā monastery, 280
Newar Buddhism as paradigmatic, 303–8
Pali scripture, 276
postcolonial Buddhist, 299–303
Prakrit canon, 281
remnant Buddhists, 296–99
saṅgha, 279, 280
semi-Sanskritic Buddhism, 312–20
technical and literary discourses, 284–90
Sanskritic civilization, 291, 292
Saruaso
gold mines in, 400
in situ inscription at, 399
Śāstra, 284–90, 299–303
Schouten, Wouter, 27
Schwab, Raymond, 108n19
Scott, James, 385
Sejarah Melayu, 183, 189
semi-Sanskritic Buddhism, 312–20
shāhbandar kōya, 157
Shafi, Mian Muhammad, 235
Shah, Sultan Muzaffar, 189
Shah-ji-ki-Dehri relics, 224, 225, 227, 232–33
Shariar, Sutan, 69n17, 69n18, 72, 80, 86
Sharif, Taufiq, 263
Sharma, Anjana, 6
Shaykh Yusuf, 206
Shelley, Percy Bysshe, 127, 139–42
Shengyousi, 345
Shilian Dashan, 369, 377–78
Shōmu (701–756), 346
Shōwa (1926–89), 335
Siberian Tatar Mosque, 350
Sinclair, Iain, 9
Singh, Aqbal, 175n1
Sinitic model, 380
Sino-Japanese Buddhism, 313
Sinosphere
Sanskrit mantra syllables in, 315
semi-Sanskritic Buddhism in, 312–20
Smith, Adam, 132
Smith, Vincent A., 239
Snaats, Cornelia, 96
socio-spatial grouping, 42
Solh, Taquiddeen, 74
Solheim, Wilhem G., 45, 45n21
Song dynasties, 343, 410
Sotaro, Araki, 380
South Asian Muslims, 251

Southeast Asian Peninsular Games, 88
Southey, Robert, 127, 134–35
Spirits and Ships (Acri), 177
Spooner, D.B., 216, 223
Śrāvakapiṭaka, 281–84
Standen, Naomi, 47
Statesman, The, 72
Steering Committee, 78
Steinberg, David Joel, 31–32
Stockdale, John, 27
Stuart, Harold, 219
Subrahmanyam, Sanjay, 37, 37n4, 100, 109, 161
Śūdras, 118–20
Sufism, 179, 196, 205
Śukasaptati, 184
Sultan, periodical, 253–58
Švagr, Jan Josef, 348, 349, 351
Sydney, Lady Morgan, 140
syncretism, 180

T

Tahir, 64n9
Taḥrīḍ, 154
Taishō (1912–26), 335
Talbot, Phillips, 80
Tanah Datar, 393
  archaeological evidence of processing gold in, 400
  excavation sites in, 405
  fertile valley of, 395
  land routes from, 398
  in West Sumatra, 394
Tang-Abbasid period, 338
Tang China, 334–35
Tang Treasure, 337
Tantrism, 183, 184, 203
Tatar Turks, 348
Taussig, Michael, 206
Taw Sein Ko, 238
Tayeb, Haji Mohammad, 255
Taylor, Keith, 359
telegram, 234n29, 234n30
Temple of Tooth Relic, 230–31
Templeman, David, 296
Thalaba the Destroyer (Southey), 134
Theosophists, 229
Theravāda Buddhism, 226, 229, 276
Thompson, Virginia, 80, 81
Thuan Quang, 373
Tibetan Buddhism, 316
Tjoa Bonatz, Mai Lin, 13
Todorov, Tzvetan, 21–29
Tokyo Mosque, 349, 350, 352
Tot den Leser, 107n17
tourism, 18–19, 18n1
Tran Kinh Hoa, 373
Treasure Trove Act, 220, 222–23, 228
Truong Minh Dat (2008), 373
Tsukamoto, Keisho, 291
Turkey, Islam in, 350–53
Turkic Tatar community, 351
Turner, Frederick, 371
Twist, Johan van, 102
Tyson, Adam D., 20, 20n4

U

ummah, 251, 261
Universal Buddhism, 290
unmanned aerial vehicle (UAV), 397
Urumqui Tatar Mosque, 349
Uttarabuddhacarita, 300

V

Vaiśyas, 114–18
Valentijn, Abraham, 96
Valentijn, François, 6, 93
  analysis of text, 104–6
  contemporary oriental discourse, 108–10
  factories, 98
  genealogy of text, 100–104
  heydendom, 94–95, 110
  life and work of, 96–98

producers and consumers, 106–8
reading text along the grain, 111–20
Verenigde Oost-Indische Compagnië, 95
Valentijn, Maria, 96
Van Bruinessen, Martin, 195
van den Brouke, Elias, 105
van den Brouke, Mattheus, 105
van Linschoten, John Huyghen, 102
van Riebeeck, Abraham, 97
Van Schendel, Willem, 385
van Warwyk, Wybrand, 98
Vasco da Gama, 155
Vellinga, M., 403
verbum dei, 299
Verenigde Oost-Indische Compagnië (VOC), 95, 98–100
Vietnam
agents, 370–76
Cochinchina, 384–85
manifest destiny, 366
networks, 376–83
regional division in, 363
spatial orientation problems in, 358–62
Vijaylakshmi Pandit, 65
Viljoen, Shaun, 206
Vining, Benjamin, 396, 419
Vink, Markus, 106

W
Wade, Geoffrey, 38, 39n11
Wahhabism, 266–67
Wang Gungwu, 41
Warren, Andrew, 141
Waterman, William, 23n7
Wavell the Viceroy, Lord, 61
Weber, Freud, 176
Weber, Max, 176
Westphalian model, 18
White, David, 182
White, Herbert Thirkell, 236, 238
"White Man's Burden", 131
Wilkins, Charles, 133
Willingdon Airport, 70
Willis, John E., 40n13
Wong, Dorothy C., 48n26

Y
Yānatraya, 281–84
Yang, Yun-yuan, 73
Yeh, George, 73
Yellow Peril, 235
yoga practitioner, 283

Z
Zamorins, 147, 149, 155–63
Zamzam, 255, 255n4
Zayn al-Dīn, Sr., 154
Zomia, 45, 385

w.ingramcontent.com/pod-product-compliance
itning Source LLC
mbersburg PA
HW052049290426
111CB00011B/1678
9 7 8 9 8 1 4 8 1 8 8 5 8 *